THE WRLD

A History Second Edition

Felipe Fernández-Armesto

UNIVERSITY OF NOTRE DAME

Volume B: From 1000 to 1800

MAPS BY

DORLING KINDERSLEY

PRENTICE HALL
Upper Saddle River   London   Singapore
Toronto   Tokyo   Sydney   Hong Kong
Mexico City

Executive Editor: Charles Cavaliere
Editorial Assistant: Lauren Aylward
Production Project Manager: Lynn Savino Wendel
Senior Development Editor: Gerald Lombardi
Editor in Chief, History: Priscilla McGeehon
Editor in Chief, Development: Rochelle Diogenes
Editorial Director: Leah Jewell
Associate Supplements Editor: Emsal Hasan
Director of Marketing: Brandy Dawson
Executive Marketing Manager: Sue Westmoreland
Senior Marketing Manager: Laura Lee Manley
Marketing Assistant: Ashley Fallon
AV Project Manager: Mirella Signoretto
Manager, Rights and Permissions: Zina Arabia

Manager, Visual Research: Beth Brenzel
Image Permission Coordinator: Craig A. Jones
Cover Image Specialist: Karan Sanatar
Photo Researcher: Francelle Carapetyan
Composition/Full Service Project Management: Rebecca Dunn, Prepare, Inc.
Director, Media & Assessment: Brian Hyland
Media Editor: Sarah Kinney
Media Project Manager: Tina Rudowski
Senior Operations Specialist: Mary Ann Gloriande
Senior Art Director: Maria Lange
Interior and Cover Designer: QT Design
Printer/Binder: Courier Kendallville
Cover Printer: Lehigh-Phoenix Color/Hagerstown

DK Maps designed and produced by DK Education, a division of Dorling Kindersley Limited, 80 Strand, London WC2R ORL. DK and the DK logo are registered trademarks of Dorling Kindersley Limited.

This book was set in 11/13 Minion.
Credits and acknowledgments borrowed from other sources and reproduced, with permission, in this textbook appear on appropriate page within text or on page C-1.

Library of Congress Cataloging-in-Publication Data
Fernández-Armesto, Felipe.
   The world : a history / Felipe Fernandez-Armesto. -- Combined vol., 2nd ed.
      p. cm.
   Maps by Dorling Kindersley.
   Includes index.
   ISBN 978-0-13-606147-2 (combined)—ISBN 978-0-205-65501-4 (exam)—ISBN 978-0-13-606148-9 (v. 1)—
   ISBN 978-0-13-606149-6 (v. 2)—ISBN 978-0-205-68347-5 (v. a)—ISBN 978-0-13-608757-1 (v. b)—ISBN 978-0-13-606150-2 (v. c)
      1. Civilization--History. 2. Human ecology. I. Title.
   CB151.F48 2007
   909—dc22   2008050926

10 9 8 7 6 5 4 3 2 1

Prentice Hall
is an imprint of

ISBN 10:   0-13-608757-4
ISBN 13: 978-0-13-608757-1

Brief Contents

Contents

"So far, we know of nowhere else in the cosmos where so much has happened and is happening today. By galactic standards, global history is a small story—but it is a good one"   xvi

PART 5   Contacts and Conflicts, 1000 C.E. to 1200 C.E.   337

11   Contending with Isolation: ca. 1000–1200   338

"In the preindustrial world, the size of states and the scope of economies were functions of time as well as distance. Messages, armies, revenues, and cargoes took a long time to travel across broken country or, by sea, through variable winds."   369

"Yet the hostility of nomads and farmers arose, less perhaps, from conflicts of interest than from mutual misunderstanding: a clash of cultures, incompatible ways of seeing the world and coping with it." 403

PART 6

The Crucible: The Eurasian Crises of the Thirteenth and Fourteenth Centuries   409

"Without the Mongol peace, it is hard to imagine any of the rest of world history working out quite as it did, for these were the roads that carried Chinese ideas and transmitted technology westward and opened up European minds to the vastness of the world." 437

"Climate and microbes belong to two rebellious realms of nature that resist human power." 444

"The world did not wait passively for European outreach to transform it, as if touched by a magic wand. Other societies were already working magic of their own, turning states into empires and cultures into civilizations." 484

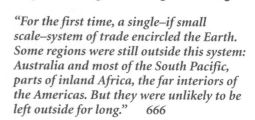

"Despite the shortcomings of their missionaries or of their congregations, the enormous extensions of the frontiers of Islam, Buddhism, and Christianity remains one of the most conspicuous features of the world of the sixteenth and seventeenth centuries." 631

"For the first time, a single–if small scale–system of trade encircled the Earth. Some regions were still outside this system: Australia and most of the South Pacific, parts of inland Africa, the far interiors of the Americas. But they were unlikely to be left outside for long." 666

"The New Europes made the West big. A culture crammed, for most of its history, into a small, remote, and beleaguered corner of Eurasia now had much of the western hemisphere and important parts of the Pacific and of Africa at its disposal."   702

Contents

THE BIG PICTURE

A CLOSER LOOK

Special Features

Projection

A map projection is used to portray all or part of the round Earth on a flat surface, which cannot be done without some distortion. The projections in *The World* show the Earth at global, continental, country, and city scale and vary with each map. The map shown here uses a Robinson projection, which uses curvature to provide a good balance between the size and shape of the lands being depicted. As any number of projections could have been selected for each map in *The World*, great care was shown in choosing projections that best serve the goals of the author.

M aps use a unique visual language to convey a great deal of information in a relatively simple form. The maps in this book use a variety of different projections—techniques used to show the Earth's curved surface on a flat map—to trace the history of humans from about 150,000 years ago to the present. This brief guide explains the different features on the maps in *The World*, Second Edition and how to interpret the different layers of information embedded in them.

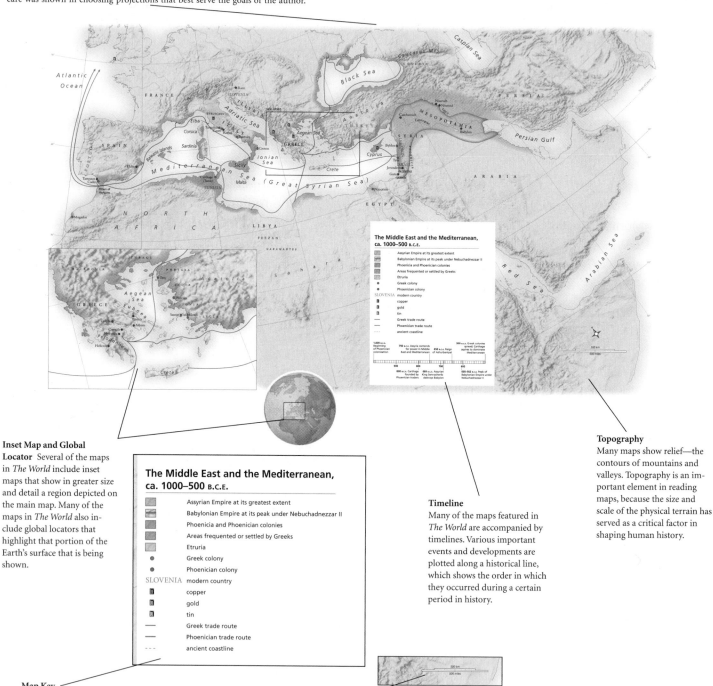

Inset Map and Global Locator

Several of the maps in *The World* include inset maps that show in greater size and detail a region depicted on the main map. Many of the maps in *The World* also include global locators that highlight that portion of the Earth's surface that is being shown.

Timeline

Many of the maps featured in *The World* are accompanied by timelines. Various important events and developments are plotted along a historical line, which shows the order in which they occurred during a certain period in history.

Topography

Many maps show relief—the contours of mountains and valleys. Topography is an important element in reading maps, because the size and scale of the physical terrain has served as a critical factor in shaping human history.

The Middle East and the Mediterranean, ca. 1000–500 B.C.E.

- Assyrian Empire at its greatest extent
- Babylonian Empire at its peak under Nebuchadnezzar II
- Phoenicia and Phoenician colonies
- Areas frequented or settled by Greeks
- Etruria
- ● Greek colony
- ● Phoenician colony
- SLOVENIA modern country
- copper
- gold
- tin
- —— Greek trade route
- —— Phoenician trade route
- --- ancient coastline

Map Key

Maps use symbols to both show the location of a feature and to give information about that feature. The symbols are explained in the key that accompanies each map.

Scalebar

When using a map to work out what distances are in reality, it is necessary to refer to the scale of that particular map. Many of the maps in *The World* (such as the one shown here) use a linear scale. This only works on equal-area maps, where distances are true. On maps with projections that are heavily curved, a special "perspective-scale graphic" is used to show distance.

KEY TO MAP FEATURES IN *THE WORLD*, SECOND EDITION

PHYSICAL FEATURES

— coastline

----- ancient coastline

— river

········· ancient river course

━━ canal

▢ glacier

▨ ancient lake

▦ marshland

▢ ice cap / sheet

▢ ice shelf

△ elevation above sea level (mountain height)

⌂ volcano

⋈ pass

LATITUDE/LONGITUDE

— equator

— lines of latitude / longitude

----- tropics / polar circles

45° degrees of longitude / latitude

BORDERS

— international border

············ undefined border

--- maritime border

— internal border

········· disputed border

COMMUNICATIONS

— major road

— minor road

▪▬▪ major railway

SETTLEMENT / POSSESSION

○ settlement symbol

◇ colonial possession

TYPOGRAPHIC KEY

REGIONS

state / political region..... LAOS

administrative region within a state..................... HENAN

cultural / undefined region / group.................... FERGHANA

SETTLEMENTS

settlement / symbol location / definition...... Farnham

MISCELLANEOUS

tropics / polar circles.......... Antarctic Circle

people / cultural group..... Samoyeds

annotation........................... **1914** British protectorate

PHYSICAL FEATURES

continent / ocean..... AFRICA

INDIAN OCEAN

landscape features.....Mekong

Lake Rudolf

Tien Shan

Sahara

Major land borders are shown using a solid line.

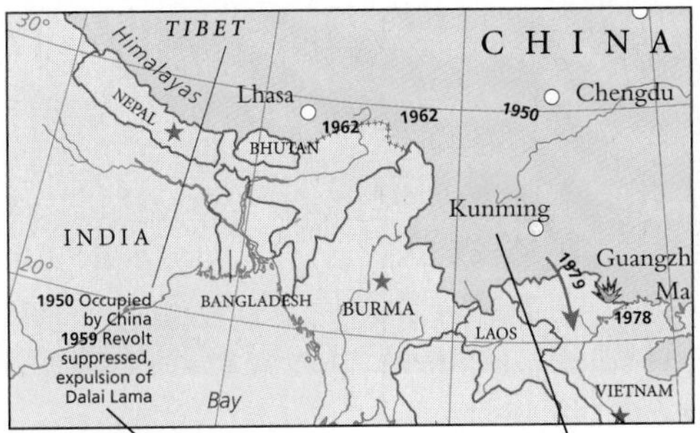

Annotations provide additional explanatory information.

Political control is identified by color.

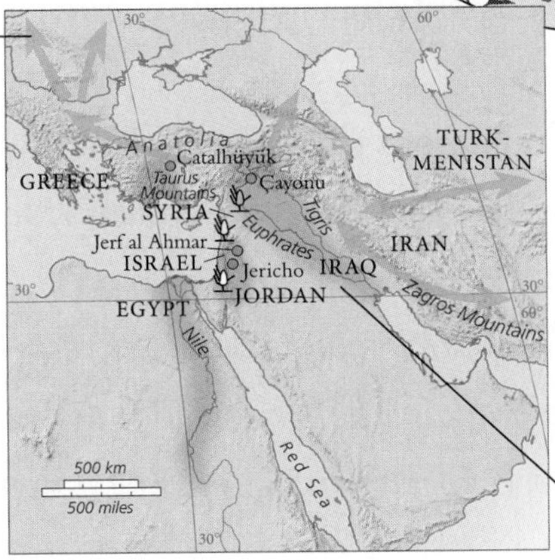

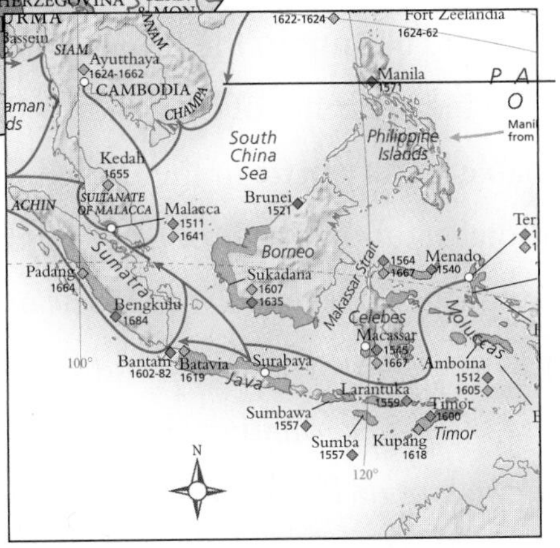

Thin arrows indicate journeys, trade routes, or campaigns.

Broad arrows indicate general movement or spread of ideas, crops, or goods.

Diffused colors are used to show a general region.

About Felipe Fernández-Armesto

Felipe Fernández-Armesto holds the William P. Reynolds Chair of History at the University of Notre Dame. He has master's and doctoral degrees from the University of Oxford, where he spent most of his teaching career, before taking up the Chair of Global Environmental History at Queen Mary College, University of London, in 2000, and the Prince of Asturias Chair at Tufts University (2005–2009). He is on the editorial boards of the History of Cartography for the University of Chicago Press, Studies in Overseas History (Leiden University), *Comparative Studies in Society and History, Journeys,* and *Journal of Global History.* Recent awards include the World History Association Book Prize (2007), Spain's Premio Nacional de Gastronomía (2005, for his work on the history of food), and the Premio Nacional de Investigación (Sociedad Geográfica Española, 2004). He has had many distinguished visiting appointments, including a Fellowship of the Netherlands Institute of Advanced Study in the Humanities and Social Sciences and a Union Pacific Visiting Professorship at the University of Minnesota. He won the Caird Medal of the National Maritime Museum in 1995 and the John Carter Brown Medal in 1999 and has honorary doctorates from La Trobe University and the Universidad de los Andes. He has served on the Council of the Hakluyt Society, on the Committee of English PEN, and as Chairman of the PEN Literary Foundation. His work in journalism includes regular columns in the British and Spanish press, and, among his many contributions to broadcasting, he is the longest-serving presenter of BBC radio's flagship current affairs program, *Analysis.* He has been short-listed for the most valuable literary prize in the United Kingdom.

Fernández-Armesto is the author, coauthor, or editor of 30 books and numerous papers and scholarly articles. His work has been translated into 25 languages. His books include *Before Columbus; The Times Illustrated History of Europe; Columbus; Millennium: A History of the Last Thousand Years* (the subject of a ten-part series on CNN); *Civilizations: Culture, Ambition, and the Transformation of Nature; Near a Thousand Tables; The Americas; Humankind: A Brief History; Ideas that Changed the World; The Times Atlas of World Exploration; The Times Guide to the Peoples of Europe; Amerigo: The Man Who Gave His Name to America;* and *Pathfinders: A Global History of Exploration.*

Dear Reader,

History is stories. There are hundreds of tales in this book about real, flesh-and-blood people—commoners and kings, sons and mothers, heroes and villains, the famous and the failed. I try to combine them in two narratives that crisscross throughout the book. One is the story of how people connect and separate, as cultures take shape and influence and change one another. Alongside this story, there is another one of how humans interact with the rest of nature—other species, the unstable natural environment, the dynamic planet.

History is global. The whole world stays in view in almost every chapter. Readers can compare and connect what was happening in every region and every continent in every period—like observers from another galaxy, gazing at the world from outer space and seeing it whole.

History is universal. This book tries to say something about every sphere of life—including science and art, suffering and pleasure, thought and imagination.

History is a problem-posing discipline. This book is full of provocations, contested claims, debated speculations, open horizons, and questions too complex and too interesting to answer easily. I employ facts not just for their own sake but also to make my readers—and myself—think.

History is evidence. Readers of this book confront the sources on every page—the words, images, and objects people really used in the past—to reveal vivid pictures of what history looked like and what it felt like to live in the past.

History enhances life. I believe that a textbook can be entertaining, even amusing, as well as instructive and accessible; challenging without being hostile; friendly without being cloying.

History isn't over. This book is about how the world got to be the way it is, confronting present problems and perspectives for the future—which is, after all, only the past that hasn't yet happened.

Felipe Fernández-Armesto

INTRODUCING THE WORLD

By the standards of astronauts, say, or science fiction writers, historians seem timid, unadventurous creatures who are only interested in one puny species—our species, the human species—on one tiny planet—our planet, Earth. But Earth is special. So far, we know of nowhere else in the cosmos where so much has happened and is happening today. By galactic standards, global history is a small story—but it's a good one.

Humans, moreover, compared with other animals, seem outward looking. Our concerns range over the universe, and beyond it, to unseen worlds, vividly imagined or mysteriously revealed. Not just everything we do but also everything that occurs to our minds is part of our history and, therefore, is part of this book, including science and art, fun and philosophy, speculations and dreams. We continually generate stories—new stories—at an amazing rate.

But the present passes instantly into the past. The present is always over, transformed into history. And the past is always with us, tugging at our memories, shaping our thoughts, launching and limiting our lives. Human history may seem narrowly self-interested, but it focuses on an undeniably riveting subject that is also our favorite subject—ourselves.

THE WAY OF HUMANKIND

Although the story of this book is a human story, it can never be merely human because, in isolation humankind does not make perfect sense. Humans are animals, and to understand ourselves thoroughly and to know what, if anything, makes us unique, we have to compare ourselves with other animals. As with other animals, we are best studied in our habitats. We cannot begin to comprehend our own history except in context. Our story is inseparable from the climates where it takes place and the other life forms that we depend on or compete with. We lord it over other species, but we remain linked to them by the food chain. We transform our environment, but we can never escape from it. We differentiate ourselves from nature—we speak loosely, for instance, of nature as if we were not natural creatures ourselves. We distance ourselves from our fellow-animals by adopting what we think are unnatural behaviors—wearing clothes, for instance, cooking food, replacing nature with culture. In short, we do what is natural to us, and all the elaborate culture we produce generates new, intimate relationships with the environment we refashion and the life forms we exploit.

We are exceptionally ambitious compared to other animals, consciously remodeling environments to suit our own purposes. We carve out fields, turn prairies into wheat lands, deserts into gardens, and gardens into deserts. We fell forests where we find them and plant them where none exist; we dam rivers, wall seas, cultivate plants, breed creatures, extinguish some species, and call others into being by selection and hybridization. Sometimes we smother terrain with environments we build for ourselves. Yet none of these practices liberates us from nature. As we shall see, one of the paradoxes of the human story is that the more we change the environment, the more vulnerable we become to ecological lurches and unpredictable disasters. Failure to establish the right balance between exploitation and conservation has often left civilizations in ruins. History becomes a path picked across the wreckage. This does not mean that the environment determines our behavior or our lives, but it does set the framework in which we act.

We are an exceptionally successful species in terms of our ability to survive in a wide range of diverse climates and landscapes—more so than just about any other creature, except for the microbes we carry around with us. But even we are still explorers of our planet, engaged in an ongoing effort to change it. Indeed, we have barely begun to change planet Earth, though, as we shall see, some human societies have devoted the last ten thousand years to trying to do it. We call ourselves lords, or, more modestly, caretakers of creation, but about 90 percent of the biosphere is too far underwater or too deep below the Earth for us to inhabit with the technology we have at present: These are environments that humans have only recently begun to invade and that we still do not dominate.

If we humans are peculiarly ambitious creatures, who are always intruding in the life of the planet, we are also odd compared to other animals in the way we generate change among ourselves. We are an unpredictable, unstable species. Lots of other animals live social lives and construct societies. But those societies are remarkably stable compared to ours. As far as we know, ants and elephants have the same lifeways and the same kinds of relationships that they have had since their species first appeared. That is not to say animals never change their cultures. One of the fascinating discoveries in primatology is that apes and monkeys develop cultural differences from one another, even between groups living in similar and sometimes adjacent environments. In one forest region of Gabon in West Africa, chimpanzees have developed a termite-catching technology. They "fish" with stripped branches that they plunge into termite nests but do not use tools to break open nuts. Chimps in a neighboring region ignore the termites but are experts in nut cracking, using rocks like hammers and anvils. In Sumatra in Indonesia, orangutans play a game—jumping from falling trees—that is unknown to their cousins in nearby Borneo. In Ethiopia in East Africa, males in some baboon groups control harems while others nearby have one mate after another. In some chimpanzee societies, hunting and meat eating seem to have increased dramatically in recent times.

These are amazing facts, but the societies of nonhuman animals still change little compared with ours. So, alongside the theme of human interaction with the rest of nature is another great theme of our history: the ways our societies have changed, grown apart from one another, reestablished contact, and influenced one another in their turn.

THE WAY OF THIS BOOK

This book, then, interweaves two stories—stories of our interactions with nature and stories of our interactions with each other. The environment-centered story is about humans distancing themselves from the rest of nature and searching for a relationship that strikes a balance between constructive and destructive exploitation. The culture-centered story is of how human cultures have become mutually influential and yet mutually differentiating. Both stories have been going on for thousands of years. We do not know whether they will end in triumph or disaster.

There is no prospect of covering all of world history in one book. Rather, the fabric of this book is woven from selected strands. Readers will see these at every turn, twisted together into yarn, stretched into stories. Human-focused historical ecology—the environmental theme—will drive readers back, again and again, to the same concepts: sustenance, shelter, disease, energy, technology, art. (The last is a vital category for historians, not only because it is part of our interface with the rest of the world, but also because it forms a record of how we see reality and of how the way we see it changes.) In the global story of human interactions—the cultural theme—we return constantly to the ways people make contact with each another: migration, trade, war, imperialism, pilgrimage, gift exchange, diplomacy, travel—and to their social frameworks: the economic and political arenas, the human groups and groupings, the states and civilizations, the sexes and generations, the classes and clusters of identity.

The stories that stretch before us are full of human experience. "The stork feeds on snakes," said the ancient Greek sage, Agathon, "the pig on acorns, and history on human lives." The only way to build up our picture of human societies and ecosystems of the past is to start with the evidence people have left. Then we reassemble it bit by bit, with the help of imagination disciplined by the sources. Anyone reading a history book needs to bear in mind that interpreting evidence is a challenge—half burden and half opportunity. The subject matter of history is not the past directly because the past is never available to our senses. We have only the evidence about it. This makes history an art, not a science, an art disciplined by respect for the sources, just as patterns impose discipline on poets or as the limitations of stagecraft discipline a play.

For a book like this, the sources set the limits of my imagination. Sometimes these are concrete clues to what people really did—footprints of their wanderings, debris of their meals, fragments of their technologies, wreckage of their homes, traces of diseases in their bones. Usually, however, the sources do not reflect the way things were but the way people wished to represent them in their arts and crafts and writings. In short, most sources are evidence of what happened only in the minds of those who made them. This means, in turn, that our picture of what went on in the world beyond human minds is always tentative and open to reinterpretation. The historian's job is not—cannot be—to say what the past was like, but rather, what it felt like to live in it because that is what the evidence tends to reveal.

One of the most admirable historians of the twentieth century, R. G. Collingwood, who was also a professor of philosophy at Oxford, said that "all history is intellectual history." He was right. History—even the environmental and cultural history that is the subject of this book—is largely about what people perceived rather than what they really saw, what they thought or felt rather than what happened outwardly, what they represented rather than what was real. The nineteenth-century philosopher Arthur Schopenhauer, one of the most pessimistic thinkers ever, who drew on Hindu and Buddhist writings for his inspiration, said that history's only subject was "humankind's oppressive, muddlesome dream." He thought that made history pointless. I think the dream makes it intriguing.

Because the evidence is always incomplete, history is not so much a matter of describing or narrating or question-answering as it is a matter of problem-posing. No one reading this book should expect to be instructed in straightforward facts or to acquire proven knowledge. The thrill of history is asking the right question, not getting the right answer. Most of the time, the most we can hope for is to identify interesting problems that stimulate debate. And we have to accept that the debate is worthwhile for its own sake, even if we have insufficient knowledge to reach conclusions.

There is no agreement among historians even about what are the right sorts of questions to ask. Some—including me—are interested in huge philosophical questions, such as how does history happen? What makes change? Is it random or is it subject to scientific laws? Do impersonal forces beyond human control—environmental factors or economics or some world force called fate or evolution or God or progress—determine it? Or is change the externalization of ideas, which arise in minds and are projected onto the world through human action? And if it's a mixture, what's the balance?

At a slightly lower level of analysis, some historians ask questions about how human societies function. How and why do societies grow and fragment and take different forms? How do some people get power over others? How and why do revolutions happen and states and civilizations rise and fall?

Other historians like to pose problems about the present. How did we get into the mess we're in? Can we trace the causes of present dilemmas back into the past and, if so, how far? Why do we have a globally connected world without global governance? Why is peace always precarious? Why does ecological overkill menace our global environment? Having accounted—or failed to account—for the present, some historians like to focus on the future. They demand lessons from history about how to change our behavior or cope with recurrences of past difficulties. Others, again, search to make sense of the past, to find an overall way of characterizing it or narrating it that makes us feel we understand it.

Yet others—the majority, in the current state of historical fashion, and again including me—like to study the past for its own sake and try to identify the questions that mattered to people at the time they first asked them. This does not mean that the sort of history found in this book is useless (although I do not necessarily think it would be a bad thing if it were). For to penetrate the minds of people of the past—especially the remote past of cultures other than your own—you have to make a supreme effort of understanding. The effort has dividends for the person who practices it. It enhances life by sharpening responses to the streetscapes and landscapes, art and artifacts, laws and letters we have inherited from the past. And understanding is what we need most today in our multicultural societies and multicivilizational world.

HOW THIS BOOK IS ARRANGED

After finding the time, accumulating the knowledge, posing the questions, stiffening the sinews, and summoning the blood, the big problem for the writer of a global history textbook is organizing the material. The big problem for the reader is navigating it. It is tempting to divide the world up into regions or cultures or even—as I did in a previous book—into biomes and devote successive chapters to each. You could call that "world history," if you genuinely managed to cover the world. But "global history" is different: an attempt to see the planet whole, as if from an immense, astral height, and discern themes that truly transcend geographical and cultural boundaries. In this book, therefore, I try to look at every continent in just about every chapter (there are a couple of chapters that, for reasons described in their place, focus only on part of the world). Each chapter concentrates on themes from the two great global stories: how human societies diverge and converge, and how they interact with the rest of nature.

Because history is a story in which the order of events matters, the chapters are grouped into 10 parts, arranged chronologically. There are 30 chapters—one for each week in a typical U.S. academic year (though of course, every reader or group of readers will go at their own pace)—and 10 parts. I hope there is plenty to surprise readers without making the parts perversely defiant of the "periods" historians conventionally speak of. Part I runs from roughly 150,000 to roughly 20,000 years ago, and, on the whole, the periods covered get shorter as sources accumulate, cultures diverge, data multiply, and readers' interests quicken. Of course, no one should be misled into thinking the parts are more than devices of convenience. Events that happened in, say, 1850, are in a different part of this book from those that happened in, say 1750. But the story is continuous, and the parts could equally well be recrafted to start and end at different moments.

At every stage, some parts of the world are more prominent than others because they are more influential, more populous, more world-shaping. For great stretches of the book, China occupies relatively more space; this is not for reasons of political correctness, but because China has, for much of the past, been immensely rich in globally influential initiatives. In the coverage of the last couple of hundred years, Europe and the United States get a lot of attention: this is not "Eurocentrism" or "Westocentrism" (if there is such a word), but an honest reflection of how history happened. But I have tried not to neglect the peoples and parts of the world that historians usually undervalue: poor and peripheral communities sometimes have a stunning impact on the world. The margins and frontiers of the world are often where world-changing events happen—the fault lines of civilizations, which radiate seismic effects.

Learning Features for the Second Edition of *The World*

The pedagogical program for the Second Edition of *The World* has been carefully devised to complement the narrative, reinforce important concepts, and prompt students to ask questions and formulate arguments.

Chapter-opening vignettes use dramatic and unusual stories to put the main themes of each chapter in relief. One-third of the chapter-opening vignettes in the Second Edition are new.

Focus Questions open each chapter and encourage students to think critically about the key questions raised in each chapter.

Making Connections tables throughout the text help students see the global linkages behind important historical developments. Praised by users of *The World,* every chapter in the Second Edition now includes at least one, and in some cases, as many as three, Making Connections tables. New Making Connections tables have been added to Chapters 9, 13, 15, 20, 21, 22, and 26. To further improve their visual efficacy, locator maps showing the regions examined in each Making Connections table have been added to the Second Edition.

A Closer Look sections, one per chapter, provide in-depth visual analysis of a specific cultural artifact. Praised by users for the way in which they connect the macro with the micro, detailed notes and tie lines draw the reader into close contact with the object, providing opportunities to pose larger questions. Users of *The World* have consistently cited the Closer Look sections as effective learning tools for their students. One-third of the Closer Look sections in the Second Edition are new. See page xxvii for a complete listing.

Maps Widely hailed by users of the First Edition, the maps in *The World* employ innovative perspectives to help the reader see world history in a fresh and dynamic way. A range of different maps—from two-page thematic maps to spot maps that pinpoint specific events—connect with the discussion on a variety of different levels. Each map in the Second Edition has been extensively checked for accuracy and/or re-drafted to improve its graphical presentation. The Second Edition includes 35 new full-size maps and 102 new locator maps. See page xxi for a listing of the maps in the Second Edition.

NEW The Big Picture Building on the success of the map program for the First Edition, each of the 10 parts in *The World* now ends with "The Big Picture," a two-page map of the world that graphically highlights an important, pivotal development in global history. Accompanied by text and questions, each Big Picture map provides the reader with a visual snapshot of what the world looked like at key intervals in human history. Interactive versions of the Big Picture maps can be found on MyHistoryLab. Short video clips of the author discussing developments in global history related to the Big Picture maps are also available on the MyHistoryLab that accompanies the text.

Visual Sources Users of *The World* consistently rank its photo program as the best found in any textbook available today. Intimately connected to the narrative, each photo provides a compelling visual record, from mammoth huts to satellite images of the Earth from space. Detailed captions, crafted by the author, explicate the meaning behind each visual source. There are over 100 new photos in the Second Edition of *The World.*

In Perspective sections conclude each chapter and do much more than summarize the preceding discussion. They put the developments covered in the chapter into historical perspective, and they make explicit for the student the process by which historians interpret the past.

Chronologies throughout each chapter arrange key historical developments in the order in which they occurred.

Key Terms are defined in the Glossary and set in boldface type in the text.

In-text Pronunciation Guides, embedded directly in the text, provide phonetic spellings for unfamiliar words.

CHANGES TO THE SECOND EDITION

The many helpful readers' reports and reviews of the First Edition by both users and non-users formed the basis for preparing the Second Edition. Every chapter was either updated with new and accepted scholarship or reorganized to clarify its presentation. In many chapters, more substantive changes were made in response to feedback and advice from teachers.

Chapters 1–15

Chapter 1 now begins with a discussion of Imo, the famous Japanese macaque. Chapter 2 examines the archaeological remains of an ancient feast to highlight the main problems of the chapter. Chapter 3 now begins with a discussion of Queen Hatshepsut's expedition to Punt. In Chapter 5, coverage of Babylon and classical Greece has been expanded. Chapter 6 now includes a new section on the Israelites and more discussion of Buddhism. Discussion of Rome has been increased in Chapter 7. Chapter 8 includes fuller treatment of Tang China. Chapter 9 now provides an overview of the main tenets of the major world religions. Chapter 10 opens with a story of Queen Gudit of Ethiopia. Both the Crusades and Ghana are examined in more depth in Chapter 12. The Renaissance receives more discussion in Chapter 15.

Chapters 16–30

The "In Perspective" section in Chapter 16 has been extensively revised and enhanced. The opening vignette for Chapter 17 now tells the story of Charles Ledger and quinine; the "In Perspective" section for this chapter has also been expanded. Chapter 18 now opens with a vignette about the experience of Siamese ambassadors in eighteenth-century France, and it examines the Protestant Reformation in more depth. The "In Perspective" sections in Chapters 19 and 20 have been expanded significantly. Chapter 21 provides more extensive treatment of the wars for independence in Latin America. Chapter 22 now includes more coverage of the French Revolution and the Napoleonic wars. Chapter 24 provides a new discussion of feminism in both Egypt and the United States. Chapter 25 has increased coverage of the Scramble for Africa. Chapter 26 includes new discussion of nationalism and state formation in Japan, Germany, Italy, and the United States. Chapter 29 now opens with the story of Dolores Jimenez and her role in the Mexican Revolution. Chapters 28 and 30 have been updated with important new information pertaining to the history of the twentieth century and the first decade of the twenty-first century: political and social developments, financial crises, and global warming.

SUPPORT MATERIALS

The World, Second Edition, comes with an extensive package of support materials for teachers and students.

For Instructors

◆ **The Instructor's Manual/Test-Item File** includes chapter outlines, overviews, key concepts, discussion questions, teaching notes, map quizzes, and suggestions for audiovisual resources, as well as approximately 1,500 test items. Particular emphasis is placed on essay questions that test students' understanding of concepts across chapters.

◆ **Test Manager** is a computerized test management program for Windows and Macintosh environments. The program allows instructors to select items from the test-item file to create tests. It also allows for online testing.

◆ **The Instructor's Resource Center** (*www.pearsonhighered.com*) Text-specific materials, such as the instructor's manual, the test-item file, map files, digital transparencies and PowerPoint™ presentations, are available for downloading by adopters.

For Instructors and Students

◆ *http://www.myhistorylab.com* MyHistory-Lab for *The World* offers students and instructors a state-of-the-art, interactive learning tool for world history. Organized by the main subtopics of *The World*, and delivered within a course-management platform, MyHistoryLab supplements and enriches the classroom experience and can form the basis for an online course. New interactive Big Picture Maps and videos of the author outlining key developments in world history now enrich the MyHistoryLab for *The World*. Audio summaries of the main concepts in each chapter are also available for downloading to MP3 players. Please contact your Pearson representative for details.

◆  **NEW** *Around the World in Sixty Minutes Video Series*. In response to overwhelming requests from instructors and students around the country, Pearson Prentice Hall and Felipe Fernández-Armesto have teamed up to produce a ten-part video series that covers key, transformative develop-

ments in world history from the beginnings of agriculture to the world we inhabit today. Each segment in the Series is approximately 4–6 minutes in length and features Fernández-Armesto discussing pivotal changes in human history: the beginnings of agriculture, the axial age, the rise of world religions, the tensions between pastoralists and settled societies, the age of the plague, human transplantations, the Enlightenment, the Industrial Revolution, and the paradoxes of the twentieth century. Shot in various locations, and interspersed with photos and historical footage, each video in the Series can serve as an ideal lecture launcher in the classroom or as a self-directed review opportunity for students. Questions at the end of each segment allow students to respond with short essays and submit electronically via MyHistoryLab. A demo video clip can be viewed at www.pearsonhighered.com/the world.

As a further enrichment to the Series, each video is part of an integrated "learning zone" that also includes an interactive version of the Big Picture map that ends each of the ten Parts in *The World*.

◆  **NEW** **Interactive Big Picture Maps** feature the same maps as those in the text, rendered as globes that can be spun. Interactive icons on the globe allow students to explore visual and textual sources, which are linked to the e-book that accompanies *The World*.

The result is a rich, dynamic, and integrated learning experience that combines video, audio, visual sources, and text documents to reinforce the inquiry-based approach that sets *The World* apart from other books. A demonstration map can be viewed at www.pearsonhighered.com/theworld.

POPULAR VALUEPACKS FOR *THE WORLD*

◆ Titles from the renowned **Penguin Classics** series can be bundled with *The World* for a nominal charge. Please contact your Pearson Arts and Sciences sales representative for details.

◆ **Connections: Key Themes in World History**. Series Editor Alfred J. Andrea. Concise and tightly focused, the titles in the popular Connections Series are designed to place the latest research on selected topics of global significance, such as disease, trade, slavery, exploration, and modernization, into an accessible format for students. Available at a 50% discount when bundled with *The World*. For more information go to www.pearsonhighered.com.

◆ Getz/Hoffman/Rodriguez, *Exchanges: A Global History Reader* introduces students to the discipline of world history. Unlike other source collections, *Exchanges* helps students look beyond strictly delineated regionalism and chronological structures to understand history as a series of ongoing debates. Available at a 50% discount when bundled with *The World*.

Clark, *A Guide to Your History Course: What Every Student Needs to Know.* This concise, spiral-bound guidebook orients students to the issues and problems they will face in the history classroom. Available at a 50% discount when bundled with *The World*.

◆ **The Prentice Hall Atlas of World History, Second Edition** includes over 100 full-color maps in world history, drawn by Dorling Kindersley, one of the world's most respected cartographic publishers. Copies of the Atlas can be bundled with *The World* for a nominal charge. Contact your Pearson sales representative for details.

For Students

◆ Extensively revised and updated, the **Primary Source: Documents in Global History DVD** is both a rich collection of textual and visual documents in world history and an indispensable tool for working with sources. Extensively developed with the guidance of historians and teachers, the revised and updated DVD version includes over 800 sources in world history—from cave art to satellite images of the Earth from space. More sources from Africa, Latin America, and Southeast. Asia have been added to this revised and updated DVD version. All sources are accompanied by headnotes and focus questions, and are searchable by topic, region, or time period.

◆ **World History Study Site** (*www.pearsonhighered.com*) This course-based, open-access online companion provides a wealth of resources for both students and professors, including test questions, flash cards, links for further research, and Web-based assignments.

◆ **CourseSmart Textbooks Online** is an exciting new choice for students looking to save money. As an alternative to purchasing the print textbook, students can subscribe to the same content online and save up to 50% off the suggested list price of the print text. With a CourseSmart eTextbook, students can search the text, make notes online, print out reading assignments that incorporate lecture notes, and bookmark important passages for later review. For more information, or to subscribe to the CourseSmart eTextbook, visit *www.coursesmart.com*.

ACKNOWLEDGMENTS

Without being intrusive, I have tried not to suppress my presence—my voice, my views—in the text because no book is objective, other than by pretense, and the reader is entitled to get to know the writer's foibles and failures. In overcoming mine, I have had a lot of help (though there are sure still to be errors and shortcomings through my fault alone). Textbooks are teamwork, and I have learned an immense amount from my friends and helpers at Pearson Prentice Hall, especially my editors, Charles Cavaliere and Gerald Lombardi, whose indefatigability and forbearance made the book better at every turn. Laura Lee Manley, senior marketing manager, and Sue Westmoreland, Executive Marketing Manager, for their creativity. I also thank the picture researcher Francelle Carapetyan, and the members of the production and cartographic sections of the team who performed Herculean labors: Ann Marie McCarthy, senior managing editor; Lynn Savino Wendel, production project manager; Mirella Signoretto, map project manager; and David Roberts, cartographer.

I also owe a debt of gratitude to the senior management team at Pearson Prentice Hall who supported this endeavor every step of the way: Bill Barke, CEO, Pearson Arts & Sciences, Yolanda de Rooy, president of the Humanities and Social Sciences division; Leah Jewell, editorial director; Priscilla McGeehon, editor-in-chief for history; Rochelle Diogenes, editor-in-chief for development; and Brandy Dawson, director of marketing.

I could not have gotten through the work without the help and support of my wonderful colleagues at Queen Mary, University of London; the Institute of Historical Research, University of London; and the History Department of Tufts University. I owe special thanks to the many scholars who share and still share their knowledge of global history at the Pearson Prentice Hall Seminar Series in Global History, and through the World History Association, the *Journal of Global History,* the *Journal of World History,* and H-NET. David Ringrose of University of California, San Diego, was a constant guide, whose interest never flagged and whose wisdom never failed. Many colleagues and counterparts advised me on their fields of expertise or performed heroic self-sacrifice in putting all of the many pieces of the book together: Natia Chakvetadze, Shannon Corliss, Maria Guarascio, Anita Castro, Conchita Ordonez, Sandra Garcia, Maria Garcia, Hector Grillone, the late Jack Betterley, Jeremy Greene, Jai Kharbanda, Ernest Tucker (United States Naval Academy), Steve Ortega (Simmons College), David Way (British Library), Antony Eastmond (Courtland Institute), Morris Rossabi (Columbia University), David Atwill and Jade Atwill (Pennsylvania State University), Stephen Morillo (Wabash College), Peter Carey (Oxford University), Jim Mallory (Queens University, Belfast), Matthew Restall (Pennsylvania State University), Roderick Whitfield (School of Oriental and African Studies, University of London), Barry Powell (University of Wisconsin), Leonard Blussé (Harvard University), Guolong Lai (University of Florida), Frank Karpiel (The Citadel), George Kosar (Tufts University), David Kalivas and Eric Martin of H-NET and the many subscribers to their service who commented on the book or posted or e-mailed queries and suggestions, and the faculty, staff, and students of the many colleges where I got the chance to discuss the book (Boston College, Colorado State University, Essex Community College, Georgetown University, Jackson State University, Northern Kentucky University, Ohio State University, Penn State University, St John's University [New York], Salem State University, San José State University, Simmons College, U.S. Air Force Academy, U.S. Naval Academy, University at Buffalo, University of California [San Diego], San Diego State University, University of Arkansas [Little Rock], and University of Memphis) as well as the many good people whose assistance I may have failed to acknowledge.

Felipe Fernández-Armesto
Somerville, Massachusett

DEVELOPING *THE WORLD*

Developing a project like *The World* required the input and counsel of hundreds of individuals. David Ringrose, from the University of California at San Diego served as *The World*'s editorial consultant, closely reading and commenting on every draft of the book. His experience and understanding of classroom issues were invaluable to the development of *The World*. Nearly 100 reviewers critiqued portions of the manuscript from the first to the final draft. In addition, the manuscript was class-tested with over 1,000 students across the country who provided invaluable feedback and advice. Additionally, fifteen focus groups were held with teachers of world history to gather feedback and test ideas. An additional 75 reviewers of critiqued portions of *The World* to help prepare the Second Edition. We thank all those who shared their time and effort to make *The World* a better book.

Reviewers of the First Edition

Donald R. Abbott, San Diego Mesa College
Wayne Ackerson, Salisbury University
Roger Adelson, Arizona State University
Alfred J. Andrea, University of Vermont (Emeritus)
David G. Atwill, Pennsylvania State University
Leonard Blussé, Harvard University
Mauricio Borrero, St. John's University
John Brackett, University of Cincinnati
Gayle K. Brunelle, California State University—Fullerton
Fred Burkhard, Maryland University College
Antoinette Burton, University of Illinois
Jorge Cañizares-Esguerra, University of Texas—Austin
Elaine Carey, St. John's University
Tim Carmichael, College of Charleston
Douglas Chambers, University of Southern Mississippi
Nupur Chaudhuri, Texas Southern University
David Christian, San Diego State University
Duane Corpis, Georgia State University
Dale Crandall-Bear, Solano Community College
Touraj Daryaee, University of California, Irvine
Jeffrey M. Diamond, College of Charleston
Brian Fagan, University of California—Santa Barbara
Nancy Fitch, California State University—Fullerton
Alison Fletcher, Kent State University
Patricia Gajda, The University of Texas at Tyler
Richard Golden, University of North Texas
Stephen S. Gosch, University of Wisconsin—Eau Claire
Jonathan Grant, Florida State University
Mary Halavais, Sonoma State University
Shah M. Hanifi, James Madison University
Russell A. Hart, Hawaii Pacific University
Phyllis G. Jestice, University of Southern Mississippi
Amy J. Johnson, Berry College
Deborah Smith Johnston, Lexington High School
Eric A. Jones, Northern Illinois University
Ravi Kalia, City College of New York
David M. Kalivas, Middlesex Community College
Frank Karpiel, College of Charleston
David Kenley, Marshall University
Andrew J. Kirkendall, Texas A&M University
Dennis Laumann, The University of Memphis
Donald Leech, University of Minnesota

Jennifer M. Lloyd, SUNY—Brockport
Aran MacKinnon, University of West Georgia
Moria Maguire, University of Arkansas—Little Rock
Susan Maneck, Jackson State University
Anthony Martin, Wellesley College
Dorothea Martin, Appalachian State University
Adam McKeown, Columbia University
Ian McNeely, University of Oregon
Margaret E. Menninger, Texas State University—San Marcos
Stephen Morillo, Wabash College
William Morison, Grand Valley State University
Laura Neitzel, Brookdale Community College
Kenneth J. Orosz, University of Maine—Farmington
Michael Pavkovic, Hawaii Pacific University
Phyllis E. Pobst, Arkansas State University
Kenneth Pomeranz, University of California—Irvine
Sara B. Pritchard, Montana State University
Norman Raiford, Greenville Technical College
Stephen Rapp, Georgia State University
Vera Blinn Reber, Shippensburg University
Matthew Redinger, Montana State University—Billings
Matthew Restall, Pennsylvania State University
Jonathan Reynolds, Arkansas State University
Richard Rice, University of Tennessee—-Chattanooga
Peter Rietbergen, Catholic University (Nijmegen)
David Ringrose, University of California—San Diego
Patricia Romero, Towson University
Morris Rossabi, Queens College
David G. Rowley, University of Wisconsin—Platteville
Sharlene Sayegh, California State University—Long Beach
William Schell, Murray State University
Linda Bregstein Scherr, Mercer County Community College
Patricia Seed, University of California, Irvine
Lawrence Sondhaus, University of Indianapolis
Richard Steigmann-Gall, Kent State University
John Thornton, Boston University
Ann Tschetter, University of Nebraska—Lincoln
Deborah Vess, Georgia College & State University
Stephen Vinson, SUNY—New Paltz
Joanna Waley-Cohen, New York University
Anne M. Will, Skagit Valley College
John Wills, University of Southern California
Theodore Jun Yoo, University of Hawaii—Manoa

Introducing The World

Reviewers of the Second Edition

Jeffrey Alexander, Douglas College/The University of British Columbia
Emma Alexander-Mudaliar, University of Winnipeg
Gerald D. Anderson, North Dakota State University
Ellen Arnold, Macalester College
Daniel Ayana, Youngstown State University
Lt. David Bachler, United States Air Force Academy
Alan Baumler, Indiana University of Pennsylvania
Cynthia Bisson, Belmont University
Robert Blackey, California State University—San Bernardino
Robert Bond, Youngstown State University
Connie Brand, Meridian Community College
Tanya Brown, Pittsburgh State University
Byron Canner, University of Utah
Robert Carriedo, United States Air Force Academy
Carole R. Carter, University of Central Arkansas
Martin Scott Catino, University of South Carolina—Aiken
Yuan-ling Chao, Middle Tennessee State University
Gregory Crider, Wingate University
Eric Cunningham, Gonzaga University
Shawn Dry, Oakland Community College
Jeffrey Dym, California State University—Sacramento
Lisa Edwards, University of Massachusetts—Lowell
Jari Eloranta, Appalachian State University
Ken Faunce, Washington State University
Jeffrey Gaab, SUNY College at Farmingdale
Trevor Getz, San Francisco State University
Peter H. Griffin, Lindenwood University
William W. Haddad, California State University—Fullerton
Laura J. Hilton, Muskingum College
Matt Hopper, California Polytechnic State University
Ahmed H. Ibrahim, Missouri State University
Robert Irwin, Grant MacEwan College
Eric Johnson, Pennsylvania State University
Lisa Kazmier, Drexel University
Keith P. Knuuti, University of Hawaii—Windward Community College
Stephen Laffer, Florida State University
Eugene Larson, Los Angeles Pierce College
Paul Lococo Jr., Leeward Community College

David Longfellow, Baylor University
M. Lois Lucas, West Virginia State University
David McCarter, Indiana State University
Tom McCarthy, United States Naval Academy
Emerson Thomas McMullen, Georgia Southern University
Gerald Mills, University of Oklahoma
Ruma Niyogi, Saint Xavier University
Bradley Parker, University of Utah
Charles Parker, St. Louis University
Robert W. Patch, University of California, Riverside
Alice K. Pate, Columbus State University
Patrick Patterson, Honolulu Community College
Patricia M. Pelley, Texas Tech University
Wendy Pojmann, Sienna College
Timothy Pytell, California State University—San Bernardino
Scott S. Reese, Northern Arizona University
Jeremy Rich, Middle Tennessee State University
Paul Richgruber, Minneapolis Community and Tech College; Inver Hills Community College
William S. Rodner, Tidewater Community College
Anthony R. Santoro, Christopher Newport University
Adam R. Seipp, Texas A & M University
Elizabeth Sharpe, Jackson State University
Jeffrey M. Shumway, Brigham Young University
James J. Simon, Genesee Community College
Phillip Luke Sinitiere, University of Houston
Timothy G. Sistrunk, California State University—Chico
Rachel Stocking, Southern Illinois University—Carbondale
Jacky Swansinger, SUNY at Fredonia
Michael Tarver, Arkansas Tech University
Patricia L. Thompson, University of Texas at San Antonio
Kate Transchel, California State University
Mary A. Valante, Appalachian State University
Gilmar Visoni, Queensborough Community College
Paul Voisey, University of Alberta
Rick Warner, Wabash College
Joshua Weiner, American River College
Claude Welch, University at Buffalo, State University of New York
Scott N. West, University of Dayton
Kristina Wilson, Morehead State University

A NOTE ON DATES AND SPELLINGS

In keeping with common practice among historians of global history, we have used B.C.E. (before the common era) and C.E. (common era) to date events. For developments deep in the past, we have employed the phrase "years ago" to convey to the reader a clear sense of time. Specific dates are only given when necessary and when doing so improves the context of the narrative.

Recognizing that almost every non-English word can be transliterated in any number of ways, we have adopted the most widely used and simplest systems for spelling names and terms. The *pinyin* system of Chinese spelling is used for all Chinese words with the exception of such words as *Yangtze*, which are still widely referred to in its Wade-Giles form. Following common usage, we have avoided using apostrophes in the spelling of Arabic and Persian words, as well as words from other languages—thus, *Quran* and *Kaaba* instead of *Qu'ran* and *Ka'ba*, and *Tbilisi* instead of *T'bilisi*. Diacritical marks, accents, and other specialized symbols are used only if the most common variant of a name or term employs such devices (such as *Çatalhüyük*), if they are part of a personal noun (such as *Nicolás*), or if the inclusion of such markings in the spelling of a word makes pronouncing it easier (*Teotihuacán*).

Throughout the text the first appearance of important non-English words whose pronunciation may be unclear for the reader are followed by phonetic spellings in parentheses, with the syllable that is stressed spelled in capital letters. So, for example *Ugarit* is spelled phonetically as "OO-gah-riht." Chinese words are not stressed, so each syllable is spelled in lowercase letters. Thus, the city of Hangzhou in China is rendered phonetically as "hahngjoh." For monosyllabic words, the phonetic spelling is in lowercase letters. So *Rus* is spelled as "roos." The table below provides a guide for how the vowel sounds in *The World* are represented phonetically.

a	as in *cat, bat*
ah	as in *car, father*
aw	as in *law, paw*
ay	as in *fate, same*
eh	as in *bet, met*
ee	as in *beet, ease*
eye	as in *dine, mine*
ih	as in *if, sniff*
o	as in *more, door*
oh	as in *row, slow*
oo	as in *loop, moo*
ow	as in *cow, mouse*
uh	as in *but, rul*

PART 5

ENVIRONMENT

1000–1300
North Atlantic warm spell

CULTURE

ca. 1000
Tale of Genji
(Japan)

1098
First Crusade

Contacts and Conflicts, 1000 C.E. to 1200 C.E.

◀ **The World Map of Al-Idrisi,** a Muslim geographer who worked in Christian-ruled Sicily in the mid-twelfth century. He tried to follow the advice of the ancient Greek geographer, Ptolemy, and constructed his map on a grid. South is at the top. The shape of Arabia is clearly recognizable to a modern eye (upper center).

1000–1200
Transfer of crops from South and Southeast Asia to Islamic world

1040s–1090
Increased steppelander migrations into Middle East

ca. 1070–1122
Chola maritime expansion

900–1200
Growing population, especially in Europe and China

1000–1200
Spread of Islam to West Africa

ca. 1125
Angkor Wat

ca. 1200
Cahokia, height of Mississippian mound building

▲ **A ferocious sea.** The pilgrimages of Buddhist monks inspired Japanese stories about the ferocity of the sea. One of the most popular tales in the late twelfth and early thirteenth centuries was about Gisho, a monk who renounced the love of a beautiful woman and set sail for Korea. But in the incident depicted here, she followed him and flung herself into the sea, where, transformed into a dragon, she protected him from storms.

JAPAN

The farewells lasted "all day and into the night." Aboard ship, the travelers prayed for a peaceful crossing. When the clouds cleared, before dawn, "oars pierced the moon's reflection." Winds lashed. Typhoons threatened. Pirates lurked. The voyagers appealed to the gods by flinging tokens, charms, and cupfuls of rice wine into the sea. When perils threatened, they even sacrificed jewels and precious mirrors. It was a routine journey along the coast of Japan in 936. The governor of Kochi—at that time, one of the remotest provinces of the Japanese Empire on southern Shikoku Island in southwest Japan—was on his way home to the capital in what is now the city of Kyoto.

A journal that the governor's wife supposedly wrote carefully recorded the events of the journey. Scholars have doubted whether a woman really wrote the work, which is full of ironies and has flashes of male humor—as when, for instance, the wind gets up the writer's skirts. But soon after the date of the diary, literature in Japan became a suitable occupation for rich, intelligent women who did not have to worry about money but were barred from Japanese public life. So the "Tosa lady," as the diarist is called, could really have been a woman. In some ways, the work is obviously a literary creation and a moral tale. The ship navigates between perils. The sea is the arena of the "gods and Buddhas." Only prayer and sacrifice can save the travelers. When clouds recede, pirates emerge. When fear turns the voyagers' hair white, "Tell us, Lord of the Islands," prays the lady to the local god, "which is whiter—the surf on the rocks or the snow on our heads?"

Despite these dramatizations and fictional conventions, the sailing conditions the diarist described were true to life. The coast was so strewn with dangers that sailors dared not sail at night, except to elude pirates. Persistent and unpredictable head winds kept the voyagers cowering in harbor, yearning for home, passing the time writing poetry. The journey from Tosa to the ship's terminal in the port of Osaka can hardly have covered more than 400 miles; yet it took nearly three months. Hostile seas penned in the Japanese, despite their skill in nautical technology. This fact helps to explain why, for most of their history, the Japanese have been confined in their own islands and remained in a relatively small country, despite considering themselves to be an empire.

The experiences of the Tosa Lady, moreover, highlight a startling truth about her times. In other parts of the world, long-range navigations were leaping oceans. For in the amount of time the Tosa Lady took to get to Osaka, an Indian Ocean

FOCUS questions

How did geography influence the spread of culture and state-building in North America and Mesoamerica?

Why was the Indian Ocean so important for the spread of culture?

Why were the land routes across Eurasia less significant than the sea routes across the Indian Ocean?

Which areas of India were most prosperous in the tenth and eleventh centuries, and what was the basis of their prosperity?

How did their relative cultural isolation affect Japan and Western Europe during these centuries?

trader, with the benefit of the reversible wind system, could get all the way from the Persian Gulf to Sumatra (in modern Indonesia): a distance of more than 5,000 miles. The lady's Persian contemporary, Buzurg ibn Shahriyar, told stories of Persian and Arab mariners in *The Book of the Wonders of India*. One Persian captain made the journey to China and back to Persia seven times. The Japanese could only imagine such journeys. Not long after the Tosa diarist wrote, a fanciful Japanese sea story told of a ship—a "hollow tree"—blown by accident nonstop all the way from Japan to Persia.

As well as by commerce, pilgrim traffic to Mecca stimulated Indian Ocean navigation, as Muslim merchant communities spread across Asia and Muslim holy men took the increasing opportunities to travel and make converts. Meanwhile, beyond the range of the monsoon, migrants from what is now Indonesia crossed the ocean across the path of the southeast trade winds and colonized Madagascar, off the east coast of Africa. Their descendants are still there, speaking the same language the navigators brought—though what inspired such an extraordinary voyage remains unknown. Meanwhile, Polynesian navigators, as we have seen, were penetrating deep into the Pacific Ocean with the aid of some of the world's most regular long-range winds (see Chapter 10). Even more remarkably, around the year 1000, Thule Inuit, as archaeologists call them, from the Pacific and Norse from Scandinavia crossed the Arctic and Atlantic oceans from opposite directions and met in Greenland.

These extraordinarily long-range migrations were part of a double dynamic, as people stretched the resources available to them in one of two ways: exploring for new resources and exploiting existing opportunities in new ways. Region by region, culture by culture, in this chapter and the next, we can see people in widely separated parts of the world using similar strategies: felling forests, extending areas of cultivation and pasture, expanding into new terrain, enhancing muscle power with new technologies.

In the eleventh and twelfth centuries, these forms of expansion were widespread themes of world history; but, as we shall see, they followed divergent courses in different regions. As was so often the case, relative isolation was usually the key to the difference between long-lasting innovation and faltering, short-lived change. Cultures that exchanged information and artifacts were relatively robust. Peoples isolated from fruitful contacts found it much harder.

Pilgrim ship. The monsoon helped to make the Arabian Sea a Muslim lake. The Indian pilgrim ship depicted in this Iraqi manuscript of the *Maqamaat* of al Hariri of 1238 is equipped with square sails to make the most of the winds on the outward and homebound crossings of the sea.

In the Americas, therefore, as so often before, experiments in new ways of life were arrested by checks, frustrated by failures, interrupted by discontinuities. Meanwhile, however, some parts of the Old World, where long-range contacts were easier and more frequent, experienced enduring transformations.

The new opportunities of the period arose partly from the environmental changes of the preceding centuries, described in the last chapter. To see how people responded, we can devote this chapter to a world tour of some of the regions most affected—starting in the Americas, before turning to the world around the shores of the Indian Ocean, including the parts of East Africa that face that ocean, and ending with the extremities of Eurasia in Japan and Western Europe. In these parts of the world, we see societies contending with isolation with varying degrees of success. It would be neat if the history of the world only reflected common themes throughout the planet; but there have always been times and places conspicuous for being different, or for allowing or encouraging people to respond to common problems in peculiar ways. Isolation makes for divergence, and the places we look at in this chapter are bound to seem different from each other.

In other regions of Africa and Eurasia—China, Central Asia, West Africa, the Byzantine Empire, and the Islamic world—the single most important source of new pressures for change arose from a common experience: the stirrings of nomadic peoples. These are the subject of the next chapter.

AMERICAN DEVELOPMENTS: FROM THE ARCTIC TO MESOAMERICA

The history of the Americas in the eleventh and twelfth centuries is scattered with stories of new frontiers, developed by new migrations or new initiatives. But the effects of isolation and, sometimes, the challenges of hostile environments checked or restricted the achievements. We can start in the north and work, patchily, southward.

Greenland and the North

About 1,000 years ago, a relatively warm spell disturbed the lives of the ice hunters all along North America's Arctic edge. Taking advantage of improved conditions for hunting and navigating, migrants worked their way across the southern edge of the Arctic Ocean, following, from west to east, the line of what we now call the Northwest Passage along the northern coast of the New World in what is today the Canadian Arctic. The Thule Inuit traveled in vessels made of walrus hides, stretched across wooden ribs and sewn with sealskin thongs. They drew their bone needles only halfway through the hides to create waterproof seams. Their vessels were shallow, so that they could hug the shore, and light, so that the voyagers could lift them from between ice floes. When ashore, their crews could camp under the upturned hulls.

The Thule people hunted at sea for whales and polar bears. They mounted their harpoons on floats made from seal bladders, which they blew up like balloons. Game could then be towed home through the sea. Alternatively, they attacked their prey on rafts of ice, which they attached to the harpooned creatures until it was time to haul them in. On land, they hunted with dogs of a breed new to North America. Their spear-armed boatmen trapped reindeer in rivers. For warfare against human enemies, they reintroduced the bow and arrow (see Chapter 1). By about 1000 they had reached Greenland and the western extremities of North America (see Map 11.1). The navigation of the Arctic was an astonishing feat, unrepeated until the twentieth century.

Inuit seacraft. European technology was unable to make a ship that could sail around the Arctic coast of North America between the Atlantic and the Pacific until 1904. But the Thule Inuit accomplished the task with hide-covered craft by about 1000 C.E. Their boats were shallow enough to hug the shore, light enough to hoist onto the ice, and buoyant enough to avoid being crushed by ice floes.

MAP 11.1

Thule Inuit and Norse Migrations to ca. 1200

→	Thule Inuit migrations to ca. 1000
●	Thule Inuit settlements
�	extent of Inuit, ca. 1200
→	assumed route of Norse settlement, late 9th century
→	assumed route of Eric the Red, late 10th century
→	conjectural route of Leif Eriksson, late 10th century
→	westerlies
--→	ocean current
CANADA	modern country
●	Norse settlement/town

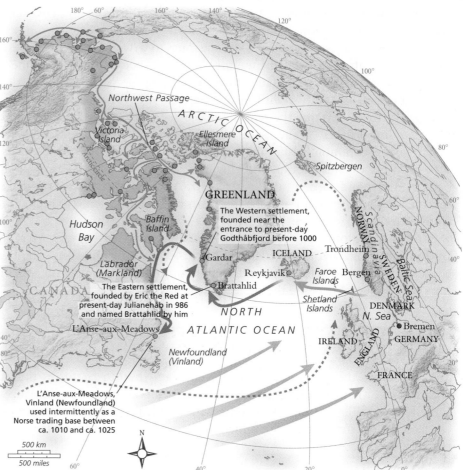

At the same time, almost equally heroic migrations were under way in the opposite direction, toward the same destinations, across the North Atlantic. A series of exploitable currents helped navigators from Scandinavia cross the ocean, via Iceland, below the Arctic Circle. It seems extraordinarily daring to risk such a long journey across the open sea, but the Scandinavians knew that the prevailing winds blew from the west in the latitudes they inhabited. So they could always hope to get home if the Atlantic venture proved fruitless. Even so, it was remarkable to navigate so far without chart or compass. The voyagers probably steered, like the Polynesians (see Chapter 10), by now-unrecoverable techniques, judging their latitude by observing the polestar with the naked eye on cloudless nights. By day, the only technical aid they had, as far as we know, was the so-called sun compass—a stump of wood with a protruding stick. The shadow it cast would tell the navigator whether his latitude had changed.

Whereas the Thule Inuit were blazing a trail of abundance, drawn by the fat-rich foods of the Arctic, the Norse—or Northmen—as the Atlantic voyagers are called, were usually escapees or exiles from poverty or restricted social opportunity. Erik the Red, traditionally celebrated as the first colonizer of Greenland, arrived there in 982, having been expelled from Iceland for murderous feuding. Most of the colonists he induced to follow him must have been extreme types—extremely desperate or extremely

Chronology: The Norse and Thule Inuit

900–1100	Warm spell in Arctic
ca. 982	Erik the Red reaches Greenland
c.a. 986	Founding of Brattahlid
ca. 1000	Thule Inuit reach Greenland
1189–1200	Construction of cathedral at Gardar

optimistic. "As to your enquiry what people go to seek in Greenland and why they fare thither through such great perils," said a medieval Norwegian book, the answer is "in man's threefold nature. One motive is fame, another curiosity, and the third is lust for gain."

In the early years of their settlement, the environment, harsh as it was, had a lot to offer the newcomers: plenty of fish and game, including luxury items valuable as potential exports to Europe, such as hunting falcons and walrus ivory. Greenland was not, however, a land the Norse cared to settle without changing the environment profoundly. They introduced grain and European grasses for grazing. They developed a breed of sheep whose wool was prized. The big wooden ships the Norse used, held together with iron nails, in a land with little timber or iron, must have seemed wildly extravagant to the Inuit in their skin canoes. The Norse town of Brattahlid in western Greenland—the remotest outpost of medieval Christendom—was heroically elaborate, with 17 monasteries and churches of stone with bells of bronze. The cathedral at Gardar was built between 1189 and 1200, of red sandstone and molded soapstone, with a bell tower, glass windows, and three fireplaces. The largest farms supported an aristocratic way of life, with big halls in which to feast dependents. But it remained an extremely precarious and isolated colony. Adam of Bremen, a canon of the cathedral of that north German city and a learned geographer of the late eleventh century, confided what little he knew: "Greenland is situated far out in the ocean opposite the mountains of Sweden. . . . The people there are greenish from the saltwater, whence, too, that region gets its name."

Brattahlid. The ruins of an eleventh-century Norse church at Brattahlid in Greenland show how ambitious—and, therefore, perhaps, ultimately how unsuccessful—the Norse colonists there were. Huge stone buildings, imported materials, dense settlements, ecologically revolutionary methods of agriculture, adherence to the culture of distant Europe in an environment where that culture could hardly be sustained—all these features of Norse life in Greenland made their colonies fragile.

The North American Southwest and the Mississippi Region

Beyond the colony in Greenland, the shore station that Greenlanders or Icelanders set up in Newfoundland off the east coast of Canada in about 1000 did not last. There were simply not enough wealthy or settled communities in the area with whom the Norse could establish contact, trade, and cultural exchange. A glance at the map of North America at the time shows similar cases, deep inland, of peoples struggling with isolation. The new way of life traveled along two routes: from the heartlands of maize in what is now Mexico into the arid lands of the North American Southwest; and from the Gulf of Mexico into the wetlands of the Mississippi valley and parts of what is now the United States' Deep South. The results included the rise of cultures with unmistakable similarities to predecessors in Mesoamerica (see Chapter 4), with urban life, irrigation, elaborate ceramics and shellcraft, gold work and copper work, ball games in some cases, and unmistakable signs of statehood (see Map 11.2).

In parts, for instance, of what are now the states of Colorado, New Mexico, and Arizona, evidence of some sort of political network spread over 57,000 square miles: from high in the drainage area of the San Juan River in the north to beyond the Little Colorado River in the south, and from the Colorado River to the Rio Grande. An extraordinary system of roadways, up to 12 yards wide,

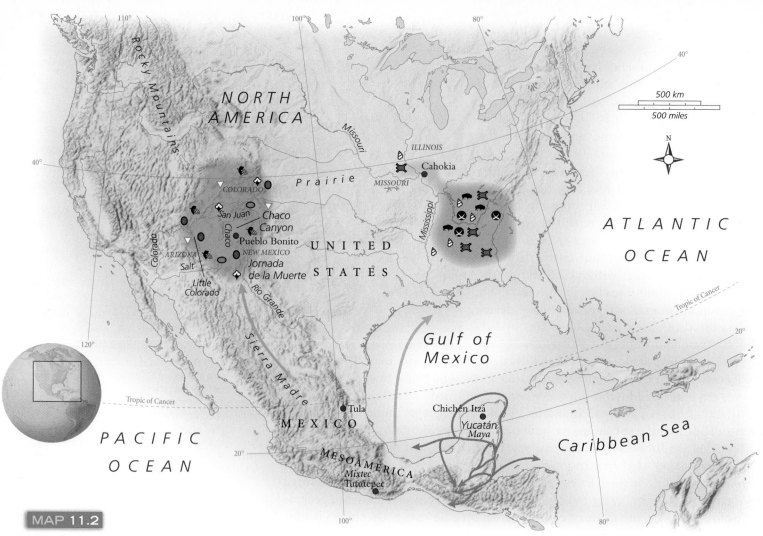

MAP 11.2

North America and Mesoamerica to ca. 1200

- canyon cultures
- ● major city or ceremonial center
- Mississippian cultures
- ➤ roads leading north from Mesoamerica
- ➤ sea route from Mesoamerica to Mississippi River valley
- → Mayan trade route
- *Mixtec* peoples
- ARIZONA modern state

Economic Basis of Canyon People

- 🌾 maize
- ● beans
- ◔ cotton
- ▽ irrigation
- ⬭ turquoise

Mississippian Trade Goods

- ♭ seashells
- ✖ deerskins
- 🦬 bison pelts
- ✪ horn

radiated from a cluster of sites around the great canyon near the source of the Chaco River. Only two needs can account for such an elaborate network. Either some unknown ritual was being enacted, demanding and reinforcing close ties between the places linked; or the roads were there to move armies.

The environment is surprising: parched and—one would think—unsuitable for settled life. Apart from turquoise, which became the basis of a limited export trade, natural wealth was scarce. But the region was densely settled, at least in patches. The canyon people built ambitious cities or ceremonial centers around irregular plazas, surrounded by large, round rooms and a honeycomb of small rectangular spaces. Massive outer walls enclosed them. The main buildings were of stone, faced with fine masonry. Roofs were made of great timbers from pine forests in the hills—a dazzling show of wealth and power in a treeless desert. To construct the ceremonial center at Chaco Canyon, 200,000 trees were felled. We do not know what the political system was. But we know it was tough. Mass executions have left frightening piles of victims' bones, crushed, split, and picked as if at a cannibal feast.

The economic basis of this civilization was fragile. Sometimes the Chaco River would flood, though not regularly enough to create rich, silty soils. Rainfall levels are likely to have been higher than now, though irrigation was essential to help crops grow in the virtually rainless summer. If water could be delivered to the fields, cotton, maize, and beans would grow predictably, without danger from the sort of fluctuating temperatures that threatened at higher altitudes. Long irrigation canals did the job.

From the twelfth century onward, the climate got drier, which put the irrigation system under a constant strain. Faced with this kind of ecological crisis, communities usually try to adapt, at first, before giving up or moving on. The rulers of the canyon people responded by expanding into new zones, building more ambitiously, organizing labor more ferociously. But decline, punctuated by crisis, shows through a series of periodic contractions of the culture area and reorganizations of the settlements. Meanwhile, the harsh peacekeeping methods seem to have stopped working. Around the mid-twelfth century, settlements withdrew to high ground, where defense was easier, but where it was much harder to make an ample living from the fields. Revivals of a similar way of life happened frequently, but the problems of isolation defeated or limited all of them until the nineteenth century.

The canyon cultures were at least as remote from Mesoamerican civilizations as the Norse of Greenland were from Europe. Roads north from Mesoamerica led across dangerous territory. Nomadic peoples patrolled the northern edges of the Mesoamerican culture area, practicing raids and conquests, like those launched in Eurasia from the steppes into China or Europe, albeit on a smaller scale. The high road north from what is now Mexico to the nearest patch of easily cultivable soil led through a 61-mile pass known in modern times as the *Jornada del Muerto*: the "dead man's march," through rock-strewn defiles and dunes where the glare was so fierce that a traveler's eyes "boiled and bulged" and seemed to burst from their sockets, and men "breathed fire and spat pitch."

It was hard to travel that road—harder still to transmit Mesoamerican crops and traditions beyond the world of Chaco Canyon. The prairie, though a flat expanse, was an ecological barrier, where few patches could sustain sedentary life. It is more likely that Mesoamerica's tool kit, food, and ways of life and thought traveled across the Gulf of Mexico, by seaborne trade, to reach the North American Southeast. In parts of this region, the environment was promising. In

Canyon Culture. The adobe-built settlement of Pueblo Bonito in New Mexico enclosed large underground ceremonial spaces and storehouses for the maize painstakingly grown by irrigation in this parched region. The builders seem to have stuck to a single, coherent plan over the many generations it took to build the complex. In the twelfth century, before drought or some unknown disaster overwhelmed the place, Pueblo Bonito was a genuine imperial center, with outlying dependent pueblos built in imitation of it and a network of roads radiating from it.

the Mississippi valley and other riverside floodplains, natural ridges accumulated over centuries, wherever the floods dumped soil. These ridges were the nurseries of the farmers' crops and the inspiration for mounds dredged from the swamps to provide gardens. A hinterland of pools and lakes provided ideal centers for fish farming to supplement the field plants, among which maize was increasingly dominant.

In this region, between the ninth and thirteenth centuries, people laid out ceremonial centers in patterns similar to those of Mesoamerica. Platforms, topped with chambered structures, were loosely grouped around large plazas. The platform mounds grew. In generation after generation, people enlarged and enhanced them, as if to commemorate their own passage through the world. Each generation piled its structures on top of those of its predecessors.

Cahokia, east of St. Louis, is the most spectacular site. Cahokia stands almost at the northwestern limit of the reach of the culture to which it belongs. Its frontier position may have allowed it to act as a commercial gateway between zones of interrelated environments and therefore of interrelated products: shells from the Gulf, deerskins from the eastern woodlands, bison pelts and horn from the prairies. It is hard to calculate its overall size, because modern developments cover much of the area, but it probably covered 5.5 square miles. Cahokia's central platform is over 100-feet high—"a stupendous pile of earth" in the opinion of one of the first explorers to record its appearance in 1810. At about 13 acres, the base of the great mound is as big as that of the biggest Egyptian pyramid.

The city first arose in the tenth century. The remains of monumental building works date from the eleventh and twelfth centuries. At its height, in about 1200, Cahokia probably had around 10,000 inhabitants in its built-up area. It was the most intensely and elaborately constructed of a great arc of mound clusters from the site of present-day St. Louis in the west to the easternmost edges of the Mississippi floodplain. Farther away, smaller, similar sites extend from the riverbanks to the uplands of Illinois and Missouri. Cahokia's size gives it the look of a focal point for this scattering of settlements. Its air of importance tempts some scholars to think of it as something like the capital of something like a state, or, at least, a cultural center from which influence radiated. The chronology of Cahokia's development is uncertain in the present state of our

Cahokia. In the eleventh and twelfth centuries, Cahokia, near modern St. Louis, Missouri, was the most ambitious city north of the Rio Grande. As this reconstruction, with huge temple mounds surrounding a central plaza, suggests, Mesoamerican influence must have been at work here. Maize—a hardy northern variety developed from strains originating in Mexico—fed over 10,000 inhabitants and sustained an imperial society. The ambition of Cahokia's rulers demanded huge efforts to work the porous clay soil, exploit nearby forests, fight wars of domination, and control floods and mudslides.

knowledge, but a spate of sudden growth and intensive building around the mid-eleventh century seems to have coincided with the abandonment or decline of smaller sites in the same region. This coincidence makes it tempting see the rise of Cahokia as an example of successful imperialism.

Graves at Cahokia have given up honored dead. Their treasures included tools and adornments of copper, bones, and tortoiseshell covered in copper. One grave had gold and copper masks. Thousands of seashells, from the Gulf of Mexico, must have possessed the highest imaginable status and value in this deeply inland place. As time went on, increasing numbers of finely made stone arrowheads were buried in elite graves. This is a precious clue to how Cahokian culture changed, but it is hard to interpret. Were the arrows trophies of success—or imputed success—in war or hunting, or simple counters of wealth? In any case, the arrows were aristocratic possessions in a society graded for status and equipped for conflict. When Cahokia lost political power in the thirteenth century, the place retained a sacred aura: its manufactures—pots, shell work, soapstone carvings, and small axe heads that presumably had a place in forgotten rites—circulated over hundreds of miles and for hundreds of years after the mound dwellers died out or dispersed.

When objects of great value are concentrated without evidence of a dwelling, grave, or warehouse, it is tempting to talk of a temple. An impressive cache of this type, found at what is now an automobile showroom, at a site somewhat to the southeast of Cahokia, contains carvings that give us glimpses into a mythic history or symbolic system that attached a high value to two themes: fertility and farming, and especially to maize and squash. One female figure tames a snake whose multiple tails are in the form of squash plants. Another female, kneeling on a mat, holds a stalk of maize. Images and fragments from other sites repeat some of these themes: female guardians of corn and serpents, some of whom also hold dishes as if offering a sacrifice.

The people who built Cahokia inaugurated a way of life that was economically successful and artistically productive for not much more than a couple of hundred years—not a bad tally for its place and time, but much shorter than the span major cities in Eurasia achieved. After a spell of stagnation or decline, their inhabitants deserted the upper Mississippi valley culture sites over a period of about four generations around the thirteenth and fourteenth centuries.

Yet culture of the kind that climaxed at Cahokia did not disappear. Rather, it was displaced and some of its more ambitious features—the huge mounds, the vast reach of trade—were abandoned. Mound building continued on a smaller scale, at sites scattered over the lower Mississippi valley and across the North American Southeast. Here, traditions of burying chiefs, with rich grave goods and sometimes with large-scale sacrifices, were also maintained.

Mesoamerica

In a similar way in Mesoamerica, the collapse of the cities of the classic Maya in the ninth and tenth centuries in Central America and southern Mexico (see Chapter 10) did not put an end to Maya experiments in civilization. Although the Maya cities of the lowlands never revived, and their peculiar culture, with its heavy

Chronology: North America and Mesoamerica, 10th to 13th Centuries	
Tenth century	Flourishing of canyon culture in American Southwest; founding of Cahokia in Mississippi River valley; founding of Chichén Itzá in Mesoamerica
Eleventh century	Mixtec first appear in historical record
1063–1125	Life of Eight-Deer Tiger-Claw
ca. 1100	Climate in American Southwest gets progressively drier
Eleventh–twelfth centuries	Maya intensively exploit Yucatán peninsula
ca. 1150	Canyon settlements withdraw to higher ground
ca.1200	Cahokia population reaches 10,000
ca. 1300	Decline of upper Mississippi valley culture sites

"Yet culture of the kind that climaxed at Cahokia did not disappear. Rather, it was displaced and some of its more ambitious features—the huge mounds, the vast reach of trade—were abandoned."

investment in inscriptions on stone, never reappeared in quite the same form elsewhere, Maya city life and state-building continued in a new environment on the limestone peninsula of Yucatán in eastern Mexico. Here the environment contrasted with the old lowland heartlands of the Maya. The climate was dry, and irrigation relied on pools and wells. But it was possible to reconstruct the old Maya way of life with remarkable fidelity. In Yucatán, lowland tradition met links with central Mexico, which was accessible through a mixture of seaborne and overland routes (see Map 11.2).

The greatest Yucatán city, Chichén Itzá, began to arise in the tenth century, at about the time the lowland Maya culture withered. Its groves of columns resemble those of Tula (see Chapter 10), which it probably influenced. Some reliefs have undecipherable inscriptions and images that recall central Mexican art. Marked cultural continuities with the former Maya world are evident in the way the buildings are arrayed in the cities of Yucatán, in layouts that reflect an abiding interest in the observation of the movements of the stars and planets, and in the huge temple facades decorated with the snouts of curl-nosed gods or the jaws of feathered serpents. The ball court of Chichén Itzá is the biggest in the Mesoamerican world, and its sides are smothered with scenes of human sacrifice. If traditions recorded later are reliable, a dynasty with imperial ambitions, the Cocom, ruled in this city, and their wars with dynasties in rival centers dominated the history of the region for centuries.

Yucatán was a new frontier for the Maya: a region of unprecedentedly intense exploitation in the eleventh and twelfth centuries. It was not the only such area in Mesoamerica. The Pacific-facing regions of Mexico, beyond the Sierra Madre, leap into the historical record in the same period. This is the region where the people known as Mixtec (MEESH-tehk) lived, in relatively small communities that one could hardly call cities but that were densely settled and famed for their specialized professions of elite craftsmen, especially in gold work and books made of bark. One of the greatest of all Mesoamerican heroes came from here: Eight-Deer Tiger-

Chichén Itzá. With the end of monumental building, inscription-making, and royal rites among the lowland Maya in the tenth century, Maya civilization did not "die out." Its centers were displaced northward to the limestone peninsula of Yucatán, where Chichén Itzá arose to be the greatest city of the region. Some ways of life continued—lavish building, city-states almost constantly at war with one another, reliance on maize as a staple food, divination, human sacrifice, and elite rituals including chocolate-drinking and ball games. But the cities all have original architectural features. Chichén Itzá, for example, has a ball court of unprecedented size, and the unique, round-chambered building known as El Caracol, shown here in the foreground.

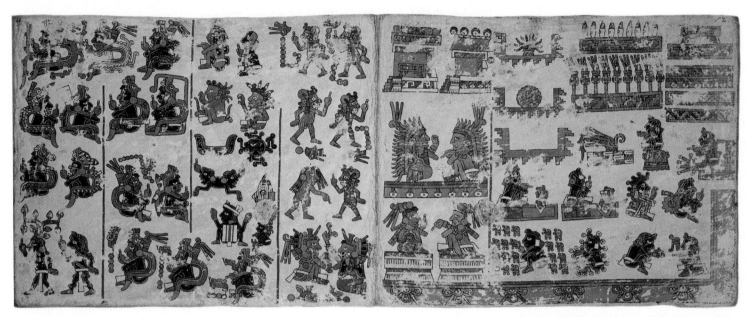

Mixtec creation myth. This Mixtec manuscript about the origins of the Earth predates the fifteenth century. Known as the Vienna Codex and painted on deer hide, it depicts Lord and Lady One-Deer, the legendary ancestors of all the Mixtec rulers, offering sacrifices of incense and tobacco to the gods.

Claw. From surviving royal genealogies, we can date his life with some confidence to the years 1063 to 1125. He came from Tututepec in the lowlands of Mexico and spent most of his career among Mixtec communities of the coastal region. His conquests have encouraged scholars to believe in an "empire of Tututepec," but we can best understand them as part of a violent power game to acquire deference, tribute, and victims for sacrifice.

Eight-Deer's wars did not necessarily lead to extensions of territorial power or of direct rule, but they did spawn a great reputation. He figures prominently in all surviving Mixtec histories. His activities show what was expected of a Mesoamerican king. He married frequently and had many children. He visited shrines, mediating between gods and men, offering sacrifices, consulting ancestors. He sent and received ambassadors, played the ball game against rival kings, negotiated peace, and—above all—made war. He died as he had lived. This model of Mesoamerican kingship was defeated, sacrificed, and dismembered by his enemies—entombed with his royal symbols in an episode vividly recorded in the genealogy of the kings of two small Mixtec towns, who wanted to be remembered as his descendants.

AROUND THE INDIAN OCEAN: ETHIOPIA, THE KHMER, AND INDIA

In the Americas, poor communications kept peoples apart and made it hard for them to exchange wealth and ideas. The Indian Ocean, by contrast, was, as we have seen, the world's great arena of exchange, crossed by trade routes and rimmed with rich societies. In the eleventh and twelfth centuries, the effects increased. In East Africa and Southeast Asia, the evidence of increasing wealth—and therefore the power of rulers able to harness that wealth—became more plentiful than ever, and new or renewed states and trading communities grew in size and influence. Meanwhile, in India, though political troubles convulsed many states, and their cultural influence shrank, trade across the ocean remained buoyant, prosperity survived, and some new or newly powerful kings emerged. We can continue our tour of the world by looking at each of these areas in turn.

"In the Americas, poor communications kept peoples apart and made it hard for them to exchange wealth and ideas. The Indian Ocean, by contrast, was, as we have seen, the world's great arena of exchange, crossed by trade routes and rimmed with rich societies."

East Africa: The Ethiopian Empire

The effects of isolation and of hostile environments, which inhibited so much long-term change in America, had also characterized the history of eastern Africa until this time (see Chapters 5 and 7). Gradually, as we have seen, links across the Indian Ocean lessened East Africa's isolation. By the twelfth century, important changes were occurring there.

Arabic-speaking geographers recorded the names of places along the east African coast as far south as the Limpopo River in Mozambique and knew of Muslim communities as far away as the island of Zanzibar. Arab traders already frequented Mogadishu (moh-gah-DEE-shoo) in modern Somalia. By 1200, Muslims from the Persian Gulf—the Shirazi dynasty—ruled it. Muslim geographers mentioned Mogadishu's transoceanic trade, bound for India and China, via the Maldive and Laccadive Islands in the Indian Ocean. Indeed, some places in Africa occur in Chinese books on geography as early as the tenth century, and East Africa, which formed part of the Indian Ocean world, bound to the trade of the ocean by the winds that linked it to Asia is well marked on thirteenth-century Chinese maps (see Map 11.3).

The increased trade of coastal kingdoms and cities could affect state-building far inland. This is important, not because state-building is necessarily good or progressive in itself, but because it is a measurable indicator of thoroughgoing, long-term change. In twelfth-century Ethiopia, a new dynasty recovered political unity and began a modest recovery. In this land, which had now been predominantly Christian for over 700 years (see Chapter 9), a time of internal crusade began, recorded in the lives of trailblazing frontier saints. On tireless pilgrimages, for instance, Takla Haymanyot made converts, dethroned idols, and chopped down forests, seizing "devils' trees" to build churches. An ideology of holy war seems to have taken hold. As early as the seventh century, some texts began to identify the ancient Ethiopian capital of Axum (see Chapter 9) as the "nursling of Zion" and her kings as "the children of Solomon," the biblical king of Israel. By the end of the twelfth century, kings regarded themselves as the heirs of Solomon and custodians of the Hebrew Ark of the Covenant, which had disappeared from the temple in Jerusalem centuries earlier. From Ziqwala, near Addis Ababa (ah-dees AH-bah-bah), the modern capital of Ethiopia, a monk called Gebre-Menfas-Qeddus challenged the surrounding Muslims and pagans to convert to Christianity.

On the Ethiopian frontier, the monastery churches of Lalibela began to emerge from the rocks: literally so, for they are hewn out of the ground. King Lalibela after whom their location is named, and who is credited with building most of them, is known only from semilegendary sources. His archives were lost in later wars or, as some scholars think, the next dynasty deliberately erased them. But the traditional tales are revealing. Emphasis, for instance, on the king's personal beauty "without defect from head to foot" reflects esteem for the artistic perfection of the buildings of his time. According to legend, a vision of heaven, which he then sought to realize on Earth, inspired Lalibela. After showing him what churches are like in heaven, God said to Lalibela, "It is not for the passing glory of this world that I will make you king, but that you may construct churches, like those you have seen, . . . out of the bowels of the earth." Stories of angels who worked on the buildings reflect the superiority of the craftsmanship. The monks who wrote Lalibela's life story emphasized that he used wage labor to supplement angelic work. Hatred of slavery was common in the writings of Ethiopian monks.

The Zagwe (ZAHG-way), as the kings of Lalibela's dynasty were called, were themselves frontiersmen. The metropolitan elites of the central highland region around Axum despised them for speaking a provincial language and regarded

"Indeed, some places in Africa occur in Chinese books on geography as early as the tenth century, and East Africa, which formed part of the Indian Ocean world, bound to the trade of the ocean by the winds that linked it to Asia is well marked on thirteenth-century Chinese maps."

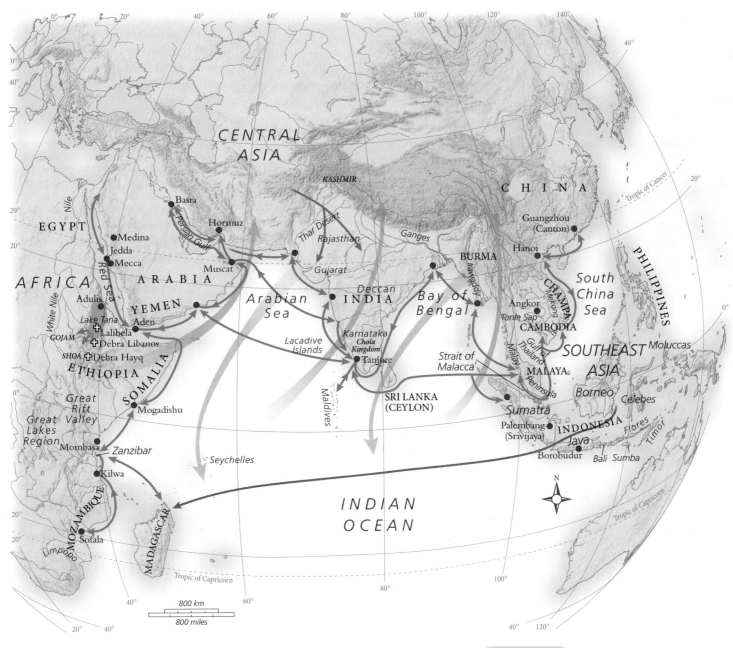

MAP 11.3

The Indian Ocean: From Ethiopia to Cambodia, ca. 1000–1200

▨	Zagwe dynasty, Ethiopia
→	Ethiopian expansion under the Solomids
✠	monastery
→	maritime trade route
→	colonization route to Madagascar
→	warm monsoon (April to September)
→	cold monsoon (October to March)
→	Muslim raids into northern India, 11th century

them as intruders. Nor perhaps did the Zagwe carry total conviction when they claimed to be heirs of Solomon. Everyone knew that they were upstarts who were not related to the old kings of Axum. Propaganda increasingly identified Ethiopia with the realm of the biblical Queen of Sheba, Solomon's concubine. Ethiopia was even proclaimed as "the new Israel." These claims to ancient roots favored rivals for the throne, who emerged in the second half of the thirteenth century, representing themselves as the rightful heirs of the Axumite monarchs, or calling themselves Solomids (meaning that they claimed to be descended from the biblical King Solomon). In 1270, they seized power. The state was organized for war, its court turned into an army, and its capital into an armed camp. The monasteries of Debra Hayq and Debra Libanos, the little world of religious communities on the islands of Lake Tana, became schools of missionaries whose task was to consolidate Ethiopian power in the conquered pagan lands of Shoa and Gojam.

Rock-cut church. Perhaps because of its relative isolation in a mountainous region, Ethiopian civilization has always shown great originality. The political and cultural revival of Ethiopia in the late twelfth and early thirteenth centuries is associated with King Lalibela, who began to build a new sacred capital in a frontier region, where masons dug churches out of the rock. Lalibela seems to have conceived this work as a place of pilgrimage, a "New Jerusalem," and an embodiment of what he claimed was a vision of heaven.

Ethiopia remained primarily an agrarian state, not a trading center. In some degree, it was always a mountain kingdom, with an ideology of defiance against neighboring states and peoples. But the multiplication of contacts across the Indian Ocean enabled Ethiopia to struggle against the effects of isolation with increasing success.

Southeast Asia: The Khmer Kingdom

At the opposite end of that ocean in Southeast Asia, the same context helps to explain the rise to fabulous wealth and power of another inland, agrarian kingdom: that of the Khmer in Cambodia. As we have seen (see Chapter 10), the Khmer homeland on the Mekong River, around the Tonle Sap, is ideal for rice growing. The fertility of the soil, enriched by silt from annual floods, nourishes three rice harvests a year. That productivity was the foundation of the kingdom's greatness. The rhythms of its rise, however, matched the growth of Indian Ocean trade, which opened outlets for the Khmer farmers' surplus. The ascent of the kingdom is documented in the growth and embellishment of its great city of Angkor.

The plan of the city reflects influences from India across the Bay of Bengal. Angkor was laid out to evoke the divine design of the world common to both Hindu and Buddhist beliefs: the central mountain or *Meru*, the mountains that ring it, the outer wall of rock, the seas flowing beyond in circlelike patterns. The royal palace built in the eleventh century centered on a tower that bore the characteristic inscription: "He thought the center of the universe was marked by Meru, and he thought it fitting to have a Meru in the center of his capital."

The architecture of the twelfth-century King Suryavarman II proclaims a new era. He had himself carved in the walls of his greatest foundation, the biggest temple in the world, Angkor Wat. Previously, monumental sculptures had only honored dead monarchs or royal ancestors. Suryavarman appears repeatedly in one of the temple galleries, surrounded by environment-defying goods: umbrellas against the sun, fans against the humidity. A dead snake dangles from his hand, perhaps in allusion to an anecdote about his accession. He seized the throne in his youth from his aged predecessor by leaping on the royal elephant and killing the king, like a god in a legend, who, "landing on the peak of a mountain, kills a serpent." Carvings he commissioned reenact the creation of the world, as if his reign were the world's renewal. They show the cosmic tug of war between good and evil gods. Scenes of the churning of the magic potion of life from the ocean suggest that the fortunate age of the world is about to begin. According to Hindu myth, peace and unity will prevail in the new age, and the various ranks of society will willingly perform their roles.

Hindu tradition predicted that this new age would last 1,728,000 years. Suryavarman's was over by 1150. But his ambitious building programs continued, especially under King Jayavarman VII later in the century. Jayavarman surrounded Angkor with shrines and palaces, way stations, and—it was said—more than 100 hospitals. A proclamation of his public health policy reads:

> He felt the afflictions of his subjects more than his own. . . . Full of deep sympathy for the good of the world, the king expresses this wish: all the souls who are plunged in the ocean of existence, may I be able to rescue them by virtue of this good work. May all the kings of Cambodia, devoted to the right, carry on my foundation, and attain for themselves and their descendants, their wives, their officials, their friends, . . . deliverance in which there will never be any sickness.

Angkor Wat. By the time of King Suryavarman II (r. 1113–1150), the great central temple of Angkor Wat, rising like the sacred mountain Hindus and Buddhists imagined at the center of the world, already dominated the skyline of Angkor. Thanks to silt deposited by the Mekong River, intensive rice cultivation generated huge food surpluses, making possible the investment of work and wealth required to build the stupendous city.

The allocation of resources for the hospitals hints at both the scale and the basis of Khmer wealth. Over 80,000 tributaries provided rice, healing spices, 48,000 varieties of fever medicines, salve for hemorrhoids, and vast amounts of sugars, camphor, and other antiseptics, purgatives, and drugs. From no other realm of the time—not even China—do we have figures of this sort or on this scale.

Even amid all this medication, the favorite remedy for illness was prayer. In 1186, Jayavarman dedicated a temple to house an image of his mother as "the Perfection of Wisdom." Again the statistics recorded in surviving documents are dazzling for their precision—which reveals the participation of meticulous bureaucrats—and the sheer volume of wealth they display. The temple received tribute from over 3,000 villages. Its endowments included vessels made of a mixture of gold and silver weighing more than 1,100 pounds and a similar set in silver. The records itemize thousands of precious stones, together with imported and locally produced luxury textiles. Daily provisions for a permanent establishment of 500 residents included rice, butter, milk, molasses, oil, seeds, and honey. Worshippers at the temple required annual supplies of wax, sandalwood, camphor, and sets of clothing for the temple's 260 cult images of Buddhas. This is all ample evidence of the penetration of Cambodia by Indian Ocean trade.

The same source adds evidence on a revolution of Jayavarman's reign: the triumph of Buddhism over Hinduism as the court religion. "Doing these good deeds," the inscription concludes,

> the king with extreme devotion to his mother, made this prayer: that because of the virtue of the good deeds I have accomplished, my mother, once delivered from the ocean of transmigration, may enjoy the state of Buddhahood.

Meanwhile, in the inner chamber of the gilded tower that the king added to the city, a Buddha replaced the Hindu images of previous reigns. The triumph of Buddhism in a state deeply rooted in Hinduism is remarkable. It owed something to the piety of the queen, who sought consolation in Buddhist devotions when her husband was away on campaign. But it was also part of a broader trend. Though Buddhism dwindled in India, it showed its potential for making converts elsewhere, slowly spreading in East, Southeast, and Central Asia.

"Though Buddhism dwindled in India, it showed its potential for making converts elsewhere, slowly spreading in East, Southeast, and Central Asia."

India: Economy and Culture

The strength of the cultural links across the Bay of Bengal, linking India and Southeast Asia, is a reminder of another problem. India had long been a fertile source of influences exerted across Eurasia: Buddhism and Hinduism; the science, logic, and technology of the Indian sages (see Chapter 6). The Indian subcontinent's central position athwart Indian Ocean trade routes guaranteed it against isolation and gave it privileged access to far-flung markets (see Map 11.3). India's long, open coasts could soak up ideas and influences from across the oceans, like the pores of a sponge.

Yet there are signs that from the eleventh century India's role in originating and recycling cultural influences began to diminish. Whereas earlier generations of Muslim scholars had looked to India as a source of useful learning, Al Biruni, who came from Persia in the 1020s, found Indian science and scholarship disappointing. He was widely regarded as the most learned man of his time, so he should have been in a position to know. Hindu science, he found, "presumed on the ignorance of the people." He found the Indian sages of his day complacent and uninterested in learning from abroad. His picture was exaggerated, and perhaps distorted by a hidden agenda: the desire to advocate the superiority of Islam over native Indian religion.

There was, however, some truth on al Biruni's side. At least in the north—the part of India he knew—political dissolution accompanied a decline in the quality and output of works of art and learning. The large states that had filled most of the subcontinent since the early ninth century collapsed under the strain of trying to compete with each other and the impact of invaders and rebellions. Much of central and northern India was not divided among territorial states but among competing royal dynasties who found it hard to sustain the loyalties of their followers. The rich Hindu temples of northern India became the prey of Muslim raiders from Afghanistan.

Nevertheless, though states provide the peace commerce requires—and, if the rulers are wise, the infrastructures that help trade thrive—economies can sometimes function well despite political troubles. In some parts of India, the economy was booming. Records of tribute paid to the temples in Rajasthan (RAH-jahs-tahn) in northwest India reveal the range of produce sold in local markets and the lively pace of trade in sugar, dyes, textiles, salt, areca nuts, coconuts, butter, salt, sesame oil. Charcoal makers, distillers, and shopkeepers had to pay taxes in cash. A local ruler in Shikar in Rajasthan in 973 levied tribute in pearls, horses, "fine garments," weapons, camphor, betel nuts, sandalwood, "and endless quantities of gold and with spirited rutting elephants, huge like mountains, together with their mates." From the eleventh century, we can reconstruct merchant lineages from inscriptions that are astonishing, because they reveal how merchants saw themselves. The Pragvata family, for instance, whose activities extended across Rajasthan and into Gujarat (goo-jah-RAHT), considered themselves warriors in a trade war against Muslim competitors and advanced loans to rulers to fight real wars. Not only the warrior caste, says one inscription, can fight in "the shop of the battlefield." This is amazingly ambitious, arrogant language for merchants, who, in most societies of the time, would not have dared to liken themselves to the warrior elite. Clearly, however turbulent the politics of the time may have been, the economy was doing well.

The most spectacular effect was the revival of Indian cities after what seems to have been a long period of relative stagnation. This effect was particularly strong in the south, where political troubles were fewer and invasions infrequent. In Karnataka (kahr-NAH-tah-kah) in southwest India, eleventh-century inscriptions mention 78 towns—three times the number recorded for the eighth century. A grant to a temple in northern Karnataka in 1204 reveals how a city was laid out, with streets leading

"The Indian subcontinent's central position athwart Indian Ocean trade routes guaranteed it against isolation and gave it privileged access to far-flung markets."

between white-plastered temples, many bazaars, water tanks, flower gardens, and food plots, with arterial roads at the city's edges. The grant lays the economy of the region and the wealth of the cities before us. It enumerates 24 city precincts, both residential and commercial. Merchants and manufacturers met in the town assembly, which decided how to tax produce passing through the town, including foodstuffs, common drugs and medicines, raw cotton, cloth, perfumes, and horses. Local manufacturers mentioned in the same text included clothiers, perfumers, and jewelers.

India: The Chola Kingdom

Far from the political disorder of the north, states in southern India could enjoy the increase of strength that the wealth of the Indian Ocean made possible. The Chola kingdom was the most remarkable. Like that of the Khmer or of Ethiopia, its heartland lay away from the coasts, in rice fields and pastures. The Chola kings almost invariably attached more importance to landward security and expansion than to the sea. A raid that touched the Ganges River did more for the prestige of the monarchy than the remotest seaborne adventure. The Chola labored to extend their landward frontiers and develop their landward resources by ruthless exploitation. Indeed, they felled forests on a gigantic scale. The founding myth of the dynasty concerns King Chola, who was out hunting antelope when, lured deep into the forest by a demon, he came to a place where there were no Brahmans to receive alms. So he cleared the forest and planted temples. His successors followed this pattern.

The power, wealth, and ambitions of the Chola kings fused with those of the merchant communities on the coast. In the kingdom's grand ports, gold was exchanged for pearls, coral, betel nuts, cardamom, loudly dyed cottons, ebony, amber, incense, ivory, and rhinoceros horn. Elephants were luxuriously warehoused and were stamped with the royal tiger emblem before being shipped out for export.

The merchants' vocation blended with the pirates'. Chola merchants had private armies and a reputation "like the lion's" for "springing to the kill." The imperial itch seemed strongest in kings whose relations with merchants were closest. King Kulottunga I (r. 1070–1122), who relaxed tolls paid to the crown, imagined himself—there is a pillar inscription to prove it—the hero of songs "sung on the further shore of the ocean by the young women of Persia." Most Chola seaborne "imperialism" was probably just raiding, though there were Chola footholds and garrisons on Sri Lanka and the Maldives and perhaps in Malaya. Its impact, however, crippled Srivijaya in Indonesia (see Chapter 10) and enriched the temples of southern India.

Hindu temples were the allies and support of the Chola kings in managing the state and the biggest beneficiaries of victories in war. While the seaward drive lasted, the registers of gifts inscribed on temple walls show its effects: a shift from livestock and produce of the soil to dazzling bestowals of exotic goods and cash, especially from about 1000 to about 1070. The treasures of the city temple of Tanjore included a crown with enough gold to buy enough oil to keep 40 lamps alight in perpetuity, and many hundreds of precious gemstones and jewels, with plenty of umbrellas and fly whisks for the comfort of the worshippers at ceremonies.

Chola temple. The great era of Chola temple building in stone began in the reign of Queen Sembiyan Mahadevi in the late tenth century. Her grandson Rajendra dwarfed her achievements with this towering example—over 200 feet high—at Tanjavur. All the villages of the kingdom had to subscribe to its upkeep.

Chronology: The Chola Kingdom

1012–1042	Reign of Rajendra; new capital to commemorate Ganges campaign
1070–1122	Reign of Kulottunga I, proponent of seaborne imperialism
Thirteenth century	Decline of Chola

When King Rajendra (r. 1012–1042) built a new capital to commemorate his campaign on the sacred river Ganges, he gave the temples an extravagant new look. Concave, sinuous forms were meant to match the supple figures of queens and goddesses, who shimmied and sashayed in the bronzes earlier kings commissioned. Into the artificial lake, 16 miles long and 3 miles wide, Rajendra poured water drawn from the Ganges. The site of the building, according to a twelfth-century poet, could overwhelm with joy "all fourteen worlds encircled by the billowing ocean. . . . The very landscape around was made invisible."

The temples are the best evidence of the grandeur of the Chola Empire and the reach of its power and trade. But they also suggest why, ultimately, the Chola withdrew from overseas ventures. The temples invested heavily in land and in the revenues of farmers whom they supplied with capital to make agricultural improvements. In consequence, they may have contributed to a shift of priorities toward agriculture and land-based wealth, and therefore, in the long term, to weakening Chola maritime imperialism—an enfeeblement that became marked in the thirteenth century. So, although India remained as rich as ever, some forms of Indian enterprise turned inward.

EURASIA'S EXTREMITIES: JAPAN AND WESTERN EUROPE

The Indian Ocean enclosed the main routes of communication around maritime Asia and between Asia and Africa. Of secondary importance were the land roads across Central Asia and the Sahara, which are subjects for the next chapter. For travelers on both the ocean roads and the land roads, Japan and Western Europe—the regions at the easternmost and westernmost extremities of Eurasia—were hard to get to and from. They were distant from the centers of the system. Europe could not communicate directly with Asia by sea. Africa was in the way. Little of the land-based trade reached the extreme west. Trade was far more intense between the relatively rich markets concentrated in the region between Byzantium in the west, India in the south, and China in the east. As we saw at the start of the chapter, the typhoon-torn seas that plagued the Tosa Lady surrounded Japan.

Societies, therefore, threatened with isolation occupied the extremities of Eurasia. But they were placed close enough to the major communications routes to tap into the great exchanges of culture of the time. During the eleventh and twelfth centuries, both areas emerged from relative isolation. For Western Europe, as we shall see in the next chapter, the revitalization even led to ambitious attempts to make conquests from the Islamic world.

Japan

While in much of the world people struggled to overcome isolation, in Japan rulers had formerly tried to make a virtue of it. Japanese rulers were fearful of losing migrants to richer regions and apprehensive of Chinese power. They had suspended diplomacy and trade with China in 838 and with Korea nearly a century later (see Map 11.4). Permission to trade abroad was hard to obtain. Even Buddhist monks had to get permission to leave the country on pilgrimage. Of course, illicit trade—or "piracy" as officials called it—went on. But self-sufficiency remained the object of government policy.

The best-known Japanese literature of the tenth and eleventh centuries focuses on a narrow, closed court society in a narrow, closed country. The fiction of Murasaki Shikibu in *The Tale of Genji*, one of the earliest realistic novels ever written, unfolds in palace chambers and corridors dark enough to make her stories of mistaken identity among lovers believable. She depicts a world in which the supreme values seem to be snobbery and sensitivity. Struggles for precedence dominate court life. The emperor grants his favorite cat the privileges "of a lady of middle rank." A nurse can tell from the sound of a visitor's cough to what level of the nobility he belongs. Murasaki's male heroes are excited to love by exquisite penmanship, a girl by the "careless dexterity of a folded note." "Sometimes, people of high rank sink to the most abject positions," muses her main character, Prince Genji, "while others of common birth rise to be high officers, wear important faces, redecorate the insides of their houses, and think themselves as good as anyone." The court is everything. Even an appointment as governor of a province is a disgrace. Court literature scarcely mentions the peasants, beaten down by famine and plague, whose rice production sustained the court aristocracy through a system of grants of "public-allowance rice" or *kugeto*.

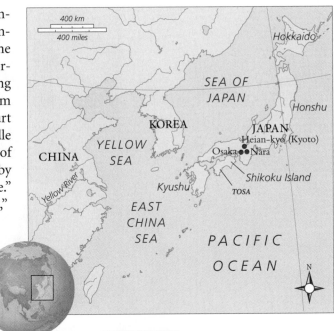

MAP 11.4

Japan, Korea, and Northern China

Murasaki was an acute observer, and her work portrayed the vices of a faction-ridden system. Genji was an underemployed prince demoted from the imperial family, like scores of surplus sons, for reasons of economy. The author was a spokeswoman for courtiers excluded from power by the man she hated, whose amorous advances she claimed to have turned down: the all-powerful courtier, Fujiwara no Michizane, who manipulated the political system by marrying his womenfolk into the imperial family and providing an effective bureaucracy from his own household. He was the brother-in-law of two emperors, uncle and father-in-law to another, uncle to one more, and grandfather to another two. After three emperors died in factional struggles, he was left as regent of the empire in 1008. He exploited his opportunities so well that, according to one embittered critic, "not a speck of earth was left for the public domain." Emperors were so preoccupied with ritual duties that the only way they could bid for power was by abdicating and attempting to control their heirs.

Provincial rule was left to administrators, supported by retinues of hired tough guys. Despised at court for their "badly powdered faces," these local leaders wielded real power and handled real wealth. Many of them, like Murasaki's Genji, were the descendants of imperial princes who had been sent to the provinces for want of employment at court, or who had opted for provincial careers to pursue autonomy, wealth, and authority of their own. Increasingly they became warriors whose authority depended on force. As the court began to lose control of the provinces, these provincial warmongers allied in rival bands. In the early twelfth century, Taira no Tadamori was a warrior-descendant of one of the most powerful clans and the son of a provincial governor. His feats against pirates, bandits, and a rebel army of disgruntled Buddhist monks won him a reception at court, but the court aristocracy despised his provincial origins and ridiculed his efforts at poetry.

In the 1070s, however, courtiers, temples, and merchants succeeded in opening Japan to foreign trade in their own economic interests. Trade with Korea resumed for a while as a result of the initiative of Korea's energetic King Munjon (r. 1046–1083). Direct relations between Japan and China followed. The results

Genji. The earliest illustrated manuscripts of *The Tale of Genji* date from the 1120s, more than 100 years after the novel was written. But they demonstrate its enduring popularity and faithfully capture its atmosphere: the leisured opulence of the imperial palace at Heian, the learning and luxury of the court ladies, and the difficulty of leading a private life—let alone conducting the complex love affairs that the story depicts—behind frail partitions that were literally paper-thin.

were dramatic: Newly rich families became players for power. The greatest profiteers were the Taira clan, who relentlessly, during the twelfth century, built up their power by acquiring provincial governorships and penetrating and, by early in the second half of the twelfth century, dominating the imperial court. In a series of civil wars, culminating in 1185, their rivals and relatives, the Minamoto clan, had replaced them as imperial "protectors" or **shoguns**. From then on the emperors never recovered real power. The renowned monk Mongaku was an adviser to successive shoguns. Invited to pray for a new shogun in 1200, he showed just what he thought of the request: "In the dwellings of those who offend, prayer is of no avail."

As the diary of the Tosa Lady shows, it was hard to get around Japan's home islands—even that relatively small part of the islands the Japanese state occupied. Overseas contacts were genuinely difficult, the surrounding seas genuinely daunting. Yet even at its most restrictive, Japan's isolation had never shut out Chinese cultural influence. Some of Murasaki's characters showed impatience with "Chinesified" styles, appealing to the "spirit of Japan." And popular literature did depict China as strange and exotic. But educated Japanese were well aware of their dependence on China for almost all their models of learning, art, and government. Chinese was the language of the upper administration as well as of all serious literature. The elite used handbooks of quotations from Chinese classics to clinch arguments. Confucian ceremonies and Chinese poetry contests (on such subjects as "the thin, solitary voice of the first cicada" and "the freshness of mountains and streams after the sky has cleared") were among the main occupations at court. Murasaki Shikibu, by her own account, repelled Fujiwara's unwanted attentions by capping his Chinese verses.

Chronology: Japan: Official Isolation

838	Trade and diplomacy with China suspended
ca. 1000	*The Tale of Genji* written
1070s	Opening of Japan to limited foreign trade; restoration of direct relations with China
1160	Taira clan ascendant
1185	Minamoto replaces Taira as shoguns

Western Europe: Economics and Politics

Nowhere else in the world were there long-range trade routes to match those of the Indian Ocean. But—though the subject is poorly documented in this period—the land routes across Eurasia, from Europe to China, and across the Sahara, between the Mediterranean and the Sahel, were probably carrying increasing amounts of traffic through the eleventh and twelfth centuries. Western Europe lay at or just beyond the western and northern extremities of these land routes.

Its relative isolation always threatened the region with backwardness. The Atlantic clouded Europe's outlook to the west. The Sahara cut it off from access to much of Africa. Europe's frontier on the east to the great civilizations of Asia was vital but hard to keep open across plains that hostile steppelanders patrolled or forests, flanked by vast marshlands, obstructed. There was no direct access to the Indian Ocean. Western European merchants rarely went there—and, when they did, they had to undertake epic overland journeys via the Nile valley or across Arabia or what are now Turkey and Iraq. Unlike in Japan, no one in Western Europe wanted to stay outside the great circuits of Eurasian exchange. But isolation was hard to overcome.

A Muslim geographer, al-Istakhri, contemplating the world from Persia in 950, hardly noticed Western Europe at all. In his map, the West was squeezed almost out of the picture, dangling feebly off the edge of the known world. Meanwhile, Latin Christians who looked out at the world in their own imaginations probably saw something like the version mapped at about the same time by the monks who drew the illustrations in the *Commentary on the Apocalypse* of Beatus of Liébana in northern Spain: Asia takes up most of the space, Africa most of the rest. Europe consists mainly of three peninsulas—Spain, Italy, and Greece, jutting into the Mediterranean—with a thin strip of hinterland above them. In 1095, urging fellow Christians to new efforts against the Muslims, Pope Urban II expressed the feeling of being under seige:

> The world is not evenly divided. Of its three parts, our enemies hold Asia . . . Africa, too, the second part of the world, has been held by our enemies for two hundred years and more. . . . Thirdly there is Europe. . . . Of this region we Christians inhabit only a small part, for who will give the name of Christians to those barbarians who live in the remote islands and seek their living on the icy ocean as if they were whales?

> *"Unlike in Japan, no one in Western Europe wanted to stay outside the great circuits of Eurasian exchange. But isolation was hard to overcome."*

A Muslim view of the world. The world, mapped by the Muslim geographer al-Istakhri in the tenth century. The map is now in the library of Leiden University in the Netherlands. Persia, the mapmaker's homeland, is in the center. Europe is the tiny triangle at the lower right. The Caspian and Aral seas are represented as two large round blobs in the middle of Asia in the lower portion. West Africa is the landmass at the top.

Otto III. The workshop of the Abbey of Reichenau in Germany was one of the finest art studios in tenth- and early eleventh-century Europe, producing the Gospel book of Emperor Otto III on gilded pages. The enthroned emperor grasps the orb of the world, stamped with the cross of Christ. He towers over clergy and aristocracy alike, while the regions of Europe, led by Rome, shuffle humbly toward him with their tribute.

Urban wanted Christendom to combine to redress what he saw as an imbalance of power. But it crumbled into competing states with no strong focus of common allegiance. It became what political scientists call a state system, with lots of interlocking territorial states, rather than an imperial system that a single state dominated or covered, as it had been in the time of the Roman Empire. From 962, the German ruler Otto I called himself—more in hope than in reality—"Roman emperor" and made a big investment to recover a sense of unity. As he understood it, his empire was "holy"—serving the whole of Christendom—and the emperor's duty was to guard and extend its frontier. When his grandson, Otto III, looked back at the reflection of himself that stared, enthroned in power, from an illustration in his gospel book, he could see lavish images of Germany, Gaul, and the Slav lands humbly bearing their tribute toward him, led by a personification of Rome. These pretensions were hollow. The empire of the Ottos was essentially a German state, covering not much more than modern Germany. Map 11.5 shows where other major states of the system took shape in the eleventh century.

The rise of the state system did not necessarily make Christendom weaker or less able to expand. On the contrary, competition between states can stimulate innovation and promote expansion. Great unitary empires, like China, are vulnerable to bad central decision making, whereas, in the complexity of a system of many states, one state may fail without incapacitating the rest.

Although Latin Christendom failed to reunite, it continued to respond to the growing sense of being under attack by outsiders. As we have just seen in the case of Ethiopia, expansion does not only happen outward. There are often inward cracks and gaps to fill, slack to take up. From the eleventh to the early fourteenth centuries, a process of internal expansion, accompanied by new economic activity, was under way in Western Europe. Latin Christendom emerged as a genuinely expanding world, as it stretched between increasingly remote horizons (see Map 11.5).

Settlement encroached on marginal soils and headed uphill. In mountain settings, Western civilization spread up slopes formerly unoccupied or abandoned to the domain of hostile highlanders, whom their lowland neighbors despised as barbarians. The new accessibility of highlands to settlement from below is intelligible

MAP 11.5

Europe, ca. 1200

○ major centers of population

▨ Muslim frontier in Spain, ca. 1200

▦ predominantly pagan lands

— Hanseatic trade route

Economic Activities

🌿 region of commercially produced cereals

🍇 region of commercially produced wine

📖 major textile area

🏛 silver mine

≡ wax

🌲 timber

⊛ salt

🐟 fish

🦫 furs

🐑 wool

against a long background of climate change: a "warm spell" that lasted from the late tenth to the mid-thirteenth centuries.

Meanwhile, other environments were transformed and ecologies disturbed. Forests fell. Bogs were drained. Farmers moved in. Church and state grasped communities formerly isolated by forest, marsh, or mountain, whose conversion to Christianity, before this period, was sometimes sketchy and whose habitats were often blanks on the map. This was more than an economic enterprise: it was a sacred undertaking—reclaiming for God part of the terrain of paganism. The forest was stained with pagan sensuality and alive with sprites, demons, and "wild men of the woods." The pious felled trees sacred to pagans.

Cistercian monastery, Catalonia. Cistercians sought to colonize wastelands, like those where John the Baptist, Jesus, and the first Christian monks withdrew from the world. But the world caught up. Peasants settled near the monasteries; rulers called upon monks to serve them; and princes chose to be buried among Cistercians, as in the monastery at Poblet, shown here, which became the pantheon of the rulers of Catalonia in northern Spain.

The most famous example is the best. Unable to sleep "on a certain night" in 1122, Abbot Suger of Saint-Denis, a monastery near Paris, rose to search the forest for 12 trees mighty enough to frame the new sanctuary he was planning for his abbey church, built—he hoped—to be full of light and "to elevate dull minds to the truth." The foresters smiled at him and wondered if the abbot was "quite ignorant of the fact that nothing of the kind could be found in the entire region"; but he found what he needed "with the courage of faith." It was a representative incident in a vast project to tame little-exploited and underexploited environments.

The Cistercians, one of the most dynamic new monastic orders of the period, directed their efforts into "deserts" where habitation was sparse and nature hostile. They disputed Suger's views on church architecture—advocating simplicity and austerity in worship—but favored building and tree felling on at least a comparable scale. They razed woodlands and "made rough places plain"—fulfilling one of the conditions the Bible specifies for the end of the world. They drove flocks and ox teams into wildernesses where today, all too often, the vast abbeys lie ruined in their turn. Sometimes, in their craving to escape the greedy secular society that put their souls at risk, Cistercians actually drove existing settlers away from their lands, extending the frontiers of colonization even farther as peasants imitated Cistercian practices on even more marginal lands.

Engineering came to the aid of environmental adaptation. Drainage helped extend the land on which people could dwell. In Holland, rapid population growth seems closely linked with the success of a project Count Floris V (r. 1256–1296) launched to reclaim waterlogged land. New embankments and canals made rivers easier to navigate. Searching out new routes and building roads and bridges were urgent tasks for the common good, for which monarchs accepted some responsibility and for which—for example—Domingo de la Calzada, who built causeways and bridges for pilgrims to the shrine of St. James at Compostela in northern Spain, was made a saint.

Behind the expanding frontiers, modest technical revolutions were boosting production. Among inventions originating in Europe at this time were windmills, ground lenses, and clocks. Others, brought there thanks to improved communications across Eurasia, were paper mills, the compass, firearms, and—a little later in the fourteenth century—the blast furnace. Large, heavy plows with curved blades

movements of peoples in the steppelands, we do not know what set them off. But once the shifts of population began, they ignited a kind of chain reaction, with some migrant groups pushing others ahead of them.

The city of Bukhara in modern Uzbekistan, once "the focus of splendor" and "the horizon of the literary stars of the world," according to an account based on the childhood recollections of a palace official's son, became for a while the headquarters of the Seljuk Turks (see Chapter 9), who overran Iran between the 1030s and the 1050s. One of Seljuk's brood seized Baghdad in 1055 and turned the caliph into a client—"a parrot in a cage." Farther east, in Afghanistan, the warlord Mahmud of Ghazni was the self-appointed guard of Islam, whose 17 raids into India gathered so many captives that prices in the slave markets of Afghanistan tumbled. He was the descendant of a Turkish adventurer. Seljuk's sons and grandsons first took service with, then turned on him. Their cavalry overwhelmed Mahmud's elephants. Muslims called them "the army of God"—not in approval but in fear. God had unleashed these ferocious pagans to punish Muslims' sins.

Turkish hostility might have shattered the Islamic world—just as the Arabs had destroyed the Persian Empire and the western barbarians had broken Rome. The Turks certainly altered the political framework of Islam. After a stunning series of conquests, however, they stopped, converted by the culture they had conquered. The first Turks to embrace Islam were a people of Central Asia known as the Karkhanids, whose conversion, according to traditional dating, occurred in 960. Their fervor set a precedent that almost all other Turkic peoples followed in placing themselves at the service of Islam.

Seljuk and his sons were among the next wave of converts. The effect was to change their whole way of life. The ruins of the capital they built at Konya in Anatolia show how thoroughly they abandoned pastoralism and absorbed the urban habits of the peoples they conquered. By the end of the twelfth century, 108 towers enclosed the city. Vast market gardens stretched far into the surrounding plain, feeding a population of perhaps 30,000. Charters of charitable foundations mention a marketplace and shops of all kinds. Inns with high-arched aisles were built to accommodate traveling merchants and their camels. But the Seljuks never entirely forgot the steppe. Their coins showed hero-horsemen with stars and haloes round their heads. Their sultans lay in tombs, shaped to recall the tents in which their ancestors dwelled.

The Seljuk experience was typical of that of pastoralists in and around the Muslim world at the time. No one knows how it happened, but the Islamic world absorbed most of the Turkic invaders and transformed them into its strength and shield. The newly converted Turks brought badly needed strength. They turned on the enemies—or alleged enemies—of orthodox, Sunni Islam. They conquered Anatolia and Armenia from Christians, Syria and Palestine from Shiites. In India and, later, on the frontiers of Europe, they began to drive back the bounds of the dominant cultures—Hindu and Christian, respectively—and advance those of Islam (see Map 12.1).

Success in attracting, converting, and domesticating pastoral peoples—and recycling their violence in Muslim

"The Turks certainly altered the political framework of Islam. After a stunning series of conquests, however, they stopped, converted by the culture they had conquered."

Caravanserai. In 1229, a Seljuk sultan built this imposing structure in Anatolia near Aksaney on the road to Konya as a place where caravans could halt. On either side of the gateway, which had to be big enough to admit laden camels, the slender columns are topped by capitals that still seem to be in the tradition of ancient Rome. There were over 200 such structures known as *caravanserai*, around the Seljuk realms, facilitating the movement of armies and officials as well as of merchants.

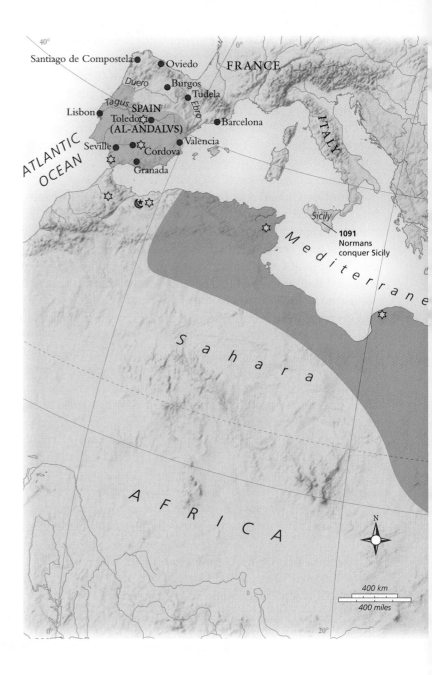

MAP 12.1

The Middle East and the Mediterranean, ca. 900–1100

	extent of caliphate, ca. 900
	area controlled by Ghaznavids, ca. 1000
➤	raids by Mahmud of Ghazni
BUWAYHIDS	Muslim dynasty with dates
➤	Seljuk conquests, ca.1040–1090
○	Seljuk capital (from 1077)
☻	Assassin stronghold
UZBEKISTAN	modern country
	Byzantine Empire, ca. 1050
----	Byzantine frontier with Seljuk Rum after 1077
⚔	battle
Karkhanids	people
✡	Jewish communities
☪	Sufi shrines, ca. 1250
✚	Christian communities
	caliphate of Cordova
	Fatimid dynasty

service—is one of the decisive and distinctive features of the history of the Islamic world. Its importance is apparent when one compares the Islamic record with those of other settled agricultural societies in Christendom, China, India, and Africa. Christendom usually dealt with steppelander threats by trying to fight them off or buy them off. The Magyars and Bulgars, who settled in Hungary and Bulgaria, respectively, were the only cases in which Europe successfully absorbed steppeland invaders. China seduced steppeland conquerors to Chinese ways of life, but was unable or unwilling to turn them permanently into a favorable fighting force. In India invading pastoralists frequently became ruling elites, sometimes adopting parts of Indian culture, but usually remaining alien intruders on the Indian scene. In none of these regions did native cultures manage to harness nomad energies for wars of aggression of their own. Yet the nomads brought new energy to the Islamic world and revitalized Muslim states' capacity for war.

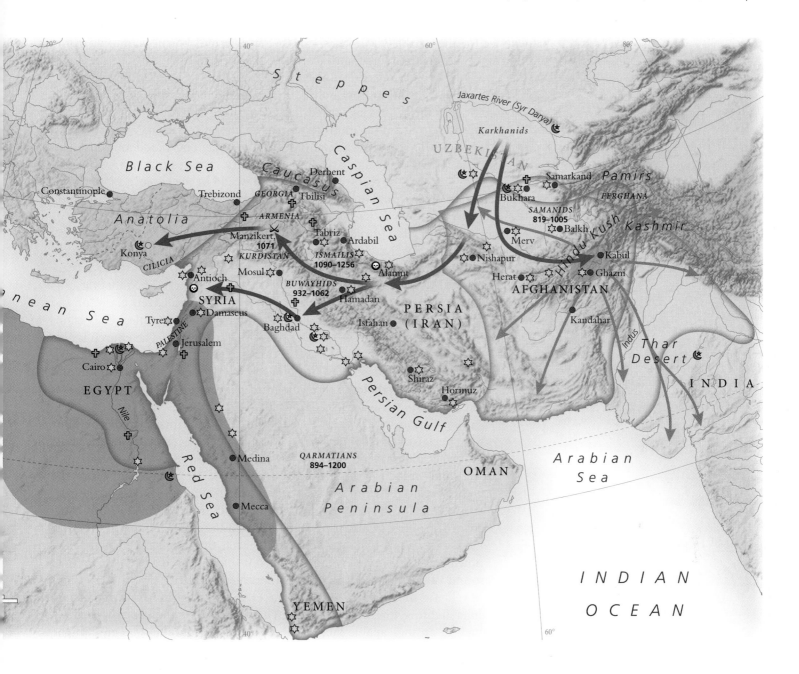

The Crusades

It is worth comparing the Islamic world's response to the steppeland invaders with the fate of the other intruders: the crusaders, who attacked from Christian Europe. Writers of world history usually give the Crusades a lot of attention, seeking signs of the vitality of the West—the capacity of Western Europeans to reach overseas and make war way beyond their frontiers. For the Islamic world, however, the Crusades were a minor nuisance. There were few crusaders. The states they founded were small and mostly short lived. Crusaders could not be converted to Islam, but—thanks to the availability of Turkish manpower and leadership—their threat to the Islamic world was neutralized or contained.

The Crusading movement started as an outgrowth from pilgrimage. Increasingly in the tenth and eleventh centuries, Christians made pilgrimages as an act of penance for their sins. Pilgrimages—in theory, peaceful journeys, on which the pilgrims relied on the mercy and charity of people whose lands they crossed—became armed expeditions. Simultaneously, Christians began to adopt what had formerly been a Muslim notion: holy war. The land where Jesus had walked, and where so many saints' bones lay buried, sanctified those who fought and died for it. Knights need no longer envy monks their easy route to salvation. Warriors could fulfill their vocation for violence and still be saved. "The blood of Muslims," declared a French poet in the early twelfth century, "washes out sins." Even if it were not holy, war for the recovery of Jerusalem would be just, according to Christian theorists: Palestine had once been Christian land, and Muslims had "usurped" it—so it was right to try to win it back.

These trends in thought and devotion came together in the 1090s. Preachers whipped up collective hysteria that sent thousands of poor, ill-armed pilgrims to their deaths in an effort to get to Jerusalem. Pope Urban II (r. 1088–1099) orchestrated a relatively well-planned military expedition. It is often claimed that the crusaders were younger sons, with inadequate inheritances, and adventurers "on the make," escaping from restricted social and economic opportunities. This claim seems false as many crusaders were rich men with a lot to lose. The church is also often thought to have encouraged the Crusades, so that it could increase its own wealth. That was one of the effects, as crusaders left property to monasteries and churches to look after in their absence, and, once they got to the East, made grants of conquered land and treasure to religious institutions there.

Association with the Holy Land and with pilgrimage made the Crusades special. But for contemporaries, especially for Muslims, they were part of a bigger phenomenon—the tide of conquest that flowed from north to south and west to east across and around the Mediterranean. From the 1060s, adventurers from Normandy in northern France conquered the central Mediterranean island of Sicily. In the 1080s, King Alfonso VI of Castile drove the frontier of his Spanish kingdom south from the valley of the River Duero to that of the Tagus. In the next decade, the Spanish mercenary chief known to tradition as El Cid carved out a short-lived realm of his own around Valencia, on Spain's Mediterranean coast. In none of these conflicts did religion motivate the conquerors. El Cid spent most of his mercenary career fighting for Muslim rulers. The outcome of the campaigns owed much to an inescapable fact of Mediterranean geography: because of the winds and currents, it is hard to defend most places in and around the sea from determined assaults from the west or north. But it so happened that the rulers on the losing sides in all these conflicts were Muslims, and religious rhetoric featured in the belligerents' propaganda. When the Crusades followed, Muslim chroniclers assumed a generalized strategy was afoot to dispossess them. They immediately dubbed it a "holy war."

The early crusaders blundered to surprising success, capturing Jerusalem in 1099 and lining the shores of the Levant with states their own leaders ruled (see Map 12.2). Muslim divisions made these successes possible. Muslim indifference and infighting prolonged them. The crusader kingdoms got support from Italian merchant-communities, which welcomed access to trade, and, occasionally, they received reinforcements from Europe. The newcomers from Europe, however, were often religious zealots who tended to disrupt the delicate tolerance between Christians and Muslims on which the crusader states relied for stability.

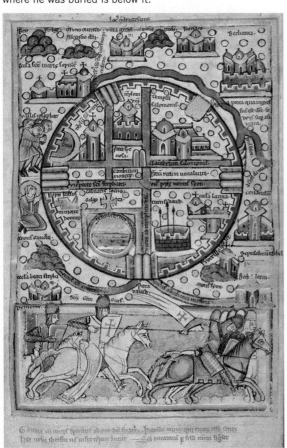

A medieval tourist-guide. This late twelfth-century guide was made to help English pilgrims find the major tourist attractions and useful spots in and around Jerusalem. The money exchange is in the center, and the food market is to its right. The Temple of Solomon occupies the upper right quarter of the city (surrounded by circular walls), and the Golden Gate "where Jesus entered sitting on a donkey" leads to it. The cross marks Golgotha where Jesus was crucified. The Holy Sepulcher where he was buried is below it.

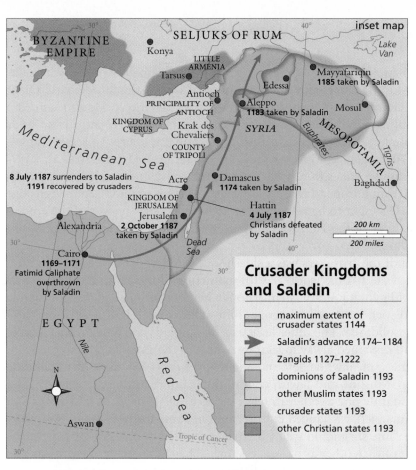

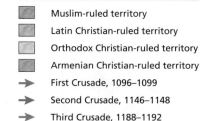

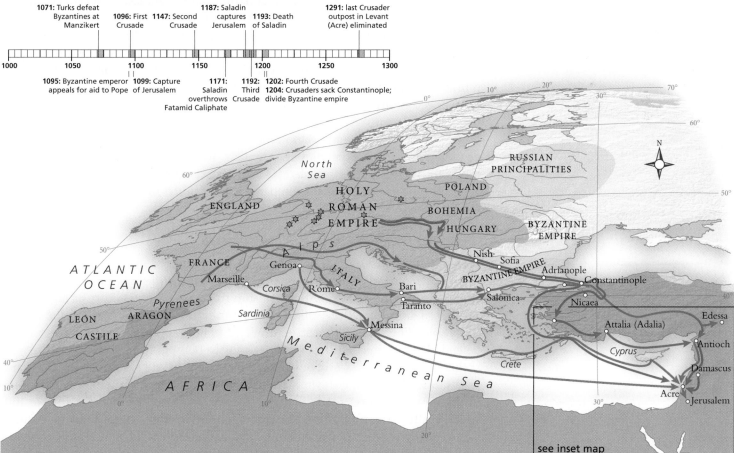

Christian and Muslim harmony. Songs in praise of the Virgin Mary, written by King Alfonso X of Castile (r. 1252–1284), could be played and enjoyed by both Christian and Muslim musicians. Both traditions upheld—and still uphold—the virginity of Jesus' mother. Food, dress, language, and even some religious practices spanned the frontier between Christian- and Muslim-ruled areas.

A Moor and a Christian playing the lute, miniature in a book of music from the 'Cantigas' of Alfonso X 'the Wise' (1221–1284). 13th Century (manuscript). Monasterio de El Escorial, El Escorial, Spain/Index/Bridgeman Art Library.

In the mid-twelfth century, Zangi—a Turkish chief who dubbed himself "pillar of the faith"—lost patience with the chaos of what we call the Middle East. Or, at least, he saw the opportunities it presented to build an empire. He proclaimed a *jihad* against infidels and Shiites. Zangi and his heirs began to reconquer the lands lost to the crusaders. Saladin, the Kurdish professional soldier who seized Zangi's empire in 1170, largely completed the job. He recaptured Jerusalem in 1187, reduced the crusader states to tiny enclaves on the coast, and beat off attempts by new crusaders from Europe to recover Jerusalem. Yet that was not Saladin's greatest achievement. He sought to be remembered above all as the "reviver of the empire of the Commander of the Faithful," a restorer of Islamic unity, a torch of Sunni Islamic orthodoxy.

The defeat of the crusaders was a sideshow. More important, in the long run, for the future of the Islamic world was the extinction of the Fatimid caliphate and the conquest of Egypt for Sunni Islam. Though heresy continued to disrupt Islamic uniformity, no such large or menacing Shiite state outside Iran ever again challenged Islamic solidarity. The other legacy of the Zangids and Saladin was Islamic militancy. Jihad remained a way to legitimize upstart dynasties and regimes.

The Crusades, meanwhile, left an equally sad legacy. For most of the Middle Ages, Christian, Muslim, and Jewish communities in the Middle East, Egypt, and Spain lived alongside one another in relative peace (see Map 12.1). Christians and Muslims intermarried, exchanged culture, and, in some frontier zones, even worshipped at the same shrines. In war, Christian and Muslim states rarely behaved as if they thought of each other as natural enemies. They often made alliances against third parties, regardless of religious affiliation. The Crusades, however, fed on religious propaganda and encouraged the two traditions to demonize each other. Crusading fervor also contributed to growing hostility in Europe between Christians and Jews, since Jews were often the victims of rioting aroused by laments over the loss of the Holy Land. In most places, Jews were the only non-Christian communities the mob found to hand (see Map 12.2).

The common opinion that the Crusades demonstrated the growing power of Latin Christendom seems—at best—exaggerated. There *was* dynamism in the Western Europe of the eleventh and twelfth centuries, but most of it was expended on inward development and on expanding the frontiers. If anything, the Crusades contributed indirectly. Their failure helped alert people in Europe to the backwardness and vulnerability of their part of the world compared to the cultures of the Near East.

The Invaders from the Sahara

It was not only in Asia that Islam successfully mobilized pastoralists for jihad. On their westernmost frontier, in Spain and Portugal, Muslims badly needed new strength. Since the eighth century, Muslim rulers had held territory as far north as the Duero and Ebro River valleys. But **al-Andalus**, as Muslims called the region, was a sprawling state, with a structure hard to hold together and frontiers hard to defend. The original Muslim settlers—mostly Berbers from North Africa—were scattered in towns or strung out around the southern and eastern river valleys and coasts, uneasily holding down large subject Christian populations. Internal communications relied on roads that the Romans had built centuries earlier to link widely scattered communities. The vast region between the rivers Tagus and Duero was a frontier in depth, strewn with fortifications, protecting the Islamic world's long flank against raids from the small Christian states that huddled in the mountains of the northwest. Wealth made al-Andalus viable: wealth gathered from the

Making Connections | THE CRUSADES

HISTORICAL BACKGROUND	➡	CAUSE FOR ACTION	➡	EUROPEAN CONSEQUENCES	➡	CONSEQUENCES IN EASTERN MEDITERRANEAN
Tradition of pilgrimage—Christians go to Jerusalem		By 1050, increased danger, disorder, and occasional persecution in Middle East		Transformation of pilgrimage into armed expeditions; adoption of Islamic idea of holy war		Transformation of Holy Land into region of continual battle
Jerusalem formerly a Christian, Muslim, and Jewish city		Muslim kingdoms control the region		Religious leaders whip up mass movement—disorganized expeditions lead to disastrous results; Pope Urban II organizes a military expedition (First Crusade)		Quick capture of Jerusalem; creation of small "crusader kingdoms"
Catholic Church most important institution in Western Europe		Church needs land, wealth to fund its clerics, infrastructure, and religious activity; new spirituality favors pilgrimages as a form of penance		Bishops and papacy help coordinate, orchestrate Crusades; crusaders left property to monasteries and churches while abroad		Conquered land and treasure often granted to church institutions
European aristocracy needs means of salvation		Development of chivalric ethos; founding of knightly orders		Aristocratic violence exported on Crusades		Crusades become ruling elite over large Muslim population
Defeat of Muslims by crusaders		Weak, disorganized Muslim kingdoms in eastern Mediterranean		Initial success of crusaders; occupation of Jerusalem and Holy Land		Proclamation of *jihad* by Zangi, Turkic chief; reconquest of Jerusalem by Saladin; overthrow of crusader kingdoms

huge agricultural surplus of rich soils in the south and east; wealth spent on the fabulous luxuries—ivory work, jewels, palaces, lavish gardens—for which Spanish art of the time is renowned.

In the late tenth century, a strong-arm general, Almanzor, kept the potentially mutinous armies and regional aristocracies of the Spanish "caliphate," as its rulers called it, busy with wars against the Christians. Almanzor died in 1002. In 1009 Berber mutineers sacked his headquarters, "wilder now than the maws of lions, bellowing the end of the world." The caliphate dissolved into numerous competing kingdoms. The Islamic world's defense in the west was divided among more and weaker hands. The Christian frontier stole and lurched southward, as the northern Christian kingdoms took advantage of the disunity in the Islamic south. By the 1080s, the Tagus valley was in Christian hands. In alarm, some of the Spanish Muslim kingdoms called on warrior ascetics from North Africa, the Almoravids, for help.

In Arabic the Almoravids' name is a pun, suggesting both hermits and soldiers. They emerged as an alliance of pastoral bands from the Sahara, who, through firebrand preaching, were aroused into self-dedication to holy war.

A CLOSER LOOK

A Cordovan Ivory Jar

Richly carved ivory jars for holding rare and costly essences, such as camphor, ambergris, and musk, show how luxurious life was in the palace of Madinat al-Zahra in Cordova in Muslim Spain in the late tenth century. This example was made for a brother of the reigning caliph.

The domed shape suggests the architecture of palaces and mosques. The missing knob would have had the form of a rich fruit, such as a pomegranate.

The scenes depict hunters picking dates, court attendants, boys stealing eagles' eggs, and lions devouring bulls. The exact meaning of the images—if there ever was any—is lost, but all hint at royal power and well-being.

The inscription reads: "Blessings from God, goodwill, happiness, and prosperity to al-Mughira, son of the Commander of the Faithful, may God's mercy be upon him," with the date, 967.

Ivory pyxis of Al–Mughira. Scene of harvesting dates. 968 C.E. From Cordoba, Spain. Inv. 4068. Photo: H. Lewandowski/Musee du Louvre/RMN Reunion des Musees Nationaux, France. Art Resource, New York.

How does this ivory jar reflect the civilization and sophistication of Muslim Spain?

From the mid-tenth century, reports began to cross North Africa of large alliances of nomads, belonging to the veiled Sanhaja (sahn-HA-jah) peoples whose territory covered most of the western Sahara. By the 1040s, the Sanhaja, apparently united in the cause of jihad, broke out of the desert to conquer Morocco. They were not the first such invaders. Nomads whom the Fatimids had expelled from southern Egypt had already wrought havoc in the region. The Almoravids, however, were apparently more numerous and more effective.

Chronology: The Almoravids and Almohads	
1040s	Sanhaja conquer Morocco
1076	Kumbi Saleh falls to Almoravid armies
1080s	Muslim kingdoms in al-Andalus call on Almoravids for help
1140s	Almoravid Empire falls to the Almohads

When they received the summons to Spain to help its Muslim rulers fend off the Christian states, the Almoravids already had a reputation for military efficiency, having created a state that spanned the Sahara. In the tradition of many Saharan tribes, they had—at least at an early stage of their history—a surprisingly egalitarian attitude to women. A woman, Zaynab al-Nafzawiya (ZAY-nab ahn-nahf-zah-WEE-yah), dominated, for a time, Almoravid politics and nominated generals. "Some said the spirits spoke to her," said orally transmitted traditions, "others that she was a witch."

In Spain, the Almoravids drove back the Christians and preserved most of the peninsula for Islam. The Almoravids spent much of their fury, however, on the rulers of the petty Muslim kingdoms, whom they swept away, first denouncing their luxury, then seizing it for themselves. The corruption to which the Almoravids submitted in their turn became a provocation and an enticement to other religiously inspired desert pastoralists. In the 1140s the Almoravids' empire was conquered by a new ascetic alliance, the Almohads—the name means "people of the oneness of God"—who again invaded Spain from North Africa and, for a while, succeeded in propping up the Islamic frontier (see Map 12.3).

These movements of desert zealots also turned south Islam's frontier with paganism in Africa. The most celebrated of Almoravid generals, Abu Bakr al-Lamtumi (AH-boo BA-kuhr ahl-lam-TOO-mee), was said to have abandoned the embraces of Zaynab herself to take up the war against the black pagans. Almoravid efforts focused on Ghana, the kingdom of the Soninke (sohn-ihn-KAY) of the upper Niger River (see Chapter 10). Ghana was enviably gold-rich, for it controlled access to the routes of trans-Saharan trade, where gold was exchanged for salt. It was also offensive to the Almoravids as the home of "sorcerers," where, according to collected reports, the people buried their dead with gifts, "made offerings of alcoholic beverages," and kept a sacred snake in a cave. Muslims—presumably traders—had their own large quarter in or near the Ghanian capital Kumbi Saleh, but were kept apart from the royal quarter of the town. The Soninke fought off Almoravid armies with some success until 1076. In that year, Kumbi fell, and its defenders were massacred. The northerners' political hold south of the Sahara did not last, but Islam was firmly implanted in West Africa.

The main reasons for Muslims to go to the "the lands of the blacks" were commercial, although they also went south to make war, to find patronage if they were scholars or artists, and to make converts to Islam. Travelers' accounts recorded in Sicily and Spain in the eleventh and twelfth centuries give us snapshots of the history of the state known as Ghana in the West African interior, in the grassland region known as the Sahel, on the trade routes where salt from the Sahara was exchanged for gold (see Map 12.3).

The most extensive account is full of sensational and salacious tales, praising the slave women, excellent at cooking "sugared nuts and honeyed donuts" and with

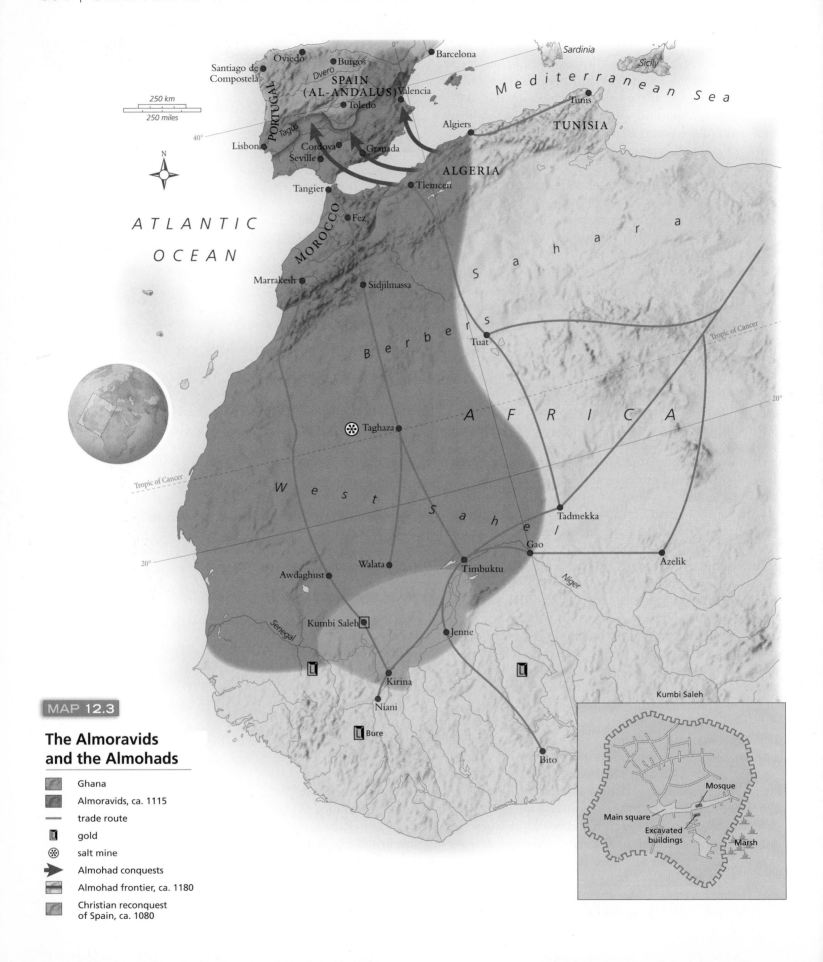

Oviedo
Burgos
Barcelona
Sardinia
Sicily
Santiago de Compostela
Dvero
SPAIN (AL-ANDALUS)
Valencia
Mediterranean Sea
250 km
250 miles
Toledo
Tunis
PORTUGAL
Tagus
40°
Lisbon
Cordova
Granada
Algiers
TUNISIA
Seville
ALGERIA
N
Tangier
Tlemcen
ATLANTIC OCEAN
MOROCCO
Fez
Sahara
Marrakesh
Sidjilmassa
Berbers
Tuat
Tropic of Cancer
AFRICA
20°
Taghaza
Tropic of Cancer
West
Sahel
Tadmekka
Gao
Azelik
Walata
Timbuktu
Niger
Awdaghust
20°
Kumbi Saleh
Jenne
Kumbi Saleh
Kirina
Niani
Bure
Bito

Mosque
Main square
Excavated buildings
Marsh

MAP 12.3

The Almoravids and the Almohads

- Ghana
- Almoravids, ca. 1115
- trade route
- gold
- salt mine
- Almohad conquests
- Almohad frontier, ca. 1180
- Christian reconquest of Spain, ca. 1080

"good figures, firm breasts, slim waists, fat buttocks, wide shoulders and sexual organs so narrow that one of them may be enjoyed as though she were a virgin indefinitely." But a vivid picture emerges of a kingdom with three or four prosperous, populous towns, productive in copperwork, cured hides, dyed robes, and Atlantic ambergris as well as gold. The authors also make clear how Islam spread in the region, partly by settlement of North African merchants in the towns and partly by the efforts of individual holy men or pious merchants who established relationships of confidence with kings. Interpreters and officials were already typically Muslims, and every town had several mosques, but even rulers sympathetic to Islam maintained their traditional court rituals, and what Muslims called "idols" and "sorcerers."

By the mid-twelfth century, Islam was clearly ascendant. Arab writers regarded Ghana as a model Islamic state, whose king revered the true caliph in Baghdad and dispensed justice with exemplary openness. They admired his well-built palace, with its objects of art and windows of glass; the huge natural ingot of gold that was the symbol of his authority; the gold ring by which he tethered his horse; his silk clothes; his elephants and giraffes. "In former times," reported a Muslim scholar based in Spain, "the people of the country professed paganism. . . . Today they are Muslims and have scholars, lawyers, and Quran readers and have become pre-eminent in these fields. Some of their chief leaders . . . have traveled to Mecca and made the Pilgrimage and visited the Prophet's tomb."

Archaeology confirms this picture. Excavations at Kumbi reveal a town of nearly 1.5 square miles, founded in the tenth century, housing perhaps 15,000 to 20,000 people, with a regular plan and evidence of large, multistoried buildings, including what excavators have designated as "mansions" of up to nine rooms, and a mosque measuring 100 feet by 140 feet. Artifacts include glass weights for weighing gold, many finely wrought metal tools, and evidence of a local form of money (see Map 12.3).

"Arab writers regard Ghana as a model Islamic state, whose king revered the true caliph in Baghdad and dispensed justice with exemplary openness."

A Quranic School in West Africa. Among the Dogon of Mali, Islamic penetration was superficial in the Middle Ages, but something of the atmosphere of the Quranic teachers who took Islam south of the Sahara in those days is detectable today in village schools kept by marabouts, who teach boys to master the Quran by heart, typically from the age of about four. Their pupils beg alms for the teacher's sustenance.

This magnificence did not last. After a long period of stagnation or decline, pagan invaders overran the Soninke state and destroyed Kumbi. But Islam had spread so widely by then among the warriors and traders of the Sahel that it retained its foothold south of the Sahara for the rest of the Middle Ages.

The Progress of Sufism

For all the achievements of the strong men who emerged from steppes and deserts to champion Islam, it is doubtful whether war alone could heal the divisions among Muslims and equip the Islamic world to expand. For that, inventive intellectuals were necessary—shapers of a religion that could appeal to a diversity of cultures and engage human sympathies and sensibilities without provoking conflict. Sufism (see Chapter 9) had enormous popular appeal. But most of the Muslim elite rejected it. In the early tenth century, for instance, ordinary people revered the great spokesman of Sufism, al-Hallaj, as a saint, but the Islamic authorities put him to death, because he claimed to have achieved self-extinction and mystical union with God. Gilani, his successor, who became one of the most popular preachers in mid-eleventh-century Baghdad, had a popular reputation as the "perfect man." He offered a simple morality of dependence on God—based on the rule, "Expect nothing from human beings"—as an alternative to the rigid legalism of Islamic scholars.

The divergence between legal-minded and mystic-minded Muslim theologians seemed unbridgeable until Abu Hamid Muhammad al-Ghazali entered the debate. He was blessed, or cursed, with an intellect he described as an "unquenchable thirst for investigation . . . an instinct and a temperament implanted in me by God through no choice of my own." At the height of a career as a conventional theologian in Baghdad, he experienced a sudden awareness of his ignorance of God. He became a Sufi, retired to his native Nishapur in Persia, and, before his death in 1111, wrote a dazzling series of works reconciling Sufism and Sunni orthodoxy. He was a master of reason and science but demonstrated, to the satisfaction of most of his readers, that human minds could not grasp some truths without direct illumination from God. Study could tell you about God, but only a mystical experience can show you who God is. Al-Ghazali likened the effect of mysticism to the difference between knowing what health is and being healthy. He valued the faith of the poor and uneducated as highly as the learning of the officials of the mosques. Al-Ghazali's rehabilitation of Sufism was vital for the future of Islam. Because Sufis were indifferent to externals, Sufi mystics could tolerate cultural differences among Muslims and between Muslims and non-Muslims in a way the legal-minded Islamic intellectuals could not. Though most people found Sufis' mystical practices as difficult to understand as any of the doctrines of the conventionally learned, Sufis' emphasis on experience, faith, and emotions was universally accessible. Their habits of holiness satisfied ordinary people's craving for saints. They were Islam's most effective missionaries in subsequent centuries (see Map 12.1).

"Though most people found Sufis' mystical practices as difficult to understand as any of the doctrines of the conventionally learned, Sufis' emphasis on experience, faith, and emotions was universally accessible."

THE BYZANTINE EMPIRE AND ITS NEIGHBORS

If the pastoralists contributed to the salvation of the Islamic world, their attacks were disastrous for the many non-Muslim states that proved less skillful at absorbing them or deflecting their power. A dramatic case in point is that of the state—

centered on Constantinople—whose rulers called it "The Roman Empire." In Western Europe, the Roman Empire was little more than a pious memory and its revival an impractical dream. But in Eastern Europe, the empire still existed—at least, in some people's perceptions. Today, historians usually balk at using the word *Roman* and prefer to call it the Byzantine Empire—from Byzantium, Constantinople's ancient Greek name. The rulers, after all, had no authority at Rome and spoke Greek rather than Latin. But the Byzantines claimed the exclusive right to regard themselves as heirs of ancient Rome. When ambassadors arrived in Constantinople in 968 from the "august emperor" Otto I in Germany (see Chapter 10), Byzantine officials laughed at "the audacity of it! To style a poor barbarian creature 'Emperor of the Romans.'" And the Byzantine emperors did maintain a principle of government that went back to the Emperor Constantine himself—they ruled both state and church. The kind of clergy the popes strove to give to the Latin Church in the eleventh century—"purified" of lay power, privileged by its own system of appointments, laws, and courts—was unacceptable in Byzantium, where emperors appointed all bishops, and the church accepted state control.

Byzantium and the Barbarians

The Roman-ness of Byzantium dwindled by degrees. Under Justinian (r. 527–565), the government at Constantinople was actively engaged in trying to reconstruct the Roman world, and Latin was still the official language (see Chapter 8). In the early seventh century, Byzantium still ruled substantial parts of the Western Roman Empire, with enclaves as far away as Spain. But events of the seventh and eighth centuries shifted its frontiers and changed its character. The Arab expansion after the death of Muhammad (see Chapter 9) stripped away the empire's territory south of the Mediterranean—Syria, Egypt, and North Africa. Meanwhile, from the sixth century to the eighth, speakers of Slav languages slowly colonized much of the Balkans, including Greece. Arabs, Bulgars, and Russians threatened Constantinople itself.

In defense of the empire, missionaries and diplomats were as important as armies. The church virtually monopolized literacy in the areas of the Balkans and Russia where Byzantine missions were active. Missionaries invented the alphabets in which Slav languages were written. They also helped to spread statehood, legitimating strong rulers, sanctifying weak ones. Many Balkan states slipped and slid between allegiance to the Latin- and Greek-speaking churches, but for a while, thanks to missionary efforts launched from Constantinople, Moravians, Croats, and Hungarians hovered in Byzantium's orbit before finally opting for the Latin Church. The greatest success for this religious diplomacy was the conversion of the rulers of much of what is now Russia (see Chapter 9). The policy was most effective when lavish gifts and the hands of Byzantine princesses, who married Bulgar khans and Russian princes, backed it. Instead of an empire like Rome's, a Byzantine "commonwealth" of Christian states was being built up—a diplomatic ring of outer defenses.

Byzantine diplomacy was exceptionally good at economizing on force by intimidating visiting barbarians with elaborate ceremonials. The Emperor Constantine VII (r. 913–959) laid down rules for courtly displays that were designed to embody imperial power and, in effect, to wield it. There was even an official whose job was to bribe paupers to line the streets for imperial processions—or, perhaps, reward those who would turn out anyway. The effect designers aimed for was unashamedly theatrical. When an ambassador arrived at Constantinople

The crown of King Geza I of Hungary. (r. 1074–1077) received from Byzantium was not a disinterested gift, but an attempt to imply that the king was a subject of the empire and dependent on Byzantium for the legitimacy of his rule. Hungary, however, remained firmly attached to the Church of Rome and to Latin culture.

in 924, the artificial roar of mechanical lions that guarded the imperial throne surprised him.

The deftness of Byzantine diplomacy, its rulers' ability to impress or intimidate surrounding "barbarians," is part of the repertoire of strategies with which all successful states managed the surge of migrations of the period. The wealth of the empire underpinned those strategies and paid for vital military backup. The Byzantine economy relied on the productivity of the peasantry of Anatolia and the trade that passed through Byzantine territory, for the empire enjoyed a privileged position, close to where great arteries of trade converged: the Silk Roads, the Volga, the Mediterranean.

Yet the system was rickety. Wealth depended on security, which was hard to guarantee. And the effectiveness of Byzantine diplomacy had its limits. While a zone of Byzantine influence took shape in the Balkans, Russia, and the Caucasus, most steppeland peoples, and the Muslims who predominated to the east and south, were indifferent to Byzantine religion and unintimidated by Byzantine methods. Caught between the Bulgars and the Turks, Byzantium seemed to lie at the eye of the steppelander storm. Byzantines tended to see their predicament as a test of faith—an episode of sacred history. In 980, the miracle at Chonae first appeared in a collection of Byzantine writings: the story of how the Archangel Michael diverted a river that evil pagans had turned to threaten his church. It is tempting to read this story as an allegory for the hoped-for, prayed-for escape of the "Roman Empire" from destruction at barbarian hands.

"The Byzantine economy relied on the productivity of the peasantry of Anatolia and the trade that passed through Byzantine territory, for the empire enjoyed a privileged position, close to where great arteries of trade converged: the Silk Roads, the Volga, the Mediterranean."

Basil II

The longed-for savior appeared from an unlikely quarter. The Emperor Basil II barely survived adolescence. Successive usurpers surprisingly allowed him to live on after his father's death until he succeeded to the throne peacefully on coming of age in 976. His image appears on a page from his surviving prayer book—heavily armed, attended by angels, while barbarians cringe at his feet. This is how he liked to see himself and wished to be remembered.

Basil ruled intuitively, as if coping with a constant state of emergency, enforcing his own will, administering rough justice, respecting no laws or conventions. In 996, he dealt with a landowner he saw exploiting peasants: "we had his luxurious villa razed to the ground and returned his property to the peasants, leaving him with what he had to begin with and reducing him to the peasants' level." This was an instance of a long conflict between great landowners and the throne. Emperors needed prosperous, independent peasants to provide bedrock taxes and manpower for the armies. Landowners wanted to control the peasants themselves. Aristocratic revolts and resistance to taxation were commonplace.

Basil dealt with the most troublesome of Byzantium's satellite peoples, the Bulgars, by blinding—so it was said—14,000 of their captured warriors and cowing them into submission. His nickname was Bulgaroctonus—the Bulgar-Slayer. He incorporated Bulgaria into the empire in 1018. On the southern front, he made peace with the Arabs, whom the Byzantines had fought, strenuously but successfully, for half a century under previous emperors. In consequence, he gave the empire virtually ideal borders, with frontiers on the Danube and the Euphrates rivers, beyond which direct rule by Byzantium seemed neither practicable nor desirable. In Bulgaria he followed up his terror stroke by a policy of conciliation, cooperating with the native elite, appointing a Bulgar as the local archbishop. In

Greece he relied on repression, forcing the empire's religion and language on the immigrant Slavs. In the Caucasus he attacked Georgia. In Armenia, his successors lost patience with diplomacy and reconquered the region (see Map 12.4).

Force was expensive by comparison with the waiting game, bribes, and tricks characteristic of traditional Byzantine policy. Basil paid for a professional army by heavily taxing the aristocracy. When he died in 1025, his treasury was full, bigger than any emperor's since the sixth century. The empire he left to his heirs exerted influence and drew deference from far away. Prayers cited Basil's name in cities as distant as Kiev and Vladimir in the lands of the Rus and Ani in Armenia. Hungary's kings deferred to the pope on religious matters, but they still felt the pull of Constantinople. As late as the 1070s, a Hungarian king accepted a crown from Constantinople. The so-called crown of St. Stephen depicts the king reverencing the rulers of the Byzantine Empire.

The Era of Difficulties

Basil's legacy was unsustainable. His methods of government were personal and arbitrary. The aristocracy could afford his taxes only while his power protected their lands from invaders. Their restiveness and rebelliousness grew even worse after his death. As Turkish migrations and invasions began to roll over Byzantine Anatolia, the revenues failed. The succession to the throne, moreover, was problematic. Basil had no children, and his brother, who succeeded him, had only daughters. These were unusual circumstances: an opportunity for strong women to come to the fore. In the background, deeper, ill-understood social changes were under way. The family—formerly, in theory, a second-best lifestyle to monastic chastity—rose in Byzantine esteem in the tenth century. Women began to be admired for fertility as well as virginity.

In the eyes of influential classes—clergy, landowners, courtiers—eleventh-century experiments did not seem to justify the empowerment of female rulers. Princesses spent their lives confined to the palace, and though they got the same formal education as men, they were denied the opportunity to accumulate useful experience of the world. Basil's niece, Zoe, regarded the throne as a family possession and responsibility. Her "family album" is laid in mosaic in her private enclosure in the gallery of Hagia Sophia, Constantinople's cathedral. Her third husband's portrait smothers that of her second, who murdered his predecessor at Zoe's behest. Zoe outraged Constantinople's snobbish elite by adopting a workman's son as her heir—an upstart "pygmy playing Hercules," said the snobs. Zoe's sister Theodora ruled alone in 1055–1056, "shamefully" and "unnaturally"—according to her opponents—refusing to marry. These judgments lack objectivity, but show the outrage the sisters provoked among the elite.

Meanwhile, relations between the Latin- and Greek-speaking churches broke down. Differences had been growing over rites, doctrines, language, and discipline between the sees of Constantinople and Rome for centuries. Underlying the theological bitterness were deep cultural differences. Language was in part to blame. The Greek-speaking Byzantine Empire could not share the common culture of the Latin-speaking elites of Western and Central Europe, while few in the Latin West could speak or read Greek with fluency. Subtle theological distinctions, inexpressible in Latin, came easily in Greek.

Basil II. This is how the Byzantine emperor Basil II (r. 976–1025) liked to see himself. Unlike the German emperor Otto III (see Chapter 11), Basil needs no human helpers. He leans on his own sword while defeated barbarians crawl at his feet and angels crown him and invest him with a scepter. Isolated above the earth, he is perfumed with incense and adorned with a halo. Images of the saints guard him on either hand. Basil may have stressed these divine sanctions for his rule because his family had peasant origins. But the proof that God was on his side was the many victories he won against the empire's foes.

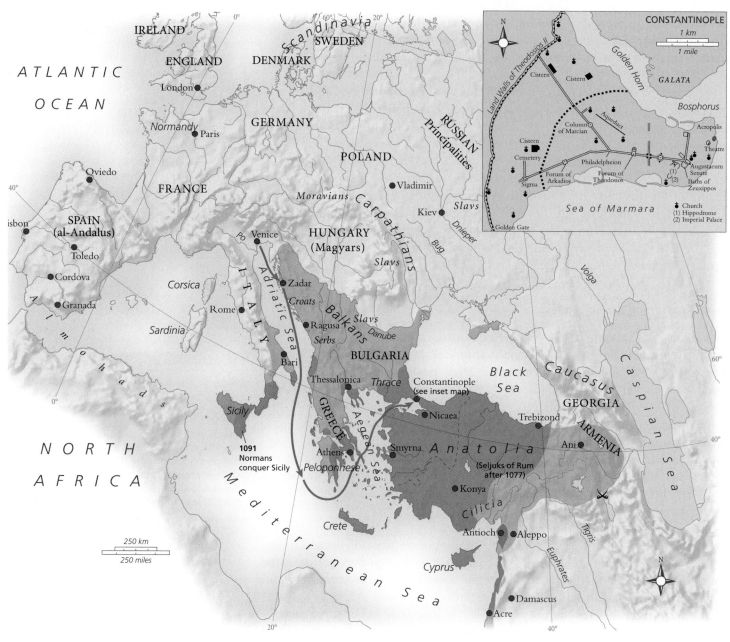

MAP 12.4

Byzantium and Its Neighbors, ca. 1050

	Byzantine empire, ca. 1050
	Byzantine empire, ca. 780
✂	battle of Manzikert, 1071
- - -	frontier with Seljuks of Rum after 1077
	maximum extent of crusader kingdoms, 1144
Croats	people
→	Fourth crusade route 1202–1204

Dogmas that were supposed to be universal turned out differently in the two tongues. For most people, religion is more a matter of conduct than of creed. In this respect, differences between the Roman and Byzantine traditions built up over centuries of relative mutual isolation. The process began as early as the mid-sixth century, when the Eastern churches resisted or rejected the supremacy of the pope. The effects were gradual but great. From the 790s, Greek and Latin congregations recited slightly different versions of the creed, the basic statement of Christian belief. By about 1000, the pope was the supreme authority regarding doctrinal questions and liturgy and the source of patronage in the church throughout Western Europe from the Atlantic to the River Bug and the Carpathian Mountains. The Western church still enclosed tremendous local diversity, but it was recognizably a single communion. Eastern Orthodox Christians felt no particular allegiance to the pope. In the West, moreover, the popes generally maintained, with difficulty, their own political independence. In the east, the patriarchs of Constantinople, as that city's bishops were titled, were the emperor's subjects and generally deferred to imperial power.

A moment when it might have been possible to restore Christian unity occurred in the mid-eleventh century. Constantinople and Rome faced common enemies. Norman invaders, the descendants of the Vikings, threatened the pope's political independence and the Byzantine emperor's remaining possessions in southern Italy and Sicily. On June 17, 1053, a Norman army cut the pope's German guard to pieces and, imploring the pope's forgiveness on bended knees, carried him off as a hostage.

Eventually, the papacy would win the Normans and turn them into its sword bearers. At first, however, the pope turned to the Byzantines for help. A Byzantine cross of the period is engraved with his message: Constantine the Great, founder of Byzantium, bows before images of the patron saints of Rome, Peter, and Paul held by a pope. Meanwhile, in 1054 in Constantinople, the patriarch, who was the head of the Byzantine church, saw an opportunity to exploit the pope's weakness. He closed the churches of the city's Latin-speaking congregations. The pope, teaching himself Greek, in the grip of a mortal sickness, sent an uncompromising mission to Constantinople. His representative, Cardinal Humbert, after weeks of bitter insults, served notice of excommunication on the "false patriarch, now for his abominable crimes notorious." The patriarch responded by excommunicating the pope. At the time, most people assumed this was just a political maneuver, soon to be rescinded or forgotten. In fact, relations between the Eastern and Western churches never fully recovered. A cultural fault line was opening across Europe.

The shenanigans of the imperial family and the quarrelsome habits of the church have given Byzantium a bad name as a society doomed by its own decadence. But it was not doomed. There are no irreversible trends in history. Nor, even when beset by difficulties, was the Byzantine Empire particularly decadent. On the contrary, the most unsuccessful emperor of the era was a model of energy and courage. Becoming emperor in 1068, Romanus IV Diogenes had to cope with aristocratic unrest while fighting on two fronts. In the west, the Normans threatened Byzantium's last possessions in Italy. In the east, Turks were penetrating Armenia and Anatolia, stealing the empire's vital food-producing zone. Romanus's military record made him look insuperable, but his generalship proved unequal to the task. In 1071, at the battle of Manzikert (MAHN-zih-kehrt), the Turks forced the emperor to kiss the ground before the feet of their leader, Alp Arslan (ahlp ahrs-LAHN)—a great-grandson of Seljuk's. Romanus could only raise a fifth of his ransom. He was released but deposed by a coup in Constantinople. Feuding at Constantinople between aristocratic factions paralyzed the government and allowed the Turks to overrun much of Anatolia.

Empress Zoe. The gallery of the great church of Hagia Sophia in Constantinople functioned as a private enclosure for members of the imperial family and was decorated with portraits of rulers and their spouses in pious attitudes. The mosaic dedicated to the Empress Zoe (980–1050) betrays the questionable complexities of her sex life. The face of Constantine IX Monomachus, her third husband, shown offering gold to Christ, was remodeled to replace the likeness of her second spouse, Michael IV, whom she had first employed to murder his predecessor, then banished to a monastery in 1041 when she tired of him. The squashed lettering above Constantine's halo to the left is clear evidence of a botched job.

Byzantium and the Crusaders

In 1097, crusaders arrived at Byzantium, ostensibly to help. But by then, the Byzantines had already begun to recover the lost ground on their own. The Byzantine princess Anna Comnena considered the newcomers more of a hindrance. Superbly educated in the classics, she was the official biographer of her father, the emperor. To her, the crusaders seemed "a race under the spell of Dionysos and Eros"—a classical way of saying they were lustful drunkards. A minority among them "undertook this journey only to worship at the Holy Sepulchre" (the tomb of Jesus at Jerusalem). Most crusaders, however, were enemies whose object was "to dethrone the emperor and capture the capital." The newcomers arrived already embittered by the religious squabbles that had divided the churches of Rome and Constantinople.

Tense cooperation between Byzantium and the crusaders, which characterized the First Crusade, broke down completely in the twelfth century. The crusaders failed to return to the empire most of the Byzantine territory they recaptured from the Muslims. Instead, they kept it for themselves. The crusaders blamed "Greek treachery" for their failures against the Muslims. The Byzantines were convinced of their own moral and cultural superiority over impious, greedy Westerners. The crusaders might have saved Byzantium, as the Turks saved the Islamic world. Instead, they undermined the empire.

Byzantium's difficulties multiplied. Agriculture was stagnant, despite the boom in other parts of Eurasia. The empire's hinterland beyond Constantinople was too insecure to prosper. In the twelfth century, in a serious reversal of earlier emperors' policy of nurturing the peasants at the landowners' expense, emperors tried to revive their rural revenues by granting control of peasant lands to great lords and encouraging monastic colonization of new lands. To some extent, this was another case of the attempt to exploit new resources, familiar in other societies of the time. The Emperor Isaac II Angelus (r. 1185–1195), for instance, gave a port to a monastery that settled a site at Vera in Thrace, formerly "devoid of men and dwellings, a haunt of snakes and scorpions, just rough ground, overgrown with spreading trees." Measures like these—which so dramatically increased the farmland of Western Christendom, Ethiopia, or, as we shall see, of China at the time—were of limited usefulness in a state whose territory was much diminished. Byzantium never recovered most of inland Anatolia from the Turks.

Increasingly, the empire was obliged to look to trade and industry for its wealth. There were, as a Byzantine poet observed, "big merchants" who "for large profits disdain terrors and defy seas." Self-made upstarts coveted money "as a polecat gazes at fat." The huge city of Constantinople, crowded and riotous as it was, benefited from its uniquely favorable position for trade, where Mediterranean and trans-Asian routes met. The Jewish merchant, Benjamin of Tudela, who visited in about 1170, celebrated "a busy city" with inhabitants so rich they "they look like princes" where "merchants come from every country by sea and land." With revenues of 200,000 gold pieces a year from rents, market dues, and the tolls on passing trade, "Wealth like that of Constantinople," Benjamin wrote, "is not to be found in the whole world. Here also are men learned in all the books of the Greeks, and they eat and drink, every man under his vine and his fig tree." For William of Tyre, a Latin bishop who visited at about the same time, the city seemed equally splendid on the surface. But William was a moralist, not a merchant. He was more aware of underlying squalor and inequalities of wealth. "The wealthy overshadow the streets," he wrote—alluding to the teetering mansions of the rich—"and leave dark, dirty spaces to the poor and to travelers." William's prejudices are obvious, but, precisely because he was so keen to criticize the city, we can trust his witness to its wealth.

A special relationship developed between Byzantium and Venice, a maritime republic near the northernmost point of the Adriatic Sea, where trade routes across the Alps converged with the main axis of north Italian commerce, the River Po. Venice's position on marshy, salty islands allowed little scope to accumulate wealth except by piracy, which Venetians practiced, mainly at the expense of Muslim shipping. In the ninth and tenth centuries, however, they began to build up enough

> *"The crusaders might have saved Byzantium, as the Turks saved the Islamic world. Instead, they undermined the empire."*

St. Mark's Basilica, Venice, is and always has been a Roman Catholic church of the Latin rite, but it looks more like a Byzantine cathedral—smothered in dazzling mosaics, a form of decoration typical of Eastern Christianity, but rare in the West. The prototype of St. Mark's was found in Constantinople. Venetian merchants supposedly stole the relics of St. Mark—whose life is narrated in the mosaic—from Egypt in the ninth century. Venice looked east for both inspiration and trade.

capital to become major traders, channeling toward Europe a share of the valuable trade in silks and spices that was concentrated at Byzantium. Culturally, as well as economically, Venice was close to Byzantium. Though Venetians belonged to the Latin Church and spoke a language derived from Latin, Byzantine models saturated their taste in art and buildings. It could not be otherwise. They knew Byzantium well, and so they had to admire it—and, in some measure, to covet what they saw there.

To would-be attackers, Byzantium's wealth was a magnet and its weakness a motive. Toward the end of the 1190s, in Western Europe, popular enthusiasm revived for a new effort to launch a Crusade to recapture Jerusalem. The Venetians agreed to ship the crusading army out at what was to prove an unaffordable price. While the army gathered, an embassy arrived from the pretender to the Byzantine throne, Alexius IV, proposing a detour. If the crusaders put Alexius on the throne, he would reward them with treasure and help them against the Turks. Gradually, faced with their inability to pay the Venetians' bill, most of the crusaders agreed to a diversion. The Fourth Crusade, launched in 1202 as a "pilgrimage" under arms to recapture Jerusalem, ended in 1204 by shedding Christian blood, capturing and sacking Constantinople and dividing most of what was left of the Byzantine Empire in Europe among the victors. The big gainer was Venice, which seized—in the words of the treaty that divided the empire—"one quarter and one half of one quarter" of Byzantine territory, achieving virtual monopoly rights in Byzantine trade and

Chronology: Byzantium	
527–565	Reign of Justinian
Sixth to eighth centuries	Colonization of Balkans by Slavs
Seventh and eighth centuries	Arabs seize Syria, Egypt, and North Africa
Ninth century	Missions to convert Balkans and Central Europe to Byzantine Christianity
1018	Bulgaria incorporated into Byzantine Empire
1054	Schism between Orthodox and Latin Churches
1071	Battle of Manzikert; Seljuk Turks defeat Byzantines and overrun Anatolia
1095	First Crusade
1204	Sack of Constantinople

suddenly becoming an imperial power in the eastern Mediterranean (see Map 12.4). Meanwhile, in the remnants of the Byzantine Empire in western and coastal Anatolia, rival dynasties disputed claims to the imperial title.

Byzantine Art and Learning

Throughout the period this chapter covers, even amid the most severe difficulties of the twelfth century, Byzantium remained a beacon of learning and art. It is easy to get starry-eyed about the excellence of Byzantine culture. In 1078, Kekaumenos, a self-educated Byzantine ex-general who took learning seriously, complained that babblers "picked passages to gossip about." The most constant and careful Byzantine work in copying and analyzing the texts of classical authors and of the fathers of the Church was probably over by the tenth century. Mystics, represented by Saint Symeon the New Theologian (as he is called), who died in 1022, proposed an alternative route to learning, through divine illumination. "Orators and philosophers" could not access the wisdom of God. Painters developed a tradition that seemed consciously unclassical, abandoning realism in favor of stylized, formal figures, usually set against abstract or sketchy backgrounds, more indebted, perhaps, to the mosaic tradition, in which Byzantine artists excelled, than to classical painting or sculpture. Most painters worked only on religious commissions and accepted the artistic vocation as a sacred obligation, aiming at work that captured the spirit of its subject and that would be revered as holy in itself. Innovation happened slowly and subtly, for artists had to treat every subject strictly in accordance with tradition and church dogma.

Nonetheless, in most arts, and in learning, Byzantium preserved and developed the classical legacy, which, in the eleventh and twelfth centuries, revived in an intellectual movement comparable with the renaissance of the same period in the West (see Chapter 11). The historian and biographer Michael Psellus (1018–1078), for instance, wrote in an antique style based on classical Greek models, interpreted the meanings of ancient art, and lectured on Plato and Aristotle (see Chapter 6). Anna Comnena's historical work was saturated in knowledge of Homer (see Chapter 5), and she commissioned commentaries on previously neglected works of Aristotle. A renaissance of classical pagan themes in art followed in the twelfth century. A famous ivory carving of that time in classical style shows Europa, a princess whom the god Zeus, in bull's guise, abducted. She plays with satyrs and

The Veroli casket. Classical stories with an erotic edge decorated Byzantine trinket boxes in the twelfth century. The panels visible in this picture of a famous example, the Veroli casket, finely carved in ivory, show Helen of Troy, Bellerophon with his winged horse, and the chaste Hippolytus on the right resisting the sexual advances of his wicked stepmother. Such were the subjects that entertained a rich lady's mind while she donned her jewels.

centaurs, pouting prettily at her pursuers. In Byzantine scholarship of the late twelfth century, nothing commanded more prestige than classical research. Michael Choniates, archbishop of Athens from 1182 to 1204, was delighted to have the famous temple of the goddess Athena, the Parthenon, as a church to preach in and classical Greek poets to read for pleasure. Another Byzantine bishop wrote commentaries on ancient Greek poetry and searched through old manuscripts to improve the texts of classical plays.

Rather than the title of Roman Emperor, or the claims to diminished power that rivals disputed after the collapse of 1204, this tradition of art and learning is Byzantium's most significant legacy. As in the Islamic world, texts and art works inherited from ancient Greece and Rome survived in the Byzantine portion of the former Roman Empire, while, in the West, they were lost among the far more destructive invasions that transformed the Roman world in the fifth century. The recovery of classical traditions in the West would probably have been impossible without cross-fertilization with the Islamic world and Byzantium.

CHINA AND THE NORTHERN BARBARIANS

Beyond the limits of the Turkish steppe, other steppeland peoples were even harder to deal with. Not even the Seljuks seemed able to win battles against them. Fortunately, however, for the Islamic world, none of these remoter nomads yet seemed willing to extend their conquests beyond the steppeland in the west. Their critical relationships lay to the east, with China. We thus need a brief account of what had happened in China in the ninth and tenth centuries.

The End of the Tang Dynasty

Superficially, the history of China, in the 800s and 900s, looks like a series of disasters. An era of political disintegration began in the ninth century. Eunuchs controlled the succession to the imperial throne. The Xuantong (shoo-ehn-tuhng) emperor, who died in 859, never named an empress or an heir lest he be "made idle," that is, murdered. Steppelander incursions continued. In 840, in a typical incident, 10,000 Uighurs (see Chapter 9), driven from their Central Asian homeland by rival nomads, arrived on the bend of the Yellow River proposing to garrison the Chinese frontier. A new menace—or, at least, one of unprecedented scale—was the rise of banditry. In a land as densely populated as China, every dislocation, invasion, war, or natural disaster had profound environmental consequences, impoverishing many peasants and driving them to survive by any available means. In the late ninth century, bandit gangs grew into rebellious armies led by renegade members of the elite—students who had failed to pass the examinations for the civil service and Buddhist clergy forced out of monasteries the government had confiscated.

An imperial decree of 877 complained that the bandit forces "come and go just as they please." The emperor's professed wish to "equalize food and clothing so that all might be prosperous" was an admission of weakness. His threat to apply "force without remorse" against those who refused to lay down their arms was empty. In 879, the bandit leader, Huang Chao (hwang chow), unified most of the gangs and crossed the Yangtze River with, reputedly, 600,000 men. He took Chang'an, the seat of the court, with effects described in the verses of one of the most striking poems of the time, the *Lament of Lady Qin*: rape, pillage, and

"In a land as densely populated as China, every dislocation invasion, war, or natural disaster had profound environmental consequences, impoverishing many peasants and driving them to survive by any available means."

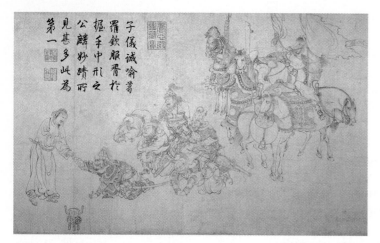

Cultural superiority. In the Confucian scale of values, superior wisdom outweighed superior strength. The cringing figures with their caps, furs, pelt banners, and armored horses are Uighurs, Turkic steppe nomads, whom General Guo Ziyi, unarmed and simply attired, graciously enlists in Chinese service. The scene supposedly depicts an eighth-century episode of the wars against Tibet. For the Song artist who painted it in the eleventh century, it represented emotions invested in the program, advocated by political theorists such as Ouyang Xiu, to use the barbarian world to benefit China (see p. 397).

bloodshed. Huang's successor, Zhu Wen (joo wehn), emerged as the most powerful man in China, effectively replacing the Tang dynasty in 907. His state fell in turn in 923 to Turkic nomads whom the Chinese had tried to use against the bandits. The Chinese Empire dissolved into "ten kingdoms."

China's situation recalls that of Western Europe, striving to maintain the ancient sense of unity and—for some rulers—even actively seeking to recover it, in times of political dissolution. The Chinese predicament also parallels those of the Islamic world and Byzantium, beset by nomadic migrants and invaders. Chinese responses, as we shall see, were also similar. They tried to fend off the "barbarians" by methods akin to those of the Byzantines: diplomacy, bribery, intimidation, displays of cultural superiority. As in the Islamic world, Chinese worked to convert invaders to their own culture, usually successfully. As in all the states we have looked at, the reexploitation of internal resources—especially by converting forest to farmland—made an important contribution.

For China, however, the outcome was different from those of other comparable regions. Throughout the period this chapter covers, the reconstruction of unity never seemed perfect or stable, but unity remained an actively pursued and—as we shall see—ultimately recoverable ideal. Divisions over religion, which deepened disunity in Christendom, or in the world of al-Hakim, had no parallel in China. China survived the invaders from the steppes but surrendered much territory to them. And, unlike the Islamic world, China never wholly succeeded in turning invading warriors into a force it could use for its own expansion.

The Rise of the Song and the Barbarian Conquests

The fight for unity after the collapse of the 920s began in 960, when a mutinous army proclaimed its general as emperor. The dynasty he founded, the Song (soong), lasted until 1279, but it always had to share China's traditional territory with steppeland invaders who created empires and dynasties of their own in parts of the north. These barbarian states adopted Chinese political ideas and bureaucratic methods and claimed the mandate of heaven—or, at least, a share in it—for themselves. But none of them were able to extend their conquests south of the Huai River, into the intricately patterned lands of rice paddies and dense population the Song retained.

First, from the early tenth to the early twelfth centuries, the Khitan state of Liao (lee-ow) loomed over China from heartlands in Mongolia and Manchuria. Under the warrior-empresses Chunjin (926–947) and Xiao (982–1009), the Liao state acquired a southern frontier across the Yellow River valley. The Khitans remained faithful to their pastoral traditions, but in the tenth century, they split their empire into two spheres, creating a Chinese-style, Chinese-speaking administration for their southern provinces. They began to build cities, following Chinese urban planning models, apparently to attract migrants. The Khitan Empire had its own civil service, selected on Confucian principles, issuing documents that scholars still do not fully understand. In a treaty of 1004, the Song conceded equality to Liao, which became known as the Northern Kingdom, alongside the Southern Kingdom of the Song. The Song paid Liao 100,000 ounces of silver and 200,000 bolts of cloth annually. This was tribute, which the Chinese disguised as "gifts" in a face-saving formula. The two dynasties affected kinship in an elaborate exchange of titles. The Liao empress mother, for instance, became the Song emperor's "junior aunt." In 1031, they jointly proclaimed "reunification of the universe," but this was a wild exaggeration. The two states lived together in uneasy equilibrium, punctuated by occasional hostilities.

Toward the end of the 1030s, a second steppeland state proclaimed itself an empire—the Tangut (tan-goot) realm of Xia (hsia). The axis of the state was a strip of grazing land, 900 miles long, squeezed between Tibet and the southern Gobi Desert. In 1044, a great Tangut victory forced another treaty out of the Song. Xia was accorded the status of a kingdom superior to all others except Song and Liao, and received annual tribute from the Song of about half the value that the Song paid to the Liao. Xia, too, had its own system of writing, its own bureaucracy, and an iron coinage much used along the Silk Roads. It also had a considerable scholarly establishment, largely devoted to acquiring and commenting on Buddhist scriptures.

The last state builders to intrude into the region were the Jurchen (juhr-chehn), who from 1115 began to build up conquests that eventually included the whole Liao Empire and covered northern China as far as the Huai River (see Map 12.5). Their homeland was in the forests of northern Manchuria. Their traditional economy relied on hunting rather than herding. They were "sheer barbarians," Chinese envoys reported, "worse than wolves or tigers." On this occasion, for once, we can be reasonably confident about the events that provoked their migration. It coincided with several years' exceptional cold and rain.

The Jurchen wars forced the Chinese to acknowledge Jurchen claims to the mandate of heaven. A treaty of 1127 imposed annual tribute on the Song of 300,000 ounces of silver, 1,000,000 strings of copper cash, and 300,000 bolts of silk. Jurchen campaigns penetrated far into the south of China. In 1161, however, the invaders despaired of creating a river navy strong enough to permanently dominate the Yangtze. The Song and Jurchen states learned to live with each other.

Meanwhile, the Jurchen adopted Chinese habits and traditions more fully than even the Khitans and Tanguts had. The Jurchen emperors were uncertain about this trend. On the one hand, they were quick to adopt Chinese bureaucracy and courtly customs themselves. On the other hand, they were afraid that the Jurchen would lose their warlike strength and will to dominate. The Jurchen, after all, were few in number—perhaps a few hundred thousand—compared with their more than 50 million Chinese subjects recorded in a census of 1207. Despite legislation forbidding Jurchen to adopt Chinese language or dress, distinctive Jurchen culture largely vanished.

Chinese thinkers found it hard to adjust to a world in which "barbarians" seemed at least their equals. On the whole, the Song coped by accepting the reality of the new distribution of power and opting for coexistence and peaceful persuasion, bribing and coaxing the foreigners into remaining quiet. One of the supplest intellects of the Song era was that of the early eleventh-century palace official, Ouyang Xiu (oh-yahng shoo). Earlier barbarian attacks, he thought, had been like "the sting of gadflies and mosquitoes." Now they were more serious and could not merely be brushed aside. He advised,

> Put away . . . armor and bows, use humble words and . . . generous gifts. ...Send a princess to obtain friendship . . . transport goods to establish firm bonds. Although this will diminish the emperor's dignity, it could for a while end fighting. . . . Who would exhaust China's resources . . . to quarrel with serpents and swine? . . . Now is

Barbarian crown. Although the scalloped form is typical of the headgear of Central Asian nomads, this Khitan cap of the eleventh century—which is so magnificent that it must have been worn by someone of very high status—shows the influence of Buddhist religion and Chinese art. From a stylized mountain, a lotus grows upward, symbolizing the ascent of the soul to enlightenment, toward a sun-like flaming jewel—a common Buddhist symbol for wisdom. Dragons, symbolizing benevolence, reach for the same goal.
Khitan headgear with repousse decoration of two dragons chasing a flaming jewel. Chinese, early 11th century Photograph © 2007 Museum of Fine Arts, Boston.

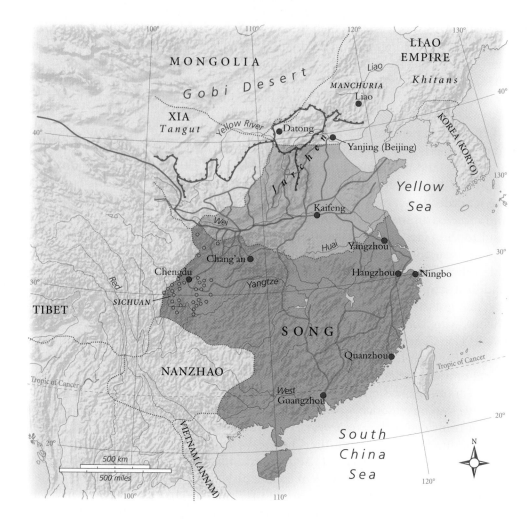

MAP 12.5

Song Empire, ca. 1150

▨	Song empire, ca.1050
▨	Song empire, 1127–1234
—	Silk Road
┅	Great Wall
●	salt mine
—	imperial highways
Khitans	people

> *"Barbarian invaders always did get seduced by Chinese ways and adopt Chinese culture. But military defeats usually preceded these cultural victories, and the adoption of Chinese ways by barbarians usually followed bloody wars and costly destruction."*

the moment for binding friendship. . . . If indeed Heaven causes the rogues to accept our humaneness and they . . . extinguish the beacons on our frontiers, which will be a great fortune to our ancestral altars.

According to Ouyang Xiu, civilization would always win encounters with savagery. Barbarians might be invincible in battle, but in the long run, they could be shamed into submission. There was a lot to be said for this point of view. China always survived. Barbarian invaders always did get seduced by Chinese ways and adopt Chinese culture. But military defeats usually preceded these cultural victories, and the adoption of Chinese ways by barbarians usually followed bloody wars and costly destruction.

In their way, Ouyang Xiu's arguments simply rewrote the old script—Chinese superiority would ultimately prevail. This kind of thinking made defeat by the Jurchen even harder to bear. The traumas the victims of the wars suffered come to life in pages by the poet Li Qingzhao (lee ching-jhao): a memoir of her life with her husband, whom she had married for love when he was a student and she was a teenager. The couple played intellectual games at teatime, rivaling each other in being able to identify literary quotations. Their books were their most cherished possessions. When the Jurchen invaded in 1127, the fleeing couple "first gave up the bulky printed volumes, the albums of paintings, and the bulkiest ornaments." They still had so many books that it took 15 carts to bear them and a string of boats to ferry them across the Yangtse. Another Jurchen raid scattered more of the collection "in clouds of black smoke." When Li Qingzhao finally got beyond danger, after the couple's parting and her husband's death, only a few baskets of books were left—and most of those were later stolen.

Economy and Society under the Song

Under pressure from the barbarian north, Song rule shrank toward the south (see Map 12.6). The Yangtze became the axis of the Song Empire. This potentially traumatic adjustment—the amputation of the ancient Yellow River heartlands, the "cradle" of Chinese civilization—was bearable because population, too, had shifted southward. About 60 percent of Chinese lived in the Yangtze valley by the last years of the tenth century. The trend continued under the impact of barbarian conquests in the north (see Map 12.6).

Away from the steppeland frontier, Chinese expansion went on. Loss of traditional territory, combined with the growth of population, stimulated colonization in new directions. The census of 1083 reported 17, 211, 713 families. By 1124, the number had grown to 20,882,258. Censuses tended to underestimate numbers, because tax evaders eluded the count. The Jurchen wars brought the growth of population to an end, but by then, Song China must have had well over 100,000,000 inhabitants—perhaps about half as many again as the whole of Europe. The state had the most basic resource: labor. It needed food and space.

The founder of the Song dynasty, Zhao Guangyin (jaow gwang-yeen), known as the Taizu (teye-tzoo) emperor, realized that China's new opportunities lay in a further shift in the center of gravity of the empire to the southwest: the vast, underpopulated region of Sichuan (seh-chwan). Colonization needed peaceful conditions. So the native tribes had to be suppressed. In a heavily forested, mountainous region, where tribal chiefs had a demonic reputation, this was not an easy task. By repute, the wildest inhabitants were the Black Bone Yi, led by a chief the Chinese called the "Demon Master." In 1001, the Song divided the region into two administrative units called "routes." A campaign in 1014 began the pacification. In 1036, the Demon Master became a salaried state official. The "forbidden hills" of Sichuan were stripped of forests and planted with tea and with mulberries for silk production. The salt mines became resources of the Chinese Empire. A land that

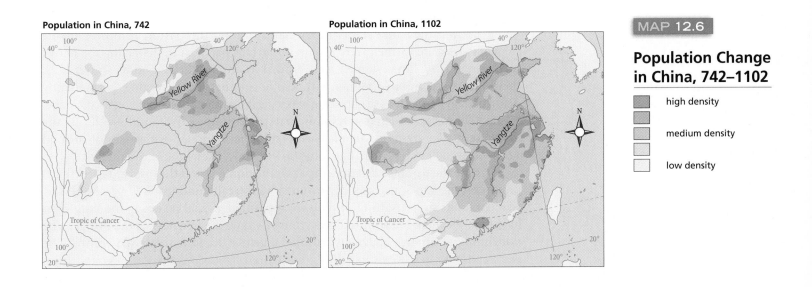

Population in China, 742

Population in China, 1102

MAP 12.6

Population Change in China, 742–1102

- high density
-
- medium density
-
- low density

Rice cultivation. In the second half of the thirteenth century, Zhen Ji illustrated poems on rice cultivation in a long series of paintings, all copied—like the poems—from twelfth-century originals. His art demonstrates the continuity of Chinese agriculture. Even after revolutionary new strains of rice were introduced in China, older varieties of the crop were still cultivated in traditional ways.

poets formerly praised as a romantic wilderness of "streams and grottoes" became China's "heavenly storehouse."

Alongside the colonization of new land, new methods of exploitation enriched China, in a process of internal expansion strikingly reminiscent of what was going on at the same time in many other regions, notably in Europe and Ethiopia (Chapter 11). Environmental change fed the growing population. Wetlands were drained. New varieties of rice arrived from Vietnam, adapted to local conditions by trial and error. Planting and harvesting two crops a year effectively doubled the capacity for food production in the Yangtze valley. From the 1040s, the state promoted agriculture by making loans to peasants for seed grain, at favorable rates. Deforestation continued, stimulated by a tax on unharvested timber. By the end of the eleventh century, the forests around the city of Kaifeng (keye-fung) had disappeared, sacrificed to huge iron-smelting works, employing 3,000 men. In 1132, a new palace at Kaifeng was built with timber from the Qingfeng (chihng-fung) Mountains, reputedly inaccessible for centuries, like the enchanted forests of fairy tales.

Meanwhile, the money economy boomed. Song mints were always busy, always pumping out new coins—a million strings of coins a year in the early years of the century, six million in 1080—and always devaluing the currency by putting less precious metal—gold and silver—into coins. Paper money became a state monopoly from 1043. Towns grew spectacularly. Until the Jurchen captured it, Kaifeng was not just a seat of government but a thriving place of manufacture and trade. A famous twelfth-century painting by Zhang Zeduan (jwang tzeh-dwan) depicts the bustling life of the city—perhaps somewhat idealistically. On a roll more than 22-yards wide, all the life of Kaifeng at festival time unfolds—craftsmen, merchants, peddlers, entertainers, shoppers, and gawking crowds. Groaning grain ships bring the extra food. A river thick with traffic intersects the criss-cross framework of the neat streets with buildings roofed with thatch. Zhang also shows restaurant diners enjoying their meals. Kaifeng had 72 large restaurants, each of up to five pavilions, three-storeys high, and connected by delicate bridges. In 1147, the poet Master Meng (mung) recalled in his *Dream of the Eastern Capital's Splendor* how in Kaifeng the entertainers' din "could be heard for miles . . . Wildman Zhao would eat and drink while hung upside down . . . Li Waining (lee weye-ning) would pop up puppets with explosives."

Women, however, rarely appear in Meng's verses or on Zhang's scroll. They never enjoyed the same status in China as among the pastoral cultures of the steppeland, where women were always important partners in managing the herds. Increasingly, in China, women were traded as commodities, and as young girls, their feet were tightly bound with cloth, so that they became permanently deformed, in a practice perhaps originally designed to hobble them against escape. It soon, however, became a fashion that men supposedly found erotic. In the *Romance of the Western Chamber*—the sublime Chinese love classic of around 1200—feet "dainty but firm, like lotus flower buds" excite the hero's interest.

Despite the troubled relationship with the nomads and the loss of the northern provinces, the late Song Empire brimmed with wealth and inspired pride and satisfaction in its subjects. In 1170, a newly appointed official set off up the Yangtze to his job in Sichuan. He admired everything he saw: the newness of the bridges, the flourishing commerce, the boats crowded together "like the teeth of a comb." The war readiness of 700 river galleys, with their "speed like flight," excited him.

He celebrated ample signs of prosperity. The province to which he was traveling possessed enviable wealth. Two districts in Sichuan had between them 22 centers of population producing annual tax revenue of between 10,000 and 50,000 strings of cash—more than any other district of the Song Empire outside the lower Yangtze. The frontier had been drawn into the empire.

Kaifeng. In this most famous of Song dynasty scroll-paintings, Zhang Zeduan captures the vitality of life on the Yellow River at the city of Kaifeng in the early twelfth century and the wonderful commercial opportunities that the approach of the Spring Festival brought. Hundreds of wares arrive by cart, mule, or camel train or on poles slung across peddlers' backs.
The Art Archive/Picture Desk, Inc./Kobal Collection.

Song Art and Learning

The era left an enduring legacy of intellectual and artistic achievement. To the eleventh-century elite, philosophy was not an occupation of luxury or leisure, but the basis and business of government. On one side of the debate, Ouyang Xiu aimed to restore "the perfection of ancient times"—an ideal age "when rites and music reached everywhere." His writings capture the agenda and atmosphere of a sort of renaissance, a revival of ancient ethics and letters. He belonged to a type familiar in almost every great courtly society: urbane, world-weary, and with highly sophisticated sensibilities. His poems in praise of singing girls and strong drink made him vulnerable to attack by moralists. During a struggle among rival groups at court in 1067, he was disgraced in a sex scandal. Ouyang Xiu retired to what he called his "old tippler's pavilion" in the country.

Wang Anshi (wahng ahn-sheh), who led the party on the other side of the debate, thought life was like a dream and valued "dreamlike merits" equally with practical results. He carried the notion of socially responsible government to extremes and consulted "peasants and serving girls" rather than relying on Confucian principles and ancient precedents. The policies he pursued, when he was in charge of the government in the 1070s, included progressive taxation, the substitution of taxes for forced labor, cheap loans for farmers, and state-owned pawnshops. Wang mistrusted Confucian confidence in China's ability to tame the steppelanders—he introduced universal conscription. To combat banditry, and prevent the desertion of young peasants to bandit

Chinese Night Revels. A female musician entertains members of the scholar-gentry in The Night Revels of Han Xizai, painted in the tenth century by Gu Hongzhong. Chinese paintings rarely show men and women together in this kind of interior setting. The elaborately laid and decorated table, the porcelain ware, and the luxury and sexual appeal of female entertainment provide an intimate glimpse of courtly life during the Song dynasty.

Misty mountains. Chinese landscape painters under the Song dynasty celebrated the mountains and caves of newly colonized lands in southwest China. Mi Fei was one of the outstanding exponents of this type of painting, developing what came to be known as the "misty mountain style." No Western artist even began to show a similar appreciation of nature before the thirteenth century, and no Westerner painted landscapes without people in them until the sixteenth century. "Mountains are rivers," says the line from Confucius that captions Mi Fei's painting, "that put forth clouds."
Pavilion of Rising Clouds, Mi Fu. Freer Gallery of Art, Smithsonian Institution, Washington, D.C.: Gift of Charles Lang Freer, F. 1908. 171

gangs, he organized village society in groups of ten families, so that each family was held responsible for the good behavior of the others.

Both parties supported reform of the examination system that produced the imperial officials with two objectives in mind: to encode in it an ethic of service to society, and to recruit the state's servants from as wide a range of social backgrounds as possible. The old examination tested only skill in composition, especially in verse, and in memorizing texts. The new test asked questions about ethical standards and about how the state could serve the people better. It was a conservative revolution.

While Wang's agenda shaped policy, Ouyang Xiu's dominated the intellectual mainstream. The dominant trend in philosophy for the rest of the Song era was the effort to reinterpret the Confucian classics for the readers' own times. The work of Zhu Xi (joo shi) (1130–1200) summarized and synthesized all previous thinking on this subject. In his own mind, he was an orthodox Confucian, but in some ways, he was what we would now call a secular humanist. He upheld the doctrine of the natural goodness of human beings. He doubted whether "there is a man in heaven judging sin" and dismissed prayer in favor of self-examination and study of the classics. Morality, he thought, was a matter of individual responsibility, not heavenly regulation. But he did accept the tradition on which the Chinese state was based: "heaven" decreed the fortunes of society according to the merits of its rulers. Zhu's synthesis was so influential that it defined what subsequent ages called Confucianism.

The intellectual and economic environment of the Song Empire was highly favorable to the arts. There was money and enthusiasm for abundant patronage of artists. In the early twelfth century, the Huidzung (hway-dzuhng) emperor, who was an accomplished painter himself, founded a school of painting and expanded the palace gallery to exhibit paintings and ceramics. The painting of the era has always attracted special admiration, not just because it was prolific and technically excellent, but also because it specialized in scenes from the natural world. Admiration for the beauty of nature, untouched by human hands, is, perhaps, a measure of the maturity of a civilization. It is doubtful, however, whether Song artists painted nature, as modern romantics do today, for its own sake. To them, the natural world was a book of lessons about humankind and from which they could make comparisons about human nature. Every subject for a painting demanded long meditation in which the artist strove to understand the essence of what he was going to paint. Su Dongpo (soo dohng-pwoh) (1036–1101) painted virtually nothing but bamboo, because its fragility suggested human weakness. Li Longmian (lee lung-mee-en) (1049–1106) favored gnarled trees, defying weather, as symbols of the resilience of the sages. Mi Fei (mee fay) (1051–1107) perfected the representation of mist—which is the breath of nature, with power to shape the image, like the spiritual dimension of human beings. With other painters of the same era, they produced some of the world's most influential, most imitated images.

In Perspective
Cains and Abels

The North African Muslim Ibn Khaldun (1332–1406), one of the world's best historians, saw history as a story of struggle between nomads and settled people. To some extent, he based his view on the experience of the eleventh and twelfth centuries, when, as far as he could make out, pastoralist invaders wrecked the peace

Making Connections | NOMADIC THREATS TO SEDENTARY PEOPLES

CHARACTERISTICS OF EURASIAN NOMADS		CONSEQUENCES
Nomadic way of life requires extensive land	▶	Constant threat of attack on sedentary peoples
Nomads ill equipped for certain economic activities and the manufacture of favored commodities	▶	Dependence on theft and tribute from, or trade with, sedentary peoples
Nomads are expert horsemen	▶	Until development of firearms and better fortifications, sedentary peoples at a disadvantage in war
Nomads cherish ideologies of superiority	▶	Clash between nomads and settled peoples
Nomads can easily exploit farmers' lands	▶	Until development of steel plows and mechanized harvesters, farmers could not exploit grasslands

and prosperity of his native region and Spain: first, Arab herders whom the Fatimids released or expelled from southern Egypt; then the Almoravids and Almohads from the Sahara. Modern historians have challenged his interpretation. The mutual disdain between tillers and herders was neither as deep nor as destructive as Ibn Khaldun thought. But the tension he perceived was real. The biblical story of Cain and Abel traces the origins of human conflict to the mutual hatred and murderous rivalry of a tiller of the soil and a keeper of flocks.

Nomads threatened their farming neighbors in various ways. The nomadic way of life demanded immeasurably more land per head of population than the intensive agriculture that fed dense farming populations. Nomads were ill equipped for some economic activities, including mining and silk manufacture, and the production of favored commodities, such as tea, fruit, and grain. For these things, therefore, they depended on theft, tribute, or trade from farming communities. The nomads were better equipped for war. Horsemanship made their way of life a preparation for battle. Sedentary peoples had not yet developed firearms or fortifications good enough to tilt the balance in their own favor. The nomads tended to cherish ideologies of superiority—variously of jihad or of divine election for empire—that clashed with the equal and opposite convictions of the settled peoples. Nomads could exploit farmers' lands, but agricultural communities did not yet have the technology—steel plows, mechanical harvesters—needed to turn the unyielding soils of the grasslands into productive farmland.

Yet the hostility of nomads and farmers arose less, perhaps, from conflicts of interest than from mutual misunderstanding: a clash of cultures, incompatible ways of seeing the world and coping with it. There is no moral difference between settled and nomadic lifeways. Each type of community, however, tended to see the other as morally inferior. This was probably because for followers of each way of life, those of the other came to represent all that was alien. Their mutual descriptions were full of incomprehension and even disgust.

Real differences underpinned this mutual revulsion. Pastoralist diets were, for farmers, literally stomach churning. Pastoralists relied on dairy foods, which most farmers' digestive systems rejected, because after early childhood they did not naturally produce lactase—the substance that makes milk digestible. It was also normal for herders to open their animal's veins for fresh blood to drink. This practice enabled nomad armies to take nourishment without halting on the march. Nomad

"Yet the hostility of nomads and farmers arose less, perhaps, from conflicts of interest than from mutual misunderstanding: a clash of cultures, incompatible ways of seeing the world and coping with it."

Chronology

907	End of Tang dynasty
960	Beginning of Song dynasty; conversion of Karkhanid Turks to Islam
1040s	Sanhaja conquer Morocco
1054	Schism between Latin and Orthodox Christianity
1071	Battle of Manzikert; end of Byzantine dominance in Anatolia
1076	Kumbi Saleh falls to Almoravid armies
1080s	Muslim kingdoms in al-Andalus call on Almoravids for help
1095	Pope Urban II calls for crusade to capture Jerusalem
1099	Jerusalem falls to crusaders
1111	Death of al-Ghazali, Sufi mystic and theologian
1140s	Almoravid Empire falls to the Almohads
1187	Crusader kingdom of Jerusalem falls to Saladin
1204	Crusaders sack Constantinople

diets tended to be short on plant foods. So to balance their intake, nomads would usually eat the raw organ meats of dead animals. This sort of food contains relatively high levels of vitamin C, which, in other cultures, people get from fruit and vegetables. Indeed, meat processed without cooking was important in the treeless environments of the steppe and the desert, where the only cooking fuel was dried animal dung. One of the great resources of the Eurasian steppe was the fat-tailed sheep, specially bred to drag its tail—as broad as a beaver's—behind it. Its fat is wonderfully soft. Even if nomads have no time to heat this fat, or no available kindling with which to cook it, they can eat it raw and digest it quickly. These were all elements of a rational food strategy for the nomadic life, but they inspired denunciations of the "barbaric" customs of eaters of raw meat and drinkers of blood. The nomads responded with equal contempt. For them, the settled life was soft and corrupted by luxury. Farming involved grubbing and groveling in mud. Cities and rice paddies were cramped and unhealthy.

After successful conquests, the nomads could usually be absorbed and induced to adopt or tolerate settled ways of life; but the conquerors kept coming. The relative success of the Islamic world in absorbing and converting the invaders of the tenth and eleventh centuries was a decisive feature of the history of the period. Byzantium, by contrast, failed to tame the intruders, while Western Christendom could recruit no more pastoralists after the Magyars. China developed no strategy to cope with the nomads, except to retreat and wait for them to adopt Chinese ways. Unprecedented changes in the steppeland, however, were about to upset the balance between nomads and settled peoples and unleash the most formidable steppeland conquerors of all, the Mongols. The outcome would transform the history of Eurasia.

PROBLEMS AND PARALLELS

1. Was the Islamic world's disunity an inevitable outcome of its vast geographic expansion by 1000? What parallels, if any, are there to earlier empires?

2. Why was the Islamic world more successful than Christian Europe or China in absorbing nomads? What strengths did the Turks bring to the Islamic world?

3. The Crusades started as an outgrowth of the tradition of pilgrimage. How was a religious process transformed into a series of violent military campaigns? What were the ultimate effects of the Crusades?

4. Why were the Almoravids and Almohads unable to prevent the decline of Islamic power in Spain Islamic power there? Why was the conversion of Ghana to Islam so significant?

5. Why did most Muslim elites and clerics reject the Sufis? Why were the teachings of Sufis like al-Ghazali important for the spread of Islam?

6. Why did the Byzantines claim to be the Roman Empire? Why was it strategically important for the rulers of Constantinople to build a Byzantine "commonwealth"? Why was Basil II so successful, and why were his successors unable to sustain his legacy? Why was there a rupture between Latin and Orthodox Christianity?

7. How did China under the Song deal with nomadic invaders? Why was Song China able to prosper despite the loss of the Yellow River valley?

8. Why did Ibn Khaldun see history as a story of struggle between nomads and settled people? Why have relations between pastoralists and sedentary peoples often been so hostile?

READ ON▶ ▶ ▶

B. Lewis, *The Middle East* (1997) is a broad introductory narrative. M. S. Hodgson, *The Venture of Islam* (1977) is as always fundamental for anything in Islamic history. L. Yaacov, *State and Society in Fatimid Egypt* (1991) is an important collection of studies on the background to the caliphate of al-Hakim. T. Talbot-Rice, *The Seljuks in Asia Minor* (1960) is important for understanding the assimilation of the Turks. The *Dede Korkut* (1974) is available in an excellent edition by G. Lewis.

T. Asbridge, *The First Crusade* (2005) is a vigorous, up-to-date account. C. Tyerman, *God's War* (2006) is an efficient general introduction, as is J. Riley-Smith, *The Crusades* (2005). J. Riley-Smith, *Atlas of the Crusades* (1990) is a useful standby. K. M. Setton, ed., *A History of the Crusades* (1969) is exhaustive. J. Pryor, *Geography, Technology and War: Studies in the Maritime History of the Mediterranean, 649–1571*, makes what happened at sea intelligible.

H. Kennedy, *Muslim Spain and Portugal*, (1997) and R. Fletcher, *Moorish Spain* (1993) are helpful as introductions. D. Wasserstein, *The Rise and Fall of the Party Kings* (1985) deals with the dissolution of the caliphate of Cordova and its successor states. For the Spanish background, R. Fletcher, *The Quest for El Cid* (1991) is scintillating and highly readable. E. W. R. Bovill, *The Golden Trade of the Moors* (1992) and *Saharan Myth and Legend* are classic works that unfold the background to the Almoravids. N. Levtzion, *Ancient Ghana and Mali* (1980) is an authoritative and concise study. On Ghana, N. Levtzion, *Corpus of Early Arabic Sources for West African History* (1981) and T. Insoll, *The Archeology of Islam in sub-Saharan Africa* (2003) provide the main sources. J. S. Trimingham, *The Sufi Orders in Islam* (1998) is the great classic treatment of its subject.

On Byzantium, as well as works recommended in earlier chapters, C. Mango, *Byzantium and Its Image* (1984) is particularly good on cultural aspects, and D. Obolensky, *The Phoenix: The Byzantine Commonwealth*, (2000), which is particularly good on diplomacy, are helpful. B. Hill, *Imperial Women in Byzantium* (1999) is an indispensable modern study. A. J. Toynbee, *Constantine Porphyrogenitus and His World* (1973) is a timeless classic by one of the great historians of the twentieth century. Among the texts referred to in this chapter, *The Embassy to Constantinople and Other Writings of Liutprand of Cremona*, ed. J. J. Norwich, is instructive, and there are many editions of the *Alexiad* of Anna Comnena and *The Itinerary of Benjamin of Tudela*. On relations with the Latin church, S. Runciman, *The Eastern Schism*, (1955) though now half a century old, is concise and readable. J. J. Norwich, *A History of Venice* (1982) is a richly detailed narrative. D. E. Queller, *The Fourth Crusade* (1999) nicely blends narrative and analysis. There are many editions of the most engaging source: G. de Villehardouin, *The Conquest of Constantinople* (2006). N. Wilson, *Scribes and Scholars* (1991) is a lively account of Byzantine learning.

On Liao, J. S. Tao, *Two Sons of Heaven* (1988) is valuable; for the Jurchen, Y. S. Tao, *The Jurchen in Twelfth-Century China* (1977) is particularly good on sinicization. R. von Glahn, *The Country of Streams and Grottoes* (1988) is scholarly and well-written, bringing the internal frontier of China to life. R. Egan, ed., *The Literary Works of Ou-yang Hsiu* (1984) is an invaluable source. J. T. C. Liu, *Reform in Sung China*, which originally appeared in the 1950s, has not been replaced as far as I know.

The World in 1200 C.E.

Hostility became routine between societies that relied mainly on tilling the soil and those that had to move frequently from one place to another with the herds they lived off. Grazing needs a lot of space, relatively speaking, to turn the plant life livestock eat into humanly edible food. So practitioners of the two types of culture became competitors for land. Their differences of culture were so marked that, as we have seen so often throughout this book, farmers and nomad herders found it easy to hate each other and hard to establish mutual understanding.

Christendom, Islam, and China had contrasting experiences of relationships with nomads. The Magyars and Bulgars settled inside Christendom, setting up states similar to those of their neighbors, but most of the herder-peoples who raided or invaded Europe remained excluded and hostile. Nomad invaders of China typically adopted Chinese ways and became vulnerable in their turn to further waves of invasion from the steppes. In Islam, however, the Turks' vocation for war outlasted conversion to Muslim religion and more settled ways of life. They became the sword-bearers of Islam, renewing manpower for defence and expansion to an extent unparalleled in Europe or China.

Despite turbulence in the steppes, contacts between China and Europe, though feeble and indirect, were never altogether interrupted. Though separated by turbulent seas, Japan was never quite out of touch with the other civilizations of east Asia. So the extremities of Eurasia were able to cope with—and, increasingly, emerge from—their relative isolation. Societies that fringed the Indian Ocean enriched and influenced each other. The relative stagnation of parts of Africa and the Americas showed, meanwhile, how isolation can inhibit change, whereas interactions between cultures exert mutual magnetism and make changes happen faster.

▶ QUESTIONS

1. How did different societies cope and contend with their relative isolation in the period from 1000 to 1200 C.E.?

2. Which settled societies were most threatened by nomadic peoples from 1000 to 1200 C.E.? Which sedentary societies were able to absorb pastoralists? In which societies did nomadic peoples remain excluded and hostile?

To view an interactive version of this map, as well as a video of the author describing key themes related to this Part, go to
www.myhistorylab.com

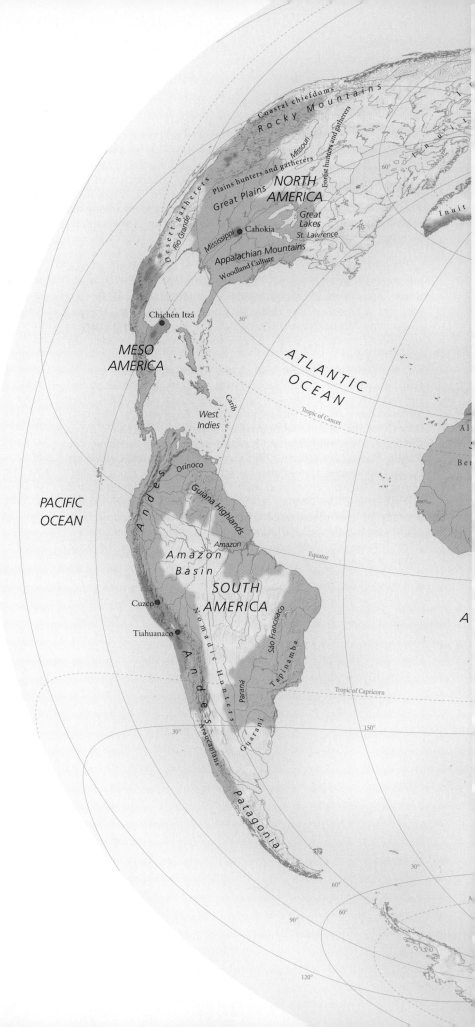

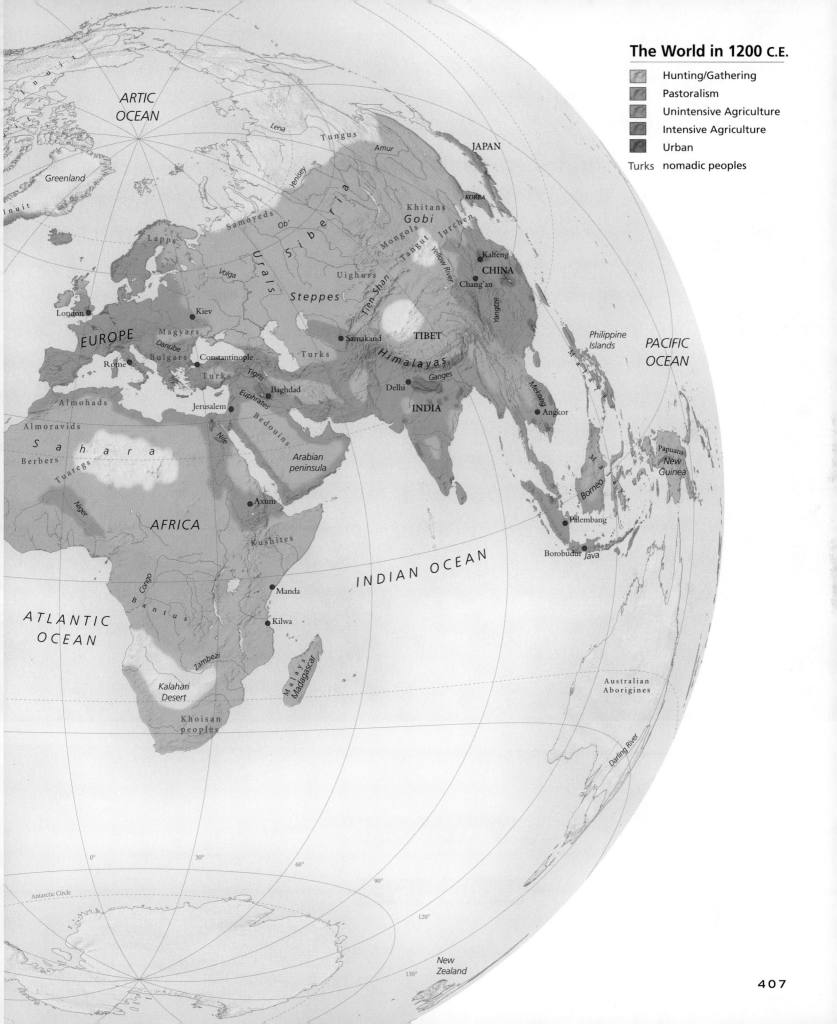

The World in 1200 C.E.

- Hunting/Gathering
- Pastoralism
- Unintensive Agriculture
- Intensive Agriculture
- Urban

Turks   nomadic peoples

ARTIC OCEAN

Greenland

Inuit

Inuit

Lapps

Samoyeds

Siberia

Tungus

Lena

Amur

Yenisey

Ob'

Urals

Volga

Khitans

Gobi

Mongols

Tangut

Jurchen

Yellow River

Kalfeng

CHINA

Chang'an

JAPAN

KOREA

London

Kiev

Magyars

Danube

Bulgars

EUROPE

Rome

Constantinople

Turks

Tigris

Euphrates

Jerusalem

Bedouins

Baghdad

Turks

Uighurs

Steppes

Samakand

Tien Shan

Himalayas

TIBET

Delhi

Ganges

INDIA

Yangtze

Mekong

Angkor

Philippine Islands

PACIFIC OCEAN

Almohads

Almoravids

Sahara

Berbers

Tuaregs

Niger

Nile

Arabian peninsula

Axum

AFRICA

Kushites

Congo

Bantus

Zambezi

Manda

Kilwa

Malays

Borneo

Palembang

Borobudur   Java

Malays

Papuans
New Guinea

INDIAN OCEAN

ATLANTIC OCEAN

Kalahari Desert

Malays
Madagascar

Khoisan peoples

Australian Aborigines

Darling River

0°

30°

60°

90°

120°

Antarctic Circle

150°

New Zealand

PART 6

ENVIRONMENT

CULTURE

1300–1800
Little Ice Age

since mid-1200s
Lenses and clocks in Europe

1206–1360s
Mongol hegemony

The Crucible: The Eurasian Crises of the Thirteenth and Fourteenth Centuries

◀ **This Korean world map,** from about 1402, known as the Kangnido, is the earliest known map of the world from East Asia. It is also the oldest surviving Korean map. Based on Chinese maps from the fourteenth century, the Kangnido clearly shows Africa (with an enormous lake in the middle of the continent) and Arabia on the lower left. The Indian subcontinent, however, has been merged into a gigantic landmass that represents China. The Korean peninsula, on the upper right, is shown as much bigger than it actually is, while Japan, on the lower right, is placed much farther south than where it is actually located.

1330s–mid-1400s (and sporadically to 1700s)
Plague in Eurasia

since mid-1400s
Growth of Atlantic navigation

from 1350s
Rise of the Ottomans

1368–1644
Ming dynasty (China)

from 1440s
Rise of Muscovy

from mid-1400s
Rise of Incas, Aztecs
Beginnings of oceanic imperialism

FRONT

BACK

FRONT

BACK

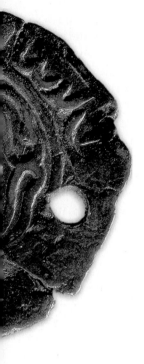

Two coins lie alongside each other in the British Museum in London. One, minted in 1230, is stamped with the name of the queen of Georgia, Rusudan, and the words, "Queen of Queens, Glory of the World and Faith, Champion of the Messiah." Beside it, another Georgian coin, minted only 17 years later, shows a figure on horseback, named as "King David, slave of the empire of the Great Khan Kuyuk." A lot had happened in Georgia in a short time. The changes the coins reflect were important not just for Georgia but for the world, for they were huge in scale, reshaping the politics, communications, and culture of Eurasia.

GEORGIA

Georgia, protected by the high Caucasus Mountains, had been remarkably successful in resisting the nomad armies of the eleventh and twelfth centuries. Though the Seljuk Turks (see Chapter 12) had briefly terrorized the kingdom and exacted tribute, the Georgians fought back. They refused to pay tribute, recovered their lost territories, and extended their frontiers over parts of neighboring Armenia. In the early thirteenth century, Georgia was a formidable state, capable of imposing rulers as far afield as the Byzantine city of Trebizond on the Black Sea coast of Anatolia and the Muslim city of Ahar in Azerbaijan on the Caspian. In the 1220s, James of Vitry, a Catholic bishop and historian of his own times, admired Georgian pilgrims he saw in Jerusalem, who "march into the holy city with banners displayed, without paying tribute to anyone, for the Muslims dare in no way molest them."

As James of Vitry noted, Georgia was "surrounded by infidels on all sides". That did not seem to matter. The Georgians even promised the pope that they would assist in a new crusade. Suddenly, however, in 1224, letters from Georgia arrived in Rome, withdrawing the promise. "A savage people of hellish aspect have invaded my realm," wrote Rusudan, "as voracious as wolves in their hunger for spoils, and as brave as lions." In the next decade, her letters got increasingly desperate. The Mongols were coming. The world would never be the same again.

◀ **The Mongols arrive in Georgia.** Two coins from the kingdom of Georgia, minted less than two decades apart, show that the Mongols had conquered that Caucasian state. The front of the top coin, minted by Queen Rusudan of Georgia in 1230, features a bust of a bearded Jesus Christ, draped in a mantle and backed by a cross-shaped halo. The Greek abbreviations for the words "Jesus" and "Christ" flank his right and left shoulders respectively. A Georgian inscription runs along the border. The back of the coin shows inscriptions in both Georgian and Arabic. In contrast, on the bottom coin, minted by King David in 1247, a figure on horse back has replaced the image of Jesus Christ (front), while the inscription on the back of the coin is exclusively in Arabic and identifies the king as "the slave of the Great Khan."

The effects of the events of the rest of the thirteenth century refashioned Eurasia, destroying old states, creating new ones, disrupting existing communications and reforging stronger, wider-ranging links. Eurasian civilizations benefited from enhanced contacts the Mongols fostered. Mongol methods were at first pitilessly bloody. They used terror and massacres to overawe their enemies. They razed cities, destroyed crops, slaughtered elites, and depleted peoples. Yet it looked as if a safer, richer, more interconnected, more dynamic, more expanding, and more enlightened world might emerge—as if something precious were to form in an alchemist's crucible, out of conflicting ingredients, flung at random and stirred with violence. Then a century of environmental disasters arrested these changes in most of Eurasia. Catastrophes reversed the growth of populations and prosperity. But previously marginal regions began to be drawn more closely into a widening pattern of contacts and cultural exchange. Some peoples, in Africa and Southeast Asia, for example, looked outward because they escaped disaster. Others, especially in Europe, did so because their reverses were so enormous that there was nothing else they could do.

THE MONGOLS: RESHAPING EURASIA

The earliest records of Mongol peoples occur in Chinese annals of the seventh century. At that time, the Mongols emerged onto the steppes of the Central Asian land now called Mongolia, from the forests to the north, where they seem to have been hunters and small-scale pig breeders. On the steppes they adopted a pastoral way of life. They became horse-borne nomads and sheepherders. Chinese and Khitan writers used versions of the names "Mongols" and "Tatars" for many different communities, with various religions and competing leaderships. One thing they had in common was that they spoke languages of common origins that were different from those of the Turks. In the early twelfth century, the bands or alliances they formed got bigger, and their raids against neighboring sedentary peoples became more menacing. In part, this was the effect of the growing preponderance of some Mongol groups over others. In part, it was the result of slow economic change.

Genghis Khan

Contact with richer neighbors gave Mongol chiefs opportunities for enrichment as mercenaries or raiders. Economic inequalities greater than the Mongols had ever known arose in a society in which blood relationships and seniority in age had formerly settled every person's position. Prowess in war enabled leaders to build up followers in parallel with—and sometimes in defiance of—the old social order. They called this process "crane catching"—comparing it to caging valuable birds. The most successful leaders enticed or forced rival groups into submission. The process spread to involve peoples who were not strictly Mongols, though the same name continued to be used—we use it still—for a confederation of many peoples, including many who spoke Turkic languages. In 1206, Temujin (TEH-moo-jeen), the most dynamic leader, proclaimed himself ruler (**khan**) "of all those who live in felt tents"—staking a claim to a steppe-wide empire. He was acclaimed by a title of obscure meaning, perhaps signifying "Ocean-King" and therefore, by implication, king of everything the ocean encloses. The title is traditionally rendered in the Roman alphabet as "Genghis Khan" (GEHN-gihs hahn).

We know maddeningly little about Temujin. Today, his memory is twisted between myths. When Mongolia was a communist state between 1921 and 1990, he was an almost unmentionable figure, inconsistent with the "peace-loving" image the communists tried to project. Now he is Mongolia's national hero. In his own day, he toyed with similarly contradictory images: a warlord who intimidated enemies into submission by massacre; an avenger of insults to his dynasty and tribe; an embodiment of Mongol convictions of superiority over sedentary peoples; a scourge of heaven, divinely appointed to chastise a wicked world; a lawgiver and architect of enduring empire.

In surviving documents, Genghis Khan addressed different audiences with conflicting messages. To Muslims, he was an instrument of God, sent to punish them for their sins. To Chinese, he was a candidate for the mandate of heaven. To Mongols, he was a giver of victory and of the treasure it brought. When he addressed monks and hermits, he stressed his own asceticism. "Heaven is weary of the inordinate luxury of China," he declared. "I have the same rags and the same food as cowherds and grooms, and I treat the soldiers as my brothers."

The violence endemic in the steppes now turned outward to challenge neighboring civilizations. Historians have been tempted to speculate about the reasons for the Mongols' expansion. One explanation is environmental. Temperatures in the steppe seem to have fallen during the relevant period. People farther west on the Russian plains complained that a cold spell in the early thirteenth century caused crops to fail. So declining pastures might have driven the Mongols to expand from the steppes. Population in the region seems to have been relatively high, and the pastoral way of life demands large amounts of grazing land to feed relatively few people. It is not a particularly energy-efficient way to provide food because it relies on animals eating plants and people eating animals, whereas farming produces humanly edible crops and cuts out animals as a wasteful intermediate stage of production. So perhaps the Mongol outthrust was a consequence of having more mouths to feed. Yet the Mongols were doing what steppelanders had always sought to do: dominate and exploit sedentary peoples. The difference was that they did it with greater ambition and greater efficiency than any of their predecessors.

Genghis Khan enforced or induced unity over almost the entire steppeland. The confederation of tribes he put together really did represent a combined effort of the steppe dwellers against the sedentary peoples who surrounded them. A single ideology came to animate, or perhaps reflect, that effort: the God-given terror-enforced right of the Mongols to conquer the world. The way events were recorded at the Mongol court in the next generation, it seemed as if from the moment of Genghis Khan's election as supreme ruler, "eternal heaven" had decreed that his conquests would encompass the world. The ruler is depicted as a constant devotee of **Tengri** (tehng-REE)—the sky, conceived as a supreme deity. The early Mongol-

Genghis Khan. Rashid al-Din (1247–1318) was a former Jewish rabbi, converted to Islam, who became the chief minister of the Mongol rulers of what is now Iran. His Compendium of Chronicles was propaganda that depicted Mongol rulers in Persian style. This is the image of Genghis Khan his successors liked to project—a lone, simple tent-dweller who was the arbitrator and lawgiver to petitioners from many nations.

"Exceptionally adaptable warmongers." This fourteenth-century Muslim painting shows the Mongols capturing Baghdad in 1258, with the help of siege craft and specialist engineers as well as their traditional cavalry. The last caliph appears behind a screen in his palace in the left background. In the center background, he emerges on a white horse to meet the Mongol leader, Hülegü. The painting seems to show the Mongols respecting the sacredness of the city and its ruler. Indeed, they showed their respect by putting the caliph to death without spilling his blood—a sign of reverence for the condemned in their culture.

inspired sources constantly insist on an analogy between the overarching unity of the sky and God's evident desire for the Earth to echo that unity through submission to one ruler.

It is more likely, however, that the sky cult was invented during the Mongol conquests to explain Genghis Khan's uniformly successful fortunes in war. The khan's imperial vision probably grew on him only gradually, as he felt his way from raiding, tribute gathering, and exacting ransom to constructing an empire, with permanent institutions of rule. Tradition alleges a turning point. When one of his generals proposed to exterminate ten million Chinese subjects and convert their fields into pasture for Mongol herds, Genghis Khan realized that he could profit more by sparing the peasants and taxing them to the tune of 500,000 ounces of silver, 400,000 sacks of grain, and 80,000 bolts of silk a year. The process, however, that turned the khan from destroyer to builder was tentative. He may have been only dimly aware of it.

Genghis Khan's initially limited ambitions are clear from the oath the Mongol chiefs swore to him at his election as khan, recorded in the earliest surviving Mongol record of the events. "If you will be our khan, we will go as your vanguard against the multitude of your enemies. All the beautiful girls and married women that we capture and all the fine horses we will bring to you." The khan acquired an unequaled reputation for lust and bloodlust. "My greatest joy," he was remembered for saying, "is to shed my enemies' blood, wring tears from their womenfolk and take their daughters for bedding." Meanwhile, he made the streets of Beijing—according to an admittedly imaginative eyewitness—"greasy with the fat of the slain." His tally of victims in Persia amounted, believably, to millions. When his army captured the city of Herat (heh-RAHT) in Afghanistan, it killed the entire population. Even after Genghis Khan had introduced more constructive policies, terror remained an instrument of empire. Mongol sieges routinely culminated in massacre. When the Mongols captured Baghdad in 1258, the last **caliph** and his sons were trampled to death—a ritual form of death reserved for rulers, which was designed to demoralize the enemy.

Wherever the Mongol armies went, their reputation preceded them. Armenian sources warned Westerners of the approach of "precursors of Antichrist . . . of hideous aspect and without pity in their bowels, . . . who rush with joy to carnage as if to a wedding feast or orgy." Rumors piled up in Germany, France, Burgundy, Hungary, and even in Spain and England, where Mongols had never been heard of before. The invaders looked like monkeys, it was said, barked like dogs, ate raw flesh, drank their horses' urine, knew no laws, and showed no mercy. Matthew Paris, the thirteenth-century English monk who, in his day, probably knew as much about the rest of the world as any of his countrymen, summed up the Mongols' image: "They are inhuman and beastly, rather monsters than men, thirsting for and drinking blood, tearing and devouring the flesh of

Chronology: The Rise of the Mongols

Seventh century	Earliest records of the Mongol people
Early twelfth century	Larger Mongol bands attack sedentary peoples
1206	Temujin proclaims himself khan

Mongol defeat. Japanese screen painters recorded the defeat of Mongol invaders. Though the Mongols adapted successfully to every kind of terrain, they were unable to continue their conquests overseas. The "divine winds"—kamikaze, as the Japanese called them—protected Japan by making it impossible for the Mongols adequately to supply or reinforce their task force.

dogs and men. . . .And so they come, with the swiftness of lightning to the confines of Christendom, ravaging and slaughtering, striking everyone with terror and with incomparable horror."

The Mongol conquests reached farther and lasted longer than those of any previous nomad empire (see Map 13.1). After Genghis Khan's death, the energy that the conquests generated took Mongol armies to the banks of the Elbe River in eastern Germany and the Adriatic Sea. Invasions of Syria, India, and Japan failed, and the Mongols withdrew from Europe without attempting to set up a permanent presence west of Russia. They completed the conquest of China, however, in 1279. At its fullest extent, therefore, the empire covered the region from the Volga River to the Pacific, encompassing the whole of Russia, Persia, China, the Silk Roads, and the steppes. This made it by a big margin the largest empire, in terms of territorial extent, the world had seen.

Efforts to explain this unique success appeal to Genghis Khan's military genius, the cunning with which the Mongols practiced feigned retreats only to encircle and destroy their advancing enemies, the effectiveness of their curved bows, the demoralizing psychological impact of their ruthless practices. Of course, they had the usual steppelander advantages of superior horsemanship and unrivaled mobility. It is likely that they succeeded, in part, through sheer numbers. Though we call it a Mongol army, Genghis Khan's was the widest alliance of steppelander peoples ever. And it is probable—though the sources are not good enough for certainty—that, relatively speaking, the steppeland was more populous in his day than ever before.

Above all, the Mongols were exceptionally adaptable warmongers. They triumphed not only in cavalry country, but also in environments where previous steppelander armies had failed, pressing into service huge forces of foot soldiers, mobilizing complex logistical support, organizing siege trains and fleets, appropriating the full potential of sedentary economies to finance further wars. The mountains of Georgia could not stop them. The Mongols captured the Georgian capital, Tbilisi (t-BEE-lee-see), in 1234, turning Georgia into a puppet kingdom. Nor, in the long run, could the rice paddies and rivers of southern China where the Mongols destroyed the Song dynasty in the 1270s. Toward the end of the century, when another supreme khan wanted to conquer Java and Japan, they were even willing to take to the sea. But both attempts failed.

"Though we call it a Mongol army, Genghis Khan's was the widest alliance of steppelander peoples ever."

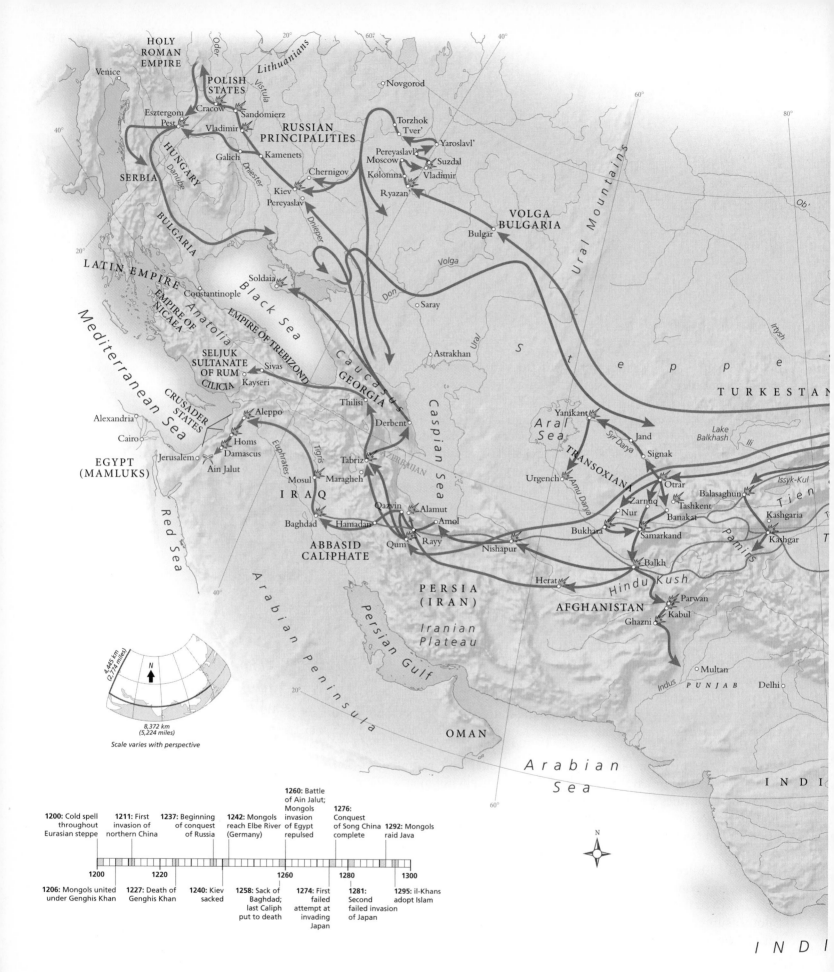

HOLY ROMAN EMPIRE

Venice

POLISH STATES

Esztergom · Cracow · Sandomierz
Pest · Vladimir

Lithuanians

Oder
Vistula

Novgorod

RUSSIAN PRINCIPALITIES

Galich · Kamenets
HUNGARY

SERBIA

Danube

BULGARIA

Dniester

Chernigov
Kiev
Pereyaslav

Dnieper

Torzhok
Tver'
Yaroslavl'
Pereyaslavl'
Moscow · Suzdal
Kolomna · Vladimir
Ryazan'

Don

Saray

VOLGA BULGARIA

Bulgar

Volga

Ural Mountains

Ob'

60°

80°

LATIN EMPIRE

Constantinople

EMPIRE OF NICAEA

Anatolia

Black Sea

Soldaia

EMPIRE OF TREBIZOND

Caucasus

GEORGIA

Thilisi

Astrakhan

Ural

Caspian Sea

S   t   e   p   p   e

TURKESTAN

Irtysh

Mediterranean Sea

SELJUK SULTANATE OF RUM

CILICIA

Sivas
Kayseri

CRUSADER STATES

Alexandria

Cairo

Aleppo

Homs
Damascus

Jerusalem

Ain Jalut

EGYPT (MAMLUKS)

Red Sea

Euphrates

Tigris

Mosul · Maragheh

IRAQ

Baghdad · Hamadan

ABBASID CALIPHATE

Derbent

AZERBAIJAN

Tabriz

Qazvin
Qum · Rayy

Alamut
Amol

Nishapur

Aral Sea

TRANSOXIANA

Syr Darya

Amu Darya

Urgench

Yanikant
Jand

Signak

Nur

Bukhara

Zarnuq
Samarkand

Balkh

Otrar
Tashkent
Banakat

Lake Balkhash

Ili

Balasaghun

Issyk-Kul

Kashgaria

Kashgar

Tien

Pamirs

PERSIA (IRAN)

Iranian Plateau

Persian Gulf

Arabian Peninsula

OMAN

Herat

Hindu Kush

AFGHANISTAN

Ghazni

Kabul
Parwan

Indus

PUNJAB

Multan

Delhi

INDIA

Arabian Sea

N

4,445 km (2,774 miles)

8,372 km (5,224 miles)

Scale varies with perspective

N

20°

60°

40°

40°

20°

40°

20°

60°

N

1200: Cold spell throughout Eurasian steppe

1211: First invasion of northern China

1237: Beginning of conquest of Russia

1242: Mongols reach Elbe River (Germany)

1260: Battle of Ain Jalut; Mongols invasion of Egypt repulsed

1276: Conquest of Song China complete

1292: Mongols raid Java

1200   1220   1260   1280   1300

1206: Mongols united under Genghis Khan

1227: Death of Genghis Khan

1240: Kiev sacked

1258: Sack of Baghdad; last Caliph put to death

1274: First failed attempt at invading Japan

1281: Second failed invasion of Japan

1295: il-Khans adopt Islam

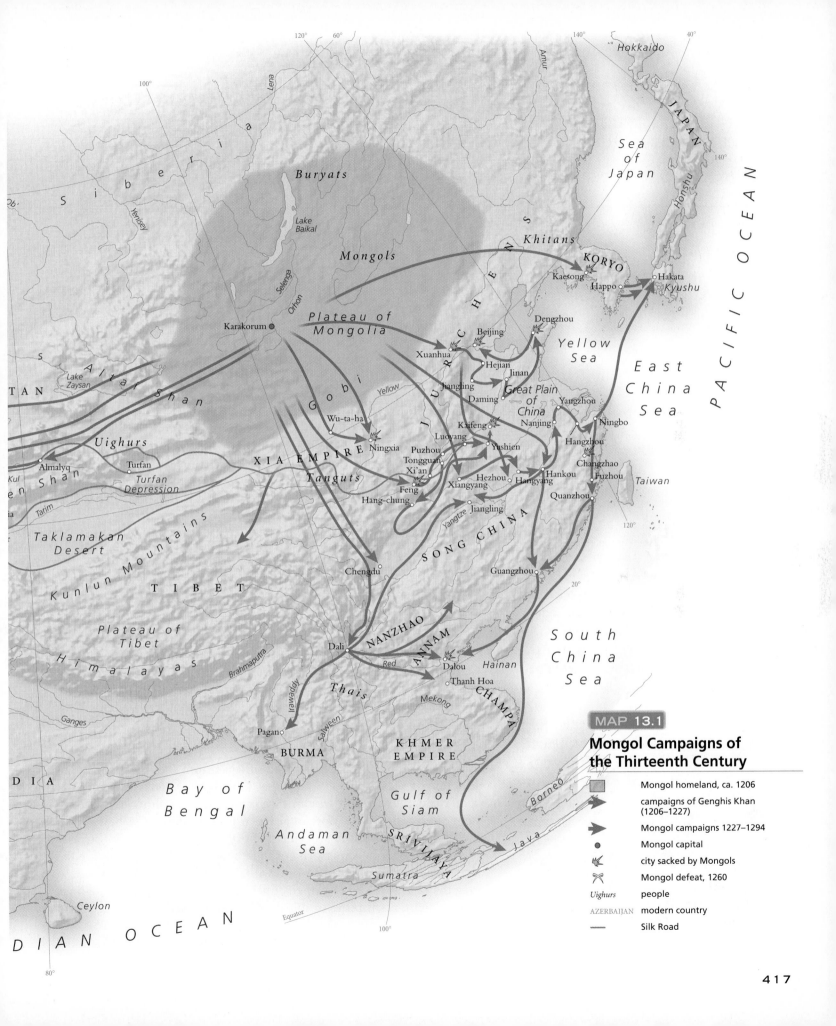

Mongol Campaigns of the Thirteenth Century

MAP 13.1

- Mongol homeland, ca. 1206
- campaigns of Genghis Khan (1206–1227)
- Mongol campaigns 1227–1294
- Mongol capital
- city sacked by Mongols
- Mongol defeat, 1260
- *Uighurs* people
- AZERBAIJAN modern country
- Silk Road

Making Connections | REASONS FOR MONGOL MILITARY SUCCESS

TACTICS/STRATEGIES	TECHNOLOGIES	PRACTICES
Psychological warfare; feigned retreats; unrivaled mobility	Superior horsemanship; curved bows; siegecraft	Ability to adapt to different environments and to overcome complex logistical obstacles; alliance formation with other steppeland peoples; recruitment of workers and administrators without favoritism

As well as for extent, the Mongol Empire was remarkable, by steppelander standards, for longevity. As his career progressed, Genghis Khan became a visionary lawgiver, a patron of letters, an architect of enduring empire. His first steps toward acquiring a bureaucracy and a judicial system more or less coincided with his election as khan. He then turned to lawmaking. Gradually, a code took shape, regulating hunting, army discipline, behavior at feasts, and social relationships, with death the penalty for murder, serious theft, conspiracy, adultery, sodomy, and witchcraft. Initially, the khan relied on Uighurs (see Chapter 9) for his administrators and ordered the adoption of the Uighur script for the Mongols' language. But he recruited as and where he conquered, without favoritism for any community or creed. His closest ministers included Muslims, Christians, and Buddhists.

In 1219, a Chinese Daoist sage, Changchun (chahng-chwuhn), answered the khan's call for wise experts. At the age of 71, he undertook an arduous three-year journey from China to meet the khan at the foot of the Hindu Kush Mountains in Afghanistan. There were sacrifices of principle Changchun would not make. He would not travel with recruits for the imperial harem, or venture "into a land where vegetables were unavailable"—by which he meant the steppe. Yet he crossed the Gobi Desert, climbed "mountains of huge cold," and braved wildernesses where his escort smeared their horses with blood to ward off demons. Admittedly, Changchun's meeting with the khan was disappointing. The question the conqueror was most eager to put was not about the art of government, but about a potion to confer longevity on himself.

The Mongol Steppe

Still, many lettered and experienced officials from the Jurchen, Khitan, and Tangut (THAN-goot) states (see Chapter 12) took service at the khan's court. The result was an exceptional, though short-lived, era in steppeland history: the **Mongol peace**. A European, who witnessed it in the 1240s, described it in an evident effort to reproach his fellow Christians with the moral superiority of their enemies: "The Mongols are the most obedient people in the world with regard to their leaders, more so even than our own clergy to their superiors. . . . There are no wranglings among them, no disputes or murders." This was obviously exaggerated, but Mongol rule did make the steppeland safe for outsiders. This was new. A previously inaccessible road through the steppes opened across

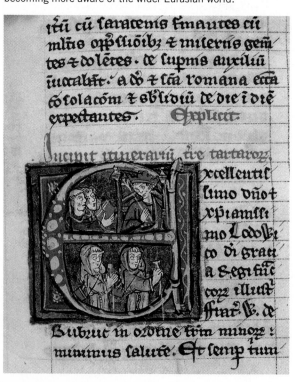

William of Rubruck. "He shall pass into the country of strange peoples. He shall try good and evil in all things." In the only surviving illumination that illustrates his report, Friar William of Rubruck looks alarmed at the instructions from King Louis IX of France to go on a mission to the Mongols. William's journey of 1253–1255 took him as far as the Mongol capital of Karakorum and generated an account full of vivid and faithful detail. The text illustrates how Western Europeans were becoming more aware of the wider Eurasian world.

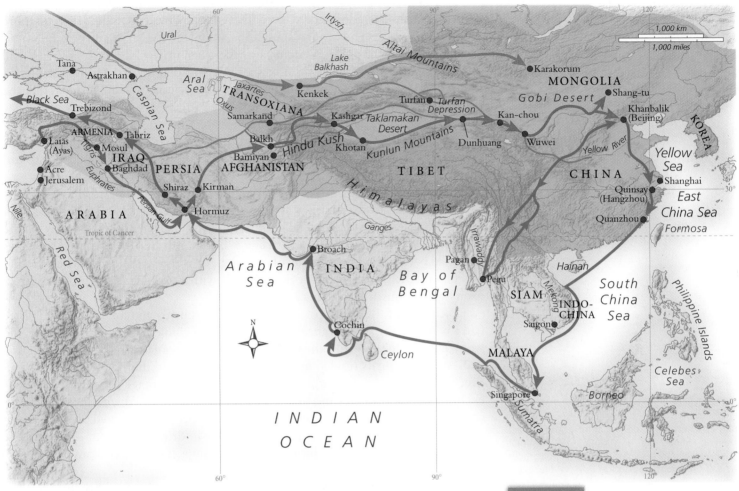

MAP 13.2

European Travelers of the Mongol Roads, 1245–1295

→ John of Piano Carpini 1245–1247 and William of Rubruck 1253–1254

→ Marco Polo 1271–1275

→ Marco Polo 1275–1295

▢ Khanate of the Golden Horde

▢ Il-Khanate

▢ Chagatai Khanate

▢ Empire of the Great Khan

— Silk Road

Eurasia north of the Silk Road. Once they had learned the benefits of peace along the steppeland road, the Mongols became its highway police. Teams of Mongol horses, for instance, took the pope's ambassador, John of Piano Carpini, 3,000 miles in 106 days in 1246. Missionaries, spies, and craftsmen in search of work at the Mongol court also made the journey in an attempt to forge friendship between the Mongols and the Christian West, or, at least, to gather intelligence (see Map 13.2).

William of Rubruck—a Franciscan envoy recorded vivid details of his mission to Mongke Khan (MOHNG-keh hahn), Genghis Khan's grandson in 1253. As well as describing the road, William also described the Mongol way of life more accurately and completely than any Western visitor until the late nineteenth century.

After taking leave of the king of France, who hoped for an alliance with the Mongols against the Muslims, William crossed the Black Sea in May and set out across the steppe by wagon, bound for Karakorum (kah-rah-KOH-ruhm), the new city in Mongolia where the khan held court. "After three days," he recorded, "we found the Mongols and I really felt as if I were entering another world." By November, he was in the middle of Transoxiana, "famished, thirsty, frozen, and exhausted." In December, he was high in the dreaded Altai Shan (AHL-tay shahn), the mountain barrier that guarded the road to Karakorum. Here he "chanted the creed, among dreadful crags, to put the demons to flight." At last, on Palm Sunday, 1254, he entered the Mongol capital.

Friar William always insisted that he was a simple missionary, but he was treated as an ambassador and behaved like a master spy. And, indeed, he had more than one objective. The Mongols might be amenable to Christianity or at least to an alliance against common enemies in the Muslim world. On the other hand, they were potential enemies, who had already invaded the fringes of Europe and might do so again. Intelligence about them was precious. William realized that the seasonal migrations of Mongol life had a scientific basis and were calculated for military efficiency. "Every commander," he noted, "according to whether he has a greater or smaller number of men under him, is familiar with the limits of his pasture lands and where he ought to graze in summer and winter, spring and autumn."

Little useful intelligence escaped William. But he also showed interest in the culture he tried unsuccessfully to convert to Christianity. His description of a Mongol tent dwelling still holds good. The layout, social space, and way of life William saw have not changed much since his day. A frame of interlaced branches stretched between supports made of branches, converging at the top. The covering was of white felt, "and they decorate the felt with various fine designs." Up to 22 oxen hauled houses on wagons 20 feet broad.

Each wife of the master of the household had her own tent, where the master had a bench facing the entrance. In an inversion of Chinese rules of precedence, the women sat on the east side, the men to the right of the master, who sat at the north end. Ancestral spirits resided in felt bags arrayed around the walls. One each hung over the heads of master and mistress, with a guardian image between them. Others hung on the women's and men's sides of the tent, adorned with the udders of a cow and a mare, symbols of the sources of life for people who relied on dairy products for their diet. The household would gather to drink in the tent of the chosen wife of the night. "I should have drawn everything for you," William assured his readers, "had I known how to draw."

Shamans' trances released the spirits from the bags that held them. Frenzied drumming, dancing, and drinking induced the shamans' ecstasies. The power of speaking with the ancestors' voices gave **shamans** enormous authority in Mongol decision making, including the opportunity to interfere in making and unmaking khans. This was a point William missed. The Mongols leaders' interest in foreign religions, and their investment in the cult of heaven, were, in part at least, strategies to offset the power of the native priests.

Outside the tent, William vividly captured the nature of the terrain—so smooth that one woman could pilot 30 wagons, linked by trailing ropes. He described a way of life that reflected steppeland ecology. The Mongols had mixed flocks of various kinds of sheep and cattle. Mixed pastoralism is essential in an environment in which no other source of food is available. Different species have different cycles of lactation and fertility. Variety therefore ensures a reliable food supply.

The horse was the dominant partner of life on the steppe. Mare's milk was the Mongols' summer food. The intestines and dried flesh of horses provided cured meat and sausages for winter. By drawing blood from the living

Yurt. The shape and decoration of a Mongol tent dwelling—known as a *yurt* or *ger*—has not changed since William of Rubruck described those he saw in the thirteenth century. In the background of this photograph are the Pamir Mountains, which travelers westward on the Silk Roads had to cross when they emerged from the Taklamakan Desert.

creatures, Mongols on campaign could refresh themselves without significantly slowing the herds. This was the basis of their reputation for blood-sucking savagery among their sedentary neighbors. They made, said William, "very fine shoes from the hind part of a horse's hide." Fermented mare's milk was the favorite intoxicating drink. The Mongols revered drunkenness and hallowed it by rites: offerings sprinkled over the bags of ancestral spirits, or poured out toward the quarters of the globe. Challenges to drinking bouts were a part of nightly entertainment. To the accompaniment of singing and clapping, the victim would be seized by the ears, with a vigorous tug "to make him open his gullet."

William related in detail his conversations with the habitually drunken Möngke Khan. Despite the khan's bluster and self-righteousness, the conversations revealed some of the qualities that made the Mongols of his era great: tolerance, adaptability, respect for tradition. "We Mongols believe," Möngke said, if we can trust William's understanding of his words, "that there is but one God, in Whom we live and in Whom we die, and towards him we have an upright heart." Spreading his hand, he added, "But just as God has given different fingers to the hand, so He has given different religions to people." Later in the thirteenth century, Kubilai Khan, another of Genghis Khan's grandsons, expressed himself to the Venetian traveler, Marco Polo, in similar terms. So this was genuinely a Mongol saying.

THE MONGOL WORLD BEYOND THE STEPPES: THE SILK ROADS, CHINA, PERSIA, AND RUSSIA

The steppeland route was ideal for horseborne travelers. Trading caravans, however, still favored the traditional **Silk Roads,** which crossed Eurasia to the south of the steppe through the Taklamakan (tahk-lah-mah-KAHN) Desert. These routes had developed over centuries, precisely because high mountains protected them from steppeland raiders. But they had never been totally secure before the Mongol peace. The new security boosted the amount of traffic the roads carried. Mongol partiality for merchants also helped. Mongols encouraged Chinese trade, uninhibited by any of the traditional Confucian prejudices against commerce as an ignoble occupation. In 1299, after the Mongol Empire had been divided among several rulers, a Persian merchant was made the ambassador of the Supreme Khan to the court of the subordinate Mongol **Il-khan** (EEL-hahn) in Persia—an elevation unthinkable under a native Chinese dynasty, which would have reserved such a post for an official educated in the Confucian classics. The khans gave low-cost loans to Chinese trading companies. Chinese goods—and with them, patterns and styles—flowed to Persian markets as never before. Chinese arts, under Mongol patronage, became more open to foreign influences.

Geography still made the Silk Roads hard to travel. Marco Polo was a young Venetian who accompanied his father and uncle on a trading mission to Mongol-ruled China in the early 1270s. "They were hard put to it to complete the journey in three and a half years," Marco Polo reported at the start of his own account, first "because of

The Silk Roads. Cresques Abraham was the finest mapmaker of his day. He painted this image of a caravan on the Silk Roads in the late 1370s or early 1380s in an atlas probably commissioned for the king of France. By that date, the Mongols no longer controlled the whole of the route, though the lances of an armed escort, presumably of Mongols, are visible behind the merchants. The caption says the caravan is bound for China, but it is heading in the opposite direction.

A CLOSER LOOK

A Mongol Passport

Although they were in use in China before the Mongols arrived, documents called *paizi*, such as the one depicted here, were used as passports to regulate communication and administration in the vast Mongol Empire. Their use, the way they were designed, and the language in which they were written help us understand the massive movements of people and the rapid exchange of ideas and technology that occurred across Eurasia during the thirteenth and fourteenth centuries when Mongol rule was at its height. William of Rubruck and Marco Polo would have carried one of these passports on their return journeys to Europe from Mongol courts in Asia.

This passport is made of iron. Thick silver bands on it form characters in the script that the Tibetan monk Phagspa, a close adviser to Kubilai Khan (r. 1260–1294), devised for writing the Mongol language in 1269.

Most *paizi* were circular or rectangular and were either fastened on clothing or suspended from a person's neck, so that customs officers could easily see them.

Above the inscription is a handle with a silver lion mask inlaid on it that shows the influence of Tibetan and Indian art.

The inscription reads:
"By the strength of Eternal Heaven, an edict of the Khan. He who has no respect [for the edict] shall be guilty."

The Metropolitan Museum of Art, Purchase, Bequest of Dorothy Graham Bennet, 1993 (1993.256) Photograph © The Metropolitan Museum of Art.

What does this passport reveal about the Mongol peace?

the snow and rain and flooded rivers and violent storms in the countries through which they had to pass, and because they could not ride so well in winter as in summer." The Taklamakan Desert was the great obstacle. The normal rule for caravans was the bigger the safer. But the modest water sources of the desert could not sustain many more than 50 men at a time with their beasts. The key to exploiting the desert routes was the distribution of water, which drains inland from the surrounding mountains and finds its way below the desert floor by underground channels. It was normal to go for 30 days without finding water, though there might be an occasional salt-marsh oasis or an unreliable river of shifting course, among featureless dunes. The worst danger was getting lost—"lured from the path by demon-spirits." "Yes," said Marco,

Demons. In Chinese and Mongol art, images of demons personify the torments of the desert—thirst, glare, sandstorms, extremes of heat and cold, the perils of being lost or attacked. William of Rubruck sang to drive away demons. Other travelers rang bells or deterred the demons with blood. In this fourteenth-century painting produced under Mongol patronage, the demon's dance evokes the swirling, stinging desert winds.

and even by daylight men hear these spirit-voices and often you fancy you are listening to the strains of many instruments, especially drums, and the clash of arms. For this reason bands of travelers make a point of keeping very close together. Before they go to sleep they set up a sign pointing in the direction in which they have to travel. And round the necks of their beasts they fasten little bells, so that by listening to the sound they may prevent them straying off the path.

As a fourteenth-century painter at Persia's Mongol court imagined them, the demons were black, athletic, and ruthless, waving the dismembered limbs of horses as they danced. As Friar William had seen, the Mongols recommended warding them off by smearing a horse's neck with blood.

A fourteenth-century guide included handy tips for Italian merchants who headed for East Asia to extend the reach of the commerce of their cities. At the port of Tana, on the Black Sea, you should furnish yourself with a good guide, regardless of expense. "And if the merchant likes to take a woman with him from Tana, he can do so." On departure from Tana, 25 days' supply of flour and salt fish were needed—"other things you will find in sufficiency and especially meat." The road was "safe by day and night," protected by Mongol police. But it was important to take a close relative for company. Otherwise, should a merchant die, his property would be forfeit. The text specified rates of exchange at each stop and recommended suitable conveyances for each stage of the journey: oxcart or horse-drawn wagon to the city of Astrakhan where the Don River runs into the Caspian Sea, depending on how fast the traveler wanted to go and how much he wanted to pay. Thereafter camel train or pack mule was best, until you arrived at the river system of China. Silver was the currency of the road, but the Chinese authorities would exchange it for paper money, which—Westerners were assured—they could use throughout China.

After the deserts, the next obstacles were the mountains on their rims. The Tian Shan, which screens the Taklamakan Desert, is one of the most formidable mountain ranges in the world: 1,800 miles long, up to 300 miles wide, and rising to 24,000 feet. The extraordinary environment these mountains enclose is odder still because of the deep depressions that punctuate them. That of Turfan (toor-FAHN) drops to more than 500 feet below sea level. Farther north, the Altai Shan Mountains guard

Chronology: Travelers during the Mongol Peace	
1245–1247	John of Piano Carpini
1253–1254	William of Rubruck
1271–1275; 1275–1295	Marco Polo
1275–1288	Rabban Bar Sauma

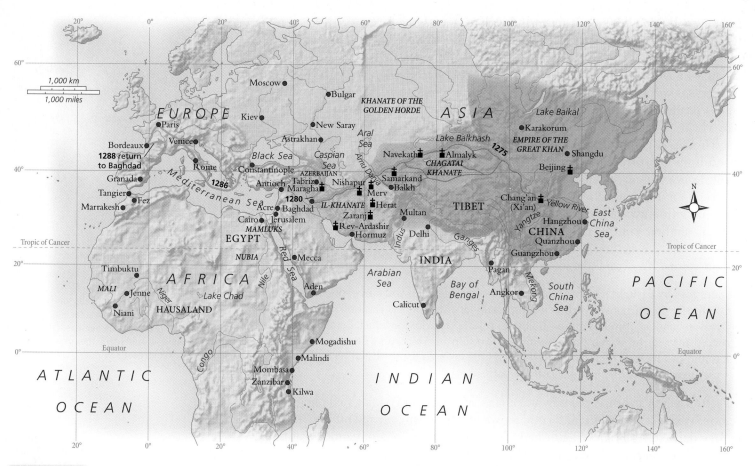

MAP 13.3

The Travels of Rabban Bar Sauma, 1275–1288

----- Silk Road

----- travels of Rabban Bar Sauma, 1275–1288

☩ Nestorian see

the Mongolian heartlands. "Before the days of the Mongols," wrote the bishop of the missionary diocese the Franciscans had established in China, "nobody believed that the Earth was habitable beyond these mountains, . . . but by God's leave and wonderful exertion the Mongols crossed them, and . . . so did I."

Europeans frequently made the journey to China. That reflects the balance of wealth and power at the time. China was rich and productive, Europe a needy backwater. We know of only one subject of the Chinese emperor who found it worthwhile to make the journey in the opposite direction. Rabban Bar Sauma was a Nestorian—a follower, that is, of a Christian tradition that had long flourished in Central Asia but the West had regarded as heretical since the fifth century (see Chapter 9).

When making a pilgrimage to Jerusalem, Bar Sauma planned a route between Nestorian monasteries, heading initially for Maragha (ma-rah-GEH) in what is now Azerbaijan, where the most respected bishop of the Nestorian church had his see. Maragha was a suitable way station: the intellectual capital of the western Mongol world, with a library reputedly of 400,000 books and a new astronomical observatory. There, Bar Sauma took service, first with the bishop, and later with the Mongol ruler of Persia, the Il-khan. He never completed his pilgrimage. In 1286, however, Bar Sauma did resume his travels. He was appointed the Mongols' ambassador to the kingdoms of the Christian West, to negotiate an alliance against Muslim Egypt (see Map 13.3).

When he got to Rome, Bar Sauma was accorded a signal honor: reception by the cardinals who had assembled to elect a pope. In Paris, he recognized the university there as an intellectual powerhouse reminiscent of Maragha, with schools of mathematics, astronomy, medicine, and philosophy. Persian was the only language in which Bar Sauma could communicate with Western interpreters. From the errors he makes in describing Western manners and politics, a lot evidently got lost in translation. He mistook diplomatic evasions for assent and vague expressions of Christian fellowship for doctrinal agreement. He returned to Persia with many assurances of friendship and exhortations to the Il-khan to convert to Christianity. The fact that he completed the journey at all shows how the Mongols made it possible to cross Eurasia.

China

The Mongols never ran their dominions as a centralized state. Nor did they apply consistent methods to govern territories as vast and diverse as theirs. Three main areas of conquest beyond the steppeland—in China, Persia, and Russia—were added after Genghis Khan's death. All were exploited in different ways, specific to the Mongols' needs and the peculiarities of each region.

The conquest of Song China was long and difficult for two reasons. It was a more powerful state than any the Mongols faced elsewhere, and it was highly defensible: compact, so that its armies could maneuver on interior lines of communication, and scored by terrain inhospitable to Mongol horsemen. But, fueled by resources from the Mongols' other conquests, and pursued with unfailing tenacity, the conquest unfolded relentlessly bit by bit. Letters from the Chinese court seeped desperation as the Mongols closed in for the kill. In 1274, the Chinese empress mother, Xie Qiao (shay chow), reflected on where the blame lay.

> The empire's descent into peril is due, I regret, to the instability of our moral virtue. . . . The sound of woeful lament reverberated through the countryside, yet we failed to investigate. The pall of hunger and cold enveloped the armed forces, yet we failed to console.

The real reasons for China's collapse lay in the superiority of the Mongols' war machine. Unlike previous steppelander invaders, the Mongols spared no resources to pursue all-out victory and hired the troops and equipment needed to subdue a country of cities, rice paddies, and rivers. Clearly, the size of the Mongols' existing empire helped. Persian engineers built the siege engines that helped overcome southern Chinese cities. The last battle was at Changzhao (chahng-jeeow) in 1275. The Chinese poet Yi Tinggao (yee teen-gow) was there, "smelling the acrid dust of the field," spying "the green irridescence of the dead." The human misery could be measured in the grief-stricken literature that survives: the suicide notes, the cries of longing for loved ones who disappeared in the chaos, massacred or enslaved. Years later, Ni Bozhuang (nee-bwo-chwang), bailiff of a Daoist monastery, recalled the loss of his wife: "I still do not know if you were taken because of your beauty, or if, surrounded by horses, you can still buy cosmetics." In 1276, with his advisers fleeing and his mother packed for

Kubilai Khan. Liu Guandao was Kubilai Khan's favorite painter. So we can be fairly sure that this is how the khan would like to be remembered: not just in the traditional inert Chinese pose (which Liu also painted), but also active, dressed and horsed like a Mongol ruler, engaged in the hunt. A woman, presumably his influential consort, Chabi, is at his side. The blank silk background evokes the featurelessness of the steppe, while also highlighting the human figures.

"For the Mongols, the conquest of China was a logical continuation of the policies of Genghis Khan and a stage in fulfilling the destiny of world conquest heaven supposedly envisaged."

flight, the young Song emperor wrote his abdication letter to the Mongol khan. "The **Mandate of Heaven** having shifted, your Servant chooses to change with it, . . . yet my heart is full of emotions and these cannot countenance the prospect of the abrupt annihilation of the . . . altars of my ancestors. Whether they be misguidedly abandoned or specially preserved intact rests solely with the revitalized moral virtue you bring to the throne."

For the Mongols, the conquest of China was a logical continuation of the policies of Genghis Khan and a stage in fulfilling the destiny of world conquest heaven supposedly envisaged. But it was also the personal project and passion of Kubilai Khan (1214–1294), Genghis's grandson, who became so immersed in China that he never asserted his supremacy against those Mongol leaders in the extreme west of the Mongol world who resisted his claims. Some of his Chinese subjects resented Kubilai's foreign ways: the libations of fermented mare's milk with which he honored his gods, his barbarous banquets of meat, the officials he chose with great freedom from outside the Confucian elite and even from outside China. Marco Polo reported that all the Chinese "hated the government of the Great Khan, because he set over them steppelanders, most of whom were Muslims, and . . . it made them feel no more than slaves." In this respect, the khan indeed broke with Chinese tradition, which was to confine administrative positions to a meritocracy, whose members were selected by examination in the Confucian classics. Kubilai showed his reverence for Confucius by building a shrine in his honor, but he needed to recruit, as Genghis Khan had, from the full range of talent the Mongol Empire supplied.

Kubilai, indeed, remained a Mongol khan. In some respects, he flouted Chinese conventions. He showed traditional steppelander respect for the abilities of women, giving them court posts and, in one case, a provincial governorship. His wife, Chabi, was one of his closest political advisers. He introduced a separate tier of administration for Mongols, who became a privileged minority in China, ruled by their own laws, and resented for it by most Chinese. In defiance of Confucian teachings, Kubilai felt obliged to fulfill the vision of world conquest he inherited from Genghis Khan. But beyond China, he registered only fleeting success. In Java, the Mongols replaced one native prince with another, without making permanent gains. In Vietnam, the Mongols were only able to levy tribute at a rate too low to meet the cost of their campaigns there. So-called *kamikaze* winds—divine typhoons that wrecked the Mongol fleets—drove Kubilai's armies back from Japan.

While upholding Mongol traditions, Kubilai also sought, emphatically, to be a Chinese emperor who performed the due rites, dressed in the Chinese manner, learned the language, patronized the arts, protected the traditions, and promoted the interests of his Chinese subjects. Marco Polo, who seems to have served him as a sort of professional storyteller, called him "the most powerful master of men, lands, and treasures there has been in the world from the time of Adam until today."

Persia

In Persia, meanwhile, the Mongol rulers were like chameleons, gradually taking on the hues of the culture they conquered. But, as in China, they were anxious to maintain a distinct identity and to preserve their own traditions. The court tended to stay in the north, where there was grazing for the kinds of herds their followers brought with them from the steppe. The Il-khans—"subordinate rulers," so called in deference to Kubilai Khan's nominal superiority—retained nomadic habits, migrating every summer and winter to new camps with palatial tents. At the end of the thirteenth century, Gazan Khan's tent took three years to make, and 200 men took 20 days to erect it. In southern Iran and Iraq, the Il-khans tended to entrust power to local dynasties, securing their loyalty by marriages with the ruling family or court nobility. In effect, this gave them hostages for the good conduct of provincial rulers.

Eventually in 1295, the Il-khans adopted Islam, after flirtations with Nestorianism and Buddhism. This marked an important departure from the tradition of religious pluralism Genghis Khan had begun and Kubilai upheld. From the moment the Il-khan Ghazan (r. 1295–1304) declared his conversion to Islam, the state began to take on a militantly religious character, excluding the Christians, Zoroastrians, Buddhists, and Jews formerly admitted to the khan's service. Moreover, the form of Islam the Il-khans finally adopted was Shiism, the prevailing tradition in Iran. Shiites (see Chapter 9) embraced doctrines most Muslims rejected: that Muhammad's authority descended by heredity from his nephew Ali; that a divinely selected leader or imam would perfect the Prophet's message; and that in the meantime the clergy had the right to interpret Islam. The Il-khan's option for Shiism ensured that eventually Persia would remain an exceptional region in the Muslim world as the only officially Shiite state.

Indeed, the religious art of the Il-khanate is strikingly unlike that of any other Muslim country. The painters freely painted human figures, especially those of Muhammad and his nephew, and even copied Christian nativity scenes to produce versions of the Prophet's birth. The Il-khans' Persia, however, was not isolated from neighboring states. On the contrary, as was usual in the Mongol world, the presence of rulers descended from Genghis Khan promoted trans-Eurasian contacts and exchanges of goods, personnel, and ideas. Persia supplied China, for instance, with engineers, astronomers, and mathematicians, while Persia received Chinese porcelain and paper money, which, however, did not take root in Persia before the twentieth century. Chinese designs influenced Persian weavers, and Chinese dragons appeared on the tiles with which Persian buildings of the time were decorated. Mongol rule ended in Persia in 1343 when the last Il-khan died without an heir.

Il-Khan art. When Mongols converted to Islam, they did not necessarily accept all the beliefs and conventions of orthodox religion. In this fourteenth-century painting from what is now Iran, the white rooster symbolizes the Muslim call to prayer—but the rooster was also a traditional Zoroastrian symbol of dawn. The prophet Muhammad, moreover, is realistically depicted at bottom right—something most Muslim painters would regard as impious today. The other figures are of angels.

Russia

Meanwhile, the Mongols who remained in their Central Asian heartlands continued to lead their traditional, unreconstructed way of life. So did those who formed the elite in the remaining areas the heirs of Genghis Khan inherited: in Turkestan and Kashgaria in Central Asia, and the steppes of the lower Volga River. From the last of these areas, where the Mongols were known as the Golden Horde, they exercised a form of overlordship over Russia, where they practiced a kind of imperialism different from those in China and Persia. The Mongols left the Christian Russian principalities and city-states to run their own affairs. But their rulers had to receive charters from the khan's court at Saray (sah-REYE) on the lower Volga, where they had to make regular appearances, loaded with tribute and subject to ritual humiliations. The population had to pay taxes

Novgorod. The cathedral of St. Sophia in Novgorod in Russia would have presented essentially the same outline in the thirteenth century that it does today. At the time, it was one of relatively few buildings in that mercantile city-state built of stone rather than wood. The tallest gilded dome shows the position of the sanctuary at the heart of the church.

directly to Mongol-appointed tax gatherers—though as time went on, the Mongols assigned the tax gathering to native Russian princes and civic authorities.

The Russians tolerated this situation—albeit unhappily, and with many revolts—partly because the Mongols intimidated them by terror. When the Mongols took the great city of Kiev in 1240, it was said, they left only 200 houses standing and strewed the fields "with countless heads and bones of the dead." Partly, however, the Russians were responding to a milder Mongol policy. In most of Russia, the invaders came to exploit rather than to destroy. According to one chronicler, the Mongols spared Russia's peasants to ensure that farming would continue. Ryazan, a Russian principality on the Volga, southeast of Moscow, seems to have borne the brunt of the Mongol invasion. Yet there, if the local chronicle can be believed, "the pious Grand Prince Ingvary Ingvarevitch sat on his father's throne and renewed the land and built churches and monasteries and consoled newcomers and gathered together the people. And there was joy among the Christians whom God had saved from the godless and impious khan." Many cities escaped lightly by capitulating at once. Novgorod, that hugely rich city (see Chapter 11), which the Mongols might have coveted, they bypassed altogether.

Moreover, the Russian princes were even more fearful of enemies to the west, where the Swedes, Poles, and Lithuanians had constructed strong, unitary monarchies, capable of sweeping the princes away if they ever succeed in expanding into Russian territory. Equally menacing were groups of mainly German adventurers, organized into crusading "orders" of warriors, such as the Teutonic Knights and the Brothers of the Sword, who took monastic-style vows but dedicated themselves to waging holy war against pagans and heretics. In practice, these orders were self-enriching companies of professional fighters, who built up territorial domains along the Baltic coast by conquest. In campaigns between 1242 and 1245, Russian coalitions fought off invaders on the western front, but they could not sustain war on two fronts. The experience made them submissive to the Mongols.

THE LIMITS OF CONQUEST: MAMLUK EGYPT AND MUSLIM INDIA

Mamluk Egypt

In the 1200s, Egypt was in chaos because of rebellions by pastoralists from the southern desert and revolt by the Mamluks, the slaves who formed the elite fighting force. It seems counterintuitive to arm slaves. But for most of the thirteenth century, the policy worked well for the heirs of Saladin who had ruled Egypt since 1192. The rulers handpicked their slave army. The slaves came overwhelmingly from Turkic peoples that Mongol rebels displaced or captured and sold. These slaves had nowhere else to go and no future except in the Egyptian sultan's service. They were acquired young. They trained in barracks, which became their substitutes for families and the source of their pride and strong sense of comradeship. They seemed, from the ruler's point of view, ideally reliable: a dependent class. Increasingly, however, the Mamluks came to know their own strength. In the 1250s, they rebelled. Their own later propaganda cites the sultan's failure to reward them fairly for their services in repelling a crusader attack on Egypt, and their outrage at the promotion of a black slave to one of the highest offices in the court. The Mamluks "threw themselves upon him like the onrush of an unleashed torrent." In 1254, the Mamluks replaced the last heir of Saladin with rulers from their own ranks.

The rebels, however, while contending with internal enemies, perceived the Mongols as a greater threat and turned to face them. In September 1260, they turned back the Mongol armies at one of the decisive battles of the world at Ain Jalut in Syria. It was the first serious reversal the Mongols had experienced since Genghis Khan united them. And it gave the Mamluk commander, Baybars (BEYE-bahrs), the chance to take over Egypt and Syria. He boasted that he could play polo in Cairo and Damascus within the space of a single week. The Mamluks mopped up the last small crusader states on the coast of Syria and Palestine between 1268 and 1291. In combination with the effects of the internal politics of the Mongol world, which inhibited armies from getting too far from the centers of power, the Mamluk victory kept the Mongols out of Africa.

Mamluk victory also marked a further stage in the Islamization of Africa. The Mamluks levied tribute on the Christian kingdoms of Nubia (see Chapter 9). Then, in the next century, they imposed Islam there. Cairo, as we shall see in the next chapter, became a normal stopping place on the pilgrimage route to Mecca for Muslim kings and dignitaries from West Africa. Islam percolated through the region of Lake Chad and into Hausaland in what is today Nigeria.

> *"It seems counterintuitive to arm slaves. But for most of the thirteenth century, the policy worked well for the heirs of Saladin who had ruled Egypt since 1192."*

Muslim India: The Delhi Sultanate

After the disruptions caused by the violent Turkic migrations of the twelfth century, it took a long time for a state in the mold of Mahmud's (mah-MOOD) to reemerge in Ghazna (GAHZ-nah) (see Chapter 12). By the 1190s, however, a Muslim Turkic dynasty and people, the Ghurids

Chronology: Rise of the Mamluks	
1254	Mamluks depose sultan of Egypt
1260	Mamluk army victorious at the battle of Ain Jalut in Syria
1268–1291	Mamluks overthrow last of the crusader states

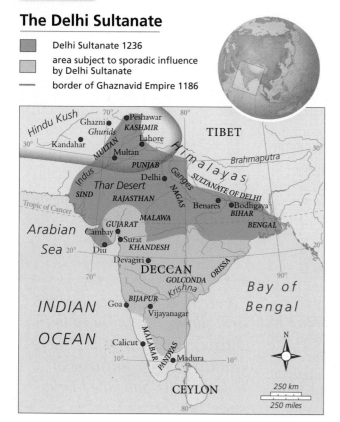

MAP 13.4

The Delhi Sultanate

■ Delhi Sultanate 1236
▢ area subject to sporadic influence by Delhi Sultanate
— border of Ghaznavid Empire 1186

(GOO-rids), had resumed the habit of raiding into Hindu India. As their victories accumulated, they began to levy fixed tribute in the Punjab and even established permanent garrisons in the Ganges valley. One of their most far-flung outposts—and therefore one of the strongest—was at the city of Delhi in northern India. The adventurer Iltutmish (eel-TOOT-mihsh) took command there in 1211. He was a former slave who had risen to general and received his freedom from his Ghurid masters. He avoided war with Hindus—which was, in essence, his job—in favor of building up his own resources. In 1216, exhibiting to his subordinates the letters that had granted him his freedom, he effectively declared himself independent. Over the next 12 years, he played the power game with skill, exploiting the rivalries of Muslim commanders to construct a state from the Indus River to the Bay of Bengal. Meanwhile, the effects of the Mongol conquests on Central Asia protected this new realm, which became known as the Sultanate of Delhi, against outside attack (see Map 13.4). The Mongols effectively eliminated any possible invader and drove many refugees to take service with Iltutmish. As one of the early chroniclers of the sultanate said, "Rulers and governors, . . . and many administrators and notables came to Iltutmish's court from fear of the slaughter and terror of the accursed Mongol, Genghis Khan."

There was no consistent form of administration. In most of the more remote territories, the Delhi sultan was an overlord, mediating between small, autonomous states, many of which Hindus ruled. Bengal was exceptional—a forest frontier, in which governors tried to promote Muslim settlement by making land grants to pioneering holy men and religious communities. But a core of lands was the sultan's personal property, exploited to benefit his treasury and run by administrators he appointed. Lands the sultan granted to warriors in exchange for military service ringed this core. For most of the rest of the century, the sultanate had a volatile history, punctuated by succession wars that were resolved at great oath-taking ceremonies, when the aristocracy of the realm—encompassing a great diversity of effectively freelance warriors and local rulers whom it was difficult or impossible for the sultan to dismiss—would make emotional but often short-lived declarations of loyalty.

Iltutmish's personal choice of successor set the tone on his deathbed in 1236. As an ex-slave, Iltutmish was no respecter of conventional ideas of hierarchy. Denouncing his sons for incompetence, he chose his daughter, Radiyya (rah-DEE-ah), as his successor. In the steppes, women often handled important jobs. In the Islamic world, a woman ruler was a form of impiety and a subversion of what was thought to be the natural order of the world. When, in 1250, a little before the Mamluks took over in Egypt, a woman had seized the throne there and applied to Baghdad for legitimation by the caliph, he is supposed to have replied that he could supply capable men, if no more existed in Egypt. Radiyya had to contend both with a brother who briefly ousted her—she had him put to death—and, what was harder, with male mistrust. Some of her coins emphasize claims to unique feminine virtues as "pillar of women." Others have modest inscriptions, in which all the glorious epithets are reserved for her father and the caliph in Baghdad. Her best strategy was to behave like a man. She dressed in male clothing, refused to cover her face, and, according to a slightly late source, "mounted horse like men, armed with bow and quiver." To conventional minds, these were provocations. She was ousted on grounds that—true or false—reflect male prejudices about female behavior. Accused of taking a black slave as a lover, she was deposed in 1240 in favor of a brother. Her real offense was self-assertion. Those modest coin inscriptions suggest that power brokers in the army and the court were willing to accept her, but only as a figurehead representative of her father, not as an active leader of men.

The sultanate had to cope not only with the turbulence of its own elite, but with its Hindu subjects and neighbors. Dominion by any state over the entire Indian subcontinent remained, at best, a dream. Frontier expansion was slow. Deforestation was an act of state, because, as a Muslim writer of the fourteenth century complained, "the infidels live in these forests, which for them are as good as city walls, and inside them they have their cattle and grain supplies of water collected from the rains, so that they cannot be overcome except by strong armies of men who go into these forests and cut down those reeds." In Bengal, the eastward shift of the Ganges River made Islamization easier. Charismatic **Sufis**, with tax-free grants of forest land for mosques and shrines, led the way.

For most of the thirteenth century, the Mongol menace overshadowed the sultanate. The internal politics of the dynasty of Genghis Khan caused dissensions and hesitancies that protected Delhi. Mongol dynastic disputes cut short periodic invasions. Moreover, a buffer state that dissident Mongols created in Delhi's western territories diminished the sultanate but also absorbed most of the khans' attacks. In the 1290s, however, the buffer collapsed. By what writers in Delhi considered a miracle, the subsequent Mongol attacks failed, faltered, or were driven off.

The Qutb Minar. The founder of the Ghurid dynasty began the Qutb Minar, near Delhi, as a monument to his own prowess in battle, toward the end of the twelfth century. Successors continued the project until, by the late fourteenth century, it was the tallest tower in India—much bigger than any minaret designed to hoist the call to prayer. The ridged form and decorative use of sandstone are typical of the stylistic traditions the Ghurids brought to India from Afghanistan.

EUROPE

With the scare the Mongol invasions caused and the loss of the last crusader states in Syria to the Mamluks, Latin Christendom looked vulnerable. Attempts were made to revitalize the crusading movement—especially by Louis IX, the king of France (r. 1226–1270) who became a model monarch for the Western world. But they all failed. A further reversal was the loss of Constantinople by its Latin rulers to a Byzantine revival. The Mongols destroyed or dominated most of the successor states that claimed Byzantium's legacy, but at the city of Nicaea in western Anatolia, rulers who continued to call themselves "Roman emperors" maintained the court rituals and art of Byzantine greatness. In 1261, they recaptured the old capital from the crusaders "after many failures," as the ruler at the time, Michael VIII, admitted, "because God wished us to know that the possession of the city was a grace dependent on his bounty."

Nevertheless, Latin Christendom grew on other fronts, extending the frontier deep into formerly pagan worlds along the Baltic in Livonia, Estonia, Prussia, and Finland. Between the 1220s and the 1260s, Christian kingdoms seized most of the Mediterranean seaboard of Spain and the Balearic Islands from the

MAP 13.5

Latin Christendom, 1200–1300

- ▨ predominantly pagan lands
- ⛫ university/cathedral schools with date of foundation
- ⛪ important churches with stained glass
- → reconquest of Spain in thirteenth century
- → campaigns of Teutonic Knights and Sword Brothers

Maritime Trade Routes
- —— Venetian
- —— Genoese
- —— Catalan

hands of Muslim rulers. Here the existing economy and population were not much disturbed. Conquests Castile and Portugal made over the same period in the Iberian southwest became a sort of Wild West of sparse settlements, tough frontiersmen, and vast cattle and sheep ranches. Meanwhile, traders of the western Mediterranean increased their commerce with northern Europe along the coasts the Spaniards conquered, through the Strait of Gibraltar (see Map 13.5). Toward the end of the century, as they became accustomed to Atlantic sailing conditions, some of them began to think of exploring the ocean for new routes and resources. In 1291, an expedition set off from the Italian city of Genoa to try to find "the regions of India by way of the ocean." The voyagers were never heard of again, but their voyage marked the beginning of a long, faltering effort by maritime communities of Western Europe to exploit the ocean at their feet.

The transforming influences, however, came from the east. The Mongol peace policing the routes that linked the extremities of Eurasia—ended Europe's relative isolation and stimulated trade and travel between Europe and China. The thirteenth century was the most intense period ever in trans-Eurasian communications, and European traditions were rechanneled as a result or, at least, guided more securely in directions they might have taken anyway. Paper, for instance, a Chinese invention that had already reached the West through Arab intermediaries, was a former luxury that came into general use in late-thirteenth-century Europe as a major contribution to what we would now call **information technology**, making written communication cheap, easy, and prolific. European maritime technology—a prerequisite of the prosperity borne by long-range trade and of the reach of most long-range imperialism—was especially primitive by non-European standards up to this time. The compass was first recorded in Europe in about 1190 in a text that explained the marvels of a pin well rubbed "with an ugly brown stone that draws iron to itself." As far as we know, the West had as yet no maritime charts. The earliest reference to such a device dates only from 1270. Gunpowder and the blast furnace were among the magical-seeming technologies that first reached Europe from China in the thirteenth and fourteenth centuries.

Meanwhile, with consequences for the future that can hardly be overestimated, Western science grew more **empirical**, more reliant on the reality of sense perceptions, more committed to the observation of nature. The renewal of this classical tradition in the West coincided with renewed contact with China, where empiricism had never been lost. At the University of Paris, which the Nestorian Rabban Bar Sauma so admired, scholars cultivated a genuinely scientific way of understanding the world. The end products were the marvelously comprehensive schemes of faith the encyclopedists of thirteenth-century Paris elaborated, especially in the work of the greatest intellect of the age, Thomas Aquinas (1225–1274), who arrayed in precise categories everything known by experience or report. In northwest Spain, an unknown, probably French artist of the thirteenth century depicted a similar vision of the whole cosmos in the stained glass windows of León Cathedral. The cosmos was measurable, portrayed between the dividers of Christ the geometer, like a ball of fluff trapped between tweezers (see page 434).

In the third quarter of the thirteenth century, Parisian teachers, of whom the most insistent was Siger of Brabant, pointed out that the doctrines of the church on the creation and the nature of the soul conflicted with classical philosophy and empirical evidence. "Every disputable question," they argued, "must be determined by rational arguments." Some thinkers took refuge in an evasive idea of "double truth," according to which things true in faith could be false in science and vice versa. The church condemned this doctrine in 1277 (along with a miscellany of magic and superstition).

Meanwhile, another professor in the thirteenth century at the University of Paris, Roger Bacon, stated that excessive deference to authority—including ancestral wisdom, custom, and consensus—was a cause of ignorance. He insisted that scientific observations could help to validate holy writ and that medical

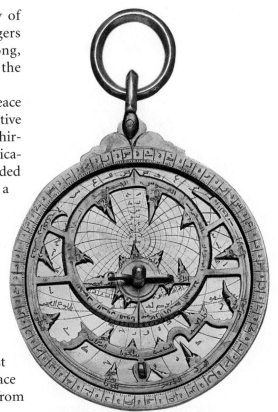

Astrolabe. The Syrian instrument maker, al-Sarraj engraved his signature on this fine astrolabe in 1230–1231. The purpose of the astrolabe is to assist in astronomy—one of the many sciences in which the Islamic world excelled at the time. By suspending the instrument at eye level and swiveling a narrow central bar until it aligned with any observed star, the user could read the star's elevation above the horizon, as well as such additional information as the latitude, the date, and even the time of day from the engraved discs.
© National Maritime Museum Picture Library, London, England. Neg. #E5555–3

The measurable cosmos. This thirteenth-century illustrator of the creation of the world shows God as a well-equipped designer, measuring creation with an architect's or mathematician's dividers. The Earth is not the center of the cosmos, but a tiny blob in the corner, surrounded by chaos and dwarfed by God.

experiments could increase knowledge and save life. He also claimed—citing the lenses with which Archimedes reputedly set fire to a Roman fleet during the siege of the Greek city of Syracuse in Sicily in 212 B.C.E.—that science could cow and convert infidels. It was part of a modest scientific revolution in Western Christendom. The most relentless experimenter of the age was the German emperor and king of Sicily, Frederick II (r. 1212–1250). He was said to have had two men disemboweled to show the varying effects of sleep and exercise on the digestion, and to have brought up children in silence "in order to settle the question" of what language human beings "naturally" speak. "But he labored in vain, for all the children died."

Bacon was a Franciscan friar, a follower of Francis of Assisi (1181–1226), and his enthusiasm for science seems to have owed something to Francis's rehabilitation of nature: because the world made God manifest, it was worth observing. Francis was a witness and maker of the new European imagination. He was a rich man's son inspired by Jesus' advice to a rich youth ("Go, sell what thou hast and give to the poor. Then take up thy cross and follow me.") to seek a life of total dependence on God. In anyone less committed and charismatic, his behavior might have been considered insane or heretical. He launched his mission by stripping naked in the public square of his native city of Assisi in northern Italy, as a sign that he was throwing himself, unprotected, on God's mercy. He relied for sustenance on what people gave him. He attracted a following and modeled his followers' way of life on the way he thought Christ and the apostles lived, refusing to accept property, sharing everything the brethren received by way of alms.

The Franciscans became the spearhead of the church's mission to the poor and inspired other orders of friars—clergy who combined religious vows of poverty, chastity, and obedience with work in the world. In an age of urbanization, this was a particularly important mission, because friars could establish bonds of sympathy with the rootless masses who gathered in towns and faced the problem of adjusting to life away from the familiar companionship of rural parishes. Friars were also a valuable counterforce to heretics who denounced the church for worldliness. Friars, if they stayed true to their vocations, could match these enemies in holiness of life and in strict self-denial.

In his attitude toward nature, Francis was representative of his time and of the convergence of Western and Chinese attitudes to nature. In China, nature was the object of reverence and the subject of art. The same values now appeared in the West. Partly to rebut heretics repelled by the disorder of creation, Francis insisted on the goodness of God's creation, which was all "bright and beautiful." Even its conflicts and cruelties were there to elicit human love. He tried to enfold the whole of nature in love. He preached to ravens and called creatures, landscapes, sun, and moon his brothers and sisters, eventually welcoming "Sister Death." He communicated his sensibilities to his followers. As a result, Franciscans were prominent in scientific thinking in the West. Love of nature made them observe it more closely and keenly and scrutinize it for good uses.

Franciscans also became patrons of increasingly naturalistic art. The art they commissioned for their churches drew the onlooker into sacred spaces, as if in eye-

Francis of Assisi. Franciscan art patronage rewarded painters like Giotto, who were interested in creating vivid versions of sacred scenes in which the actors seemed real rather than abstract. Francis preached to the birds because humans failed to heed his message—but the image suggests, too, how the Franciscans promoted awareness of the natural world. Piety and science coincided in the observation of nature.

witness of the lives of Jesus and the saints. The devotion of the rosary, introduced early in the thirteenth century, encouraged the faithful to imagine sacred mysteries, while praying, with the vividness of scenes of everyday life, as if witnessed in person. Franciscan art stirred the emotions of the devout by unprecedented realism—looking at the world with eyes as unblinking as those of the new scientific thinkers. Considered from one point of view, the realism Western painting increasingly favored was a tribute to the enhanced prestige of the senses. To paint what one's eyes could see was to confer dignity on a subject not previously thought worthy of art. So art linked the science and piety of the age.

It is hard to resist the impression that the revolutionary experiences of the West at the time—the technical progress, the innovations in art, the readjustment of notions of reality through the eyes of a new kind of science—were owed in part to influences transmitted along the routes the Mongols maintained. None of this experimentation and imagination put Western science abreast of that of China, where observation and experiment had been continuous in scientific tradition since the first millennium B.C.E. (see Chapter 6). In two technologies, however—key technologies, as they later proved to be, for their influence on world history—Western Europe came to house the world's leading centers of development and production.

The first technology was glass making. In the thirteenth century, demand for fine glassware leaped in the West because of the growing taste for using church windows made of stained glass, penetrated by light, to illuminate sacred stories and to exhibit glowingly the wonders of creation as the windows at Chartres Cathedral did. Simultaneously, glassmakers adapted their skills to meet domestic demand for glass mirrors and optical lenses. These objects were not manufactured on a significant scale anywhere else in the world, though for centuries scholars writing in Arabic had known how to make them and use them as aids to scientific observation. Now Western savants could make the same experiments themselves and even improve on them. In the thirteenth century, Robert Grosseteste, the first chancellor of the University of Oxford in England, explained the geometry of the way lenses operate. "It is obvious," he concluded, "that they can make very large objects appear very small, and contrariwise very small and remote objects as if they were large and easily discernible by sight."

Second, the West drew ahead in the technology of clockwork. Mechanical clocks had a long history in China and the Islamic world. But clockwork never caught on except in Europe. This is a hard fact to explain. Clockwork is too regular to match the movements of the heavens. It divides the day into arbitrary hours of equal length that do not match those of the sun. But this way of organizing life suited Western monasteries, where, apart from the prayers prescribed for the dawn and nightfall, the services of prayer were best arranged at regular intervals, independently of the sun. For city churches in an age of urban growth, regular

Making Connections | EUROPEAN TRANSFORMATIONS AND INNOVATIONS, THIRTEENTH AND EARLY FOURTEENTH CENTURIES

TRADE AND TRANSPORTATION	TECHNOLOGY AND SCIENCE	POLITICS	RELIGION
Increased communication across Eurasia leads to introduction of Chinese and Arabic technology, medicine, and inventions	Imported inventions such as paper, magnetic compasses, gunpowder, and blast furnace combine with focus on empiricism	Christian kingdoms seize Muslim lands in Spain, Mediterranean islands; revival of Crusades, extension of frontier north to the Baltics, Finland, and Scandinavia	Francis and his religious order place new emphasis on observing nature, serving the poor, and renouncing wealth; increased emphasis on sacred mysteries
⬇	⬇	⬇	⬇
Increased transportation and trade links within Europe aided by new infrastructure (roads, canals); growth of towns; economic and political stability leads to larger towns and cities; more productive industry	Better maritime technology expands range of sea voyages; demand for elaborate church windows spurs glassmaking and innovation in glass lenses; clocks provide regularized timekeeping for monasteries and cities; availability of paper multiplies books and empowers states with a medium for their messages	Bigger, richer states with more scope to communicate and enforce commands; more church-state competition and conflict	Mendicants prominent in scientific thinking in West; spearhead Church's mission to poor in growing towns

timekeeping was also convenient. Clockwork suited the rhythms of urban life. Civic authorities began to invest heavily in town clocks in the thirteenth and fourteenth centuries. This was the beginning of the still-familiar Western convention of an urban skyline dominated by the town hall clock tower.

The combination of lenses and clockwork mattered in the long run because eventually—not until the seventeenth century, when telescopes were combined with accurate chronometry—they gave Western astronomers an advantage over Muslim and Chinese competitors. This in turn gave Western scientists the respect of their counterparts and secured the patronage of rulers all over the world in societies interested in astronomy either for its own sake or—more often—because of astrology—the belief that events on Earth reflected the movements of the heavenly spheres.

"The importance of the Mongols' passage through world history does not stop at the frontiers of their empire. It resonated across Eurasia."

In Perspective
The Uniqueness of the Mongols

In the thirteenth century, a state arose that embraced the whole of the steppe. Like many great revolutions, the episode started bloodily and became constructive. When the Mongol alliance first challenged its neighbors, it seemed to threaten civilization with destruction—slaughtering settled peoples, razing cities, despising art and learning. Yet the Mongols came to play a unique and constructive role in the history of Eurasia. First, fear of the most devastating conquerors the interior had yet bred linked the peoples beyond the steppe, from Christendom to Japan. Then a peace that those same conquerors imposed connected them. For 100 years after the initial horror of the Mongol conquests, the steppe became a highway of fast communication, linking the extremities of the landmass and helping transfer culture across two continents. Without the Mongol peace, it is hard to imagine any of the rest of world history working out as it did, for these were the roads that carried Chinese ideas and technology westward and opened up European minds to the vastness of the world. The importance of the Mongols' passage through world history does not stop at the frontiers of their empire. It resonated across Eurasia.

The Eurasian experience was unique. Why did nothing like it happen in Africa or the Americas? Cultural exchanges across the grasslands of prairie, pampa, and Sahel never spread far until the nineteenth century. None of those regions saw conquerors like the Mongols, able to unify the entire region and turn it into a causeway of civilizations, shuttling ideas and techniques across a continent.

In the Americas, geography was an inhibiting influence. The North American prairie is aligned on a north–south axis, across climatic zones, whereas the

Chronology

1181–1226	Life of Francis of Assisi
1190	First European recorded reference to a compass
1206	Temujin proclaims himself khan
1211–1236	Reign of Iltutmish, sultan of Delhi
1225–1274	Life of Thomas Aquinas
1234	Mongols conquer Georgia
1241–1242	Mongol armies reach Elbe River, Germany
1253–1254	Mission of William of Rubruck to Mongolian court
1258	Mongols capture Baghdad, last caliph put to death
1260	Mamluks defeat Mongols at battle of Ain Jalut
1261	Byzantine Empire regains Constantinople
1268–1291	Mamluks overthrow last crusader states on coast of Palestine
1270	Earliest European reference to maritime charts
1271–1275	Marco Polo's first journey to China
1274, 1281	Failed Mongol attempts to invade Japan
1279	Mongol conquest of China completed
1286	Rabban Bar Sauma appointed Mongol ambassador to Christian West

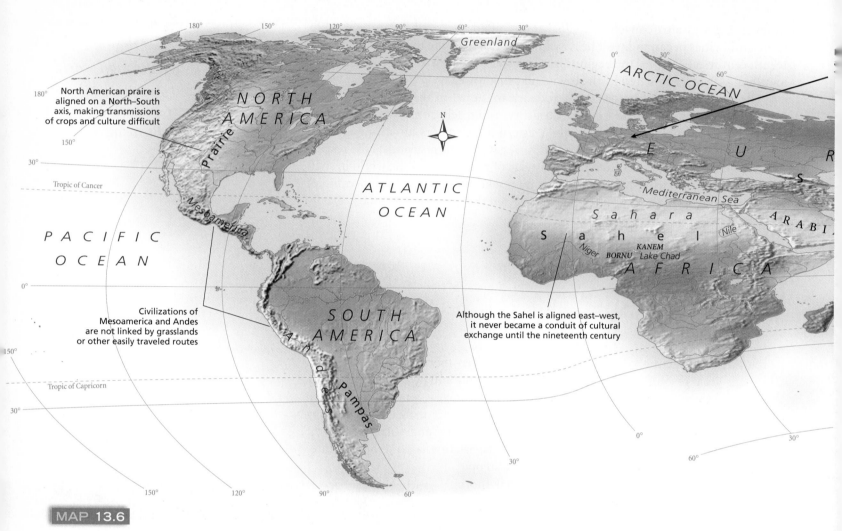

North American praire is aligned on a North–South axis, making transmissions of crops and culture difficult

Civilizations of Mesoamerica and Andes are not linked by grasslands or other easily traveled routes

Although the Sahel is aligned east–west, it never became a conduit of cultural exchange until the nineteenth century

MAP 13.6

Grassland Environments Compared

steppe stretches from east to west. Plants and animals can cross the steppe without encountering impenetrable environments. Seeds can survive the journey without perishing and without finding, at the end of the road, an environment too sunless or cold to thrive in. In North America, it took centuries longer to achieve comparable exchanges. As we have seen repeatedly—almost whenever the Americas have entered our story—transmissions of culture across latitudes are much harder to effect than those that occur within latitudes, which have relatively narrow boundaries, where climate and conditions are familiar.

Moreover, to function, an avenue of communications needs people at either end of it who want to be in touch. The Eurasian steppe was like a dumbbell, with densely populated zones and productive economies at either end of it (see Map 13.6). For people in Europe, Southwest Asia, and North Africa, access to the products of South, Southeast, and East Asia was highly desirable. For the suppliers of spices, drugs, fine textiles, and luxury products in the east, it was good to have customers who paid in silver. In the Americas, there was no chance to reproduce such relationships. The concentrations of wealth and population were in two regions—Mesoamerica and the Andes—that neither grasslands nor any other easily traveled routes linked. Though societies in other parts of the hemisphere drew lessons, models of life, technologies, and types of food from those areas, the results,

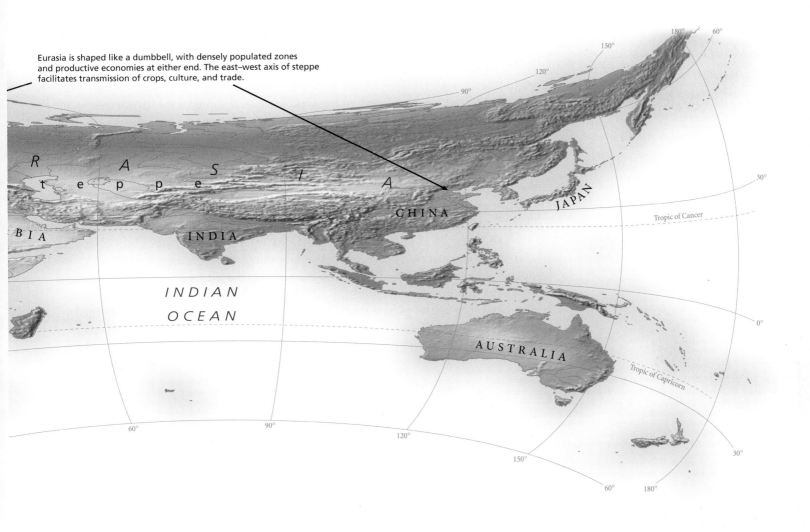

Eurasia is shaped like a dumbbell, with densely populated zones and productive economies at either end. The east–west axis of steppe facilitates transmission of crops, culture, and trade.

as we have seen (see Chapter 11) were hard to sustain because communications between these areas and outlying regions were difficult to keep up. Without the horse—extinct in the Americas for 10,000 years—the chances of an imperial people arising in the prairie or the pampa to do the sort of job the Mongols did in Europe were virtually zero. (Much later, as we shall see in Chapter 21, when European invaders reintroduced the horse in the Americas in the 1500s, experiments in grassland imperialism by peoples such as the Sioux followed.)

In Africa, the constraints were different. The **Sahel** might have played a role similar to that of the steppes in Eurasian history. There was a viable corridor of communication between the Nile and Niger valleys. In theory, an imperial people might have been able to open communications across the continent between the civilizations of East Africa, which were in touch with the world of the Indian Ocean, and those of West Africa, which the trade routes of the Sahara linked to the Mediterranean. But it never happened. For long-range empire building, the Sahel was, paradoxically, too rich compared with the Eurasian steppe. The environment of the Sahel was more diverse. Agrarian or partly agrarian states had more opportunity to develop, obstructing the formation of a Sahel-wide empire. Although pastoral peoples of the western Sahel often built up powerful empires, they always tended to run into either or both of two problems. First, as we have seen, and shall

> "The Mongol peace lasted less than 150 years. The age of plague that was now about to begin would influence the history of Eurasia, and therefore of the world, for centuries."

see again, invaders from the desert always challenged and sometimes crushed them (see Chapter 12).

Second, while they lasted, the empires of the Sahel never reached east of the region of Lake Chad. Here states grew up, strong enough to resist conquest from outside, but not strong enough to expand to imperial dimensions themselves: states like Kanem and Bornu—which were sometimes separate, sometimes united. The accounts of early Muslim visitors reviled the region for its "reed huts . . . not towns" and people clad only in loin cloths. But by the twelfth and thirteenth centuries, Kanem and Bornu commanded respect in Arab geography. Lakeshore floodplains for agriculture enriched them, together with the gold they obtained from selling their surplus millet. Around 1300, according to Arab sources, the region enclosed 12 "kingdoms."

The Mongols, after their initial bout of extreme destructiveness, brought peace and, in the wake of that peace, wealth and learning. But with increased travel, it was not only goods and ideas that circulated with increased freedom. The steppeland also became a highway to communicate disease. The Mongol peace lasted less than 150 years. The age of plague that was now about to begin would influence the history of Eurasia, and therefore of the world, for centuries.

PROBLEMS AND PARALLELS

1. How did the Mongols transform Eurasia in the thirteenth century? What techniques did the Mongols use to rule neighboring civilizations, and how successful were they?

2. How did the steppelanders' spiritual and religious life differ from that of their settled neighbors? Why did Genghis Khan believe that his empire should encompass the entire world?

3. How did the Mongol peace enable traders and travelers like Marco Polo and Rabban Bar Sauma to journey along the Silk Roads? How did Europe benefit from Chinese inventions in technology during the thirteenth century?

4. How did the civilizations of China and Persia affect the Mongols? How did Kubilai Khan combine Mongol and Chinese traditions of rulership? Why was the conversion of the Il-khans in Persia to Shiite Islam so important?

5. What were the consequences of the Mamluk victory over the Mongols at Ain Jalut? Why was the Delhi Sultanate able to survive in north India for so long?

6. How did Francis of Assisi and the Franciscan order remedy some of the social problems that medieval Europe faced? How did the Franciscans' interest in nature influence European culture?

7. What was the impact of empirical-based learning on European thinking at this time? Why were European advances in glassmaking and clockmaking so important?

8. How did geography hinder the development of continent-wide empires in Africa and the Americas? Why was it easier for ideas and trade to cross Eurasia than to cross the Americas or Africa?

READ ON▶ ▶ ▶

D. Morgan, *The Mongols* (1986) is the best history of the Mongols: concise, readable, reliable. R. Grousset, *The Empire of the Steppes* (1970) is a translation of the unsurpassed classic history of steppeland peoples in antiquity and the Middle Ages. Samuel Adshead, *Central Asia in World History* (1993) is also helpful on this period.

P. Jackson, ed., *The Travels of Friar William of Rubruck* (1990) is an outstanding and informative edition of the most vivid of sources. Extracts from sources of the same kind are in I. de Rachewiltz, ed., *Papal Envoys to the Great Khan* (1971) and C. Dawson, ed., *Mission to Asia* (1980). A. Waley, ed., *The Secret History of the Mongols* (2002) collects some Mongol sources in lively translation. There is a scholarly edition by U. Onon (2001).

M. Rossabi, *Voyager from Xanadu: Rabban Sauma and the First Journey from China to the West* (1992), and *Kubilai Khan* (1989) are the best books on their respective subjects. On the voyage of Chang Chun, J. Mirsky, *Chinese Travellers in the Middle Ages* (2000) translates the main texts.

On the Silk Roads, the exhibition catalog edited by S. Whitfield, *The Silk Roads* (2004) is the best work. R. Latham, ed., *The Travels of Marco Polo* (1958) is a convenient and accessible abridgment in translation.

On China, R. Davis, *Wind against the Mountain: The Crisis of Politics and Culture in Thirteenth-century China* (1996) is an outstanding account written with close reference to the sources. The exhibition catalog edited by M. Rossabi, *The Legacy of Genghis Khan* (1996) is the best guide to the art of the Ilkhanate and other Mongol successor-states. M. Ipsiroglu, *Painting and Culture of the Mongols* (1966) is indispensable.

J.A. Boyle, ed., *The History of the World Conqueror* (1997) and *The Successors of Genghis Khan* (1971) translates some of the most important sources on the Ilkhanate.

On the Mamluks, R.Irwin, *The Middle East in the Middle Ages: The Early Mamluk Sultanate* (1986) is the best account of the their rise, and R. Amitai-Preiss, *Mongols and Mamluks* (2005) is a superb study of the wars against the Mongols, S.A. El-Banasi, ed., *Mamluk Art* (2001) covers a wide range of revealing objects.

P. Jackson, *The Delhi Sultanate* (2003) is a splendid introduction to the subject. The best edition of Ibn Battuta is by H.W. Gibb and C.F. Beckingham for the Hakluyt Society, *The Travels of Ibn Battuta* (1956).

On the transmission of Chinese technology westward, J. Needham, *Science and Civilisation in China* (1956) is fundamental–but it is a vast work still in progress. An abridged version in two volumes–*The Shorter Science and Civilisation in China* (1980)–is available. For Western science in the period, A. Crombie, *Robert Grosseteste and the Origins of Experimental Science* (1971) is controversial and stimulating. D.C. Lindberg, *The Beginnings of Western Science* (1992) gives an efficient and comprehensive account.

Of many studies of St Francis none is entirely satisfactory, but J.H.R. Moorman, *St Francis of Assisi* (1976) and A Mockler, *Francis of Assisi* (1976) can be recommended, the first for its scholarship and brevity, the second for its vivacity. K.B.Wolf, *The Poverty of Riches* (2003) is good on St Francis's theology.

On glassmaking see G. Martin and A. MacFarlane, *The Glass Bathyscape* (2003) and, on clockwork, D. Landes, *Revolution in Time: Clocks and the Making of the Modern World* (1983). On the general background of the thirteenth-century West, D. Abulafia, ed., *The New Cambridge Medieval History*, vol. 5, (1999) is as close as one can get to a comprehensive guide.

CHAPTER 14

The Revenge of Nature: Plague, Cold, and the Limits of Disaster in the Fourteenth Century

▲ **City of the dead.** The fourteenth-century Arab traveler Ibn Battuta described Cairo's Southern Cemetery as "a place of peculiar sanctity" that "contains the graves of innumerable scholars and pious believers." The Mamluk domes and minarets visible here form part of the Sultaniyyah tomb complex that was built around 1360, a little over 10 years after the plague known as the Black Death had struck the city.

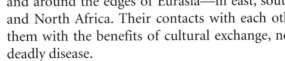

CAIRO

"The people of Cairo are fond of pleasure and amusement," wrote Ibn Battuta, when he first visited the Egyptian city in 1325. Wanderlust had made this Muslim pilgrim the world's most traveled man. Yet he had never seen, and would never see again, a city so big. Cairo had—so Ibn Battuta was told—12,000 water carriers, 30,000 donkey-rental businesses, and 36,000 river craft transporting food and goods. Among sources of pleasure he noted were "boys and maids with lustrous eyes" and the park and promenade along the Nile River, "containing many beautiful gardens." "Mother of cities, . . . mistress of broad provinces and fruitful lands, boundless in multitude of buildings, peerless in splendor. . . ." There seemed no end to Ibn Battuta's praise. The next time he visited Cairo, 23 years later in 1348, plague raged in the city, and corpses were piled in its streets. "I was told that during the plague the number of deaths there had risen to twenty-one thousand a day. I found that all the sheikhs I had known were dead. May God Most High have mercy upon them!"

Ibn Battuta was witnessing the most devastating natural catastrophe ever to have hit Eurasia: the so-called **Black Death.** This visitation of disease was not an isolated episode, but part of an enormous change, the consequences of which overtook the world. In the fourteenth century, Eurasia entered an age of plague (which would later spread worldwide), while the world entered an age of cold, as the climate got cooler. This combination of environmental disasters killed millions of people, disrupted states, and checked expansion. Themes of the story of global history, familiar from the last few chapters of this book, halted or were reversed as Eurasia's densely populated zone contracted. The growth of populations, trades, and states in Eurasia slowed or stopped. Cultural transmissions across the landmass diminished. Isolation from the main routes of trade and travel suddenly became, in some respects, an advantage.

Among the hardest-hit societies were the most ambitious—those with the longest and most active records in challenging their environments to suit themselves. Peoples that suffered most included those who had succeeded best in exploiting nature by turning land and energy sources to their own uses: those at and around the edges of Eurasia—in east, southwest, and south Asia; in Europe; and North Africa. Their contacts with each other, which had formerly enriched them with the benefits of cultural exchange, now communicated unprecedented deadly disease.

443

FOCUS questions

How did climate change globally in the fourteenth century?

Which parts of the world suffered most from the plagues of the fourteenth century?

What were the social and political effects of the plague in China, the Islamic world, and Europe?

Why did some parts of the world escape plague?

How did the absence of plague affect Japan, Java, India, Mali, and the cultures around the Pacific Ocean?

It was as if nature had struck back. Indeed, that was, more or less, how many Europeans and Muslims saw it. The weather, they thought, was a whiplash and the plague a scourge that God wielded to humble human arrogance and remind people of the unshakable power of death. One school of Muslim theologians accepted plague as God's punishment for sins, while others argued that plague, when Muslims suffered it, was "a martyrdom and a mercy from God," but "a punishment for an infidel." In China, too, conventional wisdom understood natural disasters as examples of what historian Mark Elvin calls "moral meteorology"—the corrections of heaven, unleashed to restore the balance of nature disturbed by human wickedness.

In history books, human agency tends to crowd out the rest of nature. Nonhuman life gets into the picture only as a source of analogies for human behavior, or as the means of human strategies—part of an Eden or an enemy to be used or abused. It is easy to forget that humans inhabit only a fraction of the biosphere, most of which is still outside our dominion. Currents in the ocean and the atmosphere change climate and shape our world despite us. Nor do we even control the whole of the ecosystem of which we form part. Our own bodies host microorganisms that feed on us whether we like it or not, sometimes benefiting us, sometimes doing us harm. Disease bearers can change their habits and patterns of attack with bewildering speed, leaving us unsure how to respond. Viruses, for example, are a part of the ecosystem that is largely beyond our control.

Climate and microbes belong to two rebellious realms of nature that resist human power. What happens when they combine—when sudden, unpredictable changes in both realms threaten humans simultaneously? To find out, we need only look back 700 years.

The fourteenth century was exceptional in human history because, in parts of the world, climate change and disease coincided to menace or undermine human activities. Procreation could make up the loss of life—eventually. The empires we shall see shaken and the states overthrown in this chapter and the next were restored or replaced. The regions and classes that profited from disaster—for there were some, as there are in every disaster—did not always retain their advantage for long. But the social shake-up that accompanied the changes had, for some of the people affected, irreversible effects. And it was impossible to undo the jarring psychological impact on societies that had accumulated self-confidence over a long period of expansion.

The best—or even, because of the evidence available, the only—way to approach the changes of the fourteenth century is to start in those parts of the northern hemisphere, especially in Eurasia and North Africa, where the effects of cold and plague combined. We can then turn to areas that escaped plagues, or escaped their worst consequences, in India, sub-Saharan Africa, Japan, and southeast Asia. Finally, we shall turn to far-away and out-of-touch societies in and around the Pacific to appreciate how isolation—which usually retards change—acted as a form of quarantine against disease. This should help us see some of the difference plagues made. As plagues affected some of the planet's previously most dynamic regions, other parts of the world leaped into the sight lines of global history, drawing our attention.

Readers should be aware that the distribution of material in the pages that follow reflects the distribution of sources and of scholarship. Most of what we know about the ecological disasters of the era comes from Eurasia, and, within that area, most relates to Europe. For some other areas, only scattered archaeological studies help us trace the course and character of the diseases of the time. Legal records of the kinds that help us establish the social consequences of ecological change in Europe are, at present, unavailable for most other places.

CLIMATE CHANGE

In the fourteenth century, temperatures fell. Broadly speaking, over the preceding four centuries or so, global temperatures had been relatively warm. The warm spell had been a period of expansion for most societies, with much erosion of natural environments as people converted previously underexploited land for farming or grazing (see Chapter 10). Peoples overcome by ecological disasters in the past had been victims of droughts or of their own over-exploitation of the land. Now a cool period—of fluctuating but relatively low temperatures—would last for about 500 years more. During the intense phases of the cool period, a fall in average temperatures of two or three degrees could reverse expansion, forcing people to abandon high ground, remote settlements, and northerly latitudes (such as, in the fourteenth century, parts of Greenland and of what are now Norway and Finland).

Though meteorologists scour tree rings and glaciers for evidence of weather cycles, hot and cold spells seem to alternate unpredictably. If a common cause—some cosmic rhythm—underlies all of them, we do not know what it is. Short-term fluctuations are sometimes traceable to particular causes. The middle of the second decade of the fourteenth century, for instance, was a cold period all over the Northern Hemisphere, probably because of a sudden, localized occurrence: the explosion of Indonesian volcanoes, pumping ash into the atmosphere and clouding the sun. But the fall in temperatures was not confined to a few exceptional years. It was part of a general, long-term trend.

The trend began in the Arctic in the thirteenth century. The ice cap crept southward. Glaciers disrupted shipping. From the fourteenth century, indicators of falling temperatures in the North Atlantic and parts of Eurasia are abundant, and it is fair to suppose that the Northern Hemisphere generally was registering the effects. Mean annual temperatures in China, which had stayed above 32 degrees Fahrenheit from the seventh century to the eleventh, remained below freezing from the thirteenth century—a period of abrupt fluctuations—until late in the eighteenth. Evidence of marginal glacier growth suggests that North America, too, felt the cold in the fourteenth century. Other indicators for the same century include the persistence of pack ice in summer in the seas around Greenland and the disappearance of water-demanding plants from the hinterland of Lake Chad in Central Africa from about 1300 onward. This is important, because glacier growth affects precipitation. When water ices over, less of it evaporates, and less therefore falls as rain. Weakening winds may also have contributed to changes in rainfall patterns and to the lack of moisture in deep interior regions with continental climates.

Worldwide effects—it is worth adding—of the continuing trend are detectable in glacier levels from the sixteenth century onward. A particularly marked period of glacier growth, even in low latitudes and in the Southern Hemisphere, occurred in

"The fourteenth century was exceptional in human history because, in parts of the world, climate change and disease coincided to menace or undermine human activities."

FIGURE 14.1 GLOBAL TEMPERATURE CHANGE, 1000–1900

Source: Hidore, John E. Global Environment Change: Its Nature and Impact, © 1996. Electronically reproduced by permission of Pearson Education, Inc., Upper Saddle River, New Jersey.

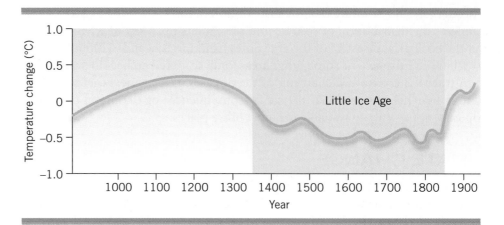

the seventeenth century. The cold therefore remained dominant, with some fluctuations, and intensified in the seventeenth century. Warming resumed gradually in the eighteenth and early nineteenth centuries, and, after a mid–nineteenth-century cold spell, has now been a constant and consistent feature of global climate probably for about the past 150 years (see Figure 14.1).

It is important to stress that the rhythms of climate change are full of fluctuating and conflicting shifts and contrasts of pace. Three levels are detectable. At one level, there is a long-term alternation between ice ages, which periodically smother great parts of the globe, and global warming, when some glacier-covered areas reemerge. We are between ice ages now. Historians, perhaps rather overdramatically, have adopted the **Little Ice Age** as a name for the protracted period of relative cold that began in the fourteenth century, but this term is misleading if it encourages readers to think of huge ice sheets spreading over the globe. All the fluctuations of the period this book covers have happened in a relatively warm era of the history of the planet.

Meanwhile, at another level, periods of a few hundred years of relative cold and warmth alternate within eras of global warming. But even within these periods, sudden changes in the winds and ocean currents can reverse the overall trend, producing spells, lasting from 10 to 50 years or so, of warmer or cooler temperatures.

Finally, there are sudden interruptions of normal conditions—occurring irregularly and, in the present state of our knowledge, unpredictably—when the normal distribution of atmospheric pressure is disturbed for unknown reasons. This produces the notorious **El Niño** effect in the tropics and the Southern Hemisphere (see Chapter 4). In Europe, reversals of normal patterns of atmospheric pressure in the North Atlantic produce longer spells, often of a decade or so, of extremely cold weather. And of course, above the deep and various rhythms of climate, the irregular lurches of the weather continue all the time.

Climate change is usually slow but can become perceptible suddenly. Contemporary descriptions show that people in Europe began to feel the cold, along with other unaccustomed weather, in the early fourteenth century. Of course, people felt the cold, and it affected their lives, because temperatures were lower than previously, not because it was cold in any absolute sense. Even after the intense global warming we have experienced recently, global temperatures have probably only recently returned to where they were when the Little Ice Age began. And European summers were probably, on average, hotter in the fourteenth century than in the twentieth.

The weather of the early fourteenth century, however, seemed hostile to people who had to endure it (see Map 14.1). In 1309–1310, the Thames River, which flows through London, froze and, wrote a chronicler, "bread wrapped in straw or other covering froze and could not be eaten unless it was warmed." Colder weather forced farmers to abandon formerly productive land above 1,300 feet in the southwest of England and 1,000 feet in the north. The cold was, an English poet wrote, "a new kind of affliction, . . . not known for a thousand years . . . . No horror left us e'er so like a ghost." Encroaching glaciers forced farmers into retreat in Norway.

During the prolonged cold of 1315–1316, before the icebergs grew sufficiently to disrupt rainfall, heavy rains were reported all over northern Europe, wrecking the crops, inflicting famine. Grain "could not ripen, nor had bread such power or essential virtue as it usually has," complained an English chronicler. A chronicler in Austria likened the rains to Noah's flood in the Bible. Fifteen or 16 people usually died each month in Bruges and Ypres in what is today Belgium. During 1316, the figure rose to 150 each month in Ypres and 190 in Bruges. From May to October, while these cities ran out of food, they lost over 5 percent and 10 percent of their population respectively. Calamitous flooding and coastal erosion became common around the North Sea, culminating in the "Great Drowning" of 1362, when the sea swallowed vast areas of Holland and 60 parishes in Denmark. On the North Sea coast of England, divers can still visit drowned villages, victims of the rips the floods of the era tore in the coastline.

Far from the sea, cooling in the Northern Hemisphere brought droughts and famines. In Central Asia, the accumulated abundance that fueled Mongol conquests in the previous century seems to have run out. The Mongol world began to contract. According to official chronicles, China experienced exceptionally severe winters for 36 of the fourteenth century's 100 years. In partial consequence, famines struck some part of China in every year of the reign of the Shun Ti emperor (r. 1333–1368).

Though the evidence is too slight for certainty, climate change at about the same time seems to have helped to destroy an impressive regional system of agriculture and urban life deep in the North American interior, between the Gila and San Juan Rivers and in the neighborhood of present-day Phoenix, Arizona. First the Hohokam (hoh–HOH–kahm) people—as archaeologists called them—re-located, from their scattered villages and small dwellings and sought for closer collaboration in relatively few, dense settlements with huge multistorey adobe houses. At Paquimé they huddled in a city with all the traditional amenities of earlier indigenous civilizations (see Chapter 11): ball courts, carved facades for temples and palaces, wells and irrigation works, workshops for copper workers and jewelsmiths. There was even a macaw hatchery to produce the ornamental feathers the elite coveted. It was a splendid effort, but it was clearly a response to stress. Every indicator shows severe population loss throughout the Southwest in the thirteenth and

"The Frozen Thames," 1677. The Thames River with old London Bridge in the middle distance and Southwark Cathedral on the right. People amuse themselves on the ice. Some shoot, and others skate. The river froze solid ten times in the seventeenth century.

Casa Grande. In the fourteenth century, Casa Grande—as this adobe structure is now called—stood five stories high. Massive outer walls and clusters of small dwellings surrounded it. It was part of the last phase of a long effort to raise monumental architecture and concentrate dense populations in what is now desert in Arizona, Colorado, and New Mexico.

PACIFIC
OCEAN

Lack of rainfall
leads to population
loss throughout the
American Southwest

North American
glaciers increase

Polar ice cap begins
to creep southward in
the thirteenth century

Phoenix *ARIZONA*

Casa Grande Paquimé

Rocky Mountains

NORTH
AMERICA

M E X I C O

Mississippi

Hudson
Bay

Greenland

Falling temperatures
force abandonment of
settlements in northerly
latitudes and on high ground

Caribbean Sea

Iceland

NORWAY

SWEDEN

FINLAND

Persistence of pack
ice in summer off
coast of Greenland

Thames River
freezes during
the winter of
1309–1310

North
Sea

ENGLAND

DEN.

RUSSIA

London

Bruges

POLAND

ATLANTIC
OCEAN

Ypres

GERMANY

S
t
e
p
p

Cold, heavy rain and
flooding destroy crops
and erode coastlines
in northern Europe

FRANCE

Salzburg

AUSTRIA

ITALY

Danube

Black Sea

SPAIN

Anatolia

A
n
d
e
s

A
n
d
e
s

Amazon

SOUTH
AMERICA

Mediterranean Sea

Euphra

MOROCCO

North Africa

EGYPT

S a h a r a

Niger

Nile

Lake Chad

AFRICA

1,000 km

1,000 miles

scale varies with perspective

N

Water-demanding
plants disappear from
the Lake Chad region

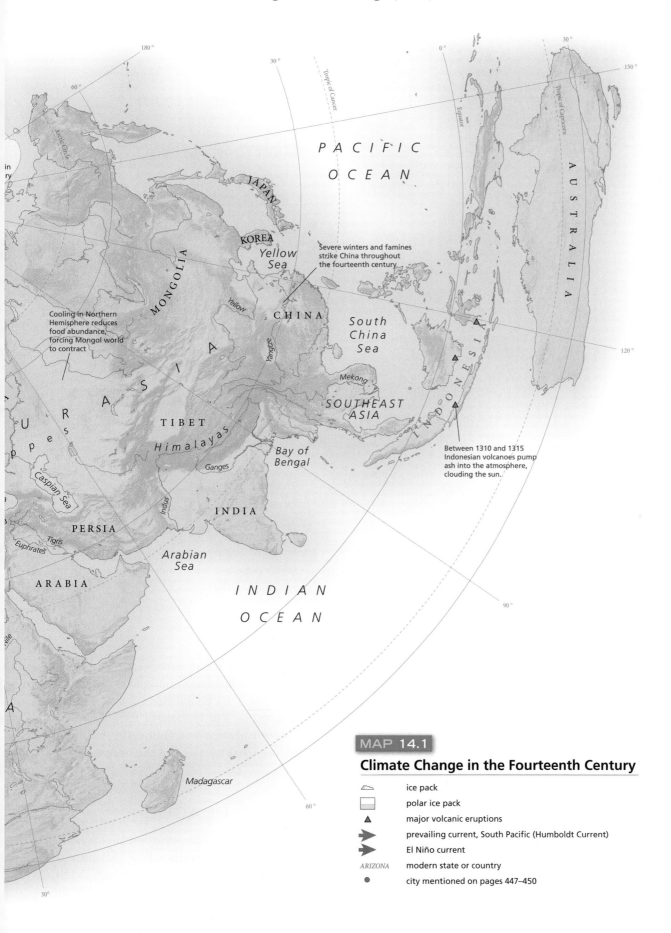

Severe winters and famines strike China throughout the fourteenth century

Cooling in Northern Hemisphere reduces food abundance, forcing Mongol world to contract

Between 1310 and 1315 Indonesian volcanoes pump ash into the atmosphere, clouding the sun.

MAP 14.1

Climate Change in the Fourteenth Century

ice pack

polar ice pack

▲   major volcanic eruptions

prevailing current, South Pacific (Humboldt Current)

El Niño current

ARIZONA   modern state or country

●   city mentioned on pages 447–450

Making Connections | CLIMATE CHANGE IN EURASIA, AFRICA, AND THE AMERICAS

REGION/PERIOD	➡	EVIDENCE AND ENVIRONMENTAL EFFECTS	➡	EFFECTS ON HUMAN SOCIETY
Arctic / 1200s		Polar ice cap in Northern Hemisphere creeps southward		Glaciers disrupt shipping
North Atlantic, Arctic Ocean / 1300s		Falling temperatures, glaciation		Pack ice in summer around Greenland disrupts sea routes
Central Africa / 1300s		Disappearance of water-demanding plants near Lake Chad		Less rainfall reduces crop yields
Europe / 1300s		Thames River freezes; glaciers encroach in Norway; flooding and coastal erosion around North Sea		Formerly productive agricultural land abandoned in England; famine and mortality increase throughout northern Europe; flooding drowns many coastal villages in Holland, Denmark, England
Central Asia, China / 1300s		More severe winters		Abundance of food that fueled Mongol advances runs out; Mongol world contracts; famines strike China
American Southwest / 1300s		Less rainfall and water		Relocation of Hohokam villages in Arizona; severe population loss; major population centers abandoned

fourteenth centuries. By around 1400, even the new settlements were abandoned. Ruins remain. Casa Grande, in Pinal County, Arizona, leaves onlookers amazed at the ambition of the builders and clueless about what befell them. Some scholars have speculated that the conditions that crushed the Hohokam may also have driven migrants southward to colonize central Mexico and found the state that later became the kernel of the Aztec world (see Chapter 15). But the only evidence for this is in later, untrustworthy legends.

THE COMING OF THE AGE OF PLAGUE

In Eurasia the cold spell coincided with the beginning of an age of plague. Starting in the 1320s, unprecedented bouts of pestilence spread over much of Eurasia, culminating, in the late 1340s, in the disaster known to Europeans as the Black Death, which, in terms of the proportion of the population it wiped out, was probably the most lethal event ever experienced in human history up to that time. Recurrences—less widespread and less intense—of similar or identical diseases remained common and frequent in Eurasia until the eighteenth century. The age of plague was so unusual and significant that we want to know what the disease was, where it came from, what caused it, and how much damage it did. All these questions are hard to answer.

Most attempts to write the history of disease have foundered on a false assumption: that we can recognize past visitations of identifiable diseases, known to modern medical science, from symptoms historical sources describe. For two reasons, this is an unrealistic expectation.

First, people in the past looked at disease with perceptions different from ours. The symptoms they spotted would not necessarily be those an observer today would note, nor would they use the same sort of language we would to describe them. The signs we look for change as culture changes. From time to time, literary and scientific literature introduces new paradigms of disease and discards or displaces old ones.

Second, diseases themselves change. They change, perhaps, more than any other aspect of history because many of the microorganisms that cause disease are subject to rapid mutations. They evolve fast because they reproduce rapidly. They respond quickly to changing environments. The plagues of the age of plague need not all have been visitations of a single disease. They could have been "cocktails" of different diseases. They may have included some diseases that today's medical handbooks identify. But we must be open to the likelihood—it is stronger than a possibility—that some of the diseases that devastated Eurasia in the age of plague were peculiar to that period. They did not exist previously in the same forms and have ceased to exist since. New pathogens are deadly because they are unfamiliar. When they strike, no one has built up immunity to them.

So what can we say about the pathology of the Black Death? Of diseases now known to medical science, bubonic plague—not, perhaps, of the same variety we know today—most likely played a part in the age of plague. Bubonic plague is a rat-borne disease. Fleas that live on rats transmit it to humans. When they bite, fleas regurgitate the bacillus, ingested from rats' blood, into the bloodstream of human victims, or communicate infection by defecating into their bites. In cases of septicemic plague (a systemic, blood-poisoning disease), one of the first symptoms is generally death. Otherwise, swellings appear—small like Brazil nuts or big and ridged like grapefruit—over the neck and groin or behind the ears. Jitters, vomiting, dizziness, and pain might follow, often accompanied by an inability to tolerate light.

Fourteenth-century sources describe all these symptoms, together with sudden fainting, before victims, as one observer explained, "almost sleeping and with a great stench eased into death." The trouble is that during the first hundred years of the age of plague, of all the sources that describe the symptoms, fewer than one in six lists symptoms of this kind. Moreover, almost everyone at the time was convinced that plague spread by infection or contagion. Rats—the normal agent for the spread of bubonic plague—play no part in the accounts in the sources. The black rat, the culprit species in the transmission of bubonic plague, seems not to have existed at the time in plague-stricken Iceland, and was rare or absent in other afflicted places. Finally, it seems most unlikely that the frequent epidemics reported in China from the 1320s to the 1360s can have been of bubonic plague in the form now familiar to us, which, as we shall see, hit an unimmunized China in the late eighteenth century. The suddenness and virulence of the visitations that afflicted China suggest the arrival of a new and previously unexperienced pathogen. For the Chinese, with their long experience in farming and animal domestication, enjoyed highly developed natural immunities to the familiar diseases that breed in farming environments.

"The age of plague was so unusual and significant that we want to know what the disease was, where it came from, what caused it, and how much damage it did. All these questions are hard to answer."

Plague victims. The illustrator of an early fifteenth-century German chronicle imagined the plague of Egypt—sent by God, according to the Book of Exodus in the Bible, to make Pharaoh "let my people go"—with the same symptoms as the Black Death. In the background, Moses brings the plague down on Egypt by prayer. By implication, prayer and obedience to the will of God could also be remedies for plague.

Many accounts of the Black Death include a bewildering variety of symptoms that are not associated with bubonic plague: complications in the lungs, spitting blood, headaches, rapid breathing, discolored urine. The emphasis of some sources on lung disorders suggests a mixture of bubonic and pneumonic plague, which primarily attacks the lungs. To judge from other surviving descriptions, outbreaks of typhus, smallpox, various kinds of influenza, and hemorrhagic fevers coincided with some visitations of plague. In the Mediterranean, the plague usually struck in summer, while in northern Europe, autumn seems to have been the deadliest season. But, looked at as a whole, the plagues of the period had no seasonal pattern and no obvious connection with any particular weather systems or atmospheric conditions. This again points to the involvement of more than one pathogen.

Anthrax may have been a contributing factor. A form of anthrax certainly existed among cattle in Europe at the time. Whether or not anthrax was a factor, domestic animals were probably an essential part of the background—as carriers of disease, as a reservoir of infection, and even as sufferers. One of the curious features about the way some early plague victims described the disease is that they were sure that their domestic animals suffered from it, just as they did themselves. A chronicler in the city of Florence in Italy listed "dogs, cats, chickens, oxen, donkeys, and sheep" among the sufferers, with the same symptoms as human victims, including swellings in the groin and armpits. At the port of Salona on the Adriatic coast, the Black Death's first victims were "horses, oxen, sheep, and goats." The Egyptian chronicler, al-Maqrizi, who was among the most observant and thoughtful witnesses, believed that the disease started, like so many others, among animals before transferring to human hosts. It had spread from grazing flocks on the steppe in 1341, after which "the wind transmitted their stench around the world." Al-Maqrizi and other Muslim commentators thought wild animals caught it, too. If any of these sources are correct, the Black Death must have been—or included—a disease unknown today.

An unresolved question is, *How, if at all, were changes in climate and disease patterns linked?* The plague pathogens, as we have seen, were remarkably indifferent to weather, striking at different seasons and in climatically different regions of Eurasia, from the cold environment of Scandinavia and rain-drenched Western Europe to the hot, dry lands of the Middle East. The plagues were less penetrative, however, in hot, moist regions and do not seem to have gotten across the Sahara to tropical Africa, even though many potential disease carriers crossed that desert to trade. It is worth bearing in mind that the plague pathogens seem to have included new arrivals in the microbial world that remained active for as long as global cooling lasted.

The Course and Impact of Plague

The nature of the plague is hard to define, but the routes by which it traveled are easier to describe (see Map 14.2). The Italian chronicler Matteo Villani said the plague came "from China and upper India," by which he meant Central Asia, for which "India" at the time was a synonym, "then through their surrounding lands and then to coastal places across the ocean." Broadly speaking, Arabic sources specify the same, or a similar, path.

The age of plague indeed seems to have started in China. But that is not the same as saying that subsequent outbreaks elsewhere were the result of communication from China, or even that they were necessarily outbreaks of the same disease or diseases. Repeated occurrences—or, perhaps, a continuous visitation—of massively lethal maladies were recorded in southwest China, and over much of central China, north of the Yangtze River, in the early 1320s. In 1331, mortality rates in parts of northeast China that had endured five reported outbreaks of plague in the previous two decades reputedly reached 90 percent. Two years later, a plague claimed 400,000 lives in the Yangtze and Huai (hway) valleys. In 1353–1354, chroniclers reported that around two-thirds of the population perished from pestilence in eight distinct Chinese districts. Most of those areas experienced repeated bouts of disease of the same sort in the late 1350s or early 1360s.

Doubt persists, however, over whether the diseases rampant in China were the cause of—or even the same as—those found farther west. From the perspective of most commentators at the time in Europe and the Middle East, plague, like the Mongols, seemed to be an invader from the steppeland. Many observers at the time noted that the Mongols transmitted plague. A lawyer in northern Italy wrote one of the most detailed and doom-laden accounts of the arrival of plague in Europe. In 1346, by his account, "countless numbers of Tatars," as he called the Mongols, and Muslims "were struck down by a mysterious illness that brought sudden death." At the time, a Mongol army was laying siege to the Genoese trading colony of Kaffa on the nothern shore of Black Sea, where Italian merchants made contact with two great trade routes: those of the Silk Roads and the Volga valley. "But behold!" he continued, "the whole army was affected by a disease. . . which killed thousands every day. . . . But they ordered corpses to be placed in catapults and lobbed into the city in the hope that the intolerable stench would kill everyone inside."

The besiegers' stratagem worked. The disease proved highly contagious. "As it happened," the account went on, "among those who escaped from Kaffa by boat, there were a few sailors who had been infected with the poisonous disease. Some boats were bound for Genoa, others went to Venice and to other Christian areas. When the sailors reached these places and mixed with the people there, it was as if they had brought evil spirits with them."

Of course, there were multiple points of entry, as the same author acknowledged:

> Almost everyone who had been in the East, or in the regions to the south and north, fell victim to sudden death after contracting this pestilential disease. . . . The scale of the mortality and the form which it took persuaded those who lived, weeping and lamenting, . . . the Chinese, Indians, Medes, Kurds, Armenians, Cilicians, Georgians, Mesopotamians, Nubians, Ethiopians, Turks, Egyptians, Arabs, Saracens and Greeks (for almost all the East had been affected)—that the last judgement has come.

A pandemic on this scale was unprecedented. The pathogens responsible had found an eco-niche as wide as Eurasia.

Chroniclers' estimates of mortality are notoriously unreliable. Historians have been reluctant to believe claims that the plague wiped out half or more—sometimes much more—of the population where it struck, but verifiable evidence bears out some of the most shocking assessments of the damage. In Barcelona on the Mediterranean coast of Spain, 60 percent of jobs in the church fell vacant. Records of the archdiocese of York in northern England suggest the first visitation of the

"From the perspective of most commentators at the time in Europe and the Middle East, plague, like the Mongols, seemed to be an invader from the steppeland."

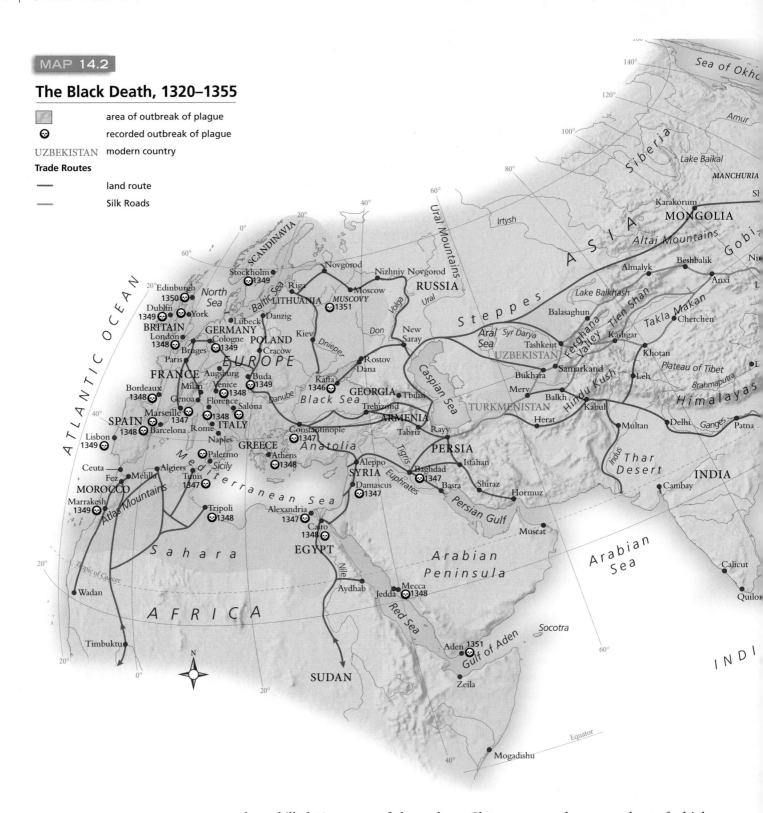

MAP 14.2

The Black Death, 1320–1355

▨ area of outbreak of plague

☺ recorded outbreak of plague

UZBEKISTAN modern country

Trade Routes

—— land route

—— Silk Roads

plague killed 40 percent of clergy there. Clergy were, perhaps, members of a high-risk profession, exceptionally exposed to infection by the need to minister to the sick. But the laity suffered just as much. In some manors in England, up to 70 percent of tenants died. Some villages in southern France lost 80 percent of their population. Towns ran out of cemetery space. The living had to pile the dead in pits with quicklime to speed decomposition and minimize rot. Half the villages of Sicily were abandoned, as were a third of those around Rome.

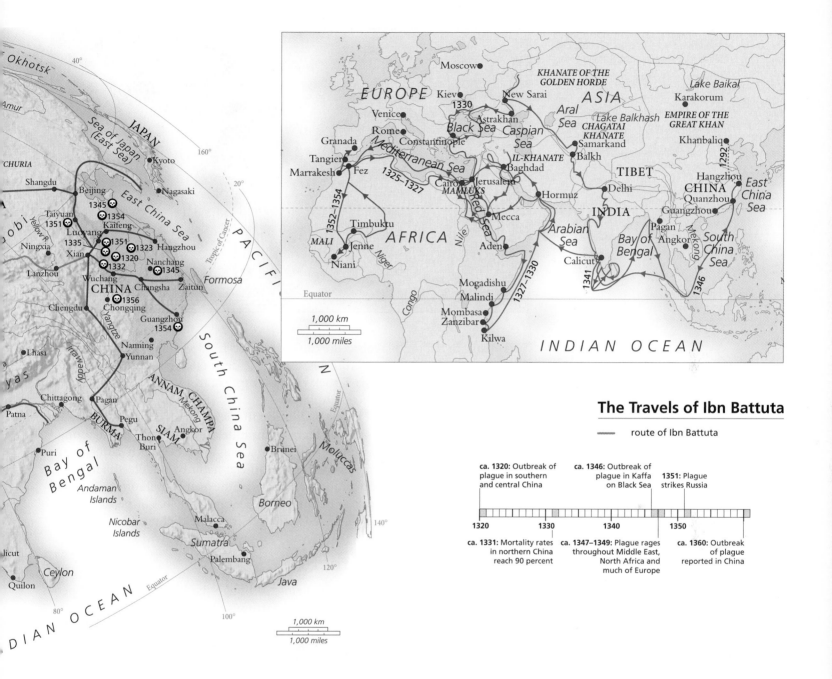

The Travels of Ibn Battuta

— route of Ibn Battuta

ca. 1320: Outbreak of plague in southern and central China

ca. 1346: Outbreak of plague in Kaffa on Black Sea

1351: Plague strikes Russia

ca. 1331: Mortality rates in northern China reach 90 percent

ca. 1347–1349: Plague rages throughout Middle East, North Africa and much of Europe

ca. 1360: Outbreak of plague reported in China

When the plague reached the Middle East, the tireless traveler, Ibn Battuta, was there to observe it, on his way back to Cairo. Arriving in Syria in May 1348, he found that deaths in the city of Damascus reached 2,400 a day. In one town, three-quarters of the public officials had died. A sheikh delayed a banquet for Ibn Battuta until a day arrived when "I did not pray over a corpse." The plague spread along the coast of North Africa, causing—so people claimed—1,000 deaths a day at its height in Tunis, and reaching Morocco, where Ibn Battuta's own mother was among the victims.

In Central Asia, where plagues bred or where microorganisms traveled between the densely populated ends of Eurasia, we can also find indications of mortality. Arab sources reported that many steppeland dynasties and Mongol warriors succumbed to plague. Nestorian headstones at Chwolson in what is now

Flagellants. In 1349, the Black Death inspired thousands of penitents to organize processions and cults of self-flagellation across Europe in an attempt to deflect God's wrath. Like many others, the Flemish chronicler whose work is depicted here denounced the flagellants for claiming that their penance was a kind of baptism, that it could wipe out sin, and that it was a sacrifice akin to Christ's death on the cross. The king of France banned flagellation, and the pope outlawed it.

Turkmenistan refer to plague as the cause of deaths in 1338 and 1339. In 1345 and 1346, according to Russian chronicles, pestilence devastated cities in the Mongol-ruled parts of southern Russia. Uzbek villages emptied. In 1346–1347, an official in Crimea reputedly counted 85,000 corpses.

In China, too little work has been done on the demographic impact of plagues to make firm assertions. In general, there seems little doubt that the population of the empire fell in the relevant period. The census of 1393, with adjustments demographers made to compensate for the official habit of underestimating the numbers, suggests a total population of perhaps a little over 80 million—compared with about 120 million in the mid–fourteenth century. The loss of people was by no means uniform. Some regions even seem to have made slight gains.

Moral and Social Effects

Natural disasters always inspire moralizing. Although the Black Death killed people indiscriminately—the vicious and the virtuous alike—it was tempting, especially for Christians, to see it as a moral agent, even a divine instrument to call the world to repentance and make people good. The plague was a leveler, attacking all sorts and conditions. For many who experienced it, the plague was a test of faith, first eliciting selfish reactions of terror and flight, profiteering and despair, then, as Matteo Villani observed, "people . . . began to help one another, so that many were cured, and people felt safe in helping others." Dice makers, claimed an abbot in northern France, turned to making rosary beads. In China, as we shall see, plague, combined with other natural disasters, helped to stir up religious movements that over spilled into political revolution (see Chapter 15). In the Islamic world, fear of plague stimulated a revival of features of popular religion the clergy normally condemned: summoning spirits, magical spells, and charms.

"Although the Black Death killed people indiscriminately—the vicious and the virtuous alike—it was tempting, especially for Christians, to see it as a moral agent, even a divine instrument to call the world to repentance and make people good."

Medicine and Morals

As well as to prayer, penance, and superstition, plague was a stimulus to science as people searched for a cure. It was normal to speak of sin as if it were the cause of the plague. But most people did not take such talk literally. Moralistic explanations of

Treating the plague. In the mid–fifteenth century, a patron who was probably a plague survivor endowed a chapel in the high Alps at Lanslevillard. The chapel was dedicated to St. Sebastian, adopted by plague victims, perhaps because his arrow wounds resembled the pockmarks and pustules of so many diseases. The scene reproduced here shows the underarm buboes that are also a symptom of bubonic plague, the indiscriminate nature of the disease, its supposed origin as a punishment from God, and physicians' efforts to cure it by lancing pustules.

disease were hardly more convincing in the fourteenth century then they are today, and scientific inquiry soon replaced lamentations. The University of Paris medical faculty blamed "a year of many fogs and damps. . . . We must not overlook the fact that pestilence proceeds from divine will, . . . but this does not mean forsaking doctors." Astrologers produced fatalistic explanations. "Corrupt air" was widely blamed, perhaps caused by polluted wells, perhaps by earthquakes. In the Islamic world, too, religious interpretations of the origin of plague never inhibited scientific inquiry into its causes and possible cures. Muslim physicians also blamed corrupt air, caused in its turn by irregular weather, decaying matter, and astrological influences.

As for how to treat plague, practices were wildly different. In Cairo, healers smeared the swellings on the bodies of the afflicted with Armenian clay. In Muslim Spain, the physician Ibn Khatib advised abstention from grains, cheese, mushrooms, and garlic. Barley water and syrup of basil were widely prescribed as remedies or ways to prevent becoming ill. Gentile of Foligno in central Italy, who died of the plague in 1348, recommended dried snake's flesh, at least a year old. This was not as silly as it sounds. Snakes, whose venom can be beneficial in measured quantities, had a long and honorable therapeutic record with the medical profession. Another Italian, Gabriele de' Mussis, favored bloodlettings and plasters made of mallow leaves. Turks sliced off the heads of the boils on the bodies of the sick and supposedly extracted "green glands."

The overwhelming medical consensus among both Christians and Muslims saw infection and contagion as the main threats to the population. Where the authorities responded accordingly in time by imposing quarantine, lives were spared. Quarantine worked in places as busy as the great city of Milan in northern Italy.

Where it could not be averted, plague shattered morale. A poet in Cairo, al-Sallah al-Safadi, described the psychological effect of the disease. Those it spared were maddened. It "spread fear and misery in the hearts of women" and convinced even the mighty of their mortality. It entered houses "like bands of thieves," dispelling people's sense of security. "God has not just subdued Egypt,"

Burying the dead. "How come you feel no sadness when you bury a fellow-creature . . . that you remain unready for your own graves . . . that you pay no heed when warnings of death reach your ears?" The twelfth-century Muslim writer al Hariri asked this question in his *Maqamat*, a collection of moralistic stories. Al Hariri had no doubt that sickness, besides being a physical affliction, also served a moral purpose. God sent it to test human virtue and compassion. When the Black Death struck in the 1300s, many Muslims and Christians also saw the plague this way and tried to minister to the sick and dying. Yet the number of deaths could overwhelm the living, and many of the dead were dumped in mass graves.

al-Safadi concluded, "he has made her crawl on her knees." The Florentine poet, Petrarch, felt the guilt of survival among the corpses. He saw "just one comfort: that we shall follow those who went before." He raged at his fellow survivors: "Go, mortals, sweat, pant, toil, range the lands and seas to pile up riches you cannot keep. . . . The life we lead is a sleep; whatever we do are dreams. Only death breaks the sleep and wakes us from dreaming. I wish I could have woken before this."

The Jews

Plague had winners and losers. In Europe, Jews were among the losers. A skeptical German Franciscan reported the common opinion that Jews started the plague by poisoning wells "and many Jews confessed as much under torture: that they had bred spiders and toads in pots and pans, and had obtained poison from overseas. . . . Throughout Germany, and in all places, they were burnt. For fear of that punishment many accepted baptism and their lives were spared." The massacres that ensued, especially in Germany, were nearly always the result of outbreaks of mob violence, which the authorities tried to restrain. In July 1348, Pope Clement VI declared the Jews innocent of the charge of well poisoning and excommunicated anyone who harmed them. In January 1349, the city council of Cologne in the Rhineland warned authorities in other cities that anti-Jewish riots could ignite popular revolt. "Accordingly we intend to forbid any harrassment of the Jews in our city because of these flying rumors, but to defend them and keep them safe, as our predecessors did—and we are convinced that you ought to do the same." Not all authorities, however, were equally vigilant, equally effective, or equally committed to the defense of the Jews, and massacres continued.

Why did some people in Europe victimize Jews? Jewish communities had existed all over the Mediterranean since Roman times (see Map 14.3). Like other migrants from the east, such as Greeks, Syrians, and Arabs, Jews were an urban and often a commercial people. The itinerary of the twelfth-century Jewish merchant, Benjamin of Tudela, whose description of Constantinople we quoted in Chapter 12, describes their close-knit world, in which a structure of family firms and the fellow feeling of co-religionists gave Jews a commercial advantage and helped them to trade between the Christian and Muslim worlds. An isolated reference to Jews in Cologne occurs as early as 321 C.E. when the Rhineland was part of the Roman Empire, but Mediterranean communities were probably the springboard for Jewish colonization of northern European cities between the sixth and eleventh centuries.

Wherever they went, Jews were alternately privileged and persecuted: privileged, because rulers who needed productive settlers were prepared to reward them with legal immunities; persecuted, because host communities resented intruders who were given special advantages. Some scholars trace **anti-Semitism** to the influence of Christianity. Indeed, medieval anti-Semitism did exploit Christian prejudices. Gospel texts could be read—as they were, for example, at the time of the First Crusade (see Chapter 12)—to saddle Jews with collective responsibility for the death of Jesus. And Holy Week, when Christians prepare to commemorate Christ's death, was at best an expensive and at worst a fatal time for Jewish communities, who had to buy security from bloody reprisals.

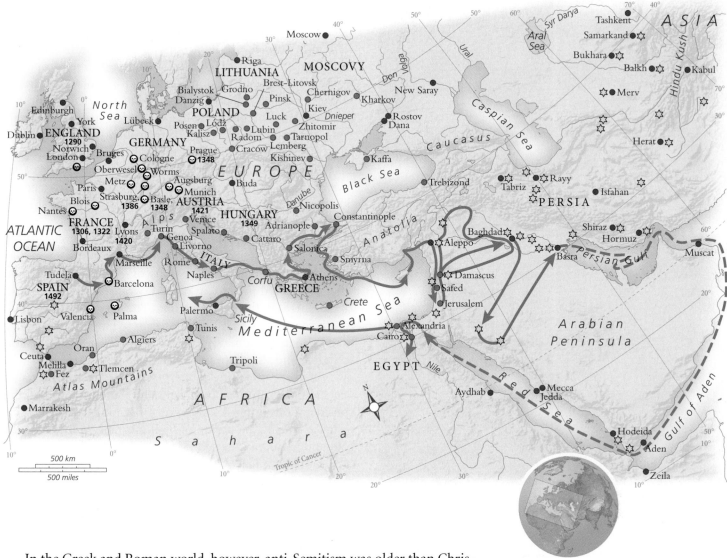

MAP 14.3

Jews in Medieval Europe and the Middle East, 1100–1400

- ● major centers of Jewish resettlement, 1200–1500
- ☺ massacres of Jews, ca. 1100–1400
- **1290** date of expulsion of Jews
- ➡ travels of Benjamin of Tuleda, ca. 1160–1173
- ▪▪➡ presumed route of Benjamin of Tuleda
- ☆ Jewish communities in Muslim world

In the Greek and Roman world, however, anti-Semitism was older than Christianity. Medieval anti-Semitism, moreover, was just one aspect of a wider phenomenon: society's antipathy for groups it could not assimilate—comparable, for instance, to the treatment of lepers, Muslims, and, later, Gypsies. Outbreaks of anti-Jewish hatred are intelligible, in part, as examples of the prejudice outsiders commonly attract. At the time of the Black Death, lepers were also accused of well poisoning. So were random strangers and individuals unpopular in their communities. We can find similar phenomena in almost every culture. The case of the Jews in Europe demands attention not because it is unique, but because it is surprising, given Western society's indebtedness to Jewish traditions, and to the individual genius of many Jews.

The increasing pace and intensity of persecution in the fourteenth century drove Jews to new centers. England had already expelled those Jews who did not convert to Christianity in 1290. The Jews were forced out of most of France in the early fourteenth century, and from many areas of western Germany in the early fifteenth century. (Spain and Portugal followed suit in the 1490s.) The effect was to shift Jewish settlement toward the central and eastern Mediterranean, Poland, and Lithuania (which first admitted Jews in 1321).

Christianity's Supremacy over Judaism. Church and Synagogue are clearly sisters, but the Church is crowned and upright, while the Synagogue is blindfold, with bare, inclined head. These examples are from Bamberg Cathedral in Germany but the pairing of Church and Synagogue appears, with remarkable consistency, all over Europe. Typically, the Synagogue has a broken staff, while the tablets of the law slip from her other hand. If the sculpture of the Church shown here were undamaged, she would almost certainly hold a cross and a chalice.

Distribution of Wealth

Though the evidence relates almost entirely to Europe, there were also people—whole groups of people—who benefited from the effects of plague. In Western Europe, propertied women were certainly among them. The aristocratic marriage market could be fatal to women who married young and faced repeated pregnancies, but it also left many young widows—the last wives of aging, dying husbands. So property law had to provide for widows by ensuring them an adequate share in their dead husbands' estates and reversion of the property the women had brought to their marriages as dowries. More widows burying more husbands could shift the balance of property ownership between the sexes.

Chroniclers, insisting on death as a leveler, often remarked that the plague carried off men and women alike. But, after the terrible devastations of 1348, contemporaries who noticed a difference in mortality rates between the sexes all saw men as the main victims. The plagues of the fourteenth century, taken as a whole, seem to have hit men harder than women, presumably because women led relatively more secluded, and therefore protected, lives than men. Rich widows, often accumulating property from successive marriages, wielded power in their own right. To some extent, the same considerations applied lower down the ranks of society. For instance, during the period of high mortality associated with cold and famine in the second decade of the fourteenth century, more than half the weddings among the peasants of the manor of Taunton in southwest England involved rich widows. After the Black Death, the lords of the manor introduced massive license fees for anyone who wanted to make such marriages, ostensibly to protect widows from predatory Romeos. In unprecedented numbers, widows became the administrators of estates. Women of leisure, education, and power played a bigger part in Western society after this. The increased prominence of women in political, literary, and religious life from the fifteenth century onward might not have been possible without the damage plague did to men.

In Western Europe peasants, if they survived the plague, also benefited from it. In the long run, owners could only keep great properties viable after plague had scythed the labor force by splitting the proceeds with their workers, or by breaking the estates up and letting peasants farm the parcels as tenants. Instead of taking orders from the lord's agent or bailiff, tenants paid rent and could manage their landholdings to their own best advantage. The trend toward "free" peasantries started long before the Black Death struck because in many cases it suited landowners, too. Peasants often made the land more productive. It made economic sense to allow them the initiative to improve their holdings. In England, where the royal courts encouraged peasant freedom to expand their own jurisdiction at aristocrats' expense, about half the peasants in the south of the country were already free when the plague arrived.

Lords wrote off their rights to labor services because, as a steward on an English estate admitted in 1351, "the lord's interest made it necessary." The contract peasant dependants of an English abbey renegotiated is revealing. "At the time of the mortality or pestilence which occurred in 1349, scarcely two peasants remained on the manor." They threatened to leave unless the abbey made a new contract. Most of their former services—including plowing, weeding, carting, and preparing soil for planting—were commuted for rent "as long as it pleases the lord—and would that it might please the lord for ever," added the scribe, "since the aforesaid services were not worth very much." It is remarkable, however, that the growth of leaseholding and the relaxation of lordly controls over peasant farmers happened on a large scale in the late fourteenth and fifteenth centuries in the parts of Western Europe plague affected. In areas the Black Death bypassed—such as Poland, much of Russia, and what is now the Czech Republic and Slovakia—the opposite happened. Peasants became tied to their lords' land and subject to the landholders' jurisdiction.

Were the effects on the European peasantry duplicated in other plague-ridden lands? Certainly, the rural population became more restive and mobile in Egypt and Syria, where, in 1370, one jurist railed against the laws that obliged justices to return peasant refugees to the places from where they had fled. Villages in Egypt often had their tax burdens reduced in acknowledgment of the loss of population. The cost of labor services rose as population fell, creating opportunities for economic mobility among peasants and urban workers, and stimulating a further decline in rural population levels as peasants migrated to towns. But these changes did not disturb landowners' grip on their holdings. Peasants and landowners seem to have suffered together the effects of declining rural productivity.

Peasant Millenarianism

Where peasants benefited, improved conditions took a long time to take effect. Combined with the effects of climate change, the immediate consequences of the plague disturbed, even subverted, the sense of security and stability associated with a traditional way of life. Moreover, most governments responded to the demographic disaster, loss of revenue, and loss of labor by raising taxes and trying to limit labor mobility. In previous centuries, ecological disasters and political oppression had often driven peasants into religious extremism or rebellion. Now, popular revolt took on a new agenda: revolutionary **millenarianism**—the doctrine that in an imminent, divinely contrived relaunch of history, God would empower the poor. This happened independently but in strikingly similar ways, in both Europe and China. A popular preacher who incited peasant rebels in England in 1381, expressed the doctrine of egalitarianism:

> How can the lords say or prove that they are more lords than we—save that they make us dig and till the ground so that they can squander what we produce? . . . They have beautiful residences and manors, while we have the trouble and the work, always in the fields and under the snow. But it is from us and our labor that everything comes with which they maintain their pomp. . . . Good folk, things cannot go well in England, nor ever shall until all things are in common and there is neither villein nor noble, but all of us are of one condition.

Prophecies helped nourish revolt. Some Franciscans (see Chapter 13), with their special vocation to serve the poor, excited expectations that the end of the world could not be far off, and that a new age was at hand when God would release riches from the bowels of the Earth and eliminate inequality. In China, a similar doctrine inspired peasant rebels in the 1350s. A new Buddha would inaugurate a golden age and give his followers power over their oppressors (see Chapter 15).

The Wife of Bath. "Thanks be to God, who is for aye alive, / Of husbands at Church door have I had five." "The Wife of Bath" was a fictional character of about 1400—shown here in a contemporary illustration to the English writer Geoffrey Chaucer's verses about her. But, like all good satire, she was representative of the society of her times: sexually shameless, irrepressibly bossy, and determined to exert "power, during all my life" over any husband "who shall be both my debtor and my slave."
"Facsimile of Ellesnere Chaucher, The Life of Bath" 1400–1410. VdA Museum, London. Picture Desk, Inc./Kobal Collection

According to both movements, a divinely appointed hero would put a bloody end to the struggle of good and evil.

The next chapter describes the politics of the ensuing revolt in China. According to popular traditions dating from soon after the time, the leader of the rebellion, the founder of the Ming dynasty, who claimed to be the prophesied hero, experienced the effects of ecological crisis himself. In one story, he rose to prominence by inventing a medicine that could cure a devastating new plague "which killed half the people and which no known medicine could combat." In another version, the plague and the great Yellow River flood of 1344 reduced him to beggary, and eventually he joined the rebellion that brought him to supreme power.

In addition to contributing to revolution and a change of dynasty in China, and to instability in Europe, the plagues helped transform the Mongol world. The region the Mongols dominated spanned the plague's trans-Eurasian corridors of transmission. Though the evidence comes from European observers, it is a safe assumption that Mongol manpower suffered and that population levels in some regions from which the Mongols levied recruits and collected taxes also fell. The loss of China in 1368 was, of course, the Mongols' most spectacular forfeiture of power. But the effects went further. Mongol control slackened in other dominions, and, on the Chinese front, it never recovered.

In general, plague-stricken societies showed more of what we now call social mobility. The ranks of aristocracies, which were always subject to rapid turnover as families died out, thinned and refilled faster than ever. This seems to have applied as much to China's scholar elite, whose hold on power lapsed and was not fully reasserted until well into the fifteenth century, as to Western European nobilities, whose composition changed. In Western Europe, the increase in the number of free peasants and tenants created a form of rural capitalism. Families formerly restricted to modest social ambitions could accumulate wealth and bid for higher status, buying education or business opportunities or more land.

THE LIMITS OF DISASTER: BEYOND THE PLAGUE ZONE

"Beyond the reach of the plagues—or, at least, beyond the zone of their most severe effects—the fourteenth century was an era of opportunity in Eurasia."

How far did the plagues of the fourteenth century reach? In terms of effects, the plague was a regional phenomenon, changing the history of China, Western Europe, the Middle East, and the steppeland empires. But much of Central and Eastern Europe escaped. So did areas that ought to have been vulnerable to a disease spread by contagion or infection, such as southeast Asia, and the parts of Africa that were in touch, by way of the Indian Ocean or the Saharan caravan routes, with affected regions. Its relative isolation protected Japan. Apart from a pestilence in the capital Kyoto in 1342, which chroniclers were inclined to attribute to the vengeful spirit of a former emperor, Japan suffered no visitations of any disease on a scale resembling that of the Black Death. The principalities and city-states of central and northern Russia suffered relatively little and late—not before 1350, which is surprising in view of Russia's openness to the steppeland and close contact with the Mongols. India was relatively little affected—references to pestilence are not much more frequent in fourteenth-century sources than for other periods, and recorded outbreaks were localized.

Beyond the reach of the plagues—or, at least, beyond the zone of their most severe effects—the fourteenth century was an era of opportunity in Eurasia. The Mongols were now troubled giants, from whom states in India, Japan, and

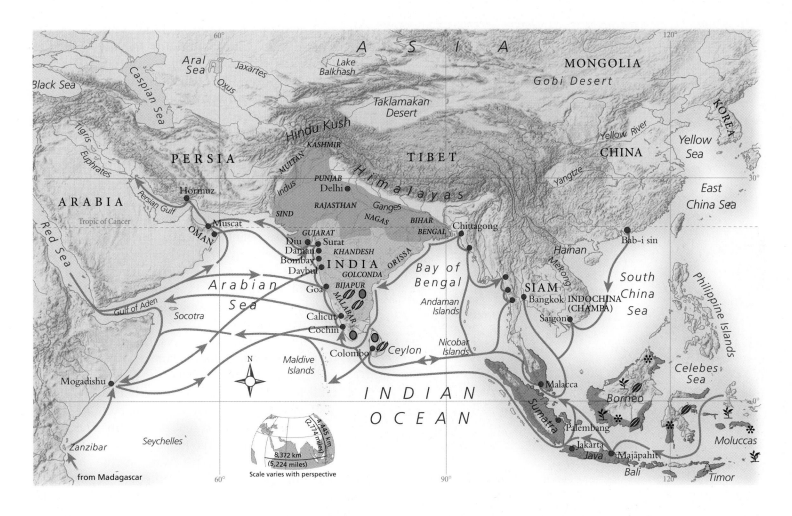

MAP 14.4

South and Southeast Asia, ca. 1350

- region where Majapahit claimed tribute
- Delhi sultanate at its greatest extent, ca. 1335
- area subject to sporadic influence by Delhi Sultanate
- main trade route
- important trade centers

Traded Goods

- pepper
- cinnamon
- sandalwood
- nutmeg
- cloves
- mace

southeast Asia were at last safe. We can look at those regions first, before turning to sub-Saharan Africa and the Pacific where, as far as we know, the plagues never penetrated.

India

In India, the sultanate of Delhi profited from the Mongols' decline. Sultan Muhammad Ibn Tughluq (r. 1325–1351) was the driving force of a policy of conquest that almost covered the subcontinent with campaigns (see Map 14.4). Ibn Battuta, who knew the sultan well, called him "of all men the most addicted to the making of gifts and the shedding of blood. His gate is never without some poor man enriched or some living man executed." Emphasis on the sultan's generosity reflects Ibn Battuta's own priorities. He was always on the lookout for rich patrons. But the key facts about Ibn Tughluq's methods are clear. He ran his court and army by balancing lavish gifts with intimidating displays of wrath.

Ibn Tughluq's administration was a machine for recycling wealth. Ibn Battuta describes the regular arrival of revenue collectors from villages, casting gold coins into a golden basin: "These contributions amount in all to a vast sum which the sultan gives to anyone he pleases." Annually, "the daughters of the infidel kings and who have been taken as captives in war during that year" were distributed among the sultan's chief supporters, after performing a sort of audition—singing and dancing, presumably to establish which girls were the most valuable.

Daulatabad. The Delhi Sultan Ibn Tughluq (r. 1325–1351) transferred his court to the strongest fortress in India, which he called Daulatabad, or "City of Riches," near the frontier of his campaigns against Hindu kingdoms in the south. He planned to relocate the entire population of the city of Delhi to the surrounding slopes. The steep ascent made the place defensible. A narrow gangway was the only approach to the palace complex.

While praising Ibn Tughluq's sense of justice, Ibn Battuta indicts him for the use of terror, abuses of power, and judicial murder. "The Sultan was far too free in shedding blood. . . . Every day there are brought to the audience hall hundreds of people, chained, beaten and fettered, and those who are for execution are executed, those for torture tortured, and those for beating beaten." He put one of his brothers to death on a charge of rebellion, which Ibn Battuta clearly felt was trumped up—the first of many judicial murders. On one occasion, the sultan executed 350 alleged deserters at once. A sheikh who accused him of tyranny was fed with excrement and beheaded. Twice, Ibn Tughluq dealt with suspected conspiracies in Delhi by expelling the classes of Muslim notables whom he suspected of disaffection.

Ibn Tughluq's was a personal empire. His own dynamism and reputation, and a policy of religious toleration held it together—the only policy workable for a Muslim elite in a largely Hindu country. But Ibn Tughluq's state was not built to last. It relied on conquest to fuel the system. The Turkic elite, who provided the muscle for revenue collection at home and for war on the frontiers, demanded constant rewards. When they did not get them, they seceded from the state. This began to happen on a large scale toward the end of Ibn Tughluq's life. Conquest is, in any case, a gambler's game. Military fortunes change, and military systems, even of the most crushing superiority, can fail unpredictably. Disaster struck Ibn Tughluq, for instance, when a plague devastated his army. "The provinces withdrew their allegiance," Ibn Battuta reported, "and the outer regions broke away."

Moreover, the Delhi sultans were under constant pressure from the Muslim establishment to impose Islam by force, launch holy war, and ease the tax burden on Muslims at the expense of "infidels." The discontent evident among sheikhs and some Muslim notables during Ibn Tughluq's reign owed something, no doubt, to fear of the sultan's arbitrary measures. But frustration with his policies of toleration also inspired much of it. Ibn Tughluq's successor succumbed to these pressures. He forfeited Hindu allegiance. Beyond the frontier, Hindu states adopted a counter ideology of resistance to Islam—at least at the level of rhetoric, since religion rarely took priority over politics. In southern India, a Hindu state with imperial ambitions arose at Vijayanagar. The conquest juggernaut of the sultanate of Delhi stopped rolling, and provincial elites in outlying regions in Gujarat and Bengal dropped out of the empire. Again, as so often happened in Indian history, both the difficulties of and the capacity for an India-wide empire had been demonstrated. But again, the problems of maintaining such a large and diverse state were obvious. Future attempts would run into the same kinds of difficulties as those that caused the sultanate's control of the outer edges of the state to unravel and its expansion to come to a halt.

Southeast Asia

Rather as Delhi did in India, a native kingdom in Java, (the main island of what is today Indonesia), exploited the opportunity that emerged as the Mongol threat waned. The offshore world of Southeast Asia produced goods the Chinese market wanted. Some states in the region were in a position to threaten or control the passage of those goods by sea: pepper and cinnamon from southern India and Sri Lanka; sandalwood from Timor; timber and aromatic spices—nutmeg, cloves, and mace—from Borneo and the Moluccas. Control of the strait between Malaya, Java, and Sumatra was strategically vital for China-bound trade, and the shipping of Java made an important contribution to the commerce of the region. That is why Kubilai Khan focused on Java when he tried to extend his empire into Southeast Asia (see Chapter 15).

The establishment of a powerful state on Java, centered on the secure, inland city of Majapahit (Mah-jah-PAH-heet), was the achievement of Kertanagara, who died in 1292. Chroniclers credited him with magic powers or saintly virtues, according to their own prejudices. In fact, he seems to have balanced the rituals of Buddhist, Hindu, and indigenous religions to keep a diverse array of followers together. Kertanagara repulsed Kubilai Khan's Mongol invasion.

The king who launched Majapahit on its own imperial career in the mid–fourteenth century was Hayan Wuruk (died 1389). He had dazzling ambitions. We know this because his childhood playmate, who became one of his chief ministers, wrote a poem in his praise. The verses reveal what the king wanted people to think of him. The poem lovingly describes the royal palace at Majapahit, which had gates of iron and a "diamond-plastered" watchtower. Majapahit was like the sun and moon, while the villages of the rest of the kingdom are "of the aspect of stars." When Hayan Wuruk traveled the country, his court filled numberless carts. Through the streets of his capital, he paraded, clad in gold, borne on a throne carved with supporting lions, to the music of lutes and drums, conches and trumpets, and singers. Ambassadors from foreign courts brought him praises in Sanskrit verse.

Hayan Wuruk was both "Buddha in the body" and "Shiva incarnate"—worshipful to Buddhist and Hindu subjects alike. He was also a master of native rituals, skilled in the theater, dance, and song. "The king's song put them under a spell," the poet assures us, "like the cries of a peacock." Hayan Wuruk's realm, according to the poet, was more famous than any country in the world except India. In reality, the kingdom occupied little more than half the island of Java. The king, however, aimed to make it bigger. The poet listed tributaries in many islands in what is today Indonesia, and "protectorates" in northern Malaya, Thailand, and Indochina. Even China and India, he claimed, defer to Hayan Wuruk. "Already the other continents," he boasts, "are getting ready to show obedience to the illustrious prince" and a state "renowned for its purifying power in the world."

That was all the exaggeration of propaganda. But a disinterested chronicler, from Samudra-Pasai, a pepper-exporting port beyond the Strait of Malacca to the west, left a description of Majapahit that confirms much of the picture:

> The empire grew prosperous. People in vast numbers thronged the city. At this time every kind of food was in great abundance. There was a ceaseless coming and going of people from the territories overseas which had submitted to the king. . . . The land of Majapahit was supporting a large population. Everywhere one went there were gongs and drums being beaten, people dancing to the strains of all kinds of loud music, entertainments of all kinds like the living theater. . . . These were the commonest sights and went on day and night in the land of Majapahit.

"When Hayan Wuruk traveled the country, his court filled numberless carts. Through the streets of his capital, he paraded, clad in gold, borne on a throne carved with supporting lions, to the music of lutes and drums, conches and trumpets, and singers."

A Javanese Queen

This fourteenth-century sculpture, carved before Islam had begun to dominate the culture of Java, depicts a Javanese queen as an incarnation of the Hindu goddess Parvati. Parvati is the wife of the supreme god Shiva, who is associated with destruction and transformation, and like him she has both benign and violent attributes.

The blooming lotus is one of the benign attributes of Parvati.

One of Parvati's sons, the elephant-headed god Ganesha, is depicted executing a dance step influenced by yoga.

Kartikkeya, another of Parvati's sons, is a god of war.

Posthumous Portrait of a Queen as Parvati. Eastern Javanese period, 14th century. Indonesia. Andesite, H. 6 ft. 8 in. (203.2 cm); W. 3 ft. 3 in. (99.1 cm). The Metropolitan Museum of Art, New York, NY, U.S.A. Image copyright ∞© The Metropolitan Museum of Art / Art Resource, NY.

Parvati is often shown riding a lion, but here she rests on Nandi, the divine bull, whom Shiva rode.

How does this sculpture reflect ideals of kingship in Java at this time?

Surviving temple reliefs show what the Java of Hayan Wuruk was like. Wooden houses, perched on pillars over stone terraces, formed neat villages. Peasants grew paddy rice, or coaxed water buffalo over dry fields to break up the soil. Women did the harvesting and cooking. Orchestras, beating gongs with sticks, accompanied masked dancers. Royal charters fill out the picture of economic activities. Industrial processes included salt making by evaporation, sugar refining, processing cured water-buffalo meat, oil pressing from seeds, making rice noodles, ironmaking, rattan weaving, and dyeing cloth. More sophisticated ceramics and textiles were imported from China. The same charters reveal the extension of royal power and impact into the hinterland. They establish direct relationships between the royal court and members of local elites. They favor the foundations of new temples and encourage the spread of communications, the building of bridges, the commissioning of ferries, and the erection of "rest houses, pious foundations, and hospitals" mentioned in the king's praise poem.

Majapahit was an expanding realm. As Mongol vigilance in the region relaxed, Majapahit's power increased. In the 1340s, a network of ports in the hands of Majapahit garrisons spread over the islands of Bali and Sumatra. Majapahit indeed seems to have annihilated commercial rivals in Sumatra and to have maintained fortified outposts on the coast of that island. In 1377, Hayan Wuruk launched an apparently successful expedition against Palembang, the major way station on the route from India to China. A struggle was on to profit from Southeast Asia's trade (see Map 14.4).

Japan

Japan, like Java, was a region that the plagues spared and the Mongols failed to conquer. Here, however, security from the Mongol menace had a contrasting effect. As the threat from the Mongols receded, so did pressure to stay united and serve the state. Potential rebels could now raise armies with increasing ease. Fourteenth-century Japan began to experience unprecedented instability. Familiar patterns in politics and social life were shaken like the contents of a kaleidoscope. Since the beginning of the rule of the shoguns, the hereditary chief ministers who controlled the government (see Chapter 11), Japan had enjoyed more than a century of stability. The warrior class had been pacified—maintained by grants of estates and their revenues. Now people at all social levels were accumulating wealth. Social status, which was supposedly protected by complicated standards of eligibility for different ranks, was up for grabs. Warriors began to diversify into new occupations, to sell or break up their estate rights, and, in increasing numbers, to resort to violence as a way of life.

At the top of this volatile society, rival branches of the imperial family contested the throne. The Emperor Godaigo (r. 1318–1339) fought to exclude family competitors and to take back the power the shoguns exercised in the emperor's name. He accused them of "drawing water from a stream and forgetting its source." Godaigo had his portrait painted showing himself with a sword—an accessory normally considered too active for an emperor, but one that signified his intentions to recover real power and keep hold of the symbols of imperial authority, which included a sacred sword.

Godaigo found, however, that he could not simply take up the reins of power himself. Traditional methods could no longer govern the country. Loyalty, though much talked of by writers at the time, became an unpredictable commodity, liable to change hands as circumstances changed. An oath the members of a warband took

"Fourteenth-century Japan began to experience unprecedented instability. Familiar patterns in politics and social life were shaken like the contents of a kaleidoscope."

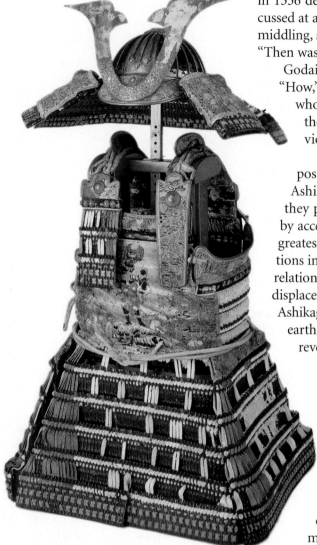

A Shogun's Armor. This armor is believed to have belonged to Ashikaga Takauji who was shogun from 1338 to 1358. The quality and costliness of the gilt copper breastplate and helmet mountings show that the armor belonged to a person of high status. Stenciled in lacquered doeskin, an image of Fudo Myo-o—the god who personified the samurai virtues of outward ferocity and inner calm—adorns the breastplate.
The Metropolitan Museum of Art, Gift of Bashford Dean, 1914 (14.100.121) Photograph © 1991 The Metropolitan Museum of Art.

in 1336 declared, "Let there be no differences of opinion. Everything shall be discussed at a council. If some disobey this, they shall suffer the punishment of all the middling, small, and great gods of the country of Japan in Heaven, Earth and Hell." "Then was then," proclaimed a saying of the time. "Now is now: rewards are lord!" Godaigo's army deserted in dissatisfaction over the rewards he could provide. "How," complained one of the officials who worked for his party, "can those who tend to have the outlook of a merchant be of use to the court?" Clearly, the new disorder was, for some, a kind of social revolution: the result of violations of the proper boundaries of class and rank.

In 1335, the most powerful of the warlords, Ashikaga Takauji, seized the position of supreme power as **shogun** in defiance of Godaigo's wishes. The Ashikaga dynasty emerged with the greatest share of authority because they promised the most rewards. They survived as shoguns almost until 1573 by accepting the realities of the changed world, withdrawing into a role as the greatest of a number of regional powers, and attempting only modest interventions in the spheres of other major warlords. The Ashikaga also restored the old relationship between shogun and emperor, in which pieties smothered the real displacement of power into the shogun's hands. "There is heaven," declared Ashikaga Takauji in his testament of 1357, "there is the sovereign, there is the earth, and there is the minister. . . . If the joint path of sovereign and subject is reversed, then there will be neither heaven nor earth, sovereign nor subject."

In 1336, the Ashikaga overwhelmed Godaigo's remaining supporters at the Battle of Minato River (see Map 14.5). Godaigo and his heirs, however, did not give up. Ashikaga victories confined them to a small enclave in the south of the country, but they resisted until the 1380s.

The chaos of the fourteenth century favored the rise of **Zen,** a tradition of Buddhism that valued personal extinction as a part of mystical experience. A twelfth-century Japanese text defined it: "a special transmission outside the scriptures, not founded on words or letters, which allows one to penetrate the nature of things by pointing directly to the mind." Zen made progress partly because of the influx of monks from China who were escaping from the Mongols, and partly because Zen ideas suited the warriors and warlords who now effectively ruled Japan. Discipline, self-denial, and willingness to die are martial virtues. The warriors recognized Zen monks as kindred spirits. Warrior families made Zen practitioners the custodians of their ancestral temples and tombs.

For the women of families of warrior and aristocratic rank, the changes of the period were oppressive. Women could attain responsible positions in the emperor's court. Hino Meishi, for instance, was in charge of the sacred imperial symbols in 1331, when the shogun tried to depose Godaigo. But changing marriage customs were unfavorable to women's personal independence. Until the fourteenth century, marriage in Japan was predominantly a private, essentially sexual relationship. Now it became increasingly formalized, as a union of two families. Wives moved into the homes of their husbands' families, instead of remaining in their own homes. Hino Meishi, for instance, started her experience of married life in 1333 in traditional manner, when her lover started visiting her openly. This publicly acknowledged the relationship as a permanent one. She worried, not because the arrangement was informal, but because her husband's family was of higher rank than her own. In the confused conditions of the civil war then raging, Meishi was forced to move house, but she ended up in her husband's home.

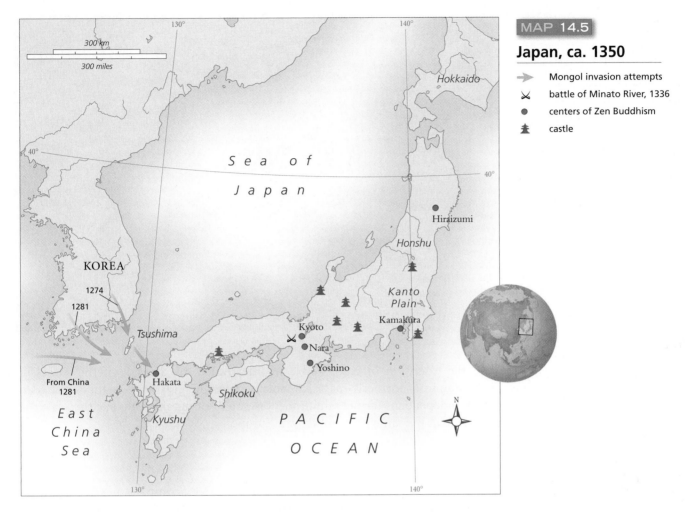

MAP 14.5

Japan, ca. 1350

→ Mongol invasion attempts

⚔ battle of Minato River, 1336

● centers of Zen Buddhism

🌲 castle

A sign of women's changed circumstances is that they stopped writing fiction and the kind of personal diaries familiar from earlier periods. Hino Meishi herself was the author of the last autobiographical memoir by a woman—which is why we know so much about her life. Self-expression was now considered inappropriate for the female sex. Wives came to be thought of as their husbands' property. In the same period, following changes in the practices of the imperial family, it became common for women aristocrats to receive a life interest in a share of family property, rather than inheriting property outright. Property rights were steered toward a single male heir. Among commoners, however, this practice failed to take hold, and women held growing amounts of property and engaged in more business in their own right.

The changes that were transforming the warrior class do not seem to have affected peasant prosperity. On the contrary, the peasants profited. Relaxation of central authority freed villagers from intrusive legislation. They could get on with improving crop yields as they saw fit. The new regime of rewards for military service meant that the landlords were always changing—dispossessed and replaced as the fortunes of war shifted. The rapid turnover of lords, who were usually absentees, also allowed the peasants to get on with their business. There were no epidemics in the fourteenth-century countryside in Japan, and serious crop failures were rare. Nor were population growth

Chronology: The Ashikaga Shogunate	
Fourteenth century	Changing marriage customs diminish women's independence
1318–1339	Emperor Godaigo seeks to regain imperial power
1335	Ashikaga Takauji defies Godaigo and seizes shogunate
1336	Godaigo's supporters defeated at Battle of Minato River

Zen garden. Zuiho-in is one of 24 temples within the temple complex of Daitokuji in Kyoto, one of the Japan's biggest Zen communities. Most temples have a garden of meditation designed to be observed from a single viewpoint to encourage solitude. The hallmarks of these gardens are the expanses of gravel raked to resemble waves, and rocks arranged like islands within it. Greenery is not a normal part of most Zen garden designs, perhaps because living plants are mutable—they change too easily with the passing seasons, whereas rocks are deceptively unchanging. But to ask what a Zen garden "means" is to invite an evasive answer.

and the extension of cultivated land interrupted. As a result of the successful exploitation of formerly marginal lands outside the great estates, the numbers of small independent farmers multiplied, though not on anything like the scale that occurred at the same time in Western Europe.

Mali

Just as Java and Japan seemed to grow in stature by comparison with the afflictions of China and the Mongols, so parts of West Africa projected an image of abundance toward the devastated Mediterranean world. A conspicuous piece of evidence for West African prosperity is the Catalan Atlas, made in the studio of the finest mapmaker in Europe, Cresques Abraham, on the Mediterranean island of Majorca, in the 1370s or 1380s. The map is smothered with gold paint, scattered with bright images in costly pigments, like the contents of a spilled jewel box. In the part of the map devoted to West Africa, a black king appears—bearded, crowned, enthroned, surrounded by depictions of rich cities of many turrets—holding a huge nugget of pure gold. "This is the richest king in all the land," says a caption.

His kingdom, Mali, occupied the Sahel region of grassland and mixed savanna between the Sahara Desert and the tropical forest. The desert sealed it from the effects of plague (see Map 14.6). According to tradition, a hero known as **Sundiata** founded the kingdom in the early thirteenth century. His story has obviously mythical features. He was a cripple, mocked and exiled, who returned home as a conqueror and avenger. The strength of his army, and those of his successors, was horsemen. Terracotta sculptures show us what they were like. Helmed and armed, with round shields and breastplates over slashed leather jackets, they kept their heads haughtily tilted and their horses on short rein, with elaborately braided bridles. Their great age of conquest came in the 1260s and 1270s when, according to the Muslim historian Ibn Khaldun, "their dominions expanded and they overcame the neighboring peoples . . . and all nations of the land of the blacks stood in awe of them."

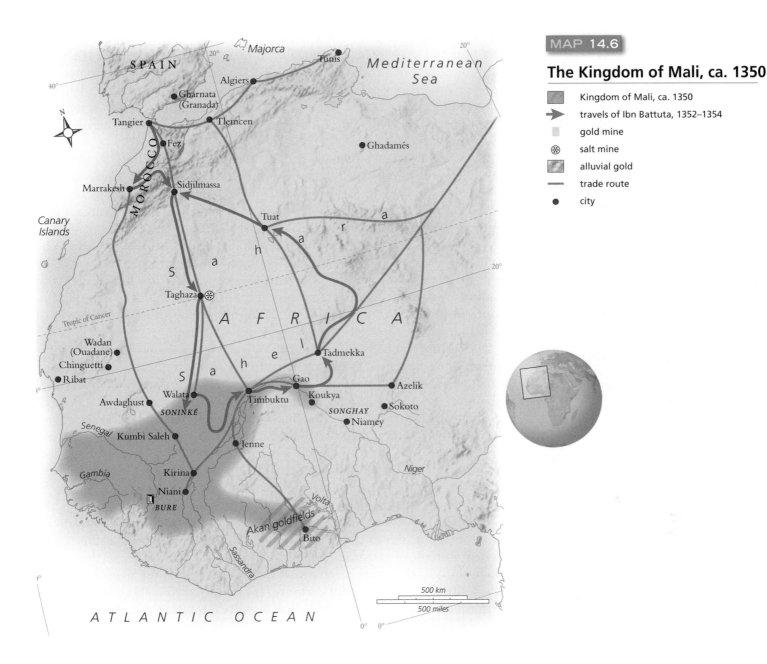

MAP 14.6

The Kingdom of Mali, ca. 1350

- Kingdom of Mali, ca. 1350
- travels of Ibn Battuta, 1352–1354
- gold mine
- salt mine
- alluvial gold
- trade route
- city

The "mansas," as the kings of Mali were titled, made pilgrimages to the Muslim holy city of Mecca via Cairo at intervals from the late thirteenth century, spreading the fame of their land. Although all Muslims are supposed to make the *hajj*, as the pigrimage to Mecca is called, at least once in their life if possible, the mere fact that the mansas could leave their country for the year-long journey shows how stable the state must have been. In about 1324, Mansa Musa stayed in Egypt for about three months on his way to Mecca. He gave 50,000 gold coins to the Mamluk sultan and distributed ingots of raw gold to officials. He endowed so many mosques and shrines that he caused inflation. By various accounts, the value of gold in Egypt fell 10 to 25 percent as a result of his stay. On his homeward journey, he raised loans that, it was said, he repaid at the rate of 700 coins for every 300 of the same value.

The location of West Africa's gold mines was a closely guarded commercial secret, but it was probably in Bure (BOO–ray), around the upper reaches of the

Mansa. "All the peoples of the land of the Blacks stood in awe of them," wrote Ibn Khaldun of the mounted warriors of the Mansas of Mali. Many fired-clay representations of these soldiers survive from the thirteenth to the fifteenth centuries. Nearly all show the same erect posture, proudly uptilted head, and elaborate helmets and bridles.

Niger River and the headwaters of the Gambia and Senegal rivers. The Volta River valley also had some gold. The merchants of Mali handled the gold trade but never controlled its production. When they tried to take over the mines, the miners refused to work. But the gold had to pass through the mansa's lands to get to trading cities, such as Walata and Timbuktu (tihm-buhk-TOO) near the edge of the Sahara. The mansa took nuggets for tribute—hence the image on Cresques Abraham's map.

In 1352, Ibn Battuta—that relentless traveler—set off to find the kingdom of Mali. He journeyed south from his home in Morocco to Taghaza, the salt-mining town on the edge of the Sahara, where "houses and mosques are built with blocks of salt." There he joined one of the merchant camel caravans that regularly crossed the desert, trading salt for gold. Mali was so rich in gold and so short of salt that the price of salt reputedly tripled or quadrupled in the kingdom's markets. Ibn Battuta and his companions crossed the desert by night marches. They ate "desert truffles swarming with lice" in a land "haunted by demons. . . . There is no visible road or track in these parts," Ibn Battuta recorded, "nothing but sand blown hither and thither by the wind." Water sources were sparse—ten days' journey apart.

Ibn Battuta reached the frontier of Mali at Walata. "It was then," he complained, "that I repented of having come to their country because of their lack of manners and their contempt for white men." He found the food disgusting, not appreciating how lucky he was to be served expensive millet at the desert's edge. Outraged to find himself watched when he relieved himself in the Niger, he failed, at first, to realize that the spectator was there to guard him from crocodiles. He found the sexual freedom of the women alarming, but approved of the way children were chained until they learned the Quran. He praised the "abhorrence of injustice" he found among black people.

The mansa's court impressed him, as it impressed other visitors in the same period. This consensus is striking, because North African Muslims rarely praised black achievements. The mansa, according to Ibn Battuta, commanded more devotion from his subjects than any other ruler in the world, though most of the court ceremonial was traditional among black kingdoms in West Africa. The mansa, for instance, spoke only through an intermediary, for to raise his voice was beneath his dignity. Supplicants had to prostrate themselves and sprinkle dust on their heads as they addressed him. When his words were relayed to the people, guards strummed their bowstrings, and everyone else hummed appreciatively. Sneezing in the mansa's presence was punishable by death. Hundreds of servants attended him with gilded rods. Court poets and scholars came to serve the mansa from Muslim Spain and North Africa.

Meanwhile, the gold of West Africa inspired heroic European efforts to get to its source. Western Europe produced only small amounts of silver, and its economies were permanently short of precious metals with which to trade. There was a longstanding adverse trade balance with more productive Silk-Road economies. To keep it going, this trade always needed infusions of cash. So, as Mali's reputation grew, the search for African gold obsessed European adventurers. Cresques Abraham depicted the fate of one of them, the Spaniard Jaume Ferrer, lost to shipwreck off the West African coast in 1346 in an attempt to find a sea route to Mali. The endeavor was hopeless. Mali was landlocked, and the African coasts had little gold until well into the fifteenth century.

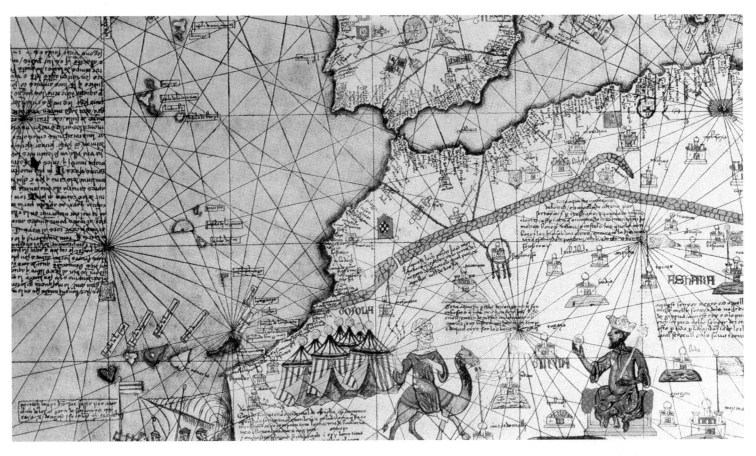

Mansa Musa. "Lord of the blacks of Guinea," reads the legend accompanying the portrait of Mansa Musa (r. ca. 1312–1327), the king of Mali in West Africa, on the fourteenth-century Catalan Atlas. "This lord is the richest and most noble lord of all this region owing to the abundance of gold which is gathered in this land." The Mansa's wealth was said to exceed that of all other kings. His European-style crown and ample beard are compliments bestowed by an artist who had not learned, as Europeans were to do in later centuries, to despise black African kingship.

THE PACIFIC: SOCIETIES OF ISOLATION

Beyond the world that escaped the worst of the Black Death lay regions contagion did not threaten. Isolation, which had arresting effects in so many cases already familiar to readers of this book, was a privilege in the fourteenth century. To understand this unaccustomed reversal of what can only be called the normal pattern of global history, we need to look at some relatively isolated societies. The vastness of the Pacific—which the technology of the time could not cross—ensured that exceptionally isolated cultures lay scattered around and about that ocean.

Easter Island

No part of the inhabited globe was more isolated than Easter Island, which lay, at the time, more than 2,000 miles away from any other human habitation. The island covers only 64 square miles of the Pacific Ocean, way off the usual routes of navigation and the usual course of the winds. It is hard to believe that the Polynesian navigators who first colonized the island, possibly over 1,500 years ago, would have stayed if they had been able to continue their journey or turn around and go home. Most of the soil is poor. Nowadays, there are no nearby fisheries, though native traditions recall a time when the island's elite feasted on porpoise and dolphin. The first settlers brought chickens and the starchy plant called taro. But not much that was edible was available to them when they arrived. Migrant birds were their renewable source of food. The oldest art on the island shows a birdman. Feasts of fowl and egg-stealing competitions greeted the annual arrival of flocks of sooty terns.

Moais. Monumental statue making on Easter Island was probably at its most intense in the fourteenth century. For a small population on a poorly provided and remote island, the investment of energy the practice required seems astounding. The images are similar to those of ancestor cults elsewhere in Polynesia, but they are exceptional in being carved from stone, rather than wood, huge, and numerous. Isolation apparently made Easter Island culture distinctive, but still recognizably like that of other Polynesian colonies.

MAP 14.7

Easter Island (Rapa Nui)

	main area of statues
◆	restored statue site
●	ceremonial center
●	settlement
◍	quarry for red topknots
◻	quarry for statues

Despite the natural poverty of the island and its isolation from other societies, in the fourteenth century it housed a people at the height of their ambition. Probably late in the first millennium, they had begun to erect monumental statues for reasons we can no longer determine. The statues, called *Moais*, resemble those other Polynesian peoples erected: tall, elongated, stylized faces hewn of stone. They were originally adorned with red topknots—sitting hatlike on their heads—and white coral eyes, looking out with a fixed stare. The Easter Island statues are unique compared with other Polynesian works of the same sort only because they are so big and there are so many of them—878 in all, including those abandoned, incomplete, in the quarries. Some 600 finished examples survive, most of them more than 20 feet tall (see Map 14.7).

It took real communal effort to make and erect the statues, each carved from a pillar of rock weighing between 30 and 40 tons. A single extended family—say, about 400 people—joining together to provide the labor and feed the workers, would have taken more than a year to complete the task. As time went on, the statues got bigger—a clear case of competition, driving up the costs of the culture, and, perhaps, condemning it to collapse, a century or two later. So an enterprising community could buck the effects of isolation, and even turn isolation to advantage—but, in an extreme case like that of Easter Island, the effort was evidently hard to sustain. Statue building slowed and, in the sixteenth or seventeenth century, stopped.

New Zealand

New Zealand was another, almost equally remote outpost of the Polynesian world, but with infinitely more resources than Easter Island, and therefore with better prospects of sustainable development. Although the date of the first settlement of New Zealand is disputed (see Chapter 11), fairly secure dates are possible for changes that were under way by the fourteenth century. Population increased. Hunting resources diminished in populated areas as the fur seal and moa began to get scarce, for the moa, a huge, flightless bird, with eggs as big as a hundred hen's eggs, was among the early settlers' main sources of food. Human overexploitation was almost certainly responsible for the moa's extinction. Its meat was processed in immense butcheries. At the biggest butchery, at the mouth of the Waitako River in South Island, up to 90,000 birds were dismembered with blades made of obsidian, a volcanic stone that can be honed to a razor-sharp edge. The same region had over 300 smaller sites, each handling at least 5,000 moa.

As the balance of the way of life shifted from hunting toward farming, mobile colonies settled down. The kind of wear the teeth of people buried in this period shows is different from that of their predecessors: fibrous foods and gritty mollusks ground their dental bites, which show fewer traces of the effects of a meat-rich diet. The results included stronger community identification with land and, therefore, more competition for cultivable resources. Part of the farming surplus was invested in war. From the fifteenth century, the number of places where weapons were made grew enormously. So did the number of fortified villages, especially in the North Island. War was only one of many forms of new or newly intensive activity that favored the power of chiefs. Farming required strong centers of power to organize collective activity and regulate the distribution of food. So did new fishing technologies with gigantic nets that needed many hands to operate them.

Ozette

Meanwhile, on the Pacific rim of the New World, people experimented with contrasting responses to isolation (see Map 14.8). Good evidence has survived for two different communities. One body of evidence comes from a community of hunters in the north of the hemisphere. Exact dates are hard to assign, but probably toward the end of the fifteenth century, a mudslide at Ozette, in Washington State, buried the homes of a community of whalers and seal fishers. The mud perfectly preserved the site. Archaeologists have revealed layers of sediment that show that ways of life had not changed here significantly for centuries before the disaster. The mud of Ozette gives us a unique glimpse into the lives of a hunting culture in what we think of in European terms as the late Middle Ages.

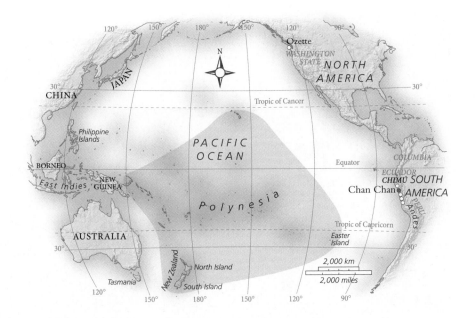

MAP 14.8

Societies of the Pacific, ca.1400

area of Polynesian settlement

PERU modern country or state

The victims of the mudslide lived in big cedarwood buildings, each more than 50 feet long and 30 feet wide. Each building housed about 40 people, divided typically by partitions into half a dozen smaller family units with their own hearths. Hanging mats helped insulate the walls. The Ozette people ate almost no vegetable matter except wild berries. Though they hunted land animals and birds, the sea was their main hunting ground. Fur seals provided nearly 90 percent of their meat. For cooking, they filled watertight cedarwood boxes with hot water and boiled or steamed their food. They hunted and fished in dugouts. Whale images dominated their art, probably because the art had a ritual or magical function in bringing good fortune to the whale hunt. Carvers also made bowls in the shape of men, depicted realistically except for big cavities, where the belly should be, to hold food or offerings. Their way of life was, broadly speaking, similar to that of the Thule Inuit centuries earlier (see Chapter 11).

Chan Chan

On the Pacific's South American edge, we can trace new activity to roughly the same period. Of course, this was not a region as isolated as New Zealand, Easter Island, or even Ozette. As we have seen many times in this book, the coasts of what are now Peru, Ecuador, and Pacific-side Colombia were always in touch with the cultures of the high Andes and, through them, with the lowlands beyond. In South America, in and around the fourteenth century, the latest experiment in state-building, intensive agriculture, and city life was under way at Chan Chan. This city was in the coastal desert region of Peru where the Moche had formerly built complex irrigation works and prosperous cities in defiance of a hostile environment (see Chapter 10). The methods of the Chimú (chee-MOO) people of Chan Chan were different. They concentrated agriculture around the city, where 30,000 people lived. The population of Chan Chan's hinterland was thinly distributed and not much greater than that of the city itself.

Cotton production was a major economic activity. Fishing seems to have mattered little. For protein, the people of Chan Chan—or, perhaps, just the elite—

Huaca del Dragón. The date of the stacked platforms of Huaca del Dragón, near the site of Chan Chan in Peru, is much disputed, but the adobe reliefs—of which a recently restored section is depicted here—are probably of Chimú workmanship. Below a frieze of warriors, a divine feast is shown. A double-headed serpent, with a rainbow-like body surrounded by clouds, devours curl-nosed victims, framing similar scenes shown in profile. Food-storage areas were built into the structure, which seems to have been both temple and warehouse—a repository, perhaps, for food of the gods.

relied on llamas. Pasture was limited, so the llamas were farmed in corrals in and around the city. Fodder supplemented grazing.

The city of Chan Chan covered almost 7 square miles. Spaces in Chan Chan served as the tombs of kings, dwellings for elites, and warehouses to store and distribute food. The layout shows that the Chimú state was oppressive, with a security-obsessed elite. High walls, fortified gateways and dog-leg corridors, designed with sharp turns to delay attackers and favor defenders, protected the rulers' quarters from their own people.

The warehouses were the most important buildings. Access to them was through chambers where costly ceremonies unfolded: sacrifices of llamas and men, deposits of precious objects. The storerooms were vital—the most vital part of the state—because El Niño periodically and unpredictably washed away the irrigation works. Stockpiling enabled the Chimú to recover when disaster struck.

The rulers' tombs were so rich that colonial-era Spaniards spoke of "mining" them. The Chimú elite favored gold for their precious ornaments and ritual objects. But gold did not occur naturally in this part of Peru. Trade or tribute must have brought it to Chimú, which was evidently an expansionist state. Perhaps it had to be to boost its resources in a difficult and depleted environment. Sites of towns built in the style of Chan Chan stretch between the Sana and Supe Rivers.

In Perspective
The Aftershock

Ibn Khaldun left an often-quoted but unforgettable description of the effects of the Black Death on the Muslim world:

> Civilization shrank with the decrease of mankind. Cities and buildings were bared, roads and signposts were abandoned, villages and palaces were deserted. Tribes and dynasties were expunged. It was as if the voice of existence in the world had called out for oblivion, and the world had responded to the call.

But how serious and enduring were the consequences? For Latin Christendom in Western Europe, the picture looked bleak. After the achievements of the previous century, and the benefits of a long period of enhanced contacts with the Islamic world and China, the West seemed poised for a great age of expansion. Now many promising initiatives of the preceding period ended. North Atlantic navigation, which Norse seafarers had developed so heroically in previous centuries, dwindled. The last Icelandic voyage to mainland America was in 1347. The Norse Greenland colonies became increasingly isolated. When a bishop's representative sailed to the more northerly of them in the 1340s, he "found nobody, either Christians or heathens, only some wild cattle and sheep, and they slaughtered the wild cattle for food, as much as the ships would carry, and then sailed home therewith themselves." When the Greenland colony was finally extinguished in the fifteenth century, it was by mysterious raiders of savage ferocity known to the Norse as Skraelingar—presumably, the Thule Inuit with whom the Norse had long shared the island. Exploration of other parts of the Atlantic virtually stopped at the time of the Black Death. In the half century preceding the onset of the plague, explorers from maritime communities in Western Europe had made considerable progress. Mapping of the African Atlantic had begun, with the Canary and Madeira Islands, and navigators had begun to investigate the pattern of the

"After the achievements of the previous century, and the benefits of a long period of enhanced contacts with the Islamic world and China, the West seemed poised for a great age of expansion. Now many promising initiatives of the preceding period ended."

Making Connections | BEYOND THE PLAGUE ZONE

REGION		TENTATIVE REASON FOR ABSENCE OF PLAGUE		CONSEQUENCES
Japan		Protected by relative isolation		Protected from Mongols; new threats emerge from prosperous provincial warlords; the imperial family divides into rival factions; new dynasty of shoguns emerges; Zen Buddhism becomes influential
Northern Russia		Unknown—interaction with Mongols should have made Russians vulnerable		Grand Duchy of Moscow begins to throw off Mongol rule in late 1300s
India		Unknown—although Silk Roads and sea trade connected it to other parts of Eurasia and Africa		Sultanate of Delhi profits from Mongols' decline, initiating policy of conquest; Turkic elite responsible for war and revenue collecting eventually secedes; Hindu/Muslim relations are always problematic
Southeast Asia		Unknown—trade routes from China, Europe, Africa should have made the region vulnerable		Establishment of powerful state on Java (Majapahit), to control trade with China and India, creating stable and prosperous society
Pacific		Isolation		Existing societies expand; shift from hunting to agriculture in New Zealand; Chimú state (Chan Chan) flourishes in Peru
Sub-Saharan West Africa		Unclear— trans-Saharan trade routes should have carried plague		Mali becomes rich and powerful from control over gold trade; European need for gold creates obsession with reaching Mali

northeast trade winds. Jaume Ferrer's shipwreck was symbolic. Few similar voyages were recorded in the second half of the fourteenth century.

Human foes supplemented the plague, famine, and cold. In 1354, an earthquake demolished the walls of the Byzantine city of Gallipoli at the entrance to the Dardanelles, which divides Europe from Anatolia. Ottoman Turks were waiting to take over the ruins, inaugurating a history of European anxiety about the defensibility of Christendom's eastern Mediterranean frontier – anxiety that would last, with fluctuations, for over 200 years. In the northeast, pagan Lithuanians eroded the conquests of the Teutonic Knights along the Baltic (see Chapter 13). To some extent, the gradual diffusion of Catholic faith, under Polish influence, into Lithuania made good these losses—for Christendom, if not for the Germans. Meanwhile, in parts of Eastern Europe, state-building continued, under rulers whose longevity helped bring stability. The period of the Black Death was spanned by the reigns of Charles the Great in Bohemia (r. 1346–1378), Casimir the Great in Poland (r. 1333–1370) and Louis the Great of Hungary (r. 1342–1382). On the whole, even in Western Europe, the effects of plague favored the state, because afflicted populations turned to monarchs as potential saviors and were willing to trust them with enhanced powers. Even peasant rebels tended to focus their resentments on the rest of the elite and appealed for aid directly—albeit, usually, unsuccessfully—to monarchs.

In the Mongol dominions, the case was different. Mongol expansion ceased. Russian principalities began to pry themselves free of Mongol control. The Mongol state in Persia fragmented, and the last Il-khan died in 1343. From the ruins of Mongol domination, a new state arose in Anatolia, under a Turkish dynasty, known as the Ottomans, whose center of operations from 1326 was at the formerly Byzantine city of Bursa, in what is now western Turkey, from where they were able to profit from the dislocation the Black Death caused (see Map 14.9). They gradually came to dominate Byzantium, invaded the Balkans, and established a close trading relationship with the Italian city of Genoa. Toward the end of the fourteenth century, they began to construct a navy, to extend their power into the Mediterranean. In China, as we shall see in the next chapter, the strain of the ecological crisis of the mid–fourteenth century contributed to the dissolution of the Mongol state and its replacement by a new regime of native Chinese rulers, under the Ming dynasty.

At a deeper level than that of the rise and fall of states and political elites, the coming of the age of plagues, made worse by unpredictable changes in climate, affected the balance of population—and therefore of power—among Eurasian civilizations. Natural disasters do not usually affect population trends for long. Population can recover with surprising speed. Recovery was harder in the wake of the Black Death because, although plagues became less ferocious, and populations built up immunity, pestilence affected the same regions for centuries to come, at a rate too rapid to enumerate. In Egypt, for instance, visitations of plague struck more than once, on average, every four years in the two centuries following the Black Death. The population of Eurasia probably remained static during the late fourteenth century and for most of the fifteenth. In the long run, of the three culture areas that suffered most, it appears that the Islamic world may have been more affected than Christendom or China, both of which seem to have recovered faster and resisted better. This can only be a tentative conclusion, because the evidence is unreliable. It does seem,

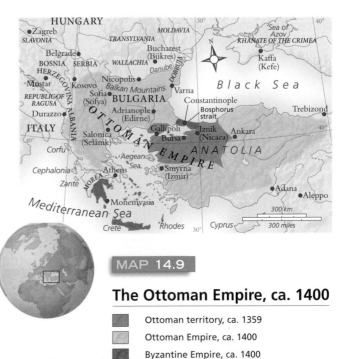

MAP 14.9

The Ottoman Empire, ca. 1400

- Ottoman territory, ca. 1359
- Ottoman Empire, ca. 1400
- Byzantine Empire, ca. 1400

Chronology	
1290	England expels Jews
Thirteenth and fourteenth centuries	Climate change in Northern Hemisphere; population rises in New Zealand and agriculture replaces hunting as way of life; rise of Chimú state (Chan Chan) in Peru
1309–1310	Thames River freezes (London)
1315–1316	Heavy rains in northern Europe
1320s	Plague epidemics in southwest and central China
1324	Mansa Musa makes *hajj* to Mecca
1325–1351	Reign of Ibn Tughluq (Delhi Sultanate, India)
1330s	Mortality rates in northeast China reach 90 percent
1335	Ashikaga Tokauji seizes shogunate (Japan)
1343	Last Il-khan dies in Persia
1346	Plague reported in Crimea (Black Sea)
1347	Last Icelandic voyage to America
1347–1349	Plague rages in Western Europe, Middle East, and North Africa
1350s	Peasant rebellions spread in China
1351	Plague strikes southern Russia
1352	Ibn Battuta sets off for Mali
1354	Ottoman Turks cross Dardanelles to occupy Byzantine city of Gallipoli
1360	Plague in China
1389	Death of Hayan Wuruk (Majapahit in Java)
ca.1400	Settlements in American Southwest abandoned

FIGURE 14.2 THE POPULATION OF EUROPE, CHINA, AND THE ISLAMIC WORLD COMPARED

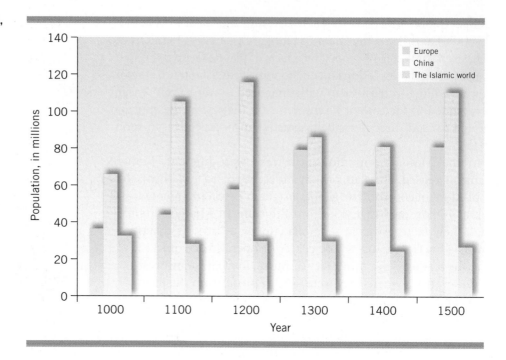

however, that the populations of Christendom and China recovered to preplague levels by the end of the fifteenth century, whereas in Egypt, Syria and, perhaps, other parts of the Islamic world, the recovery did not even begin until then. The increase of population thereafter was generally slower in the Islamic world than in Christendom and China until the twentieth century (see Figure 14.2). If correct, this conclusion may help to explain one of history's great shifts in wealth, power, and every kind of dynamism—away from the Islamic world. Whereas in what we call the Middle Ages, the Islamic world had contributed enormously—far more than Christendom—to cultural exchange in Eurasia, and had tended to win out in conflicts with Christendom, Muslim power dwindled over the succeeding centuries. The relative eclipse of the Islamic world and the relative ascent of Europe are major themes of the age of plague and, therefore, of the next two parts of this book.

PROBLEMS AND PARALLELS

1. How might Mongol rule have spread plague during the fourteenth century? How did rulers like Hayan Wuruk in Java and Ibn Tughluq in India profit from the decline of Mongol power? Why did the fading of the Mongol threat lead to political instability in Japan?

2. How did the climate change and age of plagues that began during the fourteenth century affect Western Europe, China, and the Islamic world? Why did peasants in China and Europe embrace millenarian ideas?

3. In what parts of the globe did plague and climate cause the most harm during the fourteenth century? Why was geographic isolation an advantage during the age of plague? Why was Mali under Mansa Musa so rich and powerful?

4. How was climate change related to plague? How did the onset of the Little Ice Age affect agriculture and settlement in Western Europe? How did climate change affect the people of the American Southwest?

5. Why is it difficult or impossible to understand the medical causes of the Black Death? What did West Europeans and Muslims believe caused the plague, and how did they try to treat it?

6. Who were the "winners" and "losers" in the plague years (other than the immediate survivors and victims)? Why did many Europeans blame the Jews for the Black Death? How did the status of upper-class women change in Western Europe and Japan during the fourteenth century?

READ ON ▶ ▶ ▶

H. Lamb, *Climate, History and the Modern World* (1995) is the classic work on its subject, complemented by B. Fagan's *The Little Ice Age* (2000). Classic works—now superseded on many points—on the global history of disease are H. Zinsser, *Rats, Lice, and History* (1996), and W. H. McNeill, *Plagues and Peoples* (1998). S. Cohn, *The Black Death* (2003) is indispensable for the plagues in Europe and for the epidemiology of the Black Death. N. Cantor, *In the Wake of the Plague* (2001) has some interesting material on social effects. R. Horrox, *The Black Death* (1994) is a valuable anthology of source material. M. W. Dols, *The Black Death in the Middle East* (1977)—though corrected in some respects by Cohn's work—is invaluable on its subject. As so often, the edition by H. Gibb and C. Beckingham of *The Travels of Ibn Battuta* (1994) is an indispensable guide.

On China, the *Cambridge History of China*, vols. 6–8, is fundamental, and the collection of essays edited by P. J. Smith and R. von Glahn, *The Song-Yuan-Ming Transition in Chinese History* (2003) crackles with revisionism. For Europe, M. Jones, ed., *The New Cambridge Medieval History* vi, (2000) is a comprehensive survey. On the problems of the status of women, G. Duby and M. Perrot, eds., *A History of Women* (2000) is the leading work; particularly useful work on the subjects touched in this chapter includes R. Smith, "Coping with Uncertainty: Women's Tenure of Customary Land in England," in J. Kermode, ed., *Enterprise and Individual in Fifteenth-Century England* (1997), and L. Mirrer, ed., *Upon My Husband's Death* (1992).

For Hohokam, the article by P. Crown, "The Hohokam of the American Southwest," *Journal of World History*, vol.iv (1990) is a good introduction. G. J. Gumerman, ed., *Themes in Southwest Prehistory* (1994) contains some important contributions.

On the Jews, N. Cohn, *Europe's Inner Demons* (2001) is a controversial but gripping attempt to trace the origins of anti-Semitism. P. Johnson, *History of the Jews* (1988)—though superseded in its coverage of the early period—remains the best general history. L. Kochan, *The Jew and his History* (1985) is a good introduction.

On peasant millenarianism, N. Cohn, *The Pursuit of the Millennium* (1970) remains unsurpassed. On Japan, J. Mass, ed., *Origins of Japan's Medieval World* (1997) amounts to a fine history of the fourteenth century. The Delhi sultanate is covered in R. Majumdar, *The History and Culture of the Indian People*, vol.4 (1951) and P. Jackson, *The Delhi Sultanate* (1999). On Java, T. Pigeaud, ed., *Java in the Fourteenth Century* (1960) is a marvelous edition of the poem I cite about Hayan Wuruk. D. G. Hall in N. Tarling, ed., *The Cambridge History of Southeast Asia*, vol.I (1992), provides further help. On Mali, N. Levtzion, *Ancient Ghana and Mali* (1986) is highly accessible, and D. T. Niane covers the subject expertly in *UNESCO History of Africa*, vol.iv (1998), but the classic work by E. W. R. Bovill, *The Golden Trade of the Moors* (1995), can still be read with pleasure. For the Pacific, J. van Tilburg, *Easter Island* (1995) is the only fully reliable work on that island. J. Belich, *Making Peoples* (2002) is insuperable on New Zealand. On Ozette, see R. Kirk and R. D. Dougherty, *Hunters of the Whale* (1998). On the Chimú, R. Keatinge, *Peruvian Prehistory* (1988) is standard.

CHAPTER 15

Expanding Worlds: Recovery in the Late Fourteenth and Fifteenth Centuries

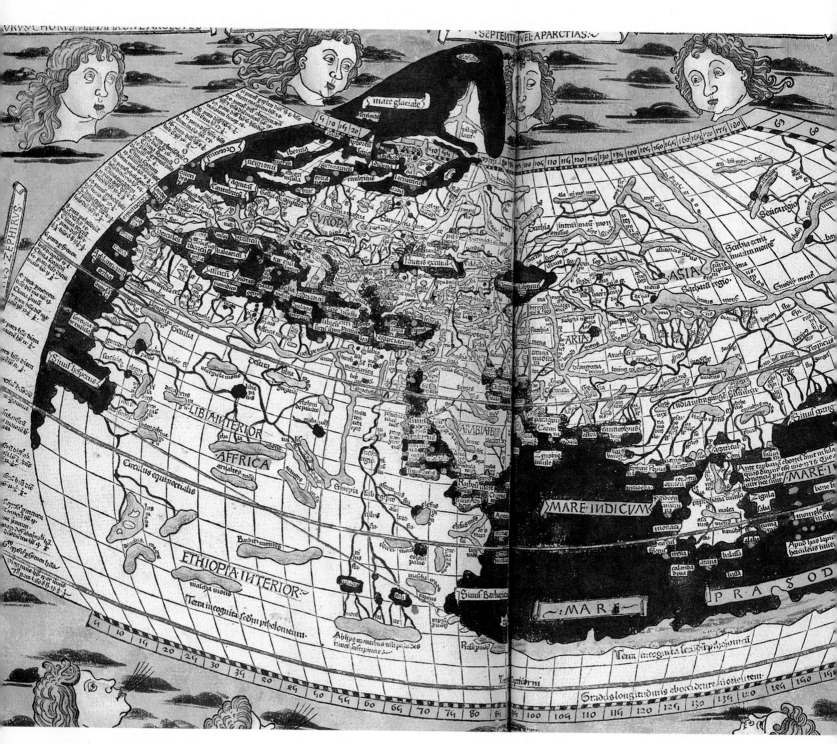

▲ **Claudius Ptolemy's Geography,** written in Alexandria, Egypt in the second century, was still the standard source for how educated Europeans saw the world in the fifteenth century. Printed editions, like this one of 1482, usually included attempts to map the world as Ptolemy described it. Common features include a grid of lines of latitude and longitude—the system Ptolemy devised for locating places in relation to one another; the exaggerated size and prominence of Sri Lanka; locating the source of the Nile in mountains beyond large lakes deep in Africa; and showing the Indian Ocean as landlocked, which undermined navigators' confidence that they could reach India and Asia by sea.

A bd-ar-Razzak was a landlubber. The stories he knew about navigation on the Indian Ocean presented the sea as God's arena, where luck changed with the wind and storms fell like divine arrows. Every story ended with a shipwreck. The thought of a voyage terrified Abd-ar-Razzak. But he had a journey to face that he could only make by sea. In 1417, he was appointed Persian ambassador to Vijayanagar (vee-jeh-yeh-NAH-gar), a powerful state in southern India, and there were too many hostile kingdoms between it and Persia for him to cross by land. But his ship sailed late,

> so that the favorable time for departing by sea, that is to say the beginning or middle of the monsoon, was allowed to pass, and we came to the end of the monsoon, which is the season when tempests and attacks from pirates are to be dreaded. . . . As soon as I caught the smell of the vessel, and all the terrors of the sea presented themselves before me, I fell into so deep a faint that for three days breathing alone indicated that life remained within me. When I came a little to myself, the merchants, who were my intimate friends, cried with one voice that the time for navigation was past, and that everyone who put to sea at this season was alone responsible for his death.

Abd-ar-Razzak's predicament, however, had a positive side. The late monsoon is so fierce that ships speed before it. He made the journey in only 19 days, about two-thirds of the time one might normally expect.

Abd-ar-Razzak's voyage demonstrates the crucial importance of winds in world history. Most of the Earth's surface area is sea. Long-range communications have to traverse wide waters. Throughout the age of sail—that is, for almost the entire history of travel—winds and currents set the limits of what was possible: the routes, the rates, the mutually accessible cultures. More particularly, Abd-ar-Razzak's experience illustrates the paradox of Indian Ocean navigation in his day. The monsoon winds made travel speedy, but the Indian Ocean was stormy, unsafe, and hard to get into and out of. Access from the east was barely possible in summer, when typhoons tore into the shores. Fierce storms guarded the southern approaches. No one who knew the reputation of these waters cared to venture between about 10 and 30 degrees south and 60 or 90 degrees east during the hurricane season. Arab legends claimed the region was impassable. Many European maps of the fifteenth century depicted the Indian Ocean as landlocked—literally inaccessible by sea. Yet it was the biggest and richest zone of long-range commerce in the world.

FOCUS questions

Why were some African empires able to expand on such an impressive scale during this period?

What role did geographic diversity play in the Inca and Aztec Empires?

What strong new empires arose on the Eurasian borderlands?

Why did China turn away from overseas expansion in the fifteenth century?

Why did Europe begin to reach out across the oceans in the late 1400s?

By the end of the fifteenth century, European navigators had found a way to penetrate it. Meanwhile, the Atlantic was developing into a rival zone, with transoceanic routes ready to be exploited. Indeed, seafaring on the Atlantic would transform the world by bringing cultures that had been torn apart into contact, conflict, commerce, and cultural and ecological exchange. The divergent, isolated worlds of ancient and medieval times were coming together to form the interconnected world we inhabit today.

How did it happen? How did the world rebound from the plagues and climate changes of the fourteenth century? For one thing, populations gradually acquired immunity against plague, as susceptible people died and those who were naturally most resistant passed on their genes. As for worsening climates, survivors relocated or just got used to colder, wetter conditions. To some extent, technological advance made up for—indeed, was a response to—decreased population. As we have seen, across Eurasia, and in parts of Africa that were in contact with Eurasia, the long period of accelerated exchange in the Song and Mongol eras had equipped expanding economies with improved technology (see Chapter 13). In regions that escaped the catastrophes of the fourteenth century, long-term population growth continued to strengthen states and economies. So it is not surprising that the world of the late fourteenth and fifteenth centuries was a world in recovery and even a world of resumed expansion.

Toward the end of the period, from about 1460 on, in states in widely separated parts of the world, expansion speeded up like springs uncoiling. An age of expansion really did begin, but the phenomenon was of an expanding world, not, as some historians say, of European expansion. The world did not wait passively for European outreach to transform it, as if touched by a magic wand. Other societies were already working magic of their own, turning states into empires and cultures into civilizations. Beyond the reach of the recurring plagues that stopped demographic growth in much of Eurasia, some of the most dynamic and rapidly expanding societies of the fifteenth century were in the Americas and sub-Saharan Africa. Indeed, in terms of territorial expansion and military effectiveness against opponents, African and American empires outclassed any state in Western Europe until the sixteenth century.

As we shall see, some European communities played big and growing roles. And their expansion did have unique features—exceptional range, above all, which enabled people from Western Europe to cross unprecedented distances on previously unexplored routes. But to appreciate what was special about Europe, we have to see it in global context and acknowledge that expansion was a worldwide phenomenon. If we start in Africa and approach Europe only after looking at the Americas and following Abd-ar-Razzak's route in Asia, we can begin to make sense of the peculiar features of the history of Atlantic-side European peoples, as they launched empires that will take up more and more space in the rest of the book.

FRAGILE EMPIRES IN AFRICA

East Africa

Ethiopia emerged relatively early from its period of quiescence following the rise and stagnation of the Solomid dynasty in the thirteenth century (see Chapter 11). In the late fourteenth century, the highland realm again began to reach beyond its mountains to dominate surrounding regions. Monasteries became schools of missionaries whose task was to consolidate Ethiopian power in the conquered pagan lands of Shoa and Gojam. Rulers, meanwhile, concentrated on reopening their ancient outlet to the Red Sea and thereby the Indian Ocean. This they accomplished by conquering the hostile lowlanders and recapturing the port of Massaweh in 1403. By then, Ethiopian rule stretched into the Great Rift valley. Trade northward along the valley was in slaves, ivory, gold, and ingredients of perfumes. Ethiopia largely controlled it. The resulting wealth funded defense of the empire and fueled expansionist ambitions. European visitors multiplied, as Ethiopia's Massaweh road became a standard route to reach the Indian Ocean.

Although Ethiopia conquered no more territory after 1469, the lives of saints, which are a major source for Ethiopian history in this period, tell of internal expansion. Wasteland was converted to farmland and settled by monks. In 1481, the Ethiopian church resumed contact with Rome, where the pope provided a church to house visiting Ethiopian monks. When Portuguese diplomatic missions began to arrive in Ethiopia—the first in the 1490s, a second in 1520—"men and gold and provisions like the sands of the sea and the stars in the sky" impressed them. As we shall see in the next chapter, however, they overestimated the empire's stability. Ethiopia had probably already overreached its resources.

"The world did not wait passively for European outreach to transform it, as if touched by a magic wand. Other societies were already working magic of their own, turning states into empires and cultures into civilizations."

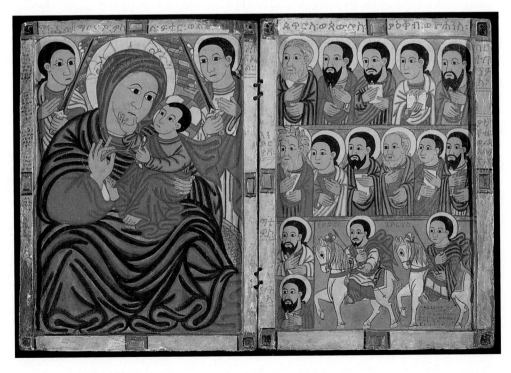

Virgin and Child. In the dynamic reign of Emperor Zara Yacob (1434–1468), Ethiopia conquered an outlet to the sea, extended and fortified its land frontier, pacified and Christianized pagan peoples, and made contact with Europe. But the enforcement of religious orthodoxy was perhaps closest to the emperor's heart. He commissioned many paintings of the Virgin and Child, often shown guarded, as here, by armed angels and worshipped by warrior saints.

Chronology: The Reemergence of Ethiopia

Late fourteenth century	Ethiopia expands into surrounding regions
1403	Recapture of port of Massaweh
1469	End of period of conquest
1481	Ethiopian church resumes contact with Rome
1490s	First Portuguese diplomatic missions arrive in Ethiopia

Southward from Ethiopia, at the far end of the Rift valley, lay the gold-rich Zambezi valley and the productive plateau beyond, which stretched to the south as far as the Limpopo River, and was rich in salt, gold, and elephants. Like Ethiopia, these areas looked toward the Indian Ocean for long-range trade with the economies of maritime Asia.

Unlike Ethiopia, communities in the Zambezi valley had ready access to the ocean, but they faced a potentially more difficult problem. Their outlets to the sea lay below the reach of the monsoon system and, therefore, beyond the reach of the normal routes of trade. Still, adventurous merchants—most of them, probably, from southern Arabia—risked the voyage to bring manufactured goods from Asia in trade for gold and ivory. Some of the most vivid evidence comes from the mosque in Kilwa (Kil-WAH), in modern Tanzania, where fifteenth-century Chinese porcelain bowls line the inside of the dome.

Further evidence of the effects of trade lie inland between the Zambezi and the Limpopo Rivers, where fortified, stone-built administrative centers—called **zimbabwes**—had been common for centuries. Now, in the late fourteenth and fifteenth centuries, the zimbabwes entered their greatest age. The most famous, Great Zimbabwe, included a formidable citadel on a hill 350 feet high, but remains of other citadels are scattered over the land (see Map 15.1). Near stone buildings, the beef-fed elite were buried with gifts: gold, jewelery, jeweled ironwork, large copper ingots, and Chinese porcelain that Arab traders brought across the Indian Ocean to Kilwa and Sofala, another great coastal city.

In the second quarter of the fifteenth century, the center of power shifted northward to the Zambezi valley, with the expansion of a new regional power. Mwene Mutapa (MWEH-nee MOO-TAH-pah), as it was called, arose during the northward migration of bands of warriors from what are now parts of Mozambique and KwaZulu-Natal. When one of their leaders conquered the middle Zambezi valley—a land rich in cloth, salt, and elephants—he took the title Mwene Mutapa, or "lord of the tribute payers," a name that became extended to the state. From about the mid–fifteenth century, the pattern of trade routes altered as Mwene Mutapa's conquests spread eastward toward the coast. But Mwene Mutapa never reached the ocean. Native merchants, who traded at inland fairs, had no interest in a direct outlet to the sea. They did well enough using middlemen on the coast and had no incentive for or experience of ocean trade. Like Mali (see Chapter 14), Mwene Mutapa was a landlocked empire, sustained by trade in gold and salt. The colonists were drawn, not driven, northward, though a decline in the navigability of the Sabi River may have stimulated the move.

Outer wall 820 feet long,
30 feet high, and 16 feet thick.

Platform area

Tower

25 yards

25 meters

MAP 15.1

Great Zimbabwe

■ stone construction
····· walls in ruin
— drain

West Africa

New states emerged in West Africa, too, but here the opportunities were the result, at least in part, of the decline of the old regional power, Mali (see Map 15.2). Like many empires of promise in out-of-the-way places, Mali became a victim of its relative isolation. From about 1360, a power struggle pitted the descendants of Mansa Musa against those of his brother, Mansa Sulayman. At

The turreted walls of Great Zimbabwe surround a 350-foot-high hill, crowned by a formidable citadel, which housed the elite, who ate beef and were buried with gifts of gold, copper, jewels, and Chinese porcelain. Though it was the biggest of the stone-built settlements of the period, Great Zimbabwe was typical, in style and substance, of other buildings in the region south of the Zambezi River during what we think of as the late Middle Ages.

about the end of the century, the Songhay, a people from lower down the Niger River, broke away and Mali lost Gao (gow). This was disastrous for Mali, because Gao was one of the great trading cities between the rain forest and the desert. Traders could now outflank Mali's trading monopoly. Mali was further weakened in the 1430s when invaders from the Sahara seized its northernmost towns.

Two decades later, in the 1450s, when Portuguese expeditions, pushing up the river Gambia, made the first recorded European contact with Mali, the Mansa's power was virtually confined to the original heartland. The result was a tragedy for the history of the world, for the absence of a strong African state undermined Europeans' view of black Africans as equals. The Portuguese expected to find a great, rich empire. Instead, they found Mali a ramshackle wreck. Their disappointment prejudiced them, and they wondered if black Africans had any capacity for political greatness. Thus, in maps, instead of the magnificent depictions of the Mansa of Mali typical of the fourteenth century—bearded and costumed in European fashion—the ruler of Mali became a figure of fun. Though some Europeans continued to treat black Africans as equals—and the Portuguese crown, in particular, maintained the affectation that black kings were fellow monarchs on a par with those of Europe—from now on, white people in Africa could nourish convictions of superiority. Although, as we shall see, other African realms or regions replaced Mali in European esteem and became famous for wealth or as places of opportunity for European adventurers, their elites never again commanded the same prestige in Europe.

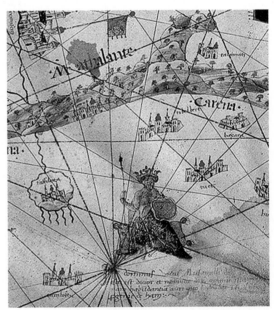

A European view of the King of Mali, ca. 1480. By the 1430s, familiarity with the West African kingdom of Mali had caused disillusionment among European visitors, who expected magnificence of the sort depicted in the previous century in the Catalan Atlas (see Chapter 14). But Mali had declined, and its ruler appeared in this map by Gabriel Vallseca of Majorca, and others of the time, as a comically dressed and even laughable figure.

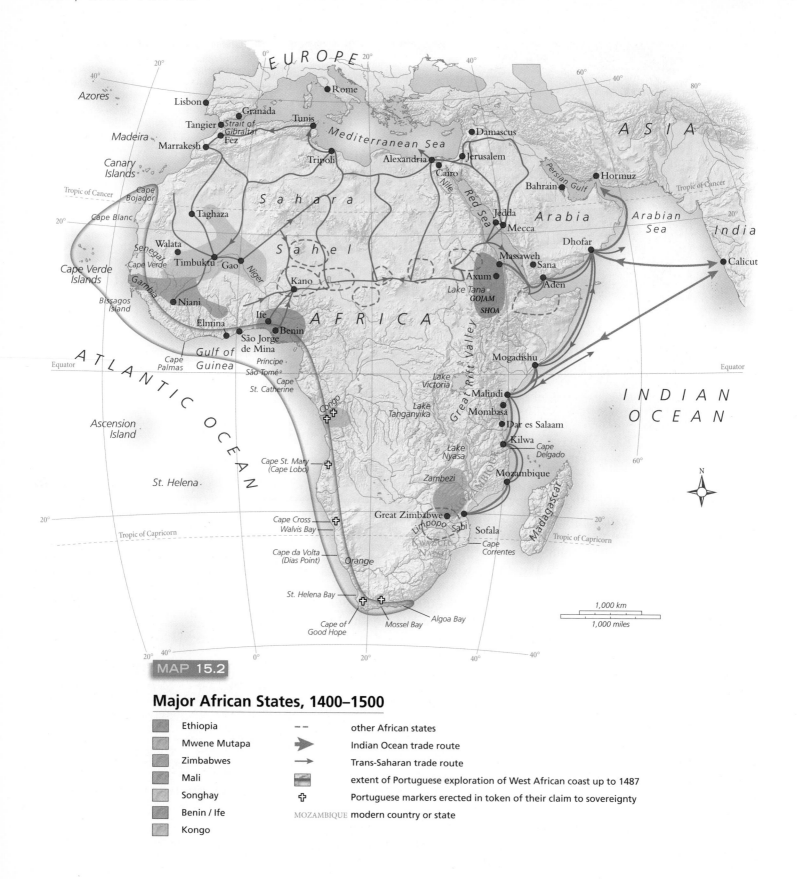

Major African States, 1400–1500

■ Ethiopia	- - - other African states
■ Mwene Mutapa	→ Indian Ocean trade route
■ Zimbabwes	→ Trans-Saharan trade route
■ Mali	▬ extent of Portuguese exploration of West African coast up to 1487
■ Songhay	✠ Portuguese markers erected in token of their claim to sovereignty
■ Benin / Ife	MOZAMBIQUE modern country or state
■ Kongo	

MAP 15.2

Songhay (SOHNG-eye) gradually succeeded Mali as the most powerful state in the region, but it never controlled as much of the Saharan trade as Mali had. At first, isolated areas were converted to Islam, but Muhammad Touray Askia, an upstart general who used Islam to justify seizing the throne, wrenched Songhay into the Islamic mainstream in the late fifteenth century. In 1497, he undertook a pilgrimage to Mecca on a scale of magnificence calculated to echo that of Mansa Musa in 1324–1325 (see Chapter 14). Askia's ascent to power represented the triumph of Islam over the pagan magic that some of his predecessors and opponents claimed to wield. His victory also ensured that Sahelian Africa—the band of dry grasslands south of the Sahara—would be predominantly Muslim. His alliance with the Muslim intelligentsia made Songhay a state "favored by God" in the eyes of religious Muslims—the class on which the state depended for administrators. He stimulated trade by imposing peace and so increasing Saharan merchants' sense of security. He promoted a modest sort of capitalism by concentrating resources in the hands of religious foundations, which had the personnel and range of contacts to maximize their holdings' potential. New canals, wells, dikes, and reservoirs scored the land. Cultivated terrain was extended, especially for rice, which had long been known in the region but never previously farmed on a large scale.

Songhay, like Mali before it, benefited from the trade routes of the Sahara, which linked the Mediterranean coast to the Niger valley. The Niger River is navigable for almost its entire length, providing access to rich goldfields and the best national communications system in Africa. At the same time, the Atlantic's adverse winds and currents limited opportunities for long-range communications by sea. The states and cultures of the tropical forest and coast in the African "bulge" were therefore limited to contending for strictly regional power and wealth. Nevertheless, they have left plenty of evidence of economic expansion and of the growing wealth and power of their kings in the fifteenth century. There are, for instance, the fortifications of the city-state of Benin and the splendid metal weapons, adornments and courtly furnishings of Benin and the Ife.

The whole African coast from Senegambia to the mouth of the Niger impressed Europeans at the time. In 1486, the Portuguese crown celebrated the baptism of a Senegambian chief in Lisbon with a lavish display. The trading post that Portugal opened at São Jorge da Mina, on the underside of the African bulge, in 1482, appeared on maps as a fantasy city. It suited the purposes of the Portuguese monarchs to exaggerate the grandeur, but their propaganda reflected the reality of a region of rich kingdoms, busy commerce, and patches of urban life.

Farther south, too, in the Congo Basin, the opportunities for states to reach out by sea were limited. The Kingdom of Kongo dominated the Congo River's navigable lower reaches, probably from the mid–fourteenth century. The ambitions of its rulers became evident when Portuguese

Chronology: The Portuguese in West Africa and the Congo	
1450s	First reported Portuguese contact with Mali
1480s	Portuguese make contact with kingdom of Kongo
1482	West African trading post of São Jorge da Mina established
1486	Senegambian chief baptized in Lisbon

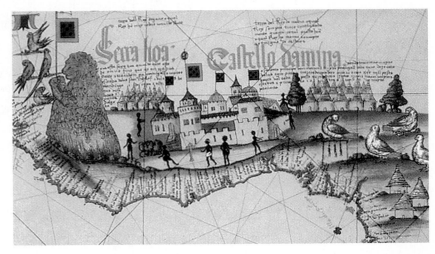

The fort of São Jorge da Mina, founded by the Portuguese in 1482 on the underside of West Africa's bulge, never really looked like this depiction on a richly decorated world map sold to an Italian ambassador in Lisbon in 1502. The turrets and spires are fanciful, but convey the image the mapmaker wanted to show: of exotic grandeur and financial success, since the fort attracted much of the region's trade in gold and slaves.

A CLOSER LOOK

A West African view of the Portuguese

The court art of Benin, in the Niger Delta of West Africa, preserves precious images of Portuguese visitors, as native artists saw them in the sixteenth century. The Obas, as the rulers of Benin were called, frequently asked for Portuguese military help, sometimes offering to adopt Christianity in exchange.

The Portuguese soldier, carved in ivory, is supporting the Oba's saltcellar. Salt was a precious commodity in Benin.

The soldier's short spear, feathered straw hat, and sweatband are local touches, but the rest of his clothes, his beard, his sword, and his pectoral cross were exotic emblems to the African artist who carved them.

African, Nigeria, Edo peoples, court of Benin, Salt-cellar: Portuguese Figure, 15th-16th century, Ivory; H. 7–1/8 in. (18.1 cm). The Metropolitan Museum of Art, Louis V. Bell and Rogers Funds, 1972. (1972.63ab) Photograph by Stan Reis. Photograph © 1984, The Metropolitan Museum of Art

How is this ivory carving evidence of West African expansion in the fifteenth century?

explorers established contact in the 1480s. Kongo enthusiastically adopted the religion and technology of the visitors. The kingdom became host to Portuguese missionaries, craftsmen, and mercenaries. The royal residence was rebuilt in Portuguese style. The kings issued documents in Portuguese, and members of the royal family went to Portugal for their education. One prince became an archbishop, and the kings continued to have Portuguese baptismal names for centuries thereafter. In emulating Portugal, the kings of Kongo were, of course, serving their own self-interest. Equipping their armies with European firepower, for example, gave the kings a military advantage over their neighbors. They gained territory and, more importantly, slaves, many of whom they sold to the Portuguese for export.

The Portuguese connection made Kongo the best-documented kingdom in West Africa in the sixteenth century. Missionary reports extolled the zeal of the "angelic" ruler Affonso I (r. 1506–1545) and commended him for "burning idolaters along with their idols," but the monarch's own letters to the king of Portugal reveal tensions with white slavers, who infringed the royal monopoly of European trade goods and seized slaves indiscriminately.

Although Ethiopia, Mwene Mutapa, Songhay, and Kongo were all formidable regional powers, and although many small states of the West African coast expanded commercially and territorially, little of this activity was on an unprecedented scale (see Map 15.2). Ethiopia's resumed rise was part of a sequence of expansion and decline that had been going on for centuries. Songhay was the latest in a series of empires in the Sahel. Trading states had long studded the underside of the West African bulge. Mwene Mutapa was the successor state of the builders of the zimbabwes. If there was something new out of the Africa at this time, it was part of a wider phenomenon. The empires grew at impressive rates and to impressive extents because they were in touch with other phenomena of commercial and political expansion: Songhay across the Sahara, Ethiopia and Mwene Mutapa across the Indian Ocean, the coastal trading cities and Kongo with the Portuguese. In the Americas, however, in the late fifteenth century, even states that had to contend with isolation could expand on a new scale.

"If there was something new out of the Africa at this time, it was part of a wider phenomenon. The empires grew at impressive rates and to impressive extents because they were in touch with other phenomena of commercial and political expansion . . ."

ECOLOGICAL IMPERIALISM IN THE AMERICAS

Since the inventive historian, Alfred Crosby, coined the term **ecological imperialism** in 1972, historians have used it to refer to the sweeping environmental changes European imperialists introduced in regions they colonized. The term also suits Native American empires, especially in mountainous regions of Mesoamerica and the Andes, where, as we have seen, the key to success in large-scale state-building lay in combining diverse regions and exploiting the complementary products of contrasting ecosystems.

The Inca Empire

In the late fifteenth century, the world's fastest-growing empire was the Inca Empire of Peru. Inca chronology is always uncertain because until the 1530s, the Incas made records in forms that are now indecipherable. Nonetheless, evidence suggests that they built their empire within a concentrated period—all during the reigns of three rulers in the late fifteenth and early sixteenth centuries.

FIGURE 15.1 MICROCLIMATES OF THE ANDES. The Andean environment packs tremendous ecological diversity into a small space, with various climatic zones at different altitudes, contrasting microclimates in the valleys, and tropical forest and the ocean close at hand.

Grassy plains: Over 13,000 ft. above sea level

Uplands: 10,500–12,500 ft. above sea level

Frost-free valleys: 7,500–10,000 ft. above sea level

Lower slopes of mountains: 2,400 ft.–7,000 ft. above sea level

Dry coastal region: 2,400 ft. above sea level

Dry coastal region

Forested eastern slopes

"The Inca realm encompassed coastal lowlands and the fringes of the Amazonian rain forest. The tribute system was based on the exchange of products between contrasting zones, as a form of insurance against disaster."

Probably early in the second half of the fifteenth century, the founders of the Inca state descended from the highlands to find fertile land. They occupied Cuzco in what is today Peru, which became their biggest city, and began subjugating their neighbors. Their story was typically Andean. They gathered many diverse environments into one state to facilitate exchanging and stockpiling a wide range of products. It was the story of Chavín de Huántar in 1000 B.C.E. (see Chapter 4). The Incas, however, took this well-established practice to new lengths. Theirs was one of the most environmentally diverse empires of the time. It was long and thin, with the Andes forming its spine and creating valleys and microclimates. Abrupt mountains multiplied microclimates, where sun, wind, and rain hit different slopes in different ways (see Figure 15.1). The Inca realm encompassed coastal lowlands and the fringes of the Amazonian rain forest. The tribute system was based on the exchange of products between contrasting zones, as a form of insurance against disaster. When the maize of the lowlands failed, for instance, potatoes from the highlands might still be abundant. The Inca uprooted populations and transferred them to new locations according to the needs of the system.

Economic security, however, came at a political price. To maintain the state, the Incas had to acquire new territories, leading to hectic and, in the long run, perhaps, unsustainable expansion. Moreover, their methods of subjugation were extreme. For example, they extinguished the coastal civilization of Chimú (see Chapter 14), razing its capital at Chan Chan almost to the ground and deporting its entire population. An Inca ruler was said to have drowned 20,000 enemy warriors when he conquered the Cañaris. The survivors became irreconcilable opponents. Many subject-peoples harbored grievances arising from memories of massacred warriors and forced migrations. Even the Incas' allies and elites were dissatisfied. The Checa, for instance, a people important to the Inca system of control, because their homeland straddled the route from Cuzco to the coast, never forgave the Inca for breaking his promise to perform ritual dances at their principal shrine in acknowledgment of their alliance. The Inca never seemed to have enough rewards to go around. The cults of dead leaders—who lay, mummified, in expensive shrines maintained by huge payrolls—existed to appease key Inca clans and factions, whose resources they boosted at the state's expense because tribute had to be diverted to meet the costs. Toward the end of the fifteenth century, the Inca Empire approached its greatest extent, from Quito (KEE-toh) in what is today Ecuador in the north, to the Valle Central in what is today Chile in the south. But at its core, the empire was shaky.

The Aztec Empire

In the same period, rapid expansion and environmental diversity characterized Mesoamerica. Here, an exceptionally dynamic state grew from the city of Tenochtitlán (teh-noch-teet-LAHN) in the valley of Mexico (and some neighboring, allied cities). Tenochtitlán stood in the middle of a lake, some 5,000 feet above sea level. It could not grow some of the staples of Mesoamerican life or any of the luxuries elites demanded for social or ritual purposes. The ground was swampy, and there was too little cultivable soil to grow enough maize and beans to feed the city. Tenochtitlán was too high and the climate too severe for cacao and cotton. Its people, whom we have traditionally called Aztecs, had only two options: poverty or warfare. They chose the latter.

Aztec expansion, like Inca expansion, was largely a late fifteenth- and early sixteenth-century phenomenon (see Map 15.3). At its peak, the Aztec Empire stretched from the Pánuco River in the north to what is now the Mexican-Guatemalan border on the Pacific coast, covering nearly 100,000 square miles and including hundreds of tributary communities.

The tribute collected demonstrated the power and reach and the ecological diversity of the regions from which the Aztecs extorted tribute. The Aztec bureaucracy meticulously listed and depicted it. From the "hot countries" in the south came ornamental feathers and jaguar pelts, jade, amber, gold, rubber for ritual ball games, and resin for incense. Overlapping regions supplied cacao, the essential ingredient of the addictive, high-status drink essential at Aztec ceremonies and parties. Ornamental shells arrived from the Gulf Coast and live eagles, deerskins, and tobacco from the mountain lands that fringed the valley of Mexico. For war and for the ball game, which was a form of mock warfare and an aristocratic exercise, Aztec nobles and priests dressed as gods, So on almost every folio of the tribute roll appear magnificent ritual garments and divine disguises. The tribute system brought necessities as well as luxuries: hundreds of thousands of bushels of maize and beans every year, with hundreds of thousands of cotton garments and quilted cotton suits of armor. Finally, there was the product that best expressed Aztec power and—perhaps in Aztec minds—supplied the blood that fueled the universe: human-sacrifice victims, captured in war or tendered in tribute. In 1487, for instance, at the dedication of a temple in Tenochtitlán, thousands of captives were said to have been slaughtered at once.

The Aztec system was complex, in the sense that tributary networks linked hundreds of communities. Some communities exchanged tribute, often collecting it from some tributaries to pass part of it on to others. Tenochtitlán was at the summit of the system, but it left most communities to govern themselves as long as they paid tribute. This was contrary to the highly interventionist politics of the Incas. According to records copied in the sixteenth century, Tenochtitlán only garrisoned or directly ruled 22 communities. The Aztecs did,

The Inca city of Machu Picchu in Peru is a miracle of urban engineering. It was built on a sharp 2,000-foot rise in the high Andes. Unrecorded in colonial times, it was discovered early in the twentieth century when the eccentric and adventurous American archaeologist, Hiram Bingham, was searching for another lost Inca city, Vilcamba. Unknown to Bingham, however, Vilcamba was in the tropical lowlands of Peru. The vast difference in climate between the two cities is stunning evidence of the environmental diversity of the Inca world.

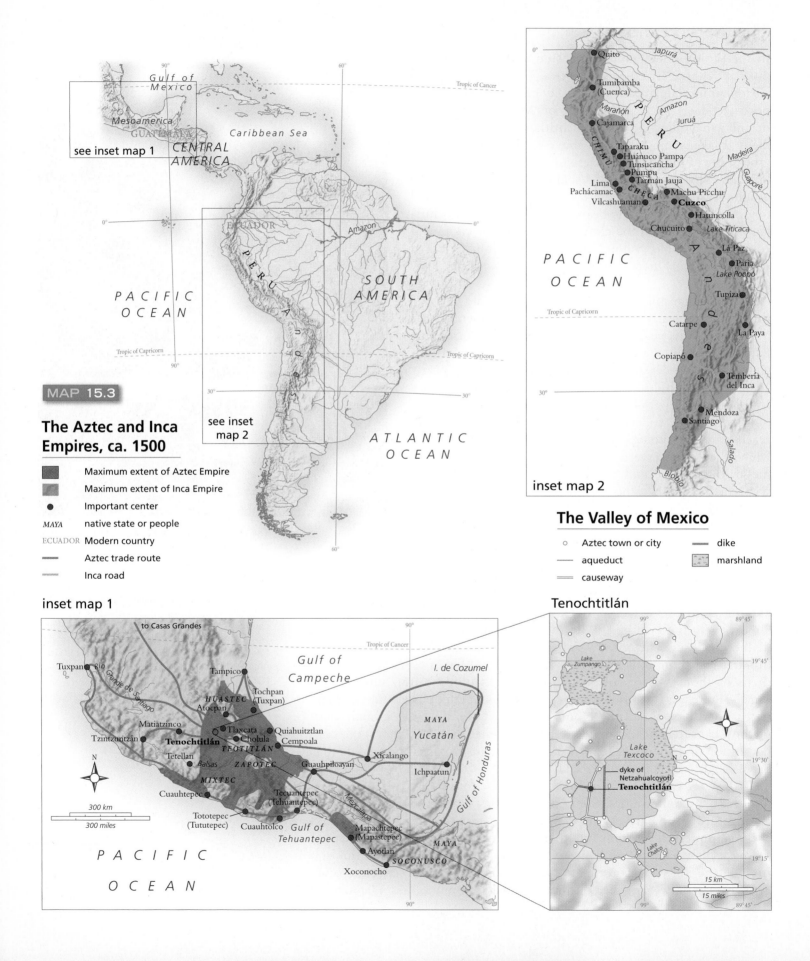

MAP 15.3

The Aztec and Inca Empires, ca. 1500

Maximum extent of Aztec Empire

Maximum extent of Inca Empire

● Important center

MAYA native state or people

ECUADOR Modern country

Aztec trade route

Inca road

The Valley of Mexico

○ Aztec town or city

aqueduct

causeway

dike

marshland

inset map 1

Tenochtitlán

inset map 2

however, share some of the same problems that afflicted the Incas. They relied on fragile alliances, bore the resentment of tributary peoples, and expanded so rapidly that their reach always threatened to outrun the available manpower and technology.

The Aztecs and Incas saw themselves as continuing the traditions of earlier empires. They recalled ruined supremacies of the past: Tula and Teotihuacán in the Aztec case, Tiahuanaco for the Incas. The reach of their power seems, however, to have exceeded anything either region had witnessed before. So how did they do it? Long-range exchanges with other cultures helped to propel empires in Eurasia and Africa into expansion, but these advantages did not apply in the Americas. Indeed, the Andean and Mesoamerican worlds were so isolated that they do not even seem to have been in touch with each other. They did not benefit from new technology. Nor, as far as we know, were people in either region bouncing back from anything resembling the demographic catastrophe of parts of the Old World in the previous century. There was no momentum of recovery behind the enormous extensions of Aztec and Inca power. The most likely explanation is that demographic growth crossed a critical threshold in both areas. Probably, only imperial solutions could command the resources and compel the exchanges of goods needed to sustain the growing cities in which the Aztecs and Incas lived. In any case, both empires, as we shall see in the next chapter, were short lived. Essentially they were empires of types traditional in the region and overreached the realistic limits of their potential.

Tribute. Early colonial Spanish administrators were careful to copy tribute records from the archives of the preconquest Aztec state. The records show both the complexity if the tributary networks that linked the Aztec world and the amazing environmental diversity of the regions from which tribute flowed. This folio, from the Codex Mendoza, shows the tribute due to Tenochtitlán—the Aztec capital in central Mexico—from the "hot country" near what is now the Mexican-Guatemalan border. Among the items depicted are ornamental feathers, bird skins, jaguar pelts, and jade beads.

NEW EURASIAN EMPIRES

The expanding states of fifteenth-century Africa and the Americas were conspicuous in their day. However, they proved relatively fragile. Sixteenth-century European conquerors swallowed the Aztec and Inca states almost at a gulp. Ethiopia barely survived in the sixteenth century, eroded by Muslim invaders and waves of pagan, pastoralist immigrants. Songhay fell to invaders from Morocco in the late sixteenth century. Finally, though Mwene Mutapa survived into the seventeenth century, having fought off would-be conquerors from Europe, it then dissolved gradually and ingloriously into numerous petty states. It was the borderlands that straddle Europe and Asia that nurtured the really big, really enduring new or resumed empires of the age, those of the Turks and Russians.

The Russian Empire

The rise of a powerful Russian state was without precedent. Previously, the geography of the region produced volatile and therefore usually short-lived empires. Its

Chronology: Incas and Aztecs	
ca. 1325	Aztecs found city of Tenochtitlán
ca. Mid-fifteenth century	Inca begin period of conquest and expansion
ca. Late-fifteenth century	Inca Empire approaches greatest extent
ca. Early sixteenth century	Aztec Empire reaches its peak

Making Connections | EXPANSION AND ITS LIMITS: AFRICA AND THE AMERICAS IN THE FIFTEENTH CENTURY

REGION/STATE OR EMPIRE	CAUSES FOR EXPANSION	EVIDENCE/EFFECTS OF EXPANSION	LIMITATIONS
East Africa / Ethiopia	Access to long-range trading routes to Indian Ocean via Red Sea ports	Recapture of coastal cities in 1400s, increased trade in slaves, ivory, gold, incense; creation of main access road to Indian Ocean	Limited agricultural land; need to control mountainous and lowland areas to access trade routes; major river systems to south and east with large populations; gradually encroaching Portuguese and Muslim influence by sixteenth century
East/Central Africa / Zambezi River Valley, Great Zimbabwe	Difficult access to Indian Ocean seaports; large populations with ivory, gold, metal resources	Manufactured goods from Asia (porcelain, silk, etc.) traded for gold, ivory; increasingly large administrative centers in stone, large amounts of coins, jewelry, gold, etc.	Landlocked; altered trade routes; decline in navigability of rivers
West Africa / Songhay Empire	Trade routes of the Sahara, linking Mediterranean and Niger valley; astute leadership (Muhammad Askia) and alliance with Muslim clerics, scholars	Canals, dikes, reservoirs; extension of cultivable land; rich trade with Niger valley goldfields	Limited long-range communication; adverse Atlantic winds/currents
Central Africa / Kongo	Domination of Congo River; alliance with Portuguese; abundant natural resources	Use of Western firearms, Christian religion and symbols to legitimate and maintain control; trading of slaves from conquered territories to Portuguese	Ultimate loss of control over slave trade to Portuguese leads to decline and fall
South America / Inca	Diversity of environments, resources; tribute system allows exchange of products between zones	Quick expansion and use of extreme methods of control; extensive road system; large shrines for dead leaders	Mass executions and other methods of subjugation alienate subject peoples and allies
Mesoamerica / Aztecs	Environmental diversity; hundreds of tributary communities; efficient recordkeeping; large array of natural resources	Intensive transformation of environment in/around capital (Tenochtitlán); abundance of commodities, both necessities (food, tools) and luxuries; widespread human sacrifice; monumental architecture	Loose administrative control; fragile alliances; alienation of tributary peoples; excessively rapid expansion

open, flat expanses of land and widely scattered populations contributed to an environment in which states could form with ease but only survive with difficulty. Most came and went quickly, vulnerable to external attack and internal rebellion.

In the fifteenth century, however, the rulers of Moscow established a state of imperial dimensions. Muscovy—as the early Russian Empire was called—has always been volatile at the edges, but it has been exceptionally enduring. One of the features that made Muscovy different was the shape of its heartland. It was based on control of the Volga River, a north–south axis of trade. Earlier empires, including the Mongols', were based on the east–west axis of the steppes, which served as highways for horse-borne armies.

The new empire's beginnings in the fourteenth century were almost imperceptible to those who experienced them or witnessed their effects. As we have seen, Russian princes could sometimes use Mongol dominance to their own advantage. Rulers of Moscow were the most adept in exploiting the Mongols to secure independence of and—increasingly—power over other Russians. Ivan I, known as Kalita or "Moneybags" (r. 1325–1340), got his nickname from his success as a tax collector for the Mongols. In 1378–1382, shortly after the collapse of Mongol rule in China, Muscovy attempted to drive the Mongols out of Russia. The challenge was premature, but Moscow's privileged relationship with the overlords survived. Mongol supremacy faded gradually.

The Russian world was expanding northward in the late fourteenth and early fifteenth centuries, as missionaries opened roads to convert people in the forests and tundra. An astonishing example of expansion by sea occurred in the 1430s. The evidence comes from a monastery on an island—bare, poor, and ice bound for much of the year—in the White Sea, on the edge of the Arctic. The monks painted their home not as it was but as they envisioned it, with a golden sanctuary and domes like candle flames. They showed the founders of their monastery rowing to the island, while whip-wielding angels expelled the original inhabitants. The paintings show merchants arriving, and monks rescuing shipwreck victims, with help from the ghosts of the monastery's saintly founders, who drive back the pack ice. Angels supply bread, cooking oil, and salt. All the ingredients of a typical story of European colonialism appear: the religious inspiration, the heroic voyage into a perilous environment, the ruthless treatment of the natives, the struggle to adapt and establish a viable economy, the quick arrival of commercial interests, and, finally, success through perseverance.

Muscovy's sudden take-off in the second half of the century, when conquests of neighboring peoples turned it into an imperial state, overshadowed early efforts at expansion. Indeed, when Constantinople fell to the Turks in 1453, Muscovites could see their city as, potentially, the "Third Rome," replacing Constantinople as Constantinople had replaced Rome, the former imperial capital (see Chapter 9). By the 1470s, Ivan the Great (r. 1462–1505) had absorbed most of Russia's other surviving principalities and was ready to throw off Mongol overlordship. He married a Byzantine princess, incorporated an imperial eagle into his coat of arms, forged a genealogy that traced his family back to the Roman Caesars, imported Italian technicians to fortify his palace complex, the Kremlin, and contemptuously dismissed an offer from the German emperor to invest him as king. "We have been sovereign in our land from our earliest forefathers," he replied, "and we hold our sovereignty from God."

"It was the borderlands that straddle Europe and Asia that nurtured the really big, really enduring new or resumed empires of the age, those of the Turks and Russians."

Russian expansion. The monastery these Russian Orthodox monks—Zosima and Savatti—founded in the White Sea off the Arctic coast of Siberia was really a modest and precarious little community, housed in wooden buildings in an icy desert. But the monks painted it as they would like it to be—big, grand, prosperous, and frequented by commerce.

During his reign, Ivan the Great more than trebled the territory he ruled—to over 240,000 square miles (see Map 15.4). His realm also took a new shape around most of the vast length of the Volga, stretching across the breadth of Eurasia, uniting the fur-rich north and the cash-rich fringes of Asia, and reaching for the Baltic and Caspian Seas. The city of Novgorod, which Muscovy absorbed in the 1470s, formed the northern pole of the state. Fur was the "black gold" of the north, inducing Russians to conquest and colonization, just as gold and spices lured other European peoples to Africa and the East.

War parties gathered pelts as tribute along a northern route that missionaries pioneered in the late fourteenth century, by way of the rivers Vym and Pechora. Repeatedly from 1465, Ivan sent expeditions to the rivers Perm and Ob to levy tribute. The expedition of 1499 numbered 4,000 men, equipped with sleds drawn by reindeer and dogs. They crossed the Ob in winter, returning with 1,000 captives from the forest-dwelling peoples who hunted for the furs. Ivan's ambassador to the rich Italian duchy of Milan boasted that his master received 1,000 gold ducats' worth of tribute annually in furs—five or six times an Italian nobleman's income. In the south, Russian dominance extended over Muslim-ruled Kazan (kah-ZAHN), near the Black Sea, Russia's great rival for control of Siberia's fur trade. While in the north missionaries, seeking to convert pagans, formed the vanguard for Russian conquests. Russian expansion therefore became a conscious crusade. Rulers justified it on religious grounds.

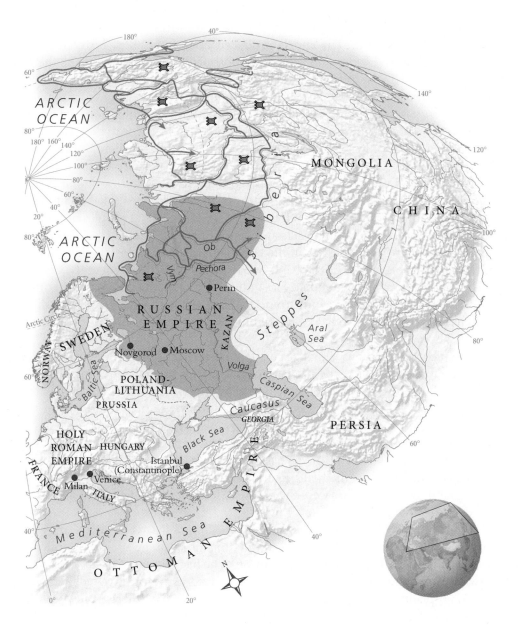

MAP 15.4

The Russian Empire, ca. 1505

Russian Empire

routes used by fur traders

fur

Timurids and the Ottoman Empire

In the early fifteenth century, Turkish—and therefore Muslim—expansion resumed in southern Europe and Asia, still under the leadership of the Ottoman dynasty. The Mongol supremacy had been a traumatic challenge to the Islamic world, shattering the reputation of Muslim armies, breaking the monopoly of Sharia or Islamic law, exposing the limitations of the clergy, and inspiring the religious minded to withdraw from the world in a spirit of resignation. The Black Death had also battered the Islamic world. In some ways, indeed, it never fully recovered. Muslims' numerical preponderance over Christians never got back to earlier levels. But, for global history, the Islamic recovery is a much bigger story than the temporary setback.

To understand recovery, we turn to one of its most brilliant Muslim observers after the Black Death, the historian Ibn Khaldun (ihb-ihn hahl-DOON). In 1377,

"Everywhere in Ibn Khaldun's day, Islamic survival and success depended on Muslims' ability to tame the invaders challenging them from the deserts and the steppes, and turn their power to the service of Islam."

he sat down in a village in what is now Algeria "with ideas pouring into my head like cream into a churn." His efforts produced one of the most justly admired works of all time on history and political philosophy, the *Muqaddimah*. Its theme was the counterpoint of herder and tiller, which Ibn Khaldun saw as the motivating force of historical change. He had plenty of opportunity to observe the often violent interplay of nomads and sedentarists, their periodic collaboration, the incorporation of herder communities into Islamic states, and the way they launched new empires of their own. The consequences were clear. Everywhere in Ibn Khaldun's day, Islamic survival and success depended on Muslims' ability to tame the invaders challenging them from the deserts and the steppes, and turn their power to the service of Islam. Despite the disasters of the Black Death, new manpower stoked the Islamic world's potential for expansion. The pastoral peoples of Central Asia continued to provide converts. Islam's unique appeal to steppelanders was one of the great formative influences in the late medieval world. Most Turkic peoples and many Mongols were converted into warriors for Islam. Consequently, Central Asia stayed Muslim, and the Indian Ocean linked mainly Muslim shores. In other words, the Silk Roads and maritime routes of Eurasia had to pass through Muslim-ruled territory. Equally important, human fuel renewed the Islamic world's capacity to wage war and expand its frontiers.

The most conspicuous mobilizer of steppeland manpower in Muslim service in the late fourteenth and early fifteenth centuries, was the self-proclaimed "world conqueror," Timur (tee-MOOR) the Lame. Western writers, who traditionally call him Tamerlane, have tended to see him, romantically, as an embodiment of the superior virtues and simple lives of pastoral peoples. In reality, Timur was a nobly born townsman from Central Asia. Unlike most steppeland upstarts, he could justly claim to be descended from Genghis Khan (see Chapter 13). His court historian represented him as "the being nearest to perfection" and a pious devotee of holy war, but his role models were the pagans, Alexander the Great (see Chapter 5) and Genghis Khan.

When Turkic nobles rebelled against their Mongol masters in his homeland, Timur emerged as their leader. Deftly eliminating his rivals, he emerged as ruler of the region by 1370. By the time he died in 1406, he had conquered Iran, halted the growth of the Ottoman Empire, captured and caged its sultan, invaded Syria and India, and planned the conquest of China (see Map 15.5). Wherever he went, he heaped up the skulls of citizens unwise enough to resist his sieges. But this destruction was for efficiency, not for its own sake. It made most conquests submit cheaply. His success was by no means uniform, but it was impressive enough and consistent enough, to seem decreed by God. He addressed enemies in terms reminiscent of Mongol tradition: "Almighty God has subjugated the world to my domination, and the will of the Creator has entrusted the countries of the Earth to my power."

The day after his death, as his heirs turned on one another, his achievements seemed transitory. Even today, Timur's impact on the Islamic world is usually seen as negative. His success against the Ottomans gave Christendom a reprieve. By humbling the Mongols, he encouraged Christians in Russia. By weakening the Muslim sultans of Delhi, he liberated millions of Hindus. These reflections, however, overlook his psychological legacy. He was a champion of Islamic orthodoxy and exerted great influence as a patron of Muslim education. He is also important as an example of the process that converted pastoralists. Having been the scourge of the Islamic world, they became its sword.

Timurid horoscope. Despite their fearsome reputation, Timurid princes—the descendants of the Muslim Turkic conqueror whom Westerners called "Tamerlane"—were great patrons of both astronomers and astrologers. This horoscope was drawn up in Shiraz, Iran, in 1411 for one of Timur's grandsons, Iskandar Sultan. The date of his birth, 1384, is given in Persian, Uighur, and Chinese.

Timur was like a hurricane—his force soon spent. The Ottomans were more like a monsoon: Their armies returned and receded as each season came and went, but they constantly made new conquests. The fate of the Mongols—expelled from China, retreating from Russia—shows how hard it was for a great Eurasian empire to survive in the aftermath of the Black Death, which jarred economies and felled manpower. Yet, falteringly in the early fifteenth century but with renewed strength thereafter, the Ottoman Empire managed to do so.

The Ottomans' great advantage was location. The heartlands of the empire were at the crossroads of some of the world's great trade routes, where the Silk Roads, the Indian Ocean routes, the Volga, the Danube, and the Mediterranean almost converged (see Map 15.5). The history of the Byzantine Empire showed the importance of holding on to this location. Byzantium flourished while it occupied these lands, faltered when its control there slackened and ceased (see Chapter 12). From their own past, the Ottomans inherited the traditions of steppeland imperialism. They were content, at first, to levy tribute and allow their tributaries to govern themselves or to exist as puppet states to be manipulated according to Ottoman needs.

Gradually, the Ottomans adapted to the conditions of the environments they conquered, which were predominantly agrarian, urban, and maritime. As their conquests grew, their methods of governing became, necessarily, more bureaucratic and centralized. As their frontiers touched formidable foes, they modified their military traditions. Other empires of nomadic origins failed when required to adapt to new military technologies, but the Ottomans' readily became a gunpowder empire. Their forces could blow away cavalry or batter down city walls.

The Ottomans even took to the sea. In the 1390s, the sultans began to build permanent fleets of their own. It was a long process and hard to catch up with

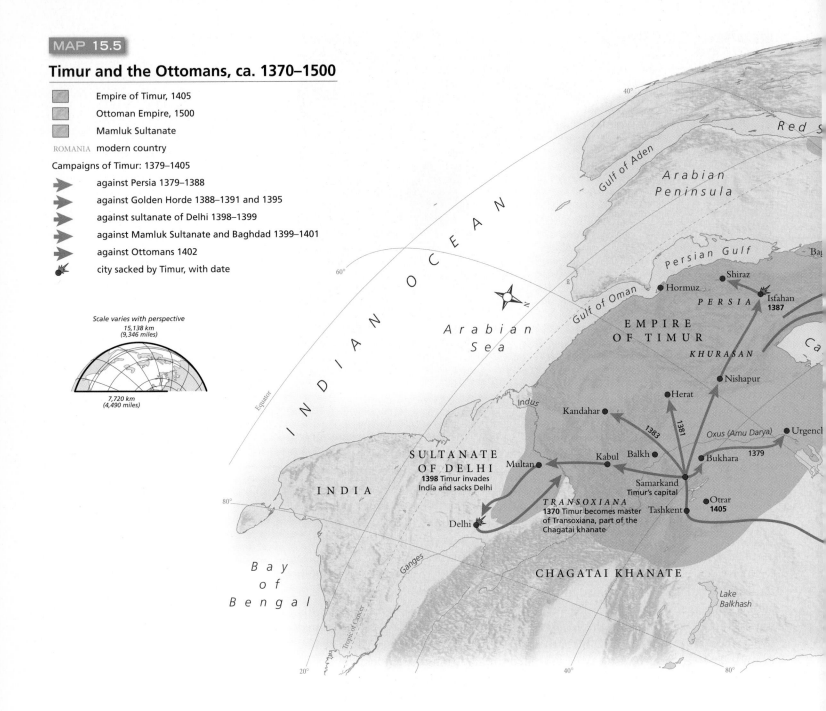

MAP 15.5

Timur and the Ottomans, ca. 1370–1500

Empire of Timur, 1405

Ottoman Empire, 1500

Mamluk Sultanate

ROMANIA modern country

Campaigns of Timur: 1379–1405

against Persia 1379–1388

against Golden Horde 1388–1391 and 1395

against sultanate of Delhi 1398–1399

against Mamluk Sultanate and Baghdad 1399–1401

against Ottomans 1402

city sacked by Timur, with date

Scale varies with perspective
15,138 km
(9,346 miles)

7,720 km
(4,490 miles)

long-established naval powers. As late as 1466, a Venetian merchant in Constantinople claimed that to win a battle Turkish fleets needed to outnumber those of Venice by four or five to one. By the end of the century, however, the Ottomans had overturned the 400-year-old Christian maritime supremacy in the Mediterranean. Never since Rome defeated Carthage (see Chapter 7) had such an unlikely candidate become a naval power.

Like other imperialists of steppeland origin, the Ottomans mastered the art of keeping subjects of diverse religions loyal to them. At the same time, Ottoman leaders, as self-appointed warriors of Islam, took whatever steps were

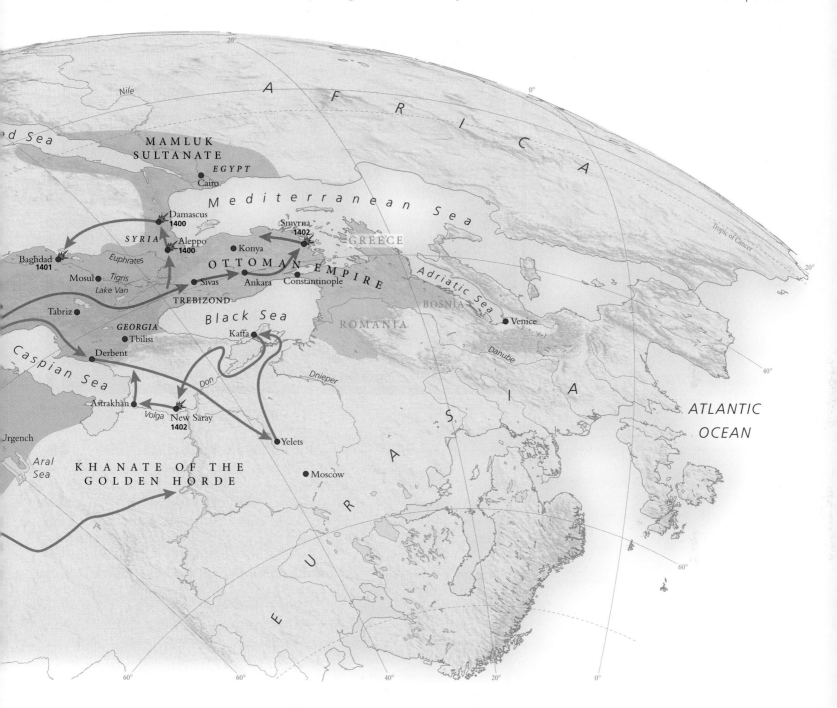

necessary to strengthen the Islamic state. They tolerated Jews, Christians, and Shiites, but had no qualms about levying punitive taxes on these minorities. On Christians, they imposed a levy of male child slaves, who were brought up as Muslims to form the **Janissaries**, an elite corps of the armed forces, and staff the ranks of the administration. The system provided servants for the state, and converts for Islam, while keeping Christian communities in submission. From the 1420s, consistently with the character of the empire as a Muslim state with people of many religions and customs, the sultan functioned as head of two linked systems of law and justice. The first consisted of secular laws and

A Turkish fleet at anchor off Toulon, in southern France, in 1543, from a chronicle written to celebrate the wide-ranging campaigns of Sultan Suleiman the Magnificent (r. 1520–1566). The Ottomans were able to wage naval war in the western Mediterranean, thanks to the many harbors along the North African coast controlled by Muslim chiefs who were subjects of the sultans.

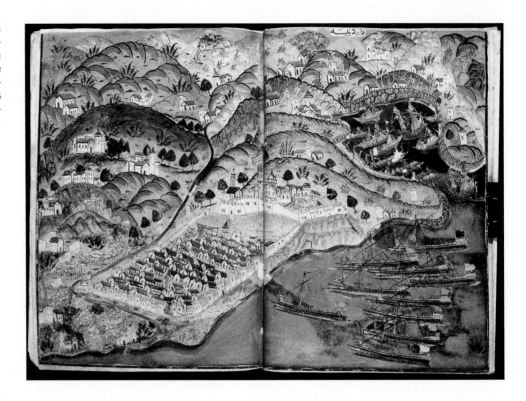

customs that the sultan's appointees administered. The second was enshrined in the Quran and the traditions of Islamic law, with a body of experts to run it, who met in the sultan's palace.

In 1451, Mehmet (MEH-meht) II became sultan at the age of 19, uninhibited by caution, committed to reform. This was a decisive step in the shift from indirect rule to centralized government. Mehmet's predecessors had prudently allowed self-rule to continue in the city of Constantinople and its few surviving dependencies—the last fragments of the Byzantine Empire that still proclaimed itself the heir of Rome. The Ottomans controlled what happened in Constantinople by threatening and bribing political factions there. But some factions in the city were determined to challenge the Turks and formed an alliance with Western Christendom. Mehmet laid siege to Constantinople. He built huge forts to command the sea approaches to the city and fired the heaviest artillery ever made at its walls. He transported ships overland in pieces to get round the great chain the defenders stretched across the entrance to the harbor. In the end, the sheer weight of numbers was decisive. The attackers climbed the walls over the bodies of dead comrades. The last Byzantine emperor, Constantine XI, fell fighting—only the eagles on his purple boots identified his corpse.

With the fall of Constantinople in 1453, Mehmet II could see his empire as a continuation of Rome. He looked westward for fashions to incorporate into his court culture and chose Italians to paint his portrait, sculpt his medals, and write some of his propaganda. The direction of Ottoman conquests tilted toward Europe as Mehmet attempted to recreate the Byzantine Empire. He extended his territory into most of what are now Greece, Romania, and Bosnia, seeking to control the shores of the Adriatic and Black seas.

THE LIMITATIONS OF CHINESE IMPERIALISM

Ottoman imperialism in the fifteenth century resumed its former course after setbacks caused by the Black Death and the rise of Timur. An observer at the time might have predicted that China, too, would resume expansion and even anticipate the Ottomans in bidding for a maritime empire. The best way to understand why such developments seemed likely—and why they were frustrated—is to look back at China's recovery from the mid-fourteenth-century plagues. Like so many decisive episodes of Chinese history, the story begins among the people on whose labor the empire depended: peasants.

The rhythms of peasant life sometimes seem slow and changeless, peasants' expectations low: deferring hope, shrugging off promises of improvement. Their response, in a surprisingly wide variety of cultural contexts, is to wait and pray for the millennium—a fabled future, when divine intervention will either perfect the world or end it. Often, however, in times of extreme disaster, peasant movements arise to try to trigger the millennium. One of the most explosive of all such movements began among Chinese canal workers in 1350.

Mid-fourteenth-century China was particularly wretched. Peasants were the victims of the slow-grinding effects of economic misery and the survivors of terrible environmental disasters. The plagues that began in the 1320s kept returning. Not until well into the 1350s did the plagues begin to lose their virulence or to encounter naturally immunized populations. In 1344, the Yellow River flooded. Persistent droughts followed. Decayed communications that prevented timely help made local famines worse. The population of the empire had fallen, by some calculations, to half what it had been at its height. In this setting, peasants were forced to repair the Grand Canal, which carried essential food supplies from southern and central China to Beijing.

The peasants' millenarianism—their hope of deliverance in a transfigured world—was based on a Buddhist myth. The lord Maitreya, the last of the earthly Buddhas, would come to prepare the world for extinction. Now, however, given the peasants' miserable lives, the myth acquired a political edge. Maitreya would put a triumphant end to the struggle of good against evildoers and give his followers power over their oppressors. A similar movement was current at the same time in Western Europe, where the Fraticelli, a group of Franciscan friars, identified with the needs and interests of the wretched of the Earth. The Franciscans predicted that a cosmic hero would come to wrest treasures from the soil and enrich the poor. Fulfilling the biblical prophecy uttered by the mother of Jesus that the prayers of the church repeated every day, he would put down the mighty from their seat and exalt the humble and meek.

In China, the mood was particularly dangerous. Along with their desire for deliverance, peasants harbored a folk memory of the Song dynasty (see Chapter 12) and a hankering for the good times supposed to have preceded the Mongol invasions of a century before. Peasant revolts are often revolutionary in the most literal sense of the word, wanting to turn the world back, "revolve" it full circle, to an imagined or misremembered golden age. Therefore, when the Mongol rulers executed a pretender to the throne who claimed to be the heir of the Song in 1351, a revolt broke out among his followers. They easily recruited thousands of peasants

Sultan Mehmet II (r. 1451–1481) extended the Ottoman Empire westward into Europe, taking great interest in the culture of lands that had once belonged to the Roman Empire—especially after he captured the old Roman capital of Constantinople in 1453. Gentile Bellini, who worked at Mehmet's court and was one of the best Venetian painters of the day, painted this portrait of the sultan in the realistic style that was popular in Italy at the time. Bellini framed the sultan's image with columns decorated in the European style.

to their cause. Some members of the elite even joined in, out of resentment at the ruling dynasty's partiality for foreign advisers.

The leader who emerged from the chaos of rebellion was Zhu Yuanzhang (joo yoo-ehn-jhang), the recruiting officer of a rebel band. By the end of the 1350s, the empire in the Yangtze region had dissolved into a chaos of small states run by similar upstarts. Between 1360 and 1363, in river warfare of reckless daring, Zhu conquered his rivals. At this stage, he was careful to represent himself as a mere servant of the rebel cause. By 1368, however, he was so powerful that he proclaimed the start of a new dynasty.

Zhu cleverly managed the coalition that had brought him to power. He juggled all the rebels' conflicting ideologies while reconciling former enemies. To please the Confucian establishment, he restored ancient court ceremonies and the examinations for public service. He kept the military command structure and even dressed in some of the same ways as the previous Mongol dynasty had. He renounced the cult of Maitreya, but only after making it clear that he had fulfilled it in his own person by adopting the name "Ming" for his dynasty. The word, which means bright, was traditionally used to describe the lord Maitreya.

Giraffe. "The ministers and all the people gathered to gaze at it and their joy knows no end," commented Zhen-tu, the Chinese court painter who recorded the arrival of one of several giraffes at China's imperial zoo in the early fifteenth century. Imperial propaganda identified giraffes with mythical beasts of good omen.
1977–42–1. Tu, Shen. "The Tribute Giraffe with Attendant". Philadelphia Museum of Art: Gift of John T. Dorrance, 1977.

Zhu had the self-educated man's typical contempt for the academic establishment. "Chewing on phrases and biting on words," he said, "they have never had any practical experience. When you examine what they do, it is nothing." But he recognized that the Confucian bureaucrats had expertise he could use. His empire—vast and literate, as it was—needed a civil service that would heed a traditional code of ethics. He also needed to keep the Confucian elite under his control. He therefore kept the traditional power centers of his court in balance: the military top brass, the eunuchs who ran the imperial household, the foreign and Muslim advisers and technicians, the Buddhist and Daoist clergies, and the merchant lobby. Together, they limited the power of the Confucian elite.

The result was a brief period when expansionist policies prevailed over Confucian caution. Zhu's son, the Yongle (yuhng-leh) emperor (r. 1402–1424) aggressively sought contact with the world beyond the empire. He meddled in the politics of Vietnam and enticed the Japanese to trade.

The most spectacular manifestation of the new outward-looking policy was the career of the Muslim eunuch-admiral, Zheng He (jehng heh). In 1405, he led the first of a series of naval expeditions. Their purpose has been the subject of long and unresolved scholarly debate, but in part, at least, it was to show China's flag all over the Indian Ocean (see Map 15.6). He replaced unacceptable rulers in Java, Sumatra, and Sri Lanka, founded a puppet state on the commercially important Strait of Malacca, and gathered tribute from Bengal in India. He displayed Chinese power as far away as Jiddah, on the Red Sea coast of Arabia and in major ports in East Africa as far south as the island of Zanzibar. "The countries beyond the horizon," he announced with some exaggeration, "and from the ends of the Earth, have become subjects." He restocked the imperial zoo with giraffes, ostriches, zebra, and rhinoceroses—all hailed as beasts bringing good luck—and brought Chinese geographical knowledge up to date.

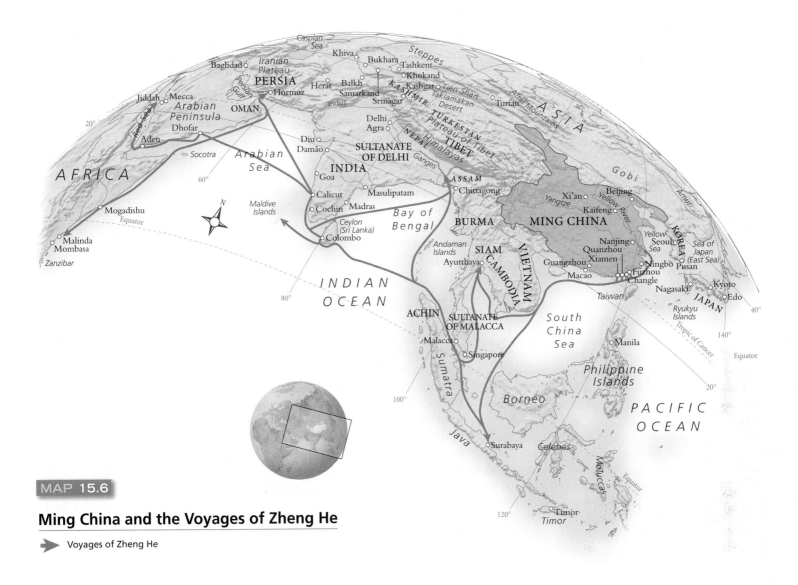

MAP 15.6

Ming China and the Voyages of Zheng He

➤ Voyages of Zheng He

Can Zheng He's voyages be called an imperial venture? Their official purpose was to pursue a fugitive pretender to the Chinese throne—but that would not have required such vast expeditions to such distant places. The Chinese called the vessels treasure ships and emphasized what they called tribute gathering (in the more distant spots Zheng He's ships visited, what happened was more like an exchange.) Commercial objectives may have been involved. Almost all the places Zheng He visited had long been important in Chinese trade. In part, the voyages were scientific missions: Ma Huan, Zheng He's interpreter, called his own book on the subject, *The Overall Survey of the Ocean's Shores,* and improved maps and data on the plants, animals, and peoples of the regions visited were among the expeditions' fruits. But flag showing is always, to some extent, about power or, at least, prestige. And the aggressive intervention Zheng He made in some places, together with the tone of his commemorative inscriptions, demonstrates that the extension or reinforcement of China's image and influence was part of the project.

Indeed, it is hard to see how else the huge investment the state made in his enterprise could have been justified. Zheng He's expeditions were on a crushing scale. His ships were much bigger than anything European navies could float at the time. His first fleet was said to comprise 66 junks of the largest ever built, 225 support vessels, and 27,870 men. The seventh voyage—probably the longest in reach—sailed 12,618 miles. The voyages lasted on average over two years each. Some silly claims have been made for Zheng He's voyages. Ships of his fleet did not sail beyond the limits of the Indian Ocean—much less discover America or Antarctica. His achievements, however, clearly demonstrated China's potential to become the center of a maritime empire of enormous reach.

But the Chinese naval effort could not last. Historians have debated why it was abandoned. In many ways, it was to the credit of Chinese decision makers that they pulled back from involvement in costly adventures far from home. Most powers that have undertaken such expeditions and attempted to impose their rule on distant countries have had cause to regret it. Confucian values, as we have seen, included giving priority to good government at home. "Barbarians" would submit to Chinese rule if and when they saw the benefits. Attempting to beat or coax them into submission was a waste of resources. By consolidating their landward empire, and refraining from seaborne imperialism, China's rulers ensured the longevity of their state. All the maritime empires founded in the world in the last 500 years have crumbled. China is still there.

Part, at least, of the context of the decision to abort Zheng He's missions is clear. The examination system and the gradual discontinuation of other forms of recruitment for public service had serious implications. Increasingly scholars, with their indifference to expansion, and gentlemen, with their contempt for trade, governed China. In the 1420s and 1430s, the balance of power at court shifted in the bureaucrats' favor, away from the Buddhists, eunuchs, Muslims, and merchants who had supported Zheng He. When the Hongxi (huhng-jher) emperor succeeded to the throne in 1425, one of his first acts was to cancel Zheng He's next voyage. He restored Confucian office holders, whom the Yongle emperor had dismissed, and curtailed the power of other factions. In 1429, the shipbuilding budget was cut almost to extinction. The scholar-elite hated overseas adventures, and the factions that favored them so much that they destroyed all Zheng He's records in an attempt to obliterate his memory. Moreover, China's land frontiers became insecure as Mongol power revived. China needed to turn away from the sea and toward the new threat.

By the late fifteenth century, the scholars' position seemed unshakable, and the supremacy of Confucian values could not be challenged. The Hongxi emperor aspired to Confucian perfection. He ordered the slaughter or expulsion of court magicians and exiled 1,000 Buddhist and Daoist monks. He resumed a Confucian priority: study of the penal code, which previous Ming emperors had neglected. He reintroduced the palace lectures, during which Confucian professors instructed the emperor. He endowed a library alongside the Confucian temple at the sage's birthplace in Qufu (choo-foo). He patronized artists whose work radiated Confucian serenity. Wu Wei (woo way), the emperor's favorite painter, had Daoist patrons, too, but his representations of ascetics meditating in sketchy landscapes demonstrate the triumph of thought over nature and, therefore, by implication, of Confucianism over Daoism.

By the end of the fifteenth century, there was little chance the Chinese would resume a strategy of expanding the empire and no chance

Wu Wei was one of the most original and influential artists of late-fifteenth-century China. But his values were those of his patrons, the conventional scholar-elite of the imperial court. This painting is typical. The scholar staring thoughtfully into the distance is drawn in delicate and flattering contrast to the heavy, blotchy ink used to depict the tree. *Wu Wei, "Scholar Seated Under a Tree," China. Ink & traces of colour on silk. 14.7 × 8.25. Chinese and Japanese Special Fund. Photograph © 2007 Courtesy Museum of Fine Arts, Boston*

that they would expand by sea. For the rest of the Ming period (1368–1644), China did not cease to be a great imperial power, but frontier stability became far more important to the ruling elite than frontier expansion. The transfer of the imperial capital from the southern citty of Nanjing to the northern city of Beijing under the Yongle emperor symbolized this concern. The state never resumed the active patronage of overseas expansion. The growth of trade and of Chinese colonization in Southeast Asia was left to the private initiative of merchants and migrants. China, the empire best equipped for maritime imperialism, opted out. Consequently, lesser powers, including those of Europe, were able to exploit opportunities in seas that Chinese power vacated.

Chronology: The Early Ming Dynasty	
1350s	Yangtze region dissolves into small warring states
1360–1363	Zhu Yuanzhang conquers his rivals
1368	Zhu Yuanzhang founds Ming dynasty
1405	Zheng He leads first naval expedition
1425	Hongxi emperor succeeds to throne; Zheng He's voyages cancelled; Confucian values ascendant

THE BEGINNINGS OF OCEANIC IMPERIALISM

Even under the Yongle emperor, China confined its seaward reach to the monsoonal seas of maritime Asia and the Indian Ocean—seas of terrible hazards and fabulous rewards. As we have seen, the Indian Ocean was relatively easy to cross but relatively hard to enter or exit. For most of history, therefore, it was the preserve of peoples whose homes bordered it or who traveled overland—like some European and Armenian traders—to become part of its world. Moreover, all the trade was internal. Merchants took no interest in venturing far beyond the monsoon system to reach other markets or supplies.

From Europe, however, access to the Indian Ocean was well worth seeking. Merchants craved a share of the richest trades and most prosperous markets in the world, especially the spices, drugs, and aromatics that were the specialities of producers in Sri Lanka, and parts of India and what is now Indonesia. These products, sold to rich buyers in China and Southwest Asia, and, to a lesser extent, in Europe, were the most profitable in the world, in terms of price per unit of weight. Many Europeans sought to find out where they came from and to take part in the trades. But the journey was too long, laborious, and hazardous to generate much profit. From the Mediterranean, merchants had either to travel up the Nile and proceed by camel caravan to a Red Sea port, or to negotiate a dangerous passage through the Ottoman Empire to the Persian Gulf. In either case, they obviously could not take ships with them. This was a potentially fatal limitation because Europeans had little to offer to people in the Indian Ocean basin except shipping services. For most of the fifteenth century, until the 1490s, Europeans were not sure if it was possible to approach the Indian Ocean by sea at all.

To understand why, until the late fifteenth century, Europeans were so backward in navigation compared with Indian Ocean peoples and unable to gain direct access to Asian markets and supplies, we must look at the wind map (see Map 15.7). For most of history, winds and currents have played a huge part in conditioning, and even determining, who and what went where in the world.

Europe's only effective access by sea to the rest of the world is along its western seaboard, into the Atlantic, which has a fixed-wind system. That is, instead of changing direction seasonally, as in monsoonal systems, the prevailing winds in the Atlantic are always the same. It took a long time to develop navigation with fixed-wind systems because, until navigators explored and decoded those winds' path-

"China, the empire best equipped for maritime imperialism, opted out. Consequently, lesser powers, including those of Europe, were able to exploit opportunities in seas that Chinese power vacated."

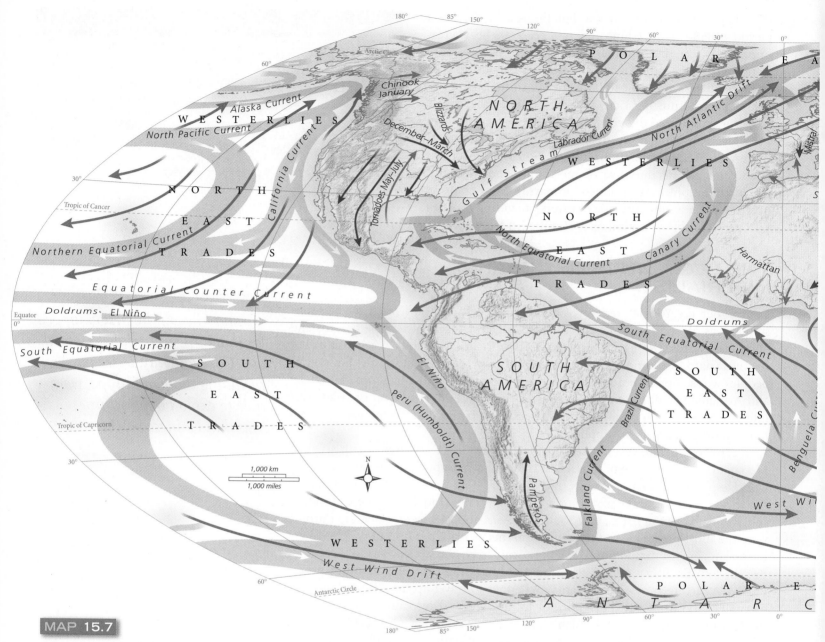

MAP 15.7

Winds and Ocean Currents Worldwide

Ocean Currents

▢ warm
▢ cold

Prevailing Winds

➤ warm
➤ cold

Local Winds

➤ warm
➤ cold

ways, adventurers could not get home. Navigators either sailed into the wind—which usually resulted in their being blown back without discovering any useful new lands or routes—or they sailed with the wind, never to be heard of again.

The Norse explorers of the North Atlantic in the tenth and eleventh centuries (see Chapter 11) overcame these limitations by sailing west with the currents that cross the Atlantic below the Arctic, and then picking up the westerlies, which took them home. But this route led only to relatively poor and underpopulated regions. For the Atlantic to become Europe's highway to the rest of the world, explorers had to develop ways to exploit the rest of the fixed-wind system. They had to discover the winds that led to commercially important destinations. There were, first, the northeast trade winds, which led to the resource-rich, densely populated regions of

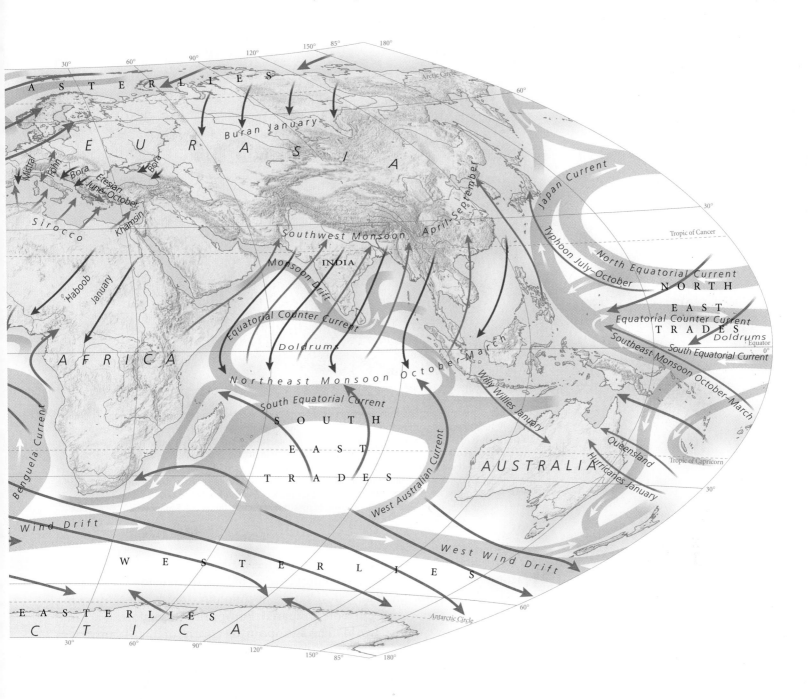

the New World, far south of the lands the Norse reached. There was also the South Atlantic wind system, which led, by way of the southeast trade winds and the westerlies of the far south, to the Indian Ocean.

The technology needed to exploit the Atlantic's wind systems only gradually became available during a period of long, slow development in the thirteenth, fourteenth, and fifteenth centuries. Like most technology, for most of history, it developed by trial and error. We know little about the process, because the work went undocumented. Humble craftsman labored to improve hull design and rigging—and therefore the maneuverability of ships—and to make water casks secure for the long voyages explorers had to undertake. Historians have traditionally emphasized the contribution of formal science in developing maritime charts and instruments

Spice box. This sixteenth-century leather box was used to house specimens of spices from Southeast Asia. Around the outer rim would have been different kinds of pepper, which accounted for as much as 70 per cent of the global trade in spices in the early modern period; cloves (the most valuable spice per unit of bulk, production of which was overwhelmingly concentrated in the islands of Ternate and Tidore); and ginger. The inner compartment would have contained nutmeg and mace (which are both products of the nutmeg tree, the former being the inner kernel of the seed, the latter its outer coating, grown in the Banda Islands in what is today Indonesia); and cinnamon (most of which came from what is now Sri Lanka, though production was widely diffused across the region as far as the Philippines).

for navigating by the stars. Now it seems that these innovations were irrelevant. No practical navigator of this period in Europe seems to have used them.

In addition to gradually developing technology, gradually improving knowledge of winds and currents prepared Europeans to explore maritime routes to the rest of the world. The European discovery of the Atlantic was launched from deep in the Mediterranean, chiefly by navigators from Genoa and the island of Majorca. They forced their way through the Strait of Gibraltar, where the strength of the adverse current seemed to stopper their sea, in the thirteenth century. From there, some turned north to the familiar European Atlantic. Others turned south into waters unsailed, as far as we know, for centuries, toward the Madeira and Canary Islands and the African Atlantic. Early efforts were long and laborious because explorers' vision was limited to the small patches of the ocean before them, with their apparently unremitting winds. Navigators were like code breakers deprived of information to work with. Moreover, the Black Death and the economic downturn of the mid–fourteenth century interrupted the effort, or at least slowed it down.

Only the long accumulation of information and experience could make a breakthrough possible. Navigators had no means to keep track of their longitude as they beat their way home against the wind. They made increasingly huge deep-sea detours to find westerlies that would take them home. Those detours led to the discovery of the Azores, a mid-ocean string of islands more than 700 miles west of Portugal. Marine charts made not later than the 1380s show all but two islands of the group. Much longer open-sea voyages now became common. From the 1430s, the Portuguese established way stations, sown with wheat or stocked with wild sheep, on the Azores, so that passing crews could find provisions.

Several attempts were made during the fifteenth century to explore Atlantic space, but most doomed themselves to failure by setting out in the belt of westerly winds. Presumably explorers chose this route because they wanted to be sure that they would be able to get home. We can still follow the tiny gains in the slowly unfolding record on rare maps and stray documents. In 1427, a Portuguese pilot called Diogo de Silves established for the first time the approximate relationship of the islands of the Azores to one another. Shortly after 1450, the westernmost islands of the Azores were reached. Over the next three decades, the Portuguese crown often commissioned voyages of exploration farther into the Atlantic, but none is known to have made any further progress. Perhaps they failed because they departed from the Azores, where the westerlies beat them back to base.

Not only was exploitation of the Atlantic slow, but at first it yielded few returns. One exception was Madeira, which paid enormous taxes to the Portuguese crown thanks to sugar planting in the mid–fifteenth century. The explorers' hope of establishing direct contact with the sources of West African gold proved false, though they were able to get gold at relatively low prices through trade with West African kingdoms. This trade also produced something that could be sold in European markets. From 1440, Portuguese desperadoes obtained increasing numbers of slaves through trading and raiding. But markets for slaves were limited because great slave-staffed plantations, of the sort later familiar in the southern United States, hardly existed in Europe, where most slaves were still domestic servants. The Canary Islands attracted investment because they produced natural dyestuffs and seemed exploitable for sugar. But their inhabitants fiercely resisted Europeans, and the conquest was long and costly.

In the 1480s, however, the situation changed, and Atlantic exploration began to pay off. In the North Atlantic, customs records of the English port of Bristol indicate that quantities of whaling products, salt fish, and walrus ivory from the ocean increased dramatically. In West Africa, the Portuguese post at São Jorge da Mina, near the mouth of the Benya River, was close to gold fields in the Volta River valley, and large amounts of gold now began to reach European hands. In 1484, sugar production at last began in the Canary Islands. In the same decade, Portuguese made contact with the kingdom of Kongo. Although voyages toward and around the southernmost tip of Africa encountered unremittingly adverse currents, they also showed that the far south of the Atlantic had westerly winds that might at last lead to the Indian Ocean. By the end of the 1480s, it was apparent that Atlantic investment could yield dividends.

Imperial marker. Portuguese explorers erected carved stone pillars to mark their route and to record their claim to have annexed territory for Portugal. Diogo Cão raised this example, the Padrão de Santo Agostinho, at Santa Maria, south of Benguela in Angola in 1482 (see Map 15.8).

The 1490s were a breakthrough-decade in Europe's efforts to reach out across the ocean to the rest of the world (see Map 15.8). In 1492–1493, Christopher Columbus, in voyages financed by Italian bankers and with backing from the Spanish 'monarchs, discovered fast, reliable routes across the Atlantic that linked the Mediterranean and the Caribbean. In 1496, John Cabot, another Italian adventurer, backed by merchants in Bristol and the English crown, discovered a direct route across the North Atlantic, using variable springtime winds to get across and the westerlies to get back. His route, however, was not reliable and, for over 100 years, was mainly used to reach the cod fisheries of Newfoundland.

European Oceanic Exploration up to 1500

→ European explorers with names and dates

→ Norse voyages of the 10th and 11th centuries

▬ extent of Portuguese exploration of West African coast up to 1487

✚ Portuguese markers erected in token of their claim to sovereignty

Thule Inuit people

Economic activity associated with early
European exploitation of the Atlantic

⬇ sugar plantation

🐟 fisheries

👤 slaves

Meanwhile, the Portuguese sought to determine whether the Indian Ocean was genuinely landlocked. In 1497–1498, a Portuguese trading venture, commissioned by the crown and probably financed by Italian bankers, attempted to use the westerlies of the South Atlantic to reach the Indian Ocean. Its leader, Vasco da Gama, turned east too early and had to struggle around the Cape of Good Hope at the tip of Africa. But he managed to get across the Indian Ocean anyway and reach the pepper-rich port of Calicut at the tip of India. The next voyage, in 1500, reached India without a serious hitch.

The breakthroughs of the 1490s opened direct, long-range routes of maritime trade across the world between Europe, Asia, and Africa. Success may seem sudden, but not if we view it against the background of slow developments in European chronology and knowledge and the accelerating benefits of Atlantic exploration in the previous decade. Was there more to it than that?

Making Connections | THE BEGINNINGS OF OCEANIC IMPERIALISM IN EUROPE

DESIRE	OBSTACLES	BREAKTHROUGHS, 1200–1500
European merchants crave access to Indian Ocean trade	Long, laborious journey across hostile territories Europeans have little to offer in exchange for the spices, drugs, and aromatics of the East Fixed-wind system of Atlantic makes oceanic voyages impractical Black Death and consequent economic downturn slow down efforts to explore Atlantic	Technology to exploit Atlantic wind system slowly develops Knowledge of winds and currents gradually improves Thirteenth century: Navigators from Genoa and Majorca force their way through the Strait of Gibraltar Portuguese discover the Azores in the late fourteenth century 1450–1480: Portuguese commission Atlantic voyages of exploration after 1480: Exploration of Atlantic begins to pay returns after 1490: Europe begins to reach out across the ocean to the rest of the world.

Was there something special about European culture that would explain why Europeans rather than explorers from other cultures discovered the world-girdling routes, linking the Old World to the New and the Indian Ocean to the Atlantic? Some European historians have argued just that—that Europeans had something others lacked.

Such a suggestion, however, seems ill conceived. Compared to the peoples of maritime Asia, Europeans were special mainly in being slow to launch long-range voyages. The Atlantic, the ocean they bordered, really was special, however, because its wind system inhibited exploration for centuries but rewarded it spectacularly once it was launched. Moreover, the breakthrough explorations were not the work of "Europe" but of people from a few communities on the Atlantic seaboard and in the Mediterranean. What distinguishes them is not that they set off with the right kind of culture, but that they set off from the right place.

THE EUROPEAN OUTLOOK: PROBLEMS AND PROMISE

In some ways, indeed, Western Europe in the fifteenth century was beset with problems. Recovery from the disasters of the fourteenth century was slow. Though plagues were less severe, they remained frequent. And though used to the severe climate of their little ice age, Western Europeans did not reoccupy the high ground and distant colonies that they had abandoned in the fourteenth century. In most places, population increase was modest and probably did not reach levels attained before the Black Death. Food supplies were unreliable, and harvests frequently failed.

Human foes joined impersonal enemies—plague, war, and famine. In 1396, a crusade to drive the Turks from the Balkans failed. It marked the beginning of a long period of Turkish advance on the Balkan and eastern Mediterranean frontiers of Christendom. Meanwhile, in the northeast, Lithuanians, most of whom remained pagan until the late fourteenth or early fifteenth century, eroded the conquests of German knightly orders along the Baltic Sea (see Chapter 12). In the early fifteenth century, Thule Inuit raiders finally obliterated the Norse colony on Greenland (see Chapter 14).

Meanwhile, hard times created opportunities for those with the skill or luck to exploit them. High mortality opened gaps in elites, which bureaucrats could fill, thanks, in part, to a revolution in government. The use of paper made it cheap and easy to transmit rulers' commands to the farthest corners of their realms. To help legitimize the newcomers' power, Western moralists redefined nobility as the product of virtue or education rather than ancestry. "Virtue is the sole and unique nobility," declared a Venetian coat of arms. A doctrine of late fifteenth-century Italian social thought invoked Greek mythology to make its point: "Neither the wealth of Croesus [reputedly the richest man in the world] nor the antiquity of the blood of Priam [the king of Troy in Homer's epics] could rival reason as an ingredient of nobility."

New economic divisions appeared. The line of the Elbe and northern Danube Rivers and the lands between became a cultural fault line. To the west of this line, underpopulation boosted the value of labor. The effects were to liberate peasants and urban communities from landowners' control, split up landholdings, encourage tenancies, and convert cropland to pasture. In the east the opposite occurred. Landholders responded to the loss of manpower and revenue by clamping down on peasants' rights and forcing formerly free towns into submission. New definitions of nobility were rejected. East of the Bohemian forest, nobility was ancient blood or acquired "by martial discipline," and that was that.

Scored by heresies, trenched by conflicting social values, and riven by economic cracks, Western Europe nevertheless showed signs of self-confidence and optimism. Scholars and artists pursued, with renewed vigor, the project of recovering the legacy of classical antiquity—the cultural achievements of ancient Greece and Rome. The movement is commonly called "**the Renaissance**" on the grounds that the civilization of classical antiquity was reborn—but "the" is a much-abused word. Scholarship has now identified renaissances in almost every century for the previous 1,000 years. No radically new departure occurred in the fifteenth century from what had gone before—merely an accentuation of long-accumulating tendencies.

An event traditionally said to be representative of the Renaissance occurred in 1400, when the Cloth Importers' Guild of Florence launched a competition for a new set of bronze doors for the greatest monument in their care: the Baptistery that faced the city's cathedral. The Baptistery had been built in the eighth century as the place where infants and converts could receive the sacrament of baptism. Urban myth, however, claimed it was orginally a Roman temple of the god Mars. Two great geniuses were the finalists in the competition: Filippo Brunelleschi and Lorenzo Ghiberti both used classical models for their startlingly realistic and dramatic trial plaques depicting the Sacrifice of Isaac. Both works represent the moment in the biblical story when God stays Abraham's hand from sacrificing his son Isaac. Ghiberti won the commission, perhaps because he was technically more ingenious, using less bronze and therefore cutting the cost. In 1425, his second set of Baptistery doors genuinely marked a breakthrough in the power of the art of bronze reliefs: "gates of paradise," as Florentines called them, which acquired the realism of an extra dimension through the use of perspective. In 1440, Donato Donatello, the most devoted student of classical art in Florence, produced his free-standing bronze statue of David, which, under the form of a sacred subject,

"Scholarship has now identified renaissances in almost every century for the previous 1,000 years. No radically new departure occurred in the fifteenth century from what had gone before—merely an accentuation of long-accumulating tendencies."

(a)   (b)

Renaissance competition. In 1400, when the Cloth Workers' Guild of Florence sponsored a competition for new designs for the doors of the baptistry in the city's cathedral, Florence's leading designers competed for the job. The subject to be portrayed was the story from the Book of Genesis when God intervened to prevent Abraham from sacrificing his son Isaac. The model entered by Filippo Brunelleschi, the cathedral's architect, was more dramatic, with an angel literally staying Abraham's hand to save Isaac from being slain (a). But Lorenzo Ghiberti's winning design was more classical. The angel's foreshortening, the musculature of Isaac's body, which was copied from ancient Greek and Roman sculpture, and the technically dazzling way in which Abraham's elbow jabs from the plaque help explain Ghiberti's success (b).

again from the Bible, seemed to bring a vanished pagan world back to life: secular, sensual, homoerotic.

For there was no notion of "art for art's sake" in fifteenth- and sixteenth-century Italy. Artists were practical. The technology of bronze casting developed along with experience in casting cannon. Many masters of the Renaissance had sidelines in gunnery. Ironically, increased demand for bronze guns starved art of a vital raw material and even led to the melting down of antique bronzes, just when artists and collectors most valued them. Similarly, painters had to be good at every kind of design, including urban planning, architectural drawing, interior decoration, jewelwork, stagecraft, party-planning, and engineering. When Leonardo da Vinci—universally hailed as one of the greatest painters of the early sixteenth century—sought new patrons, he advertised himself as skilled in every kind of handiwork, including the making of weapons and the constructions of siege engines. When he worked for the dynasty that ruled Milan, one of his jobs was to paint their coat of arms on the ceilings of their apartments.

Admirers of classical learning adopted a predominantly secular curriculum: grammar, rhetoric, poetry, history, and moral philosophy, imbided mainly from classical texts. The classics as well as—even, instead of—Christianity came to inform common ideas of morality, politics, and taste. Spreading, at first, from a few French and north Italian schools, **humanism** gradually became Europe's most prestigious form of learning. Political thinkers turned back to Greek and Roman history for instruction. Religious innovators modeled their ideas on evidence from early Christianity. Artists adopted realism and perspective from what they thought were Greek and Roman models.

Florence demonstrates humanism's power and limitations. In the fifteenth century, classical taste transformed its art and architecture. Comparisons with the Roman republic inspired its citizens to think of themselves as free and self-governing.

The Church of San Lorenzo. Filippo Brunelleschi, the trend-setting architect of Florence, got the commission to design the parish church of the ruling Medici family in 1418. He based his concept on laws of mathematical proportion that, he believed, ancient Greek and Roman architects had followed. He copied the ground plans of the most ancient churches he knew, and, to support the clergy's growing desire to make congregations participate actively in worship, he opened domes above the sacred spaces to fill them with light.

Yet power gradually fell into the hands of a single family, the Medici, who patronized art in the classical tradition but who actually spent more on jewels and on gaudy, gem-like artworks that could display their wealth. When they were temporarily overthrown in 1494, after their banking business collapsed, the state that replaced them was no Roman-style republic. Rather, it was the rule of a "godly" clique, inspired by a hell-fire preacher, who preferred piety to humanism. Botticelli (1444–1510), the great artist who had painted pagan erotica for a Medici villa, turned to biblical subjects.

Still, across Europe, the rise of humanism had lasting consequences for Christian culture. Humanists painstakingly scrutinized the language of the Bible and the historical traditions of the church, exposing incorrect translations and departures from the practices of early Christianity. New styles in church architecture reflected classical taste and, more deeply, arose from the desire to create a setting for the kind of devotion that humanism inspired. Open sanctuaries, brilliantly lit and approached through wide naves and aisles allowed worshippers to see and take part in events at the altar.

Humanism also helped arouse European interest in the wider world. Some important and provocative geographical writings of classical antiquity became widely known in the West. In the early fifteenth century, the work of the ancient Greek scholar Ptolemy, originally written in Alexandria in the second century, invited intense speculation about geography, mapping the world, and the limits of exploration. The first-century B.C.E. work of Strabo, a Greek geographer who sought to reconstruct Homer's mental map of the world, prompted questions

Chivalrous hero. When Albrecht Dürer painted an altarpiece for the family of wealthy merchants Stephan and Lucas Paumgartner in Nuremberg Germany, probably in 1498, both brothers wanted to appear as figures of chivalry. Stephan was shown as St. George, the knightly dragon-slayer, and Lucas, depicted here, took on the role of St. Eustace, displaying a banner with the image of Christ between a stag's antlers to recall the moment when Eustace, according to legend, was converted during a hunt.

about finding previously unknown continents in the ocean. Humanists' fascination with the history of language reinforced the search for "primitive" peoples who might cast light on the question of how language originated.

Magic was at least as much a part of the learned culture of the Renaissance as humanism. Florence, like everywhere else in the world at the time, as far as we know, was full of popular spells and superstitions. Three nights before the death of the Medici banker and art patron, Lorenzo the Magnificent in 1492, lightning struck the cathedral, sending stones from the famous dome crashing to the street. Florentines said Lorenzo had a demon trapped in his ring and had released it as he sensed his impending death. In 1478, when Jacopo Pazzi was hanged for his part in a conspiracy against Medici rule, heavy rains threatened the survival of the grain crop. Popular wisdom was that it was Jacopo's fault: His burial in consecrated ground had offended God; so he was dug up and dragged stinking through the streets, while the mob battered his remains before flinging them into the Arno River.

Belief in magic was not just a vulgar error. There was learned magic, too. The notion that human agency could control nature was a perfectly rational one. Promising approaches included techniques we now classify as scientific, such as observation, experiment, and the exercise of reason. Astrology, alchemy, conjuration, and sorcery had not yet proved to be false leads. For what is the difference between magic and science? Both are attempts to explain and therefore to control nature. Western science of the sixteenth and seventeenth centuries grew, in part, out of magic. The vocations of scientists overlapped with those of magicians—wielders of magical techniques for mastering nature.

In any case, chivalry was more characteristic than humanism in the values and education of most members of the elite. **Chivalry** could not, perhaps, make men good, as it was supposed to do. It could, however, win wars. In 1492, for instance, the monarchs of the Spanish kingdom of Castile extended the frontier of Christendom by conquering Granada, the last Muslim kingdom in Spain, in what the Venetian ambassador called "a beautiful war." "There was not a lord present who was not enamored of some lady," who "often handed warriors their weapons...with a request that they show their love by their deeds." Queen Isabella II of Castile (r. 1474–1504) died uttering prayers to the Archangel Michael as "prince of the chivalry of angels."

The typical chivalrous hero of the time took to the sea, conquered an island, married a princess, and became a ruler. Explorers—often men of humble social origins—tried to embody these fictions in real life. Adventurers in the service of the Portuguese Prince Henry (1394–1460), included former pirates and violent criminals. They indulged in chivalric rituals and gave themselves storybook names, like Lancelot and Tristram of the Island. They also colonized the Madeira Islands and parts of the Azores, and explored the coast of West Africa as far as Sierra Leone. The commercial sector that helped to back overseas adventures was looking for new opportunities—especially the Genoese, whose role in the eastern Mediterranean at this period was largely confined to high-bulk, low-profit shipping and trading. Marginal noblemen, shut out from advancement at home and imbued with chivalric ideas, were willing to take amazing risks. That, together with the availability of high-risk investment, helps to explain many early forays in Atlantic exploration.

Prince Henry himself—traditionally misrepresented as a navigator motivated by scientific curiosity—imagined himself a romantic hero, destined to perform great deeds and win a kingdom of his own. The truth is that he never went exploring, and his desperate efforts to make enough money to pay his retainers included slave raiding and a soap monopoly. His followers included the father-in-law of Christopher Columbus, a weaver by training who reinvented himself as a "captain of cavaliers and conquests," and who took to exploration to escape the restricted social opportunities of home.

Alongside chivalry, millenarian fantasies may have influenced overseas expansion. The first king of Portugal's ruling dynasty was actually called "Messiah of Portugal." Columbus claimed that the profits of his discoveries could be used to conquer Jerusalem and help complete God's plans for a new age. Franciscan friars who supported Columbus believed that an "Age of the Holy Spirit," which would precede the end of the world, was coming soon, and some of them came to see the New World as the place where such an age might begin.

Europe's outreach into the Atlantic was probably not the result of science or strength, so much as of delusion and desperation. This was a space race where it helped to come from behind. The prosperous cultures with access to the Indian Ocean felt no need to explore remote lands and seas for new resources. For cash-strapped Europe, however, the attempt to exploit the Atlantic for new products was like the efforts of underdeveloped countries today, anxiously drilling for offshore wealth from oil or natural gas. In some ways, it paid off.

"Europe's outreach into the Atlantic was probably not the result of science or strength, so much as of delusion and desperation. This was a space race where it helped to come from behind."

In Perspective
Beyond Empires

The imperial habit was spreading, and new empires were forming in environments that had never experienced imperialism before. Russia, for example, extended empire to the Eurasian far north. Mwene Mutapa introduced it in sub-Saharan East Africa. The Aztecs and Incas practiced it in the Americas on an unprecedented scale. Nonetheless, most of Africa and the Americas, as well as the whole of Australia and most of the Pacific island world, as far as we know, had still not experienced anything like empire. While some empires revived, most of the world remained in the hands of communities with modest political ambitions. These were still organized as kinship networks, chiefdoms, or small states. More remarkably, perhaps, some regions with an imperial past, or under imperialist threat, shied away. Instead, they developed systems in which independent states coexisted with varying degrees of mutual hostility. The world of the late fourteenth and fifteenth centuries had four such areas.

In North Africa, Mamluk Egypt was an immensely rich and productive state but remained confined to the Nile valley, unable to expand beyond the deserts that fringed it. A second area lay westward, along Africa's Mediterranean coast. Here numerous small states, founded on the profits of trade or piracy, flourished where Mediterranean and Saharan trade routes met. At the western end of North Africa, Morocco emerged as a kingdom on the edge of the Islamic world, holding Christendom at bay.

South and southeast Asia was a third empire-free region. In India, the sultanate of Delhi never fully recovered from the setbacks of the mid–fourteenth century. Hindu states proliferated, some warlike, specifically, toward Islam. The most militaristic, perhaps, was Vijayanagar—the name means "City of Victories"—with its 60 miles of sevenfold walls (see Map 15.9). This was the state, for

MAP 15.9

Vijayanagar

⬜ extent of Vijayanagar Empire, circa 1500

Absolute sovereignty. The artist of the Wilton Diptych is unknown, but it is regarded as one of the most exquisite paintings of the fourteenth century. It is a propaganda work, emphasizing the claims of King Richard II of England (r. 1377–1399), to sacred responsibilities. His heavenly patrons, St. John the Baptist, and two earlier, sainted English kings, present him to the Blessed Virgin Mary, whose angel-attendants wear Richard's badge—the emblem of the white stag—and carry the English flag. Most interpreters suppose that the message of the painting is that the Virgin is entrusting Richard with the realm of England, symbolized by the flag, but his hands seem open to receive the Christ Child himself—symbolism suitable to a traveling altarpiece, probably designed to be set up whenever the king wished to hear mass during a journey.

which Abd-ar-Razzak, the Persian ambassador mentioned at the start of the chapter, was bound in 1417. It impressed another Muslim visitor in 1443 as "such that the eye has seen nothing like it." Chinese expansion nibbled at the edges of southeast Asia, but China's renunciation of imperialism left the native states of the region free to try one another's strength. The Thai—founders of what is now called Thailand—certainly had expansionist ambitions. In the early fifteenth century, they created the region's largest state at the expense of their neighbors, the Burmese, Khmer, Mons, and Malays (see Map 15.8). Nonetheless, the region lacked a dominant empire and remained home to a state system in which a number of regional states contended with each other.

Finally, most of Europe continued to enclose a state system. East of the Vistula River, where geography favored the formation of large, unstable states by conquest, Russia, as we have seen, undertook a massive imperial enterprise. A brief union of the Polish and Lithuanian states in 1386 created what, on the map, at least, also looked like an empire of daunting dimensions, stretching from the Baltic to the Black Sea. Farther west, however, small states got stronger, and the dream of reuniting them and recreating the old Roman Empire faded—or began to look unrealistic.

Something like what we now call **nationalism** emerged. That is, group feeling developed where people's mutually intelligible speech and a common sense of identity defined by birth caused them to merge into a single community. In the fifteenth century, for instance, the kings of England began to use English, alongside

French and Latin, in official documents and correspondence. National communities adopted patron saints. At international gatherings, such as universities and church councils, people defined themselves according the nation to which they belonged and engaged in ferocious disputes over precedence. At a Council of the Church in 1415, the Castilian delegation settled such a dispute with the English by overturning the bench on which their rivals were sitting, so that the Castilians could occupy a higher place in the hall.

States increasingly asserted their absolute sovereignty, rejecting any obligation to defer to such traditionally supranational authorities as the church or the Holy Roman Emperor. When, for instance, the Emperor Sigismund visited England in 1415, a knight rode into the sea to challenge him to renounce all claim to authority in England before he was allowed to disembark. Kings of France called themselves "emperors in their own realm" and those of Castile in Spain asserted "my sovereign absolute power."

Some rulers developed ideological grounds for their claims to absolute sovereignty. French kings were supposedly endowed with divine powers to heal and able to perform "miracles in your own lifetime." Richard II of England (r. 1377–1399) had himself painted in a sumptuous image, attended by angels, opening his hands to receive the body of Christ from the hands of the Virgin Mary herself.

At the same time, the power of the state really did increase. One reason was improved communications. As paper replaced parchment, increasing the output of documents, royal bureaucracies reached more people in more parts of the realm. Changes in the concept of law also strengthened the state. Traditionally, the law was seen as a body of wisdom handed down from the past. Now it came to be seen as a code that kings and parliaments could endlessly change and recreate. The state's power also expanded over vast new areas of public life and common welfare: labor relations, wages, prices, forms of land tenure, markets, the food supply, livestock breeding, and even, in some cases, what personal adornments people could wear.

Finally, while the state was growing more powerful, the power of the church declined. Between 1378 and 1415, rulers in Latin Christendom could not agree whom to recognize as pope. The power vacuum eroded what little unity Christendom still had. Secular states became stronger as heresies arose. Under the influence of reformers who demanded—among other changes—lay control of appointments in the church and worship in everyday language instead of Latin, Bohemia for a time refused to recognize papal authority. Reformers known as conciliarists argued that the church should become a kind of republic, with power transferred from Rome to a council of bishops who would meet periodically in a kind of parliament.

Chronology

ca. 1325	Aztecs found city of Tenochtitlán
1368	Beginning of Ming dynasty
1370–1406	Reign of Timur
Late fourteenth century	Ethiopia expands into surrounding regions
1401	Lorenzo Ghiberti wins competition for the bronze doors of the Bapistery in Florence
1405	First voyage of Zheng He
1417	Voyage of Abd-ar-Razzak to Vijayanagar (India)
1430s	Portuguese establish way stations in Azores
1440s	Portuguese begin to obtain slaves from West Africa
ca. 1450	Inca begin period of expansion and conquest
1453	Ottomans capture Constantinople
1462–1505	Reign of Ivan the Great
ca. 1475	Center of power in southern Africa shifts from Zimbabwe to Mwene Mutapa
1480s	Portuguese make contact with kingdom of Kongo
1482	Portuguese establish trading post of São Jorge da Mina on West African coast
1484	Sugar production begins in Canary Islands
1490s	First Portuguese diplomatic missions arrive in Ethiopia
1492–1493	First voyage of Christopher Columbus; Spanish kingdom of Castile captures Granada, last Muslim kingdom in Spain
1496	John Cabot discovers direct route across North Atlantic
1497	Pilgrimage of Muhammed Touray Askia, ruler of Songhay, to Mecca; first voyage of Vasco da Gama
1500	Vasco da Gama reaches India; Aztec Empire at its peak

"The expanding empires of the age were reaching toward each other. Where they made contact, they became arenas of unprecedented scale for trade and for transmitting technology, ideas, sentiments, and ways of life."

How much difference did the state system make to Europe's prospects? Historians have engaged in a pointless debate over this question. On the one hand, the state system deprived Europeans of unified command, of the sort found, for instance, in the Chinese or Ottoman Empires. On the other hand, it stimulated competition among rulers, multiplying the possible sources of patronage available to innovators. For European maritime expansion, the state system was not decisive in launching most initiatives. The explorers and would-be empire builders relied on private enterprise, with little or no state backing. Columbus, for instance, got no direct financial support from the Spanish crown—the myth that Queen Isabella of Castile pawned her jewels for him is nonsense. Prince Henry's Atlantic enterprise was a private venture. Furthermore, as the example of Southeast Asia shows, a state system was not in itself sufficient to produce overseas imperialism; for that, the stimulus of coming from behind was necessary. Asian states were at the nodes of the world's richest trades. They had no need to explore new markets or conquer new centers of production, because everything came to them anyway. Europeans, on the other hand, had to expand if they were to gain access to anything worth exploiting.

For all its hesitations and limitations, fifteenth-century expansion was new and potentially world changing. The new routes pioneered in the 1490s linked the populous central belt of Eurasia to the Americas and Africa, and Europe to Asia by sea. We can see the beginnings of an interconnected globe—a **world system** able to encompass the planet. The expanding empires of the age were reaching toward each other. Where they made contact, they became arenas of unprecedented scale for trade and for transmitting technology, ideas, sentiments, and ways of life. The consequences would transform the world of the next three centuries: Worldwide encounters, commerce, conflict, contagion, and cultural and ecological exchange would follow.

PROBLEMS AND PARALLELS

1. Why was the last half of the fifteenth century an age of expansion? How did the beginnings of a world system emerge around 1500?

2. Why were African states fragile in this period? How did Muhammad Touray Askia use Islam to make Songhay the dominant power in West Africa?

3. What does the term *ecological imperialism* mean? How did the Inca exploit the many different ecosystems of their empire? What was role of tributary networks in the Aztec Empire?

4. How did the Russian and Turkish worlds expand in the fourteenth and fifteenth centuries? What was the impact of Timur's conquests on the Islamic world?

5. Why did the Chinese turn away from maritime expansionism after the voyages of Zheng He? Why was frontier stability more important than overseas expansion for China? Why did the Hongxi emperor reinstate Confucian values at the Chinese court?

6. Why were wind systems so important in world history? Why did the beginnings of European oceanic imperialism have as much to do with geography as with culture?

7. How did the rise of nationalism and the state system drive European expansion? Why were there no major empires in North Africa or in South Asia during this period?

READ ON ▶ ▶ ▶

The material on Abd-ar-Razzak comes from R. H. Major, ed., *India in the Fifteenth Century* (1964). D. Ringrose, *Expansion and Global Interaction, 1200–1700* (2001) gives the background.

On Ethiopia, S. C. Munro-Hay, *Ethiopia: the Unknown Land* (2002) and R. Pankhurst, *The Ethiopians: A History* (2001) are valuable general histories. W. G. Randles, *The Empire of Monomotapa* (1975) is excellent on Mwene Mutapa. On West Africa in this period, E. W. R. Bovill, *The Golden Trade of the Moors* (1995) is a readable classic. Songhay is not well served by books in English but a useful collection of sources is J. O. Hunwick, ed., *Timbuktu and the Songhay Empire: Al-Sa'di's Ta'rîkh al-Sudan down to 1613, and Other Contemporary Documents* (1999). Anne Hilton, *The Kingdom of Kongo* (1985) is outstanding.

Of histories of the Inca and Aztecs, J. V. Murra, *The Economic Organization of the Inca State* (1980), T.N. D'Altroy, *The Incas* (2003), and M. Smith, *The Aztecs* (2002) are particularly strong on ecological aspects.

My material on the White Sea comes from R. Cormack and D. Gaze, eds, *Art of Holy Russia* (1998). J. Martin, *Treasures of the Land of Darkness* (2004) is enthralling on the economic background to Russian expansion. I. Gray, *Ivan III and the Unification of Russia* (1972) is a businesslike introduction. Ibn Khaldun's great work is *The Muqaddimah: An Introduction to History*, tr. Franz Rosenthal (1969). B. F. Manz, *The Rise and Rule of Tamerlane* (1999) is the outstanding work on its subject.

For the Ottomans, see H. Inalcik, *The Ottoman Empire: the Classical Age* (2001). E.L. Dreyer, *Early Ming China* (1982) and *Zheng He: China and the Oceans in the Early Ming Dynasty* (2006) cover the Chinese topics of this chapter admirably. L. Levathes, *When China Ruled the Seas* (1997) is readable and reliable.

On Europe C. Allmand, ed, *The New Cambridge Medieval History, VII* (2005) is comprehensive, while M. Aston, *The Prospect of Europe* (1968) offers a short introduction. On Portuguese expansion, P.E. Russell, *Henry the Navigator* (2001) is admirable and F. Bethencourt and D. Curto, eds, *Portuguese Oceanic Expansion* (1998) provides a broad survey. P.O. Kristeller, *The Cambridge Companion to Renaissance Humanism* (1996) is an unsurpassed classic on its topic and M.H. Keen, *Chivalry* (1986) is on the way to attaining the same status.

The World in 1491

In the thirteenth century, as we pointed out in Chapter 13, the Mongol peace proved a greater stimulus to the migration of ideas and technologies across Eurasia than all previous empires had achieved. In part, the Mongols' outreach was a response to climate change, as cooling shriveled their grasslands. In the fourteenth century, observers began to notice unsteadily increasing cold. Glacial evidence shows that global cold lasted—with varying intensity—until the eighteenth century. In most of Eurasia and North Africa, climate change nourished the diseases contemporaries called plague. As long as the cold period lasted, so did frequent plagues.

The Mongol peace exceeded previous empires as a stimulus to the migration of ideas and technologies, while merchants, missionaries, and pilgrims pioneered ever more intensive communications that bound together Eurasia and parts of North, East, and West Africa. Gradually, with gathering pace in the fifteenth century and dramatic acceleration from the sixteenth century onward, convergence began to replace divergence as the dominant theme in the history of human cultures. After millennia of divergence, it seems amazing that the process should have been halted and reversed.

Explorers found routes across the Atlantic, which for the first time linked Europe and Africa to the Americas. They sailed around Africa to connect Europe by sea with the lands around the Indian Ocean, the world's richest zone of commerce. Cultural exchange stimulated Western arts and learning, though from the perspective of Islam, India, or China—Westerners remained relatively backward and poor. Over a longer period, empires and trade overleaped oceans, taking people, animals, plants, deadly microbes, and forms of culture with them. Parts of the globe that had grown unalike now began, slowly and selectively at first, to resemble each other once again as they had before the continents had drifted apart millions of years ago.

▶ QUESTIONS

1. Based on the globes shown here, which cultures were experiencing the most convergence in 1491? Which cultures were mostly divergent from other cultures?

2. In 1491, which ocean was the biggest and richest zone of long range commerce? Is there any evidence in the globes shown here that the Atlantic would emerge in the sixteenth century as a major zone of cultural and ecological exchange?

To view an interactive version of this map, as well as a video of the author describing key themes related to this Part, go to
www.myhistorylab.com

Chinese Exploration by c. 1491

- ▪ Known and mapped in detail
- ▫ Known by observation or report but not mapped in detail

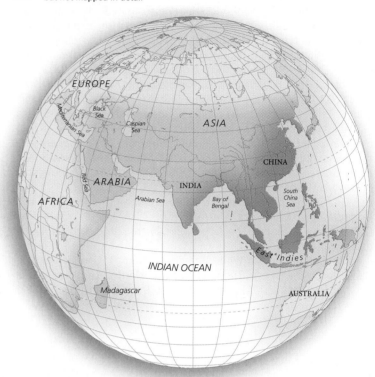

Japanese Knowledge of the World, c. 1491

- ▪ Known in detail
- ▫ Known by report

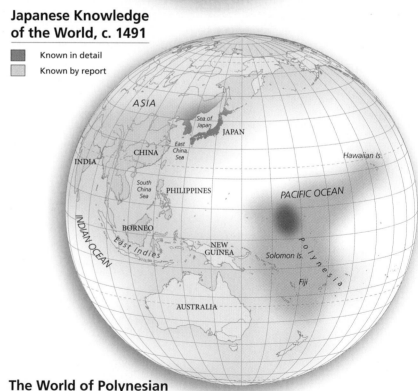

The World of Polynesian Navigators by c. 1491

- ▪ Known and mapped in detail
- ▫ Known but not mapped

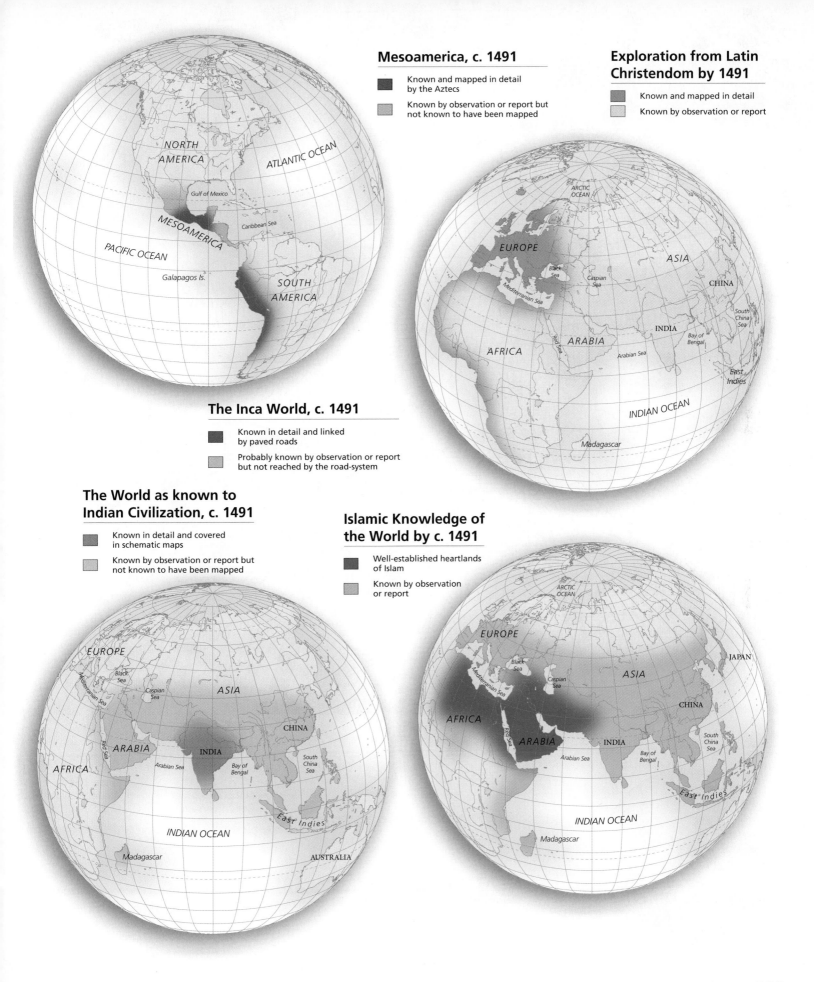

Mesoamerica, c. 1491

- Known and mapped in detail by the Aztecs
- Known by observation or report but not known to have been mapped

Exploration from Latin Christendom by 1491

- Known and mapped in detail
- Known by observation or report

The Inca World, c. 1491

- Known in detail and linked by paved roads
- Probably known by observation or report but not reached by the road-system

The World as known to Indian Civilization, c. 1491

- Known in detail and covered in schematic maps
- Known by observation or report but not known to have been mapped

Islamic Knowledge of the World by c. 1491

- Well-established heartlands of Islam
- Known by observation or report

527

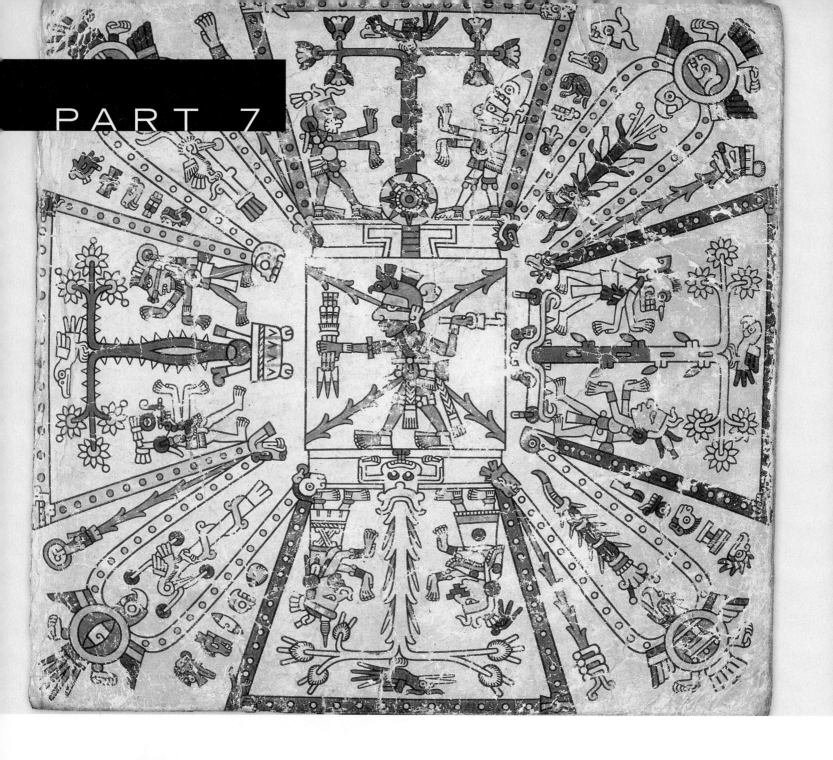

PART 7

ENVIRONMENT

CULTURE

since 1492
Columbian exchange

since 1513
Atlantic navigation—
Gulf Stream mastered

ca. 1500–1600
Portuguese maritime
empire at its height

Convergence and Divergence to ca. 1700

◄ **A Mixtec world-view,** ca. 1500, painted on deer hide. At the center of the world the god Xiutecutli or Yahui spills the life forces of fire and blood. Trees grow toward each of four directions. At the top, a sun disc, rising over temple steps, signifies east. In the west, where the sun sets, the tree is uncolored.

National Museums and Galleries on Merseyside, Liverpool, England, U.K.

since 1565
Pacific navigation—Japan current mastered

since early 1600s
Dutch navigation of "roaring 40s"

since ca. 1640
Decline of steppelands

mid–16th century
Atlantic slave trade takes off

ca. 1550–1650
Expansion of Asian empires

1640
Closing of Japan

1600–1700
Western Scientific Revolution

CHAPTER 16

Imperial Arenas: New Empires in the Sixteenth and Seventeenth Centuries

▲ **Imperial conflict.** Portuguese, armed mainly with bows, resist the attack on Hormuz, which restored the island fortress to Persian rule, in 1622. This was the first of a long series of campaigns in which indigenous powers ejected the Portuguese from their trading outposts on the coasts of Asia and East Africa.

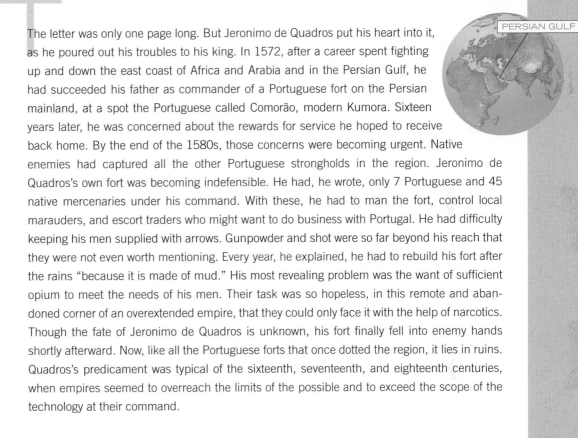

PERSIAN GULF

The letter was only one page long. But Jeronimo de Quadros put his heart into it, as he poured out his troubles to his king. In 1572, after a career spent fighting up and down the east coast of Africa and Arabia and in the Persian Gulf, he had succeeded his father as commander of a Portuguese fort on the Persian mainland, at a spot the Portuguese called Comorão, modern Kumora. Sixteen years later, he was concerned about the rewards for service he hoped to receive back home. By the end of the 1580s, those concerns were becoming urgent. Native enemies had captured all the other Portuguese strongholds in the region. Jeronimo de Quadros's own fort was becoming indefensible. He had, he wrote, only 7 Portuguese and 45 native mercenaries under his command. With these, he had to man the fort, control local marauders, and escort traders who might want to do business with Portugal. He had difficulty keeping his men supplied with arrows. Gunpowder and shot were so far beyond his reach that they were not even worth mentioning. Every year, he explained, he had to rebuild his fort after the rains "because it is made of mud." His most revealing problem was the want of sufficient opium to meet the needs of his men. Their task was so hopeless, in this remote and abandoned corner of an overextended empire, that they could only face it with the help of narcotics. Though the fate of Jeronimo de Quadros is unknown, his fort finally fell into enemy hands shortly afterward. Now, like all the Portuguese forts that once dotted the region, it lies in ruins. Quadros's predicament was typical of the sixteenth, seventeenth, and eighteenth centuries, when empires seemed to overreach the limits of the possible and to exceed the scope of the technology at their command.

Nowadays, *empire* has become one of the dirty words of politics. Politicians, exchanging abuse across the world, commonly call each other "imperialists." We recoil from the idea that any political community should be subject to another. It seems to go against our respect for principles we call freedom or self-determination. But from the sixteenth century to the eighteenth, when the unprecedented growth of empires was one of the most dramatic features of the history of the world, empires spread as much by collaboration as by conquest. They were not usually held together by force, because no state had enough resources for such a task. The moral effects of empires on their subjects were mixed. Some communities were victimized, subjugated, exterminated, or enslaved, while enhanced economic opportunities enriched others, as markets grew and trade routes lengthened. Above all, empires were arenas of exchange—and not solely or primarily of exchange of trade. They stimulated—and sometimes enforced—human migrations on a scale never previously undertaken, over unprecedented distances, and in unprecedented

FOCUS questions

How were empires the agents of change in the sixteenth and seventeenth centuries?

Why did the Dutch replace the Portuguese as the main European imperial power in Asia?

How were maritime empires different from land empires in Asia during the sixteenth and seventeenth centuries?

What roles did war and conquest play in the Mughal and Ottoman empires?

Why were Native Americans so important in the Spanish conquests of the Aztec and Inca empires?

Why did the global balance of trade begin to shift during the seventeenth century?

directions. Technologies, religions, political ideas, and artistic tastes became interchangeable across vast distances as never before.

Finally—and perhaps most importantly—**imperialism** helped to introduce a new era in evolution. Formerly, for hundreds of millions of years, ever since the continents of the world began to drift apart, the life forms of landmasses divided by uncrossable oceans developed independently of one another. Each continent had its own peculiar plant and animal life. Everything tended to be different—from human types to microbes. About 500 years ago, this long history of divergence ended. As empires crossed oceans, the continents came into mutual contact. They swapped life forms. The world we inhabit today began to take shape—in which you can find specimens of the same creatures, wherever climate permits, all over the world (see Chapter 17).

So empires offer a framework for understanding all the major long-range, long-run changes of the period. Western historians used to see the empires founded from Western Europe as the sources of the most important initiatives, and even to call the period as a whole the "Age of European Expansion." But imperialism was not a peculiarly Western vice. Asian, African, and Native American peoples created and led some of the most impressive empires of the period. And the "European" empires usually depended on non-European collaborators who saw an advantage in cooperating with the Europeans. Indeed, the numbers of Europeans involved in creating the empires and making them work were normally small compared with the numbers of native peoples or of non-European migrants from elsewhere. The influences that shaped the empires and made them different from one another generally owed more to environmental or economic circumstances than to their home countries and the traditional allegiances of their ruling elites.

MARITIME EMPIRES: PORTUGAL, JAPAN, AND THE DUTCH

Until about 500 years ago, most empires were concerned with controlling large amounts of two resources: people and land. They may have had ideological or religious reasons for wanting to extend their territorial control; or they may have engaged in conquests out of hatred or insecurity. The economic purpose underlying empire, however, was usually to gain control of, or power over, the places and people that produced valuable goods.

Less commonly, imperial communities could enrich themselves by controlling trade as well as, or even instead of, production. By land, imperialism of this kind is hard to achieve without occupying vast amounts of territory, because traders tend to find ways to outflank imperialists. At sea, however, the opportunities are better. By seizing what is often a limited number of suitable ports, or by patrolling what are often limited routes of access that winds, currents, and straits shape, imperial-minded people can obtain a stranglehold on trade in some commodities, within some climatic or geographical zones. Or they can colonize limited amounts of coastal territory that seaborne communications link, to produce and ship commercial commodities for their own profit. As we have seen, empires of these kinds flourished—briefly and at intervals—in the ancient and medieval Mediterranean and in parts of maritime Asia.

From the sixteenth to the eighteenth centuries, opportunities multiplied to found and extend such empires. Technological improvements accompanied the new opportunities. European or European-designed ships began to rival, and even excel, those of traditional Asian construction, partly thanks to borrowings from Asian technology, such as rudders, bulkheads between the ship's interior compartments, more streamlined designs for long-range commercial vessels, and technical aids that enabled navigators to determine their position by the sun and stars. Improvements in artillery and fortifications made it ever easier to defend coastal forts and trading posts. Naval powers that mustered enough shipping and shipboard firepower could use convoys to control sea lanes or even exclude rival ships by aggressive policing. Meanwhile, sea charts—which professional seamen traditionally despised because it was a matter of professional pride for them to navigate by memory and experience—gradually became an accepted and necessary part of nautical equipment. The expanding reach of exploration helped to improve these nautical maps. Gradually, too, longitude-finding techniques improved. In 1584, King Philip II of Spain decreed a prize for anyone who could solve the problem of determining longitude at sea. Other states initiated similar schemes. A long and fitful series of improvements followed, although no really reliable method was devised until the late eighteenth century.

Improved technology, however, was of little use without new routes where it could be deployed. As we saw in detail in Chapter 15, until the sixteenth century, the world's only really effective long-range, ocean-crossing routes were confined to monsoonal seas. This was chiefly because **monsoons** are seasonal. They blow toward land in summer—sucked landward by warming air, rising over large landmasses. In winter, the direction of the wind is reversed. Navigators therefore know that if they venture out to sea with a following wind, they will be able eventually to return home. By contrast, in the **fixed wind systems** of the Atlantic and Pacific oceans, the direction of the prevailing winds never shifts for long. The ambitious navigator's choice is bleak: to risk a voyage with a following wind, taking you ever farther from home, with the prospect of never being able to return; or to sail against a headwind and probably never get far. In consequence, shipping crossed and re-crossed the monsoonal seas of the Indian Ocean and maritime Asia for

Navigator. The Florentine adventurer, Amerigo Vespucci (1451–1512), presides triumphantly over this world map of 1507. The map's maker, Martin Waldseemüller, considered Vespucci as the equal of the greatest cosmographers of antiquity, and shows him here wielding a huge pair of mapmakers's dividers, alongside a map of the lands Waldseemüller called "America" in Amerigo's honor. Yet Vespucci's reputation as a navigator and explorer rested entirely on his own say-so. He campaigned for "scientific" navigation—using instruments to sail his ships, rather than relying on tradition and practical knowledge—but used instruments incompetently. He often promised to make maps of the lands he encountered in his voyages but never seems to have done so.

"As explorers cracked the wind codes of the world's oceans, previously inconceivable interconnections became possible: directly between Europe and the Indian Ocean; between America and Asia; or among Europe, Africa, and the Americas."

centuries, creating dynamic economies and generating enormous wealth, before the Atlantic or Pacific was developed as a major trading space. In the sixteenth century, however, the monopoly of the Indian Ocean ended. With the discovery of the Gulf Stream in 1513, the last major element of the wind and current system of the Atlantic became known to navigators. Thereafter, the principal routes of trade from Europe to Africa and the Americas and back were established in the form that has remained normal for seaborne commerce to the present day: outward bound with easterly trade winds, toward the Caribbean and the central zones of the Americas, then northward with the Gulf Stream to the region of westerlies that bring ships back to Europe. In the Pacific in the 1520s and 1530s, Spanish navigators explored the easterly wind corridors that link the New World to Asia, but the route back long eluded explorers. After many unsuccessful attempts to find it, an expedition of 1564–1565 solved the problem by exploiting the way the winds circulate in the northern Pacific, using the Japan Current to get back to the west coast of America from the Philippines. Finally, in the early seventeenth century, Dutch sailors began to exploit fierce westerly winds that enable sailing ships to circle the globe around 40 degrees latitude south. This made it possible to link the commerce of the Atlantic, Pacific, and Indian oceans with new speed and reliability. In particular, the Dutch opened a fast new route between Europe and the East Indies, sailing nonstop, if necessary—or with a stop or two at the island of St. Helena in the middle of the South Atlantic and at the Cape of Good Hope on the southern tip of Africa—all the way from Holland to Java in what is today Indonesia. The speediest method was to bypass the Indian Ocean to the south with the westerlies, then turn north with the Great Australia Current, skirting the coast of western Australia, and heading directly for the Sunda Strait toward the East Indies (see Map 16.1).

As explorers cracked the wind codes of the world's oceans, previously inconceivable interconnections became possible: directly between Europe and the Indian Ocean; between America and Asia; or among Europe, Africa, and the Americas.

Making Connections | LAND EMPIRES AND MARITIME EMPIRES COMPARED

TYPE OF EMPIRE	CHARACTERISTICS
Maritime	Control of international trade via strategic seizure of suitable ports, control of sea-lanes
	Colonization of limited coastal territory
	Production and shipment of high-value commodities
	Limited military confrontation and investment in imperial colonies
	Exploitation of improved maritime technology
	Expanded use of sea charts for exploration, control of far-flung regions
	Dependence on native collaborators
Land	Emphasis on control of large amounts of people and land
	Large military investment required to staff outposts and fund armies
	Land and sea access routes vulnerable unless controlled
	Massive capital investment to support imperial colonies and build infrastructure
	Superior technology needed to overcome resistance from natives
	Expanded social and cultural contacts with imperial subjects
	Dependence on native collaborators

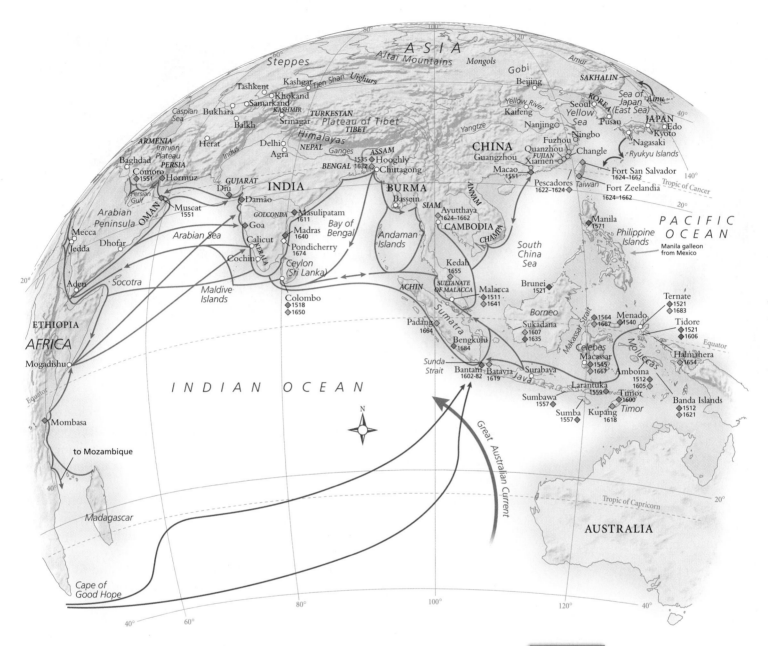

MAP 16.1

Maritime Imperialism in the Indian and Pacific Oceans, 1500–1700

◆ Portuguese trading post with date

◇ Dutch trading post with date

◆ Spanish trading post with date

◇ English trading post with date

○ major Chinese port

→ Japanese campaigns in Korea, 1592–1598

→ Japanese expansion

→ trade routes

→ Manila galleon from Mexico

→ Dutch route to the East Indies

→ Great Australian Current

The Portuguese Example

On an unprecedented scale, Europeans could now gain access to the commerce of the Indian Ocean and maritime Asia. The main motive was simple. The economies of the region were hugely richer and more productive than those of Europe. Anyone who could get ships into the region and carry some of its trade could make money here. Moreover, the region produced luxury manufactures of a quality Europeans could not produce for themselves: textiles, especially, from India and China, and increasingly, as time went on and trade developed, porcelain from China and Japan. Even more important were the foodstuffs, drugs, and spices that only grew in environments that could not be reproduced in Europe, and that were expensive because they were as much in demand in China as in Europe. Pepper dominated the spice trade because cuisine at the time in both Europe and China privileged it as a flavor and because—with other spices—it was much used in pickling processes that, along with drying and salting, were for a long time the only

ways to preserve food. Finally, eastern seas attracted European traders because their markets were highly exploitable. Gold was relatively cheap, in exchange for silver, in China, but relatively expensive in India. Canny traders could make fortunes out of the difference.

Portugal was well placed to take advantage, partly thanks to a position on the Atlantic edge, close to the place from which the trade winds spring. After dividing up zones of navigation by agreement with their Spanish neighbors, the Portuguese began to penetrate the Indian Ocean. Portuguese venturers opened direct trade with the pepper-growing region of southern India in 1500 and founded a coastal trading post nearby at Goa in 1510. They established direct access to the trading world of the islands off Southeast Asia within a few years more. They began direct contact with Thailand and China in the second decade of the sixteenth century and with Japan in the 1540s.

In some ways, the Portuguese enterprise in Asia was a classic case of maritime imperialism. Portuguese took over Malacca in modern Malaysia to try to gain an advantage in directing trade through the Strait of Malacca. They used force to compel unwilling partners to trade with them, especially in the "Spice Islands" of what is now eastern Indonesia, where low-bulk, high-value goods, such as cloves and the products of nutmeg and sandalwood and other aromatic woods were obtainable. They attacked rival shipping to damage other people's trade. They established expensive bases at the mouth of the Red Sea, on the coast of East Africa, and in the Persian Gulf—and, eventually, even on the Persian coast—in unsuccessful efforts to divert trade into their own hands and to strangle alternative routes. In 1529,

Chronology: Maritime Imperialism: Technology and Sea Routes

1513	Gulf Stream discovered
1520s–1530s	Spanish navigators explore easterly wind corridors that link the New World to Asia
1564–1565	Northern Pacific route between Asia and New World discovered
1584	Philip II of Spain offers prize for solving problem of longitude at sea
Early seventeenth century	Dutch use westerlies to circumnavigate globe

The Portuguese in India. "Unmarried Christian ladies" of contrasting complexions, with their chaperone watching from her palanquin, exchange courtesies with a gentleman in sixteenth-century Portuguese India.

they agreed with Spain to extend to the Pacific the system they had already agreed to observe in the Atlantic, in which each guaranteed the other's monopoly over selected routes, while denying access to the shipping of other powers. In effect, they divided between them seaborne routes to the non-European world. In the early seventeenth century, Portugal tried to control by force the trade of Sri Lanka—the world's main source of cinnamon (see Map 16.1).

Still, Portuguese imperialism was, by the standards of native Asian empires of the day, a feeble and shallow affair—a minor irritant, causing only local or temporary disruption. Portugal was a small country, with only 1.5 million inhabitants and few natural resources, except large salt pans and privileged access to the sea. It was poorer and less populous even than the Netherlands.

The main business of the Portuguese was to participate as shippers and traders in the existing commerce of Asia, along traditional routes. Direct trade with Europe was not significant for Asia, but was important for Europe; and it grew throughout the period. Three or four Portuguese ships a year carried the whole of the Indian pepper trade to Europe in the 1590s. In the 1680s and 1690s, when other European trading communities had joined in the business, 800 ships left Europe for Asia, most of them destined to return with Asian goods. But direct dealing with Europe was only a secondary element in the lives of most Portuguese in Asia. Most of Asia's Portuguese, indeed, lived beyond areas of Portuguese rule, as servants, mercenaries, technicians, missionaries, or commercial agents in Asian states. They were welcome, because their trading activities and their work as shippers in established trades contributed to the further enrichment of existing economies.

Francisco Vieira da Figueiredo was a representative figure. Like many poor Portuguese soldiers in the east, he resorted to trade to make a living. He was a chameleon who moved with ease through the various colorful islands between the Indian Ocean and the South China Sea. He served in 1642 as the envoy to

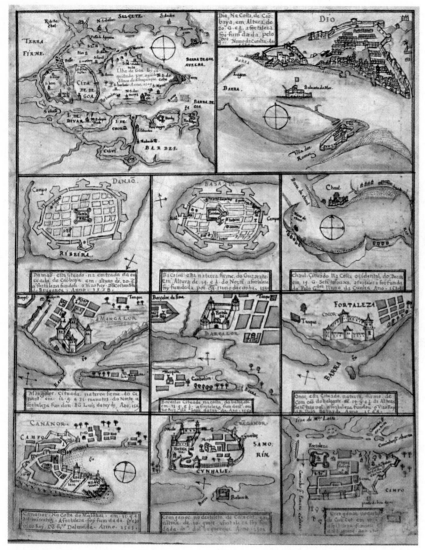

The *Estado da India*. The empire that the Portuguese called the *Estado da India* was actually a string of trading posts around the edges of the Indian Ocean and East Asia. The outposts depicted here were in India in 1630, shortly before Portugal began to withdraw from most of the region in the face of native hostility and Dutch competition. Note how lightly fortified most of these places are and how several of them include mosques—sometimes within, sometimes outside the walls. Like other European overseas expansion, that of Portugal depended on native people's willingness to collaborate with it and tolerate it.

Cambodia of a Spanish governor of Manila. He dealt with the Dutch East India Company, even when they were at war with Portugal. He became the intimate adviser of the sultan of Makassar in what is today Indonesia, the envoy of the ruler of Golconda in India, and a commercial agent for both of them. His object, according to English competitors, was "gain of wealth." Though he often talked of returning to Portugal, he was in his element in the east, where he could affect gentlemanly rank and presume on princely friends. His life was adapted for mobility. In Makassar, like other foreigners, he was forbidden to build a permanent residence. So he lived in a bamboo shack. But his real palace was his magnificently appointed yacht. As a trader, his first interest was in textiles from Coromandel in southeast India. He then specialized in aromatic woods from Indonesian islands, gold and silver from Sumatra and the Philippines, and cloves from the Molucca Islands, which were the chief item of Makassar's trade. In 1664, when the Dutch forced him out of Makassar, he went to the island of Timor and dealt in sandalwood until his death three years later.

Typically, the Portuguese blended into local society as well as local politics and regional trade by marrying or living with local women, who supported their husbands' business. Schemes to promote the supply of "eligible maidens" from Europe for Europeans living in the east were frequently launched and usually failed, or they supplied women of dubious background and morals. African or Indian wives administered their Portuguese husbands' estates while the latter were away on trading voyages. According to an English male visitor, wives acquired in the Portuguese East African possession of Mozambique excelled European women for "fidelity, behaviour to their husband, good-natured dispositions and agreeable conversation, so far as their little knowledge extends." Moralists accused some Portuguese in Goa and Bassein in Burma (today called Myanmar) of large-scale pimping, training dancing girls in their personal harems, and selling them as Hindu-temple prostitutes. The usual pattern, however, more resembled a scene engraved on a famous ivory casket from seventeenth-century Sri Lanka in which a Portuguese merchant or soldier and his Sri Lankan wife share a luxurious table of local dishes. Such marriages could be mutually beneficial. The merchant got access to valuable commercial contacts, whereas his bride acquired substantial rights to share the profits of his business under Portuguese law. Her family was often rewarded with offices in Portuguese firms or trading posts.

Until well into the second half of the seventeenth century, most European involvement in Asia was of the same sort—what some historians have called "trading-post empires." Aspiring monopolists conducted direct trades with

Europe, chiefly in spices, principally pepper. These monopolists were the Portuguese crown, and, from about the turn of the seventeenth century, English and Dutch companies. A similar trade with the New World, chiefly in Chinese silks and porcelain, traveled annually in a single Spanish galleon via Spain's colonial outpost in Manila in the Philippines. But European participation in commerce between Asian countries and in shipping ventures within Asian waters eclipsed these trades in value and extent.

Asian Examples

To understand the increased opportunities for Europeans, we need to look at the context of the enormously increased activity—as merchants, colonists, and even, occasionally, maritime imperialists—of native Asian states and communities. At either end of maritime Asia—in Japan in the east and in Oman on the coast of Arabia and the Ottoman Empire in the west—were rulers and adventurers interested in maritime imperialism (see Map 16.1).

Toyotomi Hideyoshi, the warlord who took over Japan at the end of a long era of civil war in 1585, is a case in point. He sent demands for submission to the kingdoms of Southeast Asia and to the Spanish governor in the Philippines. He vowed to ravish China "like a maiden" and "crush it like an egg." He proclaimed himself the gods' choice for mastery of the world. It sounds insane. But it was a rational strategy in the circumstances. The civil wars had militarized Japanese society. Professional warriors needed employment. Arms industries needed markets. Warlords' energies had to be redeployed. Japanese pirates had shown how vulnerable China was, sucking wealth into Japan, raiding Chinese cities far inland, and holding them to ransom.

Hideyoshi imagined his future conquests vividly. The Koreans and Chinese would "learn Japanese customs." Kidnapped children were taught Japanese. The land of China would be split among Japanese notables, and the Japanese emperor would be invested with the mandate of heaven. At first when the Japanese invaded in 1592, Korea, enfeebled by two centuries of peace, seemed easily conquerable. But the Korean navy had long experience of conflict against pirates and was equipped with startling new technology: "turtle ships" with reinforced hulls and ship-killing cannon. In combination with the typhoon-lashed seas and in collaboration with the Chinese fleet, the Korean sailors made it impossible for the Japanese to supply and reinforce their armies in Korea. Shortly after Hideyoshi's death in September 1598, the Japanese aborted their campaigns on the mainland of Asia.

It was not, however, the end of Japanese expansion. Okinawa and the Ryukyu Islands south of Japan became, in effect, a Japanese dependency by conquest in 1609. The northern land frontier of Japan gradually expanded to fill the whole of what we now think of as the Japanese home islands, at the expense of the native Ainu people, during the rest of the seventeenth century (see Chapter 19). And in the eighteenth century, Japanese expansion met that of Russia in the northern Pacific, where the two powers disputed control of the huge but barren and fog-bound island of Sakhalin. Meanwhile, although the Japanese state formally renounced southward expansion and, from the 1630s, practically forbade its subjects to travel overseas, illegal migrants and "pirates" continued to pour out of the country to take part in the new economic opportunities trade and colonization opened up in Southeast Asia. Some were Christians, fleeing from persecution after the definitive abolition of religious

> *"At either end of maritime Asia—in Japan in the east and in Oman on the coast of Arabia and the Ottoman Empire in the west—were rulers and adventurers interested in maritime imperialism."*

"Red Seal" ship. From 1592, the shogun Hideyoshi licensed foreign trading ventures by Japanese ships under the "Red Seal." Until the abolition of the trade in the 1630s, about ten voyages a year took handicrafts, copper, silver, and foodstuffs from Japan mainly to the Portuguese settlement of Macao on the coast of China, Vietnam, Thailand, and the Philippines in exchange for silk. This silk scroll of about 1630 shows Vietnamese galleys towing one of these "Red Seal ships" into a river mouth. The umbrellas indicate the market in front of the Japanese quarter. The three long houses across the river represent the Chinese quarter.

tolerance in Japan in 1639, like the community whom a Portuguese missionary met in mid-seventeenth century Burma—close-knit, hungry for the sacraments, longing to build a church. Most Japanese migration, however, was, like that of the Chinese, economically motivated. Many letters home survive, showing that the Japanese authorities were only half-hearted in suppressing the migrants' movements and content to allow them to send money home to enrich the domestic economy.

Frontiers affected cultures by changing individual lives. In the Rijksmuseum in Amsterdam, a painting of 1644 depicts the family of the rich Dutch merchant, Pieter Cnoll. His wife, Cornelia, is a beauty in an unmistakably Japanese style—daughter and fabulously wealthy heiress of one of the first officials of the Dutch East India Company and of his Japanese concubine. She called Holland "the fatherland" and corresponded with relatives in Japan. Later, she was to be a formidable businesswoman in her own right, administering her fortune after her husband's death. Then she became the tragic heroine of one of the most protracted and expensive legal cases of the seventeenth century, in her efforts to get a divorce from her grasping, tyrannical, abusive, and exploitative second husband, and to defend her fortune against him. In the background of the portrait, stealing an apple, stands her handsome Malay slave, Untung. His future would include leading a guerrilla band of runaway slaves in the backlands of Batavia, capital of the Dutch East Indies (at what is now Jakarta in Indonesia). He became king of a realm he carved out for himself in the interior of Java. Cornelia's is hardly a typical story of the overseas Japanese, but it demonstrates the fantastic range of unprecedented experiences that the empires of the time made possible.

Even greater was the outpouring of colonists from China. In many colonial outposts, in the Spanish colony of Manila, for example, though the nominal authority, the garrisons, and the guns were European—or, at least, under European officers—the real colonists, who settled the towns in large numbers and exploited the economy on a grand scale, were Chinese. Without a metropolitan government of their own committed to overseas imperialism, the migrants used Western empire builders to protect and promote their own activities.

Batavia, for example, bore the old Roman name for Holland. Its founder in 1619 was a Dutch soldier, Jan Pieterszoon Coen. Its sovereign proprietors were the

The Dutch merchant Pieter Cnoll painted in 1644 by Jacob Coeman. At one level, this seems an ordinary scene: a rich colonial trader with his elegant family and the trappings of his wealth. But the slave stealing an apple went on to become a famous bandit chief, while Cornelia, Cnoll's half-Japanese wife, became, after Cnoll's death, the richest businesswoman in the Dutch East Indies and the notorious protagonist of an agonizingly long and expensive divorce case against her second husband.

directors of the Dutch East India Company, which had a government-granted monopoly on trade between Holland and Asia. But the entrepreneurs who created its economy and attracted settlers to it in its great days were Coen's two principal Chinese collaborators: Souw Beng Kong, known as Bencon—the godfather figure of the Chinese community—and the energetic labor broker whom the Dutch called Jan Con. Lanterns inscribed, "The Original Founder of the Region" flanked the entrance to Bencon's country house. In Chinese eyes, the Dutch role was subordinate. Jan Con, who arrived from China in 1619 or 1620, rose to prominence by farming coconuts and collecting the town's taxes on gambling and cattle raising. His main business was importing labor from China, hiring Chinese laborers from Fujian (foo-jee-ehn) in southern China on annual contracts to work on canals and fortifications. He diversified into the hinterland, starting a sugar plantation and harvesting lumber. He opened salt pans and minted lead coins—giving Batavia a brief and rickety boom in the 1630s. But poor sugar yields and high salt-production costs ruined him—combined with English competitors' devastating policy of dumping lead coins in Batavia. He died, broke, in 1639. The Dutch never fully trusted Chinese businessmen again. But the Chinese character of the colony became even more marked after 1684, when the Chinese government relaxed controls on emigration. Thousands of Chinese residents enriched China by sending money home—like Jan Con himself, who never ceased to feel guilty for deserting his parents' home. Chinese shipping in Batavia's harbor normally outnumbered that of any other country by at least two and a half to one.

Overwhelmingly, the migrants were what we would now call economic refugees—escapees from poverty and contempt at home. In 1603, when the first of a long series of hate riots provoked a massacre of the local Chinese by native Filipinos in Manila, the emperor of China refused to intervene on the grounds that his murdered subjects were "scum, ungrateful to China, their land, their parents and ancestors for they had failed to return to China for so many years that such people were deemed to be of little worth." Yet the Chinese colony in the Philippines kept growing. By 1621, it had regained its premassacre level of 15,000, and it had more than doubled by the time of the next massacre in 1639.

Chinese and Japanese participated in empires—chiefly in the seventeenth century and increasingly as it went on as colonists, because their home governments, in attempts to control trade, restricted their commercial opportunities. Most merchants who operated in maritime Asia and the Indian Ocean therefore tended to come from other parts of Asia—especially from India and Armenia—and, to a limited but growing extent, from Europe. The most important single source of long-range commercial enterprise was Gujarat, in northern India. Gujaratis linked maritime trade with that of the Armenian and Indian traders dispersed throughout Central Asia and Persia. They were the biggest operators in banking as well as in commerce in the Arabian Sea. Sometimes the same individuals engaged in both types of business. Virji Vora, reputedly the richest man in the world in the early seventeenth century, was the biggest creditor of European merchants in India. He was a capitalist in the truest sense of the word, ever reinvesting his profits in commercial enterprise, so that looters who attacked his house were disappointed not to find great riches there. At times, European merchants felt oppressed by Gujarati power in key markets. In 1692, for instance, the Dutch East India Company had to sell a large cargo of nutmeg, cloves, and mace at half price to a Gujarati broker, because the company's representatives feared the power of another Gujarati—Muhammad Sahid, who was trying to control the market and was willing to undercut any competitor.

Capitalism—contrary to the traditional assumptions of Western historians—was not a European specialty. Nor—contrary to assertions still regularly made in old-fashioned history books—was it peculiar to any religious tradition. In 1904, Max Weber, one of the most influential sociologists ever, first proposed the idea that religion predisposes some communities to particular kinds of economic behavior. But in most cases, the theory does not seem to work. Jains, Christians, and Muslims were all prominent in Gujarat's trading community. In some places, despite the common belief that Hinduism generally regards commerce as a polluting and demeaning activity, even Hindus could engage in capi-

Gujerati merchant. Though most merchants in sixteenth-century Gujarat were Jains or Muslims, the Portuguese annotator of this sketch from the port city of Cambay (now officially called Khambat) calls the subject a banian—a term Europeans adopted from various languages of Sanskritic origins, usually to mean a Hindu merchant, money-changer, or loan agent. Hindus could engage in commercial occupations at the time with little danger of loss of caste, and some of them were among the richest operators in the Indian Ocean. The woman's provocative attire, make-up, jewelry, and gesture—offering the merchant an apparently symbolic flower—and the fact that the man reciprocates with a bulging purse of money leave no doubt that the scene is of prostitution. Western writers on India in the late middle ages and early modern period rarely omit references to the glamour, luxury, and abundance of brothels, and the charms of the prostitutes.

talism without losing caste. Hindus dominated the trade of Goa, although nominally this was a Portuguese-controlled city. In an auction in 1630, for instance, the local Hindu merchants numbered nearly half of the bidders and outbid their Portuguese counterparts and the government itself for about half of what was on offer. In seventeenth-century Kerala, south of Goa, most bankers were Brahmins—Hindus of the highest caste—who, according to Dutch complaints "by and large control the pepper trade."

The Dutch Connection

For over 100 years, from their arrival in the Indian Ocean in 1498, the Portuguese fitted into this Asian-dominated world without provoking seriously disruptive conflicts. At first, Spaniards were their only European rivals, and the Portuguese came to a series of advantageous arrangements with them. Gradually, however, from roughly the 1620s, the situation changed. Asian hosts lost patience with the presence of sovereign ports and offshore trading establishments, where Portuguese religious intolerance damaged trade by discriminating against Muslim and Hindu merchants. As Asian empires expanded or grew in power, or became more assertive, they eliminated key Portuguese outposts. Even after the capture of the mainland forts of which Jeronimo de Quadros was a commander, Portuguese occupation of the offshore trading post of Hormuz was tolerated until 1622, when the Portuguese were expelled from the Persian Gulf. A series of similar expulsions followed: from Hooghly—their fort in Bengal—in 1632, from Ethiopia in 1634, and from Japan in 1639. From 1640, their own attitude to their Asian interests changed. Portugal became involved in a long and destructive war against Spain that deflected Portuguese resources from the east. Atlantic priorities took over, as Portugal's Brazilian sugar plantations became increasingly profitable and the transatlantic slave trade boomed (see Chapter 20).

One reason Asian communities could become more selective about their partnerships with the Portuguese was that far more European buyers and shippers were now operating in maritime Asia. English, French, and Scandinavians all played increasing roles in the seventeenth century, but the contribution of the Dutch eclipsed them all.

The provinces of Holland and Zeeland, in what is today the Netherlands, were, like Portugal, poor communities, with relatively unproductive hinterlands, on Western Europe's ocean edge. Their people had a longstanding maritime vocation as fishermen, whalers, and shippers in northern seas, particularly in the lucrative trade in timber and dried fish with the Baltic.

In the late sixteenth century, merchants from the Netherlands broke into the trading world of the Mediterranean. In part they were driven by necessities arising from their rebellion against their ruler—who, by a series of dynastic accidents, happened also to be king of Spain. In part, too, a civil war drove them in which they were pitted against the neighboring provinces to their south in what is today Belgium. Netherlanders' contact with long-distance trade began because the Portuguese used Antwerp in the southern Netherlands as the clearing house for distributing Asian spices into northern Europe. During the war, many merchants from Antwerp migrated north to escape Spanish control. The commercial center of gravity in the Low Countries shifted with them to Holland. Meanwhile, in 1580, the king of Spain also succeeded by hereditary right to the throne of Portugal. This made Portuguese ships and possessions, potentially, fair game in the eyes of Dutch rebels.

"One reason Asian communities could become more selective about their partnerships with the Portuguese was that far more European buyers and shippers were now operating in maritime Asia."

The Netherlands. Although the Netherlands were divided into 17 provinces, all determined to preserve their own separate institutions and ways of life, the inhabitants long had a sense of common identity. This map of 1550 expresses that unity by depicting the provinces as "the Belgian lion"—which was already a traditional image—strong and warlike, clawing and snapping at Germany across the Rhine, lashing the North Sea with its tail. But it also hints at the cultural differences that divided the provinces from each other by showing how the traditional dress of Holland and Belgium, shown on the right, was different from that of the province of Frisia, shown on the left. From the 1560s to 1648, religious and political conflicts heightened the differences between the northern and southern provinces of the Netherlands and shattered their sense of unity. In consequence, two separate states emerged: a Protestant-ruled republic took shape in the seven northern provinces, while the rest of the Netherlands, which eventually became modern Belgium, remained loyal to the Catholic Habsburg dynasty.

In the 1590s, Jan van Linschoten, a Dutch servant of the Portuguese archbishop of Goa, explored the prospects of extending Dutch business into the Indian Ocean. The publication of his findings ignited a craze. In 1602, after three years of hectically free competition, leading merchants of the port of Amsterdam, who largely controlled government in the province of Holland, formed a **joint-stock company** to exploit, as a monopoly, the opportunities of trade with Asia.

Historians have generally supposed that such private limited companies were more efficient than the state monopolies by which Portugal and Spain attempted to regulate long-range trade. But the English, whose system was similar to that of the Dutch, were by comparison seriously undercapitalized and could make only a modest success of it. More important for outstripping other European trading ventures was the new outward route to the East Indies, which the Dutch began to explore in the second decade of the seventeenth century.

Even at its height, Holland's would-be monopoly of the rarer spices—cloves, nutmeg, cinnamon, and mace—was a leaky vessel. Dutch shipping never accounted for more than a seventh of the total involved in carrying the trade in these products. The Dutch never got control of pepper, which, in the seventeenth century, accounted for about 70 percent of the spice trade by value and even more by volume. Pepper demand and production grew constantly throughout the century, steadily increasing the sum of global commerce and supplying many traditional routes and handlers.

Nevertheless, the Dutch did establish a clearly dominant position as carriers of Europe's Asian trade in the seventeenth century, effectively replacing the Portuguese while keeping well ahead of other European rivals in all theaters and—in combination with political instability in Central Asia—helping to deflect trade from the Silk Roads. Four reasons underpinned Dutch success: the speed and efficiency of their route; the problems that harassed so much of the Portuguese seaborne empire in the east as some indigenous states transferred their favor to the Dutch; the selectively aggressive policies that, as we shall see, gradually brought the Dutch control of more—and more valuable—production of Asian communities than any European rivals; and above all, the privileged position they established in trade with Japan.

Overwhelmingly, the most valuable of the trading enterprises of maritime Asia led to Japan, because Japan was the world's leading producer of silver. Silver was relatively cheap in Japan. Merchants who took goods there, or performed services for Japanese businesses or rulers, could exchange it on favorable terms for profitable trade goods elsewhere. They used Japanese silver to buy pepper and cotton textiles in India and aromatic woods and spices from Indonesia. In China they acquired silks, porcelain, and rhubarb, which was prized as a laxative in Western medicine at this time. Increasingly they bought tea, which grew in importance as time went on and tastes spread, along with other aspects of culture, along new trade routes. Injections of Japanese silver supplied more cash for the world's markets, stimulating economic activity.

Chinese view of the Dutch. Jingdezhen, on the south bank of the Yangtze River, eclipsed other centers of porcelain production in China, for quality and quantity, from the eleventh century until the eighteenth. Under the Qianlong emperor (r. 1735–1796), some 60 million pieces of porcelain a year were produced there. To a Jesuit visitor in 1712, Jingdezhen had so many furnaces that at night "one thinks the whole city is on fire." Some of the output was for export, especially to Holland, but these satirical figurines of Dutch merchants—now in a French museum—seem more likely to have appealed to Chinese collectors.
Reunion des Musees Nationaux/Art Resource

However, Japan's willingness to participate in the spreading web of economic interconnections came close to collapse in the 1630s. The main reason for this was the phenomenal success of Catholic missionaries, who had accompanied Portuguese and Spanish merchants in the country and made hundreds of thousands of converts. Fears that this alien religion would undermine traditional loyalties to the state provoked an official ban on Christianity in 1597 and led to the bloody martyrdom of Catholic clergy and converts until Christianity was driven underground in 1638–1639. From 1640, Dutch merchants were the only Europeans allowed in Japan—tolerated because they were willing to let their servants take part in an annual rite called "Trampling the Crucifix." Most of the Dutch merchants were Calvinists, Protestants who repudiated "graven images" such as crucifixes anyway as contrary to the Ten Commandments (see Chapter 18). The Japanese government channeled Dutch trade through an island off the port of Nagasaki and strictly monitored the merchants' contact with Japanese subjects for more than 200 years.

Yet, to be able to continue to trade in Japan at all was an enormous bonus. For the rest of the century—until other Europeans began to build up their trade in other parts of Asia to levels at which they could generate comparable earnings—the Dutch dominated the handling of all the most valuable products of China and Southeast Asia for European markets. The Netherlands—formerly a poor, cramped, beleaguered, divided, and marginal part of Europe—experienced a "Golden Age" of wealth, art, empire-building, and military and naval power. Dutch imperialists challenged the Spanish monarchy in parts of the New World. Taking advantage of changed Portuguese priorities, and of help from some expanding Asian powers, they drove the Portuguese out of Malacca in 1641, Sri Lanka in the 1650s, and from many places in India thereafter. They resisted Spanish and French attempts at conquest in the seventeenth century. Meanwhile, they drove the English out of the Spice Islands and defeated them in the seas around England itself. Eventually, in 1688–1699 the Dutch ruler, taking advantage of internal conflicts in Britain, invaded England and became its king by deposing his English father-in-law.

A further consequence of the growing wealth and power of the Dutch was growing ambition in empire-building in Asia. Increasingly, from the 1660s, they aimed to control not only trade in valuable commodities, but also their actual

The Fall of Makassar, June 12, 1660, painted by Frederik Woldemar. The capture of Makassar in what is today Indonesia was part of the Dutch campaign to build an empire in the East Indies. Makassar was an independent sultanate whose ruler was supported by the Portuguese, and the painting shows a Portuguese ship that the Dutch had already taken. While the guns in the sultan's palace exchange fire with the Dutch ships, native troops march to the sultan's aid. The neutral English trading post flies the flag of St. George. The decisive moment of the encounter came when a Dutch landing party seized the stronghold.

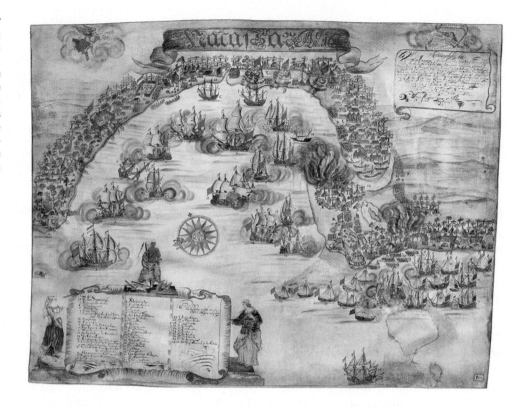

production. Refugees from Dutch aggression elsewhere poured into Makassar. Malays swelled its ships' crews. Moluccans brought their know-how in growing spices. Portuguese from Malacca introduced their long-range trading contacts. Makassar became their "second and better Malacca." According to a Dominican friar who visited in 1658, it was "one of the greatest emporia of Asia" with a ruler who collected European books and scientific instruments.

In the 1650s, the Dutch began a relentless war, first of coercion, then of conquest, in the East Indies. "Do you believe," sneered the sultan of Makassar, "that God has reserved for your trade alone islands which lie so far from your homeland?" The conquest took nearly 20 years. That of Bantam, on Java, with its big pepper output, followed in the early 1680s. Southeast Asia's age of trade was ending as native Asian cultivators abandoned cash crops, which had once enriched their cultivators but now seemed only to attract foreign predators.

The Dutch policy set a fateful example, as other European trading communities also undertook more aggressive policies. Europeans began to turn from maritime imperialism, based on control of trade, to territorial imperialism, which aimed to control production. At first their efforts were modest and unsuccessful. The Portuguese expanded outward from Goa and in the 1680s conquered the passes leading toward the Deccan, acquiring a subject population of about 30,000 people. The French crown, which had opened a permanent trading establishment at Pondicherry in southeast India in 1674, contemplated taking over Thailand but had to withdraw in humiliation. The English East India Company, founded in 1600, challenged the Mughal Empire in India to war, in an attempt to increase its share of trade, but was defeated in 1685–1688.

Chronology: European Maritime Imperialism in the Indian and Pacific Oceans, 1500–1700

1500	Portuguese begin direct trade with southern India
1510	Portuguese trading post at Goa established
1571	Spanish trading post of Manila founded
1600	English East India Company established
1602	Dutch East India Company founded
1619	Dutch found trading post of Batavia (Indonesia)
1620–1640	Portuguese expelled from trading posts in Persian Gulf and Indian Ocean
1640	Dutch merchants only Europeans allowed in Japan
1674	French establish trading post at Pondicherry (India)

Gradually, however, in the eighteenth century, Europeans would take more and more production under their own direct control, building up land empires in Asia that genuinely transformed the global economy. The profits Europeans made in Asian trade in the sixteenth and seventeenth centuries had modified Europe's age-old trading deficit with Asia in Europe's favor. Now it could be reversed, as Europeans not only influenced markets, but also manipulated production.

LAND EMPIRES: RUSSIA, CHINA, MUGHAL INDIA, AND THE OTTOMANS

The European land empires in Asia were, however, all modest affairs until well into the eighteenth century—with one exception. Russian imperialism gleams from the heavily gilded surface of a remarkable painting: the "Icon of the Hosts of the Heavenly King," made in the third quarter of the sixteenth century. Led by the biblical kings Solomon and David, Russians march across a fantastic landscape of mountains and rivers, from a city of infidels, ringed by fire, toward a shrine of the Virgin Mary. Heavenly hosts, ghostly cavalry, and the Christian founder-emperors of the Russian Orthodox tradition, Vladimir and Constantine (see Chapter 9), flank the earthly army. "Although the martyrs were born on earth," reads the commentary, "they succeeded in attaining the rank of angels." Two real leaps of Russian imperialism inspired this art. First, the conquest of Kazan in 1552 gave the **czars**—as the Russian ruler was styled in allusion to "Caesar"—command of the entire length of the Volga River, which was the great corridor of commerce at the western edge of Asia, and eliminated Russia's great rival for control of Siberia's fur trade. Furs summoned Russians to conquest and colonization, as gold lured Spaniards and spices captivated the Portuguese. The czars' next task was to conquer Siberia itself and control the production of furs as well as the trade in them (see Map 16.2). In 1555, Czar Ivan IV began to call himself Lord of Siberia. Three years later, he cut a deal with a big dynasty of fur dealers, the Stroganoffs, who were prepared to pay to turn that title into reality. The language of a chroniclers' account reflects the typical mind-set of European conquerors in new worlds: the assertion that pagans have no rights; that their lands are "empty"; that they are subhuman—bestial or monstrous; that financial privileges can promote colonization; and that the work is holy.

The Icon of the Hosts of the Heavenly King is one of the most spectacular works of Russian imperial propaganda of the sixteenth century. Mounted on a warhorse, the Archangel Michael leads a Russian army from the conquest of Kazan, shown in flames on the extreme right, into the presence of the Mother of God and her son. Constantine, the first Christian emperor, and Vladimir, Russia's first Christian ruler, carry banners.

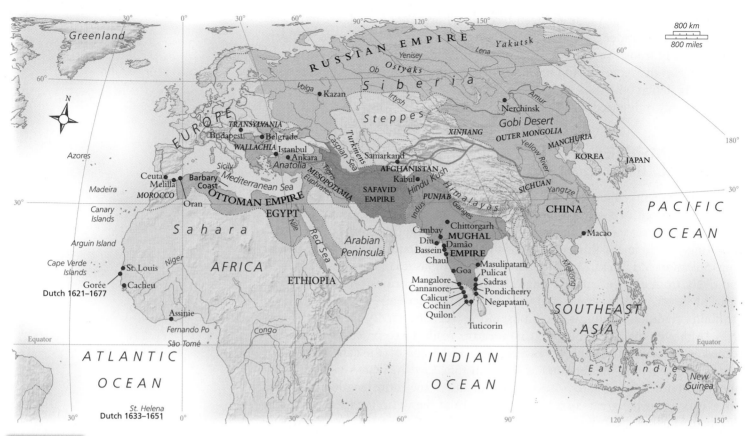

MAP 16.2

Eurasian Land Empires of the Sixteenth and Seventeenth Centuries

- Ottoman Empire
- China (Ming/Qing Empires)
- Russian Empire
- Mughal Empire
- Safavid Empire
- —— Silk Roads

Chronology: Russian Expansion Eastward

1552–1556	Russian conquest of Kazan
1555	Czar Ivan IV claims title of Lord of Siberia
ca. Late seventeenth century	Russian and Chinese expansion meet
1689	Treaty of Nerchinsk with China checks Russia's eastward expansion

From the 1570s, the "protection" of Russian armies "against the fighting men of Siberia" was proclaimed for native peoples who submitted and paid tribute in furs. Like other European military operations on remote frontiers, the Russians ascribed their success to technology: firearms mounted on river barges, from which the waterborne conquerors exchanged bullets for bowshots with defenders on the banks. The Siberian khan was said to be dismayed to hear that "when they shoot from their bows, then there is a flash of fire and a great smoke issues and there is a loud report like thunder in the sky. . . . and it is impossible to shield oneself from them by any trappings of war."

Native peoples were subjected to tribute and controlled by oaths of traditional, pagan kinds. One Siberian people, the Ostyaks, were made to swear on a bearskin on which a knife, an axe, and a loaf were spread. The oath breaker would choke to death or be cut to pieces in battle with men or bears. The Yakuts had to swear by passing between the quarters of a dismembered dog. The first object of the conquest, however, was not to vanquish these "savages" who ranged the pine forests and tundra but to eliminate the only state able to challenge Russia in the region: the Mongol khanate of Sibir, which dominated the eastern tributaries of the Irtysh River. Thus the conquest was sold as a Crusade and depicted symbolically by representations of gospel rays spread from the eyes of Christ between colonists' cities. Russians credited Khan Kuchum with a prophetic vision in October 1581: "The skies burst open and terrifying warriors with shining wings appeared. . . . They encircled Kuchum's army and cried to him, 'Depart from this land, you infidel son of the dark demon, Muhammad, because now it belongs to the Almighty.'"

China

By the late seventeenth century, Russian expansion in eastern Siberia met China's, which was preempting or pursuing Russian rivals in a war zone along the Amur River. The road that led here was kept smoother, according to a Jesuit visitor, "than Catholics in Europe keep the road on which the Sacrament is to be conveyed." The Treaty of Nerchinsk of 1689 formalized Chinese claims to vast unexplored lands of doubtful extent in northeast Asia, where some mapmakers imagined a huge land-mass pointing to or even joining America.

Much of this territory was effectively beyond any practical frontier of settle-ment. Generally, however, Chinese imperialism was of an intensive kind, compared with Russia's: dedicated not merely to economic exploitation and trade, but also to colonization and to spreading Chinese ways among native peoples. Before the end of the seventeenth century, Outer Mongolia had been crudely incorporated into the Chinese Empire, and more than 1.5 million settlers had been lured into Sichuan (seh-chwhan) in southern China by the promise of immunities from taxation. The Xinjiang (sheen-jeeahng) frontier in western China was peopled next, more thinly, by a mixture of enforced deportation and inducements to volun-tary settlers. By the end of the century, 200,000 Chinese migrants had settled there. Manchuria, homeland of the ruling dynasty, the Manchus or Qing (see Chapter 21), was normally closed to settlers, but its rich soils drew them unofficially in the hun-dreds of thousands, until the Chinese government was obliged to accept their pres-ence. Meanwhile, the people of Manchuria were progressively converted to Chinese ways. On all fronts, the pressure of intensive new settlement provoked a cycle of conflicts and solutions ominously familiar to students of European colonialism: tribal peoples reshuffled or penned in reservations; militarized agricultural colonies growing wheat, barley, peas, and maize (which had been introduced to Asia from the Americas; see Chapter 17), while keeping the natives in check. Schools were erected to spread Chinese language and values.

The Mughal Example in India

The Russian and Chinese empires practiced large-scale colonization, with attempts at new kinds of exploitation of conquered or resettled soil. That was to be the pattern of most new imperialism from this period onward. But there were still empires of what one might call an old-fashioned kind: conquest states that tended to leave the political, social, demographic, and economic structures of their conquests largely intact and to exploit them indirectly by levying tribute. The Mughal (the name means Mongol and refers to the ruling dynasty's supposed origins) Empire in India was the newest and fastest-growing empire of this type in the late sixteenth and seventeenth centuries. If we can trust its founder's mem-oirs, it began in a mood of distraction. Babur (1483–1530) was an adventurer from Central Asia, in the mold of his ancestor, Timur (see Chapter 15). In the volatile world west of the Hindu Kush, the rugged mountains that separate India from Afghanistan, he raised war bands and exchanged kingdoms with a rapidity of turnover unattainable elsewhere. His dream was to rebuild Timur's empire from the city of Samarkand in Central Asia, but after he had won and lost that city twice

"Generally, however, Chinese imperialism was of an intensive kind, compared with Russia's: dedicated not merely to economic exploitation and trade, but also to colonization and to spreading Chinese ways among native peoples."

The assault on Chittorgarh. The Mughal Emperor Akbar (r. 1556–1605) commissioned artists to record his campaigns. This painting shows a notable moment in his siege of the supposedly impregnable fortress of Chittorgarh. A tunnel mined by Akbar's engineers exploded, killing hundreds of his own men. When the fort fell, most of the defenders were massacred.

over, he turned to India. From 1519, conquering it became his obsession. India seduced him. He rebuked Afghan followers who claimed to prefer the Afghan capital of Kabul, where he had been "the sport of harsh poverty." After 1526, when he conquered Delhi in north India and made it his capital, he never left India, though he missed the "flavor of melons and grapes" of his Afghan home (see Map 16.2).

The state Babur founded remained small and unstable until the long rule of his grandson, Akbar (r. 1556–1605). The priorities of Akbar's empire emerge vividly from the account compiled by his friend and minister, Abul Fazl Allami, who begins by describing the emperor's jewel chest, then turns to the treasury, the coinage, the mints for gold and silver, the stupendous court cuisine with its gold-laced dishes, the emperor's writing room, his arsenal, his elephants, horses, cows, and camels. When he turns to what he considers the lesser aspects of government, he deals first with protocol, before insisting on a ruler's responsibilities for spiritual welfare; then come accounts of building projects, the army, revenue raising and rites (including hunting and games), lists of great nobles and court personalities.

In short, the Mughal Empire was like a business, run for profit—an investment in power and majesty, with rich returns in the form of tribute and taxes. The heartlands it ruled directly never extended much beyond the limits of Babur's conquests, in the Punjab and the Ganges valley in north India. Beyond this area, existing power structures and local rulers remained in place, supplying money and manpower for future conquests, and linked to the imperial court by every device of networking. The 800 wives Akbar assembled from the rulers who paid him tribute were, in effect, hostages and mediators of sometimes uneasy alliances. Religious tolerance was an essential ingredient of internal peace in an empire that straddled the Hindu and Muslim worlds.

The Mughal war machine was so big and costly that it was impossible to operate at a profit without the constant stream of victories that Akbar had his court artists commemorate in still ravishing, still terrifying miniature paintings. The most dramatic battle of his reign was the assault on Chittorgarh, the clifftop stronghold of a Hindu prince, in 1567–1568—recalled by a depiction of the deaths of hundreds on both sides in the accidental explosion of the mines that Akbar's engineers bored and burrowed into the cliff. Of the defending garrison of 8,000 and their 40,000 servants, 30,000 reputedly died in the last onslaught.

In some ways the Mughal Empire seems ramshackle, stumbling between victories, with no central institutions except the imperial court and army, no agreed rules of succession to the throne, and an elite divided by ethnic and religious differences and economic jealousies. The death or old age of every emperor triggered rebellion and civil war. Yet the frontier kept growing, reaching deep into south India by the time of Akbar's death in 1605, slowing during the half century that followed, and again advancing rapidly under the Emperor Aurangzeb (r. 1656–1707) to cover almost the entire subcontinent.

The Ottomans

West of India were states superficially similar to the Mughals, where Muslim rulers—the Safavid dynasty in Persia and the Ottomans, based in Turkey—dominated huge territories and diverse populations by mobilizing large armies equipped with up-to-date firepower. Historians call both of them empires, but the Safavids ruled a compact state, more or less corresponding to modern Iran and—not for want of trying—never managed permanently to annex much territory farther afield. Their story belongs in Chapter 19.

The Ottomans, by contrast, were among the most effective empire builders the world had ever known. What we have already seen of them (see Chapter 15) demonstrates that; what happened in the sixteenth and seventeenth centuries would confirm it. And although the areas they conquered had all been part of big empires before, the empire the Ottomans built up had no exact precedents. The diversity literally echoed around Lady Mary Wortley Montagu, an English ambassador's wife, in 1718, who heard her servants chatter in ten different languages. "I live," she went on, "in the perpetual hearing of this medley of sounds, which produces a very extraordinary effect upon the people that are born here. They learn all these languages at the same time and without knowing any of them well enough to write or read in it."

In the Ottoman world, boundless ambitions seemed possible. The Ottomans inherited three universalist traditions: one from their steppelander ancestors, whose aim was to make the limits of their empire match those of the sky; another from Islam, whose caliphs' legacy and title the Ottoman sultans claimed; and a third from ancient Rome, whose legacy they wrenched into their own grasp by conquering much former Roman imperial territory.

The Ottomans could afford to invest in strategies of conquest, because the sixteenth and seventeenth centuries were an era of prosperity in Turkey unprecedented at the time and unparalleled since. Their heartlands were in the Anatolian plateau. Beyond it, the Ottoman lands were grouped around three great waterways: the eastern Mediterranean, the Black Sea, and the twin rivers of Mesopotamia. Beyond what they called Rumelia, the westernmost of the provinces they ruled directly, lay a broad frontier zone that they controlled and that reached beyond Budapest in Hungary in Central Europe. In North Africa, beyond Egypt, the sultans enjoyed nominal allegiance, at least, from the principalities of the Barbary coast, as far west as what is now Algeria. They got control of most continental transit points between Asia and Europe: the western reaches of the Silk Roads, the Persian Gulf, the Red Sea, and the main ports of Egypt and the eastern Mediterranean seaboard. New trade routes from Europe to south and southeast Asia did not deflect existing trade from Ottoman territories. On the contrary, with improved communications and expanding demand, the total volume of the spice trade continued to grow, and more of this trade passed through Ottoman hands in the sixteenth century than ever before.

On the other hand, the Ottomans were, in some respects, disadvantageously placed. They had no outlets to the Atlantic or the Indian Ocean—or even to the western Mediterranean, except through narrow straits that enemies easily controlled. Wars frequently broke out on frontiers with permanently hostile neighbors—Persians in the east, Christians in the north and west. Armies shuttled back and forth across the empire in successive seasons to keep Europeans inhibited and Safavid Persians at bay. Beset, as the Ottomans were, by enemies on every side, their state needed extraordinary strength to survive. Only a state of extraordinary efficiency could expand.

Yet expand they did. They overran Egypt in 1517 and exploited it for huge annual tax surpluses that sustained campaigns elsewhere. The armies of Suleiman the Magnificent (r. 1520–1566) reached Belgrade in Serbia in the northwest Balkans in 1521 and the island of Rhodes in the Aegean in 1522. What

"The Ottomans could afford to invest in strategies of conquest, because the sixteenth and seventeenth centuries were an era of prosperity in Turkey unprecedented at the time and unparalleled since."

Ankara. The artist Jean-Baptiste Vanmour, who lived in Istanbul in the early eighteenth century, and helped to make Westerners familiar with images of the city and its people, also depicted other Turkish cities of the time, including this view of Ankara in Anatolia. Vanmour emphasized the aspects of commercial, domestic, and civic life that made the Ottoman Empire seem exotic to Western eyes.

began as a punitive expedition against Hungary in 1525 ended as the conquest of most of that country. Until Suleiman's death, the pace of conquest was enormous. He conquered Iraq from Persia and most of the shores of the Red Sea, while exerting more informal lordship over much of the rest of Arabia. Suleiman extended his rule over almost the whole southern shore of the Mediterranean, where his naval commanders, the Barbarossa brothers of Algiers, organized a seaborne empire of war galleys and pirate havens (see Map 16.2). In 1529, Suleiman was called from besieging Vienna in Austria to fight the Persians in Iraq, while a Turkish fleet raided the city of Valencia in Spain. During a single campaigning season in 1538, Ottoman forces conquered Moldavia in the northeast Balkans, besieged the Portuguese stronghold of Diu in India, and wrecked a Christian fleet off the shores of Greece. His court poet Baki hailed Suleiman as "the monarch with the crown of Alexander . . . the earth before his gate served as prayer mat for the world."

The pace of expansion was slower under Suleiman's successors, but not because the empire was running out of energy. Rather, it was because remoter conquests brought diminishing returns. The Ottoman naval effort—it is true—faltered: outgunned in the Indian Ocean by Portugal and in the central Mediterranean by Spain. But every generation brought a net gain of territory until the last years of the seventeenth century.

The degree of imperial authority could hardly be uniform in the outlying parts of so extensive an empire, but it was felt everywhere. The younger Barbarossa, who ruled the remotest outposts on the North African coast, was loosely called a king, even in Turkish accounts. He recruited ships and men with his own resources, won his victories by his own strength—so many of them that he sold Christian captives "at an onion a head." In Islamic North Africa, the sword carved the right to rule. Yet when Suleiman summoned him to Constantinople, Barbarossa did not hesitate to obey. The khans of Crimea in what is today Ukraine negotiated terms of pay—often in the form of captive slaves—for joining the sultans' campaigns and sometimes simply disobeyed the sultan. Turks garrisoned but did not directly rule Wallachia and Moldavia (in modern Romania). Transylvania, on the western edge of the empire, was a vassal state, with low taxes and a Christian prince whom its medieval parliament elected. In Arab lands, the sultans used religion as a source of legitimacy, but—with only sporadic displays of force to back it up—they found it hard to turn that legitimacy into effective allegiance. As we shall see in Chapter 19, even the parts of their empire that the sultans ruled directly were a patchwork of different methods and conventions of rule that were often hard to keep under close control.

Chronology: Mughals and Ottomans	
1517	Ottomans conquer Egypt
1519	Babur founds Mughal Empire
1520–1566	Reign of Ottoman sultan Suleiman the Magnificent
1526	Babur makes Delhi his capital
1529	Ottomans besiege Vienna
1656–1707	Aurangzeb extends Mughal Empire over most of Indian subcontinent

NEW LAND EMPIRES IN THE AMERICAS

Across the Atlantic, meanwhile, European imperialism led landward. Columbus (see Chapter 15) envisaged no more than a trading setup when he first saw what he thought was Japan, the Caribbean island of Hispaniola (modern Haiti and the Dominican Republic) in 1492, imagining a European merchant-colony under Spanish control, trading in cotton, mastic (a resin used to make varnish), and slaves. However, none of these products was available in large quantities in the Caribbean. Columbus based his initial hopes on the illusion that the riches of Asia lay only a short way farther west. But he had grossly underestimated the size of the world. Instead, therefore, the Spaniards had to focus on exploiting the gold mines of the island. Columbus's war of conquest in Hispaniola of 1495–1496 was—albeit on a small scale—the first step toward creating a Spanish territorial empire.

The settlement of more Caribbean islands and, between 1518 and 1546, the conquests of Mexico and Peru, confirmed this trend. As a result, Spaniards found themselves obeyed over huge tracts of the most densely populated territory in the Americas. Indeed, Spain—which was a relatively poor and underpopulated country—had acquired, within a few years, and in their entirety, two of the fastest-growing and most environmentally diverse empires of the age—those of the Aztecs and the Incas (see Chapter 15). This achievement was effected thousands of miles from home, with relatively primitive technology, few resources, and privately recruited bands of only a few hundred men (see Map 16.3).

How was it possible? In early colonial times, four explanations occurred to those who tried to make sense of the way the conquest had turned out. The clergy favored the view that the conquest was miraculous and providential—procured by God for his own purposes. The warriors who took part in successful expeditions, their heirs, and cronies explained it as the result of their own godlike prowess. But this was incredible and self-interested—an account designed to maximize rewards from a grateful crown. The Spaniards' Native American allies saw the overthrow of the Aztecs and Incas as their own work, with a little help from their Spanish friends. Illustrations in documents of the Tlaxcalteca (tlash-kahl-TEK-ah)—the most numerous and formidable of the Indian communities who joined the alliance against the Aztecs—show Native Americans in the vanguard of every attack and Spaniards, typically, bringing up the rear. Along with the Tlaxcalteca, the Huexotzinca (weh-hot-SEEN-kah), another people hostile to the Aztecs, claimed exemption from taxation in postconquest times on the grounds that the conquest had been mainly their own work.

Finally, according to early colonial analysts, the Native American empires were victims of their own shaky morale. Hernán Cortés (1485–1547), the adventurer who led the band that conquered Mexico, spread the claim that the Aztec Emperor

"Indeed, Spain—which was a relatively poor and underpopulated country—had acquired, within a few years, and in their entirety, two of the fastest-growing and most environmentally diverse empires of the age—those of the Aztecs and the Incas."

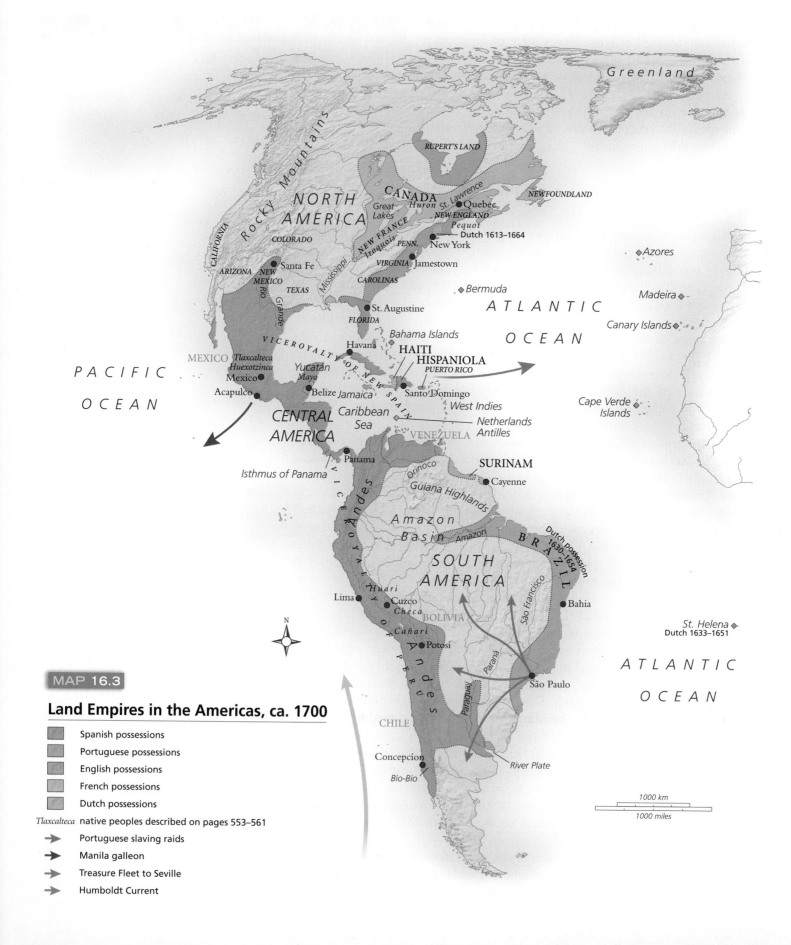

MAP 16.3

Land Empires in the Americas, ca. 1700

- ▬ Spanish possessions
- ▬ Portuguese possessions
- ▬ English possessions
- ▬ French possessions
- ▬ Dutch possessions

Tlaxcalteca native peoples described on pages 553–561

- → Portuguese slaving raids
- → Manila galleon
- → Treasure Fleet to Seville
- → Humboldt Current

Native conquistadores. The conquest of Michoacán was—apart from the capture of the Aztec capital of Tenochtitlán—the toughest and bloodiest episode of the Spanish conquest of Mexico. This account by the Spaniards' native allies, the Tlaxcalteca, made in the mid-sixteenth century, emphasizes the leading role played by Native American conquistadores. The Spaniards bring up the rear, though one of their dogs takes an enthusiastic role in the vanguard.

Moctezuma II (mok-teh-ZOO-ma) (r. 1502–1520) had surrendered power into his hands in the belief that Spanish supremacy was the fulfillment of a prophecy. This claim was almost certainly false, made up to head off awkward questions church-men and lawyers in Spain raised about whether the Spaniards had any right to rule in Mexico. In early colonial times, rumors spread that omens and signs from their gods had predisposed the Aztecs to surrender, or that they regarded the Spaniards as gods or the representatives of a departed god, destined to return as ruler. But these rumors were made up after the event, and the reported omens were bor-rowed from European books. The aggressive, confident, dynamic, and expanding Aztec state showed no signs of weak morale and resisted ferociously.

Yet similar stories were invoked to explain Spanish success elsewhere, too. To refer to Spaniards, the people of the Inca Empire used a term that was also the name of a god or legendary hero. So the notion that they mistook Spaniards for gods attracted people in that region, too. When the last independent Maya king-dom submitted to the Spanish monarchy in 1697, the priest who negotiated the surrender convinced himself that the Maya had yielded in supposed obedience to an ancient prophecy.

Historians have added other explanations. The technology gap is often assumed to have been instrumental in the conquests. And in some respects, Span-ish war technology was important. In 1521, in the final siege of the Aztec capital Tenochtitlán, Spanish-designed, gun-carrying ships patrolled the lake that sur-rounded the city. Spanish steel-edged weapons were probably more effective in dis-abling and killing enemy warriors than the blades made from volcanic glass native armorers used. Crossbows, as long as new bolts were available, could outperform Native American slings and bows. The importance of guns and horses, however, was probably slight. Horses are of limited value in mountain warfare and street

"It is worth bearing in mind that many—perhaps most—European successes were by-products of war among Native Americans themselves."

fighting—conditions in which some of the most critical episodes of the conquests occurred. It is hard to credit claims that the defenders were awestruck by these devices or inhibited by the belief that they were magical. Such claims were always linked with efforts to mock the natives' intellectual and rational powers. In practice, Native Americans quickly adapted to European styles of warfare and used horses and firearms, where these were effective, themselves.

As we shall see in the next chapter, disease was, in the long run, of enormous importance in weakening Native American resistance to European conquerors. It is more doubtful, however, whether it was decisive in the early stages of conquest. Maladies hard to identify, made worse by malnutrition, weakened and killed many of the defenders of the Aztec capital. By the time of the conquest of Peru in the 1530s, smallpox was devastating unimmunized populations. Spanish carriers unwittingly spread it wherever they went. Yet its effects cut both ways, harming the Spaniards' allies as least as much as their enemies, while still leaving formidable numbers of foes in the field. Spaniards themselves, after all, were also operating in unfamiliar and debilitating environments.

It is worth bearing in mind that many—perhaps most—European successes were by-products of war among Native Americans themselves. Some Maya communities identified more closely with the Spaniards than with their hated neighbors, exploiting Spanish help to settle feuds sometimes centuries old. The French in Canada in the next century were drawn into wars between different Iroquoian peoples. The Aztec and Inca worlds were full of conflict. Civil war wracked the Inca Empire when the Spaniards arrived. Most of its subject peoples resented Inca rule. The Huari (WAH-ree) nursed hateful memories of the Inca conquest. Only a few years before the Spaniards' arrival, the Inca had massacred thousands of recently conquered Cañari in an apparent attempt to terrorize them into obedience. Even some of the Incas' former allies had grown disenchanted. The Incas' demands for forced labor, which drove many workers hundreds of miles from their homes, were acutely resented. When the empire fell, tens of thousands of conscripted workers left their posts to return to their original communities.

The Aztecs' demands similarly alienated tributary peoples. The tribute system was both the strength and weakness of their state: strength, because it embodied their power to command resources from a vast area; weakness, because Tenochtitlán became dependent on tribute for basic necessities—the food and cotton the city could not produce for itself—and the luxuries from distant climates, needed to sustain the way of life of the elite: the ritual cacao and incense, the rubber for the ball game, the gold, the jade, the amber, the seashells, the exotic featherwork and ceremonial clothing. When the Spaniards' allies denied Tenochtitlán its tribute, they effectively starved the Aztec capital into submission.

The Spaniards' triumph was therefore less a battlefield victory than a diplomatic maneuver. In forming an alliance able to defy the Aztecs, the Spaniards enjoyed crucial advantages. The Aztecs at first treated the Spaniards' arrival as a diplomatic mission, rather than a hostile force, which gave the Spaniards time to make useful contacts in disaffected Native American communities. The Spaniards acquitted themselves so impressively in tests of battle that the Tlaxcalteca adopted them enthusiastically as allies and remained in alliance even after the Spaniards suffered a severe defeat at Aztec hands in 1520. The single most important ingredient in Spanish diplomatic success was probably their interpreter, whom they called Doña Marina. She was a native speaker of the main language of central Mexico and quickly learned Spanish. She was, at a crucial phase, the only person with the linguistic qualifications to mastermind negotiations. Tlaxcalan pictures of the conquest invariably show her center stage, mediating between Spaniards and Native Americans in peaceful scenes, and actually supervising military operations in depictions of war.

None of these explanations, however, really matches what happened in the Americas when Europeans arrived. For, usually, the transition to new kinds of European-led imperialism happened with little or no violence. Traditionally, historians have concentrated on conflicts between Europeans and their native "victims." Indeed, Spanish conquests in the New World have had a bloody reputation. Terror was a common tactic, not because the conquistadores were morally different from other warriors, but because they were subject to peculiarly intense strains of operating in hostile environments, often with little help of relief, surrounded by enemies whose cultures seemed savage and unintelligible. Yet considered from another aspect, the Spanish "conquest" seems remarkably peaceful. Most communities, especially within the regions previously subject to the Aztecs and Incas, offered the Spaniards little resistance or actively welcomed them, so eager were they to escape from their Native American overlords.

The Native American Doña Marina rather than the Spaniard Cortés directs the battle of Tenochtitlán in the Lienzo de Tlaxcala, a mid-sixteenth-century Native American portrayal of scenes from the conquest of Mexico. The same source also always shows Doña Marina center-stage negotiating alliances. Here she commands along the central causeway, where native warriors lead the attack against the Aztecs, and in the Spanish gunboat that native paddlers help propel across Lake Texcoco.

Even where no oppressive native empires existed, Native Americans were often surprisingly hospitable to European intruders, who usually seemed at first too few, vulnerable, and unused to local conditions to be much of a threat. Most European communities relied on native collaboration for food or allies, or both. Sexual alliances with native women of elite rank, especially in areas of Spanish and Portuguese operations, helped the newcomers to get established and, according to native custom in many areas, conferred on the host communities a duty to help with labor and food. Spanish friars were amazingly successful in making themselves useful as holy men, healers, arbiters of disputes, and protectors against secular exploiters. In short, the reception of Europeans owed much to a remarkably widespread feature of Native American cultures: what we might call the **stranger effect**—the tendency some peoples have to esteem and defer to strangers, whose usefulness as arbitrators of disputes, dispensers of justice, and preservers of peace, arises from the objectivity that their foreign origins confer.

Making the New Empires Work

By the end of the sixteenth century—before the French or English had established a single enduring colony anywhere in the Western Hemisphere—the Spanish monarchy in the New World effectively included all the biggest and most productive islands of the Caribbean and a continuous swathe of territory from the edge of the Colorado plateau in the north to the River Bío-Bío in southern Chile. It extended from sea to shining sea over the narrow reaches of the hemisphere, and along the Atlantic coast of what is now Venezuela, with a southerly corridor to the Atlantic, across what is now Bolivia, and along the Paraguay River and River Plate. In most areas that the Atlantic wind system made easily accessible from Europe, Spain had preempted potential rivals, except on the Brazilian coast, where, by agreement with Spain, Portugal had a series of sugar- and timber-producing

> *"The relatively late start other colonizers and would-be colonizers, in particular, the English and French monarchies, made was not the result of any inherent inferiority on their part. The best portions of the hemisphere were in other hands and only the dregs were left. It took a long time to find the will and ways to exploit them."*

colonies. The relatively late start other colonizers and would-be colonizers, in particular, the English and French monarchies, made was not the result of any inherent inferiority on their part. The best portions of the hemisphere were in other hands and only the dregs were left. It took a long time to find the will and ways to exploit them.

Unsurprisingly, therefore, in the Americas, the colonial societies of the north lived in awe of those of the south: envying their gold and silver, imitating their plantations and ranches, trying to rival their cities, coveting their territory but fearing their further expansion. English conquerors, for instance, aped those of Spain. In 1609, the first instructions to the colonists of Virginia—the first enduring English colony in North America—ordered them to maintain a pretense of divinity in dealing with the natives; and to conceal any white men's deaths to project an image of immortality. This was naive. Captain John Smith (1580–1631), the most dynamic leader of early Virginia, was a voracious reader with a storybook self-image. He claimed—in imitation of a story Columbus told about himself in Jamaica—to hold natives spellbound by his knowledge of the stars. Smith also applied methods apparently modeled on Cortés: using terror and massacre to keep natives cowed, and trying to exploit a special relationship with the natives' dominant chieftain to rule through him.

The Spanish Empire preempted European rivals in regions selected precisely because they were densely populated, with productive, established economies. In consequence, Spanish policy—rarely successful in practice—was always to preserve the Native American population. This was not the case in most other parts of the Americas, where the Indians were too few, too warlike, or too unaccustomed to large-scale production to meet the colonists' labor needs. In most colonies, once reliance on native charity was no longer necessary, Native Americans seemed at best a nuisance, unless they were needed to keep trade going (as in the parts of mainland America France nominally ruled).

Throughout British America, for instance, the native peoples were a source of conflict between frontiersmen and the representatives of the crown, who wanted the protection of Indian buffer states and the benefit of a relatively dense pool of white labor, which frontier conquests would disperse. For most colonial subjects, however, the Native Americans merely got in the way of land grabbing. Genocide was the best means to deal with them. In 1637, an explicit attempt to exterminate an entire Native American people—the New England Pequots—was half finished in a massacre on Mystic River in Connecticut, where, the governor reported, the victims could be seen "frying in the fire and the streams of blood quenching the same." The tribe's very name was banned. In defiance of official policy, a settler malcontent, Nathaniel Bacon, launched war in Virginia in 1675 with the explicit aim of destroying all Native Americans, friendly and hostile alike. This was a characteristic outrage in the late seventeenth century: a period of increasing tension—which also provoked violent clashes in areas of Spanish settlement in Florida and New Mexico—between growing colonies and threatened Native Americans. In terms of the sacrifice of life on both sides, the worst such episode was King Philip's War in New England in 1676. Launched by a Native American chief, who managed to put together an uncharacteristically big Indian coalition to stem white expansion, this resistance movement threatened to reverse the direction of extermination. The white presence was, for a few months, genuinely at risk, until Native American peoples from the interior who were willing to fight for the colonists restored the balance in the white man's favor. In areas of predominantly British

A CLOSER LOOK

The Meeting of Cortés and Moctezuma

Part of a series of canvases painted in Spain about 150 years after the fall of Mexico, The Meeting of Cortés and Moctezuma is a remarkable record of how the Spanish memorialized the conquest.

By the late seventeenth century, Spaniards in New Spain were so used to Chinese and Filipino textiles and imitations that they treated the patterns as indigenous.

For "creole" apologists, who defended the New World against jibes that America was inferior to Europe, the might and majesty of Popocatapetl were symbolic. (see p. 681)

In earlier, indigenous depictions, Doña Marina, Cortés's mistress and interpreter, occupies pride of place, receiving more honor than Cortés, who appears more or less as her assistant.

The lake-bound environment of pre-colonial Tenochtitlan is recalled, reflecting Spaniard's pride in "civilizing" the environment by smothering it with a great new city.

Spaniards who possessed armor probably did wear it to suit the sense of occasion associated with the encounter with Moctezuma. Usually, however, they preferred the native cotton armor, suited to the climate and altitude.

What does this painting say about the way the Spanish mythologized the conquest of Mexico?

The Pequot War. The capture of Fort Mystic in eastern Connecticut in May 1637 was the decisive event of the war of extermination waged by New England colonists in search of security against the Pequot people. Surprised by the ferocity of Native American resistance, the settlers burned the houses in which hundreds of Indian women and children were sheltering. This illustration, made just after the war, shows the settlers' opening volleys and the routes of their two-pronged attack.

colonization or "Anglo" rule, preconquest population levels for Native Americans have never really revived, outside the formerly Spanish-ruled Southwest of the United States.

In some places, Native Americans were useful as slaves. On the fringes of the Amazon jungles, slaving became a major industry for Portuguese based in the port of São Paulo in southern Brazil. The early economy of the Carolinas depended on the slave trade with Native Americans, who raided neighbors as far inland as the Mississippi River valley. In this part of the North American South, there were more Native American slaves than black slaves until the destructive nature of the trade led to its abandonment in the early eighteenth century.

Generally, however, the English colonies relied on imported labor—whether enslaved or not—and so could afford to massacre their Native Americans or drive them west. They had a ready-made ideology of extermination. They were the new Israel. The Native Americans were the "uncircumcized," to be dealt with as the biblical Israel dealt with its pagan enemies: smitten hip and thigh. The English, indifferent to clerical discipline, rarely endured Spanish-style agonies of conscience about the justice of their presence in America or the morality of their wars. People who left their land underexploited or unfenced deserved to lose it. Only the line of the fence or the marks of the plow proved true tenure. Native Americans in British areas of expansion were too poor to exploit for tribute. It was more economical to dispossess them and replace them with white farmers or black slaves. The only colony where this reasoning was modified was early Pennsylvania. Here moral and material considerations combined to favor a policy of friendly collaboration with the Native Americans. Thanks to the founder's Quaker high morality, supposedly just prices were paid for land purchases from the Indians, who were encouraged to stay on the frontier as buffers against hostile tribes or rival European empires.

Whether expelled, exterminated, diminished by disease, or absorbed into colonial society by marrying Europeans or adopting European ways, the Native Americans retreated to the margins of colonial life wherever European colonies were founded. European involvement in the affairs of the Western Hemisphere had begun—like European penetration of Asia—as a collaborative venture in which Native American communities and states were the newcomers' essential hosts and helpers. By the late seventeenth century, however, those relationships, almost everywhere in the Americas where European and Indian cultures confronted each other, had broken down in violence or simply been transformed as the Native American population fell. Unlike Asia, the New World was not an arena in which native and European states could coexist side by side—although, as we shall see, in the eighteenth and nineteenth centuries, short-lived attempts to found native states and empires revived beyond the frontiers of European settlement.

Chronology: Spanish and English Land Empires in the New World	
1492	Columbus arrives in Caribbean
1495–1496	Columbus begins war of conquest in Hispaniola
1518–1546	Spanish conquests of Mexico and Peru
1609	English found colony of Virginia
1675	Bacon's rebellion (Virginia)
1676	King Philip's War (New England)

In Perspective
The Global Balance of Trade

It is not generally realized that in the colonial New World precolonial patterns of exchange often remained intact. European merchants joined existing Native American trading communities, extending the reach or increasing the volume of traffic, enhancing what Indian Ocean venturers called **country trades**, which involved local or regional exchanges that never touched Europe. In North America, trade in deerskins and beaver pelts in colonial times extended precolonial practice. The French backwoodsmen and buckskin-clad frontiersmen slotted into an existing Native American framework that linked hunting grounds and routes of trade and tribute. The Huron, Native American farmers and traders who did not need to hunt, except for exercise and to supplement their diet, were the middlemen of the early seventeenth-century fur trade, supplying French buyers in Quebec in Canada. Spanish entrepreneurs took part in a profitable canoe-borne trade in local textiles, healing plants, and dyestuffs along the coast of Venezuela in the 1590s. Similarly, the economy that sustained the Spanish conquerors of Yucatán was no transoceanic affair of precious goods, but an extension of the age-old Maya trade with central Mexico, based largely on cacao for consumption in Mexico City.

Of course, Spanish activity was not confined to modest ventures of these kinds, along traditional grooves. The Spanish monarchy was a great inaugurator of new intra-American trade routes. New cities, founded in places never settled on a large scale before, especially on the Pacific and Atlantic coasts, became magnets to suppliers of foodstuffs, cotton textiles, and building materials. The conquest of Peru demanded a new transcontinental route from the Caribbean to the Pacific across the Isthmus of Panama in Central America, which became, like the alternative later opened from Bolivia to the Atlantic via the River Plate, a major silver-bearing artery of the Spanish Empire. Mule-train routes that the Native American civilizations, which had no horses or mules before the arrival of the Europeans, had never required, served the new mining ventures in remote hinterlands. The conquest of much of Chile in the mid-sixteenth century stimulated the creation of a heroic new seaborne route, far into the Pacific, to overcome the Humboldt Current. Sailing ships took longer to get from Lima in Peru to Concepción in Chile than from Seville in Spain to Santo Domingo in the Caribbean.

The slow but steady spread of Spanish frontiers brought regions formerly unknown to each other into touch. The link between Mexico and Peru is the most startling case, since it seems incredible—yet true—that the Native American civilizations of those areas never had significant mutual contact until the Spaniards arrived. Although the places Spaniards occupied in New Mexico, Arizona, and Texas showed some signs of having received cultural influences from Mexico in the past (see Chapter 10), California was a genuinely new discovery, where Spanish missions in the eighteenth century first created ventures in settlement and agriculture that made the region a potential trading partner for other parts of the Spanish monarchy (see Chapter 21). Native American merchants could have navigated the Amazon and the Orinoco rivers before the Spaniards arrived, but, as far as we know, they never did so. No one fully exploited those

"The slow but steady spread of Spanish frontiers brought regions formerly unknown to each other into touch. The link between Mexico and Peru is the most startling case, since it seems incredible—yet true—that the Native American civilizations of those areas never had significant mutual contact until the Spaniards arrived."

"The Americas were a huge bonanza—of land, of food and mineral resources, of opportunities for the productive deployment of labor, of new markets and manufactures. Western Europeans' privileged access to those resources made a new era in world history possible."

mighty and mysterious waterways as arteries of commerce until well into the seventeenth century.

Meanwhile, new commerce opened with the wider world. A system of convoys linked Spain to America and injected Europe's cash-starved economies with veins of gold and silver. The need for slaves led other European merchants to Spanish colonies and linked the Americas to Africa. The route of the Manila Galleon, a Spanish ship that made an annual crossing of the Pacific from the Philippines to Acapulco on the Pacific coast of Mexico, facilitated the direct exchange of Mexican silver for Chinese silk and porcelain. For the first time, trade girdled the world, tying the Americas, Africa, and Eurasia into a single, interconnected system.

Suppose Columbus had been right. Suppose the globe was small, and no Americas lay in the way of Europeans' westward approach to Asia. Europeans would still, of course, have taken part—presumably a bigger part—in Asia's carrying trades. They would have made money out of it and closed the wealth gap that separated them from the richer economies of maritime Asia. They would have contributed to recycling Japanese silver and helped to make the world's economy more liquid. They would probably have gone on to found the land empires that began to take shape in Asia in the late seventeenth century. The total volume of resources at their command would, however, have remained modest. The Americas were a huge bonanza—of land, of food and mineral resources, of opportunities for the productive deployment of labor, of new markets and manufactures. Western Europeans' privileged access to those resources made a new era in world history possible. The traditional poor relations of Eurasia—the formerly impoverished West—could now challenge previously towering economies,

Gathering Brazil Wood. "Because this wood is dense and hard to cut," as a French observer of Brazil's logwood trade noted, "if the foreigners who voyage over there were not helped by the savages, they could not load even a medium-sized ship in a year." The quality of this carving from Rouen, France in the 1530s, made to decorate a timber merchant's house, suggests that fortunes could be made from the trade in tropical woods. The carver glamorizes the Native Americans as innocently naked and classically posed.
Yohann Deslandes, cg76-Agence photographique des sites et musees departementaux

such as those of India and China, that had been dominant in Eurasia for thousands of years.

The dazzle of American silver, however, should not blind us to the continuing importance of the Indian Ocean as the world's major arena of large-scale, long-range trade, where the world's biggest fortunes were still made and lost, and where Europeans were interlopers, striving for toeholds. Traditionally, historians concentrated on the spice trade as an index of world-shaping changes, and especially on pepper, which accounted for as much as 70 percent of the total trade by value in the seventeenth century. It is true that by value per unit of weight, spices—especially cloves, mace, nutmeg, and cinnamon—were the world's most valuable products at the time. And it is also fair to say that by the end of the seventeenth century the major share of the trade had passed into the hands of European shipping agents, to the detriment of ancient land routes and indigenous shipping. It is important, however, to bear some qualifications in mind. China still dwarfed the rest of the world as a market for spices, and only a few ships a year carried part of the trade from the Indian Ocean to Europe. European shipping probably expended far more time and labor on moving spices around maritime Asia than on exporting them elsewhere. In this respect, the role of Europeans in the spice trade was part of a bigger picture, in which Europeans, with little to sell in Asian markets except space aboard their ships, began to accumulate wealth as suppliers of services to their richer Asian hosts. By taking advantage of the price differentials between various Asian markets—and especially, as we have seen, of the differential values of silver in Japan, China, and India—they were able gradually to take more and more of the initiative as independent traffickers in the goods, such as Indian textiles, aromatic woods of the

Chronology

1492–1493	Columbus discovers routes to and from the New World
1500	Portuguese begin direct trade with southern India
1510	Portuguese trading post at Goa established
1513	Discovery of the Gulf Stream
1518–1546	Spanish conquest of Mexico and Peru
1519	Babur founds Mughal Empire
1519–1521	Spanish navigators complete first global navigation
1520–1566	Reign of Suleiman the Magnificent (Ottoman Empire)
1521	Spanish capture Tenochtitlán; end of Aztec Empire
1529	Spain and Portugal divide Pacific seaborne routes between themselves
1530s	Spanish conquest of Peru
1552–1556	Russian conquest of Kazan
1556–1605	Mughal expansion and centralization under Akbar
1564–1565	Northern Pacific sea route between New World and Asia discovered
1585–1598	Reign of Toyotomi Hideyoshi (Japan)
1600	East India Company founded (England)
1602	Dutch East India Company founded
Early 1600s	Dutch use westerlies to circumnavigate globe
1609	English found Virginia colony
1619	Dutch found Batavia (Indonesia)
1620–1640	Portuguese expelled from trading posts in Persian Gulf and Indian Ocean
1640	Dutch merchants only Europeans allowed in Japan
1656–1707	Mughal Empire covers most of Indian subcontinent under Aurangzeb
1674	French establish trading post at Pondicherry (India)
1676	King Philip's War (New England)
1689	Treaty of Nerchinsk with China checks Russian expansion eastward

South Seas, sugar, rice, and the pharmaceuticals and porcelain of continental East Asia, which were in high demand around the Indian Ocean. As time went on, they gained more advantages by introducing products from elsewhere that were inaccessible to native Asian traders, such as African slaves, American silver, and, later, as we shall see (Chapter 25) opium. Though their activities sometimes resembled piracy, and they sometimes jeopardized their role by resorting to force in an attempt to concentrate trade in their own hands, they were, on the whole, tolerated or welcomed as a useful and exploitable addition to the shipping stocks of a region so overflowing with trade that it could absorb almost any amount of strangers, as long as they had ships. The beginning of the "rise of the West" to parity with the wealth of the East happened in the Indian Ocean as much as or rather more than in the Atlantic. It started modestly, with Westerners in a subordinate role. And its foundation was the volume and strength of intra-Asian trade: Europe generally was still economically underproductive compared with the powerhouse economies of the East.

PROBLEMS AND PARALLELS

1. How were empires agents of change in the sixteenth and seventeenth centuries?

2. What are the differences between land and maritime empires? Why were Mughal emperors such as Akbar and Ottoman sultans such as Suleiman the Magnificent so warlike?

3. How did the maritime imperialism of Japan compare with Portuguese and Dutch imperial ventures? Why did the shogun Hideyoshi try to conquer an empire on the mainland of Asia?

4. What roles did native collaborators, interpreters, merchants, and middlemen play in the empires of the sixteenth and seventeenth centuries? What does the term *stranger effect* mean?

5. What are the differences and similarities among the Russian, Chinese, Ottoman, and Mughal Empires of this period?

6. How was Spain able to achieve such a vast empire in so short a time? Why were Spain's Native American allies and collaborators such as the interpreter Doña Marina so crucial in the conquest of the Aztec and Inca empires?

7. How did a global trade network emerge in the sixteenth century? How did the Indian Ocean continue to be the major arena of large-scale, long-range trade in the sixteenth and seventeenth centuries?

READ ON ▶ ▶ ▶

The best introductions to the Portuguese maritime empire are A. J. Russell-Wood, *The Portuguese Empire, 1415–1808* (1992) and F. Bethencourt and D. Curto, eds., *Portuguese Overseas Expansion* (2007). P. Pérez-Mallaína, *Spain's Men of the Sea: Daily Life on the Indies Fleets in the Sixteenth Century* (trans. Carla Rahn Phillips, 1998) is a superb social history of shipboard life in the age of maritime expansion. C. R. Boxer, *The Dutch Seaborne Empire: 1600–1800* (reprint, 1991) is a slightly dated but still valuable and very readable account of the rise of Dutch colonial power. Its perspective on Southeast Asia should be balanced by W. Cummings, *Making Blood White: Historical Transformations in Early Modern Makasar* (2002), a sophisticated recent study of the transition from oral to literate culture in an area of increasing Dutch influence. K. So, *Japanese Piracy in Ming China during 16th Century* (1975) explores the impact of *wako* raids around the South China Sea in the sixteenth century. M. Berry, *Hideyoshi* (2001) is a superb study of that ruler. B. Walker, *The Conquest of Ainu Lands: Ecology and Culture in Japanese Expansion, 1590–1800* (2001) is important on continuing Japanese expansion.

R. L. Edmunds, *The Northern Frontier in Qing China and Tokugawa Japan: A Comparative Study of Frontier Policy* (1985) is valuable. On Qing expansion, J. Waley-Cohen, *Exile in Mid-Qing China* (1991) is important. On Batavia, L. Blusse, *Strange Company* (1986) is outstanding. J. F. Richards, *The Mughal Empire* (1996) is a fine introduction to Mughal history, while P. M. Brand and G. D. Lowry, *Akbar's India: Art from the Mughal City of Victory* (1985) explores the cultural expressions of Mughal might and ruling style. R. Murphey, *Ottoman Warfare, 1500–1700* (1999) analyzes Ottoman military power in its social, economic, and geographic contexts. K. Chase, *Firearms. A Global History to 1700* (2003) offers an overview of the dynamics of power in Eurasia whose central thesis is simplistic but whose details on the spread of gunpowder weaponry are valuable.

My material on Russian icons comes from the Royal Academy exhibition catalog *The Art of Holy Russia: Icons from Moscow, 1440–1660* (1998). On Siberia, T. Armstrong, ed., *Yermak's Campaigns in Siberia* (1975) unites the main chronicles. J. Forsyth, *A History of the Peoples of Siberia* (1994) is the best overall study.

M. Restall, *Seven Myths of the Spanish Conquest* (2003) is essential on New World imperialism. J. H. Elliott, *Empires of the Atlantic World* (2006) compares English, later British, and Spanish experience. B. E. Mundy, *The Mapping of New Spain: Indigenous Cartography and the Maps of the Relaciones Geograficas* (2000) offers an excellent scholarly analysis of the local maps and surveys collected by the Spanish government in the late sixteenth century as part of its effort to govern its new empire more effectively. A fine edition of W. Bradford, *Of Plymouth Plantation* (1999) gives a firsthand account of the creation of the Plymouth colony. E. H. Spicer, *The American Indians* (1982) is an authoritative summary of Native American history, including relations with the expanding European presence in North America.

On global trade balances in the sixteenth and seventeenth centuries, see A. Gunder Frank, *ReOrient: Global Economy in the Asian Age* (1998), a provocative study that argues forcefully for Asia, especially China, as the center of gravity of global trade right through to 1800. E. van Veen, *Decay or Defeat? An Enquiry into the Portuguese Decline in Asia* (2000) makes some important corrections, and R. Barendse, *The Arabian Seas* (2002) is extremely helpful. J. Goody, *The Theft of History* (2008) investigates the myth of the Western origins of capitalism, and much else of relevance.

CHAPTER 17

The Ecological Revolution of the Sixteenth and Seventeenth Centuries

▲ **Ledger's legacy:** the quinine plantations established in Java, thanks to the seeds Charles Ledger transplanted to the Dutch East Indies from Bolivia in the late 1850s, are now the world's major source of this antimalarial drug.

Charles Ledger's captors were taking him to the regional capital, where the Bolivian police would lock him up indefinitely if he fell into their hands. But Ledger could not afford that sacrifice of time. It was already mid-April 1855. The deadly winter of the Southern Hemisphere in the high mountains was drawing on. Ledger's men and flocks needed him. Luckily, he had a strong narcotic in his saddlebags, left over from a bout of toothache. He slipped a heavy dose into his guards' brandy, drove off their mules, and escaped into the night. Shots echoed around him as he fled, but the policemen were too dazed with the drug to aim straight.

The crime for which he was under arrest was attempting to export alpacas, small, llama-like creatures famous for their fine wool. The authorities in Peru, where Ledger began his odyssey, did not want breeding animals to fall into potentially rival hands. The law forbade anyone to drive alpacas toward the coast. Therefore, having bought hundreds of specimens and gathered them high in the Andes, near the Peruvian-Bolivian border, Ledger conceived a plan the local Indians condemned as insane. He would turn inland, drive his herd over the mountains and across deserts, via Bolivia and Argentina, to Chile. There he would board them on ships and sail them to Australia, where the government promised him a handsome reward if he could get adequate breeding stock into the country. On the way, he would cross-breed alpacas with llamas, which are much larger but have coarser coats, to improve the yield of good-quality wool.

If ever there was a nightmare journey, this was it. The authorities hunted him—alleging not unreasonably that he was breaking the spirit of the law. Rustlers mounted attacks. Indians shadowed and harried him, like hidden raptors, striving to steal animals. Ledger tried to elude his pursuers by following secretive, dangerous routes amid precipices and high passes, up to 17,000 feet above sea level. Yet he also had to organize vast amounts of fodder and water to cross high badlands where neither was available. Men he sent to gather wood for campfires froze to death in snowdrifts. More died in gunfights with pursuers. The animals perished in their hundreds from starvation or thirst or heat or cold. Ledger kept up their numbers by breeding them and replenishing them with purchases in Bolivia along his way.

Ledger spent his fortune and beggared his family. He never saw again the wife he left behind in Peru, because she died before his journey ended. So did the baby daughter with whom she was pregnant at Ledger's departure, and whom he never saw at all. It took him six years to get to the

FOCUS questions

Why was the Columbian Exchange so important, and how did it affect nutrition in Europe and Asia?

How did the introduction of new diseases by Europeans affect population levels in the Americas?

Why did the Europeans import slaves to the Americas?

Why did the balance of power change between nomads and settled peoples?

In what new ways did people around the world exploit the natural environment in the seventeenth century?

How did the European settlement in the Americas and increased contact across Eurasia redirect the course of evolution?

Chilean frontier, and even then he still had to cross the Atacama Desert—one of the most arid environments in the world. The French consul offered him a fortune for his flock, intending to send the animals to Algeria and start an alpaca textiles industry there, but Ledger persevered in what he conceived as a patriotic mission for the British Empire. When he got to Australia, the authorities reneged on their promises, dispersed the flock, and left Ledger penniless.

Ledger would have starved to death or been dependent on charity, but for the fact that the alpacas were just a sideline. Ledger's other—and even greater—contribution to world history was to discover, while he was in Bolivia, a stock of the highest-quality fever-tree seeds the world had ever seen. The tree's bark yields quinine, the universally acclaimed "miracle drug" that Jesuits had produced in Peru in the seventeenth century and had administered, with startling effects, to sufferers across the world. It supresses fevers and shivers and has regularly saved the lives of patients afflicted with malaria. Until the discovery of quinine, the only remedies known in Europe were magical mumbo jumbo—putting a peach stone in an orange and eating the fruit, for instance, or having a young virgin tie magic paper around a sufferer's neck with a long string.

In Ledger's day, efforts to propagate the miracle-seeds outside the Andean region had largely failed. But Ledger's seeds thrived in Java, where quinine kept Dutch soldiers and the Dutch Empire alive. A pension from the Dutch government sustained Ledger until his death in a suburb of Sydney, Australia, senseless with senile dementia, at the age of 87, in 1906.

Ledger's life was a small episode in the story of what was, by most standards, the greatest revolution ever to have occurred in the history of the world by means of human agency. The sheer, staggering audacity of taking Andean life forms to Australia, Algeria, or Java only became possible as a result of what historians now generally call the **Columbian Exchange**—the global redistribution of life forms, beginning in 1492 and accelerating thereafter, that accompanied the era of world-wide travel by intercontinental routes.

A divergent pattern of evolution had made the life forms of the various continents ever more different from one another from the moment, perhaps about 150 million years ago or more, when Pangaea—the unified world landmass—split and the continents began to drift apart. Relatively suddenly, by the scale of the long preceding period, the Columbian Exchange reversed that pattern. About 500 years ago, Earth-girdling travel and a mixture of deliberate and unconscious transplantation of plants, animals, and bacteria substituted a new pattern in which the life forms of different continents began to be swapped. It became possible to grow and breed plants and animals in environments that had never seen their like before. Products migrated between hemispheres, across previously impassable barriers of climate and expanses of ocean. So did people. So did pests.

Three huge transformations in humans' relationship with the environment were among the consequences or coincidences. First, the human relationship with fatal pathogens underwent puzzling lurches. At one level, as we have seen, the period from the mid-fourteenth century to the eighteenth was an age of plagues, when lethal diseases spread over the world and ravaged populations. On the other hand, the micro-organisms that were chiefly responsible seem, late in the period, to have retreated, with surprising and still unexplained suddenness, from their accustomed eco-niches. Partly as a result, a worldwide "population explosion" began toward the mid-eighteenth century.

Second, human settlement changed both its range and its nature, invading new ecological frontiers on an unprecedented scale: farming grasslands, felling forests, climbing slopes, reclaiming bogs, penetrating game preserves and deep-sea fisheries, expanding and founding cities, turning deserts into gardens and gardens into deserts. This was part of a drive for resources and energy sources in an increasingly populous and competitive world. Hunters ransacked previously unmolested wild zones for animal furs, fats, and proteins. Much of this hunting took place at sea, in pursuit of migrating fish and wandering whales. The exploration and exploitation of new frontiers created an illusion of abundance that inspired ecological overkill; yet imperialism also had positive environmental effects, as colonialists came, in some cases, to see themselves as custodians of "tropical Edens," preparing the way for a revived respect and even reverence for nature in the eighteenth-century West.

Finally, climate underwent global fluctuations: The "Little Ice Age" was in progress for most of the period and revived briefly at its end, though temperatures generally took an upward turn in the eighteenth century. The effects of the temperature changes, however, are hard to calibrate and, on the basis of present knowledge, seem surprisingly slight. We have to set them aside as an unknown quantity and look in turn at each of the other aspects of an ecological revolution, which, though its effects were global, is primarily part of the story of Western civilization, because it began as a result of world-ranging European initiatives and, in particular, changed Europe and the Americas.

THE ECOLOGICAL EXCHANGE: PLANTS AND ANIMALS

It is tempting to pick out the well-documented introductions of life forms as the highlights of the story, or focus on the legends of heroes who bore life-changing new foodstuffs across the oceans. Christopher Columbus is fairly credited with a lot of "firsts." From his first ocean crossing in 1492, he brought back descriptions and samples of New World plants, including pineapple and cassava or manioc. On his second transatlantic voyage in 1493, he took sugarcane to the island of Hispaniola—but let it grow wild. Pigs, sheep, cattle, chickens, and wheat made their first appearance in the New World on the same occasion. Other heroic firsts are the subjects of legends or fables. Juan Garrido, a black companion of Cortés, supposedly first planted wheat in Mexico. The story of Sir Walter Raleigh, the sixteenth-century poet, courtier, historian, and pirate, introducing potatoes to England is false but has an honored place in myth.

The real, though unwitting, heroes, however, are surely the plants and animals themselves, which survived deadly journeys and successfully adapted to new climates, sometimes—in the case of seeds—by accident, with little human help. They traveled in the cuffs or pleats of the clothing of carriers who didn't know they were there, or were caught in the fabric of cloth bales and sacks. In terms of volume and contribution to global nutrition, a few instances stand out. Out of Eurasia to new worlds in the Western and Southern Hemispheres went wheat, sugar, rice, bananas, coconuts, apples, pears, apricots, peaches, plums, cherries, olives, citrus fruits, and major meat-yielding and dairy livestock. The European grape variety *vitis vinifera* (the only grapes native to the Americas are Concord grapes) should perhaps be included, because of the importance that American wines made from varieties of it have attained in the world market. Yams, okra, and collard greens were among vegetables that made the crossing from Africa (see Map 17.1).

"The real, though unwitting, heroes, however, are surely the plants and animals themselves, which survived deadly journeys and successfully adapted to new climates, sometimes—in the case of seeds—by accident, with little human help."

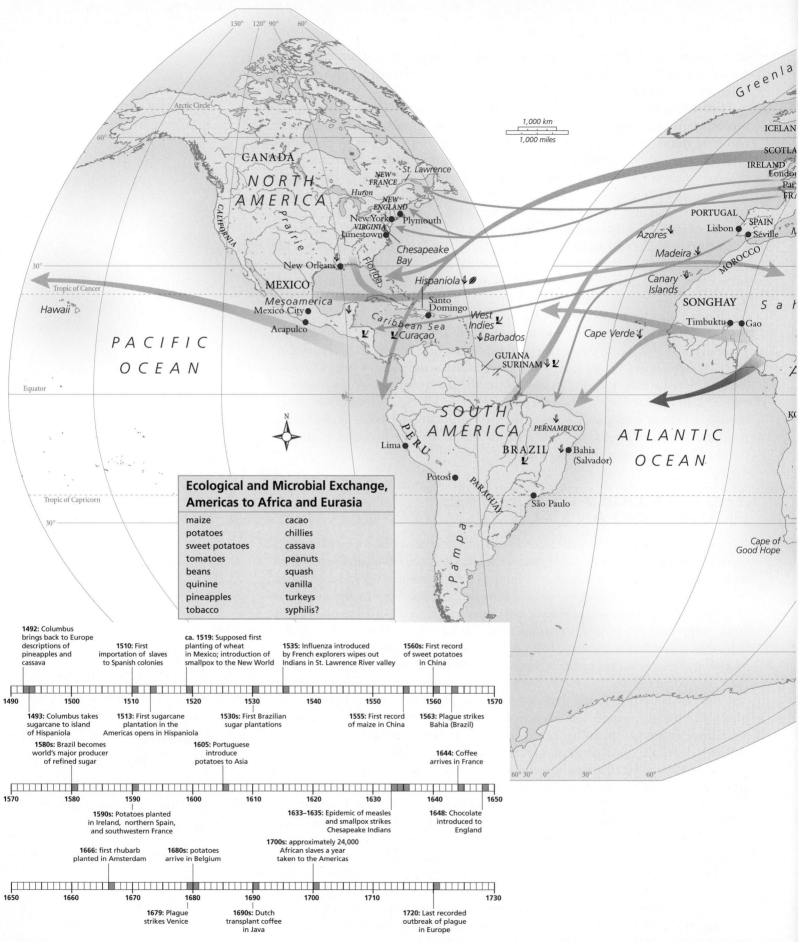

Ecological and Microbial Exchange, Americas to Africa and Eurasia

maize	cacao
potatoes	chillies
sweet potatoes	cassava
tomatoes	peanuts
beans	squash
quinine	vanilla
pineapples	turkeys
tobacco	syphilis?

1492: Columbus brings back to Europe descriptions of pineapples and cassava

1510: First importation of slaves to Spanish colonies

ca. 1519: Supposed first planting of wheat in Mexico; introduction of smallpox to the New World

1535: Influenza introduced by French explorers wipes out Indians in St. Lawrence River valley

1560s: First record of sweet potatoes in China

1490 — 1500 — 1510 — 1520 — 1530 — 1540 — 1550 — 1560 — 1570

1493: Columbus takes sugarcane to island of Hispaniola

1513: First sugarcane plantation in the Americas opens in Hispaniola

1530s: First Brazilian sugar plantations

1555: First record of maize in China

1563: Plague strikes Bahia (Brazil)

1580s: Brazil becomes world's major producer of refined sugar

1605: Portuguese introduce potatoes to Asia

1644: Coffee arrives in France

1570 — 1580 — 1590 — 1600 — 1610 — 1620 — 1630 — 1640 — 1650

1590s: Potatoes planted in Ireland, northern Spain, and southwestern France

1633–1635: Epidemic of measles and smallpox strikes Chesapeake Indians

1648: Chocolate introduced to England

1666: first rhubarb planted in Amsterdam

1680s: potatoes arrive in Belgium

1700s: approximately 24,000 African slaves a year taken to the Americas

1650 — 1660 — 1670 — 1680 — 1690 — 1700 — 1710 — 1720 — 1730

1679: Plague strikes Venice

1690s: Dutch transplant coffee in Java

1720: Last recorded outbreak of plague in Europe

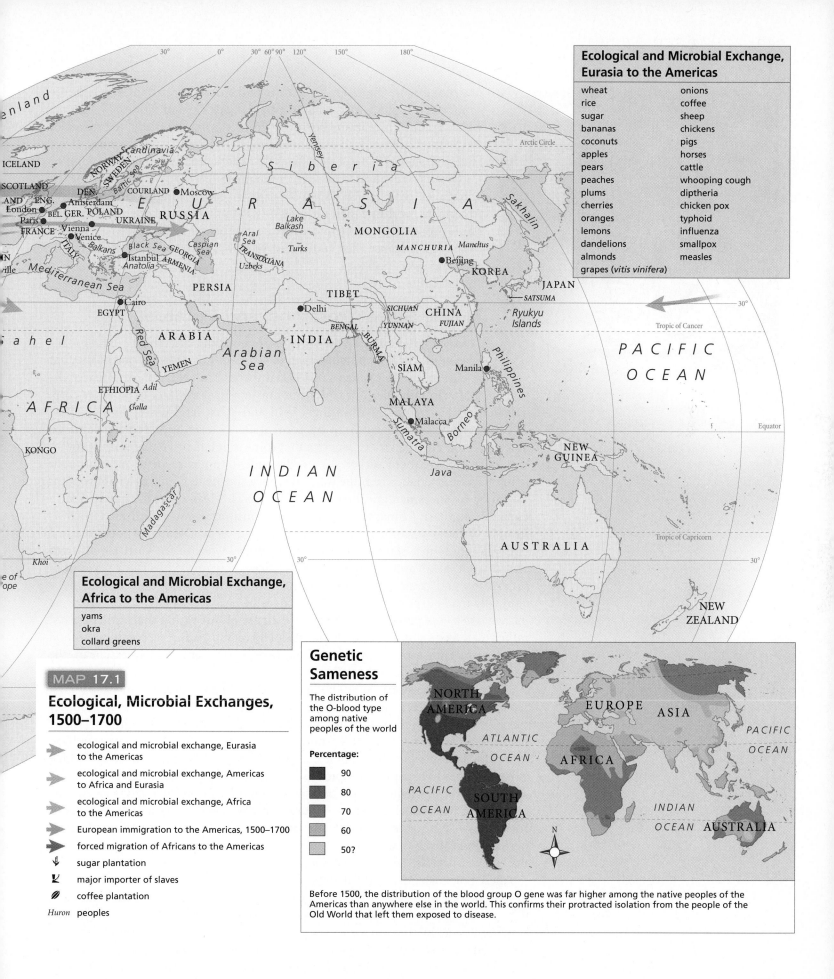

Ecological and Microbial Exchange, Eurasia to the Americas

wheat	onions
rice	coffee
sugar	sheep
bananas	chickens
coconuts	pigs
apples	horses
pears	cattle
peaches	whooping cough
plums	diptheria
cherries	chicken pox
oranges	typhoid
lemons	influenza
dandelions	smallpox
almonds	measles
grapes (*vitis vinifera*)	

Ecological and Microbial Exchange, Africa to the Americas

yams
okra
collard greens

MAP 17.1

Ecological, Microbial Exchanges, 1500–1700

➡ ecological and microbial exchange, Eurasia to the Americas

➡ ecological and microbial exchange, Americas to Africa and Eurasia

➡ ecological and microbial exchange, Africa to the Americas

➡ European immigration to the Americas, 1500–1700

➡ forced migration of Africans to the Americas

⇩ sugar plantation

↳ major importer of slaves

⊘ coffee plantation

Huron peoples

Genetic Sameness

The distribution of the O-blood type among native peoples of the world

Percentage:

- 90
- 80
- 70
- 60
- 50?

Before 1500, the distribution of the blood group O gene was far higher among the native peoples of the Americas than anywhere else in the world. This confirms their protracted isolation from the people of the Old World that left them exposed to disease.

Tobacco was thought to be good for the digestive system. In this seventeenth-century Dutch illustration, Cupid carries the smoker's pipe and pouch because tobacco, like lovemaking, is a fleeting pleasure that quickly goes up in smoke.

Along with the fancy foodstuffs and flavors already mentioned, the Americas supplied medicinal plants for Africa and Eurasia. Quinine, which Spanish physicians borrowed from among the medicinal plants of the peoples of Peru, had enormous long-term significance, because, as we have seen, it can control the effects of malaria and was therefore vital for Europeans struggling to survive in the mosquito-ridden, swampy tropics. Tobacco—"with which," said a Spanish reporter in the 1540s, Native Americans "perfume their mouths"—was thought to aid digestion. But the staple products—and therefore the most important gifts of the New World to the rest, because they could feed vast populations—were maize, potatoes, and sweet potatoes.

Maize, Sweet Potatoes, and Potatoes

Maize at first revolted Old-World taste buds but fascinated plant specialists. As the Spanish botanist Juan de Cárdenas reported in one of the first scientific studies of maize in 1591, it thrives "in cold, hot, dry, or wet climates, in mountainous regions or grasslands, as a winter or summer crop, irrigated or dry-farmed," with a high yield and short land-use cycle that made wheat seem difficult to cultivate by comparison. Maize appeared in China so quickly after it emerged from America that some scholars insist that it must somehow have arrived there earlier. Two independent routes seem to have brought maize to Asia: overland from the west, maize was borne to China as a tribute plant by Turkic frontiersmen and first recorded in 1555. Meanwhile, it came by sea to Fujian in southern China, where a visiting Spanish friar saw it cultivated in 1577. At first, Chinese welcomed it as a curiosity, not a serious source of food. It rated only a footnote in a standard Chinese agricultural work of the early seventeenth century. But its advantages over millet and rice—it required less labor per unit of production and could grow in eco-niches where those crops were unsuitable—gradually made it popular, especially in areas of new settlement. Europeans were initially even less enthusiastic than the Chinese about eating maize themselves, rather than feeding it to livestock, but it slowly established a place as human food in the eighteenth century in parts of the eastern and central Mediterranean, the Balkans, Ukraine, and southern Russia.

Like maize, the sweet potato had a transforming effect in parts of China. First reported in southern China near the Burmese border in the 1560s, it probably came overland from the south. Its flavor had a bad reputation with ethnic Chinese, but it found favor in hill country among immigrants and settlers who were obliged to occupy land previously thought marginal. Used, at first, only for horse fodder, sweet potatoes were rapidly adopted as human food. In 1594, a governor of Fujian supposedly recommended sweet potatoes when the conventional crops failed. The enthusiasm with which different cultures received the crop varied unpredictably. In Japan sweet potatoes never caught on, after following a south-to-north route perhaps indicated by variations in their name: they are called "Chinese potatoes" in the Ryukyu Islands, "Ryukyu potatoes" farther north in Satsuma in the southern Japanese home islands, and "Satsuma potatoes" in the rest of Japan.

Potatoes, which the Portuguese introduced to Asia in 1605, similarly failed to win popular favor in Japan, Korea, or China. They had remained a regionally restricted food in the Americas—cultivated at high altitudes in the Andes. Yet when Portuguese migrants took them to Bengal in India, they became an inescapable ingredient of Bengali meals. Potatoes conquered northern Europe,

Harvesting potatoes in India. Although Westerners tend to think of rice as the staple food of India, the country is now the third largest potato producer in the world, after China and Russia. Bengal—where potatoes have been an essential ingredient of the regional cuisine since the Portuguese introduced them from the New World in the 1600s—is no longer the major producer. Other provinces, especially in the highlands of northwest India have overtaken Bengal, and Andra Pradesh, shown here, is catching up.

where they gradually replaced rye as the food base of a vast swathe of humankind from Ireland across Scandinavia and Germany to Poland and Russia. War spread them, for peasants favored a crop that grew concealed in the ground and so eluded seizure by plundering troops. Tried out with success in the Basque country of northern Spain and southwest France and in Ireland before the end of the sixteenth century, the potato began its war-linked career in Belgium in the 1680s under the impact of French invasion, and spread eastward with every subsequent war. Scholars and bureaucrats promoted it because of its impressive nutritional qualities. If eaten in sufficient quantities, it is the only major staple that provides all the nutrients essential to human health.

Weeds, Grasses, and Livestock

Transplantations in the opposite direction—into the New World from the Old— turned much of the Americas into farmland for food for European palates and digestions, and ranch land for European livestock. The first stage was colonization by European weeds and grasses that made parts of the New World able to support sheep, cattle, and horses instead of just bison and llamas. European plants, such as purslane and Englishman's Foot, created what Alfred Crosby, the great historian of the ecological exchange, called "empires of the dandelion." Weeds made the revolution work. They "healed raw wounds" invaders tore in the earth, bound soil together, saved it from drying out, refilled "vacated eco-niches," and fed imported livestock.

Conscious transpositions followed. Horses and cattle came first—the New World had no similar big domesticated animals. The Spanish army that invaded New Mexico in 1598 was accompanied by thousands of head of cattle, which their masters drove over mountains and deserts—including the terrible 60-mile waterless stretch known as the March of Death. To Spanish cattlemen, the South American pampa and the North American prairie were the last frontiers of an enterprise that began in the Middle Ages, when they had adopted ranching as a way to exploit the empty, conquered lands in Spain after the Muslim population had fled or been expelled.

"To Spanish cattlemen, the South American pampa and the North American prairie were the last frontiers of an enterprise that began in the Middle Ages, when they had adopted ranching as a way to exploit the empty, conquered lands in Spain after the Muslim population had fled or been expelled."

Transporting horses. This eighteenth-century illustration from a Spanish manual of horsemanship makes it look easy. But transporting horses by sea was a delicate, hazardous, and technically demanding business. Once across the ocean, a few runaway steeds could transform the Americas. In 1536, Spaniards released 12 horses on the plains of Argentina. Within a few years, the herds "looked as dense as forests."

Embarcadero de los Cavallos.

Meanwhile, wheat arrived. The lower levels of the central valleys proved highly suitable for wheat, and although most of the Indian population continued to rely on maize, wheat bread became a badge of urban sophistication. Within a few years of the Spanish conquest, the city council of Mexico City demanded a supply of "white, clean, well-cooked and seasoned bread." The valleys of Mexico supplied Spanish garrisons all over Central America and the Caribbean with wheat flour.

Not all efforts to introduce wheat in other parts of the Americas were successful, at least at first. The Spanish colonists of Florida in 1565 brought wheat seed, together with grapevine cuttings, 200 calves, 400 pigs, 400 sheep, and unspecified numbers of goats and chickens. But the crops did not "take," and the animals went wild or died for lack of fodder or were slaughtered in desperation. By 1573, "herbs, fish, and other scum and vermin" sustained the colonists when rations were short. Corn bread and fish, foodstuffs copied from the Native American diet, were their mainstays. Similarly, the first English colonists in Virginia were unable to grow food for themselves and relied on handouts from the natives to see them through their "starving time." Investors and imperialists back home blamed colonists' moral deficiencies for these failures. But the problems of the mutual adaptation of Old World farming and New World environments were formidable, especially for settlers of exposed seaboards in an era of imperial competition. Colonies sited for defense, behind marshes or swamps, in difficult climates, needed generations of investment and long periods of heartbreakingly high rates of mortality before they could be made viable. At every stage of European colonization of new worlds, the remarkable thing is not the high rate of failure but the perseverance that led to ultimate success.

Cane Sugar

Of all the Old World arrivals in America, cane sugar was the first transplanted product to have a major impact on world markets. It is, perhaps, the first food to have conquered unaccustomed markets by the power of supply. Instead of following the usual laws of economics, according to which demand comes first and supply responds, sugar was the first of a series of tropical products that were recommended by their availability. European taste buds became enslaved to it.

Sugar rapidly became the most important item of transoceanic trade. The first sugar refinery in the Americas opened in Hispaniola in 1513. Portuguese enterprise launched the Brazilian sugar industry. For the first 30 years of their presence in Brazil, the Portuguese exploited its coasts for nothing but logwood bought in vast quantities—perhaps 19,000 tons a year—from the natives. From the 1530s, however, they began to plant sugar around Salvador and in Pernambuco in northern Brazil. It was a difficult crop to plant, harvest, and refine, greedy of capital and demanding lots of specialized labor. And it yielded surprisingly low profits for the planters—typically only 3 percent a year.

Trading in sugar, however, was highly profitable. So it was important for planters to retain an interest in the trade after the sugar left their hands. The value of the crop doubled or even quadrupled as it crossed the Atlantic. The sugar-growing area was never extensive—parts of Brazil, some Caribbean islands, patches of coasts around the Spanish Main, and French Louisiana around New Orleans—but it was highly productive. By the 1580s, four effects were evident. First, Brazil had become the world's major producer, and the economies of the older sugar islands of the eastern Atlantic—Madeira, the Azores, the Cape Verdes—(see Chapter 15) went into eclipse. Second, the need for labor in the sugar plantations and mills

A water-driven sugar mill in Pernambuco during the Dutch occupation of northern Brazil, depicted here in a Dutch atlas of 1662. Slaves carry the mill owner, slung in a hammock under a rich awning in the foreground. The sugar cane arrives by ox cart, to be ground by the power of the mill.

caused an explosion in the transatlantic slave trade. Third, the growing volume of sugar production created new American industries: refining sugar and distilling rum. In the seventeenth century, Brazilian sugar was refined locally, before export.

Finally, the competition for sugar-producing lands was becoming a major cause of imperial rivalry among European states. Dutch invaders took over the Portuguese sugar plantations in Pernambuco in 1630, then, on their expulsion nearly a quarter of a century later, concentrated on creating plantations of their own in the Caribbean and on the Guiana coast of South America, where they proclaimed a "second Brazil" in Surinam in 1667. English, French, Spaniards, Scandinavians, and even Courlanders from a duchy on the Baltic coast all set up sugar industries on Caribbean islands in the second half of the seventeenth century. Where sugar could be grown successfully, unprecedented prosperity was possible. In the 1680s, the British island of Barbados sustained a population of more than 300 people per square mile—the average figure for Western Europe at the time was 92 people per square mile. By then, the sugar trade was undergoing a further revolution that would transform it into one of the world's most popular products: the popularization of the taste for hot sugar-sweetened beverages in Europe.

Coffee, Tea, and Chocolate

For, where sugar led, coffee—and, ultimately, tea and chocolate—followed. By 1640, the coffee of Yemen rivaled or exceeded pepper as the main trading commodity of the Arabian Sea. It continued to boom, supplying markets in Persia, where coffee consumption quadrupled to nearly a million pounds a year by 1700. Even larger amounts—about 17 million pounds—went to the Ottoman Empire via the Red Sea and Egypt. Coffee arrived in France in 1644 with a returning ambassador from Turkey, along with old porcelain cups of great beauty and small napkins of fine cotton muslin, embroidered in gold, silver, and silk. The coffee-drinking habit soon found patrons. In 1657, Jean de Thévenot noticed that Parisian aristocrats hired Moorish and Italian coffeemakers. Armenian importers and street brewers popularized coffee drinking in France. Within half a century, coffee became the West's favorite addictive stimulant. In his satirical domestic comedy, the "Coffee Cantata," Johann Sebastian Bach (1685–1750) credited

Turkish coffeehouse. In the late eighteenth and early nineteenth centuries, coffee was still a luxury item in much of the world, and coffee drinking was a social ritual for the rich, as in this coffeehouse scene in Istanbul. Mass production in Java and later in Brazil, however, was already turning coffee into a cheap drink for the West's industrial workers.

Chocolate. In this canvas of about 1640—presumably intended to adorn a dining room—the Spanish painter Juan de Zurbarán (1620–1649) exalts chocolate, raising it on a silver pedestal and placing it center stage as if he were painting its portrait. In the seventeenth century, rich Europeans consumed chocolate the way the Aztec elite had—as a luxury beverage. Zurbarán here depicts a truly global experience in conspicuous consumption: expensive chocolate imported to Spain from Mexico is to be drunk in even more costly porcelain cups imported from China.

it with breaking up marriages because so many husbands stayed away from home to drink coffee in cafes, while wives sang love-songs to coffee.

Once the popularity of the new beverage was established, the next stage was to transplant it to new lands where Europeans could control the supply. The great coffee boom of the eighteenth and nineteenth centuries took it to Brazil, to the French islands of the Indian Ocean, and to the French colony of Saint-Domingue on Hispaniola, which for a while—until the black slaves there rebelled and proclaimed the Republic of Haiti in 1804—was the most productive island in the world for coffee and sugar alike. One of the most enduringly successful of the new coffee lands was Java, where the Dutch introduced the plant in the 1690s, gradually expanded production during the eighteenth century, and, in the nineteenth, fought wars to boost production on ever more marginal soils.

While coffee spread across the world from the Middle East, chocolate followed a similar path from a starting place in Mesoamerica. It took longer than coffee to penetrate European markets. In a work of 1648, credited with introducing chocolate to the English-speaking world, Thomas Gage described how colonial Mexico liked it—mixed with Old-World flavors, such as cinnamon, cloves, and almonds, as well as in the stews of bitter chocolate and chilles that were traditional Mesoamerican recipes. As the new drink became fashionable in Europe, the cacao (cah-COW) from which chocolate was made was transplanted to West Africa, where Danish plantations helped supply the growing trade in the eighteenth century. Tea also contributed to the growth of global trade, but not to the ecological exchange. China was able to supply almost the whole of world demand until the nineteenth century when the British established tea plantations in India and Sri Lanka.

Patterns of Ecological Exchange

It would be a mistake to think of the ecological exchange as merely bouncing back and forth across the oceans between the Old World and the New. Some ecological exchanges happened within the Americas. Domesticated turkeys formed no part of the first Thanksgiving meal. They were introduced to New England from Mexico later in the seventeenth century. The real maker of English economic success in Virginia was John Rolfe. He was the husband of the Indian princess Pocahontas—the forger of a kind of understanding with the natives, based on collaboration, mutual benefit, and sexual alliance that was normal in Spanish, Portuguese, and French colonies but remained rare in English colonial practice. Rolfe's vital economic contribution was to introduce "Spanish tobacco" (from the West Indies), which became Virginia's monoculture: the large-scale export crop that turned the colony from an unprofitable swamp into a field for settlers. It had to be transplanted because Europeans could not stand the taste of Virginia's native tobacco. Sweet potatoes were first recorded in Virginia in 1648, probably introduced not directly from South America, but via Europe or Africa with the slave trade.

Along the routes of transmission, gardens where plants could be adapted and bred for new climates were way stations of ecological exchange. Dutch horticulture led the way. Gardening was already a Dutch national obsession in the seventeenth century, when tulips from Turkey and chrysanthemums from Sri Lanka inspired costly "manias"—competition to grow the rarest and most spectacular varieties.

Dutch plant collectors crisscrossed the world. The Dutch Prince John Maurice of Nassau grew African and Indonesian plants in his garden in Brazil and sent Chilean monkey-puzzle trees to Germany. Nicolaas Witsen, a director of the Dutch East India Company, planted the first rhubarb in Europe in the town garden of Amsterdam in 1666—no mean achievement, as powdered rhubarb was by then one of the main products traded on the old Silk Roads. A fellow director made it his life's work, or folly, to try to grow oranges and lemons in cold, damp Holland. By the end of the seventeenth century, the company's gardens at the Cape of Good Hope on the southern tip of Africa had become the meeting place of hundreds of ornamental or potentially useful European, African, American, and Asian plants.

The result of the ecological exchange was a better-nourished world in the eighteenth century, better equipped than before with medicinal drugs derived from plants. This presumably contributed to the population explosion that then began, and has continued, with increasing pace, more or less ever since.

Human population, however, depends not only on what people do but also on how disease-bearing microorganisms behave. In the sixteenth and seventeenth centuries, a long and hazardous period of relatively low and uncertain growth preceded the upward surge of world population. Why population patterns change is still poorly understood. Clearly, social structures—and marriage disciplines above all—play a big part in explaining why people seem to breed at different rates at different moments of history. (We will discuss the global social history of the sixteenth and seventeenth centuries in Chapter 19.) Nutrition is important, because it affects fertility, and, when it improves, it keeps more people alive for more of their fertile years. But we cannot even begin to understand changing world patterns of population in the sixteenth and seventeenth centuries without looking at history under the microscope and examining the microbial world.

Dutch garden. An idealized view of the garden that Johann Maurits of Nassau created in Holland, to complement the gardens he planted in Brazil, when he was governor of the Dutch colony there from 1637 to 1644. The printed verses compare Johann Maurits with ancient Persian emperors, who were thought to have invented gardening.

THE MICROBIAL EXCHANGE

Instead of increasing population, in accordance with known precedents, colonization in the New World in these centuries provoked the worst recorded demographic disaster in history. Smallpox, in a virulent form, fatal to the immune systems of populations that had never encountered the disease, was probably the most effective killer. But some pestilence was doubtless unclassifiable in terms of current diseases, because the organisms responsible have evolved unrecognizably since that time. Symptoms often baffled their beholders. When a plague struck in Bahía, in 1563, José de Anchieta, the Jesuit "apostle of Brazil," could make no sense of symptoms that rotted the liver and produced a noxious pox, but he treated Indians by bleeding and peeling "parts of the legs and almost all their feet, cutting off the corrupt skin with scissors." Even if we assume that Native American societies were like those in the rest of the world and had suffered undocumented pestilence before the Europeans arrived, it seems incontestable that the diseases colonization brought were new and the effects unprecedented. "The breath of a Spaniard" was said to be enough to make a Native American die. The first Spanish navigators of the Amazon, in 1542, beheld cities built on stilts on the river banks, fed by aquaculture and the intensive cultivation of bitter manioc. The Spaniards did no more than pass through, yet by the time of the next European visitors a generation later, that populous world had vanished.

"But we cannot even begin to understand changing world patterns of population in the sixteenth and seventeenth centuries without looking at history under the microscope and examining the microbial world."

Smallpox victims. A native artist drew these victims of smallpox in sixteenth-century Mexico to illustrate a history that a Spanish friar wrote in Nahuatl—the language of the Aztecs. At top left, an Aztec physician is talking to his patient, who was almost certainly doomed. Hardly any Europeans died of smallpox at the time, but the disease killed millions of Native Americans, who had had no opportunity to develop immunity to it.

Demographic Collapse in the New World

Demographers have been unable to produce convincing figures for the extent or duration of the collapse, but even at the most optimistic estimates, the Indian population of Hispaniola, where New World colonization began, was virtually wiped out. In the densely settled and highly exposed regions of Mesoamerica and the Andes, Indian populations typically fell by 90 percent before they began to recover—which they did only patchily and intermittently until well into the seventeenth century and in many places not until the eighteenth.

Benevolent attitudes by colonial authorities made no difference. No empire has ever legislated so persistently, or so ineffectually, for the benefit of its victims as Spain's in the New World. It is impossible to imagine a system more benevolent—in paternalist fashion—than that of the Jesuits in the vast areas of Brazil and Paraguay that the crown separated from Spain's secular dominions for an experiment in building a self-sustaining Christian community. A picture in a work of propaganda in praise of this enterprise, published in 1700, displays its idealistic inspiration. A jaguar lies down with a tapir, and a little child leads them. Somehow, however, this paradise had got mislaid. Baptismal records show that by 1650, of the 150,000 people the Jesuits had baptized in their missions in the four most forward frontier provinces, only 40,000 survived the raids of Portuguese slavers and the visitations of plague.

The more spacious environments of North America bred equally devastating diseases. The influenza French explorers unwittingly introduced in the St. Lawrence River valley in Canada in 1535, and the nameless plague a Spanish expedition spread in what is now the American Deep South in 1538, inaugurated a history in which every attempted European settlement infected the Native Americans. The first English settlement in Virginia spread a quick-killing disease among the Indians, "so strange that they did not know anything about it or how to cure it." The next major epidemic, of 1633–1635, was recognizably of measles followed by smallpox. The Chesapeake Indians disappeared by the end of the seventeenth century. The numbers of the Huron in Canada collapsed so dramatically after contact with Europeans that one Jesuit argued desperately that it was a sign of divine favor. God was gathering his chosen to him. By the end of the seventeenth century, the Native American population in regions Europeans penetrated had fallen—according to rival estimates—by between 60 and 90 percent.

Plague and New Diseases in Eurasia

Some regions outside the Americas suffered comparable devastation. In the remoter parts of Siberia, visitors from the wider world were almost as much of a novelty as in the New World, and the unimmunized natives were equally vulnerable to unaccustomed diseases. Eighty percent of the tribespeople Russian imperialism touched east of the Yenisey River perished in the 1650s. Later, European penetration of Australia and parts of the Pacific had similar effects.

So, in a sense, the "age of plague" that started in the Old World in the late Middle Ages increased in virulence as disease-bearing microorganisms spread across the world. Microbial evolution, meanwhile, altered the patterns of disease in Eurasia. Leprosy diminished in range, but new diseases arose or old ones mutated. Tuberculosis does not seem to have been around in Europe on a significant scale—and certainly was not a major killer—until the sixteenth century when a more virulent form of the disease may have been brought back from the Americas. New strains of venereal disease developed in Europe—also perhaps as a result of transference from the New World.

Visitations of lethal sicknesses that Europeans continued vaguely to call plague remained a constant problem, holding down population growth in the seventeenth century in parts of southern Europe. The plague of Venice of 1679 left thousands of dead lying in a ditch, smothered in quicklime "like pickled game in a barrel" to dissolve the bodies. Plague in Spain in 1657 inspired terrifying paintings of lives stalked by death or focused on putrefaction. In a hospital in Seville, a carved altarpiece of the descent from the cross inspired a brotherhood of aristocrats who sought to atone for their sins by burying the plague dead and tending the plague sores of the poor with their own hands. China in the 1580s and 1640s endured more epidemics of greater virulence than in the more notorious plagues of the fourteenth century. A survivor of the plague in Hunan in 1657 claimed that nine of ten inhabitants were smitten, with a third of them breaking out in fever at midday to "become delirious in the evening and be partly eaten by rats when found dead at sunrise."

Yet for reasons that remain ill understood, the age of plagues gradually exhausted its virulence. The last recorded outbreak of plague in Europe was in the port of Marseilles on the Mediterranean coast of France in 1720. The deaths of unimmunized populations left well-adapted survivors. As a result of the ecological exchange, improved nutrition fortified increasing numbers of people. Microbes shifted their targets, perhaps, or mutated for evolutionary reasons to become less deadly. After all, it is not necessarily efficient for microorganisms to kill off their hosts. Whatever the reasons for it, deadly disease receded in the late seventeenth and early eighteenth centuries from all the areas in which it had previously been most destructive.

Of course, other diseases occupied the eco-niches retreating microbes vacated, or leaped into new ones that social, economic, or environmental change opened up. Cholera and yellow fever, for instance, broke out of their tropical heartlands to attack people in some of the fast-growing, densely populated, heavily polluted cities and ports in the industrializing West (see Chapter 29). Dysentery and typhus thrived in the undersanitized environments of rapidly growing towns. Dense concentrations of people helped tuberculosis to spread. Bubonic plague, in its modern form, may be another new disease of this period—or, at least, a recurrence of an old disease with new characteristics. As we have seen (see Chapter 14), historians' longstanding assumption that bubonic plague was the sole or main affliction of the "age of plague" in Europe is probably false. In China, there is no decisive evidence that any epidemic before the nineteenth century was of bubonic plague in its modern form. In Yunnan province, however, on China's southwest border, a new kind of environment, in which new kinds of disease had an opportunity to emerge, was taking shape in the late eighteenth century. In the last quarter of the century, mining towns mushroomed as 300,000 immigrants moved in from other parts of China. At the same time, strong similarities with modern bubonic plague characterized a particularly intense series of epidemics from the 1770s to the 1790s, followed by slightly less intense

Burial of the dead—plague-stricken or impoverished—was one of the obligations of the brethren of the religious brotherhood, or confraternity, that ran the Hospital de la Caridad in Seville, Spain. The sculptures on the high altar therefore depict the entombment of Christ. This altarpiece represents a characteristically emotional baroque theme: the paradox of inhabitants of a glorious heaven sharing the miseries and suffering of earthly life.

outbreaks until the 1820s. The most significant similarity was the presence of rats as agents of disease. Modern bubonic plague is endemic in particular kinds of rodents. It spreads to humans when rat fleas bite people and inject the bacillus into human bloodstreams. The Yunnan plague was incontestably associated with rats, according to observations made at the time, not only by physicians but also by a young poet who wrote,

> Dead rats in the East!
> Dead rats in the West!
> . . .
> A few days following the death of the rats,
> Men pass away like falling walls!

"Along with plants, animals, and germs, another life form, another ingredient of ecosystems—human beings—was swapped and shifted across the ocean and—for the most part—ended up in the Americas."

Still, the impact of modern bubonic plague was not as severe as that of the Black Death or the other scourges of the age of plague. When plague receded from Yunnan in the 1830s, it became dormant or sporadic. The next—or, by strict standards of interpretation, the first—unquestioned major outbreak in China did not occur until 1894. In any case, the new or spreading diseases of the eighteenth and nineteenth centuries generally could no longer keep pace with growing world population or, it seems, seriously restrain its growth.

Meanwhile, however, for as long as the age of plague lasted, problems of severe regional labor shortages had to be faced. The gravest of these were in the last region to suffer devastating losses of population to disease: the New World. The solution lay in transplanting human labor. This was, in a sense, yet another kind of ecological exchange. Along with plants, animals, and germs, another life form, another ingredient of ecosystems—human beings—was swapped and shifted across the ocean and—for the most part—ended up in the Americas.

LABOR: HUMAN TRANSPLANTATIONS

Even before native numbers thinned, the colonial Americas suffered from shortages of useful labor. The new economic activities Spaniards wished to promote were impossible without new sources of labor even in the most densely populated areas of Spanish rule. Native Americans were, with few exceptions, ill suited to the kind of work Europeans wanted done, such as plantation labor, domestic service, and specialist skills in mining and sugar refining. Most of them were—as a companion of Columbus commented when dismissing the idea that the native peoples of the Caribbean could usefully be enslaved—"not suited to hard work" as Europeans understood the term.

Europe, however, was unsatisfactory as an alternative labor source. Spanish schemes to introduce colonies of Spanish laborers failed in the sixteenth century. The Dutch encountered similar failure in the seventeenth. North America proved particularly hard to populate. Sixteenth-century attempts to found North American colonies almost all failed. Those founded in the seventeenth century took a long time to become viable—renewing their populations, that is, by sustainable birth rates. They could not rely, as most of Spain's early American conquests could, on native population levels to keep them viable. There are no reliable estimates of the size of the native population of North America when the Europeans arrived—well-informed guesses range from two to seven million—but there is no doubt that the region was sparsely populated. And such people as it did have were not well suited to be a labor force for colonial empires, such as the big, densely packed native populations of Mesoamerica and the Andes provided for Spain.

Immigration could not, at first, make up the deficit. Virginia was farmed mainly with a form of forced labor imported from England—"indentured" poor, escapees from social exclusion at home, who contracted with masters to serve for years at a time, on subsistence wages or payments in kind, with no hope of release. But there were never enough of them, and as the market for black slaves gradually opened up to the English, Africans replaced them. Again, the model of exploitation was found in the Spanish, Portuguese, and (by now) Dutch colonies to the south.

Until the second half of the seventeenth century, life expectancy in Virginia remained low. Few colonists survived into their 50s. The Virginia swampland, where the first permanent settlements were founded from 1607 onward, was so unhealthy that of the first 100 or so settlers, only 38 were still alive nine months after landing. Of the first 3,000, only a couple of hundred were still alive, after a bloody war with the Indians in 1622. The population did not begin to increase naturally until some 50 years after the first settlement. The breakthrough was accompanied by increased rates of immigration, which tripled from about 1650 to 1670.

New England's environment was less hostile: "endowed with grace and furnished with means," as a Puritan settler declared. From early in the 1630s (Plymouth, the first New England colony, was founded in 1620), the colonists could grow enough to feed themselves, and natural increase kept the population growing. Without valuable cash products, however, the region had little appeal for immigrants. Only 21,000 came in the whole seventeenth century, and the numbers of immigrants diminished over time—only a third of that total arrived after 1640. These were problems general to northern colonies. There were only 5,000 settlers in New Netherland when the English conquered the colony, which became New York, in 1664. New France, founded in Canada in 1608, received fewer than 4,000 immigrants in the second half of the seventeenth century. France, though densely populated by European standards in early times, never persuaded many colonists to go to America.

In the Spanish colonies, as early as 1510, the importation of slave labor began from the only source near enough and demographically buoyant enough to provide it: Africa. By the 1570s, Spanish America was importing, on average, about 2,500 African slaves a year. The average figure over the next century and a half, during which the trade to Spanish America was fairly stable, was 3,500 a year. Brazil became a major importer of slaves from the 1570s. Brazil probably had fewer than 15,000 black slaves in 1600, but numbers soared thereafter with the growth of sugar plantations, and the colony was soon absorbing more slaves than the whole Spanish Empire.

For the first 150 years or so of the colonial era, Spanish naval supremacy and Portuguese control of many of the sources of slaves denied adequate supplies of this resource to the British, Dutch, and French colonies. But as demand for slaves grew, routes of supply diversified—through piracy and illicit trading at first, then increasingly by agreement of the Spanish and Portuguese authorities with slavers of other nationalities. In the 1640s, Dutch slavers turned the island of Curaçao, off the coast of Venezuela, into a huge slaving station, supplying Spanish colonies at first and, increasingly, their own. Scandinavian traders entered the market in the 1650s. From the late 1660s, French and English companies tried to break into the slave trade. In the third quarter of the seventeenth century, nearly 15,000 slaves a year left Africa on average. In the final quarter, the number increased to 24,000 a year.

After experiments with other kinds of enforced labor, slavery became the universal method to develop the plantation crops, including the rice and cotton that, in preference to tobacco and sugar, suited some of the land the English seized in North America. The system was imitated from Spanish and Portuguese precedents

African woman and child. This painting of 1641 by the Dutch painter Albert Eckhout illustrates the range of racial types in Brazil. The woman's calm stance, her rich clothing and jewels, the lavish foodstuffs, the exotic birds, the pipe at her breast, and her son's markedly different complexion all signify an image of order, stability, variety, and abundance. In the background scaffolding rises to signal trading opportunities to passing ships.

Chronology: The Columbian Exchange: Plants, Animals, Microbes, and People

1492	Columbus arrives in the New World, beginning process of biological exchange
1500s	Horses and cattle introduced to New World
1510	Importation of slave labor in the Spanish colonies begins
1555	First record of maize cultivation in China
1570s	Brazil becomes a major importer of slaves
1580s	Brazil becomes the world's major sugar producer
1700s	Coffee becomes popular in Europe and Middle East
	Coffee production begins in Brazil and Indonesia

in areas where Native Americans were reduced by disease or refused to do plantation work. Climate drove it, as is apparent from the failure of early antislavery laws in Georgia, which was founded in 1733 as a refuge for the British poor. Subtropical America could not be made to pay without labor from Africa. No other area could supply enough workers adaptable to the climate.

WILD FRONTIERS: ENCROACHING SETTLEMENT

The slave trade was part of a bigger phenomenon: the development of new ways to exploit the soil, which, in combination with the widening of trade, hugely increased the wealth of the world. This could be called the economic dividend of imperialism: the extension of land exploited for ranching, farming, and mining, and the conversion of some land from relatively less productive to relatively more productive methods of exploitation.

Northern and Central Asia: The Waning of Steppeland Imperialism

In northern and Central Asia, the political background was of a shift of power, as steppeland imperialism waned and the growing strength and reach of settled empires in China, Persia, and Russia squeezed the pastoralists' domains. New attempts to galvanize the power of the steppelanders, by a succession of leaders who claimed descent from Genghis Khan or his heroic lieutenants (see Chapter 13), brought little success. Most new imperial initiatives remained penned inside the steppes. At the beginning of the sixteenth century, for instance, two new enemies locked horns in Southwest Asia. The pastoralist Uzbek Empire, under the Shaybanid dynasty, with its heartlands in the steppes between the Aral Sea and Lake Balkhash, celebrated the identity of "men of the steppe: all our wealth consists of horses; their flesh is our favorite food. . . . Houses have we none." The Safavid Empire of Persia, which was largely based on settled agriculture, was their neighbor to the south (see Chapter 19). To judge from the record of the previous 500 years, anyone tempted to bet on the outcome of a clash between these two states would back the steppelanders to win. But, during nearly a century of warfare, the Safavids repeatedly got the upper hand, until a final Persian victory in 1597 provoked the breakup of the Uzbek state into small khanates.

Meanwhile, at the eastern end of the steppes, the Mongols found it impossible to reunite their power for long enough, or in sufficient strength, to renew a lasting threat to China. The Mongols could not even, for much of the time, securely dominate Tibet, which in the seventeenth century became the objective of the most ambitious Mongol chiefs.

There was, however, one uncharacteristic and perhaps deceptive instance of steppeland dynamism in the period. In the 1640s, a Manchu army, which the Chinese Empire had created to help police the Mongol frontier, intervened decisively in a Chinese civil war, conquered China (see Chapter 19), and dethroned the last Ming emperor in 1644. In some ways—in practice, more or less token ways—the Manchus imposed their own values on China. One of the first commands of the new regime, which survived until 1912, was that Chinese should signify their submission by shaving their hair in Manchu fashion. According to Confucian notions of filial piety, hair was part of the sacred legacy children inherited from their parents and therefore should not be cut off. But the Manchu commander replied to objectors, "I spared your heads and now you want to keep your hair?" In most respects, however, the new dynasty rapidly adopted Chinese ways. Indeed, the great achievement of the Qing (cheeng)—the name the Manchu dynasty adopted in China—was to reverse the direction of empire. The Qing conquered much of the steppeland and spread Chinese culture deep into Central Asia.

Disputes over Tibet eventually provoked China into sustained war against the Mongols. In the 1690s, the Kangxi (kong-shee) emperor, himself a Manchu, campaigning in person on the Mongol front, described in letters home his days of early rising, "braving the sand and the dust" with "hands all blistered from holding the reins." By 1697, he was able to announce, with only a little exaggeration, "There is no Mongol principality that has not submitted to my rule." The historic pattern of imperialism in Central Asia was undergoing a kind of inversion. The Chinese Empire was reaching into the Mongol steppe, instead of lying at the periodic mercy of steppeland conquerors.

Why did the balance of power between settled life and pastoralism shift in favor of the former? The usual answer appeals to the so-called **military revolution** that accompanied the rise of firepower technology. Large forces of well-drilled, fire-armed infantry, with heavy artillery behind scientifically designed fortifications, made "gunpowder empires" invulnerable to steppeland cavalry. Demographic change also favored the settled peoples, whose populations grew faster than those of pastoralists. The progress of Islam and Buddhism in Central Asia supposedly eroded the ideologies of conquest that had animated earlier steppeland empires. Changes in the pattern of trade in the seventeenth century, when the role of the Silk Roads declined in relation to oceanic trade routes, cut off some of the liquid wealth that mobilized nomad war bands.

None of these explanations seems adequate. Steppelanders had adapted to new warfare technologies in the past. The Mongols, for instance, would never have been able to conquer China without incorporating infantry and siege engines into their armies (see Chapter 13). Settled neighbors had always outnumbered pastoral peoples, whose economic system, by its very nature, demands a lot of grazing land to feed relatively fewer mouths. Although many new trade routes carried more commerce than those of Central Asia, steppelanders still had plenty of wealth-creating opportunities to exploit. Chinese tribute lists and trading licenses show steppeland communities getting gradually richer, especially in horses, furs, and silks. Without definitive evidence, the best we can say is that all these changes, in combination, weakened the steppelanders relative to the empires that surrounded them. Whatever the reasons for it, the decline in the relative power of Eurasia's steppelanders was irreversible, as farmers from the Russian and Chinese empires colonized areas of steppeland and left the pastoralists with less territory. The retreat of the steppelanders was a conspicuous element in the making of the modern world. It formed part of a broader change: an ecological revolution that extended the range and productivity of settled farming around the world.

Steppeland defeat. The Uzbek Empire of the sixteenth century never had the power or potential to fulfill its declared aim to conquer the world. At times, the Uzbeks were even hard-pressed to defend their steppes against invaders from Persia. The late seventeenth-century Persian painter of a palace mural remembered the Uzbek Khan Shibani as the victim of defeat by Shah Ismail I (r. 1501–1524). Persia's defeat of the Uzbeks showed that the age-old pattern—in which agrarian states felt menaced by the steppelanders—had been reversed.

"The retreat of the steppelanders was a conspicuous element in the making of the modern world. It formed part of a broader change: an ecological revolution that extended the range and productivity of settled farming around the world."

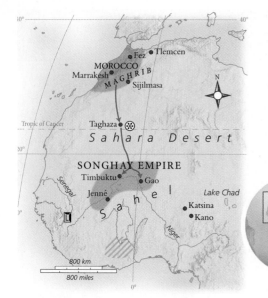

MAP 17.2

The Moroccan invasion of Songhay, 1591

- ▨ Morocco
- ▨ Moroccan occupied territory
- → Moroccan invasion route
- ▨ gold mine
- ⊛ salt mine
- ▨ alluvial gold

Pastoral Imperialism in Africa and the Americas

In some parts of the world, meanwhile, pastoralism remained or became a predominant way of life, and pastoral imperialism remained or became robust. In the African Sahel, for instance, the native tradition recovered after a challenge in the late sixteenth century from Morocco. In the 1580s, Morocco's long-cherished dreams of crossing the desert and conquering a gold-rich empire in black Africa began to look practical. The Moroccan sultan al-Mansur collected an army equipped with formidable firepower—2,500 marksmen and a train of camel-mounted artillery. The desert was not impassable, he argued. What merchant caravans could do, so could a well-organized army. From a Moroccan perspective, the Sahara was a sea of sand with an inviting shore. Like Spain's Atlantic, Morocco's Sahara was an obstacle course that could be crossed to a land of gold.

In 1588, al-Mansur declared war on Songhay. Nine thousand camels accompanied his task force on a march of 135 days across 1,500 miles, mostly of desert. Half the force may have died on the way, but the survivors dispersed the mounted hosts of Songhay as efficiently as Spanish conquerors had shattered the Aztecs and Incas (see Map 17.2). Morocco turned the western Sahel into a colony settled with 20,000 men. But the settler communities, often marrying locally, gradually slipped out of Moroccan control. After an initial bonanza, the gold shipments dwindled, and by the 1630s, Morocco's gold reserves were running out. No outside power again attempted to conquer the Sahel until the French arrived in the nineteenth century. The supremacy of the Sahel pastoralists remained secure.

The centuries-old process of expansion of arable farming from the Ethiopian highlands went into reverse in the sixteenth century, as pastoralist invaders from the east and south—pagan Oromo, Muslim Adil—seized lands and destroyed the monasteries that were the engines of Ethiopian frontier settlement. At the extreme southern tip of Africa, herding grew in economic importance. The region of the Cape of Good Hope had long been heavily grazed by thousands of head of long-horned cattle, herded by pastoralists who called themselves Khoi and who had probably themselves been driven into the region by the expansion of Bantu farmers from the north. The numbers of livestock doubled in the second half of the seventeenth century, when Dutch settlers introduced sheep following the establishment of a colony of the Dutch East India Company on the Cape in 1652. The Dutch followed Khoi strategies for selecting seasonal grazing and corralling their herds against predators. Although the Dutch also practiced arable farming, the extent of their ranching activities was incomparably greater.

In the Americas, of course, there had never been much pastoralism because there had never been large domesticable livestock herds, except for the llamas and their cousins in the Andes. In the sixteenth and seventeenth centuries, however, the introduction of horses, cattle, and sheep made new ways of life possible, raising the prospect of empires whose economy was based on herding livestock. In some ways, it is tempting to see Spanish and Portuguese imperialism in some parts of what are now Mexico and Brazil as a form of pastoral imperialism imposed on sedentary Indian peoples. Sheep and cattle, unknown before the Europeans arrived, numbered millions by the early seventeenth century and grazed hundreds of thousands of square miles of land—some of it previously unexploited, but much of it vacated by native farmers and hunters. As we shall see, in the late eighteenth and early nineteenth centuries (see Chapter 21), horse-borne Native American empire builders threatened to dominate the prairie and the pampa.

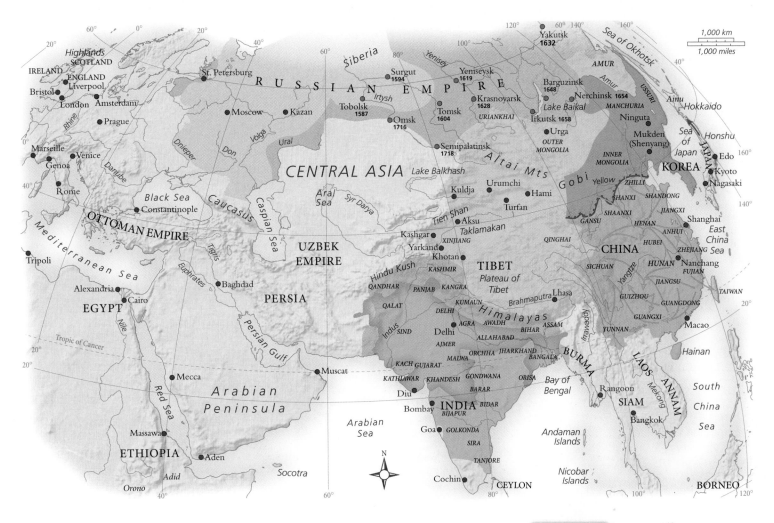

Imperialism and Settlement in Eurasia, 1600–1725

- Russian Empire, ca. 1600
- Russian Empire, ca. 1600–1725
- Russian cities founded 1587–1718
- Qing Empire in ca. 1644
- Qing Empire in ca. 1660
- Qing Empire by ca. 1770
- → internal migration in China in the 18th century
- Mughal Empire, ca. 1700
- Mughal Empire, ca. 1605
- → Japanese expansion northward
- *Ainu* people

So in some parts of the world, arable farming lost acreage or yield. In other areas, methods of exploiting the soil remained limited to hunting and gathering. Although California and parts of Australia, for instance, were highly suited to arable farming, their native inhabitants were uninterested in changing methods of feeding themselves that had worked satisfactorily for thousands of years. Not until European intrusions in the eighteenth century did ranching and tillage begin fundamentally to alter their landscapes. But the main trend of the period was the extension of new forms of exploitation—especially arable farming—onto lands where it had never before been practiced. The new empires, which encouraged colonists and drove and mined for new resources, forced the pace of this change (see Map 17.3).

IMPERIALISM AND SETTLEMENT IN EUROPE AND ASIA

The Russian conquest of Kazan in the 1550s made possible the colonization of the fertile "black earth" regions of the lower Volga River and southwest steppeland, pressing back and penning Mongol and Turkic herdsmen. By 1600, a million settlers had turned a quarter of the region to grain cultivation, turning over the heavy sod with ox-drawn plows. Although the conquest of Siberia was launched for the fur trade, the ambition to see the land colonized gradually eclipsed the original vision. The foundation of frontier cities marked the progress of colonization:

A CLOSER LOOK

The Remezov Chronicle

Several narrative accounts document the Russian conquest of Siberia. In the Remezov Chronicle, written in a monastery about 1700, and illustrated with 154 pen and ink drawings, Russian territorial expansion is depicted as an evangelizing and civilizing mission. Shown here is the title page from the Chronicle.

"From the beginning of time, our Christian God, the All-Seer ... decreed for the Gospels to be preached throughout Siberia to the ends of the universe and the limit of the mountains to the famous city of Tobolsk."

"And he will dwell in righteousness, and towns will arise to the Lord."

The hen is a motif taken from the Gospels of Luke, where it symbolizes Jerusalem's resistance to God's will. The words above it, (only partly legible), read, "Just as the hen gathers its chicks under its wing, so shall I. . . . my name."

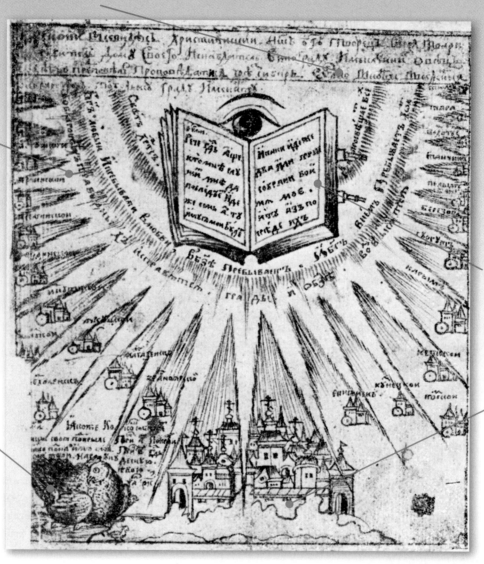

Set beneath the eye of God, the words in the open book, from the Gospels of John and Matthew, read "If any man serve me, let him follow me; and where I am there shall also my servant be. . . . where two or three are gathered together in my name, there am I in the midst of them."

Tobolsk is flatteringly depicted, while rays from the Gospel spread to 21 other towns.

How does this illustration connect territorial expansion with the Russian state's self-proclaimed mission to spread Christianity?

Tobolsk on the Irtysh River in 1587, Tomsk in 1604, Barguzinsk on Lake Baikal in 1648, Nerchinsk on the Amur River in 1654. In the mind of an eighteenth-century chronicler, Siberia had become a land of cities—22 of them, dispersed throughout the territory, depicted in an illustrative engraving as joined by rays of light to the eye of God. By then, over 300,000 peasants inhabited these settlements—outnumbering the surviving native Siberians.

Meanwhile, on a smaller scale, similar appropriations of territory by encroaching farmers displaced traditional peoples at the extremities of Eurasia, in the British Isles and Japan. The English and lowland Scots waged wars to seize land, from Ireland to the Highlands and islands of Scotland. These were, from one point of view, culture wars that self-styled civilization waged against so-called savagery, by Protestants against Catholics, by speakers of Germanic tongues against those who spoke Celtic, by feudalism against tribalism. They were also economically inspired wars fought to convert pastoral land to arable. In Japan, after the Ainu War of 1669–1672, about half of Hokkaido was set aside for Japanese peasants to settle, at the expense of the displaced Ainu natives, whom the Japanese classed as primitive and savage, using language similar to that of English and Scots propaganda about the highlanders, islanders, and Gaelic Irish.

"These were, from one point of view, culture wars that self-styled civilization waged against so-called savagery, by Protestants against Catholics, by speakers of Germanic tongues against those who spoke Celtic, by feudalism against tribalism."

China

Imperial China sponsored the biggest movements of agricultural settlers in frontier regions and new conquests. Uncultivated land was wasted land. That was what late-sixteenth-century Chinese officials thought, denouncing the "laziness" of gatherers of wild reeds on land that could be adapted to grow food. Manchu conquest of Sichuan in southern China was exceptionally savage, eliminating—so it was said—three-quarters of the people. Yet between 1667 and 1707, tax exemptions lured more than 1.5 million settlers to Sichuan. Here and on the southeast frontier, the pressure of intensive new settlement provoked a cycle of conflicts. Rebellious native tribes were penned in reservations. Militarized agricultural colonies grew wheat, barley, peas, and maize while keeping the natives obedient. Schools brought Chinese language and values to the tribes.

The civil wars of the third quarter of the seventeenth century, which pitched the last Ming loyalists against the Manchu conquerors, drove Chinese peasants out of the densely populated provinces of Fujian and Guangdong (gwahng-dohng) into Guangzxi (gwahng–jshee) and the Yangtze highlands to the tea and timber industries or to cultivate sweet potatoes or maize. Celebrating his conquests against the "half-human" natives of Guizhou (gway-joh) in the mid–seventeenth century, a Manchu general described "chiseling" through the "forests that extend beyond the horizon. . . . Every day, for our imperial court, we've developed new arable lands. . . . So these far-off wastelands and tribal domains yield us menials and serving girls."

Large-scale immigration preceded the Chinese conquest of Taiwan in the 1660s. During some four decades of Dutch rule, which preceded the Chinese conquest, Dutch colonialists rewarded Chinese migrants with land concessions, cheap seed, draft animals, and tax breaks. By the time Chinese took over the government, over 35,000 settlers had brought nearly 25,000 acres under the plow, growing mainly rice and cane sugar. When the Manchu government assumed control of the island in 1684, the "raw aboriginals" enjoyed a period of official favor. The Manchus used the native deerstalkers to repress the suspect immigrant Chinese population in an offshore province where resistance to Manchu conquest had been

Building a dike in seventeenth-century China. Peasant conscripts rig screws to drive piles into the mud to form the walls of the dike. Others use heavy wooden hammers to level the dike, or dig earth, which fellow-workers shift in baskets yoked by poles.

strong. But that did not prevent the depletion of the deer herds, as Chinese peasants continued to encroach on land officially reserved for the native Taiwanese.

To the north of traditional China, in the borderlands of Mongolia and Manchuria, colonization proceeded on a different basis. The Kangxi emperor (r. 1661–1722) tried to stop the colonization of Manchuria on the grounds that he "wished to maintain the original equestrian and hunting ways and martial virtues of the Manchus and Mongols in their home territory, which should remain a recruiting ground for soldiers." In practice, however, the frontier of settlement could not be controlled. The cultivated zone of Manchuria grew by nearly 30,000 acres in the decade following Kangxi's decree. (See Map 17.3.)

The exploitability of illegal immigrants made them welcome. The earliest colonization had a camp-life quality of roving communities of wild ginseng diggers. (Ginseng is prized in Chinese medicine.) Farmer pioneers came not far behind. In the frontier town of Ninguta (neen-goo-tah) (today known as Ning'an) on the River Hurka, in the generation after its foundation in 1660, only 400 households lived inside the ruined wall of mud. There was "no person of leisure," and the exiles' womenfolk—"descendants of the rich and honorable families of China"—slid barefoot down the icy hillside under the burden of water from the only well.

Yet even in this environment, some metropolitan values triumphed, while the winds of change overturned others or blew them away. Anyone with scholarly pretensions—let alone degrees—was prized in Ninguta. The deference the natives accorded to the Chinese and the prosperity of the settlers impressed a visitor in 1690. The older merchants even "greeted the military governor as a younger brother": in other words, they affected superiority over him. The hierarchies of home persisted alongside new rankings the emerging society of the frontier had evolved.

India

We can detect the same trends—imperial expansion, fostering new settlement, increasing the range of farming, and exploiting new resources—in the same period in India. Forest clearance was a policy the Mughal emperors (see Chapter 16) embraced determinedly, in their heartlands and new conquests alike. In Bengal, deforestation was part of a longstanding struggle to advance the frontier of settlement and of Islam by granting forested areas to Muslim holy men and communities, who planted wet rice in the cleared zones. On the edges of the Mughal heartland, deforestation was an instrument of enhanced control, uprooting the jungles where bandits and rebels sheltered, and encouraging settlement and, therefore, increasing revenues for the state. The emperor received a third of every harvest. Indian peasants were extremely efficient, producing two crops a year almost everywhere they planted—whether of millet, rice, or wheat. Lumberjacks accompanied seventeenth-century Mughal armies. Colonists who followed them to new lands received tax concessions and cheap plows. When the Mughals conquered areas from Burma in 1665, they evicted the existing population as ruthlessly as any European imperialists and introduced hundreds of Muslim religious foundations to clear the forest and plant rice.

NEW EXPLOITATION IN THE AMERICAS

The decline of the Native American population may have led to the abandonment of vast zones that the Indians had farmed before the Europeans arrived. But colonial regimes found alternative methods to exploit the land that, in total, probably made the colonial economy as productive as the Indian system had been: mining, ranching, and plantations (see Map 17.4). The arrival of plows, which had been unknown in the Americas before the Europeans brought them, meant that heavy soils could be exploited for the first time. Horses, mules, and oxen took on burdens Native American porters formerly bore on their backs.

The Spanish Empire

The Spanish Empire in the Americas had every avenue to wealth at its disposal. Suitable environments for all the new kinds of activity were available in abundance, while traditional native economies continued to produce their time-honored crops—such as maize, beans, squash, cotton, and cacao in Mesoamerica or coca, potatoes, and sweet potatoes in the Andes—and generate tribute. The most vivid mark and measure of success were the cities of Spanish America. As soon as Columbus returned from his first voyage, and news of America began to circulate in Europe, engravers imagined what they called the Indies filled with magnificent cities. In areas of Spanish rule, the vision was quickly realized, for Spanish imperialism was uncompromisingly urban minded. It is said that when two Englishmen meet on a savage frontier they found a club. Two Spaniards in the same circumstances found a city.

Spanish colonization slotted into the existing framework of Native American civilizations. In an extraordinarily productive period of expansion in the 1520s and 1530s, while the Spanish monarchy absorbed the existing great urban centers of Mesoamerica and the Andean region through conquest or diplomacy, the biggest cities of the Americas acquired new characteristics: Spanish-speaking elites, a new Native American middle class that served Spaniards' economic needs, an African American slave class for domestic service, Spanish courts and town councils, Christian religious foundations, cathedrals, and even, in Mexico City, a university and printing press. Similar developments followed Spanish colonization in other parts of the Americas in succeeding decades. Spanish colonists founded cities wherever they went. The new cities

Cuzco, home city of the Incas, never really looked like this. Built amid mountains, its monumental palaces, temples, and fortifications, constructed of huge blocks of stone, enclosed irregular spaces. But when Georg Braun and Franz Hogenberg published their views of the world's great cities in the late sixteenth century, they imagined Cuzco as a flat grid—the supposedly ideal form of Renaissance urban planning that inspired many colonial American cities.

Chronology: Founding Dates for Spanish Cities in the Americas

Caribbean and North America		South America	
Santo Domingo	1496	Cajamarca	1532
San Juan (Puerto Rico)	1509	Cartagena	1532
San Cristóbal (Havana)	1515	Cuzco	1533
Panama City	1519	Quito	1534
Mexico City	1521	Lima	1535
Guadalajara	1531	Buenos Aires	1536
Santa Fe de Bogotà	1538	Santiago	1541
Mérida	1542	La Paz	1548
Zacatecas	1546	Mendoza	1561
San Juan Bautista	1564	Caracas	1567
San Augustín (Florida)	1565		
Santa Fé (New Mexico)	1610		

rooted easily in areas where native cities and a strong urban tradition already existed. In other areas of mainland Spanish America—California, the frontier grasslands of North and South America—urbanization was harder, growing slowly from seeds that missions, military garrisons, and naval stations planted.

European styles in buildings smothered or supplemented the old angular look of Native American architectures with arches and domes. Some old Indian cities were flattened and rebuilt. Others were lightly adapted and recrafted. Some were abandoned, as a terrible demographic crisis unfolded with the collapse of the Native American population. New cities on new sites, like Lima, Peru, still perhaps the most Spanish of Spanish American cities in looks and atmosphere, replaced some Native American capitals. Parts of Old San Juan in Puerto Rico look exactly like a Spanish city of the seventeenth and eighteenth centuries, complete with walls, sea gates, courtyard gardens, and cathedral square. The civic model of life, the city-centered model of administration, was extended into new areas. From the 1570s, the Spanish crown issued exact regulations to construct new cities, with their grid plan and classically inspired buildings and monumental scale, the exact placing of cathedrals, government buildings, hospitals, and schools. The archives are full of the plans of projected cities, and many of them were actually built. But in North America in the seventeenth and early eighteenth centuries, beyond the Spanish frontier, cities of English and French construction generally remained, in a sense, in the Iroquois tradition. They were largely built of wood and, though intended for permanent occupancy, had a gimcrack air of instant shabbiness.

Brazil

Other European empires in the Americas lacked the advantage of local labor sources that they could exploit on the scale of the Spanish lands. As a result, they tended at first to expand to landward on only a modest scale, so that they could increase the areas of cultivation of the crops they introduced, such as sugar in the Caribbean, West Indian tobacco in Virginia, rice in the Carolinas, and wheat almost everywhere. In Brazil, sugar was suitable only to coastal enclaves where it could be successfully grown and easily shipped to Europe. It would never, on its own, have induced planters to create a large territorial domain in Brazil's hinterland. Rivalry with Spain to control the Amazon, however, turned Portuguese thoughts toward the Brazilian interior, especially after rival Spanish and Portuguese expeditions tested the navigability of the great Amazon River system in the 1630s. Gold and diamonds, discovered in the Brazilian province of Minas Gerais (meaning "general mines") in the 1680s, proved the incentive required for Portugal to drive its Brazilian frontier inland.

British North America

Elsewhere, though explorers scoured the Americas for natural resources in the late sixteenth and seventeenth centuries, major sources of gold, silver, pearls, and precious gems remained a Spanish monopoly. The areas left for the English and French to exploit contained only fool's gold, such as the iron pyrites Martin Frobisher found in Canada in 1576, which deceived investors into ruin and lured adventurers to their deaths. Furs were the "black gold" of the north, but, like the timber and fish that also abounded in and around North America, resources of these kinds could not alone sustain permanent or populous colonies: only the French fur trappers who lived among the Indians, migrant merchants and hunters, and seasonal visitors.

Except in the Caribbean, where sugar and, later, coffee would grow on islands seized from or ignored by Spain, it was hard to find crops suitable to sustain colonial life. Tobacco was the first such crop, introduced into Virginia in 1614. Later in the century, rice made fairly large-scale settlement practical in the coastal areas of South Carolina. Independent farmers could always cultivate small holdings for their own subsistence, as they did with remarkable success even in the inhospitably rocky soils of New England from the 1620s. But this form of exploitation could never be the foundation of prosperity. New England only really began to reveal its potential as a great world center of wealth and civilized life in the eighteenth century, not because of its own resources but because so many of the inhabitants took to the sea. Like classical Greece and ancient Phoenicia (Chapter 5), New England became a maritime civilization, making up for the poverty of its home soils by trade and the exploitation of marine resources. Three trades in particular contributed to transforming New England's economy into one of the richest, per capita, in the world by the late eighteenth century: first, the slave trade, in which New England merchants worked both as shippers and dealers; second, the export of locally produced rum and manufactured goods to the slave-producing and slave-consuming markets with which the slave trade connected the New Englanders; and finally the so-called **East India trade**—mainly with China, by way of Cape Horn on the southern tip of South America—for tea and porcelain to sell at home.

From Virginia southward, English North American colonies naturally—literally, naturally—resembled those that Spanish, Dutch, and Portuguese investors were already exploiting in Mesoamerica and South America. They were hot and wet, with torrid lowlands that could be adapted to plant cash crops with the labor of imported slaves. The first English-run sugar industry in Barbados was directly copied from the Dutch enterprise in Pernambuco, with Dutch capital and know-how. The effects on settler society were predictable. Economic reliance on large-scale, capital-intensive enterprises created huge disparities of wealth. Large-scale English planters in parts of North America and the Caribbean became, in effect, the lords of huge estates, more reminiscent of the Mediterranean or Brazil, than of England or New England. In 1700, the top 5 percent of settlers by wealth owned half of one county in Virginia.

HOME FRONTS IN EUROPE AND ASIA

New wealth-creating activities were not confined to imperial frontiers. Equal efforts were under way to exploit the homelands of the empires. Governments all over the world undertook land surveys to determine the extent of production and

A Chinese porcelain punch-bowl acquired in the East Indies trade late in the eighteenth century by the Rhode Island merchant John Brown. The decoration shows the American *hong* (or warehouse and place of business) in Guangzhou, as well as *hongs* for traders from other Western countries, overlooking the Pearl River.

Chronology: Imperialism and Coloniziation in Europe, Asia, and the Americas	
1520s–1530s	Absorption of Mesoamerican and Andean cities into Spanish Empire
1550s	Russian conquest of Kazan
ca. 1560–1650	Russian colonization of lower Volga and Siberia
1600s	Expansion, colonization, and intensive farming in Mughal India
	Outflow of Chinese and Japanese settlers to Southeast Asia
	Export of African slaves, especially to the Americas
	British colonization of North America
ca. 1620s–1660s	Large-scale Chinese immigration to Taiwan
1667–1707	1.5 million settlers arrive in Sichuan
1680s	Discovery of gold and diamonds prompts further Portuguese expansion in Brazil
Late seventeenth century	Japanese peasants displace native inhabitants of Hokkaido
1700s	New England becomes a world center of trade

Great Slave
Lake
Carrier
Chipewyan
Beaver
Lake Athabasca
Churchill
Fort
Churchill
York Factory
1682
Nelson
Severn Factory
RUPERT'S LAND
James
Bay
East
Cree
Newfoundland
Beothuk
Gulf of
St. Lawrence
Cape Breton
Island
Naskapi
Fort Albany
1670
Moose Factory
1671
Eastmain
Rupert House
1668
Montagnais
Halifax **1749**
Micmac
NOVA
SCOTIA

Saskatchewan
Cree
Lake
Winnipeg
Assiniboine
Kutenai
Nez
Perce
Flathead
Northern
Shoshoni
Bannock
Western
Shoshoni

ROCKY   MOUNTAINS
Blackfoot
Gros Ventres
Crow
Yanktonai
Teton
Arikara
Cheyenne
Dakota
Santee
Yankton

**NORTH
AMERICA**

Fort Kaministikwia
Ojibwa
Lake Superior
Michilimackinac
Menomini **1697**
Winnebago
Lake
Huron
Lake
Michigan
Sauk
Fox
Mascouten
Kickapoo
Miami

Nipissing
Algonquin
Ottawa
Huron
Penturn
Detroit
1701
Niagara
L. Ontario
L. Erie
Iroquois

NEW FRANCE
St. Lawrence
River
Quebec
1608
Montreal
1642
Lake
Champlain
Fort Orange **1624**
Albany **1664**
Mohican
Pequot
Boston **1630**
Narraganset
Newport
NEW ENGLAND

ATLANTIC OCEAN

East India Trade

Southern
Paiute
Ute
Colorado
Mojave
Western
Apache
Cocopa
Hopi
Navajo
Zuni
Queres
Acoma
Taos
Pecos
Santa Fe **1609**
Taos **1680**

Great   Plains
Kiowa
Pawnee
Oto
Kansa
Osage
Arapaho
Arkansas
Missouri
Iowa
Missouri
Illinois
Ohio
Shawnee

Kaskaskia
The
Illinois Post
1700
Quapaw
Mississippi
Chickasaw
Coosa
Caddo
Wichita
Comanche

LOUISIANA

Susquehanna
Delaware
Powhatan
New Amsterdam **1625**
(New York **1664**)
Philadelphia **1682**

Appalachian Mountains
Richmond **1733**
Jamestown
1607
Monacan
Tutelo
Yuchi
Pamlico
Tuscarora
Catawba

Cherokee
Creek
Confederacy
1672
Charleston
Savannah
1733

Imaris
Jocome
Mescalero
Apache
Jano
Suma
Concho
Opata
Lipan
Apache
Jumano
Tonkawa
Atakapa
Karankawa
Tunica
Houma
Chitimacha
Acolapissa
Choctaw
Alabama
Hitichi
Apalachee

New Orleans **1718**
Timucua
Potano **1565**
St. Augustine **1565**

Cochimi
Papago
Lower Pima
Seri
Tarahumara
Tubar
Toboso
Tepehuan

Rio Grande
Coahuilteco

1567
1567
Ais **1566**
Seminole
Calusa **1567**
Tekesta

Waicuri
Mayo
Cahita
Guasave

Zacatecan
Guachichil
Jonaz
Pame
Cuyute
Coco
Mazatec

Tampico
Tamaulipeco

Gulf
of
Mexico

Bahamas
1629

Tropic of Cancer

Tropic of Cancer

Havana
1511
Cuba
Arawak

Danish
Virgin Islands
Antigua
1632

Mérida
1542
Yucatan
Peninsula
Yucatan
Maya

NEW SPAIN
Hispaniola
San Juan **1509**
Puerto Rico

Guadeloupe
1635

Mexico City
1521
Veracruz
1519
Tlaxcaltan
Aztec
VICEROYALTY OF
SAINT-
DOMINGUE
Ciboney
Santo Domingo
1497
Martinique
1635
St Lucia
1605
Barbados
1605

1509–1655
1655
Jamaica
West   Indies
Grenada
1650

Mixe
Zoque
BELIZE
Gulf of Honduras
Trujillo
1525
Chorti
Cholutec
Paya
Mosquito
MOSQUITO
COAST
Pipil
Matagalpa
Nicarao
Xinca
Talamanca

Caribbean   Sea

Aruba
Bonaire
Curaçao
Trinidad
1577

Guaymi
Panama
1519

Cartagena
1532
Caracas
1567
VICEROYALTY OF
NEW GRANADA

PACIFIC

OCEAN

500 km
500 miles

N

Caribbean Sea

Santa Marta
1525

Panama
1519
Gulf of Darien
Cartagena **1532**
Maracaibo **1529**
Caracas **1567**
Cumaná **1521**

Gulf of Panama
AUDIENCIA OF SANTA FÉ **1548**
Lake Maracaibo
Santa Fé de Bogotá **1538**

VICEROYALTY OF NEW GRANADA **1739**

Orinoco
Rio Negro
Branco
Guiana Highlands

New Amsterdam **1627**
SURINAM
Paramaribo **1613**

Quito **1534**
PRESIDENCIA OF QUITO **1563**

Tumbes **1526**
Cuenca **1557**
Paita **1532**
MAYNAS **1638–1767**
Cajamarca **1532**
Trujillo **1525**
AUDIENCIA OF LIMA **1543**

Putumayo
Marañón
Amazon
Amazon
Juruá
Ucayali
Amazon Basin
Rio Negro
Manaus **1674**
Tapajós
Purus
Madeira

Amazon
PARÁ **1616**
Belém do Pará **1616**
São Luís (Maranhão)
MARANHÃO **1615**
Ceará
PIAUÍ **1532**
CEARÁ **1613**
Natal **1597**
DUTCH BRAZIL 1630–1654
PARAÍBA **1532**
Paraíba **1585**
Olinda
PERNAMBUCO **1532**
Recife ca.1535

VICEROYALTY OF BRAZIL

SOUTH AMERICA

Callao **1537**
Lima **1535**
Huancavelica
Cuzco **1533**
MOJOS **1659–1767**
Lake Titicaca
La Paz **1548**
Arequipa **1540**
Arica **1537**

MATO GROSSO **1748**
Vila Bela (Mato Grosso) **1752**
Planalto de Mato Grosso
CHIQUITOS **1691**

Madre de Dios
Beni
Lago Poopó
La Plata **1538**
Potosí **1545**
PRESIDENCIA OF CHARCAS **1559**
VICEROYALTY OF PERU **1543**

GOIÁS **1744**
Goiás **1744**
Minas Novas **1727**
Diamantina **1730**
MINAS GERAIS **1720**

São Francisco
SERGIPE **1532**
Fort Maurits **1637**
Sergipe del Rey
BAHIA **1532**
Bahia (Salvador) capital **1549–1763**
PORTO SEGURO **1532**
Ilhéus **1534**
Brazilian Highlands
ESPÍRITO SANTO **1532**
Vitória

ITATÍN **1609–1660**
GUAIRÁ ca.**1630–1632**
Asunción **1537**
Ciudad Real **1630**
SANTA CATARINA **1532**
Desterro **1640**
Laguna **1654**
RIO GRANDE DO SUL **1777**

SÃO PAULO **1709**
São Paulo **1532**
São Vicente **1532**
Santos **1545**
RIO DE JANEIRO **1532**
Rio de Janeiro **1565** capital from **1763**

GUARANÍ **1630–1660**
CHACO **1732–1767**
Gran Chaco
Pilcomayo
Bermejo
Paraguay
Corumbá **1788**
Paraná
Uruguay

Coquimbo **1537**
CAPTAINCY-GENERAL AND PRESIDENCIA OF CHILE **1606**
Córdoba **1573**
Mendoza **1561**
Valparaíso **1541**
Santiago **1541**
Buenos Aires **1536**
Salado
Colónia do Sacramento Portuguese **1680–1750**
Porto Alegre
Rio Grande **1737**
Montevideo **1726**
River Plate

Concepción **1550**
Valdivia **1552**
San Carlos de Ancud **1763**
Colorado
Rio Negro
Carmen de Patagones **1779**
Pampas
Araucanians
Patagonia
Golfo de San Jorge
Deseado
Golfo de Penas
Bahía Grande
Strait of Magellan
Islas Malvinas
Cape Horn

60° 80° 10° 50° 40° Equator 80° 10° Tropic of Capricorn 30° 50° 40° 60° 70° 20° Tropic of Capricorn 20° 30° 50° 40°

ATLANTIC OCEAN
ATLANTIC OCEAN

N
500 km
500 miles

MAP 17.4

Land Exploitation in the Americas up to ca. 1725

Economic Activity

	British ca. 1725		hides and deerskins
Spanish before 1650		copper
Spanish after 1650		gold
Portuguese by 1600		silver mine
Portuguese by 1750		drugs
French ca.1725		cocoa
French influence		diamonds
approximate western limit of French claim		dyes
Dutch		rice-growing region

······ fur trade routes
1682 date of foundation
Houma native people
⛪ Jesuit missions
✝ major Franciscan missions
🏰 Spanish fort

⚮ sugar-growing region
🐬 major fisheries
🌿 tobacco cultivation

***Shinsen Dainibon Zukan* (Revised Map of Japan) of 1687.** The maps of Japan that the shogun Hideyoshi commissioned have not survived, but this is one of a series based on them. Each province is marked with the name of its feudal lord or *daimyo* and the amount of his salary. The placard at the top lists each province's topographical information, including place names, temples, and shrines. The blank land to the left of it, labeled Chosenkoku, is Korea.

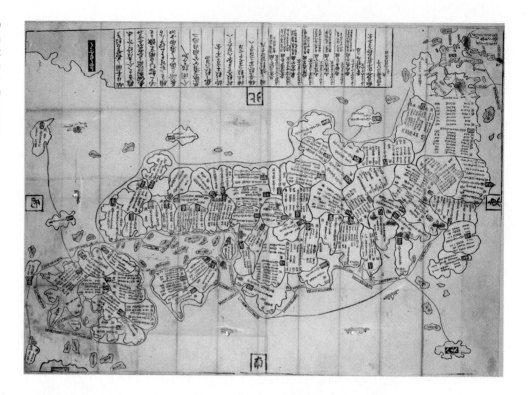

the possibilities to increase it. In the 1570s, King Philip II of Spain ordered the most comprehensive survey of his realms that any European state had ever undertaken. It was soon extended to the New World and illustrated with maps that Native Americans made. In Japan in 1580, the shogun Hideyoshi (see Chapter 16) commanded a survey of Japan that would penetrate "the deepest caves of the mountains and the reach of oars at sea." It was to include the dimensions and soil quality of every rice field and the location of every irrigation channel. Villagers who withheld information would be crucified. Landowners who failed to cooperate would be put to the sword. Begun in 1583, driven by unpitying force, the job was finished by 1598. The Mughal regime in India was not given to such bureaucratic exertions but achieved something similar in the late sixteenth century, including a tally of average yields and market prices, field by field. In 1663, frustrated by his inability to locate undeveloped resources in France, Jean-Baptiste Colbert, the chief minister of King Louis XIV, ordered the first scrupulously accurate map of the country to be made by the latest surveying techniques. It was not fully complete until 1789 on the eve of the French Revolution.

New Energy Sources

Efforts to explore the environment led to the discovery and release of new energy sources. Timber from deforestation made an enormous contribution, together with oil from aggressive whaling by European and Japanese seamen in previously unfrequented seas. Cottonseed oil and rapeseed oil in Japan came into use as oil-lamp fuel in the early 1600s. Extracting peat to be burned as fuel from the bogs of Holland became a major industry. In some places, people shifted to coal, mined in increasing quantities in Great Britain, Germany, and the southern Netherlands (modern Belgium; it was a territory of the Spanish monarchy at the time). Londoners in the mid–sixteenth century burned more than 20,000 tons of coal annually—a little less than a quarter of a ton per inhabitant. By 1700, coal imports to London totaled almost 400,000 tons for a population of about 600,000. In the late seventeenth century, miners in Kyushu, Japan, began to make a success of marketing coal: to peasants for fuel, to refiners of salt and sugar. The Japanese government, meanwhile, adopted policies to conserve and replant forests, reserving valuable timber for official purposes, excluding intruders from endangered forest zones, and rewarding tree planting. "Cherishing the mountains," for the local ruler of Tugaru in the 1660s, was essential to nurture life and reverse forest shrinkage so severe that loggers were invading the northernmost Japanese island of Hokkaido for timber. Coal was abundant in China, but the market for it remained static. Wood and charcoal were still adequate to meet China's energy needs.

Land Reclamation

Land reclamation complemented the struggle to expand and settle new frontiers. In Holland, after terrible losses of lands to the encroaching sea in the sixteenth century, reclamation became a matter of survival. New windmill-pumping technology drained 57,000 acres of land in North Holland between 1610 and 1640. In all, the Dutch added nearly 370,000 acres to the land available for farming during the century. A minor social revolution accompanied the transformation of the landscape, as smallholders lost access to the sea and were forced to sell out to big landowners. In England, the drainage of the fenlands, which lay just across the sea from Holland in the eastern counties, began in 1600. Enforced by military occupation, against the protests of the local inhabitants, who were dispossessed, the project brought about 480,000 acres under the plow by the early 1650s. In Japan, government-sponsored schemes drained the Yodfo River delta. The Nobi plain in northern Honshu was transformed from "a marshy plain of water birds" to an area with hundreds of villages. The Aka River, which once flowed through marshes, fed 12,000 acres of wet rice lands by 1650. The cultivated land area of Japan grew by 82 percent between 1600 and 1720.

FRONTIERS OF THE HUNT

Imperialism promoted more efficient—sometimes more ruthless—exploitation of the Earth. Beyond the edges of empires, we do not know enough to be sure, but improvements in the range and effectiveness of hunting, and the extension of cultivation, were happening in other parts of the world, too. When the English arrived in Virginia, they found thousand of acres under cultivation and maize stocks "of sufficient quantity to fill the holds of several ships."

The Iroquois country of northeast North America is a case in point. Toward the end of what we think of as the Middle Ages, Indians developed a form of maize suitable for latitudes as north as the Great Lakes. This zone, which extends just north of Lakes Ontario and Erie and along the southern shores of Lakes Huron and Michigan, had about 140 frost-free days a year. Increasingly in the sixteenth and seventeenth centuries, Indians planted the new crop in forest clearings between the upper Hudson River and Lake Erie, on the frontier between deciduous and evergreen trees, where ecological diversity made ambitious ways of life possible.

The very diversity of their food sources imposed a mobile way of life on the Native Americans of the region. Periodically, soil erosion and forest depletion forced them to shift the sites of their

Huron women. Published in 1664, the *History of Canada* by the Jesuit priest François du Creux summarized the vast output of the author's fellow missionaries on the subject and helped to spread a favorable image of the Huron among learned readers in Europe. Here the engraver shows industrious Huron women peacefully engaged in a civilized, agrarian activity—maize production, in an idealized setting, while an infant's cradle alludes to sentiments and social conventions that European readers would have found comforting and familiar.

towns. Maize exhausts soil more quickly than other grains. The biggest settlement in the Great Lakes region was the Illinois town of Kaskaskia, with over 7,000 people in 1680, but villages of about 1,000 people were not unusual. To make glades for planting without hard-metal tools, Native Americans cut a ring in the trunk of a tree and set it on fire until the stump burned through. The method yielded ash for fertilizer, but left a landscape strewn with stumps. Farming under these disadvantages could never entirely replace a traditional way of life based on hunting, fishing, gathering wild berries, and tapping maple trees for syrup. But, like other forest peoples of the Americas who came into contact with colonial and overseas markets, the inhabitants improved their techniques and turnover as hunters too. They adopted firearms for the kill and steel knives to skin and butcher game. Beavers, once hunted for their meat, were now more valuable for the pelts European fur traders demanded. Beavers were almost gone from southern Ontario by the mid-1630s and had virtually disappeared from New England by 1700. In southern parts of North America, below the beaver's natural range, deerskins for the European leather trade became an equally valuable product. They made suede breeches and book bindings and smooth yellow gloves. In the 1690s and early 1700s, Charleston, South Carolina, exported up to 85,000 deerskins a year, and the numbers increased until the deer herds were depleted in the 1770s.

"In some parts of the world, the effects of the ecological revolutions were delayed until the eighteenth or nineteenth centuries. But the decisive transformations had already occurred by the end of the seventeenth century. Across the densely populated belt of the world, from China to Mesoamerica and the Andes, a single network of communications transmitted the same varieties of plants and animals."

In Perspective
Evolution Redirected

In some parts of the world, the effects of the ecological revolutions were delayed until the eighteenth or nineteenth centuries. But the decisive transformations had already occurred by the end of the seventeenth century. Across the densely populated belt of the world, from China to Mesoamerica and the Andes, a single network of communications transmitted the same varieties of plants and animals. The empires that dominated the zone responded in similar ways to the problems and opportunities of the time. New crops and animals helped the great colonizing movements of the era. They enabled farmers to penetrate new environments and exploit old ones more efficiently. The results included a huge increase in the amount of food people in affected regions could coax from the fields or cull from the wild. Not only did total food production go up, but a revolution in nutrition also occurred, as a wider variety of foodstuffs became available worldwide. Sometimes, when traditional crops failed, the products of the ecological exchange could fill the gap. In some places, on the other hand, newly introduced crops displaced traditional ones without increasing people's choices. In parts of northern Europe, for instance, by the nineteenth century, people became dependent on potatoes. In parts of the Americas, wheat displaced maize, which is, in many ways, a more efficient crop.

The indirect consequences of the ecological exchanges were equally impressive. People could farm new areas with new crops, creating new communities and the kernels of new states. In southeast Europe, for instance, maize cultivators could move upcountry to higher altitudes, where the Ottoman Empire's tax gatherers and enforcers never penetrated. A global revolution in the organization and distribution of labor was among the effects, as slavers shifted manpower from Africa across the Atlantic and Indian oceans to grow transplanted crops such as sugar and coffee on a huge scale.

Making Connections | NEW WAYS OF EXPLOITING THE NATURAL ENVIRONMENT

REGION/ECOLOGICAL ZONE	NEW FORMS OF EXPLOITATION	RESULTS
Western Hemisphere (North and South America, Caribbean)	Mass importation of slaves from Africa after depopulation of Native Americans due to disease	Large areas of North, Central, and South America transformed into plantations for cultivation of sugar, cotton, rice, tobacco, and indigo; creation of large African and mixed-race populations throughout Western Hemisphere
Steppeland; mountainous regions of Asia, including Mongolia and Xianjang	Chinese takeover of traditional adversaries, exploitation of natural resources	Well-trained infantry, advanced artillery, well-designed fortifications end the nomadic threat; highland and steppe regions become source for raw materials
Cape of Good Hope, South Africa, Australia	Introduction of sheep and new breeds of cattle, extensive farming by European settlers	Displacement of natives
North and South America/lowlands, high plains	Farming pampas/prairies; felling forests	Creation of large-scale agricultural complexes focusing on wheat, maize, and other commodities for human and livestock consumption for domestic use and export
Mexico, South America	Development of silver and gold mines	Boost global supply of cash
Mexico, South America, and North America	Development of extensive livestock herding	Millions of square miles of lightly populated areas claimed for cattle and sheep herding
North America	Large-scale fur trade in American Midwest, West, and Canada	Beaver, deerskins, and other furs/skins become basis for gradual penetration, settlement of western and northern North America
Eurasia	Land reclamation projects; expansion of timber harvesting, mining	National leaders attempt to solidify control, expand state revenues through systematic exploitation of resources, beginning with thorough mapping and surveying projects

Chronology

1492	Columbus arrives in the New World, beginning process of biological exchange
1500s	Horses and cattle introduced to New World
1510	Importation of slave labor in the Spanish colonies begins
1520s and 1530s	Absorption of Mesoamerican and Andean cities into Spanish Empire
1550s	Russian conquest of Kazan
1555	First records of maize cultivation in China
ca. 1560–1650	Russian colonization of lower Volga and Siberia
1570s	Philip II of Spain orders survey of his realms
	Brazil becomes a major importer of slaves
1580s	Brazil becomes the world's major sugar producer
1580	Shogun Hideyoshi orders a survey of Japan
1600s	British colonization of North America
	Expansion, colonization, and intensive farming in Mughal India
ca. 1620s–1660s	Large-scale Chinese immigration to Taiwan
1667–1707	1.5 million settlers arrive in Sichuan
1680s	Discovery of gold and diamonds prompts further Portuguese expansion in Brazil
1690s	Charleston, South Carolina, exports up to 85,000 deerskins a year
Late seventeenth century	Japanese peasants displace native inhabitants of Hokkaido
ca. 1700	Native American population in regions penetrated by Europeans declines 60 to 90 percent
1700	Popularity of coffee booms in Europe and Middle East, and coffee production begins in Brazil and Indonesia
	New England becomes a world center of trade

Evolution, meanwhile, was launched on a new course. In one respect, at least, the ecological exchanges constituted the biggest revolution humankind had wrought in the natural history of the planet. Ever since the continents began to split apart from one another, perhaps about 130 million years ago, they had begun to nurture different life forms. Species peculiar to each continent developed in different ways, divided from each other by uncrossable seas. This divergent history now gave way to a convergent trend that has produced the world we inhabit today, when the same germs, plants, and animals occur all over the world, wherever climate permits. In a sense, human intervention began to reverse the effects of tens of millions of years of evolution.

The ecological revolution was the essential precondition for some of the global changes of the next few centuries, fueling some of the major themes of the next two parts of this book: population growth, radical breakthroughs in exploiting the globe's resources, and the globalization of empires and trade. But such effects depended on more than the physical environment. People's mental attitudes to the world changed, too, and, like the ingredients of ecological exchange, voyagers carried these new attitudes with them across the globe through long-range travel, trade, and empire-building. These mental revolutions are the subjects of the next chapter.

PROBLEMS AND PARALLELS

1. Why should the Columbian Exchange be regarded as one of the biggest revolutions in history?

2. What are some of the explanations for the "age of plagues"? Why did it suddenly end in the eighteenth century?

3. How did human settlement expand its range in the sixteenth and seventeenth centuries? What were the motives behind this expansion? What effect did it have on ecological frontiers? On the way colonialists viewed the natural world? Why did rulers like Hideyoshi in Japan initiate detailed land surveys of their domains?

4. Why was there a massive transplantation of human labor during the sixteenth and seventeenth centuries? Why did colonial America suffer from severe labor shortages?

5. Why did the balance of power between settled life and pastoralism shift in favor of the settlers? In which parts of the world did pastoralism remain a predominant way of life? Why did the Moroccan conquest of Songhay under al-Mansur ultimately fail to control the pastoralists of the Sahel?

6. What factors made Spanish colonialism in the Americas more advantageous than the ventures of the English or French?

READ ON ▶ ▶ ▶

Ledger's story can be found in G. Gramiccia, *The Life of Charles Ledger* (1988) and F. Rocco, *The Miraculous Fever-tree* (2003). The major works on the ecological exchange are A. W. Crosby, *The Columbian Exchange* (1972) and *Ecological Imperialism* (1986). J. F. Richards, *The Unending Frontier* (2003) is a superb, if necessarily selective, environmental history of the period. Classics on particular crops include N. Deerr, *The History of Sugar* (1949); S. Mintz, *Sweetness and Power* (1986); N. Salaman, *History and Social Influence of the Potato* (1985); and A. Warman, *Corn and Capitalism* (2003). M. Elvin, *The Retreat of the Elephants* (2004) is an inspiring general history of the Chinese environment. My book, *Near a Thousand Tables* (2002), puts the exchanges in the context of the history of food. R. Grove, *Green Imperialism* (1996) is an amazingly rich work that argues that European colonialism nurtured environmentalism.

On plague in general, see the works recommended in Chapter 14. The demographic disasters of the New World are the subject of intense controversy: see D. Henige, *Numbers from Nowhere*, (1998) and contrast W. M. Denevan, *The Native Population of the Americas in 1492* (1992). The most balanced general treatment is in D. N. Cook, *Born to Die*, (1998) though the author's argument that demographics explain the course of "conquest" should be considered critically. On plague in China, C. Benedict, *Bubonic Plague in Nineteenth-Century China* (1996) is important. O.J. Benedictow, *The Black Death, 1346–53* (2004) is a valuable recent contribution to plague epidemiology.

On the Atlantic slave trade, H. Thomas, *The Slave Trade* (1999) is a lively history. R. Blackburn, *The Making of New World Slavery* (1998) is an engaging introduction. J. Thornton, *Africa and Africans in the Making of the Atlantic World* (1998) is a model of scholarship and presentation. P. D. Curtin, *The Rise and Fall of the Plantation Complex* (1998); S. W. Mintz and R. Price, *The Birth of African-American Culture* (1992), B. Solow, ed., *Slavery and the Rise of the Atlantic System* (1993); D. Eltis, *The Rise of African Slavery in the Americas* (1999) are all valuable studies of the economies and societies of slave plantations.

M. Sobel, *The World They Made Together* (1989) is important on the slave world of Virginia, and L. Ferguson, *Uncommon Ground* (1995) is full of interesting material on plantation life in the North American South generally.

C. D. Totman, *Early Modern Japan* (1995) is an account particularly strong on environmental awareness. B. Walker, *The Conquest of Ainu Lands* (2001) is admirable. R. L. Edmonds, *Northern Frontiers of Qing China and Tokugawa Japan* (1985) makes an admirable comparative introduction. On Chinese expansion, R. H. G. Lee, *The Manchurian Frontier in Ch'ing History* (1970), and J. Waley-Cohen, *Exile in mid-Qing China* (1991) are indispensable. Ping-ti Ho, *Studies on the Population of China* (1959) is a valuable broad survey of its subject.

D. Twitchett and J. K. Fairbank, eds., *The Cambridge History of China*, vol. 7 (1988), is an invaluable guide to China in the period. On the Manchu conquest of China, L. Struve, *Voices from the Ming-Qing Cataclysm* (1998) is a well-selected and structured collection of sources.

There is, as far as I know, no dedicated study in English, but there are some useful pages on al-Mansur's conquest of the Sahara in A. C. Hess, *The Forgotten Frontier* (1978), and J. O. Hunwick, *Timbuktu and the Songhay Empire* (2003) contains some useful documents.

On Russian Siberia, J. Forsyth, *A History of the Peoples of Siberia* (1994) is an impressive and masterful introduction. B. Dmitrishyn et al., eds., *Russia's Conquest of Siberia* (1986) is an enormous compendium of sources. The best edition of the chronicles is T. Armstrong, ed., *Yermak's Campaigns in Siberia* (1975). J. Martin, *Treasure of the Land of Darkness* (2004) is superb on the background of the fur trade. M. Rywkin, ed., *Russian Colonial Expansion* (1988) contains some important papers.

C. Wilson, *England's Apprenticeship* (1965) is an excellent introduction to the economic history of England in the seventeenth century. For the inland see K. Lindley, *Fenland Riots and the English Revolution* (1982). J. de Vries and A. M. van der Woude, *The First Modern Economy* (1997) is the standard work on the early modern Dutch economy.

On the Mughal frontier in Bengal, R. Eaton, *The Rise of Islam and the Bengal Frontier* (1996) is of great value and importance.

On Spanish American cities V. Fraser, *The Architecture of Conquest* (1990) is a monograph (on Peru) crafted well enough to serve as an introduction.

For Brazil, J. Hemming, *Red Gold* (1978) and *Amazon Frontier* (1987) are superb and chilling accounts of the fate of the natives at the time of European conquest and colonization. S. Schwartz, ed., *Tropical Babylons* (2004) is the most up-to-date collection on the sugar colonies. G. Freyre, *The Masters and the Slaves* is a classic of such significance in Brazilian historiography that it should still be read by anyone interested in the subject. C. R. Boxer, *The Golden Age of Brazil* (1995) is almost in the same category.

B. Trigger's magnificent *A History of the Huron People*, 2 vols. (1976), is unequaled in its field.

CHAPTER 18

Mental Revolutions: Religion and Science in the Sixteenth and Seventeenth Centuries

▲ **Astronomy lesson:** from the sacred seclusion of a private chamber, King Narai of Siam listens in while Jesuits teach astronomy to his courtiers during an eclipse. Owing to the king's presence, the courtiers must attend to the lesson while lying face down on the floor. Celestial events triggered traditional royal rituals in the kingdoms of East Asia, so Jesuits' expertise in astronomy made them useful to many rulers there.

The beds were strange—"raised like thrones, girded with hangings and curtains, and with thick mattresses and covers to protect sleepers from the cold.'" That was the first thing Kosa Pan saw when he spent his first night ashore in France in 1686, as ambassador of the king of Thailand (the country Westerners used to call Siam until the twentieth century). "I am told," he went on, "that entire families sleep in one large bed, all enclosed in wooden shutters; we were spared such an indignity.'" The account that follows—which narrates the embassy's journey from the coast to Paris—is so mixed up with satirical comment intruded by a European editor that it is often hard to tell Kosa Pan's voice. Still, many comments on French customs ring true. French dancing, Kosa Pan the writer found, resembled "a military parade performed by both sexes." He literally turned his nose up at the unperfumed common people he met, for they "found our habit of bathing curious. . . . Truly I think our buffaloes smell sweeter than most French people, for we wash them more often."

When Kosa Pan at last arrived at the French king's palace, Louis XIV (r. 1643–1715) spared no effort or expense to impress the ambassador. He received him, seated on a silver throne and dressed in cloth of gold, studded with huge diamonds in imitation of Siamese royal robes. The layout and the lavish floral decorations of the audience chamber were designed to match what travelers had reported of the appearance of Siam's royal apartments. When Kosa Pan presented his credentials, Louis rose, bowed, and doffed his hat—gestures of condescension he would never have made to honor a European diplomat.

But why had Kosa Pan traveled so far? What was this Buddhist gentleman from an agrarian state in a corner of Southeast Asia doing halfway across the world, struggling across two oceans, to a continent his countrymen had only just discovered, dragging 132 crates—as he recalled—filled with gifts from his king to the king of France?

It was not the first time that King Narai of Siam had tried to forge an alliance with France. The first embassy was shipwrecked off the coast of Madagascar and never even reached the Atlantic. The second made it to Paris, initiated contacts, and caused a sensation in Europe, prompting the French court to respond with a mission to Siam. The idea for an alliance seems to have originated with a Greek adventurer whom Narai employed as a trusted confidant. Narai's objectives seem to have been twofold. First, he wanted France to supply him with soldiers, to deter other European powers from attacking Siam and keep potential rebels in awe. This alone shows that European military technology and techniques were already respected in Southeast Asia. But Narai admired another, more peaceful Western attainment, too.

FOCUS questions

Why did European elites attempt to change Christian practice and teachings during the sixteenth century?

How did Native Americans and Africans influence Christian beliefs and worship?

Where were Muslim and Buddhist missionaries most active in the sixteenth and seventeenth centuries?

How did the Mughal emperors deal with religious diversity?

Why was the spread of scientific thought important for the West?

Why were the Chinese so interested in astronomy?

A contemporary engraving shows him listening to an astronomy lesson from a visiting Jesuit missionary. Court dignitaries struggle to follow the lesson, while abasing themselves in the ritual fashion Siamese court etiquette demanded. Astronomy in parts of East Asia was more than a learned curiosity: it was a means to power. Like many other rulers who modeled their practices on those of Chinese emperors, Narai had to perform official rites at prescribed moments during the cycle of the sun, moon, and stars, to preserve—supposedly—harmony between his kingdom and the heavens. Westerners, despite their barbaric manners and offensive smell, had the advantage of mastery of two technologies—the telescope and clockwork timekeeping—that could help to guarantee the accuracy of the calendar. Kosa Pan traveled in search of knowledge as well as power—indeed, he and his king regarded the two quests as inseparable. His journey illustrates an ever more common and characteristic feature of the world of his day: the way human encounters brought cultures into contact and initiated cultural exchanges that crossed the planet.

In one respect, Kosa Pan's journey was unusual. More commonly, it was Westerners who crossed the world and initiated the contacts that brought cultural exchange, but Christianity, Islam, and Buddhism all contributed. The sixteenth and seventeenth centuries were an unprecedented era for the revitalization and spread of all three religions. They were also centuries of unprecedented development for Western science and secular values. Western science reached parts of the world where previously, like Thailand, it had been unknown. At the same time, the ways people thought, felt, and, in some respects, behaved in the West changed as a result of encounters with non-Western cultures.

CHRISTIANITY IN CHRISTENDOM

Western Christendom and, to a slightly lesser extent, the Eastern Orthodox world had developed a new sense of mission in the late Middle Ages. Fervor to renew the dynamism of the early history of the church combined with a new conviction of the obligations of the godly. Those obligations included a growing sense of the need to compel "right thinking" alongside outward conformity, and to combat heresy, unbelief, and supposedly satanic forces. People with vocations or responsibilities in the church, or with a strong personal sense of their relationship with God, increasingly took it upon themselves to spread active, committed, Christian awareness, informed by a knowledge of dogma. Among the consequences were new religious orders, new techniques of prayer, new fashions in devotion, and increased coercion and social control (see Chapter 19). But there were still parts of society and places in the world where, so far, Christianity had hardly reached or only superficially penetrated. In the sixteenth and seventeenth centuries, the mission-minded felt the need of a new conversion strategy, addressed to people low on the social scale: the poor; the rootless masses of growing cities; the neglected country folk; the peoples of forest, bog, and mountain, who had barely entered the candle-glow of the church; and the vast world that exploration and improved geographical learning revealed or suggested. Self-consciously, godly elites set themselves the task of re-Christianizing Europe, reviving the fervor of lukewarm Christians, and trying to root out pagan survivals and demonic intrusions or delusions from popular customs. Like peasants and pagans, children were part of the previously submerged world to which clerical zeal now penetrated. By the last quarter of the sixteenth century, thousands of Christian catechisms for the education of children were in print.

The countryside was Europe's pagan backyard, full of potential converts to a more intense, aware, and devout Christian life. Rural communities still lived in worlds full of spirits and demons, where natural forces were personified and placated. A miller in northern Italy in the early sixteenth century could describe a remarkably coherent universe made "of cheese and worms," from which Christian traditions about creation were entirely absent. A Jesuit priest in the city of Bordeaux in France in 1553 was appalled to find people in the nearby countryside "who have never heard of mass nor of a single word of the faith." Another Jesuit in Spain in 1615 expressed disbelief that so many of his colleagues wanted to be missionaries in Asia or America "when we have so many people here who do not know whether they believe in God." In 1628, a member of the English parliament complained of regions of the country "where God was little better known than among the Indians." In 1693, the Swedish governor general of Livonia (in the modern Baltic States) ordered the smashing of the rocks and groves people worshipped "so that not the least memorial may be left which could be used for superstition."

Campaigns like these were part of a more general attempt by ministers of religion to enforce their claim to a monopoly over ritual. For instance, in Spain, the church hierarchy had normally been happy, in the fifteenth century, to validate laypeople's claims to have experienced saintly visions. But from the early sixteenth century, the church endorsed no more such claims. The same unease was directed against the deities of local religion: the local saints and virgins, whose cults the churches swept away or replaced with the universal veneration of Christ and his mother, the Virgin Mary.

All kinds of lay competition in the clergy's proper fields became subject to attempts at control or eradication, especially such practices as fortune telling, folk healing, magic, and even fairs and festivals. The Council of Trent—a series of meetings held from 1545 to 1563 by bishops who acknowledged the pope's authority—ordered that "all superstition shall be removed" and the cults of saints and relics purged of "perversion by the people into boisterous festivities." Dancing was banned from church—and in some places forbidden altogether. Bull fighting and contests between bears and dogs were prohibited or restricted, or at least banned on holy days, not because they were torture to animals but because they were temptations for people to behave in ways of which the church disapproved—gambling, getting drunk, or having sex.

The war on popular religion was an attempt, under the constant menace of natural disasters, to wean people away from a religion of survival in this world toward one of salvation in the next. Trials of rats and exorcisms of swarms of locusts, appeals to folk healers and wisewomen, vows to saints for worldly purposes, charms to master nature, and spells to conjure the supernatural—these were the common enemies the clergy of all Christian traditions strove to control or abolish. A German law of 1669, typical of hundreds of others, condemned such magical practices as "putting pigs' hairs in fires, binding trees on New Year's Eve, and putting St. John's wort on walls to drive out spirits, and Easter bonfires

Catechism class. Balls of wool as rewards for good students, blows for the bad from the rods the schoolmaster keeps under his desk: a catechism class in progress in 1593. Thanks to printing, every student could follow the text of a lesson in a relatively cheap copy of his or her own. The illustration comes from the first catechism of the Church of England, by Alexander Nowell (ca. 1507–1602).

Witchcraft. The south German draftsman of these scenes of witchcraft turned the subject into a pretext for dark humor and social satire. Artists traditionally contrasted scenes of worldly pleasures with depictions of the pangs of hell. Here women cavort with demons in a forest clearing, where dancing hints coyly at sex, while a devil roasts meat. But the witches' executioners, stoking fires and armed with pitchforks, are almost equally demonic.

accompanied by all sorts of songs that take the name of our Lord in vain while a good deal of devilry goes on." In the seventeenth century, Catholic clergymen were prominent in reclassifying witchcraft as a psychotic delusion, but all kinds of Christians, with diminishing frequency, were inclined to persecute it.

Public rituals affect private lives. Formal religion now intruded as never before in Europe into the most private sphere of activity: sex. In the sixteenth and seventeenth centuries in most of Europe, successful campaigns brought under the supervision of the clergy all contracts in which men and women agreed to live with each other as man and wife. Ostensibly, for instance, the Spanish Inquisition, founded in 1478, was a tribunal of faith, originally designed to monitor the sincerity of former Muslims and Jews who had converted to Christianity under pressure from the Spanish authorities. In practice, most of its efforts in the second half of the sixteenth century were devoted to getting laypeople's sex lives under clerical control. Bigamy and fornication were among the most common crimes the Inquisition investigated. Church leaders had never completely approved of sex, but they were united in thinking it did least harm when they themselves licensed it. Charity, as well as power lust, motivated them. It seemed vital, as a saintly campaigner claimed in 1551, "to invalidate all marriages where there is no witness," because "an infinite number of maidens have been deceived and undone . . . trusting in the promise of marriage made to them; and some have left their parents' house and gone to their perdition."

The newly self-conscious godly elites did not, however, consist entirely of clergy. On the contrary, clerical demand for more responsive congregations and a more committed flock met lay demand for more access to the mysteries of religion. Indeed, the more the clergy weaned people from pre-Christian or non-Christian superstitions, the more they aroused lay appetites for a share in the experience of Christian devotion: prayer, the sacraments, scripture, preaching—all the means by which the Church claimed to deliver experience or knowledge of God. Different parts of Christendom met this lay demand in different ways, but always by finding forms of devotion that could connect laypeople with God: through increased access to the sacraments of the church, in some places; through preaching and translations of the Bible and liturgy in others; and everywhere by encouraging private prayer.

One of the most effective communicators of the Christian message to a wider public was the German theologian Martin Luther (1483–1546). He began with himself—a conviction of his own sinfulness and of his redemption by the grace that God freely offered to all humankind. In a personal mission that he began toward the end of the second decade of the sixteenth century, he looked first to his fellow priests, with patchy success. He was more successful in reaching secular rulers, whom he encouraged to take power over the church and to confiscate its wealth to purify it and restore it to the simplicity Jesus and his apostles had practiced. Luther's greatest effect, however, was on the lay public. For he appealed to laypeople over the heads of the church hierarchy, whose authority he gradually came to reject in favor—in practice—of his own reading of scripture. The printing press—a medium unavailable to earlier religious reformers—spread his message and illustrated it with pictures that even illiterate people could appreciate. He devised a style of writing vivid beyond crudity in images, for example, of the papacy as the whore of Rome copulating with the Antichrist foretold in the Bible, or the pope defecating lies. (Some of Luther's opponents gave as good as they got. Catholic cartoonists, for example, depicted Luther as Satan, complete with horns and tail.) What was more, Luther crafted his language out of various northern German dialects. Many communities in the German-speaking world could understand it, and it spread relatively easily around the trading zone of the North Sea and Baltic. Here, in Scandinavia and parts of Germany—assisted by rulers grateful for an excuse to take power over the churches of their realms and seize their property—Luther's version of Christianity became the majority religion. Patchily, it also spread, or was carried in even more radical forms by Luther's unruly disciples, into parts of Europe that major trade routes connected, along the corridors of the Rhine, Rhone, and Danube rivers.

Within these corners and patches of Europe, Luther not only reached places and classes where Christianity had previously been superficial, but changed the lives of individuals whose Christian awareness he touched. Rumors of his death drove the great German painter, Albrecht Dürer, to despair: "who," he asked, "will expound the gospel to us with such clearness?" Hans Sachs, the poet of Nuremberg in southwest Germany, said simply, "Luther spoke—and all was light." In some provinces, the church had anticipated his project. Cardinal Cisneros, for instance, who was head of the Spanish Inquisition from 1507 until his death in 1517, had cheap editions of devotional books published in Spanish to wean readers from the pulp fiction of the day. But Luther went further, advocating reading the Bible and conducting the liturgy of the church in languages people actually spoke instead of in Latin.

Luther, however, was politically and socially conservative. He feared social revolutionaries who claimed religious inspiration to justify rebellion against established authority. In 1525, for instance, he condemned "thieving, murderous hordes" of German peasants who claimed that his works had inspired them to rebel. The revolution of 1525 in the city of Münster alarmed him even more. Radical Christians, who claimed that God absolved them from following rules or obeying laws, seized control of the town and imposed a reign of terror, massacring their enemies and indulging—so their orthodox critics said—in orgies of looting and sex. Luther urged responsible nobles and rulers to save the town and punish the heretics. He wanted the reformed church to remain hierarchical under the rule of bishops and to adhere to the orthodoxy he preached. Some talented Protestant theologians could not accept this discipline and broke with him to found churches of their own.

The most influential in the long run were Ulrich Zwingli (1484–1531) and Jean Calvin (1509–1564). With Zwingli, Luther's main dispute was about doctrine—specifically, about what happens at communion when Christians consecrate gifts of bread and wine. Luther insisted, with modifications, on the truth of the tradition of the church: communicants really ingested the essence of Christ's flesh and blood along with bread and wine. When they met to discuss it, and Zwingli argued that flesh and blood could only be present in a metaphorical or symbolic sense, Luther chalked or carved Christ's words from the Bible—'THIS IS MY BODY'—in capital letters on the table.

Martin Luther as Satan tempting Jesus (1547). Protestant propaganda during the Reformation often depicted the pope as Satan. Here Catholic propaganda turns the tables by portraying Martin Luther as the devil (note his cloven hooves and tail.) Like Satan in the Bible, Luther asks Jesus to make bread out of stones. Implicitly, the artist is accusing Luther of warping the Church's teaching that the bread of the eucharistic becomes 'the body of Christ,' though Luther was emphatic that the bread of the sacrament was 'not bread alone' but also real flesh.
Versuchung Christi (1547), Gemalde, Bonn, Landschaftsverband Rheinland/Rheinisches Landesmuseum Bonn. Inv. Nr. 58.3.

Inextinguishable light: Pope, friar, and devil cannot blow out the candle of the Reformation lit by Martin Luther, who sits behind it surrounded by other Protestant theologians of the sixteenth century. The Frenchman Jean Calvin is next to Luther, aptly turning away from him. The standing figure touching Luther's arm is the Scots reformer John Knox. Immediately behind Luther is the Swiss Ulrich Zwingli. Luther's disciple Philip Melancthon is seated to his left. The scene is imaginary. All these reformers never gathered together, and Luther and his followers were bitterly opposed to the theological ideas of Calvin, Zwingli, and Knox. The border of the engraving alludes to Jesus' claim to be "the true Vine."

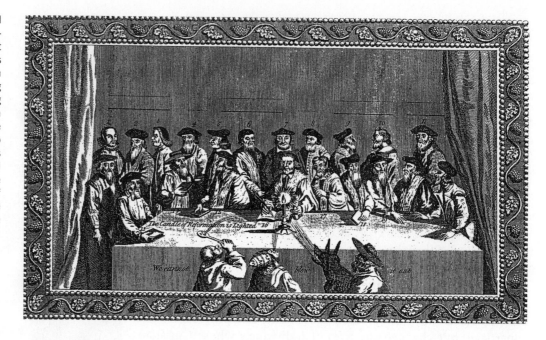

"Having broken the principle that the church was indivisible and that authority within the church was unique and binding on all Christians, the new Christian movements tended to split among themselves in often bitter and bloody disputes over Christian dogma and how to organize the church."

Calvin differed from Luther on a further point of dogma. He insisted that logically if, as Luther believed, God had chosen some people for salvation from before time began, he must have excluded others. So some people would spend eternity in hell, no matter how virtuous they were in this life. More important than this doctrine, called "predestination," in making Calvinism appealing to Christians were Calvin's gifts as a writer and administrator. His theology seems austere and chilling. Yet when he wrote about it he made it moving and humanly compelling. Strictly speaking, if everyone was saved or damned from before time began, Jesus' life and sacrifice seem pointless. Yet Calvin's writings are full of a sense of Jesus' reality and effectiveness as the focus where human and divine love meet. Calvin established a power base in the Swiss city of Geneva, where revolutionaries renounced allegiance to their ruler, the duke of Savoy, and organized missionaries who radiated from there across Europe. No state church in Europe, except those of Scotland, some German principalities, and the United Provinces of the Netherlands, adopted his teachings; but many of his followers came to occupy influential positions in the church hierarchy in England, and communities of his adherents took root in many parts of France and Switzerland, and were scattered in patches around Germany and parts of northern Italy, Hungary, and Transylvania. Having broken the principle that the church was indivisible and that authority within the church was unique and binding on all Christians, the new Christian movements tended to split among themselves in often bitter and bloody disputes over Christian dogma and how to organize the church.

The schism within Christianity endures to this day (see Map 18.1). Some national or local churches in the affected areas—northern and eastern Germany; parts of France, Switzerland, Hungary, and Holland; Scandinavia; Scotland , England, and Wales—seceded from obedience to the Church of Rome, calling themselves "Evangelical" or "Protestant," or "Reformed" (hence the term *Reformation* for the movements they formed.) A Catholic movement that historians commonly call the Counter-Reformation or the Catholic Reformation reconverted some churches to Roman obedience. Partly in reaction against Protestantism, but at a more profound level to pursue the common, underlying project to re-Christianize Europe that all Christian elites shared, new religious orders sprang up within the Catholic Church. The most significant of these for the future of world history was the Society of Jesus or Jesuits, which Ignatius Loyola (1491–1556)

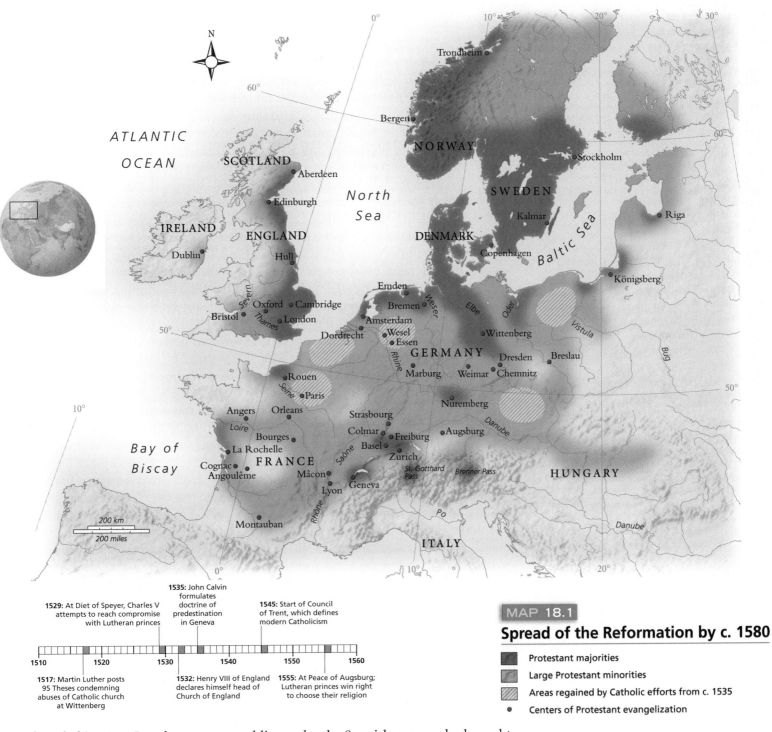

1529: At Diet of Speyer, Charles V attempts to reach compromise with Lutheran princes

1535: John Calvin formulates doctrine of predestination in Geneva

1545: Start of Council of Trent, which defines modern Catholicism

1510   1520   1530   1540   1550   1560

1517: Martin Luther posts 95 Theses condemning abuses of Catholic church at Wittenberg

1532: Henry VIII of England declares himself head of Church of England

1555: At Peace of Augsburg; Lutheran princes win right to choose their religion

MAP 18.1

Spread of the Reformation by c. 1580

- Protestant majorities
- Large Protestant minorities
- Areas regained by Catholic efforts from c. 1535
- Centers of Protestant evangelization

founded in 1540. Loyola was an ex-soldier under the Spanish crown who brought martial virtues to the movement he founded: tight discipline, comradeship, self-sacrifice, and a sense of chivalry. He was also a gifted mystic, who taught his friends and followers self-transforming techniques of prayer, and a natural intellectual, who insisted on the highest standards of learning for those who joined his order. The Jesuits became the Roman Catholic Church's most effective missionaries and educators, both in Europe and in the wider world, and the schools they established were nurseries of science and scholarship.

Having broken the principle that the church was indivisible and authority within the church was unique and binding on all Christians, the Protestant movements tended

Jesuit missionaries. The Jesuits' pride in the success of their overseas missions radiates from this eighteenth-century painting in which three of the order's sixteenth-century saints are prominently depicted. Flanked by personifications of the four continents in the foreground, the mythical giant Atlas presents the world to the Jesuits' founder, St. Ignatius Loyola. St. Francis Borja on the left-hand pedestal represents the order's preaching vocation; St. Francis Xavier, on the right, represents the ministry of the sacraments. Xavier also wears a Chinese-style vestment, a reminder of the Jesuits' long efforts to convert China. One of the leading Jesuit missionaries in China, Matteo Ricci, is in the background, among other Jesuit saints and heroes. Representatives of peoples the Jesuits converted kneel in prayer.

to split among themselves in often bitter and bloody disputes over Christian dogma and how to organize the church. A sense of hostility among the different forms of Christianity grew up in the aftermath of the schism—leading to wars justified, if not caused, by religious cant. As a result of this climate of hostility, traditional history has exaggerated the differences between Protestant and Catholic Christianity. Few people understood or cared about the subtleties of doctrine and worship that divided theologians. The doctrine most commonly said to define the Protestant reformers is that of "salvation by faith alone," according to which God imparts grace freely to anyone who professes belief in him without the sinner needing to perform pious works or obey church rules. Yet many Catholics stayed in the church while sharing Protestant views on this point, while Luther himself repeatedly insisted, in his own catechism for young Christians, "We should fear God because of his threat to those who transgress his law and love him for his promise of grace to those who keep it."

The missionary impulse within Europe produced no great revolution in spirituality. Most people remained as indifferent and shallow-minded as ever. But the language and imagery—the total communication—of the Christian faith were genuinely transformed. For Protestant clergy, services in the vernacular and the promotion of the Bible in translation were ways to help the laity become more actively involved in their faith. For Catholics, frequent communion and—to involve women in particular—the extension of the cults of the Virgin Mary and the founding of new orders of nuns who taught the young and nursed the sick served the same purpose.

Both traditions made God more intelligible, more accessible. "You seem to think that Christ was drunk," thundered Luther against radically subversive readings of the story of the Last Supper by rival Protestants like Zwingli, "and wearied his disciples with meaningless words!" This daring joke had the great virtue of treating Christ's humanity as literal and picturing him in the flesh of human weakness. In 1573, the Inquisition in Venice forced the Italian painter Veronese to re-label his painting of the Last Supper as *Dinner at the House of Levi*, because it contained scenes of feasting and mirth, but by the century's end, another Italian painter, Caravaggio, could depict the *Last Supper*, without irreverence, as an episode of tavern low life. The German artist Mathias Grünewald in the 1520s had to hide his drawing of Jesus as a low-browed, warty-faced loser, but a century and a half later, the Spanish painter Murillo could revive the ancient tradition of depicting the Christ child as a naughty boy. As a result of the church's mission to bring Christianity to the people, relevance to the lives of ordinary folk sanctified sacred subjects.

In eastern Christendom, too, reform movements led to conflicts between the Christianity of the clergy and the religion of ordinary people, and ultimately to splits in the Orthodox Church as they did in the West. A reformation parallel to that of the West began in 1621, when the Patriarch of Constantinople, Cyril Lukaris (1572–1638), renounced what he called the "bewitchment" of tradition "and took for my guide," he said, "Scripture . . . and Faith alone." The Russian priest Avvakum, "though a miserable sinner," tackled popular excesses violently. He drove mummers from his village, breaking their masks and drums, clubbing one of their dancing bears senseless, and releasing the other into the wild. In 1648, the Russian Orthodox clerical brotherhood known as the Zealots of Piety captured the czar's attention. At their insistence, the czar banished the vulgarities of popular piety from the Russian court and banned popular music as a presumed survival of paganism. Yet within 20 years, the clergy who had triumphed together in championing these changes fell out among themselves over a further proposed elimination of impurities: the standardization of texts and the harmonization of rituals. The leader of one party was exiled in 1666, the other burned at the stake in 1681.

Exaltation of the ordinary. The Italian painter Caravaggio's "Supper at Emmaus" (1599) is famous among art historians for its innovative, dramatic use of light and shade, but it is equally extraordinary for its treatment of a sacred subject: a meeting at which Jesus revealed himself to his disciples after his Resurrection. Caravaggio depicted the disciples, not as glorious saints, but as shabby, commonplace peasants.

CHRISTIANITY BEYOND CHRISTENDOM: THE LIMITS OF SUCCESS

Beyond Europe, the world that exploration and imperialism disclosed was a magnet for missionaries. "Come over and help us," said the Indian on the official seal of the trading company responsible, under the English crown, for colonizing Massachusetts in the early seventeenth century. On the whole, however, overseas missionizing was a rare vocation in Protestant Europe. There were a few exceptions. The conviction that the Algonquin Indians were a lost tribe of ancient Israel inspired John Eliot (1604–1690), who created "praying towns" in New England where Native American pastors preached and led congregations in prayers and readings from the Bible. Normally, however, only Roman Catholic religious orders had enough manpower and zeal to undertake the missions on a large scale, and outside areas of Spanish rule, their efforts were patchy.

In Asia, the contrast between the Philippines, where Spanish rule built up what is by far the biggest Christian community in Asia, and the many mission fields that proved barren or only briefly productive illustrates this patchiness. Even in the Philippines, Christian success in direct competition with Islam was limited. In the Sulu Islands, where Muslim missionaries were active within reach of protection from a strong Islamic state in Brunei, the Muslim threat could be met by force of arms, but Christian preaching could not eradicate it. In the Philippine island of Mindanao, Muslim intruders arrived from the small but spice-rich sultanate of Ternate in the 1580s. The Christian mission on Mindanao had barely begun and could not be sustained. In the late sixteenth and early seventeenth centuries, it was all Spanish garrisons could do to keep at bay Muslim hotheads who launched holy wars against the Spaniards' main base in Luzon. Yet, responding to his advisers' view that the mission was not worth the cost and effort, King Philip II of Spain (r. 1556–1598) insisted that he would rather spend all the gold in his treasury than sacrifice one church where the name of Christ was praised.

SOCIETAS ASIATICA.

P. Sebastianus Vieira Lusitanus, cum quinq, Socys Iaponibus Soc: IESV, triduano Scrobis tormento, et Subiecto igne pro Fide Christi necatus, in Iaponia Iendi. 6 Iuny A. 1634.
C. Screta d.　　　　　　　　　　　　　　　　　　　　　　Melch: Küsell.

Christian missionaries. In late sixteenth- and early seventeenth-century Japan became victims of their own success. Not only did they attract hundreds of thousands of followers, but they also established close ties to many of the daimyos, regional lords whom the central authorities distrusted. The missionaries' Spanish and Portuguese allegiance also made them suspect as potential foreign agents. A series of persecutions, beginning in the 1590s, included many martyrdoms, like that of the Jesuit Sebastião Vieira, tortured to death with some of his converts in 1634 in an episode depicted here. After 1639, the only Christians allowed in Japan were a small group of Dutch Calvinist merchants, whose servants had to trample on a crucifix in an annual ceremony, in order to prove their rejection of Christianity.

For a while, Franciscans and Jesuits in Japan encountered amazing success by targeting lords whose conversions were catalysts for the conversions of their followers. Once the missionaries had a place to say mass and a conspicuous aristocratic patron to make Christianity respectable, they could attract potential converts by displays of devotion, such as the magnificent requiem mass sung for the local ruler's wife, Lady Gracia, at Kokura that attracted thousands of mourners in 1600. By the 1630s, more than 100,000 Japanese had been baptized. Successive central governments in Japan had been suspicious of the new religion, as a source of subversive political ideas, foreign influence, and encouragement to local lords to usurp central authority. Sporadic persecution from the 1590s, however, had failed to halt the progress of Christianity. So from 1639, it was banned outright, and Christians who refused to renounce their faith were forced into exile or put to death.

China could not be converted by means similar to those the Jesuits followed in Japan. It was a relatively centralized state with no intermediate lords to serve as local flashpoints of Christian illumination. The Jesuits made most of their converts at modest social levels but focussed disproportionate efforts on the scholar officials, or mandarins, who enjoyed huge social influence. Some of their converts were impressively committed: using Christian baptismal names, passing Christianity on to their friends and families, and proclaiming their faith in public. Yang Tingyun (yahng teeng-yuhn) recalled a vivid conversion experience in the presence of one of the Jesuits' pictures of Jesus, which inspired him "with feelings of the presence of a great lord." Debates with Jesuits followed. Why could reverence for the Buddha not be accommodated alongside acknowledgment of Jesus? How could the Lord of Heaven be subject to disgrace and suffering by being crucified? How could bread and wine be turned into the body and blood of Jesus? (Answer: "My Lord's love for the world is boundless.") After much agonizing, Yang repudiated his mistress—a more impressive test, perhaps, of Christian commitment than baptism—and went on to build a church, finance the printing of Christian works, and write books explaining Christianity. His fellow Christian, Xu Guangqi (shew gwang-Kee), explained as an act of God his failure to pass the exam to enter the civil service that first brought him into contact with the missionaries and attributed to divine revelation, by way of a dream, his insight into the doctrine of the Trinity.

Despite such promising instances, the Jesuits failed to convert China for three reasons. First, as we shall see, most Chinese were more interested in the Jesuits' scientific learning and technical skills as mapmakers, astronomers, artists, clock makers, and designers than in their religious teaching. Second, the strategy the Jesuits adopted to convert China was a long-term one, and the revolutions of Chinese politics tended to interrupt it. No sooner had the Jesuits converted an empress than the Manchus overthrew the Ming dynasty in 1644 (see Chapter 17). Finally, the church lost confidence in the Jesuits' methods. This was the outcome of a conflict that began with the founder of the mission, Matteo Ricci (1552–1610). He developed a healthy respect for Chinese wisdom. Indeed, the Jesuits became mediators not only of Western culture to China but also of Chinese learning in the West. Ricci decided that the best way to proceed with Chinese converts was to permit them to continue rites of reverence for their ancestors, on the ground that it was similar to Western veneration for saints. As we have seen, this was just the sort of practice that, in the West, the clerical elite was attacking. The missionaries split over the issue, and the effectiveness of the mission suffered when Pope Clement XI ruled against the veneration of ancestors early in the eighteenth century.

In parts of South and Southeast Asia, missionary strategists targeted potential converts at various social levels. In the seventeenth century in the Molucca Islands and Sulawesi (formerly Celebes) in what is today Indonesia, Protestant and Catholic missions alike approached sultans, local notables, and village headmen, with results that usually came to embrace many ordinary people but that never seem to have lasted for long. In Manado in northern Sulawesi, Franciscans launched an intensive mission in 1619. They began by obtaining permission from an assembly of village headmen at the ruler's court. But these notables disclaimed power over their fellow villagers' religious allegiance. The friars preached from village to village, encountering universal hostility. The audience would shriek to drown out the preaching, urge their unwelcome guests to leave, and profess fidelity to their gods. They withheld food and shelter. The friars therefore withdrew in 1622. Their Jesuit successors made some progress by concentrating on the ruler and his family. When Franciscans returned to the villages in the 1640s, they enjoyed a much more positive reception. By the 1680s, under Dutch sponsorship, a Protestant mission in Manado made further headway by employing converted native schoolmasters to work among the children of the elite, wherever a local ruler would permit it. In Sri Lanka, Portuguese missionaries were more successful, but the Dutch who took over the island in 1656 were as keen to undermine Catholics as to convert Buddhists to Protestantism, and the long-term impact of Christianity proved slight.

In the New World, the bottom-up strategy of conversion was more usual. After initial contact, which, of course, often brought missionaries into touch with local leaders, ambitious programs of mass baptism and mass preaching rapidly followed. In the 1520s and 1530s, Franciscans baptized literally millions of Native Americans in Mexico, in an experiment typical of the time. It was an effort to re-create the actions and atmosphere of the early church, when a single example of holiness could bring thousands to baptism and altar as if by a miracle. Clearly, most conversions in these circumstances cannot have been profound, life-changing experiences of the kind specified in traditional definitions of conversion. The doctrinal awareness the friars succeeded in communicating was limited. The first catechism the Franciscans used in Mexico does not even refer to the divinity of Jesus, which is the central doctrine of Christian belief. Dominican friars denounced the superficiality of Franciscan

Chinese Madonna and child. When Jesuit missionaries first brought images of the Madonna and Child to China in the late sixteenth century, they were alarmed to find that the Chinese misidentified the Virgin Mary with Guanyin, goddess of mercy, who, in fertility charms, was often depicted with a child in her arms. But in a new mission field, unencumbered with local versions of Christianity, the Jesuits could not resist promoting the great universal cults of the Church: those of the Savior and his mother. Native Chinese artists began producing images of Mary with her son in her arms in the early seventeenth century, blending Western and Chinese treatment and technique.

The State Hermitage Museum, St. Petersburg. Photograph © The State Hermitage Museum

Chronology: The Revitalization and Spread of Christianity

1478	Spanish Inquisition founded
1500s	Spanish Christians compete with Muslims for dominance in the Philippines
Early sixteenth century	Martin Luther initiates Protestant Reformation in Europe
1520s and 1530s	Franciscans baptize millions of Native Americans
1540	Ignatius Loyola founds Jesuits
1545–1563	Council of Trent meets
Seventeenth century	Jesuits lead Christian missionary effort in China
1621	Reformation in Eastern Orthodox Church begins
1630s	Over 100,000 Japanese baptized
1639	Christianity banned in Japan

First book printed in the New World. "In a plain style for common understanding": the first book printed in the New World was a catechism issued by Juan de Zumárraga in Mexico City in 1543. The tasseled hat signifies that the book was published under the patronage of the archbishop of Mexico. The ornamented borders were fashionable decoration for books at the time in Europe. Zumárraga was a Franciscan friar who was committed to spreading Catholic doctrine to poor and uneducated people who knew little or nothing about the faith. The church in New Spain was not just a missionary effort directed at Native Americans, but also part of a movement active throughout the Christian world, in which the clergy and the godly tried to re-express Christian doctrine in simple terms that a wide audience could understand.

teaching, but the same problems of deficient manpower, daunting terrain, and linguistic and cultural differences hampered their own efforts.

The fear of backsliding and apostasy by new converts haunted the missions. As early as 1539, clergy in Mexico worried about the multiplication of small chapels "just like those the Indians once had for their particular gods." In central Mexico, in the mid-sixteenth century, fears that new cults disguised pagan practices convulsed the church. Doubts arose even concerning the purity of the veneration of Our Lady of Guadalupe herself—the apparition of the Virgin Mary, supposedly to an Indian shepherd boy on the site of a pre-Christian shrine, which had demonstrated the sanctity and grace of Mexican soil in the 1530s. In 1562, one of the worst recorded cases of missionary violence erupted in Yucatán, when the head of the Franciscan mission became convinced that some of his flock were harboring pagan idols. The reports that alerted him came from native informants, motivated, probably, by traditional hatred and rivalry among Indian communities, rather than by any zeal for the facts. In the subsequent persecution, 4,500 Indians were tortured, and 150 died.

In a similar case in central Peru in 1609, a parish priest was condemned for using excessive violence toward backsliders. The papers he collected include the story of a revealing trauma. Don Cristóbal Choque Casa, the son of a local Indian notable and community leader, reported that, some 30 or 40 years after a vigorous Jesuit mission had nominally converted his people, he was on his way to meet his mistress at the abandoned shrine of a tribal god, when the devil in the form of a bat attacked him. He drove out the demon by reciting the Lord's Prayer in Latin, and the following morning he summoned his fellow natives to warn them not to frequent the shrine on pain of being reported to the parish priest. But that same night, he dreamed that he was irresistibly drawn to the accursed spot himself and compelled to make a silver offering to the god. The story evokes a vivid picture of the consequences of "spiritual conquest": old shrines, so neglected that they are fit only for bats and fornicators; abiding powers, so menacing that they can still haunt the dreams, even of a sinner sufficiently indoctrinated to be able to pray in Latin.

For the rest of the colonial period, the eradication of pre-Christian devotions in Peru became the work of professional "extirpators." In most of the rest of the Spanish American world, every new generation of clergy repeated the frustrations and disillusionment of their predecessors. The Indians seemed unable to forget their old rites for appeasing nature. In the early eighteenth century, in Guatemala and Peru, priests were still making the same complaints as their predecessors a century and a half before. Indians were attached to "idols" and to their own healers and seers. They turned the saints into pagan deities. They accused each other of superstition and of working with demons. Only with extreme caution could they be trusted to revere sacred images of Jesus and the saints without idolatry.

Still, ordinary people's accessibility to the ministry of missionaries made the New World an extraordinarily rich and rewarding mission field. Aided by the tendency—exceptionally common in the Americas—of some cultures to welcome and defer to strangers, missionaries could penetrate areas otherwise untouched by any European presence, establish an honored place in their host societies, learn the languages, and guide congregations, by intimate, personal contact, into redefining themselves as Christians.

THE MISSIONARY WORLDS OF BUDDHISM AND ISLAM

Other religions paralleled Europe's mission to the infidel within.

China and Japan

In China, Zhu Hong (jew-hung) (1535–1615) and Han Shan (hahn-shahn) (1546–1623) presented Buddhism afresh as a religion people could practice "at home," eliminating the priestly character that had formerly made it seem inaccessible and unintelligible to lay followers. Lay devotees could perform the same rituals at home as monks did in a monastery. Laymen could worship the Buddha, fast, adopt vegetarianism, and even don the saffron robe that signified a religious vocation. In the eighteenth century, Peng Shaosheng (pahng show-shuhng) took the same line of reform further by explaining techniques of mental prayer, unprompted by images of gods. This emphasis on direct religious experience, unmediated through a priestly class, strikingly resembled what was going on in Europe.

In seventeenth-century Japan, comparable movements, embracing both Buddhism and native religion, began with the reexamination of ancient texts, just as Christian reformers began by going back to the Bible. The monk Keichu (1640–1701) was a pioneer in recovering authentic texts of the *Manyoshu*, poetic native scriptures of the eighth century. These scriptures, along with other old myths known as the *Kojiki*, became the basis of a born-again local religion, stripped of the additions of intervening centuries and of influences from outside Japan. Among Keichu's successors in the following century, Motoori Morinaga (1730–1801) used the *Manyoshu* as Protestants used the Gospels—to reconstruct a model of purity and to denounce the degeneracy of the latter days. Meanwhile, the suppression of Christianity in Japan created an opportunity for Buddhism. Wealthy lords, merchants, and peasants endowed many new Buddhist foundations.

The Mongols

The decisive initiative in reenergizing missionary Buddhism came from within Mongolia in the 1570s. Altan Khan (1530–1583) ruled a swathe of territory along the northern loop of the Yellow River to the border of Tibet. He founded Koke Khota—the "Blue City"—to be a permanent Mongol capital near the present border of Inner and Outer Mongolia. The Chinese called it Guihua—"Return to Civilization." He was a determined pagan, who treated his gout by sacrificing a human victim and paddling inside the victim's split open body. Realizing that Buddhist help would be vital to his schemes to extend his realm by conquest, he founded monasteries, sent for scriptures to Beijing, and had them translated on tablets of polished apple wood. Shrines and monasteries filled the slopes above his capital. Cultivation of Buddhism gave his khanate a distinctive profile among the client-states on China's northwest border.

At Altan Khan's invitation, the ruler of Tibet, known as the **Dalai Lama,** visited Mongolia in 1576 and 1586. Tibet was a priestly Buddhist state, and the Dalai Lama was, by unalterable convention, the head of the Buddhist establishment. He guided reform of Mongol customs. Human sacrifices were forbidden, and blood sacrifices of all sorts stopped. The ongons—the felt images in which spirits resided, except

The Ongons, or Ongghot, small figures of cloth or wood kept in a box or—like these, which once dangled from a tent pole in a pouch—are the most conspicuous feature of Mongolian shamanism. In traditional Mongol belief, the souls of the dead "become ongghot" with the power both to help and harm living people. Using the little images, the shaman, in his ecstasy, can transmit the presence and power of these spirits into himself. In the late sixteenth and seventeenth centuries, Buddhist missionaries tried with varying success to stamp out shamanism and belief in the Ongons.

Chronology: The Spread of Buddhism and Islam

Fifteenth and sixteenth centuries	Merchants and missionaries spread Islam
1570s	Mongol ruler Altan Khan stimulates the revival of missionary Buddhism in Mongolia
Late sixteenth century	Zhu Hong and Han Shan stress direct experience of Buddhism in China
Seventeenth century	"Jihad of the sword" takes on greater importance in spread of Islam
1630s	Missions initiated by Prince Neyici Toyin bring Buddhism to Manchuria
1690s	Torokawa scholars incite revival and jihad in Hausaland in modern Nigeria

when the rites of shamans liberated them (see Chapter 13)—were to be burned and replaced by Buddhist statues. The new religion was at first limited to the aristocracy. But over the next century, Buddhism spread through society and outward across the Mongol dominions. The next Dalai Lama was the son of a Mongol prince. His training for his role in the 1590s took place in Mongolia, amid scholars engaged in the systematic translation of the vast body of Buddhist scriptures into Mongolian. Young noblemen joined the priesthood. Altan Khan had 100 of them ordained as priests to celebrate the Dalai Lama's first visit. Increasingly in the late sixteenth and early seventeenth centuries, the documents Mongol chiefs issued during diplomatic exchanges contain allusions to Buddhism, and when they made alliances with pagan peoples, Buddhist and pagan language and ceremonies marked the occasions.

From the 1630s, a mission that Prince Neyici Toyin (1557–1653) organized took the Buddhism of Tibet beyond Mongolia into Manchuria, building the great Yellow Temple in Shenyang (shehn-yahng) to house an antique statue of the Buddha. Toyin worked by "miracles" of healing that may have owed something to the superiority of Tibetan and Chinese medicine over the unscientific therapies of the shamans. Manchu political power, after they conquered China in 1644, reinforced the mission. The Manchu emperors perceived Buddhist missionaries as pacifiers and potential agents of imperial policy. They appointed Tibetan lamas to instruct the Mongols, presumably in part to reconcile the Mongols to Chinese rule.

Like Catholic missions in the New World, political conquests and violence shadowed and disfigured Buddhist missions in northern Asia. Neyici Toyin burned before his tent a bonfire of ongons ten tent-frames high. The following advice was given to Buddhist missionaries in the extreme west of Mongolia in the mid-seventeenth century: "Whoever has worshipped ongons, burn their ongons and confiscate their cattle and sheep. From those who let the shamans and shamanesses perform fumigations, take their horses, fumigate the shamans in their turn with dog dung." In practice, the old gods reemerged as Buddhist deities, just as in Christian America the Native American gods survived as saints and representations of the Virgin Mary. In both Mongolia and the Americas, the old gods continued to mediate between humans and nature.

Islam

The trend to what might be called low-level strategy—missionary efforts targeting ordinary people—also seems to have affected Islamic missions (see Map 18.2). In Southeast Asia (in what were to become Malaysia and Indonesia) and Africa, which were the two great arenas of Islamic expansion at the time, the means of conversion were fourfold: commerce, deliberate missionary effort, holy war, and dynastic links. As in Southeast Asia, on the Islamic world's African front, the arrival of Christian Europeans hardly affected the retreat of paganism. Except in the coastal toeholds of Christendom, the same combination of merchants, missionaries, and warmongers ensured the dominance of Islam.

Merchants and missionaries spread Islam together. Trade shunted pious Muslims from city to city and installed them as port supervisors, customs officials, and agents to local rulers. Missionaries followed: scholars in search of patronage, discharging along the way the Muslim's obligation to convert unbelievers; spiritual

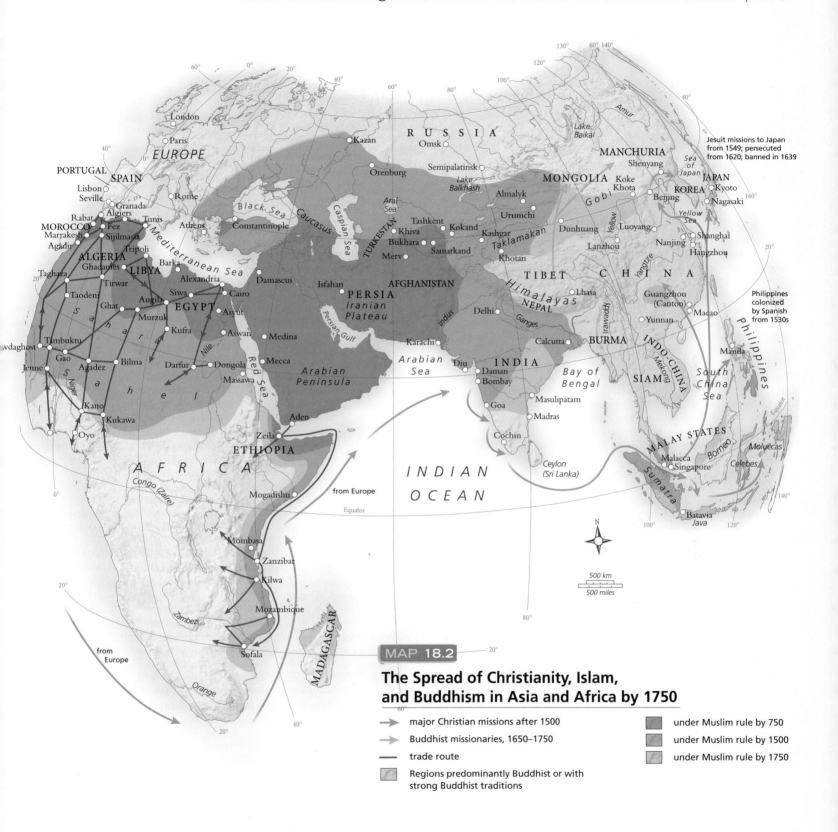

MAP 18.2

The Spread of Christianity, Islam, and Buddhism in Asia and Africa by 1750

→ major Christian missions after 1500

→ Buddhist missionaries, 1650–1750

── trade route

Regions predominantly Buddhist or with strong Buddhist traditions

under Muslim rule by 750

under Muslim rule by 1500

under Muslim rule by 1750

athletes in search of exercise, anxious to challenge native shamans in contests of conspicuous austerity and supernatural power. In some areas, **Sufis**—mystics, with a feel for popular worship of natural forces, for whom, as one of them said, God was "closer than the veins of my neck"—made crucial contributions. In Southeast Asia, Sufis congregated in Melaka, and after the city fell to the Portuguese in 1511,

The Chronicles of Java. Islam in Southeast Asia has often been mixed with elements from other religions. This illustrated manuscript tells the history of the island of Java in what today is Indonesia and the spread of Islam there by Sufi saints and rulers up to 1647. Written in Javanese, it seeks to give the Muslim rulers of the state of Mataram legitimacy by telling of how one of their ancestors had ties to three different religious traditions: He was blessed by a Muslim saint, practiced Hindu asceticism, and married the goddess of the southern ocean.

they fanned out from there through Java and Sumatra. In the late sixteenth and seventeenth centuries, the sultanate of Aceh in northwest Sumatra in modern Indonesia was a nursery of Sufi missionaries of sometimes dubious Islamic orthodoxy, such as Shams al-Din, who saw himself as a prophet of the end of the world and whose books were burned after his death in 1630. Even peaceful Muslim missionaries tended to see themselves as warriors of a sort, waging a "jihad of words." During the seventeenth century, perhaps under the goad of competition from Christianity, the "jihad of the sword" grew in importance, and the extension of the frontier of the Islamic world depended increasingly on the aggression of sultans, especially from central Java.

In West Africa, merchant clans or classes, like the Saharan Arabs known as Kunta, who made a habit of marrying the daughters of holy men, were the advanced guard of Islam. The black wandering scholars known as the Torokawa incited revivalism and jihad in Hausaland in modern Nigeria from the 1690s. Schools with a wide curriculum played a vital part in diffusing Islam among the Hausa, scattering pupils who in turn attracted students of their own. A sheikh who died in 1655 was able, at school in Katsina, near the present border of Niger and Nigeria, to "taste to the full the Law, the interpretation of the Quran, prophetic tradition, grammar, syntax, philology, logic, study of grammatical particles, and of the name of God, Quranic recitation, and the science of meter and rhyme." Paid by donations according to pupils' wealth, the master of such a school sat on a pile of rugs and sheepskins before his niche of books, equipped with his tray of sand for tracing letters with his finger. He might have his brazier filled with burning charcoal to warm him in winter and his spittoon for the husks of kola nuts that were eaten for their caffeine content. Students' manuscripts survive, smothered in annotations from the teacher's commentary, which was often in a native language instead of Arabic, the language of the Quran. At the end of this course, the student

Making Connections | REVITALIZATION OF WORLD RELIGIONS

RELIGION	REASONS FOR REVITALIZATION	CONSEQUENCES	NEW ADHERENTS
Christianity	To renew dynamism of early church To combat heresies, paganism, witchcraft To engage unevangelized and underevangelized people	New religious orders; new techniques of prayer; new types of devotion; increased coercion and social control by church–state alliances; sharp restrictions on localized beliefs and rituals; emphasis on missionary efforts	Lower-class Europeans, urban and country; colonized peoples in America, Africa, Asia
Buddhism	To popularize Buddhism in China and Japan To adapt to native religious beliefs (China and Japan) As a vehicle for strengthening political control (Mongolia, Manchuria)	Eliminating the need for priestly leadership; simplified rituals; emphasis on direct religious experience via meditation, ritual; creation of new systems of monasteries throughout Asia; Tibetan lamas restructured Mongol spiritual practices	Laymen, peasants, and other social classes throughout Japan, China, Central Asia
Islam	To spread belief to Southeast Asia, Africa To adapt to native religious beliefs To enhance Muslim spirituality	Use of merchants, Sufi missionaries, holy war (jihad), and dynastic alliances to expand Islamic influence; intermarriage as a method of advancing Islam; spread of Islamic schools increases literacy	Ordinary people, especially in Southeast Asia, Africa

acquired a certificate, emblazoned with a long pedigree of named teachers going back to Malik ibn Anas, the eighth-century codifier of Islamic law.

THE RESULTING MIX: GLOBAL RELIGIOUS DIVERSITY—AMERICAN AND INDIAN EXAMPLES

The forms of Catholic Christianity that became characteristic of Spanish America were, in their way, every bit as different from the Catholic mainstream as was the Protestantism of most of the English colonies. In part, this was because of the imperfections of the "Spiritual Conquest" of Spanish America by Catholic missionaries. Missionaries were few. Cultural and linguistic obstacles impeded communication. Pre-Christian religion was probably too deeply rooted to be destroyed. In partial consequence, Native American features ripple Latin American Catholicism to this day.

Secular scholars, and Protestant critics of Catholic missionaries, sometimes call these Native American influences **syncretic** features or pagan survivals because Christianity and paganism seemed to fuse in a new religion that was not quite either but was a blend of both. Yet the proper comparison for colonial religion is not—or not solely—with the religion of the Native American past but with that of Europe of the same era, where clerical bafflement at the stubborn survival of popular religion was just as great. The Christianity of the American countryside was deficient in similar ways to that of the European countryside. Anxiety about how to survive in this world interfered with people's concern about their salvation in the next. Rites to induce rain, suppress pests, elude plague, and fend off famine drove Scripture and sacraments into neglected corners of ordinary lives. As the programs of reform unfolded in Europe, clergy and educated laity acquired ever-higher standards of doctrinal awareness, ever-deeper experiences of Christian self-consciousness. Their expectations of their flocks increased accordingly—which accounts for the continual renewal of their dissatisfaction. The more Christianized the elite became, the more Christian the clergy expected ordinary people to behave. Meanwhile, the Christianity of Indians in Spanish America had as much variety as that of Europeans in Anglo-America.

Black America

The religion of black people in the Americas—though it varied a lot from place to place, molded into conflicting traditions by the influence of Protestantism and Catholicism, respectively—always had one thing in common: it was always black— different, that is, from the religion of white people. Brazil is the best-documented area and has a characteristic profile. Here, in colonial times, black artistic vocations and religious devotion were centered on cult images that charitable associations of black Catholic laypeople often supported financially. These **confraternities,** as they are called, were vital institutions for colonial society generally, melding the culturally uprooted into a coherent community, renewing their sense of identity and belonging. They were even more important for black people, who were compulsory colonists, traumatically transferred as slaves from Africa to an alienating environment on another continent. Confraternities cushioned and comforted them in a white world. The confraternities were unstable organizations, "created and dissolved with extraordinary rapidity," as one of their most distinguished historians has said. Encouraged by the church, and especially by the Jesuits and Franciscans, the black brotherhoods were hotbeds of disorder.

For the guardians of the colonial power structure, the confraternities' choice of patron saints, whose statues they paraded through the streets and elevated in shrines, was often self-assertive, sometimes defiant. St. Elesbaan, for instance, was a warrior-avenger, a black crusading emperor of Ethiopia, who led an expedition to avenge the massacre of Christians by a Jewish ruler in Yemen in 525. He was easily reinterpreted as a symbol of resistance to the many plantation owners of Portuguese-Jewish ancestry. St. Benedict of Palermo, perhaps the favorite patron of black confraternities, was born the son of Nubian slaves in Sicily in 1526. He became a hermit in his youth, to escape taunts about his blackness. Then, as a Franciscan lay brother, he rose to become guardian of his friary and worked miracles after his death in 1583. The cult of St. Iphigenia, a legendary black virgin, who resisted the spells of her suitor's magicians with the help of 200 fellow virgins, embodied the triumph of faith over magic. But it had its subversive aspect,

Shamans still burn incense on the steps of the church of Saint Thomas at Chichicastenango in the Guatemala highlands, where worshippers leave offerings of flowers and rum. The steps—a mound similar to pre-Hispanic Maya temples—seem to rival the church interior as a place of devotion. Is this paganism, Christianity, or a mixture of the two? Most local shamans now serve as officials of societies dedicated to Christian saints, and the religion of Chichicastenango may be best understood as one of the many local forms of Christianity that developed in the colonial New World.

too, sanctifying virginity in a slave society where women wished sterility on themselves in order not to produce children who would become slaves. Veneration of the Mother of God was closer in spirit to the fertility religions supposedly traditional among migrants from Africa and more consistent with the interests of slaveowners, who wanted their human livestock to breed. Black Catholicism was an excitant, not an opiate. Rather than playing the role commonly assigned to religion—keeping believers in their place—it inspired hopes of betterment in this world. A commonly depicted scene in black religious art was that of black tormentors torturing white Judas in hell.

Colonial black Catholicism really was different from that of white people. Masters excluded slaves from mass, ostensibly "on account of the [slaves] smell," but really to keep them away from dangerously radical clergy. White confraternities reviled black people "with their guitars and drums, with their *mestizo* prostitutes," and with their revolutionary pretensions, "just as though they were no different from honest white people." Fugitive black slaves who set up their own backwoods communities and independent kingdoms were formally excommunicated. The church hierarchy usually refused their requests for chaplains.

Missionary activity in Brazil began in the early sixteenth century before the Counter-Reformation, when the clergy were still content with superficial levels of Christian teaching. It continued in an era of growing Catholic sensitivity to the native heritage of potential converts, who were not always called on to renounce all their culture to become Christians. The mulatto priest António da Vieira (1608–1697), who became a royal chaplain in 1641, imported "masks and rattles to show the heathen that the Christian religion was not sad." In partial consequence, Brazilian Catholicism is an umbrella term for a bewildering range of styles of devotion. Outside the Spanish and Portuguese colonies—and especially in those of the British and Dutch, where plantations were inaccessible to Catholic religious orders—the lack of missionary activity was even more marked. As a result, African religions persisted, and syncretism happened because the slaves on these plantations often learned Christianity by themselves and blended it with African religious beliefs.

"As a result, African religions persisted, and syncretism happened because the slaves on these plantations often learned Christianity by themselves and blended it with African religious beliefs."

White America

As for the religion of white Americans in colonial times, its great common—albeit not constant—feature was enthusiasm. Refugees from religious persecution in Europe, who took religion seriously, formed or infiltrated many colonies: Catholics and radical Protestants in British North America, Jews or so-called New Christians—descendants of Jews, whose Christianity Judaism deeply influenced—in Spanish and Portuguese colonies. Even hard-headed laymen could prove open to religious enthusiasm in the heady atmosphere of a New World where everything seemed possible and a new church might be constructed from scratch, without the corruption and distortions that had warped Jesus' teaching in the Old World. Columbus and Cortés—neither of whom showed much interest in religion in their early lives—both had visions of a restored apostolic age in the lands they explored and conquered.

The most extreme form of enthusiasm is **millenarianism**. Millenarianism is, in some ways, the characteristic form of religious fervor of the Americas. It can be detected in pre-Christian Native American religions. In central Mexico, most peoples celebrated rites of renewal of the Earth in fire every 52 years and nourished

The Cult Image of St. Elesbaan

Devotion to St. Elesbaan, shown here in an early eighteenth-century statue from the Confraternity of Our Lady of the Rosary, was one of a number of politically charged, socially subversive cults that attracted black worshippers in colonial Brazil.

Black saints were inspiring models for the black confraternities, lay Christian brotherhoods that flourished in Brazil.

Elesbaan is dressed as priest and emperor, ruler of the Christian kingdom of Ethiopia in East Africa.

Elesbaan supposedly led an Ethiopian invasion across the Red Sea to Yemen in southern Arabia in 525 to dethrone a Jewish ruler who was persecuting Christians. The many black slaves in Brazil felt persecuted by their masters, many of whom were of Jewish or allegedly Jewish ancestry.

How does this statue show the uniqueness of black Christianity in colonial Brazil?

myths of the destruction of the world in a divine furnace. But for these and other Native American cultures we know about, time was cyclical. Each destruction was the start of a new cycle. For Native Americans, the end of time—which for Christians would be the climax of history—was unimaginable.

Franciscans introduced Christian millenarianism to the New World in the sixteenth century. Most of the early missionaries came from a few Franciscan communities in southern Spain, where friars nurtured obsessions with the coming end of the world, which would be preceded by a cosmic war between good and evil leading to the Age of the Holy Spirit.

Fantasies of this kind unhinged unorthodox minds at frequent intervals. The Spanish adventurer Lope de Aguirre, during a harrowing navigation of the Amazon in the 1560s, imagined himself as the embodiment of God's wrath. His Franciscan contemporary, Francisco de la Cruz, was the self-proclaimed universal pope and emperor of the last days. The fervor of the spiritual Franciscans mingled with whatever forms of millenarianism were inherited from Native American tradition. In Mexico in 1541, an Indian chief called Don Martín Ocelotl (oss-ehl-OT-el) proclaimed the second coming of Christ, embodied in himself. In 1579, in Paraguay, another Indian chief, Oberá the Resplendent, launched a rebellion against Spanish rule with a similar message. In Peru, so-called *Inkarrí* (een-kah-REE) movements kept legendary memories of the Inca Empire alive into modern times and fused them with expectations of the coming of a "Last World Emperor."

North America merged similar traditions with the original forms of millenarianism that grew up in Protestantism. Because millenarianism was generally considered heretical, or was associated with heresies, it became common in America, driven there by persecution, nourished there by toleration. Anabaptism (the belief that only adults should be baptized), world's-end biblical fundamentalism, and sects invented by prophets who preached that the last days of the world were at hand have all contributed to the formation of the United States. The founders of Massachusetts saw the colony as a refuge for those God intended "to save out of general destruction." The Puritan minister John Cotton predicted the end would come in 1655. Another Puritan minister, Increase Mather, felt he could hear God's "murdering pieces go off" as he watched the comet of 1680. The Shakers, another Protestant sect, called themselves "The United Society of Believers in Christ's Second Coming."

"Because millenarianism was generally considered heretical, or was associated with heresies, it became common in America, driven there by persecution, nourished there by toleration."

India

Religious frontiers, where rival creeds and communions meet, are often places of conflict. But they can also stimulate creative thinking, as contrasting religious groups strive to understand and live with each other. Sixteenth-century India produced an enduring new religion: **Sikhism,** which blended elements of Hindu and Muslim tradition—or, as Sikhs would say, went beyond both. Neither Hindu nor Muslim paths to God suffice, said Guru Nanak (1469–1539), the Sikh founder, "so whose path should I follow? I shall follow the path of God."

Nanak was a widely traveled pilgrim of enormous learning. The Mughal Emperor Akbar (r. 1556–1605), who was illiterate and traveled mainly on military campaigns, sought to outdo him by founding a religion of his own. Like Nanak he recognized that in a religiously plural world, it made better sense—and better served the peace of his realm—to look at what religions had in common rather than at what divided them. "God should be adored with every form of adoration,"

Religious debate. The Mughal Emperor Akbar (r. 1556–1605) devised his own religion in an attempt to defuse conflicts among his subjects, who were mostly Muslims and Hindus. He also presided over debates—like the one shown here from his album of paintings of the life of his court—in which Muslims, Hindus, Buddhists, Sikhs, and Christians (represented by black-robed Jesuits, whom Akbar greatly admired) were supposed to reconcile their differences. But the debates ended in bitterness and mutual antagonism.

he said, according to a Jesuit who lived at his court. And indeed, he exhibited broad-mindedness unparalleled in Christendom in his day. Awestruck by the realism of a European painting of the Virgin Mary in the chapel he gave to the Jesuits in his palace, Akbar and his courtiers "could not contain their joy at seeing the infant Jesus in his mother's arms and it seemed as if they would like to play with him and talk to him." The emperor acquired European prints for his own painters to copy. Catholic religious imagery became part of the decor of his court.

Akbar promoted debates between teachers of rival religions in an attempt to establish a synthesis, which he called the "Faith of God"—the Din-i-ilahi. In what sounds like a standard story of saintly conversion, enlightenment came to him while he was hunting, in the late 1570s. Unsurprisingly, the new religion seemed like an attempt to make the Mughal state itself sacred. Akbar came to see himself as a manifestation, even an embodiment of God. Most Muslims were repelled and resolved never to try to accommodate other religions again. Later Mughal emperors felt torn between strategies of tolerance and of hostility toward non-Muslim faiths. The need to appease Hindus caused a mid-seventeenth century revival of Akbar's efforts by Dara Shukoh, a pretender to the Mughal throne, who proposed "the mingling of the two oceans" of Muslim and Hindu teaching. But his fanatically Muslim brother, Aurangzeb (r. 1658–1707), beat him to the throne and promoted Islam aggressively. He executed the Sikh leader, Guru Hari Rai, for blasphemy and discriminated against Hindus in distributing offices and rewards. The result was a backlash. When a Sikh prince seized the city of Jodhpur, for example, in 1707, he banned Islam and burned the mosques.

THE RENAISSANCE "DISCOVERY OF THE WORLD"

In the long run—according to traditional readings of world history—religious diversity, which arose from the splitting and mingling of religions in the sixteenth century, made the world more secular. People became less committed to their religions because they had to live at peace with neighbors of different faiths. The mutual challenges of rival religions weakened all of them by comparison with other godless or materialistic ways of looking at the world.

But these changes, if they happened at all, took a long time to take effect. In Europe, for instance, in the sixteenth and seventeenth centuries, most of the ideas contemporaries denounced as atheism turn out, on close examination, to have been challenges to traditional Christian descriptions of God. Secular subjects did become more common in art, and religious subjects less so. But this may have had less to do with changing ideologies than with the economics of art. As wealth spread, so did art patronage. The church's dominance of the art market weakened. Religions did become more mutually tolerant, in some places where they mingled, and forfeited their claims to exclusive truth. In other cases, however, the opposite occurred and, overall, on a global scale, religious warfare and persecution probably became more bitter and more widespread.

In the first half of the sixteenth century, fashions in learning, art, and letters informed by the inspiration of classical Greece and Rome, leaped from Italy, where they had originated, across Europe, in a movement traditionally called the Renaissance (see Chapter 15). During his invasion of Italy in 1515, King Francis I of France saw "all the best [art] works"; he began to collect casts of ancient sculptures and acquire the services of Italian artists, including Leonardo da Vinci (1459–1519). The sixteenth-century courts of Henry VIII of England, the Habsburg Archduchess Mary of Hungary (who ruled the Low Countries for her nephew, the Emperor Charles V), Sigmund I and II in Poland and Lithuania, and Ferdinand I and Maximilian II in Austria and Bohemia became similar centers for spreading the Renaissance. In the 1520s, returning poets took Italian verse forms to Spain, Portugal, and England. In Spain, the great new buildings of the period—the cathedral and royal palace of Granada, the town hall of Seville, the hospital in Toledo—introduced a new look, based on classically inspired shape, harmony, proportions, space, and light. Beyond royal courts, the trade in engravings, the migrations of artists and scholars, and the taste of civic patrons, took the same classicizing tradition to the great cities of Germany and Switzerland.

Poets who scoured the era of the Roman Emperor Augustus (r. 27 B.C.E.–14 C.E.) for models and churchmen who looked back to the time of Christ shared the same perspective. Virgil (70–19 B.C.E.), Augustus's favorite poet, was generally, if mistakenly, credited with having prophesied the birth of Jesus. Fusions of Christianity with classical philosophy became popular as never before since the fourth century, when Christianity conquered the thinking classes of the Roman Empire. Christian Platonism and Christian stoicism (see Chapter 6) were characteristic fashions of the era, and the most influential thinker of the first half of the sixteenth century, Erasmus of Rotterdam (1466–1536), made "the philosophy of Christ" a current term. Benvenuto Cellini the Florentine (1500–1571) sculpted a *Crucifixion* that expresses serene stoicism, rather than the searing passion earlier sculptors had represented. In a series of sculptures by Michelangelo (1475–1564), "captives" in human shape emerge from the coarse particularity of rocks. Michelangelo seems to have been trying to embody the notion that matter hides reality—which is spiritual—from our senses and that we need genius or grace to see it.

Meanwhile, the discoveries of explorers transformed the way Europeans pictured the world. They confirmed the vastness of the globe and disclosed the existence of a New World in the Western Hemisphere. In particular, the discoveries challenged European notions of what it means to be human, as encounters unfolded with a previously unsuspected range of cultures and civilizations.

The most exciting moment of all occurred when Christopher Columbus first glimpsed what he called "naked people," on Friday, October 12, 1492, on an island he called San Salvador, which most scholars identify with Watling Island in the Bahamas. The natives were therefore probably Lucayos—a people of whom little is known, though archaeological evidence endorses Columbus's account of their material culture. His description deploys many of the categories, comparisons, and images available in his day to help Westerners understand other cultures. Many of his observations cut two ways. The natives' ignorance of warfare established their innocent credentials but also meant they would be easy to conquer. Their nakedness evoked a primitive Eden or an ideal of dependence on God, but also suggested savagery and similarity to beasts. Their lack of commercial skills showed that they were both morally uncorrupted and easily fooled. Their rational faculties made them identifiable as human and exploitable as slaves. Columbus seemed genuinely torn between conflicting ideas about the Native Americans. After all, he and his men were undergoing an experience no European had ever had before.

Michelangelo's "captives" are often described as unfinished. But they illustrate an idea of the ancient Greek philosopher Plato: Like captives from their bonds, or reality from the shadows, true forms emerge struggling from the rocks that enclose them.

Columbus's Encounter with Indians. One of the engravings that illustrated an early edition of the first printed report of Columbus's first transatlantic voyage illustrates a scene that never happened but that Columbus himself imagined and described. Asian traders do business with the naked, timid people Columbus met on Hispaniola. The image was designed to bolster his claim that he had reached a point close to and in touch with the riches of Asia.

Throughout his journeys to the New World, Columbus remained undecided between rival perceptions of the people—as potential Christians, as types of pagan virtue, as exploitable slaves, as savage, as civilized, as figures of fun. A long quest began to understand the diversity of humankind. Discoveries in the natural world complicated it. In the seventeenth century, as Europeans increasingly got to know the great apes of Africa and other primates, the problem of where to draw the limits of humankind grew increasingly puzzling. Discoveries about the human body kept pace with those of human cultures. Traditional ideas of human nature reeled under the impact of discoveries on every side.

Eyes adjusted slowly to the newly revealed realities. Influenced by missionaries eager to save souls among newly encountered peoples, the church took a positive view of their natural qualities to protect them from secular exploitation and extermination. The question of whether the native peoples of the New World were fully human, endowed with rational souls, was settled—at least for Catholics—affirmatively by Pope Paul III in the 1530s, but their status needed frequent shoring up against slippage. Missionary scholars in the Americas built up files to demonstrate the social and political sophistication of native societies. A case like that of the Aztecs posed typical problems. Cannibalism and human sacrifice tarnished the record of a people who otherwise appeared highly "civil." In evidence—vividly painted by native artists at the court of the Spanish Viceroy of Mexico—compiled under missionary guidance in the 1540s, one can still see the range of qualities the clergy held up for admiration. The training of an Aztec candidate for the priesthood of the pre-Christian gods is shown in gory detail, as his teachers beat his body to bleeding. But this was evidence not of barbarism but of the similarity of Aztec values to those of their Franciscan evangelists, who also practiced devotional whipping and tortured their own flesh. The Aztec state was depicted as a well-regulated pyramid, symmetrically disposed to administer justice, with an emperor at the top, counselors below him, and common pleaders at the lowest level: a mirror image of the society the missionaries had left in Spain. The Aztecs' sense of justice was shown to conform to the standards Europeans deemed natural. An adulterous couple, stoned to death, suggested a comparison with the ancient Jews and, therefore, openness to the milder Christian message. Justice was tempered with mercy. Though drunkenness among the Aztecs was punishable by death, the aged were depicted as enjoying exemption. Mild restraint took the place of execution. When the Aztecs went to war, provocations on their enemies' part were shown to precede hostilities, which followed only after diplomatic efforts had been rebuffed. The natives, it seemed, practiced "just" war by traditional Christian standards—something that the Spanish monarchy strove to do with imperfect success. Missionaries could cite examples like these for every native community where they worked.

In the mid-sixteenth century, a Spanish bishop, Bartolomé de Las Casas (1474–1566), was the loudest spokesman for broadening the definition of humankind to include Native Americans. He was a convert to conscience—an exploiter of Indian labor on Hispaniola, who reformed when he heard a Dominican preacher's challenge: "are the Indians not human beings, endowed with rational souls, like yourselves?" He joined the Dominicans and became the official Protector of the Indians. In effect, despite unsuccessful spells as a missionary and a frontier bishop, he was a professional lobbyist who managed, albeit briefly, to get the Spanish crown to legislate for Indian rights. Human sacrifice, according to Las Casas, should be seen rather as evidence of the misplaced piety of its practitioners, or of their pitiable state as victims of the devil, than as an infringement of natural law. His conclusion—"All the peoples of mankind are human"—sounds self-evident, but it was a message important enough to bear repetition. It was applied patchily at first. Black people hardly felt the benefits for centuries. It made possible a new view of history, according to which all peoples were created equal, but passed through various universal stages of historic development. Broadly speaking, this model prevailed in educated European minds in the seventeenth and eighteenth centuries.

THE RISE OF WESTERN SCIENCE

Partly because of privileged access to the recycled learning of classical antiquity and partly owing to the new data accumulated during the exploration of the world, Western science registered leaps in the seventeenth century that science in other parts of the world could not match.

If secularism did not displace religion to any great extent in the West, science did, in some degree, probably displace magic. Just by offering this opinion, we raise a problem: What is the difference between magic and science? Both are attempts to explain and therefore to control nature. The Western science of the sixteenth and seventeenth centuries grew, in part, out of magic. Starting with Marsiglio Ficino (1433–1499), an Italian priest and physician who worked for the Medici, Renaissance writers argued that magic was good if it was used to heal or to accumulate knowledge of nature, and that some ancient magical texts were lawful reading for Christians.

The most influential text was the work supposedly written by an ancient Egyptian known as "Hermes Trismegistos" (Hermes Thrice-Blessed), but which was actually composed by an unidentified Byzantine forger. It arrived in Florence in 1460 among a consignment of books bought from the Balkans after the fall of Constantinople to the Turks in 1453 for the Medici library, and it caused a sensation. Renaissance scholars felt inspired to pursue "Egyptian" wisdom in search of an alternative to the austere rationalism of classical learning—a fount of older and supposedly purer knowledge than could be had from the Greeks or Romans. The distinction between magic and science as means of attempting to control nature almost vanished in the sixteenth century.

Doctor Faustus, who sold his soul to the devil in exchange for magical access to knowledge, was a fictional character, but he symbolized a real yearning. In his world, wisdom was supernatural knowledge. The Habsburg Emperor Rudolf II (r. 1576–1612), who patronized mysterious arts in his castle in Prague in what is now the Czech Republic, was hailed as the new Hermes. Here magicians gathered to probe the secrets of nature and to practice astrology, alchemy, cabbalism (the ancient mystical and magical wisdom of the Jews), and *pansophy*—the attempt to classify all knowledge and so unlock access to mastery of the universe.

None of this magic worked, but the effort to manipulate it was not wasted. Alchemy fed into chemistry, astrology into astronomy, cabbalism into mathematics,

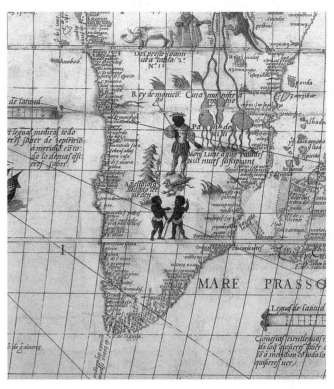

Renaissance view of Africans. The world map of Italian navigator Sebastian Cabot of the 1540s includes positive images of black Africans. The manicongo—the ruler of Kongo—appears with crown, scepter, and elegant European clothes. Pygmies, though small and poorly clad, carry sticks to prove their rational ability to use tools and "understand each other"—as the inscription on the map puts it—in civilized conversation.

and pansophy into the classification of nature. Would-be wizards constructed what they called "theaters of the world" in which all knowledge could be divided into compartments and displayed and "wonder chambers" where specimens of everything in nature could be gathered. The eventual outcome of this work included the methods for classifying plants, animals, and languages that we still use today. Wonder chambers developed into museums. Many of the great figures of the scientific revolution in the Western world of the sixteenth and seventeenth centuries either started with magic or maintained an interest in it. Johannes Kepler (1571–1630), who worked out the path of the planets around the sun, was one of Emperor Rudolf's favorites. Sir Isaac Newton (1642–1727) was a part-time alchemist. The philosopher and mathematician Gottfried Wilhelm Leibniz (1646–1716) studied ancient Egyptian hieroglyphs (though he could not read them) and cabbalistic notation.

If Western science of the time owed a lot to magic, it gradually developed a direction of its own: toward empirical methods, rational explanations, and verifiable facts. One of the most conspicuous examples is the abandonment of the image of the universe centered on the Earth that appeared in the Bible and was generally accepted in the ancient world. In 1543, the Polish astronomer and churchman Nicolaus Copernicus (1473–1543) proposed reclassifying the Earth as one of several planets revolving around the sun. His theory was formulated tentatively, advocated discreetly, and spread slowly. He received the first printing of his great book on the heavens when he was on his deathbed. It took nearly a century after his death to remold people's vision of the universe. In combination with Kepler's work on the mapping of orbits around the sun published early in the seventeenth century, the Copernican revolution expanded the limits of the observable heavens, substituted a dynamic for a static system, and wrenched the universe into a new shape around the paths of the planets, accurately represented. This shift of focus

Wonder chamber. In Europe in the late sixteenth and seventeenth centuries, art collection expanded to include the "curiosities" of nature and science. This seventeenth-century painting records the splendors of a Dutch gentleman's collection. Portraits of the owner and his wife preside over an array of objects that is modestly representative of the world: scenes from nature, the Bible, classical myth, and antique ruins—all the traditional sources of wisdom—are on the walls. A personification of the Tiber River—representing ancient Rome—is over the door. Wonders of nature—coral and shells—mingle with classical statues. On the tables, learned visitors contemplate the sphere of Earth and the heavens, and the new wonders revealed by exploration. In the center, the artist warns against religiously inspired vandals who destroyed art and learning.
Adriaen Stalbent (1589–1662) "The Sciences and the Arts." Wood, 93 x 114 cm. Inv. 1405. Museo del Prado, Madrid, Spain. Photograph © Erich Lessing, Art Resource, NY

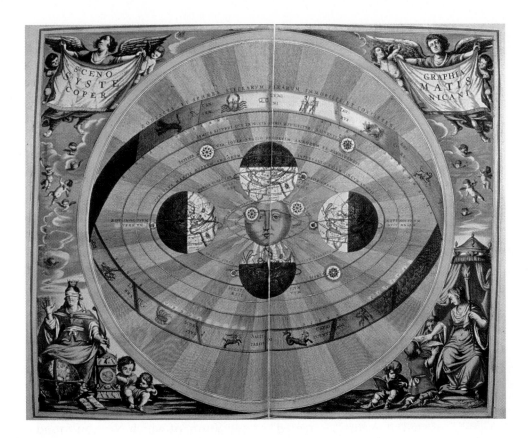

The Copernican Universe. Personifications of Justice and Learning flank a vision of the cosmos, as late seventeenth-century European scientists imagined it. A rim of stars, signified by the signs of the Zodiac, surrounds the six planets that were known at the time. The planets move around the sun in the elliptical orbits discovered by Johannes Kepler (1571–1630). The Earth, with moon attached, is no longer at the center of the universe. But as the most important planet, it is shown in detail, with emphasis on how day, night, and the seasons change as the Earth moves.

from the Earth to the sun was a strain on eyes adjusted to an outlook that made the Earth the center of the universe. Every subsequent revelation of astronomy has reduced the relative dimensions of our dwelling place and ground its apparent significance into tinier fragments.

Scientific reasoning grew more systematic. Two particularly influential styles of thinking are illustrated—and were first fully formulated—in the work, respectively, of the English experimenter, Francis Bacon (1561–1626), and the French philosopher and logician, René Descartes (1596–1650). Bacon took from the Dutch scientist, J. B. van Helmont (1577–1644) the motto, "Logic is useless for making scientific discoveries." Bacon prized observation above tradition and was said to have died a martyr to science when he caught a chill while testing the effects of low temperatures on a chicken. He devised the method by which scientists turn observations into general laws: the so-called **inductive method** by which a general inference is made from a series of uniform observations and is then tested. The result, if it works, is a scientific "law." Scientists can then use this law to predict how natural phenomena will behave under similar circumstances.

Descartes, who affected laziness and detested the restless lives of men such as Bacon (who also pursued an ambitious career in politics), made doubt the key to the only possible certainty. Striving to escape from the suspicion that all appearances are false, Descartes reasoned that the reality of his mind was proved by its own self-doubts. His starting point was the age-old problem of **epistemology**: How do we know that we know? How do we distinguish truth from falsehood? Suppose, he said, "some evil genius has deployed all his energies in deceiving me." Then nothing in the world might be certain except that "without doubt I exist

"This shift of focus from the Earth to the sun was a strain on eyes adjusted to an outlook that made the Earth the center of the universe. Every subsequent revelation of astronomy has reduced the relative dimensions of our dwelling place and ground its apparent significance into tinier fragments."

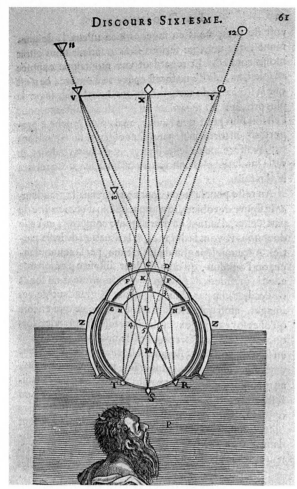

A vision of vision. The French philosopher René Descartes (1596–1650) described how we see things in his *Optics,* which was published in 1637. Light travels—in waves, Descartes guessed—between object and eye. The eye itself works like a lens, bending the light to form an impression. Science, like magic, had the power to make humans "masters and possessors of nature."

[even] . . . if he deceives me, and let him deceive me as much as he will, he will never cause me to be nothing so long as I think that I am something." This left a further problem: "What then am I? A thing which thinks. What is a thing which thinks? It is a thing which doubts, understands, conceives, affirms, denies, wills, refuses, which also imagines and feels."

The work of Isaac Newton (1643–1727) typified the achievements of seventeenth-century Western science. In a bout of furious thinking and experimenting, beginning in the 1660s, Newton seemed to discover the underlying "secret of the universe" that had eluded the Renaissance wise men. He imagined the universe as a mechanical contrivance—like the wind-up models of the heavens in brass and gleaming wood that became popular toys for gentlemen's libraries. It was tuned by a celestial engineer and turned and stabilized by a universal force—gravity—observable in the swing of a pendulum or the fall of an apple, as well as in the motions of moons and planets.

Newton was a traditional figure: an old-fashioned humanist and an encyclopedist, obsessed by trying to determine the chronology of the Bible. He was even, in his wilder fantasies, a dabbler in magic, hunting down the secret of a systematic universe, an alchemist seeking the Philosophers' Stone, which legend said could turn base metals into gold. He was also a representative figure of a trend in the thought of his time: **empiricism,** the doctrine beloved in England and Scotland in his day, that reality is observable and verifiable through our senses. The universe consisted of events "cemented" by causation, of which Newton found a scientific description and exposed the laws. "Nature's Laws," according to the epitaph the eighteenth-century poet Alexander Pope wrote for Newton, "lay hid in Night" until "God said, 'Let Newton be!' and there was Light."

If so, it turned out to be an act of divine self-withdrawal. Newton thought gravity was God's way of holding the universe together. Many of his followers disagreed. Belief in a supreme being (though not necessarily in God as Christianity describes him) thrived in eighteenth-century Europe, partly because the mechanical universe could dispense with the divine "Watchmaker" after he had given it its initial winding. By the end of the eighteenth century, the French astronomer and mathematician Pierre-Simon de Laplace (1749–1827), who interpreted almost every known physical phenomenon in terms of the attraction and repulsion of atomic particles, could boast that he had reduced God to "an unnecessary hypothesis."

WESTERN SCIENCE IN THE EAST

It would be wrong, however, to speak of the rise of science at the expense of religion. There is no necessary conflict between the two, and no one in the sixteenth or seventeenth centuries, as far as we know, even suspected that there could be. Science did prove, however, in one respect, to be more powerful than any single religion. It showed more cultural flexibility, appealing more widely across the world. The spread of Christianity, Buddhism, and Islam was among the great movements of the age—but they all ran up against cultural limits. Buddhism grew mainly in Central Asia. Islam registered little appeal in Europe outside of the Turkish-controlled Balkans. Christianity was rejected in most of China and India and all but wiped out in Japan. The new Western science, however, had the power to penetrate everywhere. The cultural exchange that took Christianity to Asia also took Western science across Eurasia. Indeed, the same Jesuit scholars were the agents of both transfers.

In some respects, the intellectual climate in Eastern Asia was unwelcoming to Western ideas. In the seventeenth century, a Confucian revival in China, Japan, and Korea impeded Western thought because it spread ancient Confucian prejudice against Western "barbarians." The Dutch, on whom, from 1639, Japan depended exclusively for information about the West, were generally regarded—said one of their few Japanese admirers—as "scarcely men, a sort of beast." According to the Korean Confucian scholar Yi T'oegye (1501–1570), "It is no exaggeration to liken [Westerners] to birds and beasts." In some ways, Japanese scholars welcomed the Western view of the world as undermining Chinese claims to cultural superiority and to China being the center of the world, but they hesitated to adopt Western ideas as uniquely true. When the Zen monk Ishin Suden (1569–1633) explained the nature of Japan as a "divine land," he used all the traditional language. In Confucian terms, Japan was "born of Earth and Heaven"; by Daoist thought, it was "grounded in the opposing principles of Yin and Yang"; and it was a "Buddha-land" for good measure.

In China, the change of dynasty in 1644 from the Ming to the Qing stimulated the Confucian revival. Because he did not want to serve rulers whom he considered to be usurpers, Wang Fuzhi (wahng foo-jih) (1619–1692) withdrew to the hills of Hunan in the distant south. There he celebrated the values of eleventh-century Confucians and dreamed of "the order of heaven" restored on Earth. Gu Yanwu (goo yehn-woo) (1613–1682), similarly alienated from the new dynasty, returned to Confucian guidelines for life: "study all learning" and "have a sense of shame." Like any determined Renaissance scholar in Europe, he dedicated himself to "the search for antiquities." "Anything legible I copied by hand, and when I saw an inscription unseen by my predecessors I was so overjoyed that I could not sleep." He and his fellow scholars consciously guarded the spoils of time against erosion, damage, and oblivion.

This Chinese renaissance was comparable in kind with that of Europe, but did not achieve the same effects. For the first time in recorded history, China slipped behind Europe, in some fields, in the rate of scientific achievement. On the whole, the global history of technology up to this time reflected consistent Chinese superiority. World-shaping innovations typically happened first in China. Take a few key examples. Printing and paper, the bases of modern communications until the late twentieth century, were Chinese inventions. So was paper money—without which modern capitalism would be unthinkable. So was gunpowder, the key to modern warfare. So were the rudder and the method of shipbuilding that protected the vessel against sinking by dividing the hull into separate compartments—these were vital innovations in the development of global shipping. The blast furnace, essential for modern industrialization, also came from China. In what we think of as the late Middle Ages, however, Western technology edged ahead in two areas: clockwork and lens-making (see Chapter 13). These came together in the science of astronomy.

The impact of Western astronomy in China is immediately visible in one of the world's most extraordinary books, the *Tianwen Lue* (tee-ehn-wen lehw) *(A Treatise on Astronomy)* that Manuel Dias, a young Jesuit missionary, wrote in Latin and, with native help, in Chinese in 1610—the year after the great Italian astronomer Galileo Galilei (1564–1642) first used a telescope to study the heavens. "Lately," Dias told Chinese readers, "a famous Western sage has constructed a marvelous instrument." Through the telescope, he said, "the moon appears a thousand times

"This Chinese renaissance was comparable in kind with that of Europe, but did not achieve the same effects. For the first time in recorded history, China slipped behind Europe, in some fields, in the rate of scientific achievement."

The Observatory at Beijing. In 1674, the Chinese government handed over the observatory at Beijing to the Jesuits for reorganization. Among the results was a new observatory, shown in this eighteenth-century engraving, that the Jesuits set up on the roof of the imperial palace using instruments built to European specifications. Some of these instruments have survived and have only recently been removed to a museum.

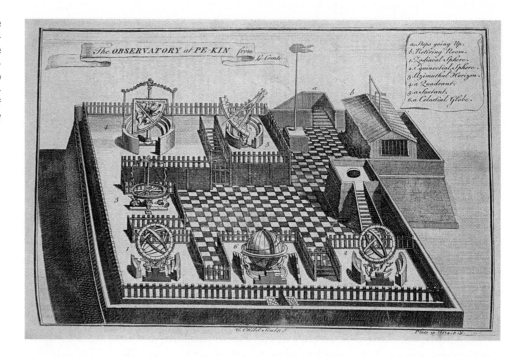

larger"; Saturn's rings become visible; "Jupiter appears always surrounded by moons. . . . The day this instrument arrives in China we shall give more details of its admirable use."

For a simple reason, Jesuit mastery of astronomy was the most important of the many technical skills with which they impressed the Chinese. The Chinese Board of Astronomy, an official department of the Chinese imperial court, existed not for the disinterested study of the heavens but to devise a ritual calendar. The ceremonies of the imperial court, like those of King Narai of Thailand, were attuned to the rhythms of the stars, so that earthly order should reflect heavenly harmony. To perform the rites for movable feasts and unique occasions, the stars had to be favorable. The Chinese believed that the success of imperial enterprises, the survival of the dynasty, and the life of the empire depended on it. The environment of a star-struck court stimulated scientific knowledge. Though the Board of Astronomy was young—created in the early seventeenth century—the Chinese tradition in astronomy was ancient, and it had been practiced at court for centuries. The imperial observatory had a continuous history of some 400 years behind it, and the number and quality of recorded observations available to Chinese astronomers had been unequaled anywhere in the West until well into the sixteenth century.

Yet when the Jesuits arrived, their superiority over the Muslim personnel who then ran the observatory seemed so marked that the imperial court abandoned the entire native Chinese tradition and turned the practice of astronomy over to the newcomers. After a couple of false starts, the Jesuit Ferdinand Verbiest took over the Board of Astronomy in 1669 and systematically reformed the calendar. In 1674, at the emperor's request, the observatory was re-equipped with instruments of Jesuit design. The rooftop observatory, with the instruments erected like shrines on little platforms, provided European engravers with one of their most popular Chinese pictures. The astronomy lesson of King Narai had parallels in many parts of Asia.

Influences from the East reflected back at the West. Gottfried Wilhelm Leibniz, was one of the greatest admirers of China in his day, devouring everything he could learn about the country from Jesuit writings. In 1679, he published his own book on Chinese learning. He believed that Chinese wisdom was superior to Europe's in civilized values, ethics, and politics: "I almost think," he wrote, "that Chinese missionaries should be sent to us to teach us the aims and practices of natural theology, as we send missionaries to them to instruct them in revealed religion." But he thought Europe was ahead in mathematics and what we would now call physics. The reversal in the balance of technical skill in Eurasia had begun. In succeeding centuries, similar reversals in historic patterns of power and wealth would elevate the West in other respects.

In Perspective
The Scales of Thought

Despite the shortcomings of the missionaries or of their congregations, the enormous extension of the frontiers of Islam, Buddhism, and Christianity remains one of the most conspicuous features of the world of the sixteenth and seventeenth centuries. Buddhism and Islam expanded into territories that bordered their existing heartlands. By overleaping the Atlantic and Pacific oceans, Christianity registered a spectacular difference. Islam, however, had the advantage of expanding in the demographically vigorous worlds of Africa, Malaysia, and Indonesia, whereas the territories Buddhism won in northern Asia were vast but sparsely populated. As we saw in the last chapter, the millions Christianity won in the Americas quickly withered with the rapid decline of the Native American population.

In the long run, however, the sheer size of the New World counted for most. Because of the exclusion of Islam from the Western Hemisphere, Muslim predominance among world religions slipped in the eighteenth and nineteenth centuries, when the Americas made up and exceeded their lost population. In the balance of resources, Christendom acquired potentially vast extra weight. For reasons no one has ever been able fully to explain, Christianity proved more flexible—more adaptable to more cultures—than Islam or Buddhism did. Islam continued to spread, but only within a relatively narrow band of the world, bounded on the north by the Mediterranean basin and the Eurasian steppelands and in the south by the tropics and the Indian Ocean. The expansion of Buddhism into Central Asia was a conspicuous triumph by earlier Buddhist standards: the religion had not spread far and had even retreated from some of its former heartlands, in the previous 500 years or so. But by the standards of Christian and Muslim expansion in the sixteenth and seventeenth centuries, the Buddhist achievement was modest. It is worth reflecting on how much the conditions governing the spread of these religions seem to have changed today. Christianity still exhibits remarkable adaptability, with dramatic levels of conversions and rates of growth in parts of Asia and sub-Saharan Africa. Islam has begun to overleap its traditional boundaries, thanks mainly to the wide-ranging migrations of Muslims, especially from parts of North Africa and South and Southeast Asia. Buddhism has developed a new appeal, attracting adherents for the first time in cultural environments it never penetrated before, especially in Europe and North America.

Equally remarkable, in the period this chapter has covered, and equally significant for the history of the world over the following few centuries, was the spurt of Western science and the recognition it achieved, in some respects, in China. Although China, the Islamic world, and, to some extent, India, had rich scientific

"Despite the shortcomings of the missionaries or of their congregations, the enormous extension of the frontiers of Islam, Buddhism, and Christianity remains one of the most conspicuous features of the world of the sixteenth and seventeenth centuries."

Chronology

Fifteenth century	Study of classical Greece and Rome provides foundation for the rise of Italian humanism
Fifteenth and sixteenth centuries	Merchants and missionaries spread Islam
Early sixteenth century	Martin Luther initiates Protestant Reformation in Europe
1500s	Spanish Christians compete with Muslims in the Philippines
Sixteenth and seventeenth centuries	Royal courts in northern Europe spread humanism; Contact with Native Americans challenges European notions of what it means to be human; elites take on task of "re-Christianizing" Europe
1520s and 1530s	Franciscans baptize millions of Native Americans
1540	Ignatius Loyola founds Jesuit order
1543	Nicholas Copernicus proposes heliocentric theory
Mid-sixteenth century	Catholic Church begins Counter-Reformation
1545–1563	Council of Trent meets
1596–1650	René Descartes, French philosopher and proponent of deductive reasoning
1570s	Mongol ruler Altan Khan stimulates the revival of missionary Buddhism in Mongolia
Late sixteenth century	Mughal emperor Akbar attempts to establish the "Faith of God"
Seventeenth century	Jesuits lead Christian missionary effort in China
1621	Reformation in Eastern Orthodox Church begins
1630s	Missions initiated by Prince Neyici Toyin bring Buddhism to Manchuria
1639	Christianity banned in Japan
1669	Jesuit Ferdinand Verbiest takes over the Chinese Board of Astronomy
1687	Sir Isaac Newton publishes *Principia Mathematica*

traditions of their own, and although the Islamic world, like the West, had privileged access to the scientific legacy of the ancient Greeks and Romans, Westerners now caught up and pushed ahead in some fields. Of these fields, astronomy was of key importance in the seventeenth century because it won acceptance for Westerners in other cultures. The only two major fields of innovation in which Western technicians exceeded those of China in the Middle Ages were glasswork, especially lens-making, and clockwork. In astronomy, these fields came together, giving Western sages an advantage in competition with indigenous rivals in China, India, and Southeast Asia. Meanwhile, Westerners absorbed and developed technologies of Chinese origin that would ultimately multiply Westerners' advantage in competition with Asian states and economies, including those of China. Printing and paper-making (the insuperable ingredients of modern communications until the twentieth century) were Chinese inventions. So were paper money and the blast furnace (without which capitalism and industrialization would have been impossible). So were gunpowder and vital direction-finding and shipbuilding techniques, without which the West might never have caught up with China in nautical or military endeavors. In the eighteenth century, as we shall see, Western superiority in some military, naval, and industrial technologies would begin to have an impact. The resulting shift in the world balance of power and resources is the subject we have to tackle next.

PROBLEMS AND PARALLELS

1. Why were the sixteenth and seventeenth centuries an unprecedented era in the revitalization of Buddhism, Christianity, and Islam? How did the missionary strategies of these different faiths compare? What strategies did the Jesuits use to try to convert China and Japan? Why did Altan Khan patronize Buddhist missionaries in Mongolia?

2. Why did pre-Christian religious practices persist among Native Americans? Why has millenarianism been so important in American Christianity? How did Guru Nanak and the Emperor Akbar seek to bridge the rivalry between Hinduism and Islam in India?

3. How did the Renaissance "discovery of the world" influence European thinking and spirituality? How did their encounters with non-Western cultures transform the way Westerners saw the world? Why were Christopher Columbus's attitudes toward Native Americans so conflicted?

4. Why were the sixteenth and seventeenth centuries significant in the development of Western science and secular values and in the transmission of Western science to other parts of the world? How did the relationship of Western science to magic evolve over time?

5. What Western ideas were most welcome in the East and which were not? Why was King Narai of Siam so interested in astronomy?

READ ON▶ ▶ ▶

The Diary of Kosa Pan (2002) is available, edited by M. Smithies and D. van der Cruysse. J. D. Tracy, *Europe's Reformations* (1999) is a reliable account, but J. Bossy, *Christianity in the West* (1985) and J. Delumeau, *The Catholic Church from Luther to Voltaire* (1977) are radical and searching. My account follows F. Fernández-Armesto and D. Wilson, *Reformations* (1997). On China and Indonesia, respectively, I am indebted to W. J. Peterson, *Why Did They Become Christians?* Y. T'ing-yün, L. Chih-tsao, and H. Kuang-ch'i' in J. W. O'Malley et al., eds., *The Jesuits: Cultures, Sciences and the Arts, 1540–1773,* which is an important collection generally, and A. Meersman, *The Franciscans in the Indonesian Archipelago, 1300–1775* (1967). L. M. Brockey, *Journey to the East* (2007) reveals the extent of the Jesuits' work in China. M. C. Ricklefs, *A History of Modern Indonesia: c. 1300 to the Present*, (1981) is an excellent general history that traces Islamic missionary efforts in Indonesia in the seventeenth century. On Buddhist missions, W. Heissig, *The Religions of Mongolia* (2000) is fundamental, as is M. Hodgson, *The Venture of Islam* (1977) on Islam.

R. Ricard, *The Spiritual Conquest of Mexico* (1966) is an enduring classic. P. U. Bonomi, *Under the Cope of Heaven: Religion, Society, and Politics in Colonial America* (1986) and S. Schwartz, *"A Mixed Multitude": The Struggle for Toleration in Colonial Pennsylvania* (1987) explicate the emergence of religious diversity in North America's Middle Atlantic colonies in the seventeenth century. M. Deren, *Divine Horsemen: The Living Gods of Haiti* (1985) is the best introduction to the Afro-Caribbean religion A. Métraux, *Black Peasants and Their Religion* (1960) is an enduring classic.

J. Rubiés, *Travel and Ethnology in the Renaissance. South India through European Eyes, 1250–1625* (2000) is a brilliant analysis of European perceptions of religious diversity in India during the Renaissance. L. Jardine, *Worldly Goods: A New History of the Renaissance* (1998) reexamines the cultural achievements of the Renaissance in the context of the material and commercial world that produced them. L. Jardine and J. Brotton, *Global Interests: Renaissance Art between East and West* (2000) sets the global context.

S. Shapin, *The Scientific Revolution* (1998) examines how the world of seventeenth-century scientists shaped their understanding of nature. A. Grayling, *Descartes* (2006) is up-to-date, readable, and provocative; L. Jardine and A. Stewart, *Hostage to Fortune: The Troubled Life of Francis Bacon* (1999) is masterly. J. Waley-Cohen, "China and Western Technology in the Late Eighteenth Century." *American Historical Review* (1993) traces the reception of various Western technologies, including gunpowder, in China. M. Jacob, *Scientific Culture and the Making of the Industrial West* (1997) offers a detailed analysis of how the cultural dissemination of Newtonian mechanics affected the emergence of industrial technology, especially in Britain.

CHAPTER 19

States and Societies: Political and Social Change in the Sixteenth and Seventeenth Centuries

▲ **Queen Nzinga.** In 1622, before she came to the throne of Ndongo, Nzinga made a treaty with the Portuguese. This contemporary engraving shows her conducting negotiations, seated on a slave's back to avoid standing in the presence of a white man of lower rank than herself.

At an uncertain date, sometime in the 1640s, Queen Nzinga of Ndongo, in southwestern Africa, announced that she would "become a man." Her husbands, of whom she had several, were labeled as concubines, dressed in women's clothes, and made to sleep among her maids (under pain of instant beheading, should any illicit sex ensue). Her ladies-in-waiting were re-equipped as bodyguards. Henceforth she led her troops into battle. She could still handle weapons skillfully as late as 1662, at the age of 80, when an Italian visitor to her court witnessed a military parade. Like many other female pretenders to thrones that men normally occupied, she had overcome challenges to her right to rule by reclassifying herself as masculine.

The decision to switch gender was not the first challenging transformation in Nzinga's life. She came to power as regent for her nephew, the rightful king according to the normal rules of succession, in 1615, but, fearful of having to surrender power, she killed him and declared herself queen. In 1622, she adopted Christianity, less—it seems—out of conviction than to secure Portuguese help against the enemies who sought to dethrone her. She used the ferocious mercenaries known as Imbalanga—private war bands that grew by kidnapping boys—to fight her battles. When they cheated her, she vowed to "become an Imbalanga" herself and lead her own war band. As this involved bloody rituals of sacrifice, cannibalism, and child killing, she had to renounce Christianity. But she returned to the faith in the 1640s to obtain more reliable help again from the Portuguese.

Hers was a surprising and bizarre career. In one respect, however, it was a representative episode of early modern politics. All Nzinga's self-transformations were strategic moves in her struggle for power in Ndongo—a hard-fought series of wars, in which she repeatedly clawed her way back from defeat and repeatedly returned victorious after being driven from her realm. That struggle was part of a longer, broader, deeper story of political change that many parts of the world echoed: the rise of strong, central monarchies, the subduing of unruly aristocracies, the shift of power from the hands of nobles into those of royal dependants. In the 1560s, when Portuguese explorers, slavers, and missionaries first described Ndongo, it was a loosely defined kingdom, where big landowners wielded the most power and claimed the right to elect the monarch. Over the next few decades, kings asserted their hereditary right to the throne, without the need to consult the nobility. They also used slaves as administrators, wrenching authority away from aristocrats and confiding it to their own creatures. Nzinga was the slaves' candidate for kingship. Her first rivals in the wars she fought to secure the throne were nobles. Her attachment to the hereditary principle was passionate. Twice she lost control of the burial grounds of her ancestors. Twice she defied military priorities to win them back and defend them at heavy cost. Her effort to assert the legitimacy of female rule was successful. Her nominee, her sister, Barbara, succeeded her as queen. Women occupied the throne of Ndongo for 75 of the 100 years that followed Nzinga's death.

FOCUS questions

How did European rulers strengthen their power in the sixteenth and seventeenth centuries?

Why were the Ottomans able to build such a successful and long-lasting empire?

What role did Shiite Islam play in Safavid Persia?

How did Chinese society change under the Qing dynasty?

How did the Tokugawa shoguns govern Japan?

How did the "creole mentality" affect Spanish America?

What roles did African states play in the Atlantic slave trade?

What common features affected the development of states all over the world during this period?

Nzinga's realm was small but fiercely contested. As we look around the world of political and social change in the sixteenth and seventeenth centuries in this chapter, first at Europe, then at parts of Asia and the Americas before returning to Africa, we see similar conflicts unfold, albeit with many differences from region to region and state to state, as monarchs searched and struggled to redistribute power to their own advantage, and new or newly empowered classes contended for a share in the growing might and resources of states. Though many of the problems rulers and elites faced were similar world-wide, the variety of responses cannot be crushed to fit an easy formula: we have to acknowledge the diversity and make the best sense of it we can. Global history is difficult and delightful because, although, as I hope this book shows, there is a single story that encompasses the world, there are also contrasting and sometimes conflicting stories within it, which fit into the framework in different ways.

POLITICAL CHANGE IN EUROPE

Europe already had a state system (see Chapter 11). Events of the sixteenth and seventeenth centuries enshrined that system and made the political reunification of Western Europe—which had been a dream or mirage since the fall of Rome—unthinkable for centuries. There were three principal reasons for this.

First, the ideal of Western political unity faded as the various European states solidified their political independence and exerted more control over their inhabitants. In the Middle Ages, hopes of such unity had focused on the prospect of reviving the unity of the ancient Roman Empire. The term *Roman Empire* survived in the formal name of the group of mainly German states—the Holy Roman Empire of the German Nation—that an elected emperor ruled. When King Charles of Spain was elected to be Emperor Charles V in 1519, the outlook for uniting Europe seemed favorable. Through inheritance from his Habsburg father, Charles was already ruler of the Netherlands (modern Belgium, Holland, and Luxembourg), Austria, and much of Central Europe (see Map 19.1). His propagandists speculated that Charles V or his son would be the "Last World Emperor" foretold by prophecy whose reign would inaugurate the final age of the world before the Second Coming of Christ. Naturally, however, most other states resisted this idea, or tried to claim the role for their own rulers. Charles V's attempt to impose religious uniformity in the form of Roman Catholicism on his empire failed, demonstrating the limits of his real power. After his abdication in 1556, no one ever again convincingly reasserted the prospect of a durable universal state in the tradition of Rome.

Second, the power of individual European states increased rulers' power against rivals to their authority and the states' power over their own citizens. In 1648, almost all European states signed the **Treaty of Westphalia**, which ended a long war that had devastated much of Central Europe in the name of religion. The treaty gave rulers the right to impose their religions on their subjects. Though most European states experienced civil wars in the sixteenth and seventeenth centuries, monarchs usually won them. Cities and churches surrendered most of their

The map shows European territories with labels including:

IRELAND, ENGLAND, London, NETHERLANDS, BELGIUM, GERMANY, LUXEMBOURG, Paris, FRANCHE-COMTE, FRANCE, AUSTRIA, Milan, Venice, NAVARRE, PORTUGAL, Lisbon, ARAGON, Barcelona, Madrid, CASTILE, Granada, SWEDEN, DENMARK, POLAND, SILESIA, MORAVIA, Vienna, TRANSYLVANIA, HUNGARY, Mohacs, RUSSIA, OTTOMAN EMPIRE, Istanbul, ITALY, Corsica, Rome, Sardinia, Sicily, Balearic islands, NORTH AFRICA

Water bodies and rivers: North Sea, Baltic Sea, ATLANTIC OCEAN, Bay of Biscay, Mediterranean Sea, Adriatic Sea, Aegean Sea, Rhine, Elbe, Oder, Seine, Loire, Rhône, Douro, Tagus, Guadalquivir, Danube, Dniester

Scale: 300 km / 300 miles

MAP 19.1

The Dominions of Charles V

Habsburg lands of Charles V

boundaries of the Holy Roman Empire

privileges of self-government. Aristocracies—their personnel transformed as old families died out and rulers elevated new families to noble status—became close collaborators in royal power, rather than rivals to it, as aristocrats had been so often in the past. Offices under the crown became increasingly profitable additions to the income that aristocrats earned from their inherited estates. Countries that had been difficult or impossible to rule before their civil wars became easy to govern when their violent and restless elements had been exhausted or became dependent on royal rewards and appointments. England and Scotland had been particularly hard for their monarchs to tax in the sixteenth and early seventeenth centuries. The so-called Glorious Revolution of 1688–1689, which its aristocratic leaders represented as a blow against royal tyranny, actually turned Britain into Europe's most fiscally efficient state. In place of a dynasty committed to peace, the revolution installed rulers who fought expensive wars. Taxation trebled during the reign of the monarchs the British revolutionaries crowned.

Finally, Spain, the only power capable of imposing unity on Europe, failed. Spain seems, in retrospect, an unlikely superpower. It was a weakly united monarchy, consisting of several distinct states, each with its own languages and laws, linked only by imperfect allegiance to a single dynasty. The biggest of these states— Castile and Aragon—permanently shared the same monarchs only from 1516.

Castile acquired two other realms—Granada in the south and Navarre in the north—in conquests as late as 1492 and 1511, respectively. Spain's internal resources were small compared with those of France, which probably had, at the start of the sixteenth century, a population twice as big, substantially more territory, a more favorable climate, and enormously more productive farmland. About a third of the surface of Spain is mountainous or virtually desert.

Yet Spain was unrivaled for military and naval effectiveness in Europe throughout the sixteenth century and well into the seventeenth, while also maintaining, man for man and woman for woman, Europe's best-educated population—rivaled or excelled only in parts of the Netherlands and Italy—and generating some of the continent's most vibrant art and literature. Knowledge of Spanish became, like English today, a mark of education among Europe's elites.

How was Spain's strength possible? It was the result, in part, of the feebleness of its potential competitors. France spent much of the period racked by civil wars between aristocratic factions and did not fulfill its potential until the late seventeenth century, after the last of the wars was over. England, crippled by a low tax yield and split by religious dissent, failed to exploit the maritime advantages of its strategic position between the Atlantic and the North Sea. Germany was only a geographical expression, a loose collection of semi-independent states, incapable of working together. Poland, though vast in area, had insecure frontiers and a powerful nobility that defied or crippled royal power. Italy was a muddle of small states that no one could unify and only Spain could dominate. As a result, smaller, less naturally favored states had moments as major powers: Sweden for much of the seventeenth century, Holland in the second half of it.

Spain had the advantage of privileged access to the silver mines of Mexico and Peru. But the importance of the silver sent back to Spain was not so much in its total value as in its predictability. While these shipments remained regular, until the second or third decade of the seventeenth century, they gave Spanish kings much better credit ratings than other rulers of the time. The total contribution silver imports made to the cost of sustaining Spanish power was small compared with the yield from taxation in the realm of Castile. Moreover, in contrast to most of the rest of Europe, where rivalry for power among monarchs, church, nobles, and city authorities caused frequent breakdowns and occasional wars, Castile was exceptionally united in loyalty to its monarchs. The close collaboration of crown and aristocracy began in war against Muslim Granada, from 1480 to 1492, solidified in the early 1520s, when crown and aristocracy combined to suppress rebellion in some cities, and lasted until the 1640s, when the aristocratic spirit of service to the crown collapsed—and tax revenues collapsed along with it. While religious conflicts divided other parts of Western Europe, Spain became increasingly united in religion. Almost all minority religious communities—Jews, Muslims, the few Protestants—were subjected to forcible conversion, or persecuted out of existence. Finally, Spain's opportunity resulted in part from a factor ever present in monarchical state systems: dynastic accident. Throughout the period, the ruler of Spain also ruled southern Italy and Sicily. From 1519 to 1556, Castile's king happened also to be ruler of the Holy Roman Empire. From

Potosí in Bolivia—the world's most productive silver mine in the late sixteenth and seventeenth centuries. The "Silver Mountain" really does have an abrupt, conical outline, but all early modern representations exaggerate that shape and emphasize its dominance over the puny dwellings and almost ant-like workers.

1504 until 1648, Spanish monarchs were nominally rulers of the Netherlands—though substantial parts of those countries were permanently in revolt from the 1570s. Between 1580 and 1640, kings of Spain were also undisputed kings of Portugal and of its vast overseas possessions in Africa, Asia, and Brazil.

There was a moment in the 1580s and 1590s when Spain seemed able to bid for the role of arbiter of Europe, or even—in the minds of some Spaniards, who fantasized about conquering Cambodia, China, and Japan—of the world (see Map 19.2). In 1588, Spain sent the first of a series of invasion fleets, the Spanish Armadas, against England, and although all of them were turned back or wrecked by bad weather, they demonstrated England's vulnerability to invasion. In the early 1590s, the uniform success of Spanish armies in mainland Europe made the conquest of France and the suppression of Netherlandish rebels seem likely. And all this happened while the frontiers of the Spanish monarchy continued to advance in the Americas and Asia.

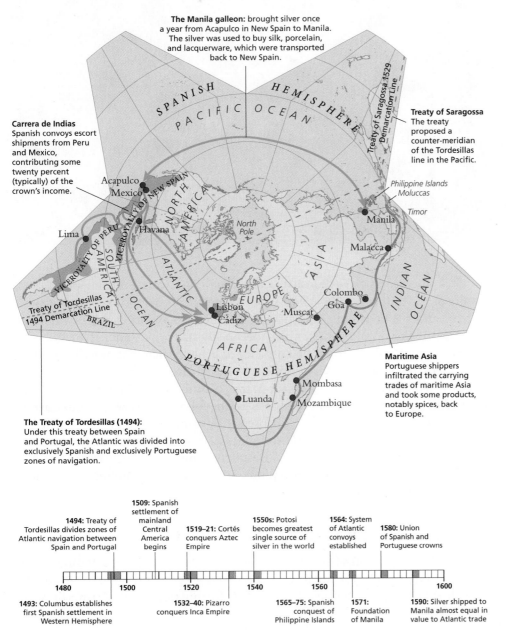

The **Manila galleon:** brought silver once a year from Acapulco in New Spain to Manila. The silver was used to buy silk, porcelain, and lacquerware, which were transported back to New Spain.

Carrera de Indias
Spanish convoys escort shipments from Peru and Mexico, contributing some twenty percent (typically) of the crown's income.

Treaty of Saragossa
The treaty proposed a counter-meridian of the Tordesillas line in the Pacific.

Maritime Asia
Portuguese shippers infiltrated the carrying trades of maritime Asia and took some products, notably spices, back to Europe.

The Treaty of Tordesillas (1494):
Under this treaty between Spain and Portugal, the Atlantic was divided into exclusively Spanish and exclusively Portuguese zones of navigation.

MAP 19.2

The Spanish Monarchy in 1600

- Dominions of the king of Spain
- Carrera de Indias
- Portuguese trade with maritime Asia

1494: Treaty of Tordesillas divides zones of Atlantic navigation between Spain and Portugal

1509: Spanish settlement of mainland Central America begins

1519–21: Cortés conquers Aztec Empire

1550s: Potosi becomes greatest single source of silver in the world

1564: System of Atlantic convoys established

1580: Union of Spanish and Portuguese crowns

1480 **1500** **1520** **1540** **1560** **1600**

1493: Columbus establishes first Spanish settlement in Western Hemisphere

1532–40: Pizarro conquers Inca Empire

1565–75: Spanish conquest of Philippine Islands

1571: Foundation of Manila

1590: Silver shipped to Manila almost equal in value to Atlantic trade

The Surrender at Breda. Diego Velázquez (1599–1660), the greatest painter of the Spanish Baroque, leaves us in no doubt who won the struggle in 1624–1625 for the fortress city of Breda in the Netherlands. The Spaniards' lances are proudly erect. Those of the defeated Dutch are in disarray. The pain of war, however, is shared. No one is triumphant. The symmetry of the canvas gives almost equal space to both sides. The Spanish commander, Ambrosio Spinola, shown on the left foreground, seems to be consoling a colleague rather than humbling a defeated enemy.

Still, the success proved unsustainable. The 1590s were a turning point, as the loyalty of Philip II's (r. 1556–1598) subordinate kingdoms showed signs of strain, state revenues ebbed, and a catastrophic decline of population, which would last for most of the seventeenth century, began. By the time Philip II died, he had already decided to leave to his heir a policy of peace. When that peace broke down in a general renewal of conflicts in Western Europe in the 1620s, the strain proved unbearable. Spanish naval supremacy in the Atlantic wavered in the late 1620s and faltered in northern Europe in the 1630s. In the following decade, Spanish armies' long unbroken record of victory collapsed with major defeats by the French.

Meanwhile, serious rebellions broke out in Naples and Catalonia, and Portugal recovered its independence in 1640. Despite an impressive recovery in the eighteenth century from this critical low point, Spain never again attempted to outclass all Europe's other powers.

WESTERN POLITICAL THOUGHT

Along with the growth of the power of the state, the way people thought about politics changed. They came to take the sovereignty of the state for granted. A French political philosopher, Jean Bodin, formulated the doctrine of sovereignty in 1576. Sovereignty defined the state, which had the sole right to make laws and distribute justice to its subjects. Sovereignty could not be shared. There was no portion of it for the church, or any sectional interest, or any outside power.

More radically, in 1513, the Florentine historian and office seeker, Niccolò Machiavelli, challenged traditional thinking about the purpose of the state. Political theorists of antiquity and the Middle Ages recommended various kinds of state, but they all agreed that the state must have a moral purpose: to increase virtue or happiness or both. Even the Legalist school in ancient China (see Chapter 6) advocated oppression in the wider interest of the oppressed. When Machiavelli wrote *The Prince*, his rules for rulers, the book shocked readers not just because the author recommended lying, cheating, ruthlessness, and injustice, but because he did so with no apparent concession to morality.

Machiavelli cut all references to God out of his descriptions of politics and made only mocking references to religion. The only basis for decision making was the ruler's own interest, and his only responsibility was to retain his power. He should keep faith only when it suits him. He should pretend virtue. He should also pretend to be religious. Machiavelli's other books are strongly republican in sentiment, and he may have intended *The Prince* to be ironical. Irony, however, can be the hardest form of rhetoric to detect. Later thinking borrowed two influences from *The Prince*: first, the doctrine of **realpolitik**, which says that the state is not subject to moral laws and serves only itself; second, the claim that the end justifies the means and that any excesses are permissible to ensure the survival of the state, or public safety, or national security, as some later formulations put it. Meanwhile, among moralists, *Machiavel* became a term of abuse, and the devil became known as "old Nick."

In the absence of any overriding authority or mechanism for sharing sovereignty, the European state system needed international laws. When Thomas Aquinas (see Chapter 12) summarized the previous state of thinking in the Western world in the thirteenth century, he distinguished the laws of individual states from what he called the **law of nations**, which all states must obey and which governs the relationships between them. Yet he never said what this law was or where or how it could be codified. Many jurists assumed it was just natural law or the basic, universal principles of justice—but this is also hard to identify in complex cases. The Spanish Jesuit theologian Francisco Suárez (1548–1617) solved the problem in a radical way. The law of nations "differs in an absolute sense," he said, "from natural law" and "is simply a kind of positive human law." It says whatever people agree it should say.

This made it possible to construct an international order along lines first proposed earlier in the sixteenth century by one of Suárez's predecessors at the University of Salamanca in Spain, the Dominican Francisco de Vitoria, who advocated laws "created by the authority of the whole world"—not just pacts or agreements between states. In 1625, the Dutch jurist Hugo Grotius worked out the system that prevailed until the late twentieth century. Natural law obliged states to respect each other's sovereignty. The commercial and maritime laws that they formally ratified or traditionally embraced, and the treaties they made between themselves regulated relations among them with the strength of contracts, enforceable by war. This system did not need the support of any particular ideology or religion to back it. It could embrace the world beyond Christendom. It would remain valid, Grotius said, even if God did not exist.

> *"When Machiavelli wrote The Prince, his rules for rulers, the book shocked readers not just because the author recommended lying, cheating, ruthlessness, and injustice, but because he did so with no apparent concession to morality."*

WESTERN SOCIETY

Modern societies are divided into horizontally stacked classes that are defined according to their income or wealth—upper class, middle class, working class. But in the sixteenth and seventeenth centuries, classes intersected with other structures, in which most people were more likely to situate themselves: vertical structures—interest groups, professions, trades, the entourages and clients of powerful noblemen and officials, social orders, such as the nobility or the peasantry, religious sects, clans—whose members' sense of mutual belonging depended on the differences they felt between themselves and outsiders rather than on shared values, wealth, priorities, or education (see Figure 19.1). The elite estates or social groups, the nobility and clergy, were not classes in any sense that a modern market researcher or opinion pollster would recognize. They were communities of privilege uniting people of hugely different degrees of wealth whose tax privileges and legal advantages marked them out from the rest of society. A prince-bishop ruling a semi-independent state like Cologne in Germany or Liège in Belgium belonged to the same clerical estate as a penniless priest who wandered from parish to parish saying mass for a fee. Nobility embraced a duke with an income exceeding a king's and a rural nobleman whose only possession was a lance for hire.

Cities formed communities of a similar kind, jealous of their jurisdiction, walled against the world, and fortified in their civic identities by the enjoyment of economic "liberties"—such as the right to hold markets or fairs, or levy tolls on travelers or merchandise. In most countries, Jews formed similar communities, also distinguished by economic and legal privileges as well as disabilities. So did the Protestant minorities in France and Poland. The kinsmen and retinues of noble families had some of the same characteristics, often embracing poor and remote relations as well as retainers at every level of wealth and rank, tenants, servants, and other dependants, who gathered for festivals or accounting days and sometimes lived together in considerable numbers under a single vast roof, eating their meals in common. On a smaller scale, the "families," as they were usually called, or extended households of urban artisans, with generations of apprentices sharing their roofs, had the same characteristics.

A vast, slow process of erosion changed this way of organizing society. In most of Europe, the family was redefined as an ever-smaller knot of close kin. Between the sixteenth and eighteenth centuries, in aristocratic households, family dining rooms came to provide a privileged retreat from the communal life of the great hall of the medieval castle. This was true even for kings. Court portraits of Philip IV (r. 1621–1665) of Spain and Charles I (r. 1625–1649) of England reveal a world of nuclear families, in which the royal children and parents cluster together. In Protestantism, the family grew in importance because so many other structures of life—religious brotherhoods, guilds, and monasteries—were abolished. The glittering courts of monarchs sucked provincial aristocracies away from their estates and hereditary followings, breaking the bonds of vertical structures. "Take but degree away," as a character says in a play of William Shake-

FIGURE 19.1 ORGANIZATION OF WESTERN SOCIETY IN THE SIXTEENTH AND SEVENTEENTH CENTURIES COMPARED TO MODERN SOCIETIES

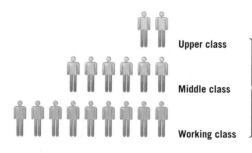

(a) Modern societies

Upper class

Middle class

Working class

Classes of people differentiated by income, wealth, shared values, or education

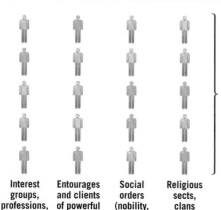

(b) Societies in sixteenth and seventeenth centuries

Widely varying groups whose sense of mutual belonging depends on differences between themselves and outsiders

Interest groups, professions, trades

Entourages and clients of powerful noblemen and officials

Social orders (nobility, peasantry, etc.)

Religious sects, clans

speare's, written around 1602, "untune that string and hark! What discord follows!" Everywhere that string was retuned to the clink of moneybags, as monarchs put titles up for sale. "Ducats make dukes," quipped an early seventeenth-century Spanish satirist. Women's status was transformed. In Padua in northern Italy in the 1550s, the anatomist Gabriele Falloppio sliced open women's cadavers and found that they worked in unsuspected ways. Women were not just nature's bungled attempts to make males, as earlier medical theory claimed. In the late Middle Ages, there had been isolated and discouraging examples of women in power as regents or sovereign queens. Now women rulers appeared in unprecedented numbers in Europe. Some—like the flighty Mary, Queen of Scots (r. 1512–1567), or Catherine de' Medici (1519–1589), Regent of France—reenacted in their lives cautionary tales of the biblical Eve: submitting to lovers or favorites, manipulating men. To the Scots Protestant preacher John Knox (ca. 1513–1572)—expressing a common opinion strongly—women in power were a "monstrous" aberration. But most women rulers earned praise for what Elizabeth I of England (r. 1558–1603) called her "heart and stomach of a king." In other words, men praised them for ruling like men even though they were women.

In ordinary homes, struggles between different forms of Christianity gave new importance to women's traditional domain—as the guardians of household routine. Mothers were the hearthside evangelists who transmitted simple religious faith and devotional practice from one generation to the next. Their choices ensured, in some places, the survival of Catholicism, in others the rapid progress of Protestantism. Women who married according to the clergies' new rules (see Chapter 18) could be better protected against male predators and more secure in keeping their property when their husbands died. In late seventeenth-century Massachusetts, the Puritan preacher Cotton Mather believed women were morally superior beings, because of their constant fear of death in childbirth.

There could, however, be no corresponding increase in what feminists today call women's "options." New economic opportunities on a sufficient scale were unavailable until industrialization that began in the late eighteenth century. Widowhood remained the best option for women who wanted freedom and influence. The most remarkable feature of this situation, which might have tempted wives to murder, is that so many husbands survived it. In most of sixteenth- and seventeenth-century Europe, husbands committed more detected domestic murders than wives. And women, despite their improved status, were still often victims: beaten by husbands, scolded by confessors, repressed by social rules, and cheated by the courts. "Long Meg of Westminster"—hero of an English story of 1582—proves her superiority over men in a series of fair fights, but "never let it be said," she announced when she married, "that Long Meg shall be her husband's master."

Conflicts along class lines were rare. The so-called Wars of Religion between Catholics and Protestants in sixteenth-century France resembled old-fashioned civil wars, in which aristocrats recruited private armies from their retainers, relatives, and tenants to battle each other. Other sixteenth-century rebellions were of the same character, or else were the protests of threatened minorities, such as Catholics in England, or descendants of Moors in Spain. Or else they were assertions of provincial identity, like those Aragonese who rioted against Spanish royal power in defense of their provincial liberties in 1590, or Netherlanders who rose up

Married Charity. As an allegory of the love of God, "which is called Charity," according to the inscription, Hans Holbein painted his wife, Elsbeth, with their children, Philip and Catarina, during a rare moment at home in the Swiss city of Basle in 1529, after a trip to England, where commissions from the king and the court bought the painter a spell of prosperity. But he spent most of his life grubbing for commissions far afield, and Elsbeth was left to bring up the family on her own for years at a time. She eventually sold this painting to make ends meet.

Chronology: Early Modern Europe: Politics, Ideas, and Society

Sixteenth through eighteenth centuries	Nuclear family grows in importance
1513	Machiavelli writes *The Prince*
1519	Charles V becomes Holy Roman Emperor
Mid- to late sixteenth century	French Wars of Religion
1576	Jean Bodin formulates doctrine of sovereignty
1588	Defeat of the Spanish Armada
1618–1648	Thirty Years' War
1640s	Strain of empire precipitates decline of Spanish power
r. 1682—1725	Peter the Great attempts Westernization of Russia

in 1568 against the foreign methods and officials of an absentee monarch, Philip II of Spain. The English Civil Wars of 1640–1653 used to be held up as a classic case of class revolution—the birth pangs of bourgeois society, struggling to emerge bloody from the womb of feudalism. But the war seems better understood as a mixture of a traditional aristocratic rebellion, a provincial revolt against intrusive central government, a struggle of "ins" and "outs," and a genuine war of religion.

Patterns of social change were not uniform across Europe. From the fifteenth century, an economic divide opened in Central Europe. The fault line ran roughly along the Elbe and upper Danube rivers. In the west, peasants could take advantage of intense demand for labor and a relative glut of exploitable land. Forms of land tenure grew more diverse. Traditional limitations on peasants' freedom to move and acquire property weakened. Similar conditions prevailed selectively in Eastern Europe. In parts of Brandenburg in Germany, for instance, the countryside had so few people in the fifteenth century that noble landlords took to the plow themselves. Generally, however, as Eastern Europe gradually took over the Mediterranean Basin's former role as grain supplier to the continent, landlords increasingly restricted peasants' freedom to sell their labor.

This was a remarkable reversal of the course of history as conventionally understood. In the Middle Ages, such restrictions on peasants had not been a characteristic institution of the regions where it now began to take root. Indeed, at modest social levels, colonization beyond the Elbe had been the work of peasant escapees from a society of restricted opportunities and lordly oppression in the west. Now even the free towns, in what are now Poland, eastern Germany, the Czech Republic, Slovakia, and Hungary, lost their rights of jurisdiction on a massive scale to aristocrats and rulers. In Poland, Hungary, and Bohemia, the nobility reclaimed or enforced their right to elect the king. A world of aristocratic dominance was emerging.

Traditional notions about nobility became entrenched. According to István Werbočky, Hungary's key theorist on this issue in the early sixteenth century, only the nobles were the nation. Their privileges were rights of conquest, inherited from presumed Hunnic and Scythian ancestors. Other classes descended from natural slaves or criminals. Werbočky did acknowledge that new men could join the aristocracy "by the exercise of martial discipline and other virtues and gifts of mind or body." But to him these were means to strengthen a hereditary caste—not, as most Westerners maintained, methods to open up a social group to outsiders.

Despite these growing differences between east and west, Peter the Great of Russia (r. 1682–1725) tugged and wrenched the frontier of Europe eastward by striving to make Russia more like Western Europe. It was an information revolution—a transfer of technology as well as fashion and taste from west to east. Peter's reforms redesigned his empire. He moved the capital from Moscow to the new city of St. Petersburg that he built on the Baltic, redrafted the Russian alphabet, and remodeled the aristocracy's facial hair. A popular print showed a demon barber executing Peter's command that the Russian nobility shave off their beards to make them look like "modern" European aristocrats. Preachers called Peter the sculptor and architect of Russia, remolding the country, carving the palace furni-

Making Connections | FACTORS CONTRIBUTING TO EUROPEAN STATE-BUILDING

HISTORICAL DEVELOPMENTS	INFLUENTIAL CONTRIBUTING FACTORS	SOCIAL AND POLITICAL CONSEQUENCES
Renaissance: development of Western political thought	Sovereignty becomes dominant way to identify the state Retaining power becomes dominant political motivation Need for international cooperation leads to commercial, maritime laws	Machiavelli's *The Prince* becomes handbook for gaining and maintaining power Law of nations becomes important factor in states honoring each other's sovereignty The "ends justify the means" to ensure states' survival
Spanish dominance 1500–1600	Access to silver mines of Mexico, Peru Relatively unified monarchy; aristocracy ennobled by service; religious hierarchy Developed superior military and naval forces Dynastic connections	First wealthy colonial superpower controls Portugal, much of Africa, Asia, Central and South America; challenges England, France; controls much of Italy, Netherlands, Germany Economic, military decline in seventeenth century leaves opening for other European states
Social transformation of Europe	Smaller family units become primary social unit Intermarriage between aristocratic, royal families Expansion of the role of women as moral exemplars	Religious conflicts supercede class conflict Increasing economic freedom, opportunity for urban dwellers Traditional notions of nobility become entrenched Western "progress" becomes a model for Peter the Great of Russia and others

ture with his own hands. He allowed women out of the home where traditional Russian practice had tried to confine them. He made two great journeys through Europe in semidisguise to learn Western ways. His role models were foreign: Dutch, German, Swedish. He aimed to be for his country both Romulus and Numa—the founder, that is, of ancient Rome and the king who supposedly crafted its laws. He appeared in engravings in Roman tradition, baton-wielding on a rearing horse, with the title "Imperator" engraved in Roman letters. He seriously considered making Dutch the official language of his court. He became an honorary Danish admiral and a member of the French Academy of Sciences. But rebels regarded him as Antichrist or, at best, the, satanic imposter of a true czar. Western admirers saw him as Russia's modernizer, but the report of a visit to St. Petersburg illustrates the uneasy, short-term impact of his reforms. High society there, said the report, was just like those of Paris or London, except that Russian ladies still put cosmetic blacking on their teeth. Henceforth, Russia was permanently part, by wars or alliances, of European politics. Peter the Great's daughter, Elizabeth (r. 1741–1762) was the last ruler of her dynasty, the Romanovs, in the male line. Thereafter, all the czars were products of the European dynastic marriage market.

Peter's policy, and, in particular, his decision to relocate the capital of Russia on the Baltic, should be considered in a further context: the northward shift of

Demon barber: Czar Peter the Great (r. 1682–1725) enforces conformity to the religion of the state in Russia. The Old Believers, religious dissidents who split from the Russian Orthodox Church in the 1660s, believed that beards were part of the image of God, and that therefore it was a sacrilege to shave. Peter saw beards as signs of Russia's backwardness and of resistance to his rule, and he imposed a tax on facial hair.

Europe's center of gravity. The newly rising powers of the seventeenth century—the Netherlands, Sweden, England, France—were all in the north. So were some of the most spectacularly growing cities—Amsterdam, Paris, London. The Mediterranean seemed stagnant by comparison. It was in the north that the great global trading companies and banks arose. There were undeniable advantages to being in business in northern rather than southern Europe in the sixteenth and seventeenth centuries. Inflation flowed from south to north—stimulated by new sources of gold and silver, by new forms and expanded levels of credit, and by the demand an increase of population created. This meant goods were cheaper in the north. Northerners used that price advantage to break into the Mediterranean in the late sixteenth century. Demand for their shipping helped—to bring in grain to meet food shortages and to counter losses to Turkish and North African piracy. From shipping, northerners diversified into slaving and banking, handling—and creaming off—the wealth of the cash-rich empires of Spain and Portugal, diverting the trade of Venice and the eastern Mediterranean.

THE OTTOMANS

Europe's shifting axis of wealth affected the Ottoman Empire, a partly Mediterranean power. Yet this was a state that straddled Europe and Asia and, as we saw in Chapter 16, combined diverse traditions of political thought. The nerve center of the empire was the sultan's palace in Constantinople, the Topkapi Saray. Its layout embodies much of the way the sultans thought about their role and is a guide to how politics worked. The throne room is a pavilion, and many apartments are scattered through the grounds, like the tents of a nomad camp. The imperial stool is big enough for a sultan of the most morbid obesity. This was an empire that sustained memories of its ancient nomadic origins through centuries of settled life.

The harem could accommodate 2,000 women, the stables 4,000 horses. The scale of everything in the Topkapi Palace attests to the size of the empire and the effectiveness of Ottoman authority. The grounds of 7,500,000 square feet enclosed 10 mosques, 14 bathhouses, and 2 hospitals. The kitchens were equipped to serve 5,000 diners daily and 10,000 on holidays.

The Topkapi was a fortress, a sanctuary, and a shrine. The bustle of the outer courts, where the kitchen noise competed with the clatter of the guards, contrasted with the inner silence of the sacred spaces where the sultan was cocooned, close to his vast collection of relics of the Prophet Muhammad. Here, according to a visitor in 1700, "even the horses seem to know where they are."

Inside the sultan's private quarters, with its lavish alleys and secret hideaways, we can sense the hidden methods of government. Here talk was of politics: pillow talk and conversation in the baths, as well as the diplomatic encounters and the sultan's meetings with his ministers. In the absence of rules of succession to the throne, women and eunuchs conspired to manipulate the transfer of power from one sultan to the next. Sultans commonly exercised their privilege to put their brothers to death as security against rebellion, or confined them in the luxurious prison quarters known as the cages. A knock on the door might be a summons to become sultan or the rap of an executioner: Sultan Ibrahim I (EE-brah-heem) (r. 1640–1648) heard both and mistook each for the other. Access to a sultan's mother or favorite concubine was an avenue of politi-

The sultan's birthday party. Members of the imperial family, officials, and dignitaries line up, one by one, in strict order of protocol, to congratulate Ottoman Sultan Selim III (r. 1789–1807) in the Topkapi Palace in Istanbul. Konstantin Kapidagli, the painter, was highly favored at the sultan's court and imitated by painters in the West.
Dagli Orti/Picture Desk, Inc./Kobal Collection

cal influence. For much of the seventeenth century, the effective chief executives of the state were queen mothers who knew little of the world beyond the harem walls, but who learned much from spies and servants, and who can be seen in paintings of court life, listening, from behind elaborate screens, to audiences with ambassadors and political council meetings. "Although Western visitors all went away heady with the exotic scents of palace life, the efficiency of the Ottoman state from the fifteenth to the seventeenth centuries could rival any Western competitors, many of whose traditions it shared." Other empires of nomadic origins failed to keep up with advances in the technology of war, but the Ottomans could float a vast navy, batter the walls of Byzantium with cannons in 1453, or blow away the Safavid cavalry of Persia with gunpowder. The modernization of the army influenced social change. The traditional aristocracy, the mounted "protectors"—cavalrymen who served in war and were maintained by tribute—lost roles and revenues.

The direction and balance of the conquests, which, in the fifteenth and sixteenth centuries, tilted toward Europe, gave the sultans access to huge numbers of Christian subjects, who paid discriminatory taxes and supplied a quota, the **devsirme** (dehv-SHEER-meh), of their male children to serve as Muslims in the elite slave army, the **Janissaries**, or in the sultan's administration. In the seventeenth century (see Chapter 15), the Janissaries became a hereditary corps, probably at the cost of their military efficiency, and conquests on the Christian front ceased.

To Western observers, the sultan seemed a model of despotism. He made and unmade laws, both religious and secular, at will. His subjects had no rights against his anger. And unlike Christian rulers, sultans had no need of a Reformation to curb the power of clergy. Though they had to be wary of the moral vigilance of the Islamic clerical establishment, as caliphs as well as sultans, they controlled the power structure of Sunni Islam themselves. Westerners regarded Ottoman government as disturbingly alien, but in the 1570s, the Ottoman jurist Ebu us-Suud

"Although Western visitors all went away heady with the exotic scents of palace life, the efficiency of the Ottoman state from the fifteenth to the seventeenth centuries could rival any Western competitors, many of whose traditions it shared."

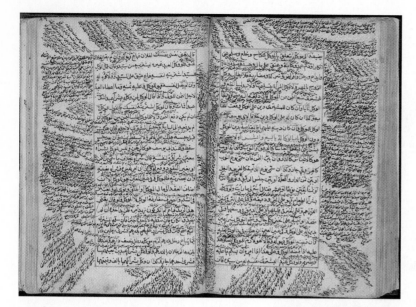

Ottoman law book. Written in Arabic in Istanbul in 1517 by Ibrahim al Halabi, the Islamic legal textbook known as *Multaqa al-Abhur (Confluence of the Currents)* remained an authoritative guide to the laws of the Ottoman Empire for 300 years. It contains rules for almost every human activity: spiritual rites, domestic relations, inheritance, commercial transactions, and crimes. The section shown here refers to buying and selling done by third parties. Various commentators made notes on this copy of the text.

produced a justification of the ruler's power that revealed a thorough command of Roman law and was not unlike Jean Bodin's near-contemporary theory of sovereignty in France. Still, the Ottoman system was unquestionably more autocratic than anything European "absolute" monarchs could manage. Even allowing for the inefficiencies that arise when preindustrial technology transmits commands over vast distances, the dominions of Sultan Murad IV (r. 1623–1640) were more tightly reined to the center than those of his counterparts in most of Europe. His Spanish contemporary, Philip IV, for instance, was generally regarded as the most powerful Christian king of his day. He ruled multiple kingdoms with the aid of an up-to-date bureaucracy, but without an overarching source of authority. In different places, his rule was known by different titles, legitimized by different theories, embodied in different institutions, and constrained by different laws. Not so Murad's.

In most of the Ottoman Empire, for instance, the sultan's representatives were chosen in a remarkably uniform way. It is not true, as Europeans used to say, that these men were all in a formal sense the sultan's slaves. The head of the civil service, the Grand Vizir was indeed a slave, but lesser officials and provincial governors were drawn from every class and every part of the empire. Typically, in the sixteenth century, they trained as pages in the sultan's household before taking provincial commands, where they were maintained by revenues from designated areas. They rose through the administrative ranks of the provinces to which they were assigned.

Military and administrative life was incomparably the best route to wealth in the empire. Provincial governors made more out of their offices than even the richest merchants made from trade. The emphasis was not quite on plunder to the same extent as in Mughal India. Suleiman the Magnificent (r. 1520–1566; see Chapter 16) regulated the fees courts charged to litigants and practiced restraint in taxation and exploitation as part of the ideology of the state. Still, rational exploitation of subjects' wealth was the aim of the rulers of the empire. *Dirlik* (DEER-leek)—the term applied to provincial government—literally meant "wealth."

Increasingly, in the seventeenth century, the need to make the state efficient in war, in the face of the mounting costs of modern weaponry, drove changes in administrative practices. The lower ranks of the provincial administration became a career dead end, as governors came more and more from the army. The result was the rise of enormously powerful provincial governors. When some of them rebelled in 1658, the state barely mustered the resources to beat them.

Despite the central training of the ruling elite, and its close dependency on the sultan, it is easy to overrate the degree of control the empire exercised in the provinces. The system could perhaps best be characterized as centralization tempered by chaos. Rival governors, for instance, sometimes got simultaneous letters of appointment to the same place and were left to fight it out. Banditry usurped authority—fed with manpower by deserters from the army and peasants whom immoderate tax gatherers forced into outlawry. In a typical incident in 1606, Canboladolu Ali Pasha (jahn-boh-LAHD-oh-loo AH-lee PAH-shah), a notorious bandit chief, proposed to police the eastern front on the Persian border with 16,000 men in exchange for lucrative governorships for himself and his kin. The sultan granted his request.

The following year, the army overthrew him, but his success shows at once a weakness of the state and a form of internal diplomacy sultans had to practice. Many states of the time faced problems with bandits, but most tried to deal summarily with them. The Ottomans negotiated with them and tried to manipulate them. This was typical of the Ottoman approach, which was always flexible and adaptable. There was one law, but it could always be modified to take into account local custom. The sultan derived his authority from religious principles, but these could be emphasized in different ways to suit different communities. Uniform rules, in theory, governed taxation, but in practice it was arbitrary and changeable. Historians always tend to date "decline" too early, because they know what follows. To speak of Ottoman decline in the seventeenth century seems premature. It might be fairer to say that the Ottomans ceased to expand. In 1683, an attempt to capture the Habsburg capital Vienna failed, and in subsequent treaties, the Ottomans gave up further ambitions in Europe. If they faltered, it was not so much because of imperfections in their system of government—which, after all, had proved itself in the past—as because of an unexplained stagnancy in the population of their empire. Its growth did not match that of the populations of Europe, India, China, or Japan. And in the eighteenth century, Ottoman population growth slowed, relatively speaking, even more.

MUGHAL INDIA AND SAFAVID PERSIA

Like the empire of the Ottomans, that of the Mughals in India thrived on the economic success of the people they ruled. Or perhaps it would be fairer to say that the Mughals and their subjects enriched each other. The Mughals' fantastic demand for revenues stimulated economic inventiveness and forced peasants to produce for urban markets. Spectacular spending on war, buildings, and luxuries recycled wealth and stimulated an economy that high taxation might otherwise have stifled.

The Mughals' understanding of the nature of sovereignty was rooted in their conviction that they descended from Timur and ultimately from Genghis Khan (see Chapters 13 and 15). The names they gave their children and their dynasty reflect their Mongol and Islamic heritage. They ran their empire as a conquest—which, of course, it was, but it is more usual for conquerors to come to identify with the realms they rule. As we have seen (see Chapters 16 and 17), outside the relatively small, centrally administered core of the empire, Mughal methods of control relied on dividing tribute among a network of their relations, followers, clients, and allies. Like the Mongols and the Ottomans, they never established clear rules of succession to the throne. Every reign saw dynastic rebellions and wars of succession. Rivalries and alliances shifted unstably. The Mughals had always to balance the conflicting claims of rival aristocracies—the descendants of Timur, the Afghans and Persians who helped establish the dynasty in the 1520s, and the native Indian warrior chiefs on whom they relied increasingly to keep their empire together and extend it. A painting for the Emperor Akbar (r. 1556–1605) captures a familiar scene. A chain gang of captured rebels—some of them clad as beasts, others stripped naked— appears at his palace, shaking their chains defiantly, while their captors exult.

Captive rebels arrive at the palace of the Mughal Emperor Akbar (r. 1556–1605) in 1573, wearing animal skins to symbolize the unnatural perversity and bestiality of the act of rebellion. The emperor is offstage to the right, because it would diminish his dignity to depict him in the company of rebels. The painting is one of a series Akbar commissioned to commemorate the great events of his reign.

The Emperor Aurangzeb (r. 1658–1707) found the formula to keep the system going for a time: constant war to keep the aristocracies occupied, and continual conquests to multiply their rewards. A new generation of leaders arose, "born in the camp," as one of his ministers observed. New nobles, recruited from the frontier regions of the Deccan in south India as Aurangzeb's conquests grew, were promoted above old ones, getting the choicest shares of tribute. Newcomers composed nearly half the upper ranks of the aristocracy by the end of the reign. Restlessness and rebellion in the heartlands and older conquests were among the results as ambitious or disaffected nobles clashed with each other and fought with the imperial administration. Rural disruption and loss of revenues followed. In part, the Mughal Empire was a victim of its success. It expanded too fast to sustain the system of keeping nobles dependent by assigning them revenues. Still, when he died in 1707, Aurangzeb left a treasury stuffed with reserves greater than Akbar's.

Squeezed between the Ottomans and the Mughals, the Safavids of Persia (1501–1773) ran, in some respects, a similar state to both of them, with universalist rhetoric, a nominally all-powerful ruler, and flexible relationships between the ruler and subordinate sources of authority. Like the Ottomans, the Safavids benefited from the growth in trade across Eurasia: especially, in the Safavid case, in the silk trade of the lands they ruled. Like the Ottomans, they drew on ancient traditions of kingship, as well as Muslim political thought, to legitimize their rule. The first ruler of the dynasty commissioned a lavishly illustrated history of the ancient Persian kings. Their rules of succession were, like the chaotic systems that prevailed among the Ottomans and Mughals, divisive and bloodily enforced. Shah Abbas I (ah-BAS), the Great (r. 1588–1629) imprisoned his sons and exterminated his remoter relations. Isfahan, his capital, resembled a great Indian or Ottoman city, full of unmistakable evidence of power, wealth, confidence, and energy. Its central plaza was seven times the size of St. Mark's Place in Venice. The goalposts installed there for games of polo were of marble. At one end, the great mosque was offset at an angle to guarantee a good view of the domes and minarets, displayed behind a gate 90 feet high. There were 273 public baths and 1,802 inns for commercial caravans.

Nevertheless, Safavid rule never relied on the kind of uniform bureaucracy the Ottomans used. Practices resembling those of the Mughals kept them in power. Except in some frontier regions, where they relied on accommodations with local rulers, the Safavids deployed a hereditary class of warrior horsemen of Turkic origin, known as the Qizilbash (KIH-zihl-bahsh), to enforce taxation and repress rebellion. As time went on, however, the Qizilbash tended to put down roots in the regions they ruled and frequently became rebels themselves. To tie elite loyalties firmly into the center, the Safavids used marriage, distributing the womenfolk of the ruling house around the provinces. Where possible, rulers exterminated

Isfahan, a vital center of trade, provides unmistakable evidence of the power, wealth, and dynamism of Safavid Persia. In this illustration, from the 1725 edition of *Voyages to Moscow, Persia, and the East Indies* by the Dutch traveler Cornelis de Brun (1652–1726), a camel caravan approaches the city.

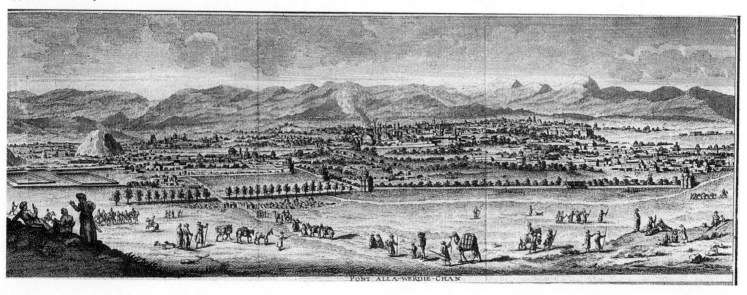

PONT ALLA-WERDIE-CHAN

troublesome Qizilbash clans or replaced them with their own personal representatives. But the dynasty rarely had the power to put these devices into practice.

The Safavids, however, practiced politics that were unique in two respects. First, they were fiercely Shiite. They contemplated neither the religious pluralism of the Mughals nor the toleration of the Ottomans. They wanted to rule an exclusively Shiite Muslim people. Shiism was the basis of their claim to legitimacy. Religious minorities were forced to convert or were persecuted toward extinction. Second, the Safavids had no nostalgia for a mythic steppelander past. On the contrary, they claimed to be enemies of the nomads, and as we saw in Chapter 17, defeated the Uzbek steppelanders (see Map 19.3).

The Safavids' religious policies are hard to understand, since—at the start of the period—most of the people they ruled were not Shiites. A desire to have a distinctive ideology, in opposition to that of the Ottomans, seems to have impelled them. Or perhaps, like Akbar in India, they wanted a religion of their own. Like so many dynasties—like Islam itself—the Safavid line started with warrior holy men, who turned tribesmen from deserts and mountains into formidable armies. The first Safavid shah, Ismail I (ihs-mah-EEL) (r. 1501–1524), was a visionary who conversed with a vision of Muhammad's nephew Ali (see Chapter 8) and who appears, from his powerful, egocentric poetry, to have considered himself to be an incarnation of God. To a Venetian traveler, it seemed that throughout Iran "the

MAP 19.3

The Safavid Empire, 1501–1736

- Safavid Empire, 1722
- territory under Ottoman rule, 1722
- Mughal Empire, 1722
- easternmost limit of area contested by Ottomans to 1736
- ➤ Uzbek invasion, 1587

Uzbeks steppe people

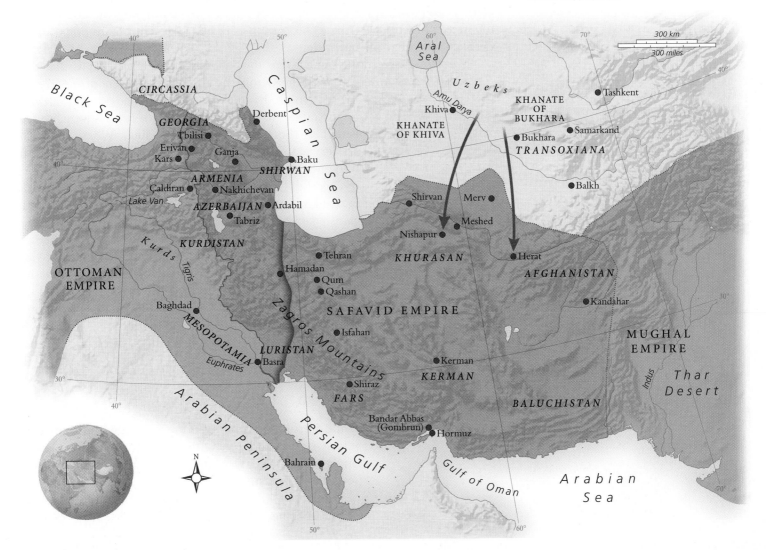

Flagellants. Iranians shout religious slogans and beat themselves with iron chains in Tehran during the Shiite religious festival of Ashura in March 2004. Ashura marks the day when Imam al Hussein, the "leader of the martyrs" and grandson of the prophet Muhammad, was killed in Karbala in 680 C.E. in what is today Iraq.

name of God is forgotten and only that of Ismail remembered." Ismail imposed Shiism by force. But force is never enough to change emotional allegiances. In subsequent reigns, dazzling, frightening ceremonials impressed Shiism on the people's minds. In 1641, a visiting Western observer described a typical ritual, designed to commemorate the death of one of the great martyrs of Shiism: a terrifying mock conflict, a melee of horses, camels—some painted black to appear more fearsome—and "naked persons who struggled and screamed as if in despair, gashed with wounds, which they beat to make them spurt blood." An accompanying parade featured mourning women, and children, dressed in hides that were pierced with arrows and smeared with blood. Throughout such ceremonies, messages of hatred were directed against the supposed heirs of the martyr's murderers—the Safavids' Sunni Ottoman neighbors.

Paradoxically, perhaps, Safavid rulers never seemed very pious—tending to exempt themselves from Islamic rules about drink and sex—until one of the last shahs of the dynasty, Husain (r. 1694–1722), who engraved Islamic law in stone, smashed the 6,000 wine bottles in the imperial cellars, forbade song, dance, coffee, games, and prostitution, and banished even respectable women from appearing in the streets. In retrospect, these commands seem like a desperate attempt to capture the allegiance of an alienated clergy.

It is remarkable not so much that the Safavids ultimately failed as that they succeeded for so long. Whereas the Ottomans and Mughals were able to renew their strength by making new conquests, the Safavids' opportunities to match that means of success were limited. Ismail I thought himself invincible. When Ottoman artillery stopped his cavalry at the Battle of Chaldiran in Iraq in 1514, he flew black banners inscribed with the word *revenge*. But he never achieved it and withdrew into a world of drinking and womanizing. The Safavids did make some gains against the Turks later in the sixteenth century, and Safavid armies won impressive successes well into the seventeenth century. They raided Ottoman Baghdad twice. Scores of thousands of Georgian, Armenian, and Circassian prisoners were drafted into the slave corps that served the shahs as administrators. Portuguese intruders were turned out of the Persian Gulf. But the strength of the Ottomans to the west and of the Mughals to the east left the Safavids nowhere to expand.

CHINA

While Europe became ever more divided among competing states, and the Ottoman, Mughal, and Safavid empires consolidated, the unity of China survived potentially devastating threats.

Under the Ming dynasty (1368–1644), sixteenth-century China enriched its subjects. Fernão Mendes Pinto, a

Chronology: Islamic Empires: The Ottomans, Safavid Persia, and Mughal India	
Fifteenth and sixteenth centuries	Ottomans create an elite slave army, the Janissaries
1501–1722	Safavid dynasty in Persia
r. 1501–1524	First Safavid ruler, Shah Ismail I, imposes Shiism by force
1520s	Afghans and Persians help establish Mughal power in India
1570s	Ottoman jurist Ebu us-Suud justifies the Sultan's power
1658	Rebellion of provincial governors against Ottoman authority
1683	Ottomans fail to capture Vienna and cease conquests on the Christian front
r. 1658–1707	Emperor Aurangzeb engages in almost constant warfare in India
r. 1694–1722	Last Safavid ruler, Husain, imposes strict Islamic law
ca. Eighteenth century	Mughal power begins irreversible decline
1857	End of Mughal Empire

A CLOSER LOOK

A Safavid Battle Tunic

Throughout the Muslim world from the fifteenth century onward, soldiers wore talismanic shirts, designed to protect them in battle and ensure victory over enemies. This Safavid battle tunic, most likely from the late sixteenth century, was worn next to the warrior's skin and is embroidered with verses from the Quran.

"Help is from God and speedy victory. So give the good news to the believers." (61:13)

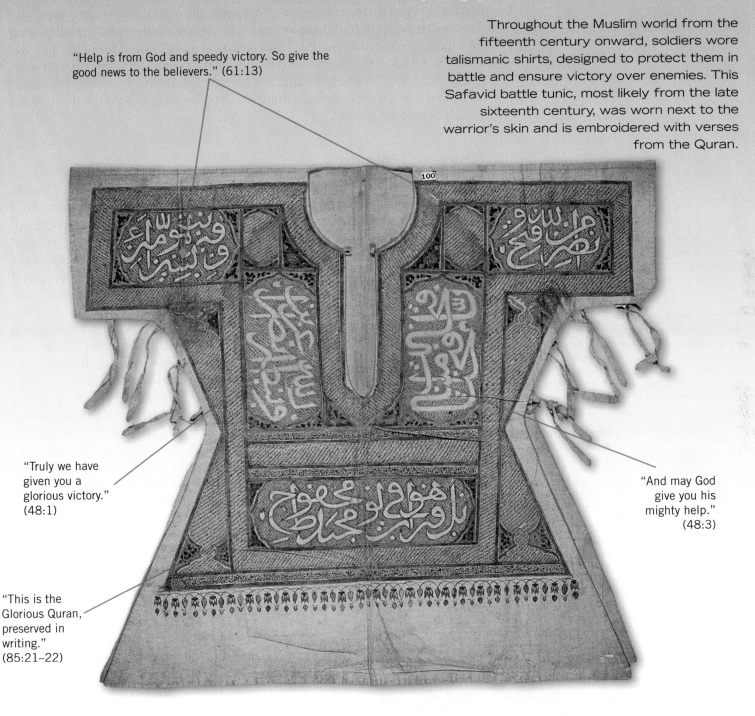

"Truly we have given you a glorious victory." (48:1)

"And may God give you his mighty help." (48:3)

"This is the Glorious Quran, preserved in writing." (85:21–22)

Why was there a close connection between Islam and war in Safavid Persia?

Portuguese window shopper in Beijing, walked around markets "as if in a daze" at the "silk, lace, canvas, clothes of cotton and linen, furs of marten, musk ox, and ermine, delicate porcelain, gold- and silver plate, seed pearls and pearls, gold dust and gold bullion." And as for the base metals, gems, ivory, spices, condiments and foods—"well, all these things were to be had in such abundance that I feel there are not enough words in the dictionary to name them all." The wealth gap between China and most of the rest of the world probably went on increasing over the next two centuries, as demand soared for newly popular goods in which China dominated world markets: porcelain, fine lacquerware, tea, ginseng, and rhubarb. By the mid-seventeenth century—before prolonged civil wars limited its growth—China probably contained about a third of the population of the world.

Chinese Politics

The emperors' authority, unlimited in theory, was restricted in practice by the power of the 20,000 or so scholar **mandarins** who ran the administration. They qualified for their jobs by passing competitive examinations in knowledge of classical Confucian texts. In consequence, most of them never questioned Confucian ideas. They wanted emperors to stick to the performance of sacred rites and the administration of justice. The empire, they felt, was best left in a state of peaceful balance, without undertaking the risks of aggression against its neighbors. Traditionally, emperors had escaped the control of bureaucrats by appealing to other factions, such as the Buddhist clergy, the court eunuchs, and the army. In the sixteenth century, however, the supremacy of the mandarins appeared unshakable. The emperor was not allowed to leave the capital—ostensibly, to prevent the delegation of power into profane hands while he was away. For example, the Zhengde (jehng-duh) emperor (r. 1505–1521) moved out of the palace and surrounded himself with eunuchs and monks. In a series of incidents beginning in 1517, he insisted on going on campaign on the Mongol frontier, in defiance of the mandarins, to escape the suffocating presence of his ministers. But he was obliged to abandon the expeditions when the scholars, in effect, went on strike, crippling the administration.

The gravest crisis arose in 1587, when the Wanli (wahn-lee) emperor (r. 1572–1620) resolved to defy the mandarins. Evidence of widespread corruption in the civil service had undermined his confidence in the moral order traditional Confucianism recommended. He proposed to assert his power by altering the rules of succession, passing over his eldest son in favor of a son by his favorite concubine. Factions supporting the rivals traded accusations of witchcraft and distributed pamphlets among the people. After 10 years of stalemate, in which government effectively came to a halt, the emperor backed down. Intellectual trends reflected the shift in the location of power. The philosopher Li Zhi (lee jeh) wrote a new version of Chinese history, in which emperors counted for nothing, and the heroes were mandarins. Ming government was never fully effective after this crisis.

Chinese porcelain. Ming dynasty porcelain bowls from China, with their distinctive blue and white glazes, make superb ceiling ornaments. Two hundred sixty of them decorate a room in the Santos Palace in Lisbon, Portugal. The ceiling dates from the 1660s, but some of the bowls are more than a century and a half older.

The Ming Empire seemed unable to cope with ecological disasters—floods and famines—in the 1630s. Peasant rebellions became civil wars as independent army commanders fought each other to control or even capture the throne. Meanwhile, from about 1590, the Ming delegated defense on the Mongol frontier to the northwest to Nurhaci, a chief of a pastoral war band in Manchuria (see Chapter 17). Chinese support enabled him to unite the Manchus. He began to call himself emperor and to represent himself as the spiritual heir of Manchu ancestors who had conquered northern China in the twelfth century. In 1636, Nurhaci's successor, Abahai, decreed a new ideology, which he called "Qing." The name was an allusion to "pure" water, which would quench the "bright" flame of "Ming." After intervening decisively in China's civil wars, the Manchus methodically and bloodily took over the country, proclaiming the Qing (chihng) dynasty. It was a long drawn-out business. The last Ming claimant to the throne was executed in 1662. The last Ming loyalists were not rooted out from their nests on the island of Taiwan until the 1680s. Yet the partisans of the defeated dynasty dictated ideology to the newcomers.

The shock of conquest by the Manchus made Chinese intellectuals rethink the whole basis of political legitimacy. The most startling and innovative result was the development of a doctrine of the sovereignty of the people, similar to that of Western Europe. Huang Zongxi (hwang dzohng-shee) (1610–1695) thought that a state of nature had once existed when "each man looked to himself" until benevolent individuals created the empire. Corruption set in, and "the ruler's self-interest took the place of the common good. . . . The ruler takes the very marrow from people's bones and takes daughters and sons to serve his debauchery." Lü Liuliang (loo lee-o-lee-ahng) (1629–1683) went further: "The common man and the emperor are rooted in the same nature." "It might seem as though social order was projected downwards to the common man," but, from the perspective of heaven, "the principle originates with the people and reaches up to the ruler. . . . Heaven's order and Heaven's justice are not things rulers and ministers can take and make their own."

"Unlike the West with the memory of ancient Greece and Rome, China had no examples of republicanism or democracy to look to in its history or idealize in myth."

Yet, whereas in the West, this sort of thinking helped to justify republics and generate revolutions, nothing comparable happened in China until the early twentieth century, when a great deal of Western influence had done its work. There were plenty of peasant rebellions under the Qing whose rule lasted until 1912, but, as throughout the Chinese past, these revolts aimed to renew the empire and replace the dynasty, not end the imperial system and transfer the **mandate of heaven** from a monarch to the people. Unlike the West with the memory of ancient Greece and Rome, China had no examples of republicanism or democracy to look to in its history or idealize in myth. Still, the work of Huang, Lü, and similar theorists passed into Confucian tradition. It helped to keep radical criticism of the imperial system alive and prepare Chinese minds for the later reception of Western revolutionary ideas.

Chinese Society

China experienced a sometimes violent revolution in the ownership of land. Peasant revolts in the 1640s challenged landowners' privileges. An incident from 1645 shows what was going on. A powerful clan's poor relation called Huang Tong (hwang tohng) roused tenants "for the pleasure of working off their petty grievances"—as a hostile court official put it—into attacking his rich kinsmen. He broke into the county capital and, after looting and bloodletting, tore down the

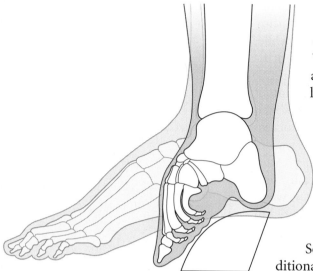

Erotic Deformity. There is a market in body shapes, as in everything else. In Qing China, the feet of women deformed by binding in childhood—typically at about five or six years old—became increasingly popular among families who could afford to remove their womenfolk from the workplace. Erotic literature enhanced the appeal of the practice, which also served patriarchy by making women less mobile and more dependent on men.

walls. Over the next few decades, the government gradually abolished limitations on peasants' freedom to sell their labor. In 1681, peasants could no longer be sold along with the land they farmed but were free to "do as they please." The last restrictions on peasant freedom were swept away in the early eighteenth century. As a result, the landlord life became less attractive. Land was still valued as a source of prestige or security, but agriculture was despised as "the labor of fools," while peasant fierceness made rent collection "a task to be feared." Individuals determined to reacquire ancestral lands no longer sought to restore estates that had been broken up by dividing the property among all the heirs. China became increasingly a land of peasant smallholders. Rural investment took the form of pawnbrokering by urban loan sharks who lent money to peasants to buy seed grain. A history of hatred between city and country began that still endures.

So in China, as in Europe, economic change broke down some of the traditional structures of society. Migrations probably contributed to the effect. The clan, or extended family that persisted from one generation to another, however, was a social structure that could not be destroyed. Ancestor worship made the clan into a religion. The administrative system perpetuated its role because Chinese clans, thousands strong, combined to select the best candidates from among their members to take the exams to enter the civil service and become mandarins. The rich members of the clan would pay for the education of the children of their poorest relations, if there was a chance that some bright young boy (girls could not take the exams) would rise to an office of influence in the state and favor his kin. Men normally married women from outside their own clan, and these wives then came to support the interests of their husbands' clan. There are signs that the restriction and even oppression of women got worse in seventeenth-century China. Female foot binding literally hobbled its victims and restricted their mobility (see Chapter 12). Widow suicide, though it never attained the degree of compulsion that it did in Hindu India, was increasingly encouraged. Widows who stayed alive often prospered in business, but remarried much less often than in Europe, where the remarriage of widows and widowers was a standard way to cope with the effects of high mortality.

Elements in China's seventeenth-century experience combined to strengthen and spread the sense of Chinese identity. This may seem surprising. We might expect the disruptions caused by civil war and the Manchu conquest, the dislocations of mass migrations over vast distances, the spillage of population by immigration overseas to Taiwan and Southeast Asia, or migration to the plains of Mongolia on an unprecedented scale to have weakened allegiance to the state. The vastness of the empire meant that China's new rulers had to exhibit great skill in adapting their legitimacy: as Manchus in Manchuria, as khans in Mongolia, as protectors of the Buddhist establishment in Tibet. Only on their extreme western frontier, where their subjects were Muslims, did the Qing emperors show hostility to the local culture. In the rest of the empire, however, their policy was to favor the adoption of Chinese culture. By the end of the eighteenth century, China's ethnic minorities had largely come to think of themselves as Chinese. Internal migra-

Chronology: Ming and Qing China: Politics and Society

1368–1644	Ming dynasty
1500s	Commercial economy booms
1587	The Wanli emperor precipitates a crisis by challenging the mandarins
1630s	Ecological disasters undermine Ming power
1640s	Peasant revolts challenge landowners' privileges
1644–1912	Qing dynasty
Seventeenth and eighteenth centuries	Mandarins reconciled to Qing power
Early eighteenth century	Last restrictions on peasant freedom eliminated

tions helped. They induced minorities to leave their traditional homelands and encouraged a sense that everyone within the empire was Chinese. Meanwhile, the overseas Chinese found themselves thrust into communities composed of migrants from many parts of China. As a result, they increasingly felt—paradoxically, perhaps—a common sense of belonging to the same community, which they projected home in their letters.

Qing strategy was to reconcile the different Chinese elites, especially the scholar-gentry, from among whom the mandarins were mostly recruited, to Manchu rule with generous rewards and with complete deference to the Confucian point of view that was deeply rooted among the Chinese elites. The Kangxi emperor (r. 1661–1722), who was the second Manchu to rule China, took lessons in the Confucian classics daily before dawn. The Qing avoided the impasse with the mandarins, in which late Ming rule had been mired, for three reasons. First, the scholars clung to the Qing as guarantors against disorder. Second, the dynasty and the bureaucracy had a common enemy in the warlords whose armies survived the civil wars that had brought down the Ming and who ruled vast areas with little input from the central government. The Kangxi emperor overthrew them in 1673. Finally, the Qing had their own power base in the Manchu warrior-elite. A twofold problem arose: how to perpetuate the martial readiness of Manchus, softened by adopting Chinese ways, and how to preserve a balance in the dynasty between Chinese and Manchu identities. Though the Qing emperors spoke and wrote Chinese, they kept up their knowledge of the Manchu language, privileged Manchus who remained loyal to their traditional culture, and founded schools of martial virtue for Manchu sons.

TOKUGAWA JAPAN

Compared with the multiethnic, religiously and socially diverse societies that the Qing, Ottomans, or Mughals ruled, the Japanese already had a remarkably uniform set of notions about themselves. The only ethnic minority in the Japanese islands was the Ainu people of the far north, and most of them lived outside the boundary of the Japanese Empire in 1600. The Japanese treated those Ainu whom they did conquer with deep suspicion and forbade them to mix with Japanese people. In any case there were relatively few Ainu.

Nevertheless, in other respects, the dynamic features of the period affected Japan as sweepingly as any of the other newly or lately interconnected regions in Eurasia that we have been discussing. Historians have always regarded the seventeenth century as a period of deepening Japanese isolationism. And Japanese governments did try increasingly to exclude foreign culture—but only that of "barbarian" Westerners. Chinese and Korean arts and ideas remained welcome, and, indeed, Confucianism revived spectacularly in the Japanese elite's scale of values (see Chapter 18). Imperial expansion went on. Although the government severely controlled merchants and shipping, this was not to prevent trade. On the contrary, Japan's overseas commerce grew throughout the seventeenth and eighteenth centuries, partly through the Dutch and Chinese agents who were allowed restricted trading privileges in Japan, and partly through illegal trade that the Japanese authorities condemned as piracy but never wholly suppressed. In any case, Japan was big and booming enough to generate its own internal commercial revolution. The area under cultivation doubled in 100 years from the mid sixteenth century. Population rose from something like 12 million in about 1550 to 30 million, according to a census of 1721.

Manchu warrior. "The bandits' heads were strung together. . . . Without even combing his horse's mane, he returned to make his report." The poem about this portrait of Zhanyinbao, of the Chinese Imperial Guard, in 1760, praises his prowess in law enforcement, but the artist shows him in hunting dress, armed with the bow that the Qianlong emperor, in the Manchu tradition, favored for the hunt. The realism and animation with which the subject's face is portrayed suggest that one of the Jesuit court artists painted this picture.
The Metropolitan Museum of Art, Purchase, The Dillon Fund Gift, 1986 (1986.206) Photograph © The Metropolitan Museum of Art

Racing to Edo. The harbor of Osaka, in about 1670, where ships laden with the new cotton crop are about to sail for the imperial courtly city of Edo (modern Tokyo). Merchant's warehouses line the way. It was an annual race: whoever got to the capital first would sell at the highest price.

Peasants and merchants were the big gainers from the new prosperity, as peasants switched to surplus production to feed the growing cities, and merchants exploited the expanding markets. Edo (EH-doh), the old name for Tokyo, was one of the biggest cities in the world, with at least 600,000 people in 1700. A service-industry bourgeoisie of merchants, clerks, and craftsmen thrived in booming cities. Peasant prosperity eased the former cycle of famine and rebellion. In an atmosphere of social peace, governments encouraged people to concentrate on getting rich. The writer of novellas, Saikaku, was the spokesman of the age. "Heaven says nothing," announces his most famous book, *The Japanese Family Storehouse* (1688), "and the whole earth grows rich beneath its silent rule." He collected stories about money making and "placed them in a storehouse to serve each family's prosperity." Most of his stories tell of self-enrichment by hard work or intelligence. A street scavenger who picks up sticks becomes a chopstick-manufacturing millionaire. A desperate widow makes a fortune by raffling off her own house. "Now, if ever, trade is an exciting venture. So let none of you risk slipshod methods in earning your livings." The new economic climate had losers, too. Peace was bleak for the traditional warrior class, the samurai, who suffered from effects of the commercial boom: relatively low land values, high interest rates, and stagnation in the amount of rice the peasants had to provide to pay samurai pensions. Many samurai were reduced to the role of ronin—underemployed freelance soldiers, drifting between service to different lords. Lords (called **daimyo**) rarely paid samurai proper salaries. Exploitative pay was sometimes masked as "emergency reductions," sometimes as loans from the samurai that the daimyo never repaid.

Korea experienced similar problems with impoverished members of its noble class, or *yangbans*, as they were called. Traditionally, they discharged responsibilities in war and administration and, in official positions, could obtain land and wealth. But those excluded from office led lives of impoverished idleness, amid prostitutes and low-life hangers-on, satirized in popular literature and art.

Clearly, however, for those who shared it, Japanese prosperity was founded on what Japanese call the Great Peace: the era of internal peace that followed the reunification of Japan early in the seventeenth century under a dynasty of chief ministers, the Tokugawa, who ruled as *shoguns* in Edo, while the emperors remained secluded figureheads, performing sacred rites in a provincial court at

Making Connections | CHINA AND JAPAN: STABILITY AND CHANGE, 1500–1700

STATE AND SOURCES OF STABILITY	CHALLENGES	SOCIAL, CULTURAL, AND POLITICAL ADAPTATIONS
China / Confucianism; scholar mandarins run the state regardless of emperor, dynasty	Ecological disaster—floods and famines in the 1630s Peasant rebellions, civil wars resulting from natural disasters Conquest by Manchus Pressure for land reform, challenges to landowners	Development of the docrine of sovereignty of the people Elimination of right to sell peasants along with land Breakup of large estates Continuation of clan loyalty, ancestor worship amid social, economic change
Japan / ethnic homogeneity; imperial system of rule; stable population and economic prosperity	Christian missionaries convert many people Disenfranchisement of traditional warrior class (samurai) Need to maintain peace between shoguns and provincial rulers (daimyo)	Enforced isolationism from West balanced by continuing trade with Asia New emphasis on Confucian, Buddhist beliefs Encouragement of commercial revolution, urbanism

the old capital in Kyoto. The key to stability was management of relations between the shoguns and the 260 or so daimyo who ruled Japan's provinces. The daimyo had to be drawn from a limited number of noble families, but the shogun appointed and frequently transferred them from one domain to another. Some daimyo, however, effectively managed to secure hereditary succession in their chosen regions. The Shimazu lords of the huge domain of Satsuma in southern Japan, for instance, built up enough regional power to exercise effective autonomy (and, eventually, in the nineteenth century to challenge the shoguns.) Normally, the Tokugawa obliged daimyo to maintain houses—and, in effect, leave hostages—at the shogun's court in Edo and reside there for part of each year. The shoguns also arranged marriages between daimyo families. In these respects, the system resembled the way many European monarchs dealt with their most powerful nobles.

THE NEW WORLD OF THE AMERICAS

Historians' favorite question about European overseas colonization is whether it created frontier societies—removed from models of society in the European homelands by generation gaps and pioneer radicalism—or exact duplications of home: transplanted Old Worlds. The answer of course is that the colonies were both. Molded and changed by new challenges and opportunities, settler communities usually tugged at nostalgic images of a home they aped or mirrored. An early apologist for the Spanish Empire conceived it as the colonists' obligation to rebuild New Spain in the image of the old Spain. Hence Spaniards built European-style arches in earthquake zones in the Americas, even though earth tremors could—and did—easily reduce such structures to ruin. Even Puritans, who did consciously want to make something new of New England, went about it by fencing and planting to create English-style fields.

Yet the results nearly always did mark the beginning of something that was different from Europe. Colonies had to adapt to new environments and, in many cases, to the presence of new neighbors. Sectarian religious communities, democratic commonwealths, and plantation economies were all new, for instance, to the English experience. A bureaucratic state, with little delegation of authority to nobles and towns, was unknown in Spain. While slaves had existed in Europe in the Middle Ages, slavery on the American scale was unprecedented. Huge mixed-race populations, of the kind that filled Spanish and Portuguese America, had never before had a chance to emerge outside the Muslim world. The new colonies were products of their environments, which changed the people who lived in them.

The New World really was new. The Spanish experience there was one of the biggest surprises of history: the creation of the first great world empire of land and sea, and the only one, on a comparable scale, erected without the aid of industrial technology. A new political environment took shape. Historians have scoured sixteenth-century Europe for the origins of the "modern state," in which the authority of the aristocracy shrank to insignificance, the crown enforced an effective monopoly of government jurisdiction, the independence of towns withered, the church submitted to royal control, and sovereignty—formerly definable in terms of the right to pronounce justice—became increasingly identified with supreme legislative power, as laws multiplied.

States in Europe developed along those lines, but only the Spanish Empire in the New World fully matched all the criteria. Great nobles were generally absent from the Spanish colonial administration, which was staffed by professional, university-trained bureaucrats whom the crown appointed and paid. Town councils were largely composed of royal nominees. Church patronage was exclusively at the disposal of the crown. With a few exceptions, feudal tenure—combining the right to try cases at law along with land ownership—was banned. Though Spaniards with rights to Native American labor or tribute pretended to enjoy a sort of fantasy feudalism, speaking loosely of their "vassals," they were usually denied formal legal rights to govern or administer justice and the vassals in question were subject only to the king. Meanwhile, a stream of legislation regulated—or, with varying effectiveness, was supposed to regulate—the new society in the Americas. The Spanish Empire was never efficient, because of the vast distances royal authority had to cover. Remote administrators could and did ignore royal commands. But this was a modern state because it was a bureaucratic state and a state governed by laws.

It also threw up new kinds of social effects, new microsocieties: the shipboard world of to-ing and fro-ing across the Atlantic and Pacific; the missions; the slave plantations; the little kingdoms runaway slaves called **maroons** set up; the households Spanish conquerors founded with pretensions to nobility and native wives or concubines. In Spanish colonies, **creole** consciousness arose at an early stage among persons of at least partly European descent who were born in the colonies. In some ways it was evident in the first generation of the conquerors. Pride in mixed ancestry—or false claims to it, especially claims to be descended from Indian nobility—was one sure sign of creole self-assertion. So was the use of Native American languages alongside or instead of Spanish. In the late sixteenth and early seventeenth centuries, Fernando de Alva Ixtlilxochitl's was a typically self-conscious creole voice: a historian of his community in Texcoco in Mexico, an interpreter of Native American language in the law courts, a government representative on municipal councils, a promoter and collector of Aztec literature. In the same period in Peru, the royal Inca blood of Garcilaso de la Vega made him highly

> *"The New World really was new. The Spanish experience there was one of the biggest surprises of history: the creation of the first great world empire of land and sea, and the only one, on a comparable scale, erected without the aid of industrial technology."*

sought after as a godparent by young families in the Spanish town where he lived.

Historians have often supposed that the trauma of conquest and the catastrophic effects of the unaccustomed diseases Europeans introduced shocked Native Americans into docility. In many ways, however, it is remarkable how much—and how long—their society survived. Sometimes it simply evaded the Europeans. The Inca state, for instance, withdrew in the 1530s to a new, lowland environment centered on the fortress city of Vilcabamba (veel-kah-BAM-bah) in Peru, until a further Spanish conquest uprooted it in 1572. Independent Native American states survived for generations and sometimes for centuries beyond the reach of Spanish power in the rain forests of Guatemala, the Mexican desert, the Florida swamps. In other cases, Native American communities survived by forming partnerships with Spanish religious orders as their protectors, or— especially in the former Aztec and Inca subject areas— by collaborating with the Spanish monarchy and simply continuing to pay to the new elite the tribute they had formerly paid to Native American imperialists.

Mixing of the races. One of the most popular subjects for painters in eighteenth-century Spanish America was the vast range of skin complexions that intermarriage among Europeans, Native Americans, and black Africans produced. Hundreds of sets like this one survive, each consisting of many portraits of couples and their children, with every imaginable gradation of skin color. No one knows exactly what these paintings were for, but Spaniards who returned to Europe brought them home as souvenirs.

In some places, the substitution of new elites, not conquest, transformed politics and society. The new elites were not just composed of Europeans but also of newly elevated Native American individuals and communities. In the Aztec world, for instance, where war and disease wiped out much of the former generation of leaders, Spaniards—especially missionaries—formed new relationships with surviving youngsters, who became committed to Christianity and new values under the influence of mission schools. In urban environments a new class of opportunistic Native American *ladinos* arose—who learned Spanish and earned Spanish trust. In Panama the Spaniards elevated new local big men, mistrustful of the ritual functions of the leaders they displaced and whom they identified as "demonic." Everywhere, the children of marriages between Spaniards and Indians assumed a potentially advantageous place in colonial society. Because people at the time were more sensitive to differences of class than of race, these *mestizos*, as the descendants of Europeans and Native Americans were called, had access to positions of power and opportunities of wealth.

Of all the new kinds of society the global interconnections of the period created, the most novel were surely those of "the world the slaves made" in the Americas. From Virginia to Bahía in Brazil, much of Atlantic-side America became, in early colonial times, a world that was more African than European. In 1553—when black people in Mexico were doing little more than domestic labor—the viceroy, the representative of the king of Spain, was afraid that they would swamp white settlers. Black people rarely came to form a majority in the Spanish colonies— Cuba and Santo Domingo were two exceptions. Elsewhere, however, Africans were often the largest part of the population. By the end of the seventeenth century, England's Caribbean colonies had over 120,000 black slaves and only about 15,000 white inhabitants. The slaves practiced their own religions (see Chapter 18), maintained their own household patterns, and ate their own food. They created languages of their own to bridge the communication gaps among people from so many different parts of Europe and Africa. One of the earliest documented of these

Sranan, Dutch, and English Compared

Sranan	Dutch	English
brada	broder	brother
buku	boek	book
datra	doctor	doctor
faya	vuur	fire
gado	god	god
ingi	Indiaan	Indian
kerki	kerk	church
masra	meneer	mister
noso	neus	nose
omeni	hoeveel	how much
skribi	schrijven	write
srudati	soldaat	soldier
trow	trouwen	marry

new languages is Sranan, still the main language of Surinam, the former Dutch colony in South America. Slaves invented it in an amazingly short time, under a brief period of British rule, in the 1650s and early 1660s. Despite high mortality and rapid turnover in the slave population, they stuck to it through the subsequent 300 years of Dutch rule—adopting some Dutch words, but maintaining Sranan essential structures and vocabulary.

Even in tightly controlled plantations, slave communities often created autonomous institutions. In Jamaica, the British could never eliminate the secret power of the *obeah-men*, whom they denounced as sorcerers, or curb the "benches" of elders, who were the self-regulating judges of the slaves. Though specialists debate the issue, the evidence from British North America suggests that slaves themselves seem to have evolved the social order of plantation life—the family structures, the regulation of relationships, the norms of behavior. Their African culture was only slowly transformed, because most owners resisted Christianizing their slaves. The Bible might give them subversive ideas about the equality of men. Clergy might interfere with owners' rights of abuse.

As well as African ways of life, there were African political structures in America: independent states established by runaways, sometimes in collaboration with Native Americans. Colonial authorities were forced to recognize the most successful maroon kingdoms. It was easier to establish a working relationship than run the risks of war and of inflaming slaves' grievances. The best-known case is that of a maroon kingdom in Esmeraldas in the hinterland of what is today Colombia, which signed a treaty with the Spanish crown in 1599. The Spanish viceroy commissioned a commemorative painting of the event from Alonso Sánchez Galque, the best painter in the colony at the time. It shows a maroon leader and his sons, richly attired as Spanish gentlemen, but bejeweled with ear and nose ornaments of gold in Native American fashion.

Beyond the reach of British colonies, too, in the seventeenth and eighteenth centuries, maroon states in South Carolina and Jamaica enjoyed arrangements with the colonial authorities that guaranteed their peaceful toleration in exchange for joint regulation of the fate of new fugitives from the plantations (see Map 19.4). In the backcountry of Surinam, a maroon state was established in 1663 (the year the maroons of Jamaica received the first treaty acknowledging their autonomy), with the connivance of planters who sent their slaves there to evade the head tax on them

Don Francisco Arove and his sons, leaders of a maroon kingdom in Esmeraldas, who submitted to the Spanish crown by treaty in 1599. A government official commissioned the painting for presentation to King Philip III. The mixed culture of this community of runaway slaves is reflected in the appearance of its leaders: their black faces, their rich clothing in the style of Spanish noblemen, the costly ear and nose ornaments borrowed from Native American tradition.

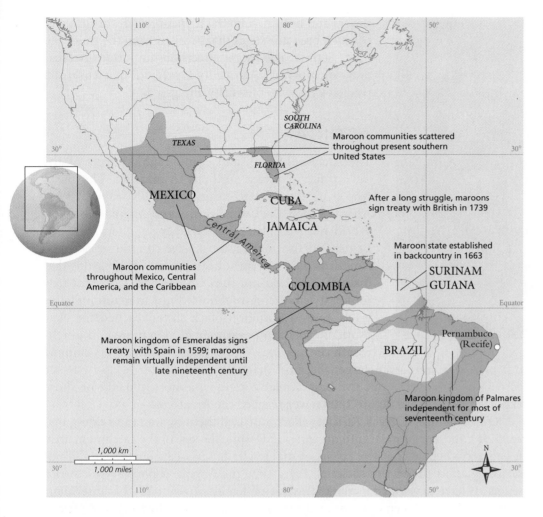

MAP 19.4

**Maroon Communities
in the Americas, 1500–1800**

Spanish territory after 1650
Portuguese territory by 1750

Maroon communities scattered throughout present southern United States

After a long struggle, maroons sign treaty with British in 1739

Maroon state established in backcountry in 1663

Maroon communities throughout Mexico, Central America, and the Caribbean

Maroon kingdom of Esmeraldas signs treaty with Spain in 1599; maroons remain virtually independent until late nineteenth century

Maroon kingdom of Palmares independent for most of seventeenth century

1,000 km
1,000 miles

that they were required to pay to the colonial government. The best documented and longest lasting of the runaways' states was upcountry from Pernambuco (pehr-nam-BOO-koh) in Brazil, where the kingdom of Palmares (pal-MAHR-eshs) defended its independence from Portugal for almost the entire seventeenth century. At its height, under King Zumbi, in the late seventeenth century, it had a royal guard 5,000 strong, an elaborate court life that impressed visiting Portuguese, and a black elite rich enough to have many slaves of their own.

Europeans dealing in the slave trade convinced themselves that slavery represented a civilizing process: the recovery of one of the virtues of the ancient Greek and Roman worlds, which slave energy had fueled, and the removal of slaves from the supposedly "barbarous darkness" of Africa to the "light" of Christian European civilization. In practice, it is hard to imagine anything more destructively barbarizing. Slavery nourished its own forms of lies and cant: racism, which depicted blacks as inherently inferior to whites, or claimed that they were better off enslaved than at home. It corrupted owners, by giving them power over the lives and bodies of their slaves and encouraging them to abuse it. It corrupted shippers, who overcrowded their cargoes to maximize their profits and, in verifiable incidents, tossed slaves overboard for the insurance ship owners could earn for dead "cargo." It kept black and white people in mutual fear and loathing, driving black rebels to horrific and despairing acts to find refuge or gain revenge, and trapping colonial governments in policies of inhuman rage and repression. It let loose predatory gangs of

"Europeans dealing in the slave trade convinced themselves that slavery represented a civilizing process: the recovery of one of the virtues of the ancient Greek and Roman worlds, which slave energy had fueled, and the removal of slaves from the supposedly 'barbarous darkness' of Africa to the 'light' of Christian European civilization. In practice, it is hard to imagine anything more destructively barbarizing."

Archibald Dalzel's *History of Dahomey* of 1793 was a slaver's defense of the slave trade, and the engravings in it reflect the author's prejudice against black Africans. The royal court of Dahomey in West Africa is presented as a contemptible blend of despotism, silliness, and immorality.

FIGURE 19.2 THE ATLANTIC SLAVE TRADE, FIFTEENTH TO EIGHTEENTH CENTURIES

From Cañizares-Esguerra, Jorge; Seeman, Eric, The Atlantic in Global History: 1500–2000, © 2007. Electronically reproduced by permission of Pearson Education, Inc., Upper Saddle River, New Jersey.

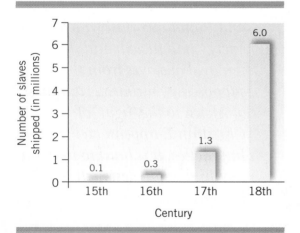

slavers and bounty hunters. It encouraged war in Africa between predator states that profited from the trade and their victims. The moral effects are important because every memory of inhumanity is precious in a world still riddled with vices of cruelty and greed.

AFRICA

The social, political, and demographic effects of the slave trade in Africa are hard to measure. The slaves who crossed the Atlantic came especially from the West African bulge, the Congo Basin, and Angola. The New World needed substantial numbers of them. Outside British North America, most slave communities in the Americas did not reproduce naturally, for reasons that historians still do not fully understand. Constant new imports were therefore required just to maintain labor levels. Over 1.5 million black slaves reached the New World by 1600, and nearly six million more in the eighteenth century (see Figure 19.2). The numbers shipped out of Africa were even larger, because many slaves died during the passage across the Atlantic. From the best available figures, almost 400,000 of those exported from Africa before 1800 never reached the Americas.

Overwhelmingly, black African sellers procured them by war and raiding that reached hundreds of miles into the interior. Despite the size of the catchment area, it is hard to believe that the export of manpower on the scale demanded did not seriously affect the victim societies. For a time the Angola region of West Africa seems to have developed a marked excess of females over males because many more men than women were shipped across the Atlantic. On the fringes of African slave-trading societies, some areas may have been depopulated.

Dahomey—one of many slave-trading states that sprang up or grew in West Africa during the slaving era (see Map 19.5)—illustrates the political effects. The kingdom arose in the interior of the present state of Benin in the early seventeenth century. Europeans already called the region the Slave Coast. Dahomey lived by war, and subordinated all other values to a ferocious warrior cult. Guests at the king's table dined with silver-handled forks on food European-trained cooks prepared, but they had to approach the king's palace over a path paved with skulls and were obliged to witness the human sacrifices with which Dahomeyans celebrated royal funerals and annual commemorations of former kings. Around the midseventeenth century, Dahomey began to accumulate muskets in exchange for slaves it obtained by raiding farther north. The 18 trading communities subject to Dahomey in the 1680s grew to over 200 within 20 years. Dahomey acquired a strip of coast—so King Agaja told European traders—to control outlets for slaves.

Yet with a productive territory in an area of varied commerce, Dahomey did not depend on slaving, which, by the best available calculations, accounted for perhaps 2.5 percent of its economy. Slaving apologists frequently pointed out that a war ethic motivated Dahomeyan aggression and that Dahomey prized captives more as potential human sacrifices than as slaves. White slave traders claimed that they performed a work of mercy by redeeming their victims from certain death. Dahomey's wars were not

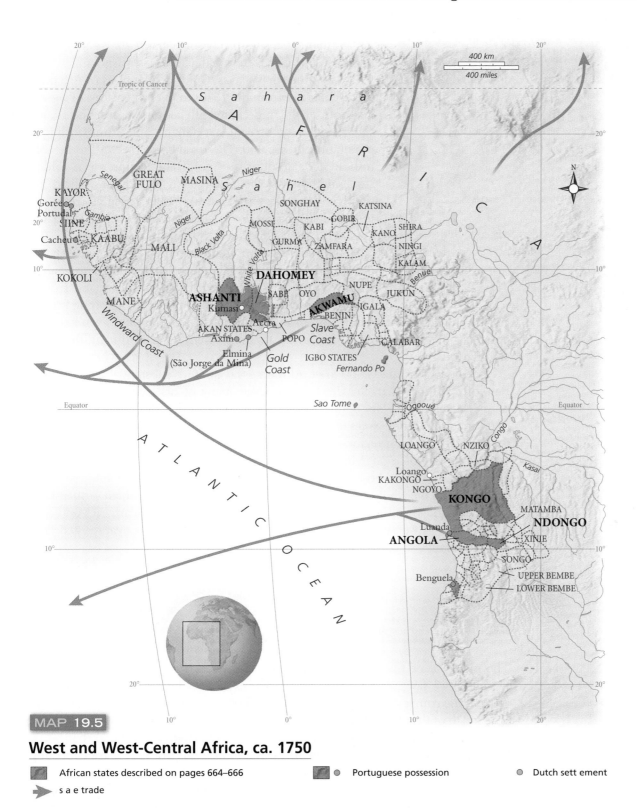

MAP 19.5

West and West-Central Africa, ca. 1750

- African states described on pages 664–666
- s a e trade
- Portuguese possession
- Dutch sett ement

fought primarily for slaves. Indeed, only a third of the campaigns acquired enough victims to cover the costs. Still, some facts are clear. Dahomey rose and fell with the rhythms of the slave trade, and its cult of ferocity coincided with the market for captives of war. The economics of the slave trade obliged African suppliers to be warriors or bandits, because the prices Europeans paid made it worth raiding for slaves, but not worth raising them.

Chronology: Africa, the Americas, and the Slave Trade

Late sixteenth century	Maroon kingdom of Esmeraldas
Seventeenth and eighteenth centuries	Slave states proliferate in West Africa; Maroon states in South Carolina and Jamaica
Late seventeenth century	Black slave population of British Caribbean reaches 120,000
	Maroon kingdom of Palmares reaches its height
ca. 1700	Number of slaves shipped to New World reaches 1.5 million
ca. 1800	Number of slaves shipped to New World reaches 7.5 million

Farther west, the history of Ashanti shows that state-building on an even greater scale was possible with resources other than slaves. Gold was the basis of Ashanti's spectacular rise from the 1680s to the dimensions of a great kingdom by the mid-eighteenth century, occupying 10,000 square miles of present-day Ghana and commanding a population of 750,000. The royal chest was said to be able to hold 400,000 ounces of gold. The throne was a golden stool said to have been called down from the sky. The court sheltered under ceremonial umbrellas as big as trees. For the annual yam ceremony, when the king's tributaries gathered with their followers, the capital at Kumasi housed 100,000 people. More adaptable than Dahomey, Ashanti used firepower to defeat mounted armies from the Sahel, while coping with a variety of environments and fronts. Part of its armies' success was owed to outstanding intelligence and logistics, with fast runners operating along cleared roads. Even Ashanti, however, increasingly relied on slaving to supplement its gold during the eighteenth century.

To the east of the Gold Coast, Akwamu was another substantial slave-stealing state of a distinct character. Its ruler enslaved many of his subjects by arranging phoney denunciations for adultery—a crime many African states punished by servitude—and mobilizing gangs of "smart boys" to kidnap victims. Similarly, in the other main slave-producing region—the Congo Basin and Angola—the profits of slaving enabled ambitious monarchs to consolidate and centralize states. Kongo became a hereditary kingdom, whose rulers appointed the chiefs of subordinate states, and who succeeded, on the whole, in preventing, or at least limiting, enslavement of their own subjects. Ndongo, in the interior of what is now Angola, grew similarly rich and centralized and, as we saw, under the formidable warrior queen, Nzinga, resisted Portuguese attempts at conquest for most of the seventeenth century.

In Perspective
Centuries of Upheaval

The upheaval of the sixteenth and seventeenth centuries affected much of the world. As we saw in Chapter 18, ecological exchanges had reversed, in a crucial respect, the course of evolution. Empires had overflowed like tidal waves and covered much of the globe. The balance of power between pastoral and settled peoples in Eurasia had shifted definitively toward the latter. Migrations and exchanges of culture crossed oceans and continents, sometimes with profoundly transforming effects. For the first time, a single—if small-scale—system of trade encircled the Earth. Some regions were still outside this system: Australia and most of the South Pacific, parts of inland Africa, the far interiors of the Americas. But they were unlikely to be left outside it for long.

Increasing demand was the result of gradually rising population and of huge increases of cash, which the silver mines of Japan and the Americas unlocked. New economic opportunities enriched new countries and new classes. A military revolution, as scholars now call it, introduced new technology to war: firearms that a peasant could handle with little training; fortifications that were proof against traditional horse-borne warriors; armies disciplined in the routines of battle rather than being trained, like knights of old, in individual combat. These changes started in Europe, but they transformed warfare in all the "gunpowder-empires" of the Old World. The military revolution loosened aristocracies' hold on one of the most basic forms of power, creating easily drilled armies of massed infantry, equipped with guns. Stronger states emerged in Europe and Africa; stronger empires in Asia; unprecedented empires in the Americas.

Although empires still seemed to dominate the map of the world, and although small chieftaincies and tribal states continued to occupy much of it, there was some evidence, in some regions, of a trend toward the kind of state familiar today: the relatively small and self-contained state, with internal sovereignty. In Europe, the Habsburg dynasty failed to turn Spanish preponderance into imperial control. Even in Germany, Habsburg power waned and, though Habsburg emperors continued to speak of their empire, it was transformed into a mass of loosely linked, small, effectively sovereign entities. In Southeast Asia, many rulers dreamed of creating an empire that would stretch from the Indian Ocean to the Pacific, and from India to China, but the traditional state system survived largely intact. In western Africa, while slaving states grew in strength, none reconstructed the extensive sway Mali had enjoyed in the fourteenth century or Soghay, for a while, in the sixteenth (see Chapters 14 and 15). Safavid Persia, though historians usually refer to it as an empire, more closely resembled a compact and—by the standards of its neighbors—a relatively homogeneous state. Although the Tokugawa imposed peace on Japan, there were limits to the political unification they imposed: in many ways, the daimiyos functioned like the rulers of loosely confederated states.

It is tempting to seek a connection between political instability, especially in the spell of civil wars and revolts that afflicted many states in the mid- to late seventeenth century, and the environmental changes described in Chapter 17. Although the ecological revolution and the spread and intensification of agriculture were sweepingly global phenomena, their effects took a long time to register. The seventeenth century was generally, as far as we can tell, a period of demographic stagnation in most of Eurasia and Africa, and even of decline in some places, posing a challenge for states that had to raise money and men for war. The concentrated aggravation of Eurasia's age of plague in the seventeenth century (see Chapter 17) made the problem worse. Like visitations of plagues in Eurasia in the fourteenth century (see Chapter 14), it accompanied protracted freak weather and abruptly falling temperatures, as a spell of unusually dense sunspots coincided with many volcanic eruptions, spraying the atmosphere with dust and shrouding the planet from solar energy. The period from the end of the 1640s to the 1680s was particularly hard. In the same decades, some of the most spectacular political revolutions of Eurasia occurred, including the collapse of the Ming Empire, the fragmentation of the Spanish monarchy, the temporary dissolution of the Polish Commonwealth, the splitting of the Netherlands, a major re-casting of the Holy Roman Empire, and, in England and the Ottoman Empire, revolutions in which rulers were killed. At the least, it seems likely that environmental changes added to the strains of war that disrupted these states.

Remarkably, however, they all emerged strengthened. The Qing, who dethroned the Ming in 1644, renewed the Chinese Empire and made it more effective militarily. The northern Netherlands became the launch-pad of a great global empire and the nursery of a "Golden Age" of wealth and art. Germany more or less split into many small states—but individually they were stronger than ever. The Poles recovered sufficiently to challenge the Ottomans, whose empire was barely affected by the palace revolution. Although Spain lost control of Portugal and the Netherlands, rebellions elsewhere failed, and the Spanish crown emerged with a tighter hold on

"For the first time, a single—if small-scale—system of trade encircled the Earth. Some regions were still outside this system: Australia and most of the South Pacific, parts of inland Africa, the far interiors of the Americas. But they were unlikely to be left outside it for long."

Chronology

1368–1644	Ming dynasty
Fifteenth and sixteenth centuries	Ottomans create an elite slave army, the Janissaries
Sixteenth through eighteenth centuries	Nuclear family moves to the center of European society
1500s	Chinese commercial economy booms
1501–1722	Safavid dynasty in Persia
r. 1501–1524	First Safavid ruler, Shah Ismail I, imposes Shiism by force
1513	Machiavelli writes *The Prince*
1519	Charles V becomes Holy Roman Emperor
1520s	Afghans and Persians help establish Mughal power in India
1570s	Ottoman jurist Ebu us-Suud justifies the Ottoman Sultan's power
1576	Jean Bodin formulates doctrine of sovereignty
1603–1868	Tokugawa shogunate
1618–1648	Thirty Years' War
1630s	Ecological disasters undermine Ming power
1640s	Strain of empire precipitates decline of Spanish power
1644–1911	Qing dynasty
Seventeenth and eighteenth centuries	Mandarins reconciled to Qing power
1658	Rebellion of provincial governors against Ottoman authority
1658—1707	Emperor Aurangzeb engages in almost constant warfare
r. 1682–1725	Peter the Great attempts Westernization of Russia
1683	Ottomans fail to capture Vienna and cease conquests on the Christian front
Late seventeenth century	Maroon kingdom of Palmares reaches its height
Seventeenth and eighteenth centuries	Slave states proliferate in West Africa; Japan undergoes a "commercial revolution"
Eighteenth century	Last restrictions on freedom of Chinese peasants eliminated; Mughal power begins irreversible decline
1721	Population of Japan reaches 30 million
ca. 1800	Number of slaves shipped to New World reaches 7.5 million

what was still a vast and—overall—growing empire. England's convulsions were traumatic, but in the course of them, the English crushed the independence of the Irish and Scots. France's time of troubles ended with the reign of Louis XIV (r. 1643–1715), whose image ever since has stood for royal power and the pursuit of gain and glory by war.

Growing state power went hand in hand with social changes. Rulers in Christendom and Islam challenged clergies for control of their subjects' private lives, especially their marriages. Where aristocratic government had formerly prevailed, bureaucrats and courtiers tended to replace local and provincial aristocrats as the main props of monarchical power. Remarkably, this trend was especially marked in Spain's American empire, where royal commands waned in effectiveness with the distance they traveled and the time it took. Although it would be going too far to speak of "the rise of the bourgeoisie," it is true that over much of the world—encompassing most of Europe, much of Asia, and significant parts of Africa and the Americas—new social configurations took shape, as the old vertical structures of society grew weaker, in which people identified with each other on the basis of kinship or local or provincial allegiance, or caste, or membership of an order or estate, or adhesion to a religious tradition. Instead, or alongside them, new sources of common interest grew in strength, with people identifying with others of similar wealth—or lack of it—and way of life. The trend was particularly strong in Europe, where family life grew ever more intimate and ever more narrowly focused on the home. Longstanding traditions dissolved or weakened, while new contexts for creating wealth and wielding power emerged, making possible the developments to which we must turn in the next part of the book: startling innovations in the global distribution of wealth and power, and revolutionary ways of thinking and behaving that became conspicuous in the eighteenth-century West and—as we shall see—then spread over the world.

PROBLEMS AND PARALLELS

1. How did the power of the state grow in the sixteenth and seventeenth centuries? How did monarchs such as Queen Nzinga seek to redistribute power to their own advantage? Which newly empowered classes contended for a share in the growing might and resources of states?

2. What were the sources of Spanish power in the sixteenth and seventeenth centuries? Why did Charles V fail to establish a dominant state in Europe? Why did Spain eventually lose its preeminent position in Europe?

3. How did the way Westerners think about sovereignty and international law change in this period? Why was Machiavelli's advice to rulers so shocking? How did European society change during this period?

4. What are the similarities and differences among the Ottoman, Mughal, and Safavid empires during this period? Why did Shah Ismail I impose Shiism on Persia?

5. What economic and social changes occurred in China during the early Qing dynasty? How did these changes affect Chinese politics? How did Japanese society change under the Tokugawa shoguns?

6. In what ways were European colonies in the Americas products of their environments? In what ways was the Spanish Empire a modern state? How did the creole mentality affect colonial societies?

7. How did slave communities in the Americas create autonomous institutions? What effect did the slave trade have on African states during this period?

READ ON ▶ ▶ ▶

The account of Queen Nzinga is indebted to work by J. K. Thornton, whose *Africa and Africans in the Making of the Atlantic World* (1995) is fundamental. A very readable introduction to the social transformation of early modern Europe is G. Huppert, *After the Black Death: A Social History of Early Modern Europe* (2nd ed., 1998). G. Parker, *The Military Revolution: Military Innovation and the Rise of the West, 1500–1800* (1988) is a vastly influential, though technologically oriented, statement of the connection between military and political change in Europe and globally. B. Downing, *The Military Revolution and Political Change* (1992) takes a closer, regionally differentiated look at political transformation. R. Carr, ed., *Spain: A History* (2000) is the best introduction to its subject. R. Harrison, *Hobbes, Locke, and Confusion's Masterpiece: An Examination of Seventeenth-Century Political Philosophy* (2002) is a masterful explication of seventeenth-century political philosophy. O. Hufton, *The Prospect Before Her* (1996) and I. Maclean, *The Renaissance Notion of Woman* (1983) are important for understanding the role of women in the West.

I. M. Kunt, *The Sultan's Servants: The Transformation of Ottoman Provincial Government* (1983) looks at the local and bottom-up forces affecting Ottoman governance, while H. Inalcik, *The Middle East and the Balkans under the Ottoman Empire: Essays on Economy and Society* (1993) explores the mutual impact of rulers and ruled in the most ethnically and religiously diverse area of Ottoman control. K. Barkey, *Bandits and Bureaucrats: The Ottoman Route to State Centralization* (1994) studies Ottoman state formation from the perspective of the central government.

I. Gallup-Diaz, *The Door to the Seas and the Key to the Universe. Indian Politics and Imperial Rival in Darien, 1640–1750* (2002) takes an ethnohistorical perspective on Indian responses and resistance to European encroachment in this period. Peter Jackson and Lawrence Lockhart, eds., *The Cambridge History of Iran: Volume 6, The Timurid and Safavid Periods* (1986) is the standard history of Persia during this period.

R. Huang, *1587: A Year of No Significance* (1982) tells the story of the crisis of that year in China. My account of the rise of the Qing is indebted to L. Struve, *Voices from the Ming-Qing Cataclysm* (1998). F. Wakeman, Jr., *The Great Enterprise* (1985) looks at the social bases of early Qing political and military power. Pak Chi-won, *Tale of a Yangban* (1994) offers a story of Chinese influence in Korea. C. Totman, *Politics in the Tokugawa Bakufu* (1967) is the classic study of the political transformations of Japan after unification. S. Morillo, "Guns and Government: A Comparative Study of Europe and Japan," *Journal of World History* (1995) uses Japan as a case study in the primacy of social over military change, challenging Parker's "military revolution" thesis.

P. P. Boucher, *Cannibal Encounters. Europeans and Island Caribs, 1492–1763* (1999), traces cultural interactions in the Caribbean and demonstrates the effectiveness of Carib resistance to Europeans.

The intense instability of the mid-seventeenth century is studied in G. Parker and L. Smith, eds., *The General Crisis of the Seventeenth Century*. G. Parker, *The World Crisis: Climate, Collapse and Recovery in the Seventeenth Century* (forthcoming) brilliantly sets the phenomenon in a global context.

The World in 1700

The way life-forms began to cross the world in the sixteenth century halted one of the longest-standing trends on the planet. Scores of millions of years of divergent evolution, continent by continent, were reversed. But the big effects on the diversification of food and the increase of global population had not yet been felt. The lurches of climate sped transformations of states—leading to retreating aristocracies, encroaching bureaucracies, and the multiplication of laws—but the transformations were patchy and incomplete. The worldwide reach of explorers, traders, missionaries, and conquerors from Atlantic-side Europe demonstrated the imperial potential of Europe, but the empires were still feeble, outclassed by those of indigenous Asian powers. Prowess in astronomy and cartography won Europeans new respect in parts of Asia where they had formerly longed in vain for access. The global balance of wealth and power, however, remained undisturbed: indeed, China benefited most from the growing range and scale of global trade. Christianity was reaching previously unevangelized populations in Europe and around the world—but the spread of Islam and Buddhism echoed and, in some regions matched or exceeded, that of Christianity.

From inside a European *Wunderkammer* or Memory-Theater, such as the one shown on this map, the world did look different. Riches were pouring into Europe as never before, thanks above all to previously unexploited resources in the Americas. Maps, reports, curiosities, and exotica garnered from all over the globe were beginning to give European science a privileged view of the world and to stimulate imperial imaginations. Glimmeringly, the prospects of "the rise of the West" to global hegemony were beginning to be discernible.

▶ QUESTIONS

1. If the ecological revolution was the essential precondition for the major global changes of the sixteenth and seventeenth centuries, why was Europe better able to take advantage of these new resources?

2. How did mental attitudes to the world change as the result of ecological exchange?

To view an interactive version of this map, as well as a video of the author describing key themes related to this Part, go to www.myhistorylab.com

670

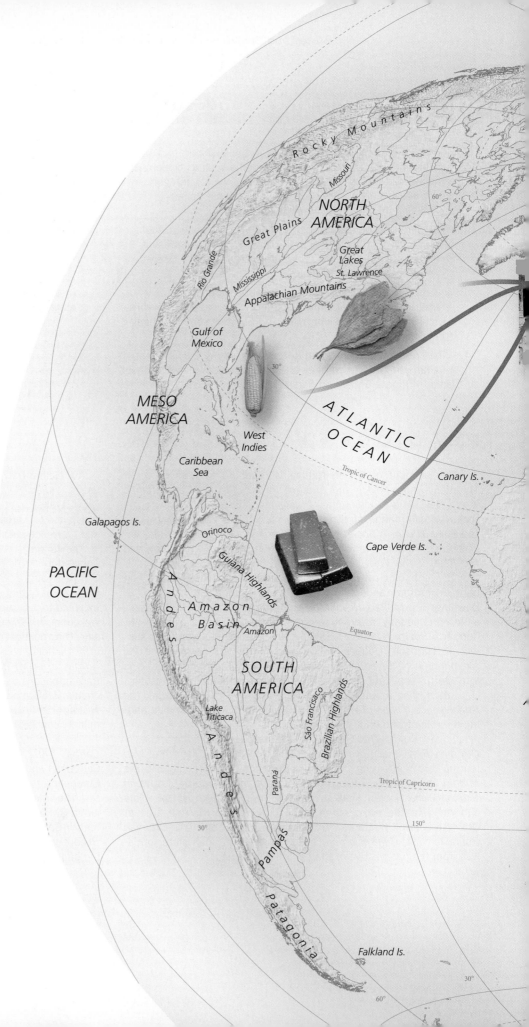

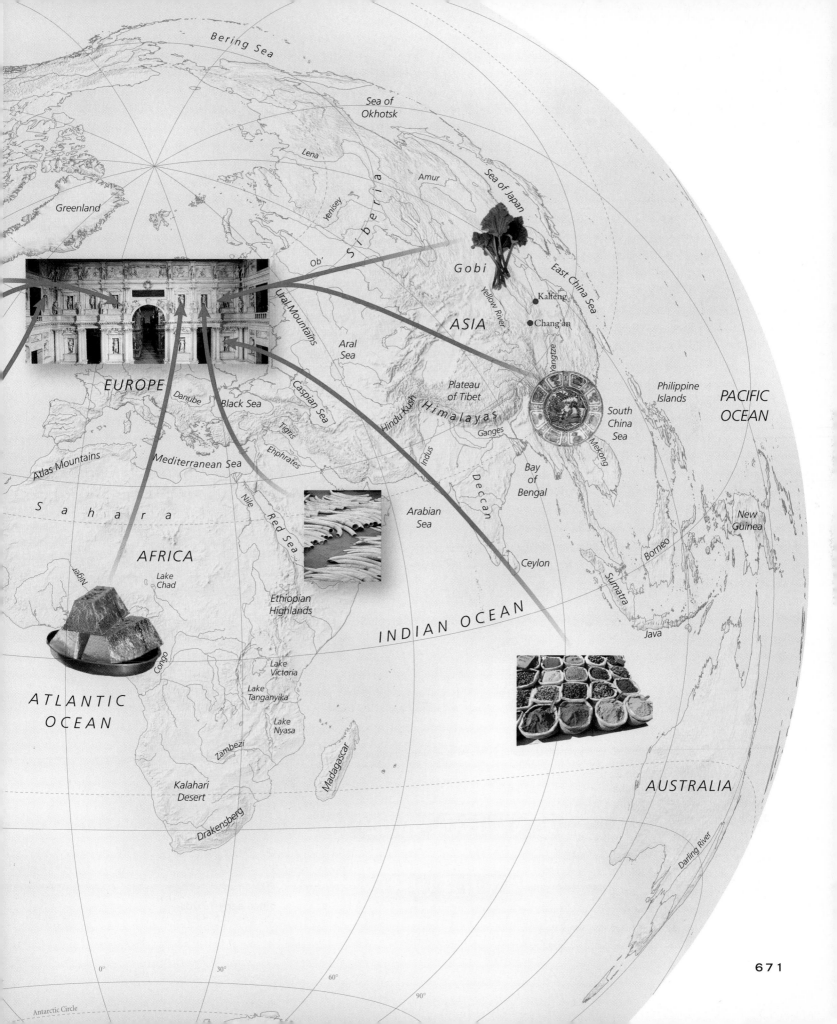

Bering Sea

Greenland

Sea of
Okhotsk

Lena

Amur

Sea of Japan

Siberia

Yenisey

Gobi

East China
Sea

Ob'

Ural Mountains

Kaifeng

Yellow River

ASIA

Chang'an

EUROPE

Danube

Black Sea

Caspian Sea

Aral
Sea

Philippine
Islands

PACIFIC
OCEAN

Yangtze

Plateau
of Tibet

Atlas Mountains

Mediterranean Sea

Tigris

Euphrates

Hindu Kush

Himalayas

South
China
Sea

Mekong

Ganges

Sahara

Nile

Red Sea

Indus

Deccan

Bay
of
Bengal

Arabian
Sea

New
Guinea

AFRICA

Niger

Lake Chad

Ethiopian
Highlands

Ceylon

INDIAN OCEAN

Sumatra

Borneo

ATLANTIC
OCEAN

Congo

Lake
Victoria

Lake
Tanganyika

Java

Lake
Nyasa

Madagascar

Zambezi

AUSTRALIA

Kalahari
Desert

Drakensberg

Darling River

0°

30°

60°

90°

Antarctic Circle

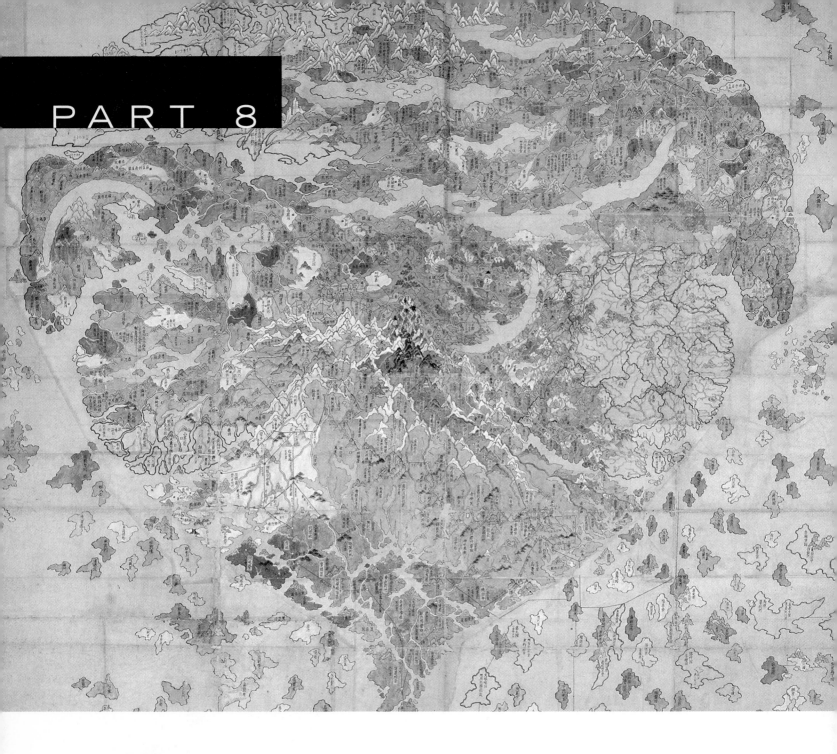

PART 8

ENVIRONMENT

since ca. 1700
Global navigation and trade

CULTURE

since early 1700s
Decline of Asian
empires

Global Enlightenments, 1700–1800

◀ **A Buddhist world map** by the Japanese monk-painter Sokaku, ca. 1709. In the worldview of Buddhists and Hindus, the Earth is divided into seven island continents, each separated by an encircling sea, and each continent double the size of the preceding one. This example shows the continent of Jambudvipa, which forms the innermost circle of continents. The map incorporates European geographical knowledge, including Europe itself in the upper-left corner.

since 1720s
Rise of global horticulture

ca. 1750
Population boom starts: Europe, China, and the Americas

since ca. 1760
British industrialization

1780–1800
Peak of Atlantic slave trade

ca. 1720–1790
European
Enlightenment

1756–1757
British conquest of
Bengal

1776–1783
American
Revolution

1789–1795
French Revolution

CHAPTER 20

Driven by Growth: The Global Economy in the Eighteenth Century

▲ **Shaken and stirred:** Avenging angels soar through the dust-filled sky over Lisbon, Portugal after the earthquake of 1755. The themes highlighted by the painting are echoed in the literature of the time: the revival of religion in the aftermath of horror, divine righteousness, the moral opportunity for displays of charity, the leveling effects of the disaster, which reduced the rich to the same destitution that the poor suffered.

H ere is a tale of an optimist and a pessimist. Both were brilliant mathematicians, fascinated by statistics. The optimist was a French nobleman: Marie Jean Antoine Nicolas de Caritat, Marquis de Condorcet, born in 1743, who adopted with enthusiasm every radical cause that came his way. The pessimist was an English clergyman, Thomas Malthus, born in 1766, whose skepticism about human nature grew bleaker as the events of his time in Europe flung shadows and gushed blood. Condorcet believed humankind was heading for perfection. Malthus believed it was heading for extinction.

For Condorcet, in *The Progress of the Human Mind*, published shortly after his death in 1794, one of the proofs of progress was the growth of population: evidence—he thought—that people were growing happier, healthier, more fertile, longer lived, and more willing to bring children into the world. Indeed, he correctly spotted the broad global population trends of his day. In the second half of the eighteenth century, world population was booming. Between about 1750 and 1850, the population of China doubled, that of Europe nearly doubled, and that of the Americas doubled three times. The overall figures are hard to compute and mean nothing, of course, for anywhere in particular, but they expose a vivid backdrop to the events of the time. In 1700, world population was perhaps a little over 600 million. By 1800, it had climbed to around 900 million. The global population explosion of modern times had begun.

Among Condorcet's contemporaries, virtually no one believed there could be any such thing as overpopulation. Increased population promised more economic activity, more wealth, more manpower, more strength. But what, to Condorcet, seemed reason to rejoice, Malthus reinterpreted as the beginning of catastrophe. In his *Essay on the Principle of Population* of 1798, Malthus drew the statistical basis of his thinking from Condorcet's work but refiltered it through his own pessimistic vision. He concluded that population was rising so much faster than food production that humankind was bound for disaster. "The power of population is indefinitely greater than the power in the earth to produce subsistence for man," he wrote. "Population, when unchecked, increases in a geometrical ratio. Subsistence only increases in an arithmetical ratio." Only "natural checks"—famine, plague, war, and catastrophe—could keep numbers down to a level at which people could be fed.

Condorcet and Malthus were in their own ways typical of their time. For the intellectual and moral climate of Europe changed abruptly in the 1790s when revolution and war undermined confidence in reason and in basic human goodness. Ironically, Condorcet was a victim of changes he was incapable of recognizing. He

FOCUS questions

Why did the world's population rise in the eighteenth century?

Why did rising population stimulate economic activity in parts of Europe?

Why was China's position as the world's richest economy threatened in the late eighteenth century?

How did British exploitation affect India's economy?

How did imperial expansion stimulate economic activity?

wrote his great work during 1792, while hiding from revolutionaries who wanted to chop off his head, and he died in prison shortly after they captured him. So his was a heroically defiant voice, insisting on the goodness of his persecutors and a future better than the present and the past. Malthus was an earnest, honest observer, peering with anxious charity into a grave new world of overpopulation tempered by disaster.

Malthus wrote so convincingly that he panicked the elites of the West into believing him. His view, according to the influential English writer William Hazlitt (1778–1830), was "a ground on which to fix the levers that may move the world." Among the disastrous consequences Malthus's book may have encouraged were the wars and imperial ventures that people's fear of running out of space and resources provoked. But Malthusian anxieties proved false. Populations rise and fall, and trends never last long. Overpopulation is rare in history. Experience suggests that people breed less when they attain prosperity. Despite the huge increase of world population since Malthus's day to over 6 billion, food production has matched or exceeded it.

Condorcet was closer to being right than Malthus was about the stimulating effects of population increase in the world of his day. We cannot fully understand anything else in the history of the eighteenth century without it: the speeding up of economic activity; the extension of settlement into new lands; the huge increases in production as empires grew in pursuit of resources; the drive of science to find new ways to understand and exploit nature; the intellectual challenges that accompanied all this ferment. On the whole, with exceptions, shifts in the balance of wealth and power also reflected demographic change. Rising regions, like Europe, China, and parts of North America and Africa, were those that experienced sharp population increases, whereas areas of relatively stable population, such as the Ottoman Empire, housed stagnant or declining states (see Map 20.1).

POPULATION TRENDS

Population growth took two forms: dispersal on underexploited frontiers, and concentration in growing cities and denser agricultural settlements. Around 1500, there were perhaps 80 million people in Europe. Modest, faltering growth in the sixteenth and seventeenth centuries raised the overall figure to about 120 million. It rose by about 50 percent to 180 million in the next 100 years.

Some areas hugely exceeded this rate. Russia's population doubled. We can see similar patterns in China and India. China had nearly 350 million people by 1800, India some 200 million. No reliable figures exist for Central and northern Asia, but the incoming colonists who arrived to turn suitable patches of steppe and forest in these areas into grassland on which their herds could graze made a significant difference in what were—in relation to their enormous size—sparsely populated regions.

Although figures are unavailable for Africa, evidence of restless migration suggests that the population was increasing there, too. In East Africa, for example, Oromo herdsmen (see Chapter 17) spread over much of Ethiopia. The cattle-rearing Masai of what is now Kenya expanded to fill all the land available for the kind of herding economy that suited them. In Central Africa, the Mongo people from equatorial Zaire in what is today the Congo colonized the lower Kasai and Sunkuru valleys and the forest fringe. In the far south, settlers of Dutch origin spread ever farther into the interior from the Cape. It is hard to see how the relentless growth of the slave trade in the seventeenth and eighteenth centuries could have been sustained without a rising population in the West African regions the slavers most frequented. East Africa, meanwhile, supplied slaves on a lesser scale to markets in Muslim Asia and to new European plantations in the Dutch East Indies and the islands of the Indian Ocean.

In the Americas, the effects of Old World diseases had penetrated most areas by the seventeenth century. Disease still had destructive work to do in previously protected places, particularly in the American West, where smallpox and measles decimated Native Americans in the early nineteenth century. On the whole, however, a population boom replaced the Americas' era of demographic decline. In Spanish America, while indigenous populations showed signs of recovery, increased numbers of settlers and slaves were moving inland. By the end of the eighteenth century, Spain's American empire probably contained 14.5 million people. The population of British North America increased fivefold in the first half of the century, and nearly tenfold to 2.5 million in the second half. Numbers of white and black people rose, while the numbers of Native Americans dwindled, as they were driven from their lands or exposed to unaccustomed diseases (see Figure 20.1). Immigrants replenished and overflowed the space the Native Americans left behind. In the Caribbean, slaves accounted for most of the increase. During the eighteenth century the slave population in the British West Indies grew from about 120,000 to nearly 750,000, mainly because so many new slaves were brought from Africa, and they lived alongside about 100,000 white people.

Some parts of the world lagged behind in population growth or experienced it in different ways. Japan's demographic surge ended before the mid-eighteenth century, when it had over 30 million inhabitants. Japanese censuses of 1721 and 1804 reveal hardly any change. The population was disproportionately concentrated in a small part of the country, around and between Osaka and Ise Bays, where there was perhaps genuine pressure of overpopulation, or at least a sense that space was tight. Indeed, the census figures show outward movement from the heartland into the islands of Shikoku, Kyushu, and western Honshu. Japanese families seem to have practiced a wide variety of measures to restrain fertility, including delayed marriage, infanticide, and contraception. In Europe, the French were taking similar measures. The most populous country in Europe, France was also the first to experience a slowdown in the rate of population increase, which was already noticeable before the end of the eighteenth century. The Ottoman and Persian Empires were the other main areas exempt from spectacular population growth. They seem, for unknown reasons, to have registered only small increases. It helps to understand the fading of the Ottoman Empire, among the great powers of the world, to know that the ratio of its population relative to that of Europe as a whole dropped from perhaps about 1:6 in 1600 to about 1:10 in 1800.

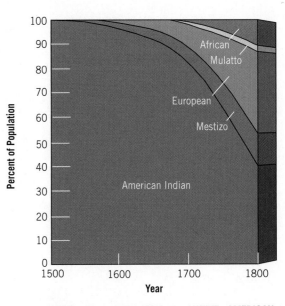

FIGURE 20.1 THE AFRICAN, NATIVE AMERICAN, EUROPEAN, AND MIXED RACE POPULATION OF THE AMERICAS, 1500–1800
Colin McEvedy and Richard Jones, Atlas of World Population History, p. 280. Reproduced with permission of Curtis Brown Group Ltd, London on behalf of the Estate of Colin McEvedy. © Copyright Colin McEvedy 1978.

Urbanization

Irrespective of the overall trends in population, urbanization—the growth of cities and towns—increased during this period over most of Eurasia and the Americas, though, of course, cities large in their day were small by present standards. China,

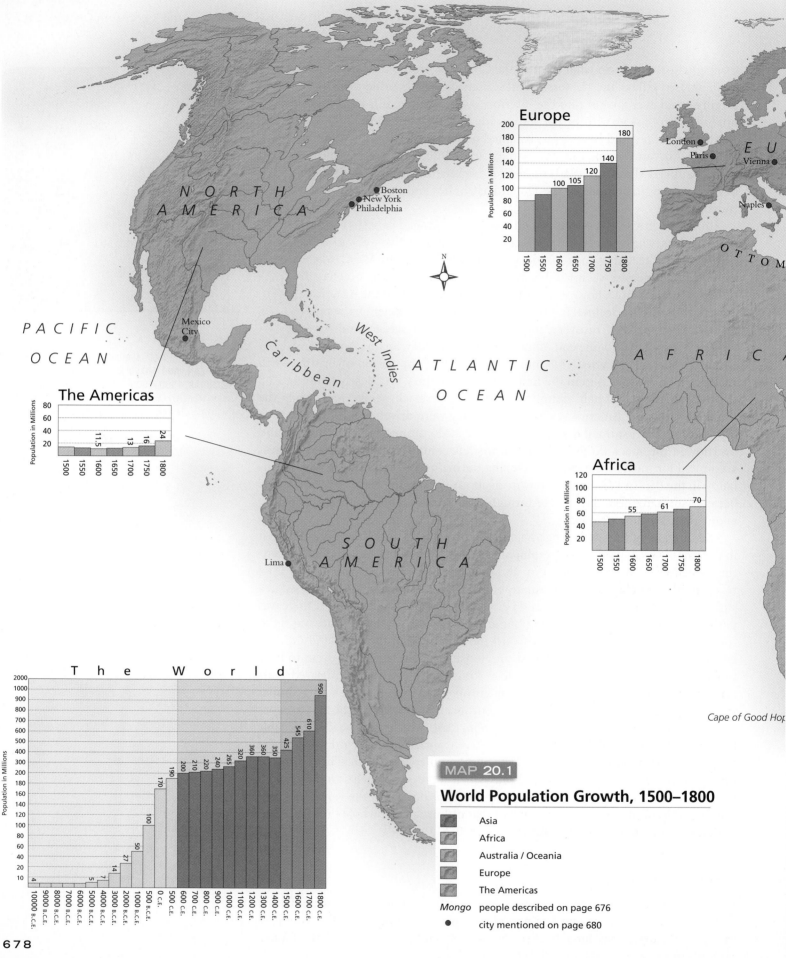

Europe

Population in Millions

1500	1550	1600	1650	1700	1750	1800
		100	105	120	140	180

The Americas

Population in Millions

1500	1550	1600	1650	1700	1750	1800
		11.5		13	16	24

Africa

Population in Millions

1500	1550	1600	1650	1700	1750	1800
		55		61		70

The World

Population in Millions

10000 B.C.E.	9000 B.C.E.	8000 B.C.E.	7000 B.C.E.	6000 B.C.E.	5000 B.C.E.	4000 B.C.E.	3000 B.C.E.	2000 B.C.E.	1000 B.C.E.	500 B.C.E.	0 C.E.	500 C.E.	600 C.E.	700 C.E.	800 C.E.	900 C.E.	1000 C.E.	1100 C.E.	1200 C.E.	1300 C.E.	1400 C.E.	1500 C.E.	1600 C.E.	1700 C.E.	1800 C.E.
4					5	7	14	27	50	100	170	190	200	210	220	240	265	320	360	360	350	425	545	610	950

MAP 20.1

World Population Growth, 1500–1800

- Asia
- Africa
- Australia / Oceania
- Europe
- The Americas

Mongo people described on page 676

● city mentioned on page 680

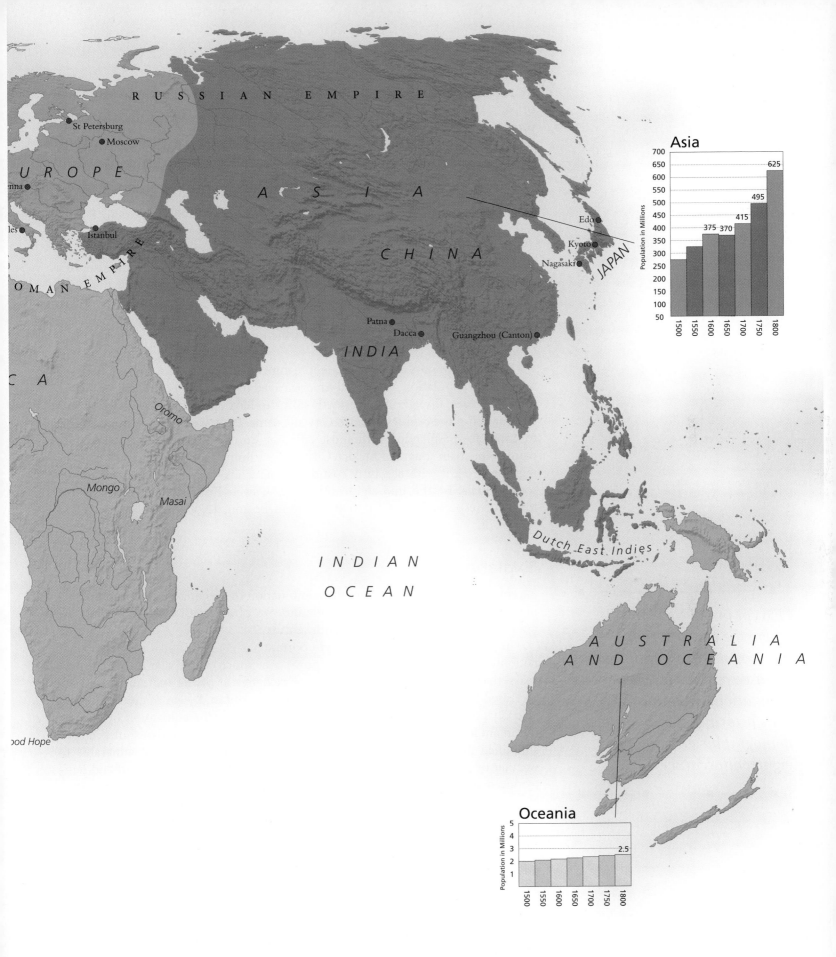

RUSSIAN EMPIRE

St Petersburg

Moscow

EUROPE

enna

les

Istanbul

OMAN EMPIRE

ASIA

CHINA

CA

Oromo

Mongo

Masai

Patna

Dacca

INDIA

Guangzhou (Canton)

Edo

Kyoto

Nagasaki

JAPAN

Asia

Population in Millions

700	
650	625
600	
550	
500	495
450	
415
400	
375	370
350	
300	
250	
200	
150	
100	
50	

1500 1550 1600 1650 1700 1750 1800

INDIAN

OCEAN

Dutch East Indies

AUSTRALIA
AND OCEANIA

Oceania

Population in Millions

5	
4	
3	
	2.5
2	
1	

1500 1550 1600 1650 1700 1750 1800

ood Hope

India, and Japan housed the most urbanized societies. The vast extended urban area of which Guangzhou (gwang-joh) in southern China was the center had as many people as all the capitals of Western Europe put together. By the best available estimates, at the end of the eighteenth century, Dacca in what is today Bangladesh, the world's greatest center of textile production, had over 200,000 people, and Patna in northern India had over 300,000. In Japan, the population was, to an exceptional degree, concentrated in cities, with at least 6 percent of Japanese living in urban concentrations of over 100,000 inhabitants. The corresponding figure in Europe was only 2 percent.

But Europe also experienced intensified urbanization and, in pockets, exceeded even Japan's rate. Britain had only one big city, but it was a monster of a place. London approached a million inhabitants by the beginning of the nineteenth century. Paris at the same time had over 500,000, and Naples in southern Italy not many fewer. Moscow, Vienna, and Amsterdam each exceeded 200,000, as did Russia's new capital St. Petersburg, which did not even exist until 1703 (see Chapter 19).

Urbanization was also a prominent feature of change in the Americas. Nearly a third of the population of Spanish America lived in settlements officially classed as towns or cities, though urban growth seems to have slowed in many areas in the last quarter of the century. Mexico City and Lima, Peru, were colonial capitals able to compete in splendor with most cities of Europe. Cristóbal de Villalpando painted the main square of Mexico City in 1695, lining the scene with lavish buildings, peopling it with elegantly costumed characters, costly coaches, and snooty social rituals. By the mid-eighteenth century, even British North America had towns of respectable size—15,000 people in Boston, 12,000 in Philadelphia and New York.

Explanations

Except in the New World, where the combination of arriving migrants and receding disease accounts for rising population, we cannot satisfactorily explain the demographic growth of the eighteenth century.

Improved food supply played an important part, but it is not a sufficient explanation on its own. Nutrition did improve over much of the world during these years, thanks to the worldwide ecological exchange of plants and animals, which increased farmers' options and extended the amount and yield of cultivable land (see Chapter 17). Over the long term, **monocultures** (the cultivation of a single dominant food crop, such as potatoes or rice) have increased food output, but have simplified human food chains and have made large populations vulnerable to weather or political crises. The ecological exchanges reversed that trend and reintroduced complexity and diversity into the human food chain. A wider range of crops, with different harvest times and different tolerances for changes in the weather, ensured that the food supply was proof against variable conditions. If bad weather hit one crop, other crops remained available.

Urbanization, on the other hand, made the diet of the poor worse. It interposed middlemen between poor city dwellers and farmers, raised the cost of food, and separated consumers from fresh local produce. In China and India, increased food production does not seem to have kept pace with population growth. Still, concentrated markets for anything, including food, are more efficient than dispersed ones. Improved shipping, canals, and coastal trade made the distribution of bulk foods easier, notably in China, Japan, and Europe—areas that already had

"Except in the New World, where the combination of arriving migrants and receding disease accounts for rising population, we cannot satisfactorily explain the demographic growth of the eighteenth century."

A CLOSER LOOK

Mexico City in 1695

"The capital of the New World." Seventeenth-century Mexico City sought, in the words of one commentator, to be "an imperial city of great size, space, concourse, and population." Cristóbal de Villalpando's painting of the city's main square in 1695 captures this vision and emphasizes order, geometry, and European-style elegance. Yet the painting also shows why critics claimed to find Mexico City chaotic and confusing. By this date, uncontrolled growth had raised its population to nearly 100,000.

Water carriers fill their pitchers at a famous fountain, around which Native American women sit under elegant umbrellas.

Fancy carriages and elaborate manners suggest the wealth, status, and European tastes of the city's elite.

Elegant shops in the Spanish market.

In the native market, vendors sell foodstuffs in their thatched stalls.

How does this painting document the size, importance, and roles of cities in the eighteenth century?

Gin Lane, London. For the poor in the foul, cruel slums of industrializing cities, drink was the only affordable escape. 'Drunk for a penny. Dead Drunk for tuppence,' proclaims an ad depicted in William Hogarth's characteristically blunt engraving of London's St. Giles's district in 1751. Hogarth did not imagine the syphilitic woman too drunk to see that her baby is falling to certain death: the courts heard similar cases frequently. *Hogarth, William (1697–1764). "Gin Lane." Published in London, 1751. Engraving. British Museum. London, Great Britain. © British Museum/Art Resource, NY*

relatively good transport networks. Ultimately, while many people may not have eaten better food in the eighteenth century (and may even have gotten less healthy food), more people around the world did get more food, ate more regularly, and survived longer to work and reproduce.

Improved hygiene may have helped increase populations, but it is not likely to have been decisive. Urbanization bred ever more unsanitary conditions, even in the most technically ambitious and sophisticated societies, until well into the nineteenth century (see Chapter 24). An age of typhus and cholera succeeded the age of plague because bigger cities meant that more people were exposed to water contaminated by human sewage and to the lice that spread typhus. Typhus and cholera only began to disappear in the West in the nineteenth century when European and American cities constructed sewage systems and provided clean water for their inhabitants to drink and bathe in. Typhus, typhoid, and other fevers, some of tropical origin, colonized econiches in growing cities and could reenact scenes reminiscent of the age of plague. A particularly deadly series of local epidemics in England in the 1720s killed 100,000 people. In Japan, however, the remarkable absence of cholera in this period may have been the result of exceptional standards of sanitation and of the use of human waste as fertilizer—which ensured that Japanese streets, unlike those in other parts of the world, were kept clean of human feces.

We can group other existing explanations for the new demographic trend under two main headings. First, there is what we might loosely call the theory of *progress*, which represents population growth as the result of successes in the struggle against death—successes that postponed early mortality and extended people's fertile lives. According to this theory, human health improved because of better medical and public health strategies. Second, environmental conditions may hold the key. The survivors of plagues and epidemics developed immunities to diseases, for instance, or—some historians have argued—the microorganisms that carried diseases fatal to humans may have evolved into less deadly forms. We can look at each of these in turn, seeing what they contributed and trying to identify possible factors that have not yet received adequate attention.

Medicine

Some improvements in health were clearly the result of improved medical science or care. But most medicine remained useless and ignorant, and nothing that was new in medicine affected the plague. In some parts of Europe, professionals—doctors and trained midwives—handled childbirth, babies were freed from tight swaddling clothes, and breast-feeding was praised. But these practices were still the exception and are unlikely to have had much effect on population statistics. In most places, a declining death rate among people in their fertile years seems to have been crucial, rather than any reduction in infant mortality.

The exchange of ideas about cures, methods for treating the sick, and medicinal plants was part of the great cultural exchange across Eurasia and between

Europe and the Americas. It boosted the variety of medicinal drugs and plants of every society it touched. Eighteenth-century European medicinal drugs looked—by today's standards—increasingly effective as time went on. Such ingredients as spider's webs, unicorn horn, powdered snake flesh, and moss scraped from human skulls disappeared from medical textbooks in favor, for instance, of opium, quinine, and chemical remedies. But these expensive preparations probably did no good to most people and only a little good to a few. In the West, the theory of medicine, inherited from the ancient Greeks (see Chapter 6), which attributed ill health to imbalances in the body between basic juices or fluids called *humors*, gradually receded. But nothing particularly scientific replaced it. Diet and exercise—or lack of them—were still considered fundamental both to the causes and treatment of disease. Contagion was suspected as a cause, but no one had any idea how it worked. Environmental circumstances got an increasing share of blame, as medical theorists condemned *miasmas* or "corrupt air" from mists and gases from the earth as unhealthy. No one yet recognized germs or microbes as dangerous or knew anything about viruses.

Still, despite the deficiencies of medicine, two diseases were conquered or contained: scurvy (the vitamin C deficiency that particularly afflicted long-range seafarers) and smallpox. A crisis in the history of scurvy occurred in 1740–1744, when the British naval commander George Anson lost almost 1,400 out of a complement of over 1,900 men during a round-the-world voyage. Scurvy was only the worst of a plague of deficiency diseases, including beriberi, blindness, and "idiotism, lunacy, convulsions," that afflicted Anson's crews. But the terrible death toll provoked a systematic inquiry by the British navy into how to treat it. James Lind, a naval surgeon who had seen service in the West Indies, tried out a large selection of possible remedies on a sample of 12 patients at sea. "The consequence was," he recorded, "that the most sudden and visible good effects were perceived from the use of the oranges and lemons; one of those who had taken them, being at the end of six days fit for duty."

Lind had discovered a cure for scurvy, but not a preventive. Unlike the case with other vitamins, the human body cannot store more vitamin C than it needs in a day, and there was still no way to preserve oranges and lemons at sea for long enough to secure the health of the crews. The only effective remedy was to replenish ships with fresh supplies at every opportunity and to eat as many fruits and green vegetables as crews could find wherever a ship could land, ravaging desert islands for the barely edible weeds sailors called scurvy grass. The Spanish-sponsored voyage of Alessandro Malaspina, the most ambitious scientific expedition of the eighteenth century, from 1789 to 1794, virtually banished scurvy from the fleet with ample supplies of oranges and lemons (see Chapter 22). Other navies, however, that lacked the Spaniards' advantage of a large colonial empire with frequent ports of call, remained desperate for alternative diagnoses and easier cures. A surgeon with experience of Russian Arctic exploration advised "warm reindeer blood, raw frozen fish, exercise," and any edible greens that might come to hand. During his Pacific voyages from 1785 to 1788, the French explorer Jean-François de La Pérouse mixed quinine and extract of spruce trees in the crew's drinking water. The eighteenth-century British explorer of the Pacific, Captain James Cook, put his faith in sauerkraut. Yet despite these discoveries, official resistance to new ideas meant that the issue of citrus-juice rations to English sailors did not begin until as late as 1795. Even then, of course, although doctors knew that doses of citrus juice worked, they did not know why because vitamins had not yet been discovered.

Scurvy was not a major killer. More important, for the population statistics, was progress in containing smallpox—still a significant taker of young lives. China, India,

The Anatomy of Man's Body as govern'd by the Twelve Constellations. Almanacs provided a wide range of information, self-improvement advice, and wisdom—practical, religious, and scientific—to eighteenth- and nineteenth-century Americans. First published in 1732, Benjamin Franklin's *Poor Richard's Almanack* was a huge success, selling nearly 10,000 copies a year. As this woodcut from 1750 indicates, many people still clung to the ancient belief that the movement of the planets and the position of the stars influenced the well-being of the parts of the human body.

Vaccination. When Louis Léopold Boilly painted this scene of a smallpox vaccination in 1807, the procedure still seemed curious and alarming. But it had become a routine part of doctors' domestic visits across much of Europe and the Americas.

and the Middle East had long known about inoculation as a means of prevention. Now the practice spread to Europe. In 1718, Lady Mary Wortley Montagu, wife of the British ambassador in Constantinople, volunteered her six-year-old son to be a guinea pig in an inoculation experiment by an "old Greek woman, who had practised this way for many years." After injection, the boy was covered in pustules, with swollen arms, dry mouth, and an urgent fever. Yet the experiment was a success, and when London was threatened with an epidemic in 1721, Lady Mary repeated it on her daughter. King George II (r. 1727–1760) had his daughters inoculated, and British high society adopted the practice. Lady Mary had achieved an ambition she conceived as a patriotic duty: "to bring this useful invention into England." Cheap, mass methods of inoculation soon followed. In 1796, Edward Jenner substituted cowpox for smallpox in the inoculation process. This was a considerable improvement, since cowpox had the same immunizing effect, but carried almost no risk of harming inoculated persons.

The Ecology of Disease

The success of this campaign against smallpox was remarkable. More remarkable still was the way the global profile of disease changed on its own without humans doing anything to affect it. Part of this was a consequence of ecological exchange. Fewer populations suffered from lack of natural immunization. Global communications meant that more and more people could contract the same diseases, just as they made the same plants and animals familiar over a vast range of the world. Still, migrations of disease-bearing organisms remained dangerous. Yellow fever crossed the Atlantic from Africa and spread beyond the tropics, hitting cities as far north as Philadelphia repeatedly in the eighteenth century. Cholera became a frequent visitor to European cities. Tropical forms of malaria were deadly to European visitors and would-be colonists. The European cocktail of diseases that despoiled the Americas of native peoples in the sixteenth and seventeenth centuries continued to wreak havoc on new discoveries. Toward the end of the eighteenth century, Hawaii suffered much as the Americas had done. Tahiti's population declined from 40,000 in 1769 to 9,000 in 1830. When European colonization began in Australia in 1788, smallpox wrought havoc there among the Aboriginal population.

Yet in terms of global population, a remarkable fact more than balanced these losses. In the eighteenth century, the age of plague ended. The last European pandemic of a disease its victims called "plague" occurred from 1661 to 1669, rolling from Turkey across Europe to Amsterdam, where it killed 34,000 people in 1663–1664. In 1665, it emptied London—more people fleeing in panic than dying of plague. Ascending the Rhine River, it ended by filling mass graves in Spain and Italy. Thereafter, Europe suffered only local outbreaks. The last outbreak of a level of severity characteristic of the age of plague occurred in 1711 in eastern Germany and Austria, with over 500,000 deaths. The last occurrence of any sort in Western Europe was the outbreak in the French Mediterranean port of Marseilles in 1720. Between corpse-strewn gutters and mass plague pits, the Archbishop of Marseilles strode, comforting the afflicted, with a bundle of herbs under his nose in hopes of warding off the disease, or leading the population in penitential processions and prayers to the Sacred Heart of Jesus. Eleven of his twelve companions were infected and died at his side.

After that, plague never returned to Europe. Changes in the distribution of carrier species of rats, fleas, and lice may have played a part (see Chapter 14). But the demise of plague could be like most other forms of species extinction: a product of evolution. The microorganisms that bear disease are more volatile, more apt to evolve, than other, bigger organisms, because they are individually short lived. They go through many generations in a relatively short span of time. Viruses are especially mutable. So species come and go much faster in the microbial world than among the great, lumbering plants and animals whose evolution we normally observe. We think of evolution as a slow-working process. Microbes experience it fast. Those that kill off their hosts are obviously not adaptively successful. They need to find new eco-niches to ensure their own survival, or they are self-condemned to disappear. For reasons we do not know—but which must be connected with their own evolutionary advantage— hostile microorganisms may sometimes switch their attention away from one set of victims to another. Historically, our improving health may owe less than we suppose to our own cleverness and more to the changing habits and nature of microbes.

"Historically, our improving health may owe less than we suppose to our own cleverness and more to the changing habits and nature of microbes."

ECONOMIC TRENDS: CHINA, INDIA, AND THE OTTOMAN EMPIRE

More population means more economic activity. That is not surprising. But eighteenth-century economic activity did mark a new departure from long-prevailing global patterns, as the gap in production, and therefore in wealth, began to narrow. The West began to catch up with China and India. The new rich among the world's economies began to emerge in Europe and America. By the end of the eighteenth century, India went into sharp relative decline. China maintained its supremacy, but signs suggested that its days as the world's richest society were numbered.

China

The distribution of the world's most productive and profitable industries indicates what was going on. The most intensive concentrations of industrial activity were still in East and South Asia. Take the case of the Beneficial and Beautiful wholesaling firm, founded in the seventeenth century in the city of Hangzhou (hahng-joh) on the coast of central China. According to records collected in the early nineteenth century, the firm built up its cloth sales to a million lengths a year by making bold rebates to tailors. In the early eighteenth century, the firm employed 4,000 weavers and several times that number of spinners. The dyeing and finishing were concentrated in a specialized suburb of the city, where in 1730 10,900 workers were gathered under 340 contractors and, claimed the firm's publicity, "for two hundred years now there has been no place, either north or south, that has failed to consider Beneficial and Beautiful cloth to be lovely."

The tale of the Beneficial and Beautiful Company was an exceptional but not an uncharacteristic story. A porcelain center in eighteenth-century Jiangxi (jee-ahng-shee) province in southern China "made the ground shake with the noise of tens of thousands of pestles. The heavens are alight with the glare from the furnaces, so that one cannot sleep at night." Farther south were ironworks that employed 2,000 to 3,000 men, and water-driven hammers pounded incense "without any expenditure of muscular effort." In the southwest provinces, similar machines for husking rice were lined up by the hundred, while water-driven paper-makers hummed "like the whirr of wings." The great city of Nanjing had three imperial textile factories at the start of the eighteenth century, employing 2,500 artisans and 664 looms. Near what is today Shanghai, in 1723, there were about 20,000 textile workers and dyers. The imperial government appointed the entrepreneurs in state factories, and they could make fabulous private fortunes without cheating the throne. A typical example, Zaoyin, whose career was largely spent managing imperial factories, was a shy, modest man who pretended to read as he was carried in his litter to screen his eyes from the sight of the common people rising in respect as he passed. But he made a famous collection of rare art works and curiosities, "without speaking of silver, treated like mud," as his own nurse reported. "No matter what thing there is on earth, there it was piled up like mountains or the waters of the sea."

The sheer size of China's internal market guaranteed a dynamic economy (see Map 20.2). In about 1800, over 10 percent of grain production was for sale rather than eaten by the farmers who grew it, together with more than a quarter of the raw cotton produced throughout the empire, and over half the cotton cloth—amounting to 3 billion bolts of cloth a year. Nearly all the silk, tea, and salt in the empire likewise were sold on the market.

Foreign trade, against this background, was of relatively small importance to China. It was vital, however, for the economies of much of the rest of the world. In the foreign trading posts (called **factories**), of Guangzhou, the world clamored for admittance at China's barely open door. All the trade of Europeans and Americans in search of Chinese tea, silk, rhubarb, and porcelain was funneled through this narrow opening. A privileged group of Chinese merchants controlled the trade. China's favorable trade balance, moreover, continued to expand, thanks to the growth of the European tea market. Dutch tea purchases in Guangzhou rose from about 1.5 million guilders (in Dutch currency) in 1729–1733 to nearly 16.5 million in 1785–1791. By that time, the British had taken over as the main customers, transporting nearly 300 million pounds of tea in the 20 years after Britain reduced the tea tax in 1784.

The "barbarians," as the Chinese called the Europeans, still paid almost entirely in silver. Eventually, Western merchants found a commodity they could market in China. Opium was the only foreign product Western suppliers con-

Guangzhou. In 1800, Guangzhou harbor still carried more international trade than any other port in the world. European traders were not allowed anywhere else in the Chinese Empire. Their residential quarters and warehouses are the white buildings in the center foreground. A European merchant probably commissioned the painting as a souvenir of his stay in China.
Photograph courtesy Peabody Essex Museum.

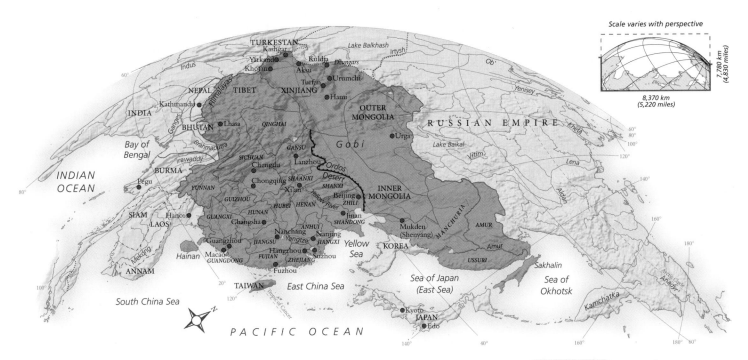

Scale varies with perspective

8,370 km
(5,220 miles)

7,780 km
(4,830 miles)

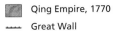

MAP 20.2

China in the Late Eighteenth Century

Qing Empire, 1770

Great Wall

trolled that Chinese consumers wanted, or came to want, in large quantities. The poppies from which opium was derived were grown in northern India under British rule. As with the milder drug China exported in exchange—the tea that banished sleep or, at least, promoted wakefulness—supply seems to have led demand. When China first banned the opium trade, in 1729, imports were reckoned at 200 of what the Chinese called "chests" a year. Each "chest" contained about 170 pounds of opium. One thousand chests were recorded in 1767. In 1773, the British East India Company imposed a monopoly on the opium trade in India. By the early nineteenth century, 10,000 chests of opium were entering

China annually. This was a significant new element in global trade. Foreigners now had, for the first time in recorded history, a chance to narrow their habitual trade gap with China (see Chapter 25).

China's economic supremacy had lasted a long time, but it was vulnerable to erosion in three ways. First, foreign suppliers could exploit the opium market. Second, they could find substitutions for their imports from China—making their own porcelain and silk, growing their own rhubarb, finding alternative places, such as India and Sri Lanka, where they could plant tea. Finally, they could outstrip Chinese production by mechanizing their industries. All these changes would occur in the nineteenth century. In the long run, the last of these changes made the greatest difference. For China could not mechanize production. The empire was caught in what the historian Mark Elvin has called a "**high-level equilibrium trap**." Industries that were meeting huge demands with traditional technologies had no scope to increase output. An economy with a vast pool of labor had no means or incentive to replace human muscle with machines.

Comparison with Britain illustrates the point. Starting from a low threshold, Britain could triple cotton-cloth production between the 1740s and 1770s. A similar rise in Chinese output would have glutted the world. The entire world supply of raw cotton would have been insufficient to meet it. In about the 1770s or 1780s, a single Chinese province imported yearly, on average, six times as much raw cotton as the whole of Britain. Cheap labor is good for industrialization, but cheap capital is better. In the teeming worlds of India and China, the cost of labor relative to that of capital may have been too low for industry's good. The trap was typified by the experience of a Chinese official in 1742 who proposed to save peasants in his charge four-fifths of their labor by installing expensive copper pumps at a wellhead. Aghast at the immobilization of so much hard wealth, the peasants continued to prefer to draw water by hand. China's unwillingness to mechanize is not surprising. The frustration some of us feel today at our continued dependence on the internal combustion engine and fossil fuels shows how the inertia of inferior technologies can arrest progress.

India

The Indian economy was even more vulnerable than China's to manipulation by foreign imperialism and competition from mechanizing systems. Yet Indian industries in the eighteenth century were scarcely less impressive than those of China. In Bengal, where it seemed to a British observer that "every man, woman, or child in every village was employed in making cloth," each major type of textile was the specialist product of a particular subcaste. A Dutch silk factory in Bengal, with 700 or 800 workers, was modeled less on European precedents than on the official textile factories the Mughals sponsored to supply the imperial wardrobe with fine cloth. Other kinds of economic specialization concentrated vast amounts of manpower and produced goods of outstanding quality and high value. Kurnool, a town of only 100,000 people on the Krishna River, is said to have had 30,000 to 60,000 iron ore workers. Until Benjamin Huntsman perfected the manu-

Dutch trading post. With its huge fluttering flag, formal grounds, spacious quarters, and splendid gates in the Mughal style, the Dutch trading post at Hoogly in northeast India looks like an outpost of empire. In fact, however, it represents how dependent European merchants of the seventeenth century were on the wealth of the East. The post opened for trade in 1635, so that the Dutch East India Company could acquire relatively cheap silk in India and exchange it at a handsome profit for silver in Japan.

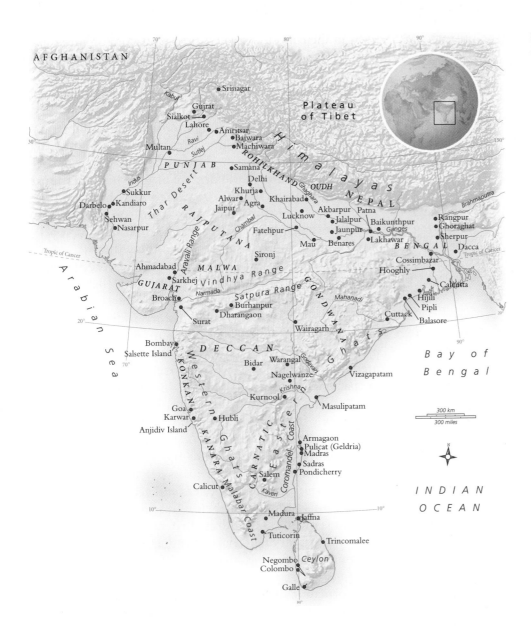

MAP **20.3**

India in the Eighteenth Century

● important city or trading center

facture of cast steel in the 1760s, "the finest steel" in Britain "was made by the Hindoos" in India and imported at £1,000 per ton (which was more than 40 times the annual wages of a skilled British worker). By the conventional economic standards of Europe, the Mughals' tax demands—exacting perhaps 50 percent of the gross product of the empire—might seem depressing to any developing industrial spirit. But high taxation created a huge administrative class with surplus spending power (see Chapter 21). Their demand may have stimulated the concentration of production. Mughal India was almost certainly the world's most productive state in terms of manufacture for export, despite the modest technical equipment with which its industries were generally supplied (see Map 20.3).

Against this background, India's industrial collapse is astonishing. The ancient drain of Westerners' silver into India, which had been going on since pre-Roman times (see Chapter 7), was reversed in Bengal by the 1770s, In 1807, John Crawfurd reported that "kite makers, falconers, astrologers, and snake-charmers" had replaced useful trades in Bengal. A French missionary claimed, "Europe is no longer dependent on India for anything, having learned to beat the Hindus on their own ground,

Chronology: Global Population and Economic Trends

ca. 1500	Population of Europe reaches 80 million
Eighteenth century	Urbanization increases in Europe and the Americas; most intense concentrations of industry found in East and South Asia
ca. 1750–1800	Indian industry goes into decline
	Population of China doubles; population of the Americas increases sixfold
1784–1814	British import 300 million pounds of tea from China
Late eighteenth century	Ottoman Empire loses control of its shipping industry
1794	Condorcet's *The Progress of the Human Mind* published
1796	Edward Jenner improves smallpox vaccine
1798	Malthus's *Essay on Population* published
ca. 1800	Population of Europe reaches 180 million

even in their most characteristic manufactures and industries, for which from time immemorial *we* were dependent on *them*. In fact the roles have been reversed and this revolution threatens to ruin India completely."

How did this collapse happen? Indian industry may have been caught, like China's, in an equilibrium trap. But it was more fragile in any case: less high powered, less technically advanced. The decline of Indian industry probably started with the decline of the Mughal Empire in the eighteenth century—skewered at its heart by Persian and Afghan invaders who sacked the capital, and shredded at its edges by usurping officials and rebellions. The impoverishment of the Mughal court deprived native industry of its best market. After Persian invaders looted the imperial treasury at Delhi in 1739, the nobles could no longer buy the products of Bengal. Then, with an exactness rare in history, India's industrial debacle coincided with one of the dramatic new developments of the next chapter of this book: the establishment of British rule or influence over most of India and, in particular, over its former industrial heartlands. Between the 1760s and the 1780s, in the early years of British rule in Bengal, silver imports into India virtually ceased. Instead, the British used tax revenues they extracted from the country to pay for the goods they exported to it. The British East India Company and its servants shamelessly exploited their monopoly by cutting prices to suppliers and acquiring allegedly low-quality Indian goods at confiscatory prices before reselling them to Indians and Europeans at enormous profits. Nor did the British neglect the opportunity to impose high prices for primary materials on Indian manufacturers. In 1767, for instance, the company's representative sold silk yarn to weavers at double the price he paid for it.

The rapidity of the transformation of India from an economic powerhouse to a declining economy surprised contemporaries. For the Irish statesman, Edmund Burke (1729–1797), it was one of the "stupendous revolutions that have happened in our age of wonders." The dual nature of India's predicament, political and commercial, decorates the ceiling of the East India Company's headquarters in London, where Britannia, enthroned, receives the riches of the East from an abject procession led by India.

The Ottoman Empire and Its Environs

As in India, some of the same inducements and problems affected the industrial development of the Ottoman Empire. Here, too, raw materials were abundant. The vitality of the luxury market impressed every European visitor. But the selectivity of Turkish talent for industry and the lack of technical inventiveness in important trades made the empire as vulnerable as India to European competition. According to a voyager in the Persian Gulf in the mid-eighteenth century, the expensive spending habits of local notables mainly benefited French importers. In the second half of the eighteenth century, the carrying trade of the Ottoman Empire passed entirely into foreign hands—mainly French, English, and Venetian. In 1775,

Making Connections | ECONOMIC TRENDS: CHINA, INDIA, AND THE OTTOMAN EMPIRE

REGION	TRANSFORMATIONS IN ECONOMIC ACTIVITY	POLITICAL/SOCIAL EFFECTS
China	increased scale of traditional crafts/industry; employment of thousands of urban workers; Westerners clamor for entry into dynamic market seeking tea, silk, porcelain via trading posts in South China; development of opium as viable commodity	increased supply = increased demand for opium, greater dependence of Chinese population; gradual decline of Chinese power after Westerners mechanize traditional industries (textiles, porcelain, etc.)
India	increased scale of textile industries spread throughout subcontinent; other economic specialization also booms (iron-ore mining, steel making, etc.); high taxation and large administrative class with surplus spending power	Britain's colonization of India, taxation, and confiscation of goods leads to decline of Indian power
Ottoman Empire	abundance of raw materials, limited industry leads to competitive disadvantage with Europe by late 18th century; lavish lifestyles of Ottoman elites benefit European importers of luxury goods; decline of Persian silk, Egyptian linen as trade goods	gradual encroachment of European powers; decline of sultan's power, and prestige

Tunisian shippers (Tunis in North Africa was nominally part of the Ottoman Empire) abandoned a heroic effort to compete with French shippers, whose home government supported them with tax breaks and naval protection. Persian silk, previously transmitted through Ottoman territory, and Egyptian linen disappeared from the export lists of the empire, as British, French, and Italian manufacturers produced cheaper alternatives. A critical observer of the Turks in 1807 admitted that "Europe certainly cannot surpass them in several of their manufactures"—essentially fine textiles—and that "in many of the inferior trades," Turkish workmen were equal to those of France. But he added that from laziness or lack of enterprise they "have not introduced or encouraged several useful arts of later invention."

THE WEST'S PRODUCTIVITY LEAP

The overall picture is clear. In the eighteenth-century world, economies in Western Europe were becoming more developed, catching up with, and, in some respects, surpassing the parts of Asia that had previously been enormously more productive. At first sight, **industrialization** in Europe looks like one of those great transformations of history that just happen beyond human control because of economic, demographic, and environmental forces—necessities that mother invention. No one in Europe thought about it until the process had already begun to unfold. Yet a conspicuously active and fruitful period in the history of Western science preceded and accompanied—though it did not cause—industrialization (see Chapter 18). Science and technical innovation were parallel results from growing curiosity about the real world and growing interest in tinkering with things to see how they work. It makes sense to look into the realm of ideas to try to find the origins of Europe's leap in production.

"Science and technical innovation were parallel results from growing curiosity about the real world and growing interest in tinkering with things to see how they work."

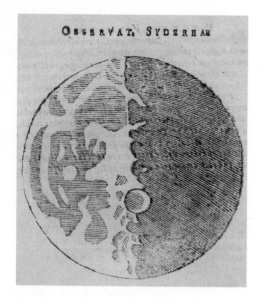

The moon. By the time Galileo published the results of his astronomical observations through a telescope in 1610, the instrument was famous throughout Europe, and a Jesuit missionary had even written a book about it in Chinese. The telescope revealed that the moon, formerly perceived as being a perfect sphere, was in fact ridged and pitted.

Demonstrations of the power of invisible forces in nature were domestic entertainments for rich people in eighteenth-century Europe. Intently, and with indifference to suffering, the scientist who dominates this painting of such a scene by Joseph Wright of Derby, in 1768, proves the vital necessity of air by depriving a bird of it. As the bird dies, a girl is revolted. Lovers carry on regardless. A father tries to explain science; a young man is enraptured by it.
Joseph Wright of Derby (1734–1797). "An Experiment on a Bird in the Air Pump." Oil on canvas. National Gallery, London, UK/The Bridgeman Art Library.

The Scientific Background

The scientific revolution that occurred in the West during the seventeenth and eighteenth centuries extended the reach of human knowledge to subjects that had formerly been too remote or too difficult to understand. Galileo Galilei (1564–1642) could see the moons of Jupiter through his telescope. Anton van Leeuwenhoek (1632–1723) saw microbes through his microscope. Marin Mersenne (1588–1648) measured the speed of sound. Robert Hooke (1635–1703) could sniff what he called "nitre-air" in the acrid smell of vapor from a lighted wick, before Antoine Lavoisier (1743–1794) proved the existence of oxygen by isolating it and setting it on fire. Isaac Newton (1642–1727) could wrest the rainbow from a shaft of light or feel the force that bound the cosmos in the weight of an apple (see Chapter 17). Luigi Galvani (1737–1798) could feel the thrill of electricity in his fingertips. Friedrich Mesmer (1734–1815) thought hypnotism was a kind of detectable animal magnetism. Through life-threatening demonstrations with kite and keys, Benjamin Franklin (1706–1790) claimed to show that lightning is a kind of electricity. Their triumphs made believable the cry of philosophers: "Nothing that we do not sense can be present to the mind!"

These discoveries accustomed Europeans to the idea that barely detectable forces can have enormous power, just as the strength of the body reposes in threadlike muscles. Nature was full of invisible powers that could replace human effort. The idea of harnessing natural energy arose unsurprisingly in the context of scientific thought. Steam, the first such power source in nature to be harnessed to replace muscles, was a fairly obvious case. You can see it and feel its heat, even though it takes imagination to believe that it can work machinery and make things move. But engineers in late eighteenth-century Britain used a discovery of "pure" science—atmospheric pressure, which is invisible and only an experiment can detect—to make steam power exploitable. Still, it is not enough to have a good idea. Conditions have to be right before good ideas get applied. The principles of the steam engine had been known in ancient Rome, and the science of the West had largely been anticipated in China. But, just as conditions in China restrained industrial output in the eighteenth century, conditions in parts of Europe promoted it. Population was rising fast enough to boost demand, without activating a high-level equilibrium trap. The global context favored economies that had privileged access to the Atlantic sea lanes of global commerce. And, within Europe, new energy sources were being explored and released. The most conspicuous case is Britain's, where, in the second half of the eighteenth century, industrial output exhibited the most dynamic increases of any economy in the world (see Map 20.4).

The British Example

Britain, in population terms, was puny compared with the industrial giants of Asia. Britain still had fewer than 9 million people in 1800. But this was a dramatic increase from the 5.3 million recorded in 1731. To make up for the lack of manpower, Britain had unrivaled resources of untapped energy just below the surface of its soil. Coal production throughout Western Europe rose dramatically in the

MAP 20.4

Industrial Britain, ca. 1800

iron works
shipbuilding
major urban growth
pottery
cutlery
woolens/cloth/cotton
silk
coalfields
turnpike road network, 1750
Manchester 33 journey time from London, in hours

eighteenth century, but the biggest supplies, of the best quality, were in Britain. In the late seventeenth century, the annual output of British coal miners was less than 3 million tons. By 1800, it had reached almost 14 million tons. Part of the increase was due to steam pumps, which enabled miners to dig deeper, below the water table, into shafts that could be drained. In turn, the pumps got people thinking about wider applications of steam-driven technology.

Britain, moreover, was an outstanding example of success in exploiting a position on the Atlantic. Britain tightly controlled the economies of its colonies in and across the Atlantic, so that their trade enriched British shippers and suppliers. British-ruled Ireland's agricultural surplus helped feed England and Scotland. Some of the profits of the slave economy of the West Indies went into agricultural improvement in Britain or investment in the infrastructure of roads, canals, and docks. The same shippers handled slave transfers and raw cotton imports, and exported the produce of the first major industrialized sector of the economy: cotton textile manufacture. By the 1770s, the Atlantic world of Africa and the Americas absorbed more of Britain's exports than Europe or Asia did and almost the entire export output of the British cotton and iron industries. The merchant marine tripled to nearly 700,000 tons by 1776. Investment in infrastructure transformed the road network and stagecoach services. During the century, the time it took to get to London from Scotland was cut from 256 to 60 hours, and the journey from London to the city of Manchester fell by about 75 percent to 33 hours (see Map 20.4).

The cumulative effect of all these changes was a sharp increase in Britain's national product in the 1780s. For the rest of the century, annual output grew at 1.8 percent compared with 1 percent previously. Pig-iron production doubled and then doubled again. Exports, which had more than doubled in the first three-quarters of the century to over £14 million in value, reached £22 million by the century's end.

It would be an exaggeration, however, to speak—as historians used to do—of an eighteenth-century Industrial Revolution. In most industries, development was piecemeal, and methods remained traditional. Huge gains in productivity resulted simply by supplying traditional methods with more manpower and more capital investment to meet rising demand. In England, between 1785 and 1800, beer production rose by about a third, as did that of tallow candles. Soap manufacture rose by over 40 percent in the same period. Overwhelmingly, these industries grew without significant mechanization, and the spectacular growth of London provided their market. In the same period, sales of imported commodities, which required little processing, grew comparably or even more impressively. Tobacco sales increased by over half. Tea sales more than doubled.

The great exceptions—where transformed methods did boost production—were the textile and iron industries. Improved smelting techniques using coke, made from coal, drove changes in how the iron and steel trades were organized. By eliminating charcoal smelting and producing iron goods to replace wooden ones, these techniques doubly relieved pressure on failing timber resources. Output of iron rose from 17,350 tons in 1740 to over 125,000 tons in 1796. The first iron bridge spanned the River Severn in 1779. The first iron ship sailed in 1787. In 1767, Richard Arkwright patented a machine that enabled a single operative to spin 16 threads of yarn at once. In 1769, he adapted it to be powered by a water mill, turning—with improvements achieved over the next few years—100 spindles at a time. In 1779, Edmund Crompton found a way to use water or steam to power a machine to weave the yarn into cloth. In consequence, the cost of processing 100

The first iron bridge. The Iron Bridge spanning the River Severn at Coalbrookdale in England was the world's first cast-iron bridge. Completed in 1770, it has come to be regarded as a symbol of the beginning of the Industrial Revolution. The Iron Bridge is also one of the last of its type to have survived intact. It was erected in just three months using sections made in a local foundry.

pounds of raw cotton into cloth was cut by more than half in 20 years. The first steam-powered textile mill opened in 1785. Raw cotton imports, which amounted to under 3 million pounds weight in 1750, reached nearly 60 million pounds in 1800. A new way of working evolved in mechanized factories, with huge concentrations of workers, a pattern that would revolutionize the societies it affected in the next century.

Historians have always wondered and often asked whether there was anything special about British values or mind-sets or "spirit" that might help to explain why Britons took up the opportunities of the age with so much enthusiasm and effectiveness. Commercial values may have occupied a relatively high priority in British culture. Certainly, people thought so at the time. Napoleon—who developed intense hatred for Britain after he became ruler of France in 1799—sneered at "a nation of shopkeepers," but Britons accepted the sneer with pride. Early in the eighteenth century, the English novelist Daniel Defoe exulted in the incalculably huge number of British tradesmen. You may as well, he said, "count the stars in the sky." The agricultural writer Arthur Young (1741–1820) jokingly advised his sons to "get children" because "they are worth more than ever they were."

There was a serious theory behind Young's joke. The British economist David Ricardo (1772–1823) recognized a principle of economics—that labor adds value to a product. He went further. Value, he argued, is proportional to the labor invested in it, "labor . . . being the foundation of all value, and the relative quantity of labor . . . almost exclusively determining the relative value of commodities." In its crude form, the theory is wrong. Goods are not always exchanged at values proportionate to the labor invested in them. Capital plays a part (and is not always just stored-up labor, since raw natural assets can be sold for cash). So does the way the goods are perceived. Rarity value—which Ricardo did recognize, citing objects of art and "wines of a peculiar quality"—is the most obvious example. Advertising and recommendation can also add value. Still, the principle is right. Ricardo drew from it a counterintuitive conclusion. If labor makes the biggest contribution to profits, one would expect high wages to reflect this (as generally, in modern industrial societies, they do). Ricardo, however, thought that to maximize profits, capitalists would always keep wages low. "There can be no rise in the value of labor without a fall in profits." In fact, wages were static in England and rose a little in Scotland. Industrialization did not drive wages down, because the growth of population and of trade continually drove demand upward.

In broad context, however, Britain's eighteenth-century experience seems more characteristic than extraordinary—just a more pronounced case of an effort to maximize the use of resources that was happening all over Western and northern Europe. By the time the French Revolution began in 1789, for instance, similar, if smaller, industrial complexes were emerging in France, Belgium, eastern Germany, and northern Spain. This effort was most widely generalized in the case of land—universally recognized, along with labor, as the most basic resource of all. In Britain, landholdings were considerably consolidated during the eighteenth century, with important consequences for efficiency. By 1790, over a quarter of the land in England was concentrated in estates of over 3,000 acres. In much of the highland zone of Scotland, landlords expelled or exterminated smallholders to make way for large sheep-grazing estates. Over most of the country, landowners adopted a common program: reducing labor costs, replacing inefficient grain farming with grazing, improving soils by draining and fertilizing, enhancing livestock by scientific stockbreeding, diversifying crops to maximize use of the earth, and, perhaps most importantly, by "enclosing" land—fencing off underexploited land that had been open to anyone in the community for their own use. French agriculturalists who called themselves "physiocrats" recommended ways to improve agriculture to enrich France. Agricultural improvement societies promoted English-style changes in Spain and Spanish America. Similar approaches spread over much of Europe, as far east as Poland and as far south as northern Italy.

Agricultural improver. Thomas Coke of Norfolk (1752–1842), shown on the left, was an exemplary British agricultural improver, whose work with sheep was particularly influential. He boosted his flock from 800 to 2,500 without increasing the amount of grazing land the sheep needed, thanks in part to the scientific improvement he made in the South Down breed, depicted here, which produced highly prized mutton.

These European changes had parallels in East Asia beyond the reach of the equilibrium trap. In Korea and Japan, many works of popular agricultural advice were published to satisfy a passionate market for agricultural improvement. In Korea, farmers began to sow barley after the rice harvest to boost grain production. As in England, small landholdings were consolidated into huge farms for cash crops: ginseng, tobacco, and cotton. A measure of the Korean economic boom was the 1,000 new markets that sprang up in the first half of the eighteenth century. In Japan, too, agriculture became commercialized, as peasant subsistence agriculture virtually disappeared. Cotton cultivation spread from Osaka almost throughout the country. Osaka also lost its monopoly of oil lamp and soy sauce production, and Kyoto its dominance over silk output. The new crops that ecological exchange made available also played their part. In 1732, for instance, a locust plague in Kyushu destroyed the grain, but people had sweet potatoes to fall back on. Famines still occurred, but now local communities could afford social-welfare schemes to mitigate their effects. Landowners paid a wealth tax to supply emergency rice stocks, make loans to new businesses, and support the elderly. The leveling off of Japanese population trends looks like a classic case of prosperity having a restraining effect on birthrates. In Okayama, over the century as a whole, the average size of a household declined from seven persons to five.

THE EXPANSION OF RESOURCES

The effort to coax more food from the soil was only one aspect of a worldwide search for new food resources—a search in which Western Europeans occupied a privileged place.

Global Gardening

In the late eighteenth century, the botanical garden of Madrid in Spain was the nursery of a uniquely widespread empire. In the half-century after its foundation in 1756, it was one of the grand ornaments of European science, forming the last link in a chain of such gardens in Manila in the Philippines, in Lima in Peru, in Mexico City, and in the Canary Islands off the coast of Africa. At least in theory, samples of the plant life of every climate the Spanish monarchy occupied could be centralized in a single place of research. From Peru, for instance, in 1783, came 1,000 colored drawings and 1,500 written descriptions of plants. Perhaps the most important collections were those of Hipólito Pavón, whose expedition to Chile and Peru in 1777–1788 allowed him to indulge his personal passion—the study of the healing properties of plants—and to produce the most complete study of quinine yet attempted. Another prolific contributor was José Celestino Mutis, who presided over scientific life in one of the heroic outposts of the Spanish Empire at Bogotá, in what is today Colombia, from 1760 until his death in 1808.

The Botanical Garden of Madrid. By establishing a series of botanical gardens on both sides of the Atlantic, the Spanish monarchs in the eighteenth century promoted the transplantation of scientifically interesting or useful plants—including species good for health or nutrition—between continents. Today, the Botanical Garden of Madrid is little more than a park, but it retains reminders of its original functions, including the eighteenth-century plant house in the background of this photograph and the bust of the great Swedish botanist, Carolus Linnaeus (1707–1778), in the foreground.

At their best, empires could gather useful specimens from an astonishing diversity of climes and make their flowers bloom together in scientific proximity. The Botanical Garden in Paris performed a comparable role. The French Jesuit missionary, Pierre Nicolas le Chéron d'Incarville, sent rare Chinese and Japanese plants there with Russian caravans across Asia. In England, the Royal Botanical Gardens at Kew, London, and the garden of the University of Oxford had similar functions, as, in the Netherlands, did the town gardens of Amsterdam and Utrecht and the University Garden of Leiden.

The plants of the world could gather in Europe and be redistributed around European empires, because only these empires were scattered widely enough around the globe, and had the environmental range, to exploit the opportunities to the full. European empires became laboratories of ecological exchange. Pierre Poivre, for instance, launched one of the most breathtaking experiments in France's Indian Ocean island colonies in 1747. Until he transformed them, the islands were economically unsuccessful—diminishing assets, wasted by deforestation and repeated attempts to introduce plantation monocultures. Poivre trained to be a Jesuit but, too young for ordination, filled in his time by traveling widely in Asia to study natural history. He smuggled 3,000 valuable spice plants out of Southeast Asia and planted them in the island of Mauritius off the east coast of Africa, where they eventually became the basis of a commercially successful operation in cloves, cinnamon, and pepper. When he became governor of France's Indian Ocean colonies 20 years after his first introductions, he combined the policy of diversifying crops with a strategy to restore the islands' forests to maintain rainfall levels.

Similar transplantations occurred to and fro, as the ecological exchange became more systematic and planned. Coffee is a case in point. Southern Arabia had long enjoyed a world monopoly of coffee. But in 1707, the Dutch introduced it into Java, the main island of what is today Indonesia, as part of a system of political control in which local rulers guaranteed to deliver it at prices that exploited producers, who had to be forced to grow it. Coffee was one of the most commercially successful products of the eighteenth century. The French planted it in the island of Bourbon (modern Réunion) in the Indian Ocean and in Saint-Domingue (modern Haiti) in the Caribbean, and the Portuguese in Brazil (see Chapter 17). By mid-century, the Arabian coffee trade had ceased to grow, and the British East India Company no longer sent regular ships there (see Map 20.5). Since almost all coffee drinkers of the era took their cups heavily sweetened, the sugar and coffee trades grew together, and sugar, of course, had wider applications. The expansion of sugar lands in the seventeenth-century Atlantic was followed, in the eighteenth century, by a similar expansion around the Indian Ocean. By 1800, sugar had probably replaced pepper as Southeast Asia's major export.

Even places too isolated for the global ecological exchange to affect could achieve high levels of productivity. Hawaii is a case in point, since it remained outside the range of European navigation until 1778. The earliest European accounts of Hawaii were full of praise for the native farmers. Expeditions from the late 1770s to the 1790s recorded fields outlined with irrigation ditches and stone walls, "made with a neatness approaching to elegance," planted with taro, breadfruit, sweet potato, sugarcane, and coconut, and laid out in a pattern calculated to impress readers at home as civilized. The roads "would have done credit to any European engineer." An engraving made on the basis of reports from the expedition of the British navigator, George Vancouver, early in the 1790s shows a field system of a regularity that arouses one's suspicions that it was made up to present a picture attuned to European ideals. Yet the same array of farmers' geometry is visible today, under the surface of fields no longer tilled, in the noon sunlight on the slopes of Hualalai and the Kohala Mountains on the Big Island of Hawaii. Only in Hawaii, moreover, among Polynesian settlements, was fish farming fully developed. Into the grid of fields and pools, other constructions were slotted. Massive platforms of stone supported temples of exact symmetry, and the wall-building techniques were adaptable to the demands of fortifications two or three times the height of a man. Early European visitors could recognize not only institutions of statehood but also an islandwide empire in the making—a process completed in 1795, when the first king, Kamehameha I, defeated the last of his enemies and extended his rule over all the Hawaiian islands.

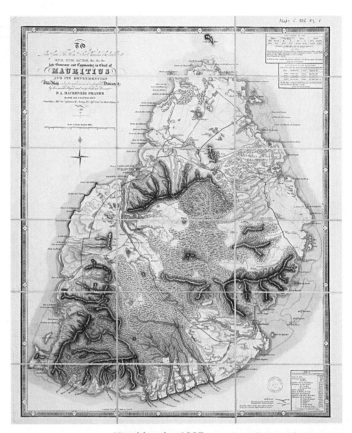

Mauritius in 1835. In the eighteenth century, French administrators introduced forest conservation to the Indian Ocean island and banned colonists there from growing what were thought to be ecologically unsuitable crops, such as cotton and wheat. The map shows the surviving forests in the center and the lower left.

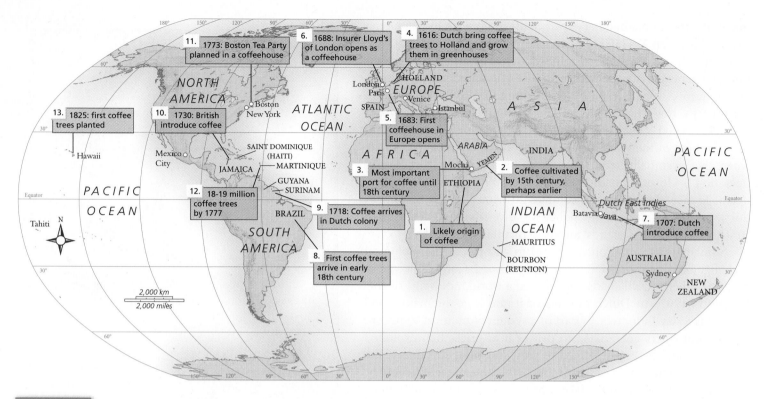

MAP **20.5**

The Spread of Coffee Worldwide

The Pacific generally was a latecomer to the great ocean-borne exchange of foodstuffs. In 1774, a Spanish expedition tried to annex Tahiti. It failed, but left Spanish hogs behind, which first improved, then replaced, the native breed of pigs. By 1788, the small, long-legged, long-snouted native pigs had disappeared. In consequence, Tahiti had an advantage in the pork trade that soon transformed the Pacific as a result of two developments. First, Captain James Cook (1728–1779) perfected a method to keep salt pork edible after a long sea voyage. Second, Australia became a British colony. In 1792, George Vancouver shipped 80 live pigs from Tahiti to Sydney in Australia to create a food source for the colonists. But it proved more economical for Australia to import pork ready salted from Tahiti than to breed its own pigs. In the first year of the trade, 1802–1803, merchants in Sydney—Australia's first middle class—handled 300,000 pounds of the meat. By the time the trade waned in the late 1820s, ten times that amount had changed hands. The muskets that paid for the pork stimulated civil war and turned Tahiti into a monarchy.

The breadfruit was an eye-catching part of the abundance that made the South Sea islands wonderful to eighteenth-century European sailors: places of restoration that supplied the long-felt wants of seaboard life. Along with the sexual license of Tahitian life, on an island where "the only god is love," ample fresh food helped to make the South Seas seem "certainly the paradise of the world," according to a British visitor in 1787. In the lingo of modern economists, this was a world of "subsistence affluence," where there was little specialization in food production and limited trade in food products, but where, in normal times, abundance was spectacular.

In most islands, yams, taro, and plantains contributed most to the basic diet, but when in season, breadfruit was the making of every feast, the starchy complement to the festive meats: pigs, turtles, dogs, chicken, fish, and some prestigious larvae, such as the grubs of the longhorn beetle, which infests coconuts. The most widely favored way to prepare breadfruit was to bake it whole in hot embers or in pits with hot stones. It was also eaten in fish stews, cooked in coconut milk. Because it is a seasonal product, and—unlike taro—rots if not harvested when it is ripe, it was also dried, fermented, and smoked. It helped to communicate an illusion of nutritional richness and became a fixture in Europeans' mental picture of the South Sea–island Eden in the eighteenth century.

William Hodges' vision of Tahiti, remembered from his experiences as resident artist with Captain Cook's expedition of 1772: "a voluptuaries' paradise . . . a habitat for nymphs."

The "inestimable benefit" of this "new fruit" was among the prizes that lured the French explorer, the Count de La Pérouse, to his death in the South Pacific in 1788. The same search inspired the voyage that ended with events Hollywood turned into the most famous episode of eighteenth-century naval history: the mutiny on the *Bounty*. Captain William Bligh's mission as commander of the British warship *Bounty* in 1787 was to pluck a bit of the paradise of the South Pacific in the form of breadfruit tree seedlings and transfer it to the slave hell of the Caribbean. On Jamaica, Bryan Edwards, a planter who was always on the lookout for ways to improve the slave economy, believed that breadfruit could energize slaves and turn his island into a hive of industry. So the British government sent Bligh to Tahiti.

Bligh brought his single-minded, demonic energy to the task. In the South Pacific, most of his men mutinied. The captain and the loyal survivors were cast adrift in midocean and saved, after terrible deprivations, only by Bligh's startling ability as a navigator. Meanwhile, some of the mutineers lived in self-condemned exile with their Tahitian women on Pitcairn, an uncharted island where predictable quarrels led to feuding in which most of them were killed. The Royal Navy hunted down and executed others. After six years' bloodshed and hardship and with a new ship, Bligh completed his mission. But there was an ironic twist—the breadfruit experiment proved disastrous. Breadfruit is not a particularly useful food. It has few nutrients. It does not keep well. The slaves would not eat it.

Other food transfers were more successful. Captain James Cook, the explorer who was responsible for so many more famous initiatives in Pacific history, was also the prophet of pigs and potatoes in New Zealand. The Dutch had discovered New Zealand in 1642, but it was then forgotten. Cook rediscovered the islands in 1769. The native inhabitants of New Zealand, the Maori, who preferred their own food, resisted his first efforts to introduce new foodstuffs (see Chapter 14). "All our endeavours for stocking this country with useful animals are likely to be frustrated by the very people we mean to serve." But Maori in the north of New Zealand were trading potatoes by 1801, and pigs became a trading item by about 1815. Other attempted introductions, such as goats, garlic, cattle, and cabbage, failed because they did not fit into traditional Maori ways of farming. Cook's shipboard scientist, Johann Reinhold Forster, suffered for his efforts to introduce sheep and goats to the islands, especially from the smell their manure produced when they were stabled in the cabin next to his to protect them from the weather. Potatoes, however, proved popular in New Zealand because they were sufficiently like the kumara or sweet potatoes that had long been familiar to the Maori, who also welcomed Europe's pigs, which could be grazed and eaten.

The same expedition succeeded in a series of other introductions. Forster reported:

> We have imported goats into Tahiti and laid the foundations of a numerous breed of animals most excellently calculated for the hills occupying the inland parts of this isle . . . and in all the isles we made presents of garden seeds and planted potatoes in Queen Charlotte's Sound with a good quantity of garlic: so that future navigators may be refreshed in these seas more than they would expect.

"The breadfruit was an eye-catching part of the abundance that made the South Sea islands wonderful to eighteenth-century European sailors: places of restoration that supplied the long-felt wants of seaboard life."

Sydney. Crowned by brushland, with natives in canoes in the foreground, this is what the harbor of Sydney, Australia looked like soon after the colony of New South Wales was founded in 1788. The governor's house is high on the hillside to the left, and fields are taking shape around the cove.

A View of Sydney Cove Port Jackson March 7th 1792

New Zealand was an outstanding example of what Alfred Crosby called **Neo-Europes** (New Europes): lands in other hemispheres where the environment sufficiently resembled Europe's for European migrants to thrive, European plants to take root, and a European way of life to be transplanted. Even with help from the climate, however, it was not easy to catch reflections of home in such distant mirrors. The strenuous efforts the British had to apply to adapt in the Australian colony of New South Wales are vividly documented. Take, for instance, the case of James Ruse. He was a pardoned convict who had been a farmer in England. In 1789, he received a grant of 30 acres at Parramatta in Australia. The "middling soil," it seemed to him, was bound to fail for want of manure. He burned timber, dug in ash, hoed, clod molded the earth, dug in grass and weeds, and left the soil exposed to sun for sowing. He planted turnip seed "which will mellow and prepare it for next year" and mulched it with his own compost, made from straw rotted in pits. He and his wife did all the work themselves.

Success with such untried soils depended on experimentation with varied planting strategies. Early Australia was a strange sort of New Europe at first—made with yams, pumpkins, and maize. On the warm coastal lowlands where the first settlers set up, maize did better than the rye, barley, and wheat that the founding fleet shipped from England in 1788. Firs and oaks were planted, but the food trees were more exotic: oranges, lemons, and limes grew alongside indigo, coffee, ginger, and castor nut. On the outward voyage, the fleet acquired tropical specimens, including bananas, cocoa, guava, sugarcane, and tamarind. In 1802, visitors could admire "the bamboo of Asia" in the governor's garden in Melbourne, the capital of New South Wales. The most successful early livestock were introduced from Calcutta in India and the Cape of Good Hope in South Africa, which also supplied fruit trees.

In the long run, a European model did prevail, but it was primarily a Mediterranean one. Sir Joseph Banks, the British botanist who equipped the founding expedition, believed that over most of its extent the Southern Hemisphere was about 10 degrees cooler at any given latitude than the Northern. He therefore expected Botany Bay in southern Australia to resemble southwest France and sent over citrus fruits, pomegranates, apricots, nectarines, and peaches. "All the vegetables of Europe" fed the colonists in the 1790s, but Mediterranean colors predominated in visitors' descriptions. The first governor had oranges in his garden, "as many fine figs as ever I tasted in Spain or Portugal," and "a thousand vines yielding three hundredweight of grapes." Watkin Tench, whose study of the soils was vital to the colony's success—his samples can still be seen, dried to powder, in a Sydney museum—commended the performance of grape "vines of every sort. . . . That their juice will probably hereafter furnish an indispensable article of luxury at European tables has already been predicted in the vehemence of speculation." He also spotted the potential of oranges, lemons, and figs. By the time of a French visit in 1802, peaches were so plentiful that they were used to fatten the hogs. The French commander saw, in the governor's garden, "the Portugal orange and the Canary fig ripening beneath the shade of the French apple tree." The Mediterranean world also provided Australia with an exportable staple—wool. The first consignment of merino sheep, a Spanish breed, left for New South Wales in 1804. Only five rams and one old ewe survived the journey, but these were enough to begin the stocking of the country, which today has more sheep than people.

This Australian experience set the pattern for the colonial New Europes of the nineteenth century, where "the roots are European but the tree grows to a different pattern and design." The North American West, New Zealand, and to a lesser extent, the "cone" of South America—Uruguay, Argentina, and Chile—were all settled, displacing the native cultures with dynamic, outward-going, and relatively populous economies. All defied their original planners and developed their own distinctive characters—tricks that the alchemy of settlement worked in the crucible of new environments.

Transplanting breadfruit. Thomas Gosse, the official artist of the British expedition that took breadfruit from Tahiti to Jamaica in the 1790s, gave pride of place to the Tahitians in the pictures he painted of the voyage. He depicted the British in a marginal, subordinate, and passive role. The breadfruit was supposed to provide cheap food for Jamaica's slaves, but the slaves rejected it.

Making Connections | EXPANDING RESOURCES IN THE EIGHTEENTH CENTURY

TYPE OF FOOD RESOURCE	METHODS OF SPREADING	RESULTS
Botanical Garden of Spain, Madrid and similar gardens throughout Spanish empire (Peru, Mexico, Canary Islands, Manila); Botanical gardens in Paris, London, Netherlands	via naval expeditions of exploration, trading expeditions	cultivation of exotic plants previously confined to specific areas (spices in Indonesia, for example) now able to be dispersed to colonized regions for economic gain
Coffee	Dutch introduction to Java; French introduction to Indian ocean and Caribbean colonies; Portuguese to Brazil	growth of worldwide coffee industry via systematic planning, growth of supply
Pork	new forms of salting, preserving pork leads to introduction of pigs on Pacific islands to provision European ships	Pacific islands become increasingly important as strategic stops for provisions
Potatoes	spread to New Zealand, other Pacific islands by James Cook and other explorers	successful introduction because of similarity to native sweet potato (kumara)
Maize, yams, wheat, oranges, lemons, limes	spread to New Zealand, Australia by James Cook and early settlers	creation of "new Europes" with crops, climate similar to Europe, but also able to grow citrus, coffee, indigo near coasts and in sub-tropical areas

In Perspective
New Europes, New Departures

"There was never," observed Samuel Johnson (1709–1784), the English man of letters, contemplating his own era, "from the earliest ages a time in which trade so engaged the attention of mankind, or commercial gain was sought with such general emulation." The world was encircled by a cycle that was speeding up: growing population, growing demand, growing output, growing commerce, all stimulated by each other. The big gainers were economies that bordered the Atlantic, where traders and shippers could participate in the increasing opportunities worldwide. For the Atlantic led to the wind systems of the world and, by relatively easy access, to exploitable empires.

Overseas colonies were an unmixed blessing for the states that founded them. Colonies demanded heavy investment and paid modest returns. They drained manpower from home countries without always adding much to long-term demand. On the contrary, colonies tended to develop regional economies, "creole mentalities," and—as we shall see in the next chapter—independence movements. The biggest, most precocious, and, in terms of cash yield, richest of the empires—that of Spain—never stimulated much of a commercial or industrial revolution in Spain itself. Yet gradually, in less obvious ways, overseas imperialism did contribute to European world dominance.

The New Europes made the West big. A culture crammed, for most of its history, into a small, remote, and beleaguered corner of Eurasia, now had much of the Western Hemisphere and important parts of the Pacific and Africa at its disposal. Even without the technical and scientific advantages the West was beginning to build up, the growing resources available to Western economies were enough to change the world.

Silver was of special importance among the products for which Europeans exploited the New World, because the critical shortage from which Westerners had suffered, in their efforts to penetrate Asian markets, had always been a shortage of cash. But the new plants of American origin that crossed the world and enhanced the productivity of other regions grew in importance. So did the sheer extent of exploitable terrain the Americas added to the resources of European empires, once they solved their labor problems by enslaving millions of Africans. The plantations and ranchlands of the Americas helped the West to even up the traditional imbalance of global resources that had formerly favored Asian economies.

Chronology

ca. 1500	Population of Europe reaches 80 million
Seventeenth and eighteenth centuries	Scientific revolution in the West
ca. 1700	Population of Europe reaches 120 million
Eighteenth century	Urbanization increases in Europe and the Americas; concentration of landholdings in Britain; most intense concentrations of industry found in East and South Asia; economic boom in Korea and Japan
1721–1804	Population of Japan stabilizes
ca. 1750–1800	Indian industry goes into decline
1750–1850	Population of China doubles; population of the Americas increases sixfold
1756	Botanical Garden of Madrid founded
1769	Captain James Cook rediscovers New Zealand
1760–1808	José Celestino Mutis leads scientific study in Colombia
1770s	The Atlantic world absorbs more British exports than Europe or Asia
1777–1788	Hipólito Pavón's expedition to Chile and Peru
1780s	Sharp increase in Britain's national product
1784–1814	British import 300 million pounds of tea from China
1787	*Bounty* begins journey to South Pacific
Late eighteenth century	Ottoman Empire loses control of its shipping industry
1794	Condorcet's *The Progress of the Human Mind* published
1796	Edward Jenner improves smallpox vaccine
1798	Malthus's *Essay on Population* published
ca. 1800	British coal production reaches 14 million tons; population of Europe reaches 180 million; 10,000 "chests" of opium imported into China annually
1805	Merino sheep introduced to Australia

China and Japan were also big gainers from the economic and demographic changes of the eighteenth century. But a future in which the West would be increasingly dominant was already visible. In the late eighteenth and early nineteenth centuries, the industrialization of Britain would keep rough pace with the deindustrialization of India at British bayonet point. Domination of India acquired even greater significance in the nineteenth century when the British turned Indian land over to the production of tea and opium, which destroyed China's trade balance, and ultimately to the farming of quinine in industrial quantities, which enabled European armies to treat malaria, one of the most deadly hazards of tropical environments. Meanwhile, other eighteenth-century developments, which are the subjects of the next two chapters, contributed to reshaping world history: the growth, strain, instability, and—in some cases—collapse of land empires, and the increasing exchange of ideas between parts of Asia and the West.

> *"The world was encircled by a cycle that was speeding up: growing population, growing demand, growing output, growing commerce, all stimulated by each other."*

PROBLEMS AND PARALLELS

1. Why is the population increase of the eighteenth century central to understanding the history of this period? What are the various explanations for the demographic growth of the eighteenth century? How did increased urbanization affect the demographic trends of this period?
2. How did global economic patterns change during the eighteenth century? Why did the disparity in productivity and wealth between China and India and the West begin to narrow? Why did Ottoman economic activity decline?
3. How did the demographic changes and the speeding up of economic activity affect the global balance of power? Why did Europe's productivity leap in the eighteenth century? How did science contribute to European technical innovation in this period?
4. How did "global gardeners" like Pierre Poivre and Captain James Cook affect the economies and societies of islands in the Indian Ocean and the Pacific? What does the term *New Europes* mean? How did European plants and animals transform Australia?
5. What are the social, economic, and political reasons for the rise of Britain as a world power in the eighteenth century? What factors led to its military and economic strength?

READ ON ▶ ▶ ▶

On the great eighteenth-century thinkers about population, see J. Avery, *Progress, Poverty and Population: Re-Reading Condorcet, Godwin and Malthus* (1997). Robert Duplessis, *Transitions to Capitalism in Early Modern Europe* (1997) contains much nuanced information on European demographics and is a good overview of the run-up to industrialization, distinguishing Britain from the Continent. Margaret Jacob, *Scientific Culture and the Making of the Industrial West* (1997) shows the cultural conduits through which Newtonian mechanics influenced technological progress. See also Joel Mokyr, *The Lever of Riches: Technological Creativity and Economic Progress* (1990), which is perhaps overly optimistic.

On China during the eighteenth century, Pamela Crossley, *The Manchus* (1997) is useful, as is Joanna Waley-Cohen, "China and Western Technology in the Late Eighteenth Century," *American Historical Review* (1993). But now fundamental are Kenneth Pomeranz, *The Great Divergence: China, Europe, and the Making of the Modern World Economy* (2001) and Andre Gunder-Frank, *ReORIENT: Global Economy in the Asian Age.* For a contrasting view, see David Landes, *The Wealth and Poverty of Nations* (1998). Huri Islamoglu-Inan, *The Ottoman Empire and the World Economy* (1987), puts the Ottoman economy in perspective. Seema Alavi, ed., *The Eighteenth Century in India* (2002) collects the most significant work on the Indian economy and the impact of British commercial and political interventions.

Richard Grove, *Green Imperialism: Colonial Expansion, Tropical Island Edens and the Origins of Environmentalism, 1600–1860* (1996) is excellent for the development of resources. *The Journals of Hipólito Ruiz: Spanish Botanist in Peru and Chile, 1777–1788*, trans. Richard Schulte et al. (1998) provides a fascinating first-hand account. Ernest Dodge, *Islands and Empires: Western Impact on the Pacific and East Asia* (1976) is useful, while Alfred Crosby, *Ecological Imperialism: The Biological Expansion of Europe, 900–1900* (1993) is a classic.

Abolitionism Belief that slavery and the slave trade are immoral and should be abolished.

Aborigine A member of the indigenous or earliest-known population of a region.

Aborigines Indigenous people of Australia.

Afrikaans An official language of South Africa, spoken mostly by the Boers. It is derived from seventeenth-century Dutch.

Age of Plague Term for the spread of lethal diseases from the fourteenth through the eighteenth centuries.

Ahriman The chief spirit of darkness and evil in Zoroastrianism, the enemy of Ahura Mazda.

Ahura Mazda The chief deity of Zoroastrianism, the creator of the world, the source of light, and the embodiment of good.

Al-Andalus Arabic name for the Iberian Peninsula (Spain and Portugal).

Alluvial plains Flat lands where mud from rivers or lakes renews the topsoil. If people can control the flooding that is common in such conditions, alluvial plains are excellent for settled agriculture.

Almoravids Muslim dynasty of Berber warriors that flourished from 1049 to 1145 and that established political dominance over northwest Africa and Spain.

Alternative energy Energy sources that usually produce less pollution than does the burning of fossil fuels, and are renewable in some cases.

Alternative medicine Medicines, treatments, and techniques not advocated by the mainstream medical establishment in the West.

Americanization The process by which other cultures, to a greater or lesser degree, adopt American fashions, culture, and ways of life.

Anarchists Believers in the theory that all forms of government are oppressive and undesirable and should be opposed and abolished.

Animal rights Movement that asserts that animals have fundamental rights that human beings have a moral obligation to respect.

Anti-Semitism Hostility or prejudice against Jews or Judaism.

Arthasastra Ancient Indian study of economics and politics that influenced the Emperor Asoka. The Arthasastra expresses an ideology of universal rule and emphasizes the supremacy of "the king's law" and the importance of uniform justice.

Artificial intelligence The creation of a machine or computer program that exhibits the characteristics of human intelligence.

Arts and Crafts Movement Nineteenth-century artists and intellectuals who argued that the products produced by individual craftsmen were more attractive than and morally superior to the mass, uniform goods produced by industry.

Assassins A secret order of Muslims in what is today Syria and Lebanon who terrorized and killed its opponents, both Christian and Muslim. The Assassins were active from the eleventh to the thirteenth centuries.

Atlantic Slave Trade Trade in African slaves who were bought, primarily in West Africa, by Europeans and white Americans and transported across the Atlantic, usually in horrific conditions, to satisfy the demand for labor in the plantations and mines of the Americas.

Atomic theory The theory that matter is not a continuous whole, but is composed of tiny, discrete particles.

Australopithecine (Trans.) "Southern ape-like creatures." Term used to describe prehuman species that existed before those classed under the genus *Homo*.

Axial Age A pivotal age in the history of world civilization, lasting for roughly 500 years up to the beginning of the Christian era, in which critical intellectual and cultural ideas arose in and were transmitted across the Mediterranean world, India, Iran, and East Asia.

Axial zone The densely populated central belt of world population, communication, and cultural exchange in Eurasia that stretches from Japan and China to Western Europe and North Africa.

Aztecs People of central Mexico whose civilization and empire were at their height at the time of the Spanish conquest in the early sixteenth century.

Balance of trade The relative value of goods traded between two or more nations or states. Each trading partner strives to have a favorable balance of trade, that is, to sell more to its trading partners than it buys from them.

Bantu African people sharing a common linguistic ancestry who originated in West Africa and whose early agriculture centered on the cultivation of yams and oil palms in swamplands.

Big bang theory Theory that the universe began with an explosion of almost infinitesimally compressed matter, the effects of which are still going on.

Black Death Term for a lethal disease or diseases that struck large parts of Eurasia and North Africa in the 1300s and killed millions of people.

Boers Dutch settlers and their descendents in southern Africa. The first Boers arrived in South Africa in the seventeenth century.

Bon Religion that was Buddhism's main rival in Tibet for several centuries in the late first millennium C.E.

Brahman A member of the highest, priestly caste of traditional Indian society.

British East India Company British trading company founded in 1600 that played a key role in the colonization of India. It ruled much of the subcontinent until 1857.

Bureaucratization The process by which government increasingly operates through a body of trained officials who follow a set of regular rules and procedures.

Business Imperialism Economic domination and exploitation of poorer and weaker countries by richer and stronger states.

Byzantine Empire Term for the Greek-speaking, eastern portion of the former Roman Empire, centered on Constantinople. It lasted until 1453, when it was conquered by the Ottoman Turks.

Cahokia Most spectacular existent site of Mississippi Valley Native American civilization, located near modern St. Louis.

Caliph The supreme Islamic political and religious authority, literally, the "successor" of the Prophet Muhammad.

Canyon cultures Indigenous peoples of the North American Southwest. The canyon cultures flourished beween about 850 and 1250 C.E.

Capitalism An economic system in which the means of production and distribution are privately or corporately owned.

Caste system A social system in which people's places in society, how they live and work, and with whom they can marry are determined by heredity. The Indian caste system has been intertwined with India's religious and economic systems.

Centralization The concentration of power in the hands of a central government.

Chaos theory Theory that some systems are so complex that their causes and effects are untraceable.

Chicago economics The economic theory associated with economists who taught at the University of Chicago that holds that low taxes and light government regulation will lead to economic prosperity.

Chimú Civilization centered on the Pacific coast of Peru that was conquered by the Inca in the fifteenth century.

Chinese Board of Astronomy Official department of the Chinese imperial court created in the early seventeenth century that was responsible for devising the ritual calendar.

Chinese diaspora The migration of Chinese immigrants around the world between the seventeenth and nineteenth centuries.

Chivalry The qualities idealized by the medieval European aristocracy and associated with knighthood, such as bravery, courtesy, honor, and gallantry.

Chola Expansive kingdom in southern India that had important connections with merchant communities on the coast. Chola reached its height around 1050 C.E.

Christendom Term referring to the European states in which Christianity was the dominant or only religion.

Cistercians Christian monastic order that built monasteries in places where habitation was sparse and nature hostile. Cistercians practiced a more ascetic and rigorous form of the Benedictine rule.

Citizen army The mass army the French created during the Revolution by imposing mandatory military service on the entire active adult male population. The army was created in response to the threat of invasion by an alliance of anti-Revolutionary countries in the early 1790s.

Civilizing mission The belief that imperialism and colonialism are justified because imperial powers have a duty to bring the benefits of "civilization" to, or impose them on, the "backward" people they ruled or conquered.

Clan A social group made up of a number of families that claim descent from a common ancestor and follow a hereditary chieftain.

Class struggle Conflict between competing social classes that, in Karl Marx's view, was responsible for all important historical change.

Climacteric A period of critical change in a society that is poised between different possible outcomes.

Code Napoleon Civil code promulgated by Napoleon in 1804 and spread by his armies across Europe. It still forms the basis for the legal code for many European, Latin American, and African countries.

Cold war Post–World War II rivalry between the United States and its allies and the Soviet Union and its allies. The cold war ended in 1990–1991 with the end of the Soviet Empire in Eastern Europe and the collapse of the Soviet Union itself.

Columbian Exchange Biological exchange of plants, animals, microbes, and human beings between the Americas and the rest of the world.

Commune Collective name for the citizen body of a medieval and Renaissance Italian town.

Communism A system of government in which the state plans and controls the economy, and private property and class distinctions are abolished.

Confraternities Lay Catholic charitable brotherhoods.

Confucianism Chinese doctrine founded by Confucius emphasizing learning and the fulfillment of obligations among family members, citizens, and the state.

Constitutionalism The doctrine that the state is founded on a set of fundamental laws that rulers and citizens make together and are bound to respect.

Consumerism A system of values that exalts the consumption and possession of consumer goods as both a social good and as an end in themselves.

Coolies Poor laborers from China and India who left their homelands to do hard manual and agricultural work in other parts of the world in the nineteenth and early twentieth centuries.

Copernican revolution Development of a heliocentric model of the solar system begun in 1543 by Nicholas Copernicus, a Polish churchman and astronomer.

Council of Trent A series of meetings from 1545 to 1563 to direct the response of the Roman Catholic Church to Protestantism. The council defined Catholic dogma and reformed church discipline.

Counter Reformation The Catholic effort to combat the spread of Protestantism in the sixteenth and seventeenth centuries.

Countercolonization The flow of immigrants out of former colonies to the "home countries" that used to rule them.

Country trades Commerce involving local or regional exchanges of goods from one Asian destination to another that, while often handled by European merchants, never touched Europe.

Covenant In the Bible, God's promise to the human race.

Creoles People of at least part-European descent born in the West Indies, French Louisiana, or Spanish America.

Crusades Any of the military expeditions undertaken by European Christians from the late eleventh to the thirteenth centuries to recover the Holy Land from the Muslims.

Cubism Artistic style developed by Pablo Picasso and Georges Braque in the early twentieth century, characterized by the reduction and fragmentation of natural forms into abstract, often geometric structures.

Cultural relativism The doctrine that cultures cannot be ranked in any order of merit. No culture is superior to another, and each culture must be judged on its own terms.

Cultural Revolution Campaign launched by Mao Zedong in 1965–1966 against the bureaucrats of the Chinese Communist Party. In lasted until 1976 and involved widespread disorder, violence, killings, and the persecution of intellectuals and the educated elite.

Culture Socially transmitted behavior, beliefs, institutions, and technologies that a given group of people, peoples, or animals share.

Cuneiform Mesopotamian writing system that was inscribed on clay tablets with wedge-shaped markers.

Czars (Trans.) "Caesar." Title of the emperors who ruled Russia until the revolution of 1917.

Dada An early twentieth-century European artistic and literary movement that flouted conventional and traditional aesthetic and cultural values by producing works marked by nonsense, travesty, and incongruity.

Dahomey West African slave-trading state that began to be prominent in the sixteenth century.

Daimyo Japanese feudal lord who ruled a province and was subject to the shoguns.

Daoism Chinese doctrine founded by Laozi that identified detachment from the world with the pursuit of immortality.

"Declaration of the Rights of Man and Citizen" Declaration of basic principles adopted by the French National Assembly in August 1789, at the start of the French Revolution.

Decolonization The process by which the nineteenth-century colonial empires in Asia, Africa, the Caribbean, and the Pacific were dismantled after World War II.

Deforestation The process by which trees are eliminated from an ecosystem.

Democracy Government by the people, exercised either directly or through elected representatives.

Devsirme Quota of male children supplied by Christian subjects as tribute to the Ottoman Sultan. Many of the boys were drafted into the janissaries.

Dharma In the teachings of Buddha, moral law or duty.

Diffusion The spread of a practice, belief, culture, or technology within a community or between communities.

Dirlik (Trans.) "Wealth." The term applied to provincial government in the Ottoman Empire.

Divine love God's ongoing love for and interest in human beings.

Dominicans Order of preaching friars established in 1216 by Saint Dominic.

Druze Lebanese sect that regards the caliph al-Hakim as a manifestation of God. Other Muslims regard the Druze as heretics.

Dualism Perception of the world as an arena of conflict between opposing principles of good and evil.

Dutch East India Company Dutch company founded in 1602 that enjoyed a government-granted monopoly on trade between Holland and Asia. The company eventually established a territorial empire in what is today Indonesia.

Dutch East Indies Dutch colonies in Asia centered on present-day Indonesia.

East India Trade Maritime trade between Western Europe and New England and Asia (predominantly India and China) between 1600 and 1800. Westerners paid cash for items from Asia, such as porcelain, tea, silk, cotton textiles, and spices.

Easterlies Winds coming from the east.

Ecological exchange The exchange of plants and animals between ecosystems.

Ecological imperialism Term historians use for the sweeping environmental changes European and other imperialists introduced in regions they colonized.

Ecology of civilization The interaction of people with their environment.

Economic liberalism Belief that government interference in and regulation of the economy should be kept to a minimum.

Edo Former name of Tokyo when it was the center of government for the Tokugawa shoguns.

El Niño A periodic reversal of the normal flow of Pacific currents that alters weather patterns and affects the number and location of fish in the ocean.

Elan vital The "vital force" hypothesized by the French philosopher Henri Bergson as a source of efficient causation and evolution in nature.

Empiricism The view that experience, especially of the senses, is the only source of knowledge.

Emporium trading Commerce that takes place in fixed market places or trading posts.

Enlightened despotism Reforms instituted by powerful monarchs in eighteenth-century Europe who were inspired by the principles of the Enlightenment.

Enlightenment Movement of eighteenth-century European thought championed by the *philosophes*, thinkers who held that change and reform were desirable and could be achieved by the application of reason and science. Most Enlightenment thinkers were hostile to conventional religion.

Enthusiasm "Religion" of English romantics who believed that emotion and passion were positive qualities.

Epistemology The branch of philosophy that studies the nature of knowledge.

Eugenics The theory that the human race can be improved mentally and physically by controlled selective breeding and that the state and society have a duty to encourage "superior" persons to have offspring and prevent "inferior" persons from reproducing.

Eunuchs Castrated male servants valued because they could not produce heirs or have sexual relations with women. In Byzantium, China, and the Islamic world, eunuchs could rise to high office in the state and the military.

European Union (EU) Loose economic and political federation that succeeded the European Economic Community (EEC) in 1993. It has expanded to include most of the states in Western and Eastern Europe.

Evolution Change in the genetic composition of a population over successive generations, as a result of natural selection acting on the genetic variation among individuals.

Examination system System for selecting Chinese officials and bureaucrats according to merit through a series of competitive, written examinations that, in theory, any Chinese young man could take. Success in the exams required years of intense study in classical Chinese literature. The examination system was not abolished until the early twentieth century.

Existentialism Philosophy that regards human existence as unexplainable, and stresses freedom of choice and accepting responsibility for the consequences of one's acts.

Expressionism Term describing a work of art in which forms are created primarily to evoke subjective emotions rather than to portray objective reality.

Factories Foreign trading posts in China and other parts of Asia. The chief representative of a factory was known as a "factor." Though the earliest trading posts were established by the Portuguese in the sixteenth century, the number of factories grew rapidly in the eighteenth and nineteenth centuries, with European and American merchants trading for silk, rhubarb, tea, and porcelain.

Fascism A system of government marked by centralization of authority under a dictator, stringent socioeconomic controls, and suppression of the opposition through terror and censorship.

Fatimids Muslim dynasty that ruled parts of North Africa and Egypt (909–1171).

Feminism The belief that women collectively constitute a class of society that has been historically oppressed and deserves to be set free.

Final Solution Nazi plan to murder all European Jews.

Fixed-wind systems Wind system in which the prevailing winds do not change direction for long periods of time.

Fossil fuels Fuels including peat, coal, natural gas, and oil.

Franciscans Religious order founded by Francis of Assisi in 1209 and dedicated to the virtues of humility, poverty, and charitable work among the poor.

Free trade The notion that maximum economic efficiency is achieved when barriers to trade, especially taxes on imports and exports, are eliminated.

French Revolution Political, intellectual, and social upheaval that began in France in 1789. It resulted in the overthrow of the monarchy and the establishment of a republic.

Fulani Traditional herdsmen of the Sahel in West Africa.

Fundamentalism The idea that a sacred text or texts contains fundamental truths that cannot be questioned, either by critical inquiry or by scientific evidence.

Futurism Artistic vision articulated by Emilio Filippo Marinetti in 1909. He believed that all traditional art and ideas should be repudiated, destroyed, and replaced by the new. Futurists glorified speed, technology, progress, and violence.

Gauchos Argentine cowboys.

General will Jean-Jacques Rousseau's concept of the collective will of the population. He believed that the purpose of government was to express the general will.

Genetic revolution Revolution in the understanding of human biology produced by advances in genetic research.

Genocide The systematic and planned extermination of an entire national, racial, political, or ethnic group.

Ghana A medieval West African kingdom in what are now eastern Senegal, southwest Mali, and southern Mauritania.

Global gardening The collecting in botanical gardens of plants from around the world for cultivation and study.

Globalization The process through which uniform or similar ways of life are spread across the planet.

Glyph A form of writing that uses symbolic figures that are usually engraved or incised, such as Egyptian hieroglyphics.

GM Crops that have been *genetically modified* to produce certain desired characteristics.

Golden Horde Term for Mongols who ruled much of Russia from the steppes of the lower Volga River from the thirteenth to the fifteenth centuries.

Grand Vizier The chief minister of state in the Ottoman Empire.

Greater East Asia Co-Prosperity Sphere Bloc of Asian nations under Japanese economic and political control during World War II.

Green revolution Improvements in twentieth-century agriculture that substantially increased food production by developing new strains of crops and agricultural techniques.

Greenhouse effect The increase in temperature caused by the trapping of carbon in the Earth's atmosphere.

Guardians Self-elected class of philosopher-rulers found in Plato's *Republic*.

Guomindang (GMD) Nationalist Chinese political party founded in 1912 by Sun Yat-Sen. The Guomindang took power in China in 1928 but was defeated by the Chinese Communists in 1949.

Habsburgs An Austro-German imperial family that reached the height of their power in the sixteenth century under Charles V of Spain when the Habsburgs ruled much of Europe and the Americas. The Habsburgs continued to rule a multinational empire based in Vienna until 1918.

Haj The pilgrimage to Mecca that all faithful Muslims are required to complete at least once in their lifetime if they able.

Han Dynasty that ruled China from ca. 206 B.C.E. to ca. 220 C.E. This was the period when the fundamental identity and culture of China were formed. Chinese people still refer to themselves as "Han."

Hanseatic League Founded in 1356, the Hanseatic League was a powerful network of allied ports along the North Sea and Baltic coasts that collaborated to promote trade.

Harem The quarters reserved for the female members of a Muslim household.

Herders Agriculturalists who emphasize the raising of animals, rather than plants, for food and products, such as wool and hides.

High-level equilibrium trap A situation in which an economy that is meeting high levels of demand with traditional technology finds that it has little scope to increase its output.

Hinduism Indian polytheistic religion that developed out of Brahmanism and in response to Buddhism. It remains the majority religion in India today.

Hispaniola Modern Haiti and the Dominican Republic.

Hohokam People Native American culture that flourished from about the third century B.C.E. to the mid–fifteenth century C.E. in south-central Arizona.

Holocaust Term for the murder of millions of Jews by the Nazi regime during World War II.

Holy Roman Empire A loose federation of states under an elected emperor that consisted primarily of Germany and northern Italy. It endured in various forms from 800 to 1806.

Homo erectus (Trans.) "Standing upright." Humanlike tool-using species that lived about 1.5 million years ago. At one time, Homo erectus was thought to be the first "human."

Homo ergaster (Trans.) "Workman." Humanlike species that lived 800,000 years ago and stacked the bones of its dead.

Homo habilis (Trans.) "Handy." Humanlike species that lived about 2.5 million years ago and made stone hand axes.

Homo sapiens (Trans.) "Wise." The species to which contemporary humans belong.

Human rights Notion of inherent rights that all human beings share. Based in part on the assumption that being human constitutes in itself a meaningful moral category that excludes nonhuman creatures.

Humanism Cultural and intellectual movement of the Renaissance centered on the study of the literature, art, and civilization of ancient Greece and Rome.

Hurons A Native American confederacy of eastern Canada. The Huron flourished immediately prior to contact with Europeans, but declined rapidly as a result of European diseases such as smallpox. They were allied with the French in wars against the British, the Dutch, and other Native Americans.

Husbandry The practice of cultivating crops and breeding and raising livestock; agriculture.

Ice-Age affluence Relative prosperity of Ice-Age society as the result of abundant game and wild, edible plants.

Icon A representation or picture of a Christian saint or sacred event. Icons have been traditionally venerated in the Eastern, or Orthodox Church.

Il-Khanate A branch of the Mongol Empire, centered in present-day Iran. Its rulers, the Il-Khans, converted to Islam and adopted Persian culture.

Imam A Muslim religious teacher. Also the title of Muslim political and religious rulers in Yemen and Oman.

Imperator A Latin term that originally meant an army commander under the Roman Republic and evolved into the term *emperor*.

Imperialism The policy of extending a nation's authority and influence by conquest or by establishing economic and political hegemony over other nations.

Incas Peoples of highland Peru who established an empire from northern Ecuador to central Chile before the Spanish conquest in the 1530s.

Indian National Congress Political organization created in 1885 that played a leading role in the Indian independence movement.

Indirect rule Rule by a colonial power through local elites.

Individualism Belief in the primary importance of the individual and in the virtues of self-reliance and personal independence.

Indo-European languages Language family that originated in Asia and from which most of Europe's present languages evolved.

Inductive method Method by which scientists turn individual observations and experiments into general laws.

Industrial Revolution The complex set of economic, demographic, and technological events that began in Western Europe and resulted in the advent of an industrial economy.

Industrialization The process by which an industrial economy is developed.

Information technology Technology, such as printing presses and computers, that facilitates the spread of information.

Inquisition A tribunal of the Roman Catholic Church that was charged with suppressing heresy and immorality.

Iroquois Native American confederacy based in northern New York State, originally composed of the Mohawk, Oneida, Onondaga, Cayuga, and Seneca peoples, known as the Five Nations. The confederation created a constitution sometime between the mid-1400s and the early 1600s.

Isolationism Belief that, unless directly challenged, a country should concentrate on domestic issues and avoid foreign conflicts or active participation in foreign affairs.

Jainism A way of life that arose in India designed to free the soul from evil by ascetic practices: chastity, detachment, truth, selflessness, and strict vegetarianism.

Janissaries Soldiers in an elite Ottoman infantry formation that was first organized in the fourteenth century. Originally drafted from among the sons of the sultan's Christian subjects, the janissaries had become a hereditary and militarily obsolete caste by the early nineteenth century.

Jesuits Order of regular clergy strongly committed to education, scholarship, and missionary work. Founded by Ignatius of Loyola in 1534.

Jihad Arabic word meaning "striving." Muhammad used the word to refer to the inner struggle all Muslims must wage against evil, and the real wars fought against the enemies of Islam.

Joint-stock company A business whose capital is held in transferable shares of stock by its joint owners. The Dutch East India Company, founded in 1602, was the first joint-stock company.

Kaaba The holiest place in Islam. Formerly a pagan shrine, the Kaaba is a massive cube-shaped structure in Mecca toward which Muslims turn to pray.

Keynesianism Economic policy advocated by J. M. Keynes, based on the premise that governments could adjust the distribution of wealth and regulate the functioning of the economy through taxation and public spending, without seriously weakening free enterprise or infringing freedom.

Khan A ruler of a Mongol, Tartar, or Turkish tribe.

Khedive Title held by the hereditary viceroys of Egypt in the nineteenth century. Although nominally subject to the Ottoman sultans, the khedives were, in effect, sovereign princes.

Khmer Agrarian kingdom of Cambodia, built on the wealth produced by enormous rice surpluses.

Kongo Kingdom located in west central Africa along the Congo River, founded in the fourteenth century. The Portuguese converted its rulers and elite to Catholicism in the fifteenth century.

Kulturkampf (Trans.) "The struggle for culture." Name given to the conflict between the Roman Catholic Church and the imperial German government under Chancellor Otto von Bismarck in the 1870s.

Laissez-faire An economic policy that emphasizes the minimization of government regulation and involvement in the economy.

Latin Church Dominant Christian church in Western Europe.

Latitude The angular distance north or south of the Earth's equator, measured in degrees along a meridian.

League of Nations International political organization created after World War I to resolve disputes between states peacefully and create a more just international order.

Legalism Chinese school of thought that emerged in the fourth century B.C.E. Legalists believed that morality was meaningless and that obedience to the state was the supreme good. The state thus had the right to enforce its laws under threat of the harshest penalties.

Levant The countries bordering on the eastern Mediterranean from Turkey to Egypt.

Liberation theology Religious movement in Latin America, primarily among Roman Catholics, concerned with justice for the poor and oppressed. Its adherents argue that sin is the result not just of individual moral failure but of the oppressive and exploitative way in which capitalist society is organized and functions.

Little Ice Age Protracted period of relative cold from the fourteenth to the early nineteenth centuries.

Logograms A system of writing in which stylized pictures represent a word or phrase.

Longitude An imaginary great circle on the surface of the Earth passing through the north and south poles at right angles to the equator.

Lotus Sutra The most famous of Buddhist scriptures.

Low Countries A region of northwest Europe comprising what is today Belgium, the Netherlands, and Luxembourg.

Magyars Steppeland people who invaded Eastern Europe in the tenth century and were eventually converted to Catholic Christianity. The Magyars are the majority ethnic group in present-day Hungary.

Mahayana One of the major schools of Buddhism. It emphasizes the Buddha's infinite compassion for all human beings, social concern, and universal salvation. It is the dominant branch of Buddhism in East Asia.

Mahdi A Muslim messiah, whose coming would inaugurate a cosmic struggle, preceding the end of the world.

Maize The grain that modern Americans call "corn." It was first cultivated in ancient Mesoamerica.

Mali Powerful West African state that flourished in the fourteenth century.

Malthusian Ideas inspired by Thomas Malthus's theory that population growth would always outpace growth in food supply.

Mamluks Egyptian Muslim slave army. The mamluks provided Egypt's rulers from 1390 to 1517.

Mana According to the Polynesians, a supernatural force that regulates everything in the world. For example, the mana of a net makes it catch a fish, and the mana of an herb gives it its healing powers.

Manchurian Incident Japanese invasion of Manchuria in 1931, justified by the alleged effort of the Chinese to blow up a Japanese train. In fact, Japanese agents deliberately triggered the explosion to provide a pretext for war.

Manchus A people native to Manchuria who ruled China during the Qing dynasty.

Mandarins High public officials in the Chinese Empire, usually chosen by merit after competitive written exams.

Mandate of Heaven The source of divine legitimacy for Chinese emperors. According to the mandate of heaven, emperors were chosen by the gods and retained their favor as long as the emperors acted in righteous ways. Emperors and dynasties that lost the mandate of heaven could be deposed or overthrown.

Manichaeanism A dualistic philosophy dividing the world between the two opposed principles of good and evil.

Manifest destiny Nineteenth-century belief that the United States was destined to expand across all of North America from the Atlantic to the Pacific, including Canada and Mexico.

Manila Galleons Spanish galleons that sailed each year between the Philippines and Mexico with a cargo of silk, porcelain, and other Asian luxury goods that were paid for with Mexican silver.

Maori Indigenous Polynesian people of New Zealand.

Marathas Petty Hindu princes who ruled in Maharashtra in southern India in the eighteenth century.

Maritime empires Empires based on trade and naval power that flourished in the sixteenth and seventeenth centuries.

Maroons Runaway slaves in the Americas who formed autonomous communities, and even states, between 1500 and 1800.

Marshall Plan Foreign-aid program for Western Europe after World War II, named after U.S. Secretary of State George C. Marshall.

Marxism The political and economic philosophy of Karl Marx and Friedrich Engels in which the concept of class struggle is the determining principle in social and historical change.

Material culture Concrete objects that people create.

Matrilineal A society that traces ancestry through the maternal line.

Maya Major civilization of Mesoamerica. The earliest evidence connected to Maya civilization dates from about 1000 B.C.E. Maya civilization reached its peak between 250 and 900 C.E. Maya cultural and political practices were a major influence on other Mesoamericans.

Meiji Restoration The overthrow of the Tokugawa *bakufu* in Japan in 1868 and the "restoration" of power to the imperial government under the Emperor Meiji.

Mercantilism An economic theory that emphasized close government control of the economy to maximize a country's exports and to earn as much bullion as possible.

Mesoamerica A region stretching from central Mexico to Central America. Mesoamerica was home to the Olmec, the Maya, the Aztecs, and other Native American peoples.

Messiah The anticipated savior of the Jews. Christians identified Jesus as the Messiah.

Mestizos The descendents of Europeans and Native Americans.

Microbial exchange The exchange of microbes between ecosystems.

Militarization The trend toward larger and more powerful armed forces and the organization of society and the economy to achieve that goal.

Military revolution Change in warfare in the sixteenth and seventeenth centuries that accompanied the rise of fire-power technology.

Millenarianism Belief that the end of the world is about to occur, as foretold in the biblical Book of Revelation.

Minas Gerais (Trans.) "General Mines." Region of Brazil rich in mineral resources that experienced a gold rush in the early eighteenth century.

Ming Dynasty Chinese dynasty (1368–1644) noted for its flourishing foreign trade and achievements in scholarship and the arts.

Mongols Nomadic people whose homeland was in Mongolia. In the twelfth and thirteenth centuries, they conquered most of Eurasia from China to Eastern Europe.

Monocultures The cultivation of a single dominant food crop, such as potatoes or rice. Societies that practiced monoculture were vulnerable to famine if bad weather or disease caused their single food crop to fail.

Monroe Doctrine The policy enunciated by President James Monroe in 1823 that the United States would oppose further European colonization in the Americas.

Monsoons A wind from the southwest or south that brings heavy rainfall each summer to southern Asia.

Mound agriculture Form of agriculture found in pre-Columbian North America.

Mughals Muslim dynasty founded by Babur that ruled India, at least nominally, from the mid–1500s until 1857.

Multiculturalism The belief that different cultures can coexist peacefully and equitably in a single country.

Napoleonic Wars Wars waged between France under Napoleon and its European enemies from 1799 to 1815. The fighting spilled over into the Middle East and sparked conflicts in North America and India and independence movements in the Spanish and Portuguese colonies in the Americas.

Nationalism Belief that a people who share the same language, historic experience, and sense of identity make up a nation and that every nation has the right to assert its identity, pursue its destiny, defend its rights, and be the primary focus of its people's loyalty.

Natural selection The process by which only the organisms best adapted to their environment pass on their genetic material to subsequent generations.

Nature versus nurture Debate over the relative importance of inherited characterizes and environmental factors in determining human development.

Nazis Members of the National Socialist German Workers' Party, founded in Germany in 1919 and brought to power in 1933 under Adolf Hitler.

Neanderthal (Trans.) "Neander Valley." Humanlike species, evidence for whose existence was found in the Neander River valley in northern Germany in the mid–nineteenth century. Neanderthals disappeared from the evolutionary record about 30,000 years ago.

Negritude The affirmation of the distinctive nature, quality, and validity of black culture.

Nestorianism The Christian theological doctrine that within Jesus are two distinct and separate persons, divine and human, rather than a single divine person. Orthodox Christians classed Nestorianism as a heresy, but it spread across Central Asia along the Silk Roads.

New Europes Lands in other hemispheres where the environment resembled that of Europe and where immigrants could successfully transplant a European way of life and European culture.

New Rich Rich people whose wealth was acquired in the recent past, often in industry or commerce.

New World Term Europeans applied to the Americas.

Nirvana The spiritual goal of Buddhism, when a person ends the cycle of birth and rebirth and achieves enlightenment and freedom from any attachment to material things.

Noble savage Idealized vision that some people in the West held about certain non-Europeans, especially some Native Americans and Polynesians. It was based on the notions that civilization was a corrupting force and that these peoples lived lives more in tune with nature.

Northwest Passage Water route from the Atlantic to the Pacific through the Arctic archipelago of northern Canada and along the northern coast of Alaska. For centuries, Europeans sought in vain for a more accessible route to the Pacific farther south in North America.

Obsidian Volcanic glass used to make tools, weapons, and mirrors.

Old regime Term for the social, economic, and political institutions that existed in France and the rest of Europe before the French Revolution.

Old World Term for the regions of the world—Europe, parts of Africa and Asia—that were known to Europeans before the discovery of the Americas.

Ongons Tibetan images in which spirits are thought to reside. Shamans claimed to communicate with the ongons.

OPEC The Organization of Petroleum Exporting Countries, an alliance of the world's major oil producers.

Oracle A person or group that claims to be able to have access to knowledge of the future by consulting a god. Ancient rulers often consulted oracles.

Oriental despotism Arbitrary and corrupt rule. Eighteenth-century Europeans saw it as characteristic of Asian or Islamic rulers.

Orthodox Church Dominant Christian church in the Byzantine Empire, the Balkans, and Russia.

Ottoman Empire Islamic empire based in present-day Turkey, with its capital at Istanbul. At its height in the sixteenth century, the Ottoman Empire stretched from Iraq across North Africa to the borders of Morocco and included almost all the Balkans and most of Hungary. The empire gradually declined, but endured until it was dismembered after World War I.

Pampas A vast plain of south-central South America that supports huge herds of cattle and other livestock.

Pan-African Congress A series of five meetings held between 1919 and 1945 that claimed to represent all black Africans and demanded an end to colonial rule.

Pangaea A hypothetical prehistoric supercontinent that included all the landmasses of the Earth.

Partition of India The division in 1947 along ethnic and religious lines of the British Indian Empire into two independent states: India, which was largely Hindu, and Pakistan, which was largely Muslim. The division involved widespread violence in which at least 500,000 people were killed.

Paternalism A social or economic relationship that resembles the dependency that exists between a father and his child.

Patrilineal A society that traces ancestry through the paternal line.

Philosopher's stone A substance that was believed to have the power to change base metals into gold.

Physiocrats Eighteenth-century French political economists who argued that agriculture was the foundation of any country's wealth and recommended agricultural improvements.

Plantation system System of commercial agriculture based on large landholdings, often worked by forced labor.

Polestar Bright star used for navigation.

Positivism Doctrine that asserts the undeniability of human sense perception and the power of reason to prove that what our senses perceive is true.

Pragmatism Philosophy advocated by William James that holds that the standard for evaluating the truth or validity of a theory or concept depends on how well it works and on the results that arise from holding it.

Proletariat The working class, which according to Karl Marx, would overthrow the bourgeoisie.

Protectorate A country or region that, although nominally independent and not a colony, is in fact controlled militarily, politically, and economically by a more powerful foreign state.

Protestantism The theological system of any of the churches of Western Christendom that separated from the Roman Catholic Church during the Reformation. The advent of Protestantism is usually associated with Martin Luther's break from the Catholic Church in the 1520s.

Psychoanalysis Technique developed by Sigmund Freud to treat patients suffering from emotional or psychological disorders by making them aware of their subconscious conflicts, motivations, and desires.

Public sphere Sites for the public discussion of political, social, economic, and cultural issues.

Qing dynasty Last imperial Chinese dynasty (1644–1912), founded when the Manchus, a steppeland people from Manchuria, conquered China. It was succeeded by a republic.

Quantum mechanics Mechanics based on the principle that matter and energy have the properties of both particles and waves.

Quran The sacred text of Islam dictated from God to the Prophet Muhammad by the Archangel Gabriel. Considered by Muslims to contain the final revelations of God to humanity.

Rape of Nanjing Atrocities committed by the Japanese during their occupation of the city of Nanjing, China, in 1937.

Rastafarianism A religious and political movement that began among black people in Jamaica in the 1930s. Its adherents believe that former Emperor Haile Selassie of Ethiopia (r. 1930–1974) was divine and the Messiah whose coming was foretold in the Bible.

Rationalism The doctrine that reason by itself can determine truth and solve the world's problems.

Realpolitik Political doctrine that says that the state is not subject to moral laws and has the right to do whatever safeguards it and advances its interests.

Reformation The Protestant break from the Roman Catholic Church in the sixteenth century.

Remittances Transfers of money by foreign workers to their home countries.

Renaissance Humanistic revival of classical art, architecture, literature, and learning that originated in Italy in the fourteenth century and spread throughout Europe.

Renewable energy Energy that is not derived from a finite resource such as oil or coal.

Rig Veda A collection of hymns and poems created by a sedentary people living in the area north of the Indus valley where northern India and Pakistan meet. The Rig Veda provides evidence for the theory that invaders destroyed Harappan civilization.

Romanticism Intellectual and artistic movement that arose in reaction to the Enlightenment's emphasis on reason. Romantics had a heightened interest in nature and religion, and emphasized emotion and imagination.

Rus A Slavic-Scandinavian people who created the first Russian state and converted to Orthodox Christianity.

Safavids Shiite dynasty that ruled Persia between 1501 and 1722.

Sahel A semiarid region of north Central Africa south of the Sahara Desert.

Saint Domingue A French colony on Hispaniola that flourished in the eighteenth century by cultivating sugar and coffee with slave labor. It became the modern republic of Haiti after a protracted struggle that began in the 1790s.

Samurai The hereditary Japanese feudal-military aristocracy.

Sati In Hinduism, the burning of a widow on her husband's funeral pyre.

Satyagraha (Trans.) "The force of truth." Nonviolent movement launched by Mohandas K. Gandhi, with the goal of achieving Indian independence.

Savanna A flat grassland of tropical or subtropical regions.

Scientific revolution The sweeping change in the investigation of nature and the view of the universe that took place in Europe in the sixteenth and seventeenth centuries.

Scientism The belief that science and the scientific method can explain everything in the universe and that no other form of inquiry is valid.

Scramble for Africa Late nineteenth-century competition among European powers to acquire colonies in Africa.

Sea Peoples Unknown seafaring people that contributed to the instability of the eastern Mediterranean in the twelfth century B.C.E., attacking Egypt, Palestine, Mesopotamia, Anatolia, and Syria.

Second Vatican Council Council of the Roman Catholic Church that convened at intervals in the 1960s and led to major changes in church liturgy and discipline.

Secularism Belief that religious considerations should be excluded from civil affairs or public education.

Self-determination Principle that a given people or nationality has the right to determine their own political status.

Self-strengthening Mid–nineteenth-century Chinese reform movement initiated in response to Western incursions.

Seljuks A Turkish dynasty ruling in Central and western Asia from the eleventh to the thirteenth centuries.

Serf Agricultural laborer attached to the land owned by a lord and required to perform labor in return for certain legal or customary rights. Unlike slaves, serfs could not usually be sold away from the land.

Shaman A person who acts as an intermediary between humans and spirits or gods. Such a person functions as the medium though which spirits talk to humans.

Sharia Islamic law The word *sharia* derives from the verb *shara'a*, which is connected to the concepts of "spiritual law" and "system of divine law."

Shiites Members of the most important minority tradition in the Islamic world. Shiites believe that the caliphate is the prerogative of Muhammad's nephew, Ali, and his heirs. Shiism has been the state religion in Iran since the sixteenth century.

Shinto A religion native to Japan, characterized by veneration of nature spirits and ancestors and by a lack of formal dogma.

Shogun A hereditary military ruler of Japan who exercised real power in the name of the emperor, who was usually powerless and relegated to purely ceremonial roles. The last shogun was removed from office in 1868.

Sikhism Indian religion founded by Nanak Guru in the early sixteenth century that blends elements of the Hindu and Muslim traditions.

Silk Roads Key overland trade routes that connected eastern and western Eurasia. The route first began to function in the aftermath of Alexander the Great's expansion into Central Asia at the end of the fourth century B.C.E.

Sioux A nomadic Native American people of central North America who, with the benefit of horses introduced to the Americas by the Spanish, formed a pastoralist empire in the late eighteenth and mid–nineteenth centuries.

Social Darwinism The misapplication of Darwin's biological theories to human societies, often to justify claims of racial superiority and rule by the strong over the weak.

Socialism Any of various theories or systems in which the means of producing and distributing goods is owned collectively or by a centralized government.

Socialist realism An artistic doctrine embraced by many communist and leftist regimes that the sole legitimate purpose of the arts was to glorify the ideals of the state by portraying workers, peasants, and the masses in a strictly representational, nonabstract style.

Sociobiology The study of the biological determinants of social behavior.

Solidarity Polish trade union founded in 1980 that played a key role in bringing down Poland's communist regime.

Solomids Dynasty that seized power in Ethiopia in 1270 C.E. and claimed descent from the Biblical King Solomon.

Song dynasty Dynasty (960–1279) under which China achieved one of its highest levels of culture and prosperity.

Songhay An ancient empire of West Africa in the present-day country of Mali. It reached the height of its power around 1500 C.E.

Soninke West African kingdom on the upper Niger River.

Soviet Russian term for a workers' collective.

State system Organization of early modern Europe into competing nation-states.

Steppe A vast semiarid, grass-covered plain, extending across northern Eurasia and central North America.

Stoicism Philosophy founded on the belief that nature is morally neutral and that the wise person, therefore, achieves happiness by accepting misfortune and practicing self-control.

Stranger effect The tendency some peoples have to esteem and defer to strangers.

Stream of consciousness A literary technique that presents the thoughts and feelings of a character in a novel or story as they arise in the character's mind.

Subsidiarity Doctrine that decisions should always be made at the level closest to the people whom the decisions most affect.

Suez Canal Canal linking the Mediterranean and the Red Sea. It was built by French engineers with European capital and opened in 1869.

Sufis Members of Islamic groups that cultivate mystical beliefs and practices. Sufis have often been instrumental in spreading Islam, but Muslim authorities have often distrusted them.

Sundiata Legendary hero said to have founded the kingdom of Mali in West Africa.

Sunnis Members of the dominant tradition in the Islamic world. Sunnis believe that any member of Muhammad's tribe could be designated caliph.

Surrealism Literary and artistic movement that attempts to express the workings of the subconscious.

Syllogisms A form of argument in which we can infer a necessary conclusion from two premises that prior demonstration or agreement has established to be true.

Syncretic Characterized by the reconciliation or fusion of differing systems of belief.

Taiping Rebellion Rebellion (1852–1864) against the Qing Empire that resulted in tens of millions of deaths and widespread destruction in southern China.

Tang dynasty Chinese dynasty (618–907) famous for its wealth and encouragement of the arts and literature.

Tengri "Ruler of the sky." The supreme deity of the Mongols and other steppeland peoples.

The Encyclopedia Twenty-eight volume compendium of Enlightenment thought published in French and edited by Denis Diderot. The first volume appeared in 1751.

The Mongol Peace Era in the thirteenth and fourteenth centuries when Mongol rule created order and stability in Central Asia and enabled goods and ideas to flow along the Silk Roads.

Theory of value The theory that the value of goods is not inherent, but rather determined by supply and demand.

Theravada A conservative branch of Buddhism that adheres to the nontheistic ideal of self-purification to nirvana. Theravada Buddhism emphasizes the monastic ideal and is dominant in present-day Sri Lanka and southeast Asia.

Third Rome Term Russians used for Moscow and Russian Orthodox Christianity. It expressed the belief that the Russian czars were the divinely chosen heirs of the Roman and Byzantine emperors.

Thule Inuit Indigenous Native American people who crossed the Arctic and arrived in Greenland around 1000 C.E.

Tillers Agriculturalists who emphasize the cultivation of plants for food and products, such as timber and cotton.

Tokugawa A family of shoguns that ruled Japan in the name of the emperors from 1603 to 1868.

Trading-post empires Term for the networks of imperial forts and trading posts that Europeans established in Asia in the seventeenth century.

Treasure Fleets Spanish fleets that sailed from the Caribbean each year to bring gold and silver from mines in the Americas back to Europe.

Tundra A treeless area between the ice cap and the tree line of Arctic regions.

Turks A member of any of the Turkic-speaking, nomadic peoples who originated in Central Asia. The Turks eventually converted to Islam and dominated the Middle East.

Uncertainty principle Niels Bohr and Werner Heisenberg's theory that because observers are part of every observation their findings can never be objective.

United Nations International political organization created after World War II to prevent armed conflict, settle international disputes peacefully, and provide cultural, economic, and technological aid. It was the successor to the League of Nations, which had proved to be ineffectual.

Universal love Love between all people, regardless of status, nationality, or family ties.

Upanishads The theoretical sections of the Veda (the literature of the sages of the Ganges civilization). The Upanishads were written down as early as 800 B.C.E.

Urbanization The process by which urban areas develop and expand.

Utilitarianism System of thought devised by Jeremy Bentham, based on the notion that the goal of the state was to create the greatest happiness for the greatest number of people.

Utopianism Belief in a system or ideology aimed at producing a perfect or ideal society.

Vaccination Inoculation with a vaccine to produce immunity to a particular disease.

Vernacular languages The languages that people actually spoke—as opposed to Latin—which was the language used by the Roman Catholic Church and was, for a long time, the language of scholarship, the law, and diplomacy in much of Europe.

Virtual reality A computer simulation of a real or imaginary system.

Wahhabbism Muslim sect founded by Abdul Wahhab (1703–1792), known for its strict observance of the Quran. It is the dominant form of Islam in Saudi Arabia.

Westerlies Winds coming from the west.

Westernization The process by which other cultures adopt Western styles or ways of life.

World system The system of interconnections among the world's population.

World War I Global war (1914–1918) sparked by the assassination of Archduke Francis Ferdinand of Austria by a Serb terrorist in June 1914.

World War II Global conflict that lasted from 1939 to 1945 and ended with the defeat and occupation of Fascist Italy, Nazi Germany, and Japan.

Zen A school of Mahayana Buddhism that asserts that a person can attain enlightenment through meditation, self-contemplation, and intuition.

Ziggurat A tall, tapering Mesopotamian temple. Ziggurats were the physical and cultural centers of Mesopotamian cities.

Zimbabwes Stone-built administrative centers for rulers and the elite in southern Africa. The zimbabwes flourished in the fifteenth century.

Zoroastrianism Iranian religious system founded by Zoroaster that posited a universal struggle between the forces of light (the good) and of darkness (evil).

CHAPTER 11

1. G. Coédès, Angor: *An Introduction* (1963), pp 104–105.

2. G. Coédès, Angor: *An Introduction* p. 96.

3. Patrologia Latina, cli, col. 0572; William of Malmesbury, *Chronicle of the Kings of England*, 68 IV, ch. 2 (ed. J. A. Giles [1857], p. 360).

CHAPTER 12

1. J. T. C. Liu, *Reform in Sung China: Wang An-Shih and His New Policies* (Cambridge, MA: Harvard University Press, 1957), p. 54.

CHAPTER 13

1. P. Jackson, ed., *The Travels of Friar Willam of Rubruck* (London, 1981), pp. 113–114.

2. R. Latham, ed., *The Travels of Marco Polo* (Harmondsworth, 1972), p. 85.

3. R. L. Davis, *Wind Against the Mountain: The Crisis of Politics and Culture in Thirteenth-Century China* (Cambridge, MA: Harvard University Asia Center, 1996), p. 62.

4. J. Fennell, *The Crisis of Medieval Russia* (Longman Publishing Group, 1983), p. 88.

CHAPTER 14

1. R. Horrox, *The Black Death* (Manchester University Press, 1994), p. 16.

2. N. Cantor, *In the Wake of the Plague* (New York: Perennial/Harper Collins, 2002), p. 199.

3. D. Hall in *Cambridge History of Southeast Asia*, ed. N. Tarling (Cambridge University Press, 1992), i. 218.

4. F. Rosenthal ed. *The Muqaddimah*, 3 vols. (New York: Pantheon Books, 1958), i, 64–65.

CHAPTER 16

1. T. Armstrong, ed., *Yermak's Campaign in Siberia* (London, 1975), pp. 38–50, 59–69, 108, 163; B. Bobrick, *East of the Sun: The Epic Conquest and Tragic History of Siberia* (London, 1993), p. 43.

CHAPTER 18

1. *Principes de la philosophie* Bk I, 8,7; Discours sur la méthode, ch 4.

CHAPTER 20

1. M.E. Itoare, ed., *The Resolution Journal of John Reinhold Forster*, 4 vols. (London, 1982), ii, 409.

Index